Writing Apache Modules
with Perl and C

Writing Apache Modules with Perl and C

Lincoln Stein and Doug MacEachern

O'REILLY®

Beijing · Cambridge · Farnham · Köln · Paris · Sebastopol · Taipei · Tokyo

Writing Apache Modules with Perl and C
by Lincoln Stein and Doug MacEachern

Copyright © 1999 O'Reilly & Associates, Inc. All rights reserved.
Printed in the United States of America.

mod_perl Quick Reference Card by Andrew Ford, Copyright © 1998, 1999 Ford & Mason, Ltd.
All rights reserved.

Published by O'Reilly & Associates, Inc., 101 Morris Street, Sebastopol, CA 95472.

Editor: Linda Mui

Production Editor: Melanie Wang

Printing History:

March 1999:   First Edition.

ISBN: 1-56592-567-X   [6/99]

Table of Contents

Preface

One of the minor miracles of the World Wide Web is that it makes client/server network programming easy. With the Common Gateway Interface (CGI) anyone can become a network programmer, creating dynamic web pages, frontends for databases, and even complex intranet applications with ease. If you're like many web programmers, you started out by writing CGI scripts in Perl. With its powerful text-processing facilities, forgiving syntax, and tool-oriented design, Perl lends itself to the small programs that CGI was designed for.

Unfortunately the Perl/CGI love affair doesn't last forever. As your scripts get larger and your server more heavily loaded, you inevitably run into the performance wall. A 1,000-line Perl CGI script that runs fine on a lightly loaded web site becomes unacceptably slow when it increases to 10,000 lines and the hit rate triples. You may have tried switching to a different programming language and been disappointed. Because the main bottleneck in the CGI protocol is the need to relaunch the script every time it's requested, even compiled C won't give you the performance boost you expect.

If your application needs go beyond simple dynamic pages, you may have run into the limitations of the CGI protocol itself. Many interesting things go on in the heart of a web server—things like the smart remapping of URLs, access control and authentication, or the assignment of MIME types to different documents. The CGI protocol doesn't give you access to these internals. You can neither find out what's going on nor intervene in any meaningful way.

To go beyond simple CGI scripting, you must use an alternative protocol that doesn't rely on launching and relaunching an external program each time a script runs. Alternatives include NSAPI on Netscape servers, ISAPI on Windows servers, Java servlets, server-side includes, Active Server Pages (ASP), FastCGI, Dynamic HTML, ActiveX, JavaScript, and Java applets.

Sadly, choosing among these technologies is a no-win situation. Some choices lock you into a server platform for life. Others limit the browsers you can support. Many offer proprietary solutions that aren't available in other vendors' products. Nearly all of them require you to throw out your existing investment in Perl CGI scripts and reimplement everything from scratch.

The Apache server offers you a way out of this trap. It is a freely distributed, full-featured web server that runs on Unix and Windows NT systems. Derived from the popular NCSA *httpd* server, Apache dominates the web, currently accounting for more than half of the servers reachable from the Internet. Like its commercial cousins from Microsoft and Netscape, Apache supports an application programming interface (API), allowing you to extend the server with extension modules of your own design. Modules can behave like CGI scripts, creating interactive pages on the fly, or they can make much more fundamental changes in the operation of the server, such as implementing a single sign-on security system or logging web accesses to a relational database. Regardless of whether they're simple or complex, Apache modules provide performance many times greater than the fastest conventional CGI scripts.

The best thing about Apache modules, however, is the existence of *mod_perl*. *mod_perl* is a fully functional Perl interpreter embedded directly in Apache. With *mod_perl* you can take your existing Perl CGI scripts and plug them in, usually without making any source code changes whatsoever. The scripts will run exactly as before but many times faster (nearly as fast as fetching static HTML pages in many cases). Better yet, *mod_perl* offers a Perl interface to the Apache API, allowing you full access to Apache internals. Instead of writing Perl scripts, you can write Perl extension modules that control every aspect of the Apache server.

Move your existing Perl scripts over to *mod_perl* to get the immediate performance boost. As you need to, add new features to your scripts that take advantage of the Apache API (or don't, if you wish to maintain portability with other servers). When you absolutely need to drag out the last little bit of performance, you can bite the bullet and rewrite your Perl modules as C modules. Surprisingly enough, the performance of Apache/Perl is so good that you won't need to do this as often as you expect.

This book will show you how to write Apache modules. Because you can get so much done with Perl modules, the focus of the book is on the Apache API through the eyes of the Perl programmer. We cover techniques for creating dynamic HTML documents, interfacing to databases, maintaining state across multiple user sessions, implementing access control and authentication schemes, supporting advanced HTTP methods such as server publish, and implementing custom logging systems. If you are a C programmer, don't despair. Two chapters on writing C-language modules point out the differences between the Perl and C APIs and lead you through the process of writing, compiling, and installing C-language modules. This book includes complete reference guides to both the Perl and C APIs and multiple appendixes covering the more esoteric aspects of writing Apache modules.

We think you'll find developing Apache modules to be an eye-opening experience. With any luck, you won't have to worry about switching web application development environments for a long time to come.

What You Need to Know to Get the Most out of This Book

This book was designed for application developers who already have some experience with web programming. We assume that you understand CGI scripting, know how to produce HTML pages dynamically, and can create fill-out forms and process their contents. We also assume that you know the basics of web server administration—if not with the Apache server itself, then with another Unix or Microsoft Windows–based web server.

A knowledge of the Perl programming language is definitely required! We use the Perl version of the Apache API to illustrate the central concepts of module design and implementation, and most of our example code is written in Perl as well. We chose to do it this way because we think there are more people who are comfortable developing web applications in Perl than in C or C++. You don't have to be a Perl guru to read this book, but there will be places where you'll find the going tough if you don't understand Perl syntax. We make particularly heavy use of the current features of Perl (Version 5.004 and higher), particularly in regard to Perl's object-oriented syntax. If you know Perl Version 4 but haven't gotten around to reading about the Version 5 features, now's the time to start learning about hash references, blessed objects, and method calls.

If you're an experienced C programmer, you can probably get what you need from the Perl chapters without necessarily understanding every line of the example code. Be forewarned, however, that our discussion of the C-language API tends toward terseness since it builds on the framework established by earlier chapters on the Perl API.

Apache and *mod_perl* both run on Unix machines and Windows NT systems, and we have endeavored to give equal time to both groups of programmers. However, both authors are primarily Unix developers, and if our bias leaks through here and there, please try to forgive us.

We've used the following books for background reading and reference information. We hope they will be useful to you as well:

Web site administration, maintenance, and security

How to Set Up and Maintain a Web Site: The Guide for Information Providers, 2nd ed., by Lincoln Stein (Addison-Wesley Longman, 1997).

Web Security: A Step-by-Step Reference Guide, by Lincoln Stein (Addison-Wesley Longman, 1998).

Web Security and Electronic Commerce, by Simpson Garfinkle with Gene Spafford (O'Reilly & Associates, 1997).

The Apache web server

Apache: The Definitive Guide, by Ben Laurie and Peter Laurie (O'Reilly & Associates, 1997).

Apache Server for Dummies, by Ken Coar (IDE, 1998).

CGI scripting

The Official Guide to CGI.pm, by Lincoln Stein (John Wiley & Sons, 1998).

CGI/Perl Cookbook, by Craig Patchett and Matthew Wright (John Wiley & Sons, 1998).

The HTTP protocol

The HTTP/1.0 and HTTP/1.1 protocols page at the WWW Consortium site: *http://www.w3.org/Protocols*.

Web client programming

Web Client Programming with Perl, by Clinton Wong (O'Reilly & Associates, 1997).

Perl programming

Programming Perl, 2nd ed., by Tom Christiansen, Larry Wall, and Randal Schwartz (O'Reilly & Associates, 1996).

Perl Cookbook, by Tom Christiansen and Nathan Torkington (O'Reilly & Associates, 1998).

Advanced Perl Programming, by Srinam Srinivasan (O'Reilly & Associates, 1997).

Effective Perl Programming, by Joseph Hall (Addison-Wesley Longman, 1998).

C programming

The C Programming Language, 2nd ed., by Brian Kernighan and Dennis Ritchie (Prentice-Hall, 1988).

C: A Reference Manual, by Samuel Harbison and Guy Steele (Prentice-Hall, 1987).

HTML

> *HTML: The Definitive Guide*, 3rd ed., by Chuck Musciano and Bill Kennedy (O'Reilly & Associates, 1998).

> *HTML 3*, by Dave Raggett, Jenny Lam, and Ian Alexander (Addison-Wesley Longman, 1996).

How This Book Is Organized

Chapter 1, *Server-Side Programming with Apache*, talks about general issues of web application programming and shows how the web server APIs in general, and the Apache server API in specific, fit into the picture.

Chapter 2, *A First Module*, shows you the mechanics of getting your system ready for Perl and C module development. It describes how to lay out the directory structure, install required files, and configure the Apache web server for maximum flexibility. It then leads you through the steps of installing two simple modules, one written in Perl and the other in C.

Chapter 3, *The Apache Module Architecture and API*, paints a broad overview of the Apache API, taking you through the various phases of the HTTP transaction and the process of server startup, initialization, and cleanup. It shows how API modules fit into this process and how they can intervene to customize it.

Chapter 4, *Content Handlers*, is all about the request phase of the transaction, where modules create document content to be transmitted back to the browser. This chapter, and in fact the next three chapters, all use the Perl API to illustrate the concepts and to provide concrete working examples.

Chapter 5, *Maintaining State*, describes various techniques for maintaining state on a web server so that a user's interaction with the server becomes a continuous session rather than a series of unrelated transactions. The chapter starts with simple tricks and slowly grows in sophistication as we develop an Internet-wide tournament version of the classic "hangman" game.

Chapter 6, *Authentication and Authorization*, shows you how to intervene in Apache's authentication and authorization phases to create custom server access control systems of arbitrary complexity. Among other things, this chapter shows you how to implement an authentication system based on a relational database.

Chapter 7, *Other Request Phases*, is a grab bag of miscellaneous techniques, covering everything from controlling Apache's MIME-typing system to running proxy requests. Featured examples include a 10-line anonymizing proxy server and a system that blocks annoying banner ads.

Chapter 8, *Customizing the Apache Configuration Process,* shows how to define runtime configuration directives for Perl extension modules. It then turns the tables and shows you how Perl code can take over the configuration process and configure Apache dynamically at startup time.

Chapter 9, *Perl API Reference Guide,* is a reference guide to the Perl API, where we list every object, function, and method in exhaustive detail.

Chapter 10, *C API Reference Guide, Part I,* and Chapter 11, *C API Reference Guide, Part II,* show how to apply the lessons learned from the Perl API to the C-language API, and discuss the differences between Perl and C module development. These chapters also provide a definitive reference-style listing of all C API data structures and functions.

This book also contains the following appendixes:

Appendix A, *Standard Noncore Modules*
> A reference guide to a number of useful Perl modules that come with the standard *mod_perl* distribution but are not part of the official Apache API.

Appendix B, *Building and Installing mod_perl*
> A complete guide to installing *mod_perl,* including all the various installation options, bells, and whistles.

Appendix C, *Building Multifile C API Modules*
> Help with building C API modules that use the dynamic shared object (DSO) system.

Appendix D, *Apache:: Modules Available on CPAN*
> A listing of third-party Perl API modules that can be found on the Comprehensive Perl Archive Network (CPAN).

Appendix E, *Third-Party C Modules*
> A guide to the third-party C API modules that can be found at *http:// modules.apache.org/.*

Appendix F, *HTML::Embperl—Embedding Perl Code in HTML*
> An introduction to *HTML::Embperl,* a popular HTML template-based system that runs on top of *mod_perl.*

Conventions

The following typographic conventions are used in this book:

Italic
> is used for filenames, directories, command names, module names, function calls, command-line switches, and Apache file directives. It is also used for email addresses and URLs.

`Constant Width`
> is used for code examples. It is also used for constants and data structures.

`Constant Width Bold`
> is used to mark user input in examples.

`Constant Width Italic`
> is used to mark replaceables in examples.

The Companion Web Site to This Book

This book has a companion web site at *http://www.modperl.com/*. Here you can find all the source code for the code examples in this book—you don't have to blister your fingers typing them in. Many of the code examples are also running as demos there, letting you try them out as you read about them.

Here you'll also find announcements, errata, supplementary examples, download-ables, and links to other sources of information about Apache, Perl, and Apache module development.

Using FTP and CPAN

The Apache web server is available for download from the web. To obtain it via the web, go to the Apache home page, *http://www.apache.org/*, and follow the links to the most recent version.

mod_perl and all the various Perl modules and helper utilities mentioned in this book are available via anonymous FTP from any of the sites on the Comprehensive Perl Archive Network (CPAN). This is a list of several hundred public FTP sites that mirror each others' contents on a regular basis.

To find a CPAN site near you, point your web browser to Tom Christiansen's CPAN redirector services at *http://www.perl.com/CPAN/*. This will automatically take you to an FTP site in your geographic region. From there, you can either browse and download the files you want directly, or retrieve the full list of CPAN sites and select one on your own to use with the FTP client of your choice. Most of the modules you will be interested in obtaining will be located in the *modules/by-module* subdirectory.

Once you've downloaded the Perl module you want, you'll need to build and install it. Some modules are 100 percent Perl and can just be copied to the Perl library directory. Others contain some component written in C and need to be compiled. If you are using a Win32 system, you may want to look for a binary version of the module you're interested in. Most of the popular modules are available in precompiled binary form. Look in the CPAN *ports/win32* directory for the version suitable for your Win32 Perl build. Otherwise, if you have a C compiler and the *nmake* program installed, you can build many modules from source, as described in this section.

Building a Perl module and installing it is simple and usually painless. The following shows the traditional way to download using an old-fashioned FTP command-line client:

```
% ftp ftp.cis.ufl.edu
Connected to ftp.cis.ufl.edu.
220 torrent.cise.ufl.edu FTP server ready.
Name (ftp.cis.ufl.edu:lstein): anonymous
331 Guest login ok, send your complete e-mail address as password.
Password: your email address here
230 Guest login ok, access restrictions apply.
Remote system type is UNIX.
Using binary mode to transfer files.
ftp> cd /pub/perl/CPAN/modules/by-module
250 CWD command successful.
ftp> cd MD5
250 CWD command successful.
ftp> binary
200 Type set to I.
ftp> get Digest-MD5-2.00.tar.gz
local: Digest-MD5-2.00.tar.gz remote: Digest-MD5-2.00.tar.gz
200 PORT command successful.
150 Opening BINARY mode data connection for Digest-MD5-2.00.tar.gz (58105
bytes).
226 Transfer complete.
58105 bytes received in 11.1 secs (5.1 Kbytes/sec)
ftp> quit
221 Goodbye.
```

Perl modules are distributed as gzipped *tar* archives. You can unpack them like this:

```
% gunzip -c Digest-MD5-2.00.tar.gz  | tar xvf -
Digest-MD5-2.00/
Digest-MD5-2.00/typemap
Digest-MD5-2.00/MD2/
Digest-MD5-2.00/MD2/MD2.pm
...
```

Once unpacked, you'll enter the newly created directory and give the *perl Makefile.PL*, *make*, *make test*, and *make install* commands. Together these will build, test, and install the module (you may need to be root to perform the final step).

```
% cd Digest-MD5-2.00
% perl Makefile.PL
Testing alignment requirements for U32...
Checking if your kit is complete...
Looks good
```

```
Writing Makefile for Digest::MD2
Writing Makefile for Digest::MD5
% make
mkdir ./blib
mkdir ./blib/lib
mkdir ./blib/lib/Digest
...
% make test
make[1]: Entering directory `/home/lstein/Digest-MD5-2.00/MD2'
make[1]: Leaving directory `/home/lstein/Digest-MD5-2.00/MD2'
PERL_DL_NONLAZY=1 /usr/local/bin/perl -I./blib/arch -I./blib/lib...
t/digest............ok
t/files.............ok
t/md5-aaa...........ok
t/md5...............ok
t/rfc2202...........ok
t/sha1..............skipping test on this platform
All tests successful.
Files=6,  Tests=291,  1 secs ( 1.37 cusr  0.08 csys =  1.45 cpu)
% make install
make[1]: Entering directory `/home/lstein/Digest-MD5-2.00/MD2'
make[1]: Leaving directory `/home/lstein/Digest-MD5-2.00/MD2'
Installing /usr/local/lib/perl5/site_perl/i586-linux/./auto/Digest/MD5/MD5.so
Installing /usr/local/lib/perl5/site_perl/i586-linux/./auto/Digest/MD5/MD5.bs
...
```

A simpler way to do the same thing is to use Andreas Koenig's wonderful CPAN shell. With it you can download, build, and install Perl modules from a simple command-line shell. The following illustrates a typical session:

```
% perl -MCPAN -e shell

cpan shell -- CPAN exploration and modules installation (v1.40)
ReadLine support enabled

cpan> install MD5
Running make for GAAS/Digest-MD5-2.00.tar.gz
Fetching with LWP:
   ftp://ftp.cis.ufl.edu/pub/perl/CPAN/authors/id/GAAS/Digest-MD5-2.00.tar.gz
CPAN: MD5 loaded ok
Fetching with LWP:
   ftp://ftp.cis.ufl.edu/pub/perl/CPAN/authors/id/GAAS/CHECKSUMS
Checksum for /home/lstein/.cpan/sources/authors/id/GAAS/Digest-MD5-2.00.tar.g
z ok
Digest-MD5-2.00/
Digest-MD5-2.00/typemap
Digest-MD5-2.00/MD2/
Digest-MD5-2.00/MD2/MD2.pm
...
Installing /usr/local/lib/perl5/site_perl/i586-linux/./auto/Digest/MD5/MD5.so
Installing /usr/local/lib/perl5/site_perl/i586-linux/./auto/Digest/MD5/MD5.bs
Installing /usr/local/lib/perl5/site_perl/i586-linux/./auto/MD5/MD5.so
Installing /usr/local/lib/perl5/man/man3/./MD5.3
...
```

```
Writing /usr/local/lib/perl5/site_perl/i586-linux/auto/MD5/.packlist
Appending installation info to /usr/local/lib/perl5/i586-linux/5.00404/perllo
cal.pod

cpan> exit
```

Comments and Questions

Please address comments and questions concerning this book to the publisher:

O'Reilly & Associates, Inc.
101 Morris Street
Sebastopol, CA 95472
800-998-9938 (in the U.S. or Canada)
707-829-0515 (international or local)
707-829-0104 (fax)

You can also send us messages electronically. To be put on our mailing list or to request a catalog, send email to:

info@oreilly.com

To ask technical questions or comment on the book, send email to:

bookquestions@oreilly.com

Acknowledgments

This book was a bear to write, a pachyderm to edit, and a mule to get delivered on time. However, our technical reviewers were angels throughout, patiently helping us to get the details right and to transform the manuscript from a beastly beast into a well-groomed animal. We hope the end product justifies the image that graces its cover.

Two of our reviewers must be singled out from the crowd for their extra efforts. Andrew Ford, for his amazingly concise *mod_perl Quick Reference Card*, and Gerald Richter, for contributing the appendix on Embperl. Our other technical reviewers, in no particular order, were Manoj Kasichainula, Jon Orwant, Mike Stok, Randal Schwartz, Mike Fletcher, Eric Cholet, Frank Cringle, Gisle Aas, Stephen Reppucci, Doug Bagley, Jim "Woody" Woodgate, Howard Jones, Brian W. Fitzpatrick, Andreas Koenig, Brian Moseley, Mike Wertheim, Stas Bekman, Ask Bjoern Hansen, Jason Riedy, Nathan Torkington, Travis Broughton, Jeff Rowe, Eugenia Harris, Ken Coar, Ralf Engelschall, Vivek Khera, and Mark-Jason Dominus. Thank you, one and all.

Our editor, Linda Mui, was delightful to work with and should be a model for book editors everywhere. How she could continue to radiate an aura of calm collectedness when the book was already running three months behind schedule and showing continuing signs of slippage is beyond our ken. Her suggestions were insightful, and her edits were always right on the money. Kudos also to Rob Romano, the O'Reilly illustrator whose artwork appears in Chapters 3 and 6.

Lincoln would like to thank his coauthor, Doug, whose *mod_perl* module brought together two of the greatest open source projects of our time. Although it sometimes seemed like we were in an infinite loop—Lincoln would write about some aspect of the API, giving Doug ideas for new *mod_perl* features, leading Lincoln to document the new features, and so on—in the end it was all worth it, giving us an excellent book *and* a polished piece of software.

Lincoln also wishes to extend his personal gratitude to his wife, Jean, who put up with his getting up at 5:30 every morning to write. The book might have gotten done a bit earlier if she hadn't always been there to lure him back to bed, but it wouldn't have been half as much fun.

Doug would like to thank his coauthor, Lincoln, for proposing the idea of this book and making it come to life, in every aspect of the word. Lincoln's writing tools, his "scalpel" and "magic wand" as Doug often called them, shaped this book into a form far beyond Doug's highest expectations.

Doug would also like to thank his family, his friends, and his girlfriend for patiently putting up with months of "Sorry, I can't, I have to work on the book." Even though the book may have been finished sooner, Doug is glad they didn't always accept no for an answer. Otherwise, he may have forgotten there is more to life than book writing!

Finally we'd like to thank everyone on the *modperl@apache.org* mailing list for their enthusiastic support, technical fixes, and fresh ideas throughout the process. This book is our gift to you in return for your many gifts to us.

—Lincoln Stein and Doug MacEachern
November 12, 1998

Server-Side Programming with Apache

Before the World Wide Web appeared, client/server network programming was a drag. Application developers had to develop the communications protocol, write the low-level network code to reliably transmit and receive messages, create a user interface at the client side of the connection, and write a server to listen for incoming requests, service them properly, and transmit the results back to the client. Even simple client/server applications were many thousand lines of code, the development pace was slow, and programmers worked in C.

When the web appeared in the early '90s, all that changed. The web provided a simple but versatile communications protocol standard, a universal network client, and a set of reliable and well-written network servers. In addition, the early servers provided developers with a server extension protocol called the Common Gateway Interface (CGI). Using CGI, a programmer could get a simple client/server application up and running in 10 lines of code instead of thousands. Instead of being limited to C or another "systems language," CGI allowed programmers to use whatever development environment they felt comfortable with, whether that be the command shell, Perl, Python, REXX, Visual Basic, or a traditional compiled language. Suddenly client/server programming was transformed from a chore into a breeze. The number of client/server applications increased 100-fold over a period of months, and a new breed of software developer, the "web programmer," appeared.

The face of network application development continues its rapid pace of change. Open the pages of a web developer's magazine today and you'll be greeted by a bewildering array of competing technologies. You can develop applications using server-side include technologies such as PHP or Microsoft's Active Server Pages (ASP). You can create client-side applications with Java, JavaScript, or Dynamic

HTML (DHTML). You can serve pages directly out of databases with products like the Oracle web server or Lotus Domino. You can write high-performance server-side applications using a proprietary server application programming interface (API). Or you can combine server- and client-side programming with integrated development environments like Netscape's LiveWire or NeXT's WebObjects. CGI scripting is still around too, but enhancements like FastCGI and ActiveState's Perl ISAPI are there to improve script performance.

All these choices can be overwhelming, and it isn't always clear which development system offers the best tradeoff between power, performance, compatibility, and longevity. This chapter puts a historical perspective on web application development and shows you how and where the Apache C and Perl APIs fit into the picture.

Web Programming Then and Now

In the beginning was the web server. Specifically, in the very very beginning was CERN *httpd*, a C-language server developed at CERN, the European high-energy physics lab, by Tim Berners-Lee, Ari Luotonen, and Henrik Frystyk Nielsen around 1991. CERN *httpd* was designed to serve static web pages. The server listened to the network for Uniform Resource Locator (URL) requests using what would eventually be called the HTTP/0.9 protocol, translated the URLs into file paths, and returned the contents of the files to the waiting client. If you wanted to extend the functionality of the web server—for example, to hook it up to a bibliographic database of scientific papers—you had to modify the server's source code and recompile.

This was neither very flexible nor very easy to do. So early on, CERN *httpd* was enhanced to launch external programs to handle certain URL requests. Special URLs, recognized with a complex system of pattern matching and string transformation rules, would invoke a command shell to run an external script or program. The output of the script would then be redirected to the browser, generating a web page on the fly. A simple scheme allowed users to pass argument lists to the script, allowing developers to create keyword search systems and other basic applications.

Meanwhile, Rob McCool, of the National Center for Supercomputing Applications at the University of Illinois, was developing another web server to accompany NCSA's browser product, Mosaic. NCSA *httpd* was smaller than CERN *httpd*, faster (or so the common wisdom had it), had a host of nifty features, and was easier than the CERN software to configure and install. It quickly gained ground on CERN *httpd*, particularly in the United States. Like CERN *httpd*, the NCSA product had a facility for generating pages on the fly with external programs but one that differed in detail from CERN *httpd*'s. Scripts written to work with NCSA *httpd* wouldn't work with CERN *httpd* and vice versa.

The Birth of CGI

Fortunately for the world, the CERN and the NCSA groups did not cling tenaciously to "their" standards as certain latter-day software vendors do. Instead, the two groups got together along with other interested parties and worked out a common standard called the Common Gateway Interface.

CGI was intended to be the duct tape of the web—a flexible glue that could quickly and easily bridge between the web protocols and other forms of information technology. And it worked. By following a few easy conventions, CGI scripts can place user-friendly web frontends on top of databases, scientific analysis tools, order entry systems, and games. They can even provide access to older network services, such as gopher, whois, or WAIS. As the web changed from an academic exercise into big business, CGI came along for the ride. Every major server vendor (with a couple of notable exceptions, such as some of the Macintosh server developers) has incorporated the CGI standard into its product. It comes very close to the "write once, run everywhere" development environment that application developers have been seeking for decades.

But CGI is not the highest-performance environment. The Achilles' heel of a CGI script is that every time a web server needs it, the server must set up the CGI environment, read the script into memory, and launch the script. The CGI protocol works well with operating systems that were optimized for fast process startup and many simultaneous processes, such as Unix dialects, provided that the server doesn't become very heavily loaded. However, as load increases, the process creation bottleneck eventually turns formerly snappy scripts into molasses. On operating systems that were designed to run lightweight threads and where full processes are rather heavyweight, such as Windows NT, CGI scripts are a performance disaster.

Another fundamental problem with CGI scripts is that they exit as soon as they finish processing the current request. If the CGI script does some time-consuming operation during startup, such as establishing a database connection or creating complex data structures, the overhead of reestablishing the state each time it's needed is considerable—and a pain to program around.

Server APIs

An early alternative to the CGI scripting paradigm was the invention of web server APIs (application programming interfaces), mechanisms that the developer can use to extend the functionality of the server itself by linking new modules directly to the server executable. For example, to search a database from within a web page, a developer could write a module that combines calls to web server functions with calls to a relational database library. Add a dash or two of program logic to transform URLs into SQL, and the web server suddenly becomes a fancy database front-end. Server APIs typically provide extensive access to the innards of the server itself, allowing developers to customize how it performs the various phases of the HTTP transaction. Although this might seem like an esoteric feature, it's quite powerful.

The earliest web API that we know of was built into the Plexus web server, written by Tony Sanders of BSDI. Plexus was a 100 percent pure Perl server that did almost everything that web servers of the time were expected to do. Written entirely in Perl Version 4, Plexus allowed the webmaster to extend the server by adding new source files to be compiled and run on an as-needed basis.

APIs invented later include NSAPI, the interface for Netscape servers; ISAPI, the interface used by Microsoft's Internet Information Server and some other Windows-based servers; and of course the Apache web server's API, the only one of the bunch that doesn't have a cute acronym.

Server APIs provide performance and access to the guts of the server's software, giving them programming powers beyond those of mere mortal CGI scripts. Their drawbacks include a steep learning curve and often a certain amount of risk and inconvenience, not to mention limited portability. As an example of the risk, a bug in an API module can crash the whole server. Because of the tight linkage between the server and its API modules, it's never as easy to install and debug a new module as it is to install and debug a new CGI script. On some platforms, you might have to bring the server down to recompile and link it. On other platforms, you have to worry about the details of dynamic loading. However, the biggest problem of server APIs is their limited portability. A server module written for one API is unlikely to work with another vendor's server without extensive revision.

Server-Side Includes

Another server-side solution uses server-side includes to embed snippets of code inside HTML comments or special-purpose tags. NCSA *httpd* was the first to implement server-side includes. More advanced members of this species include Microsoft's Active Server Pages, Allaire Cold Fusion, and PHP, all of which turn HTML into a miniature programming language complete with variables, looping constructs, and database access methods.

Netscape servers recognize HTML pages that have been enhanced with scraps of JavaScript code (this is distinct from client-side JavaScript, which we talk about later). Embperl, a facility that runs on top of Apache's *mod_perl* module, marries

HTML to Perl, as does PerlScript, an ActiveState extension for Microsoft Internet Information Server.*

The main problem with server-side includes and other HTML extensions is that they're *ad hoc.* No standards exist for server-side includes, and pages written for one vendor's web server will definitely not run unmodified on another's.

Embedded Interpreters

To avoid some of the problems of proprietary APIs and server-side includes, several vendors have turned to using embedded high-level interpretive languages in their servers. Embedded interpreters often come with CGI emulation layers, allowing script files to be executed directly by the server without the overhead of invoking separate processes. An embedded interpreter also eliminates the need to make dramatic changes to the server software itself. In many cases an embedded interpreter provides a smooth path for speeding up CGI scripts because little or no source code modification is necessary.

Examples of embedded interpreters include *mod_pyapache,* which embeds a Python interpreter. When a Python script is requested, the latency between loading the script and running it is dramatically reduced because the interpreter is already in memory. A similar module exists for the TCL language.

Sun Microsystems' "servlet" API provides a standard way for web servers to run small programs written in the Java programming language. Depending on the implementation, a portion of the Java runtime system may be embedded in the web server or the web server itself may be written in Java. Apache's servlet system uses co-processes rather than an embedded interpreter. These implementations all avoid the overhead of launching a new external process for each request.

Much of this book is about *mod_perl,* an Apache module that embeds the Perl interpreter in the server. However, as we shall see, *mod_perl* goes well beyond providing an emulation layer for CGI scripts to give programmers complete access to the Apache API.

Script Co-processing

Another way to avoid the latency of CGI scripts is to keep them loaded and running all the time as a co-process. When the server needs the script to generate a page, it sends it a message and waits for the response.

The first system to use co-processing was the FastCGI protocol, released by Open Market in 1996. Under this system, the web server runs FastCGI scripts as separate

---

* ActiveState Tool Corp., *http://www.activestate.com/*

processes just like ordinary CGI scripts. However, once launched, these scripts don't immediately exit when they finish processing the initial request. Instead, they go into an infinite loop that awaits new incoming requests, processes them, and goes back to waiting. Things are arranged so that the FastCGI process's input and output streams are redirected to the web server and a CGI-like environment is set up at the beginning of each request.

Existing CGI scripts can be adapted to use FastCGI by making a few, usually painless, changes to the script source code. Implementations of FastCGI are available for Apache, as well as Zeus, Netscape, Microsoft IIS, and other servers. However, FastCGI has so far failed to win wide acceptance in the web development community, perhaps because of Open Market's retreat from the web server market. Fortunately, a group of volunteers have picked up the Apache *mod_fastcgi* module and are continuing to support and advance this freeware implementation. You can find out more about *mod_fastcgi* at the *www.fastcgi.com* website. Commercial implementations of FastCGI are also available from Fast Engines, Inc. (*www.fastengines.com*), which provides the Netscape and Microsoft IIS versions of FastCGI.

Another co-processing system is an Apache module called *mod_jserv*, which you can find at the project homepage, *http://java.apache.org/*. *mod_jserv* allows Apache to run Java servlets using Sun's servlet API. However, unlike most other servlet systems, *mod_jserv* uses something called the "JServ Protocol" to allow the web server to communicate with Java scripts running as separate processes. You can also control these servlets via the Apache Perl API using the *Apache::Servlet* module written by Ian Kluft.

Client-Side Scripting

An entirely different way to improve the performance of web-based applications is to move some or all of the processing from the server side to the client side. It seems silly to send a fill-out form all the way across the Internet and back again if all you need to do is validate that the user has filled in the Zip Code field correctly. This, and the ability to provide more dynamic interfaces, is a big part of the motivation for client-side scripting.

In client-side systems, the browser is more than an HTML rendering engine for the web pages you send it. Instead, it is an active participant, executing commands and even running small programs on your behalf. JavaScript, introduced by Netscape in early 1995, and VBScript, introduced by Microsoft soon afterward, embed a browser scripting language in HTML documents. When you combine browser scripting languages with cascading style sheets, document layers, and other HTML enhancements, you get "Dynamic HTML" (DHTML). The problem with DHTML is that it's a compatibility nightmare. The browsers built by Microsoft and Netscape implement different sets of DHTML features, and features vary even between browser version numbers. Developers must choose which browser to support, or use mind-bogglingly awkward workarounds to support more than one type of browser. Entire books have been written about DHTML workarounds!

Then there are Java applets. Java burst onto the web development scene in 1995 with an unprecedented level of publicity and has been going strong ever since. A full-featured programming language from Sun Microsystems, Java can be used to write standalone applications, server-side extensions ("servlets," which we discussed earlier), and client-side "applet" applications. Despite the similarity in names, Java and JavaScript share little in common except a similar syntax. Java's ability to run both at the server side and the client side makes Java more suitable for the implementation of complex software development projects than JavaScript or VBScript, and the language is more stable than either of those two.

However, although Java claims to solve client-side compatibility problems, the many slight differences in implementation of the Java runtime library in different browsers has given it a reputation for "write once, debug everywhere." Also, because of security concerns, Java applets are very much restricted in what they can do, although this is expected to change once Sun and the vendors introduce a security model based on unforgeable digital signatures.

Microsoft's ActiveX technology is a repackaging of its COM (Common Object Model) architecture. ActiveX allows dynamic link libraries to be packed up into "controls," shipped across the Internet, and run on the user's computer. Because ActiveX controls are compiled binaries, and because COM has not been adopted by other operating systems, this technology is most suitable for uniform intranet environments that consist of Microsoft Windows machines running a recent version of Internet Explorer.

Integrated Development Environments

Integrated development environments try to give software developers the best of both client-side and server-side worlds by providing a high-level view of the application. In this type of environment, you don't worry much about the details of how web pages are displayed. Instead, you concentrate on the application logic and the user interface.

The development environment turns your program into some mixture of database access queries, server-side procedures, and client-side scripts. Some popular environments of this sort include Netscape's "Live" development systems (LiveWire for client-server applications and LiveConnect for database connectivity),* NeXT's

---

* As this book was going to press, Netscape announced that it was dropping support for LiveWire, transforming it from a "Live" product into a "dead" one.

object-oriented WebObjects, Allaire's ColdFusion, and the Microsoft FrontPage publishing system. These systems, although attractive, have the same disadvantage as embedded HTML languages: once you've committed to one of these environments, there's no backing out. There's not the least whiff of compatibility across different vendors' development systems.

Making the Choice

Your head is probably spinning with all the possibilities. Which tool should you use for your own application development? The choice depends on your application's requirements and the tradeoffs you're willing to accept. Table 1-1 gives the authors' highly subjective ranking of the different development systems' pros and cons.

Table 1-1. Comparison of Web Development Solutions

	Portability	Performance	Simplicity	Power
CGI	++++	+	+++	++
FastCGI	++	+++	+++	++
Server API	+	++++	+	++++
Server-side includes	++	++	++++	++
DHTML	+	+++	+	++
Client-side Java	++	+++	++	+++
Embedded interpreter	+++	+++	++	++++
Integrated system	+	+++	++	++++

In this table, the "Portability" column indicates how easy it is to move a web application from one server to another in the case of server-side systems, or from one make of web browser to another in the case of client-side solutions. By "Performance," we mean the interactive speed of the application that the user perceives more than raw data processing power of the system. "Simplicity" is our gut feeling for the steepness of the system's learning curve and how convenient the system is to develop in once you're comfortable with it. "Power" is an estimate of the capabilities of the system: how much control it provides over the way the application behaves and its flexibility to meet creative demands.

If your main concern is present and future portability, your best choice is vanilla CGI. You can be confident that your CGI scripts will work properly with all browsers, and that you'll be able to migrate scripts from one server to another with a minimum of hardship. CGI scripts are simple to write and offer a fair amount of flexibility, but their performance is poor.

If you want power and performance at all costs, go with a server API. The applications that you write will work correctly with all browsers, but you'll want to think twice before moving your programs to a different server. Chances are that a large chunk of your application will need to be rewritten when you migrate from one vendor's API to another's.

FastCGI offers a marked performance improvement but does require you to make some minor modifications to CGI script source code in order to use it.

If you need a sophisticated graphical user interface at the browser side, then some component of your application must be client-side Java or DHTML. Despite its compatibility problems, DHTML is worth considering, particularly when you are running an intranet and have complete control over your users' choice of browsers.

Java applets improve the compatibility situation. So long as you don't try to get too fancy, there's a good chance that an applet will run on more than one version of a single vendor's browser, and perhaps even on browsers from different vendors.

If you're looking for ease of programming and a gentle learning curve, you should consider a server-side include system like PHP or Active Server Pages. You don't have to learn the whole language at once. Just start writing HTML and add new features as you need them. The cost of this simplicity is portability once again. Pages written for one vendor's server-side include system won't work correctly with a different vendor's system, although the HTML framework will still display correctly.

A script interpreter embedded in the web server has much better performance than a standalone CGI script. In many cases, CGI scripts can be moved to embedded interpreters and back again without source code modifications, allowing for portability among different servers. To take the most advantage of the features offered by embedded interpreters, you must usually write server-specific code, which sacrifices portability and adds a bit of complexity to the application code.

The Apache Project

This book is devoted to developing applications with the Apache web server API, so we turn our attention now to the short history of the Apache project.

The Apache project began in 1995 when a group of eight volunteers, seeing that web software was becoming increasingly commercialized, got together to create a supported open source web server. Apache began as an enhanced version of the public-domain NCSA server but steadily diverged from the original. Many new features have been added to Apache over the years: significant features include the ability for a single server to host multiple virtual web sites, a smorgasbord of authentication schemes, and the ability for the server to act as a caching proxy. In some cases, Apache is way ahead of the commercial vendors in the features wars. For example, at the time this book was written only the Apache web server had implemented the HTTP/1.1 Digest Authentication scheme.

Internally the server has been completely redesigned to use a modular and extensible architecture, turning it into what the authors describe as a "web server toolkit." In fact, there's very little of the original NCSA *httpd* source code left within
Apache. The main NCSA legacy is the configuration files, which remain backward-
compatible with NCSA *httpd.*

Apache's success has been phenomenal. In less than three years, Apache has risen
from relative obscurity to the position of market leader. Netcraft, a British market
research company that monitors the growth and usage of the web, estimates that
Apache servers now run on over 50 percent of the Internet's web sites, making it
by far the most popular web server in the world. Microsoft, its nearest rival, holds
a mere 22 percent of the market.* This is despite the fact that Apache has lacked
some of the conveniences that common wisdom holds to be essential, such as a
graphical user interface for configuration and administration.

Apache has been used as the code base for several commercial server products.
The most successful of these, C2Net's Stronghold, adds support for secure commu-
nications with Secure Socket Layer (SSL) and a form-based configuration manager.
There is also WebTen by Tenon Intersystems, a Macintosh PowerPC port, and the
Red Hat Secure Server, an inexpensive SSL-supporting server from the makers of
Red Hat Linux.

Another milestone was reached in November of 1997 when the Apache Group
announced its port of Apache to the Windows NT and 95 operating systems
(Win32). A fully multithreaded implementation, the Win32 port supports all the
features of the Unix version and is designed with the same modular architecture as
its brother. Freeware ports to OS/2 and the AmigaOS are also available.

In the summer of 1998, IBM announced its plans to join with the Apache volunteers to develop a version of Apache to use as the basis of its secure Internet commerce server system, supplanting the servers that it and Lotus Corporation had
previously developed.

Why use Apache? Many web sites run Apache by accident. The server software is
small, free, and well documented and can be downloaded without filling out
pages of licensing agreements. The person responsible for getting his organization's web site up and running downloads and installs Apache just to get his feet
wet, intending to replace Apache with a "real" server at a later date. But that date
never comes. Apache does the job and does it well.

---

* Impressive as they are, these numbers should be taken with a grain or two of salt. Netcraft's survey
techniques count only web servers connected directly to the Internet. The number of web servers running
intranets is not represented in these counts, which might inflate or deflate Apache's true market share.

However, there are better reasons for using Apache. Like other successful open source products such as Perl, the GNU tools, and the Linux operating system, Apache has some big advantages over its commercial rivals.

It's fast and efficient

The Apache web server core consists of 25,000 lines of highly tuned C code. It uses many tricks to eke every last drop of performance out of the HTTP protocol and, as a result, runs faster and consumes less system resources than many commercial servers. Its modular architecture allows you to build a server that contains just the functionality that you need and no more.

It's portable

Apache runs on all Unix variants, including the popular freeware Linux operating system. It also runs on Microsoft Windows systems (95, 98, and NT), OS/2, and even the bs2000 mainframe architecture.

It's well supported

Apache is supported by a cast of thousands. Beyond the core Apache Group developers, who respond to bug reports and answer technical questions via email, Apache is supported by a community of webmasters with hundreds of thousands of hours of aggregate experience behind them. Questions posted to the Usenet newsgroup *comp.infosystems.www.servers.unix* are usually answered within hours. If you need a higher level of support, you can purchase Stronghold or another commercial version of Apache and get all the benefits of the freeware product, plus trained professional help.

It won't go away

In the software world, a vendor's size or stock market performance is no guarantee of its staying power. Companies that look invincible one year become losers the next. In 1988, who would have thought the Digital Equipment whale would be gobbled up by the Compaq minnow just 10 years later? Good community software projects don't go away. Because the source code is available to all, someone is always there to pick up the torch when a member of the core developer group leaves.

It's stable and reliable

All software contains bugs. When a commercial server contains a bug there's an irresistible institutional temptation for the vendor to cover up the problem or offer misleading reassurances to the public. With Apache, the entire development process is open to the public. The source code is all there for you to review, and you can even eavesdrop on the development process by subscribing to the developer's mailing list. As a result, bugs don't remain hidden for long, and they are usually fixed rapidly once uncovered. If you get really desperate, you can dig into the source code and fix the problem yourself. (If you do so, please send the fix back to the community!)

It's got features to burn

> Because of its modular architecture and many contributors, Apache has more features than any other web server on the market. Some of its features you may never use. Others, such as its powerful URL rewriting facility, are peerless and powerful.

It's extensible

> Apache is open and extensible. If it doesn't already have a feature you want, you can write your own server module to implement it. In the unlikely event that the server API doesn't support what you want to do, you can dig into the source code for the server core itself. The entire system is open to your inspection; there are no black boxes or precompiled libraries for you to work around.

It's easy to administer

> Apache is configured with plain-text configuration files and controlled with a simple command-line tool. This sounds like a deficiency when compared to the fancy graphical user interfaces supplied with commercial servers, but it does have some advantages. You can save old copies of the configuration files or even commit them to a source code control system, allowing you to keep track of all the configuration changes you've made and to return to an older version if something breaks. You can easily copy the configuration files from one host machine to another, effectively cloning the server. Lastly, the ability to control the server from the command line lets you administer the server from anywhere that you can telnet from—you don't even need web connectivity.

> This being said, Apache does provide simple web-based interfaces for viewing the current configuration and server status. A number of people are working on administrative GUIs, and there is already a web interface for remotely managing web user accounts (the *user_manage* tool available at *http://stein.cshl.org/~lstein/user_manage*).

It makes you part of a community

> When you install an Apache server you become part of a large virtual community of Apache webmasters, authors, and developers. You will never feel that the software is something whose use has been grudgingly granted to you by a corporate entity. Instead, the Apache server is owned by its community. By using the Apache server, you automatically own a bit of it too and are contributing, if even in only a small way, to its continued health and development. Welcome to the club!

The Apache C and Perl APIs

The Apache module API gives you access to nearly all of the server's internal processing. You can inspect what it's doing at each step of the HTTP transaction cycle and intervene at any of the steps to customize the server's behavior. You can arrange for the server to take custom actions at startup and exit time, add your own directives to its configuration files, customize the process of translating URLs into file names, create custom authentication and authorization systems, and even tap into the server's logging system. This is all done via modules—self-contained pieces of code that can either be linked directly into the server executable, or loaded on demand as a dynamic shared object (DSO).

The Apache module API was intended for C programmers. To write a traditional compiled module, you prepare one or more C source files with a text editor, compile them into object files, and either link them into the server binary or move them into a special directory for DSOs. If the module is implemented as a DSO, you'll also need to edit the server configuration file so that the module gets loaded at the appropriate time. You'll then launch the server and begin the testing and debugging process.

This sounds like a drag, and it is. It's even more of a drag because you have to worry about details of memory management and configuration file processing that are tangential to the task at hand. A mistake in any one of these areas can crash the server.

For this reason, the Apache server C API has generally been used only for substantial modules which need high performance, tiny modules that execute very frequently, or anything that needs access to server internals. For small to medium applications, one-offs, and other quick hacks, developers have used CGI scripts, FastCGI, or some other development system.

Things changed in 1996 when Doug MacEachern introduced *mod_perl*, a complete Perl interpreter wrapped within an Apache module. This module makes almost the entire Apache API available to Perl programmers as objects and method calls. The parts that it doesn't export are C-specific routines that Perl programmers don't need to worry about. Anything that you can do with the C API you can do with *mod_perl* with less fuss and bother. You don't have to restart the server to add a new *mod_perl* module, and a buggy module is less likely to crash the server.

We have found that for the vast majority of applications *mod_perl* is all you need. For those cases when you need the raw processing power or the small memory footprint that a compiled module gives you, the C and Perl forms of the API are close enough so that you can prototype the application in *mod_perl* first and port it to C later. You may well be surprised to find that the "prototype" is all you really need!

This book uses *mod_perl* to teach you the Apache API. This keeps the examples short and easy to understand, and shows you the essentials without bogging down in detail. Toward the end of the book we show you how to port Apache modules written in Perl into C to get the memory and execution efficiency of a compiled language.

Ideas and Success Stories

To give you an impression of the power and versatility of the Apache API, here are some examples of what people have done with it. Some of the modules described here have been incorporated into Apache and are now part of the standard distribution. Others are third-party modules that have been developed to solve particular mission-critical tasks.

A movie database

The Internet Movie Database (*http://www.imdb.com/*) uses *mod_perl* to make queries against a vast database of film and television movies. The system rewrites URLs on the fly in order to present pages in the language of the user's choice and to quickly retrieve the results of previously cached searches. In 1998, the site won the coveted Webby award for design and service.

No more URL spelling errors

URLs are hard things to type, and many HTML links are broken because of a single typo in a long URL. The most frequent errors are problems with capitalization, since many HTML authors grew up in a case-insensitive MS-DOS/Windows world before entering the case-sensitive web.

mod_speling [*sic*], part of the standard Apache distribution, is a C-language module that catches and fixes typographical errors on the fly. If no immediate match to a requested URL is found, it checks for capitalization variations and a variety of character insertions, omissions, substitutions, and transpositions, trying to find a matching valid document on the site. If one is found, it generates a redirect request, transparently forwarding the browser to the correct resource. Otherwise, it presents the user with a menu of closest guesses to choose from.

An on-campus housing renewal system

At Texas A&M University, students have to indicate each academic year whether they plan to continue living in campus-provided housing. For the 1997–1998 academic year, the university decided to move the process from its current error-prone manual system to a web-based solution. The system was initially implemented using ActiveWare's PerlScript to drive a set of Microsoft Internet Information Server Active Server Pages, but with less than two weeks to go before deployment it was clear that the system would be too slow to handle the load. The system was hurriedly rewritten to use *mod_perl* on top of the NT version of Apache, resulting in a measured 60-fold increase in performance. The system went online in the nick of time and functioned without a hitch, serving 400,000 documents generated on the fly to 10,000 people over the course of the four-day registration period.

Scripting languages embedded in HTML

The PHP system (*http://www.php.net/*) is a powerful scripting language that processes programs embedded within HTML documents. The language provides support for persistent connections to ODBC and Unix databases, on-the-fly graphics, and LDAP searches. The language is implemented both as a CGI script that can run on top of any server and as a high-performance C-language module for Apache.

The ePerl (*http://www.engelschall.com/sw/eperl/*) and Embperl (*http://perl.apache.org/embperl/*) systems are like PHP, but use *mod_perl* to embed snippets of Perl code directly inside HTML pages. They can do anything that Perl can do, including opening network connections to other Internet services, accessing databases, and generating dynamic documents based on user input.

An advertising banner server

No web application needs higher performance than banner ad servers, which are pummeled by millions of requests per day. One banner ad vendor, whose conventional CGI-based system was topping out at 1.5 banners per second, moved its system to *mod_perl* and experienced a greater than 10-fold performance boost. The vendor is now serving 10 million banners a week from a single host.

A dynamic map server

The *www.stadtplandienst.de* site uses the *mod_perl* API with the ImageMagick graphics library to create dynamic searchable tourist maps for Berlin and other German cities. The system is fast and responsive, despite the computationally intensive nature of its job and its frequently heavy load.

A commodities trading system

Lind-Waldock & Co. (*http://www.lind-waldock.com/*), the world's largest discount commodities trading firm, uses *mod_perl* running under the Stronghold version of Apache to generate live and delayed quotes, dynamic charts, and late-breaking news, as well as a frontend to their online order entry system. The system is tightly integrated with the company's relational database system for customer authentication and transaction processing.

Brian Fitzpatrick, a member of the consulting team that designed and implemented the system, was pleasantly surprised at how smooth the process was: "*mod_perl* allowed us to work the web server and code around our design— not the other way around."

A document management system

The Advanced Computer Communications company maintains more than 1500 documents in various formats scattered among multiple NFS-mounted file systems in its internal network. Their document management system periodically indexes the scattered documents by document name, creation date, and content, then uses the *mod_perl* interface to the Apache API to allow users to search and retrieve documents of interest to them. The system automatically performs document format conversion. Some are sent to the browser for download, others are precompressed with PKZIP to reduce transmission time, and still others are converted into formats that can be displayed directly in the browser window.

These applications represent only a few of the possible uses for the Apache module API. What you can do with it is limited only by your imagination. The rest of this book shows you how to turn your ideas into reality.

2

A First Module

This chapter covers the mechanics of developing Apache extension modules in the Perl and C APIs. First we'll show you how to install *mod_perl*, which you'll need for all Perl API modules, and how to write a simple "Hello World" script. Then we'll show you an equivalent C module implemented both as statically linked code and as a dynamic shared object.

We won't go into the gory details of Apache internals in this chapter—that's deferred until Chapter 3, *The Apache Module Architecture and API*—but by the end you'll understand the mechanics of getting a new Apache module up and running.

Preliminaries

Before you can start hacking away at your own Apache modules, there are a number of preliminaries to take care of. This section discusses what you need and how you can get it if you don't have it already.

A Working Apache Web Server

You'll need a working version of Apache, preferably a recent release (the version we used to prepare this book was Version 1.3.4). If you do not already have Apache, you can download it, free of charge, from *http://www.apache.org/*.

Users of Windows 95 and NT systems (henceforth called "Win32") who want to write modules using the Perl API can download precompiled binaries. You will need two components: the server itself, available at *http://www.apache.org/dist/*, and *ApacheModulePerl.dll*, which is *mod_perl* implemented as a dynamically loadable module. *ApacheModulePerl.dll* has been made available by Jeffrey W. Baker. You can find it on the Comprehensive Perl Archive Network (CPAN) in the directory *authors/Jeffrey_Baker/.** Win32 users with access to the Microsoft Visual C++ development environment can also compile *ApacheModulePerl.dll* from *mod_perl* source code.

This book will not try to teach you how to install and maintain an Apache-based web site. For the full details, see the Apache server's excellent online documentation or the reference books listed in the preface.

A C Compiler and make Utility

To use the C API, you'll need a working C compiler and its associated utilities. Most Unix systems come with the necessary software development tools preinstalled, but sometimes the bundled tools are obsolete or nonstandard (SunOS and HP-UX systems are particularly infamous in this regard). To save yourself some headaches, you may want to install the GNU *gcc* compiler and *make* programs. They are available via anonymous FTP from *prep.ai.mit.edu*, in the directory */pub/gnu*, or via the web at *http://www.gnu.org/*.

Win32 users are not so lucky. To develop C API modules, you will need the Microsoft Visual C++ 5.0 development package. No other development environment is guaranteed to work, although you are certainly welcome to try; Borland C++ is reported to work in some people's hands. If you are primarily interested in the Perl API, you can use the precompiled binaries mentioned in the previous section.

A Complete Perl Installation

To use the Perl API, you will need a full installation of Perl, Version 5.004 or higher. In many cases, this means that you will have to download and install Perl yourself. We have found that some systems that come with Perl preinstalled are missing some of the essential parts of the library hierarchy needed to create and install new Perl modules. This includes certain Linux distributions. Find the Perl source distribution at any of the CPAN sites, download it, and install it according to the directions. This book was prepared using Perl Version 5.004_04.

During installation Perl creates a library file containing all its core routines. On some Unix systems, Perl will offer you the choice between building a statically linked library (usually named *libperl.a*) or building a shared library (named *libperl.so* or *libperl.o*). Unless you're going to be linking many different executables to Perl, there's no compelling reason to create a shared library. Most sites will

---

* See the preface for instructions on finding and using a CPAN site close to you.

have only two executables linked to Perl: the Apache server daemon and the *perl* program itself. Under these circumstances the memory saved by using the shared version is inconsequential compared to the execution overhead of using the shared library. We recommend that you build the statically linked library unless you are going to build multiple embedded Perl systems.

Recent Versions of CGI.pm and LWP

While not strictly necessary, your life will be easier if you have recent versions of the Perl CGI.pm and LWP modules installed. CGI.pm is a collection of utilities that makes conventional CGI scripts easier to write. It also comes in handy for modules written with the *mod_perl* API. We recommend using Version 2.42 or higher.

LWP (Library for WWW access in Perl) is a collection of modules for creating web robots, agents, and browsers in Perl. LWP is invaluable for creating web proxies, and we make use of it in later chapters. More important, *mod_perl* uses LWP during installation for regression testing. We recommend using LWP Version 5.36 or higher.

Both CGI.pm and LWP can be found on CPAN, in the subdirectories *modules/by-module/CGI* and *modules/by-module/LWP*. Complete installation directions can be found in the packages themselves.

Directory Layout Structure

We refer to a variety of special files and directories throughout this book. Although there is a standard Apache server layout, this standard has changed over time and many sites have extensively customized their layout. Furthermore, some operating systems which come with Apache preinstalled choose a nonstandard directory structure that is more consistent with the OS's way of doing things. To avoid potential confusion, we explain the directory structure we use in this book. If you are installing Apache and *mod_perl* for the first time, you might want to follow the suggestions given here for convenience.

Server root directory
> This is the top of the Apache server tree. In a typical setup, this directory contains a *bin* directory for the *httpd* Apache executable and the *apachectl* control utility; the configuration and log directories (*conf* and *logs*); a directory for executable CGI scripts, *cgi-bin*; a directory for dynamically loaded modules, *libexec*; header files for building C-language modules, *include*; and the document root directory, *htdocs*.*

---

* The directory layout we describe here is the default Apache layout. Other predefined layouts may be configured with the Apache configuration option `--with-layout=Type` where `Type` can be GNU or another user-defined layout. Consult the Apache installation documention for more details.

The default server root directory on Unix machines is */usr/local/apache*, which we'll use throughout the book. However, in order to avoid typing this long name, we suggest creating a pseudo-user named *www* with */usr/local/apache* as its home directory.* This allows you to refer to the server root quickly as *~www*.

On Win32 systems, the default server root is *C:\Program Files\Apache Group\ Apache*. However, many people change that to simply *C:\Apache*, as we do here. Readers who use this platform should mentally substitute *~www* with the path to their true server root.

Document root directory

This is the top of the web document tree, the default directory from which the server fetches documents when the remote user requests *http://your.site/*. We'll assume *~www/htdocs* in our examples (*C:\Apache\htdocs* on Win32 systems).

Apache and mod_perl build directory

This is a directory where you can build Apache and *mod_perl* from their source distributions. There's no standard place for this. Different people use */usr/src*, */usr/build*, */usr/tmp*, or their home directories. In order to keep the various packages in one place, we recommend *~www/build* for this purpose.

httpd.conf, srm.conf, access.conf

These are the three important configuration files for the Apache server. There are three separate configuration files for historical reasons (to support backward compatibility with NCSA *httpd*). Any configuration directive can go into any of these files. Many sites have forcibly desegregated their directives and placed all their site's configuration directives into a single large *httpd.conf* file; in fact, this is the default as of Version 1.3.4 of Apache. Other sites use separate files for each virtual host and use the *Include* directive to load them all at configuration time.

We use a slightly modified version of the lump-everything-into-*httpd.conf* approach. All the core Apache directives are kept in *httpd.conf*, including virtual hosts and per-directory configuration sections. However, we like to pull all the Apache Perl API directives into a separate file named *perl.conf* and then load it at server startup time with the following set of directives:

```
<IfModule mod_perl.c>
   Include conf/perl.conf
</IfModule>
```

---

* If you do set up the *www* pseudo-user, be sure to forbid login for this user by locking the account password. You can make the *httpd* executable and its auxiliary files owned by this user if you wish, but the server should continue to run with the permissions of the "nobody" user as recommended by the default configuration. It's also sometimes handy to create a *www* group to which the webmaster and other users authorized to work in the server root belong.

The *<IfModule>* conditional directive allows us to use the same *httpd.conf* file for servers that include the embedded Perl interpreter as well as those that do not. Notice that the argument to *<IfModule>* is the name of the module source code file, so you have to use *mod_perl.c* here, rather than *mod_perl.*

httpd.conf and its sibling configuration files all live in *~www/conf.*

.htaccess

This is the file extension for the per-directory configuration files that can be located throughout the document tree. Although the name implies a role in access control, this is just another historical artifact. These files are more frequently used as a way to change per-directory configuration options without modifying the central configuration files. Some sites change the name of the *.htaccess* file to something more meaningful (or more obscure). We use the default name in our examples and, in fact, use the term ".htaccess file" somewhat generically rather than the longer, but more accurate, "per-directory access control and options file."

cgi-bin

This is the location of the server's executable CGI scripts, usually *~www/cgi-bin.* We assume the default.

perl

This is the location of Perl scripts running under *mod_perl*'s *Apache::Registry* module (which we talk more about later in this chapter). Perl source files located in this directory are executed as if they were CGI scripts but load and run much faster because they are interpreted directly by the server. We use *~www/perl* in this book.

Module library tree

You need a convenient place to put any library files used by modules written under the Perl API and any dynamically loadable modules written with the C API (*.o* and *.so* files under Unix, *.dll* files on Win32). The standard location for C API modules is *~www/libexec* on Unix systems (*C:\Apache\libexec* on Win32 systems).

There is no standard location for Perl API modules, so we recommend creating a directory named *~www/lib/perl* for this purpose.

"Perl module" and "Apache Perl module"

Speaking of which, there is a nasty potential ambiguity in the word "module" when referring to Apache modules written using the Perl API. Perl itself makes extensive use of loadable library modules (*.pm* files) that have nothing to do with running a web server. Making things even more confusing is the fact that the Apache modules written in Perl are usually *.pm* files themselves.

We try to minimize the ambiguity by referring to "Perl module" when we mean plain old Perl modules that are not involved in the web server and

"Apache Perl module" when we mean Perl modules written to run under the Apache Perl API. In addition, all Apache Perl modules are named beginning with the word "Apache::". Here are some examples:

Type of Module	Examples
Apache module	*mod_mime, mod_rewrite*
Apache Perl module	*Apache::AuthenDBI, Apache::Traffic*
Perl module	*Text::ParseWords, IO::File*

Perl library tree

This is the location of the Perl5 library tree, which was created when you (or someone else) installed Perl on your system. It contains Perl modules, Plain Old Documentation (POD) files, loadable library objects, and header files used for compiling new Perl modules. This directory can be located in a variety of amusing and surprising places, but on most systems it can be found in */usr/lib/ perl5*, */usr/local/lib/perl5*, or *C:\perl5* (Win32).

Installing mod_perl

In order to use the Perl API, you'll need to download and install *mod_perl* if you haven't done so already. This section will describe the simplest way to do this. If you've already installed *mod_perl* you'll want to skip this section or jump directly to Appendix B, *Building and Installing mod_perl*, where we give you the low-down on *mod_perl*'s advanced installation options.

If you are a Win32 user, you can skip to the section "Win32 Installation" and download the precompiled *ApacheModulePerl.dll* loadable module. We'll show you how to activate *ApacheModulePerl.dll* at the end of the section.

The Installation Process

mod_perl is part of the CPAN archive. FTP to a CPAN site close to you and enter the directory *modules/by-module/Apache/*. Download the file *mod_perl-X.XX.tar.gz*, where *X.XX* is the highest version number you find.

It is easiest to build *mod_perl* when it is located at the same level as the Apache source tree. Change your working directory to the source directory of the server root, and unpack the *mod_perl* distribution using the *gunzip* and *tar* tools:*

```
% cd ~www/build
% gunzip -c mod_perl-X.XX.tar.gz | tar xvf -
```

---

* If you don't have *gunzip* and *tar*, you can find the freeware GNU versions of these tools at *ftp:// prep.ai.mit.edu/pub/gnu*.

```
mod_perl-X.XX/t/
mod_perl-X.XX/t/docs/
mod_perl-X.XX/t/docs/env.iphtml
mod_perl-X.XX/t/docs/content.shtml
mod_perl-X.XX/t/docs/error.txt
  ....
% cd mod_perl-X.XX
```

Now, peruse the *README* and *INSTALL* files located in the *mod_perl* directory. These files contain late-breaking news, installation notes, and other information.

The next step is to configure, build, and install *mod_perl*. Several things happen during this process. First, an installation script named *Makefile.PL* generates a top-level *Makefile* and runs Apache's *configure* script to add *mod_perl* to the list of C modules compiled into the server. After this, you run *make* to build the *mod_perl* object file and link it into a new version of the Apache server executable. The final steps of the install process are to test this new executable and, if it checks out, to move *mod_perl*'s support files and documentation into the Perl library directory.

If you have other third-party modules to add to Apache, such as PHP, you can add them during the *mod_perl* build process by providing arguments to the installation script that will be passed through to Apache's *configure*. Alternatively, you can separate the *mod_perl* build from the Apache build and run *configure* yourself.

The outline of the whole process is as follows:

```
perl Makefile.PL options          # run installation script
make                              # make httpd executable
make test                         # run tests (optional)
make install                      # install mod_perl
```

The `perl Makefile.PL` line is supplemented by a series of tag=value pairs that control a bewildering array of options. The full list of options is given in Appendix B. Most options are concerned with activating handlers for various phases of the HTTP transaction. For example, to enable the handlers for the authentication and log phases (which we explain in more detail later), you would configure *mod_perl* with this command:

```
perl Makefile.PL PERL_LOG=1 PERL_AUTHEN=1
```

You'll probably want to enable all the handlers in order to get access to the full Apache API. The easiest way to do this is by issuing this command:

```
perl Makefile.PL EVERYTHING=1 APACHE_PREFIX=/usr/local/apache
```

EVERYTHING=1 enables all the handlers and activates a variety of other neat features, including server-side includes written in Perl and support for *<Perl>* sections in the Apache configuration files. Providing an *APACHE_PREFIX* option with the location of the server root allows the install script to automatically copy the new version of the Apache server and its support files into the server root. If you don't provide this option, you can still copy the files manually after they're built. More details on these options can be found in the *mod_perl* manual pages and in Appendix B.

Other configuration options are not involved in building *mod_perl* itself, but are passed through to Apache's *configure* script to control other aspects of Apache's configuration. The most frequently used of these is *ADD_MODULE*, which accepts a comma-delimited list of additional modules to compile into Apache. Use this if there are optional modules such as the *mod_status* and *mod_proxy* that you wish to build Apache with.

When run, *Makefile.PL* will search the immediate vicinity for the Apache source tree. When it finds it, it will print the path and ask you for confirmation. If the search fails, *Makefile.PL* will prompt you to type in the path. You should type in the full path to the Apache *src* directory. Next you'll be asked whether *httpd* should be built during the *make*. You should answer "y" to this question. At this point, *Makefile.PL* will run Apache's own *configure* script and you'll see a series of messages from *configure*.

After running *configure*, *Makefile.PL* will display a list of the options that are enabled. Then it checks for the presence of the LWP and CGI.pm packages and warns you if one or both are absent or outdated. Neither package is essential to successfully install *mod_perl*, but LWP is required to run the regression tests. If you wish, you can install *mod_perl* without running the tests. If at some later date you wish to run the regression tests, just install LWP and run *Makefile.PL* again.

Here's an example configuration session:

```
% perl Makefile.PL EVERYTHING=1 APACHE_PREFIX=/usr/local/apache

ReadLine support enabled
Configure mod_perl with ../apache_1.3.3/src ? [y] y
Shall I build httpd in ../apache_1.3.3/src for you? [y] y
cp src/modules/perl/perl_PL.h ../apache_1.3.3/src/modules/perl/perl_PL.h
... many similar lines deleted ...

Will run tests as User: 'johnd' Group: 'users'
Configuring for Apache, Version 1.3.3
 + activated perl module (modules/perl/libperl.a)
Creating Makefile
Creating Configuration.apaci in src
      + id: mod_perl/1.16
      + id: Perl/5.00404 (linux) [perl]
... many similar lines deleted ...

PerlDispatchHandler.........enabled
PerlChildInitHandler........enabled
PerlChildExitHandler........enabled
PerlPostReadRequestHandler..enabled
PerlTransHandler............enabled
... many similar lines deleted ...
```

```
Writing Makefile for Apache
Writing Makefile for Apache::Connection
Writing Makefile for Apache::Constants
Writing Makefile for Apache::File
Writing Makefile for Apache::Log
Writing Makefile for Apache::ModuleConfig
Writing Makefile for Apache::Server
Writing Makefile for Apache::Symbol
Writing Makefile for Apache::Tie
Writing Makefile for Apache::URI
Writing Makefile for Apache::Util
Writing Makefile for mod_perl
```

If something goes wrong during configuration, there should be a diagnostic warning that will point to the problem (for example, "no Apache source directory found"). Correct the problem and try again. If you need to pass a long series of configuration options, you will probably find it convenient to turn the configuration command into a short shell script along these lines:

```
#!/bin/sh
# mod_perl configuration 9/28/98
perl Makefile.PL EVERYTHING=1 \
    ADD_MODULE=unique_id,status,proxy,info \
    APACHE_PREFIX=/usr/local/apache
```

This makes it easy to edit the configuration and run the command again. Plus, you'll have a record of the configuration you used the next time you upgrade Apache or *mod_perl*.

The next step is to run *make*. A new Apache server with an integrated *mod_perl* will now be built in front of your eyes. At the end of the process you'll find a brand-new *httpd* in the Apache source tree. It will look just like the old one, except significantly larger (fourfold increases in size are not uncommon). This is because the Perl interpreter has just been made part of *httpd*. It's unlikely that you'll encounter any problems during the make if you were previously successful in compiling both Apache and Perl, but if the make process does abort because of a fatal error, you'll have to do some detective work to determine where things went wrong. It helps to redirect the messages from the build process into a file for later perusal:

```
% make |& tee make.out
```

You can now run the optional tests. This step is recommended. During the tests the newly built server will be launched and a series of scripts will barrage it with requests to determine whether it produces the expected answers. Because the server listens to a nonstandard port during the tests, you can run the tests on the same machine that already hosts a web server. You do not need to be the super-user (or Administrator) in order to run the tests; however, you do need to have the LWP library installed. Otherwise, the tests will abort at an early stage.

To run the tests, run *make test* from within the *mod_perl* directory:

```
% make test
cp t/conf/mod_perl_srm.conf t/conf/srm.conf
../apache-1.3/src/httpd -f `pwd`/t/conf/httpd.conf -X -d `pwd`/t &
httpd listening on port 8529
will write error_log to: t/logs/error_log
letting apache warm up...done
/opt/perl5/bin/perl t/TEST 0
modules/actions.....ok
modules/cgi.........ok
modules/constants...ok
modules/embperl.....ok
modules/eperl.......ok
... many similar lines deleted ...

All tests successful.
Files=35,  Tests=350, 35 secs (26.13 cusr  2.56 csys = 28.69 cpu)
kill `cat t/logs/httpd.pid`
rm -f t/logs/httpd.pid
rm -f t/logs/error_log
```

Don't worry about any tests that are skipped. This just indicates that you haven't installed one of the optional *mod_perl* features. You can always install the feature and rerun the tests later. Any messages about failed tests, however, are cause for concern. If you see such a message, you should rerun the tests with the verbose flag (`make test TEST_VERBOSE=1`). You can try to track down the problem yourself, or post the results to the *mod_perl* mailing list (which we'll discuss presently).

Provided that all goes well, you can now finish the installation. You may need to have superuser or Administrator privileges in order to do this. Run *make install* to move *mod_perl*'s support files and documentation to the main Perl library directory. You will see a long series of copy commands. If you specified the *APACHE_PREFIX* option, then *make install* will also install the Apache side of things, including *httpd*, its configuration files, document, and log trees. Otherwise, change to the Apache source directory and copy the new *httpd* by hand to your server root directory. Make sure to keep a copy of the old *httpd* binary around, just in case.

Win32 Installation

For Windows users, download the ApacheModulePerl binary distribution from CPAN, in the subdirectory *authors/Jeffrey_Baker/*. The Win32 distribution file uses a very long name, following the CPAN conventions for binary distribution file names.* Make sure you download the one with the highest version number, and unpack it with your favorite ZIP file extractor.

---

* The binary distribution filename conventions can be found on the CPAN: *http://www.cpan.org/modules/05bindist.convention.html.*

Now copy the contents of the *lib* subdirectory into your Perl library tree, usually *C:\perl5\lib* (be careful to copy the contents of *lib*, not the directory itself, or you run the risk of clobbering your Perl library tree!). Next, move the file *ApacheModule-Perl.dll* to the Apache loadable modules directory, usually *C:\Apache\modules.* Open *httpd.conf* with your favorite text editor and add the following line:

```
LoadModule perl_module modules/ApacheModulePerl.dll
```

Kill and restart the server if it's already running. *mod_perl* should now be installed. Should you wish to build *mod_perl* from source code, consult the *INSTALL.win32* file located at the top of the *mod_perl* distribution directory.

The mod_perl Mailing List

If you have trouble running or installing *mod_perl*, be sure to read over the *SUPPORT* document located at the top of the *mod_perl* distribution directory. It contains tips and pointers to other tips for solutions to common problems.

If you cannot find a solution to your problem, you should post a message to the *mod_perl* mailing list requesting help. To subscribe to the mailing list, send an email message to *majordomo@apache.org* with the message "subscribe modperl" in the mail body (*not* the subject line). You will receive confirmation by return mail along with instructions for unsubscribing from the list should you ever wish to withdraw. Save this message for future reference.

You can now email your request for help to *modperl@apache.org*. Be sure to include the output of the VERBOSE regression tests, along with the following details:

- *mod_perl* version
- Perl version
- Apache version
- Operating system and version

There's also a searchable archive of the full mailing list at *http://forum.swarthmore.edu/epigone/modperl*. Before posting a question, you might want to check the archive first to see if someone else has ever had a similar problem. Also be sure to check the *mod_perl* FAQ (frequently asked questions list) at *http://perl.apache.org/faq/*.

If you are just getting started with *mod_perl* or find yourself stuck at times, consult Stas Bekman's *mod_perl* Developer's Mini Guide at *http://perl.apache.org/guide/*. The guide was designed to help you overcome possible obstacles when using *mod_perl* as a replacement for CGI. It is a collection of tips and tricks from *mod_perl* developers around the globe, which will save any developer a great deal of time and headache medicine. Many areas covered by the guide are not covered in this book, so be sure to read it! If you are only interested in receiving announcements about new versions of *mod_perl* and add-on modules, you should subscribe to the *modperl-announce* mailing list. The subscription procedure is the same, except that the mail body should read "subscribe modperl-announce."

"Hello World" with the Perl API

Now that you have *mod_perl* installed, it's time to put the Perl API through its paces.

First you'll need to create a location for your Apache Perl modules to live. If you haven't done so already, create a directory in some convenient place. We suggest creating a *lib* subdirectory within the server root, and a *perl* directory within that, making the full location *~www/lib/perl* (Unix), or *C:\Apache\lib\perl* (Win32). Within this directory, create yet another directory for modules that live in the *Apache::* namespace (which will be the vast majority of the modules we write), namely *~www/lib/perl/Apache.*

You'll now have to tell Apache where to look for these modules. *mod_perl* uses the same include path mechanism to find required modules that Perl does, and you can modify the default path either by setting the environment variable `PERL5LIB` to a colon-delimited list of directories to search before Apache starts up or by calling `use lib '/path/to/look/in'` when the interpreter is first launched. The first technique is most convenient to use in conjunction with the *PerlSetEnv* directive, which sets an environment variable. Place this directive somewhere early in your server configuration file:

```
PerlSetEnv PERL5LIB /my/lib/perl:/other/lib/perl
```

Unfortunately this adds a little overhead to each request. Instead, we recommend creating a Perl startup file that runs the *use lib* statement. You can configure *mod_perl* to invoke a startup file of common Perl commands each time the server is launched or restarted. This is the logical place to put the *use lib* statement. Here's a small startup file to get you started:

```
#!/usr/local/bin/perl

# modify the include path before we do anything else
BEGIN {
    use Apache ();
    use lib Apache->server_root_relative('lib/perl');
}

# commonly used modules
use Apache::Registry ();
use Apache::Constants();
```

```
use CGI qw(-compile :all);
use CGI::Carp ();

# put any other common modules here
# use Apache::DBI ();
# use LWP ();
# use DB_File ();
1;
```

This example startup file first modifies the include path to point to the location of the Apache Perl module directory. It uses the *Apache::server_root_relative()* method to turn the relative path into an absolute path that *use lib* will honor. It then loads up some commonly used libraries, including *Apache::Registry* (a fast CGI-like environment), *Apache::Constants* (various constants used by Apache modules), and the *CGI* and *CGI::Carp* modules.

If most of your modules are going to use these libraries, loading them once at startup time makes sense and assures the absolute fastest performance of your modules. Loading less-frequently used libraries should be deferred to the time you actually need them.

Save the startup file to some logical place. We recommend *~www/conf/startup.pl*, so that it lives alongside Apache's other configuration files. If you can you should make this file owned and only writable by root (Administrator on Win32 systems). This is because during the server startup phase the code in this file is executed as the superuser, so anyone with write permissions to this file (or the directory that contains it) effectively has superuser privileges.

We'll need to tell Apache to run the startup file at launch time. Open *perl.conf* (actually, any of the configuration files will do) and add the following lines to the bottom:

```
PerlRequire        conf/startup.pl
PerlFreshRestart   On
```

The first directive tells Apache to load and run the startup script when it is first launched. Like other file paths in Apache's configuration files, partial paths are treated as relative to the server root. The second directive tells the server to repeat this process every time it is restarted. This allows changes to the startup script (and other Apache Perl modules) to take effect without bringing the server completely down.

You should now start or restart the server. On Unix platforms, the easiest way to do this is to use the *apachectl* script located in *~www/bin*. The command *apachectl graceful* will send the server a polite USR1 signal to ask it to restart when it is finished processing all current requests, while *apachectl restart* will issue the server a more imperative HUP signal to command it to cancel all pending transaction and immediately restart. In either case, the server will be launched if it isn't already running. Users of the Win32 port can restart the server by issuing the command *apache –k restart* (Versions 1.3.3 and higher). If Apache is installed as a Windows NT service, you may also restart it using the Services control panel or by issuing the commands *NET STOP APACHE* and *NET START APACHE* from within a command window.

Watch the server *ErrorLog* during this process. If there are any errors in the configuration file or the Perl startup file, you'll see messages to that effect. Be particularly alert for messages like "Invalid Command 'PerlRequire'." This message means that you haven't actually launched a *mod_perl*-enabled version of Apache. Are you sure that you launched the new executable?

Now that everything's configured properly, you can write a module using the Apache Perl API. Example 2-1 gives a basic one named *Apache::Hello* for you to try out:

Example 2-1. A First Apache Perl Module

```
package Apache::Hello;
# File: Apache/Hello.pm

use strict;
use Apache::Constants qw(:common);

sub handler {
    my $r = shift;
    $r->content_type('text/html');
    $r->send_http_header;
    my $host = $r->get_remote_host;
    $r->print(<<END);
<HTML>
<HEAD>
<TITLE>Hello There</TITLE>
</HEAD>
<BODY>
<H1>Hello $host</H1>
Who would take this book seriously if the first example didn't
say "hello world"?
</BODY>
</HTML>
END
    return OK;
}

1;
```

We'll go into the details in later chapters, but essentially, this module contains the definition for a single subroutine named *handler()*. When the time comes, Apache will invoke *handler()* to handle the request, passing it an Apache request object stored in the variable $r. The request object is the primary interface between subroutine and server.

Using methods provided by the request object, our module first sets the MIME content type of the outgoing data to *text/html* and then sends the HTTP headers by calling *send_http_header()*. It retrieves the DNS name of the remote host by making another call to the request object and incorporates this value into a short HTML page that it sends to the browser by calling the request object's *print()* method. At the end of the subroutine, the module returns a value of OK (defined in the library module *Apache::Constants*) to signal to Apache that execution was successful.

To install this module, save it as *~www/lib/perl/Apache/Hello.pm* (*C:\Apache\lib\ perl\Apache\Hello.pm* on Win32 systems). This makes it accessible to *mod_perl*. The next step is to associate the module with a URI by mapping it to a portion of your document tree.* The simplest way to do this is by adding an Apache *<Location>* directive to *perl.conf* (or any of the other configuration files, for that matter). This entry will do the trick:

```
<Location /hello/world>
  SetHandler  perl-script
  PerlHandler Apache::Hello
</Location>
```

The first directive, *SetHandler perl-script*, tells Apache to invoke *mod_perl* to handle the phase of the HTTP transaction that produces the content of the page. The second directive, *PerlHandler Apache::Hello*, tells *mod_perl* to load the *Apache::Hello* module and execute its *handler()* subroutine. Without this directive, you would get a "File not found" error. The URI specified in *<Location>* can be any arbitrary path on your system and doesn't (and probably shouldn't) refer to a real file already in the document tree. If there already is a physical document at that location, the Perl module will supersede it.

You will have to restart the server again in order to have the new *<Location>* section take effect. Later we will discuss how to install new modules without restarting the server. Fire up your favorite browser and fetch the URI */hello/world*. You should be greeted by the page shown in Figure 2-1.

If you get a server error of some sort, don't despair. Look in the server error log for helpful messages from the Perl interpreter. They may be bare messages, or if you are loading *CGI::Carp* in the Perl startup file, they may be preceded by a timestamp and *–e* in the filename field, indicating that the error occurred within a Perl *eval()* statement. Most of what *mod_perl* does occurs within the context of an *eval()*.

---

* In the context of incoming Apache requests, we use "URI" (Uniform Resource Identifier) rather than "URL" (Uniform Resource Locator) throughout this book. URI is the more general term, so it can refer to partial documents as well as to fully qualified URLs. The main reason, however, is that URI is used in the Apache online documentation and in the names of API function calls, and who are we to buck tradition?

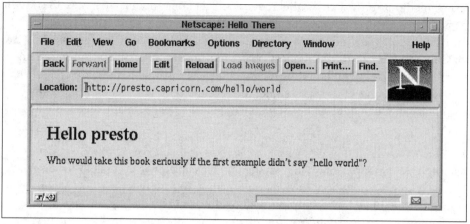

Figure 2-1. Apache::Hello results

Most commonly you'll see messages about syntax errors. Fix the errors, restart the server, and try again. If you get messages about not being able to find the *Apache::Hello* module, most likely your include path is screwed up. Check that the Perl startup script is setting the include path correctly, that *Apache/Hello.pm* is installed in the correct subdirectory, and that the permissions of *Hello.pm* and all its parent directories give the Apache server user read access. Then restart the server and try again.

These are the basic steps for creating and installing a module using the Apache Perl API. Later chapters will give you a more in-depth understanding of what's going on here and how you can take advantage of it to do wonderful stuff.

"Hello World" with the C API

In this section we will create the same "Hello World" module using the C API. This will show you how closely related the two APIs really are. Many of the details in this section are specific for Unix versions of Apache. For differences relating to working in Win32 environments, be sure to read the section "Building C Modules in the Windows Environment."

The preparation for writing C API modules is somewhat simpler than that for the Perl modules. You just need to create a subdirectory in the Apache source tree to hold your site-specific source code. We recommend creating a directory named *site* in the *modules* subdirectory. The complete path to the directory will be something like *~www/src/modules/site* (*C:\Apache\src\modules\site* on Win32 systems).

To have this new subdirectory participate in the server build process, create a file within it named *Makefile.tmpl*. For simple modules that are contained within a single source file, *Makefile.tmpl* can be completely empty. The Apache *configure* script does a pretty good job of creating a reasonable default makefile. *Makefile.tmpl* is there to provide additional file and library dependencies that Apache doesn't know about.

The next step is to create the module itself. Example 2-2 shows the source for *mod_hello*. Create a file in the *site* subdirectory named *mod_hello.c* and type in the source code (or better yet, steal it from the source code listings in *http:// www.modperl.com/book/source/*).

Example 2-2. A First C-Language Module

```c
#include "httpd.h"
#include "http_config.h"
#include "http_core.h"
#include "http_log.h"
#include "http_protocol.h"
/* file: mod_hello.c */

/* here's the content handler */
static int hello_handler(request_rec *r) {
  const char* hostname;

  r->content_type = "text/html";
  ap_send_http_header(r);
  hostname = ap_get_remote_host(r->connection,r->per_dir_config,REMOTE_NAME);

  ap_rputs("<HTML>\n"                            ,r);
  ap_rputs("<HEAD>\n"                            ,r);
  ap_rputs("<TITLE>Hello There</TITLE>\n"        ,r);
  ap_rputs("</HEAD>\n"                           ,r);
  ap_rputs("<BODY>\n"                            ,r);
  ap_rprintf(r,"<H1>Hello %s</H1>\n"             ,hostname);
  ap_rputs("Who would take this book seriously if the first example didn't\n",r);
  ap_rputs("say \"hello world\"?\n"              ,r);
  ap_rputs("</BODY>\n"                           ,r);
  ap_rputs("</HTML>\n"                           ,r);

  return OK;
}

/* Make the name of the content handler known to Apache */
static handler_rec hello_handlers[] =
{
    {"hello-handler", hello_handler},
    {NULL}
};

/* Tell Apache what phases of the transaction we handle */
module MODULE_VAR_EXPORT hello_module =
{
  STANDARD_MODULE_STUFF,
  NULL,                  /* module initializer              */
  NULL,                  /* per-directory config creator    */
```

Example 2-2. A First C-Language Module (continued)

```
    NULL,                /* dir config merger                    */
    NULL,                /* server config creator                */
    NULL,                /* server config merger                 */
    NULL,                /* command table                        */
    hello_handlers,      /* [9]  content handlers                */
    NULL,                /* [2]  URI-to-filename translation     */
    NULL,                /* [5]  check/validate user_id          */
    NULL,                /* [6]  check user_id is valid *here*   */
    NULL,                /* [4]  check access by host address    */
    NULL,                /* [7]  MIME type checker/setter        */
    NULL,                /* [8]  fixups                          */
    NULL,                /* [10] logger                          */
    NULL,                /* [3]  header parser                   */
    NULL,                /* process initialization               */
    NULL,                /* process exit/cleanup                 */
    NULL                 /* [1]  post read_request handling      */
};
```

We'll go into the sordid details on how this module works later. Essentially, all the real work is done in the content handler subroutine *hello_handler()* which accepts an Apache request record pointer as its argument and returns an integer result code. The subroutine first changes the *content_type* field of the request record to *text/html*, promising the remote browser that we will be producing an HTML document. It then calls the Apache *ap_send_http_header()* subroutine to send the HTTP header off.

The *hello_handler()* subroutine now fetches the DNS name of the remote host by calling the *ap_get_remote_host()* function. It passes various parts of the request record to the function and specifies that our preference is to retrieve the remote host's DNS using a single DNS lookup rather than a more secure (but slower) double lookup.* We now build the HTML document using a series of calls to *ap_rputs()* and *ap_rprintf()*. These subroutines act just like *puts()* and *printf()*, but their output is funneled to the browser by way of the Apache server. When the document is finished, we return a status code of OK, indicating to Apache that execution was successful.

The rest of this module consists of bookkeeping. First we create a **handler_rec** array. As discussed in more detail later, this data structure is used to associate certain document types with the handler subroutines that process them. A document type can be referred to by certain magic MIME types, such as *application/x-httpd-cgi*, but more frequently it is just a handler name for use in Apache's *AddHandler* and *SetHandler* directives. In this module, we associate the subroutine *hello_*

---

* Note that if *HostNameLookups* is configured to be *Off*, the *ap_get_remote_host()* function will return the IP address of the client. See Chapter 8, *Customizing the Apache Configuration Process*, and Chapter 9, *Perl API Reference Guide*, for more details on the *ap_get_remote_host()* function.

handler() with the handler name *hello-handler*. Although in theory a single module could declare several content handlers, in practice they usually declare only one.

After this is another data structure created using the *module* type definition. This data structure is essentially a list of the various phases of the Apache HTTP transaction (described in the next chapter), with empty slots where you can place your handlers for those phases.

In *mod_hello* we're only interested in handling the content generation part of the transaction, which happens to be the seventh slot in the structure but is the ninth phase to run. There's no rhyme or reason in order of the slots because new transaction phases were invented over time. The bracketed numbers in the slot comments indicate the order in which the handlers run, although as we explain in the next chapter, not all handlers are run for all transactions. We leave all the slots NULL except for the content handlers field, in which we place the address of the previously declared `handler_rec` array.

Now the new module needs to be configured with Apache. This can be accomplished with little effort thanks to Apache's *configure* script. The *--activate-module* argument is used to add third-party modules to the server, that is, modules not included with the Apache distribution. Its value is the path to the source or object file of the module to be included, in this case *src/modules/site/mod_hello.c*. Once activated, the *--enable-module* argument works just as it does with standard modules, in this case, linking *mod_hello* with the new server. From the top of the Apache distribution directory (which contains the *ABOUT_APACHE* file) type this command:

```
% ./configure --activate-module=src/modules/site/mod_hello.c \
         --enable-module=hello

Configuring for Apache, Version 1.3.3
 + activated hello module (modules/site/mod_hello.c)
Creating Makefile
Creating Configuration.apaci in src
Creating Makefile in src
 + configured for Linux platform
 + setting C compiler to gcc
 + adding selected modules
 + checking for system header files
 + doing sanity check on compiler and options
Creating Makefile in src/support
Creating Makefile in src/main
Creating Makefile in src/ap
Creating Makefile in src/regex
Creating Makefile in src/os/unix
Creating Makefile in src/modules/standard
```

You can now run *make* and a new *httpd* will be built. If you watch the build process carefully, you'll see *mod_hello.c* first compiled into an object file named *mod_
hello.o,* and then added to a library archive named *libsite.a. libsite.a,* in turn, is
statically linked into the *httpd* executable during the final link phase. If anything
goes wrong during compilation and linking, you'll need to go back to see what
you might have done wrong.

To test the module, you'll need to associate it with a URI. The simplest way to do
this is to use *SetHandler* to map it to a part of the document tree. Add a *<Loca-
tion>* directive to *perl.conf* (or one of the other configuration files) that looks like
this:

```
<Location /hey/there>
   SetHandler  hello-handler
</Location>
```

Stop the Apache server if it is already running, and launch the new *httpd.* Better
yet, you can keep the existing server running and just launch the new *httpd* with
the *–f* flag to specify an alternate *httpd.conf* file. Be sure to change the *Port* directive in the alternate *httpd.conf* so that it listens on an unused port. Now fire up a
browser and fetch the URI *http://your.site/hey/there.* You should get the same page
that we saw in Figure 2-1.

When you want to make changes to the *mod_hello.c* source code, just edit the file
and run *make* again. You only need to run *configure* when adding a new module
or completely removing an old one. You won't break anything if you run
configure when you don't need to, but you will cause the entire server to be
recompiled from scratch, which might take a while.

Building a Dynamically Loadable Module

It can be a pain to relink and reinstall the server executable every time you make
a change to a custom module. As of Version 1.3, Apache offers a way to build
dynamically loadable modules. You build the module as a shared object, place it
somewhere handy, add a *LoadModule* directive to *httpd.conf,* and send the server
a restart signal. After the module is loaded, it's indistinguishable from any other
module.

Dynamic loading is available on most systems, including Linux, FreeBSD, Solaris,
BSDI, AIX, and IRIX systems. To configure your server for dynamic loading,
recompile it with the *mod_so* module installed. *mod_so* is a standard Apache module, found in *src/modules/standard,* but it is not compiled in by default. From
within the Apache source tree, rerun the *configure* script, adding *mod_so* to the
list of modules you wish to enable:

```
% ./configure --enable-module=so --enable-module=other_module ...
```

Now you must run a full *make* to rebuild the *httpd*. This is only for the purpose of installing the statically linked *mod_so*. You won't need to rebuild *httpd* to add new dynamically loadable modules. You can install and launch the new *httpd* now if you wish, or wait until the dynamically loadable *hello_module* is ready to go.

You now have an *httpd* with *mod_so* installed, but you still need to build *mod_hello.so*. This can be done in one of two ways. One way is to use the *configure* script to build a new dynamically loadable module. From the top of the Apache distribution (where the *ABOUT_APACHE* file is located) run the *configure* command again, replacing the *--enable-module* option with *--enable-shared*:

```
% ./configure --activate-module=src/modules/site/mod_hello.c \
        --enable-shared=hello
```

When the *--enable-shared* argument is present, this implies that *mod_so* should be built with the server, so there's no need to use *--enable-module=so*.

Now you'll need to run *make* to create the file *src/modules/site/mod_hello.so*. When this is done, just copy the shared object file to Apache's *libexec* directory:

```
% cp src/modules/site/mod_hello.so ~www/libexec/
```

Open *httpd.conf* and add the following line:

```
LoadModule hello_module libexec/mod_hello.so
```

The *LoadModule* directive, available only when *so_module* is installed, takes two arguments. The first is the name of the module to load at runtime, and the second is the path to the shared object file to load. You can use a path relative to the server root, as shown here, or an absolute file path.

A second, and possibly easier way to build a module as a DSO is to use the *apxs* program, the "APache eXtenSion" tool. With a single command, our *mod_hello* module can be compiled, installed, and configured. The *−c* option specifies which module to compile. The *−i* option tells *apxs* to install the module and the *−a* option adds the *LoadModule* directive to your *httpd.conf* file.

```
% ~www/bin/apxs -c -i -a mod_hello.c
   gcc -DLINUX=2 -DHAS_BOOL -DUSE_HSREGEX -I/usr/local/apache/include
   -c mod_hello.c -o mod_hello.so mod_hello.o
   cp mod_hello.so /usr/local/apache/libexec/mod_hello.so
   chmod 644 /usr/local/apache/libexec/mod_hello.so
   [activating module 'hello' in /usr/local/apache/conf/httpd.conf]
```

The main advantage of *apxs* is that you do not need to store your C language module source files underneath the Apache source tree but can keep them anywhere you wish. *apxs* has numerous other options, the handiest of which are the *−g* and *−n* options, which together create a dummy "template" directory that you can use as a skeleton on which to build your own modules. The full details can be found in the *apxs* manual page, located in the *man* subdirectory under the server root.

Regardless of whether you built *mod_hello* using *configure* or *apxs*, you should now start or restart *httpd* and watch the error log for messages. Provided that *LogLevel* is set to *debug* (see Chapter 4, *Content Handlers*), you should see a message to this effect:

```
[Tue Mar 24 07:49:56 1998] [debug] mod_so.c(234): loaded module hello_module
```

You should now be able to fetch *http://your.site/hey/there*, and see the familiar page produced by this example script.

Building Large C Modules

If your C module consists of more than a single source file, or if it requires linking with shared libraries, see Appendix C, *Building Multifile C API Modules*.

Building C Modules in the Windows Environment

As of this writing, Apache does not provide any special support tools for building third-party modules in the Win32 environment. We'll show you how to build an Apache module DLL (Dynamic Link Library) using Microsoft Visual C++. The naming convention for module source files is the same in Win32 systems as it is in Unix, but the DLL library names generally replace the *mod_* prefix with *ApacheModule*. In our example, we will build an *ApacheModuleHello.dll* from our *mod_hello.c* source file. The source file doesn't have to be changed in the slightest to compile under Win32.

To ensure that this procedure works, you'll have to compile everything on a Windows NT system (Windows 95/98 doesn't work, although you can run the resulting binaries on 95/98). You may also have to build Apache and Perl from source. The binary distributions are not guaranteed to interoperate correctly with modules you build yourself.

Here is the blow-by-blow procedure:

1. Create a new project.

   Select the File → New menu to bring up the Projects window. Select "Win32 Dynamic-Link Library" and enter "ApacheModuleHello" as the project name and *C:\build\ApacheModuleHello* (or the build location of your choice) as its location. See Figure 2-2.

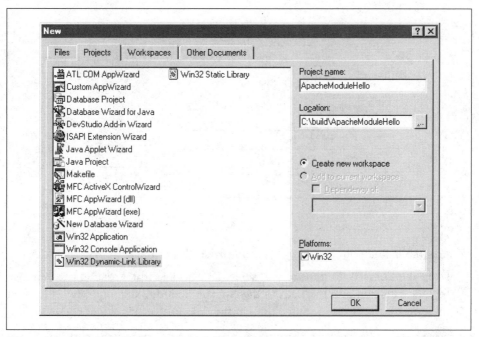

Figure 2-2. Select "Win32 Dynamic-Link Library" to create a new Apache module project.

2. Add the module source files.

   From the Project menu, select Add To Project → Files. Add *mod_hello.c* to the list (Figure 2-3).

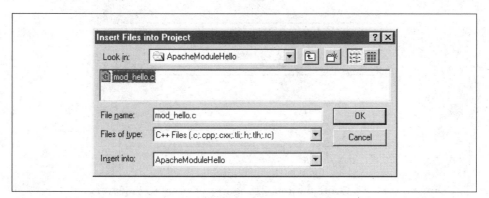

Figure 2-3. Add the module source files to the Visual C++ project.

3. Add Apache Runtime Library.

   Repeat the previous step, adding the Apache core library, *C:\Apache\ApacheCore.lib* (Figure 2-4).

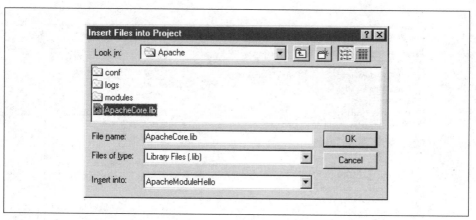

Figure 2-4. Add the Apache runtime library to the build.

4. Add the include directory for Apache header files.

   From the Tools → Options menu, select Directories. In the dialog box, choose
   Include files and add the path to the Apache include directory. This is located
   underneath the Apache source tree, in the directory *src\include* (Figure 2-5).

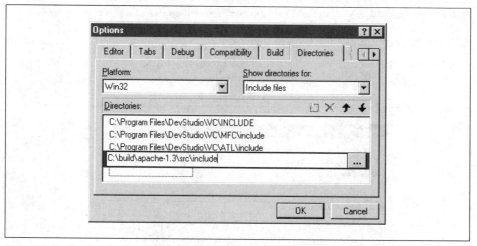

Figure 2-5. The Apache include path must be added to the project directories.

5. Change the Active Configuration setting from Debug to Release.

   From the Build → Set Active Configuration menu, select Win32 Release. This
   will enable optimizations and turn off debugging code (Figure 2-6).

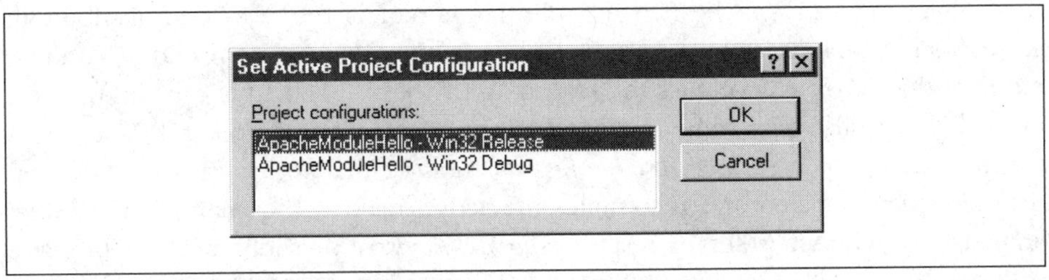

Figure 2-6. Set the Active Configuration.

6. Compile.

From the Build menu, select Build ApacheModuleHello.dll. The compiler will fire up and, if all goes well, create the DLL library. If you get any error messages during this process, go back and fix the problems.

7. Install the DLL.

Copy *ApacheModuleHello/Release/ApacheModuleHello.dll* to the *C:\Apache\ modules* directory.

8. Configure *httpd.*

Add the following lines to *httpd.conf*:

```
LoadModule hello_module modules/ApacheModuleHello.dll
<Location /hi/there>
    SetHandler hello-handler
</Location>
```

Fire up your favorite browser and request the URI *http://your.site/hi/there.* With luck, *ApacheModuleHello* will run and you'll see the page from Figure 2-1.

Instant Modules with Apache::Registry

By now, although it may not be obvious, you've seen two of the problems with using the Apache APIs. The first problem is that you can't make changes to modules casually. When using the Perl API, you have to restart the server in order to have your changes take effect. With the C API, you have to rebuild the module library or completely relink the server executable. Depending on the context, this can be a minor annoyance (when you're developing a module on a test server that gets light usage) to a bit of a headache (when you're trying to apply bug fixes to an installed module on a heavily used production server).

The second problem is that Apache API modules don't look anything like CGI scripts. If you've got a lot of CGI scripts that you want to run faster, porting them to the Apache API can be a major undertaking.

Apache::Registry, an Apache Perl module that is part of the *mod_perl* distribution, solves both problems with one stroke. When it runs, it creates a pseudo-CGI environment that so exactly mimics the real thing that Perl CGI scripts can run under it unmodified. It also maintains a cache of the scripts under its control. When you make a change to a script, *Apache::Registry* notices that the script's modification date has been updated and recompiles the script, making the changes take effect immediately without a server restart. *Apache::Registry* provides a clean upgrade path for existing CGI scripts. Running CGI scripts under *Apache::Registry* gives them an immediate satisfying performance boost without having to make any source code changes. Later you can modify the script at your own pace to take advantage of the nifty features offered only by the Apache API.

Be aware that *Apache::Registry* is intended only for Perl CGI scripts. CGI scripts written in other languages cannot benefit from the speedup of having a Perl interpreter embedded in the server.

To install *Apache::Registry* you'll need to create a directory to hold the scripts that it manages. We recommend a *perl* directory within the server root, such as *~www/perl*. Now enter the following directives into *perl.conf*:

```
Alias /perl/ /usr/local/apache/perl/
<Location /perl>
    SetHandler      perl-script
    PerlHandler     Apache::Registry
    PerlSendHeader  On
    Options         +ExecCGI
</Location>
```

The *Alias* directive makes URIs beginning with */perl* part of the virtual document tree and associates it with the physical path */usr/local/apache/perl*. Change this as appropriate for your site. The meaning of the various directives inside *<Location>* are explained fully in Chapter 4.

Restart the server, and give *Apache::Registry* a try by creating the script shown in Example 2-3. Name it *hello.pl*, make it executable, and move it into *~www/perl/*. With your browser, fetch *http://your.site/perl/hello.pl*. You should see the familiar page that we first saw in Figure 2-1.

Example 2-3. "Hello World" Using Apache::Registry

```
#!/usr/local/bin/perl
# file: hello.pl

print "Content-Type: text/html\n\n";

print <<END;
<HTML>
<HEAD>
<TITLE>Hello There</TITLE>
```

Example 2-3. "Hello World" Using Apache::Registry (continued)

```
</HEAD>
<BODY>
<H1>Hello $ENV{REMOTE_HOST}</H1>
Who would take this book seriously if the first example didn't
say "hello world"?
</BODY>
</HTML>
END
```

As you can see, *hello.pl* looks identical to a normal CGI script, even down to the use of $ENV{REMOTE_HOST} to fetch the CGI environment variable that contains the name of the remote host. If you make changes to this script, they will take effect immediately without requiring a server restart. Plus, if you press the browser's reload button a few times in quick succession, you may notice that it reloads much faster than a normal Perl CGI script would. That's because the script's compiled code remains in memory between fetches. There's none of the usual overhead for loading and running the Perl interpreter.

If you are used to using the CGI.pm module, you'll be heartened to learn that under *Apache::Registry* you can create and process fill-out forms in exactly the way you would in standard CGI scripts. Example 2-4 shows the code for *hello_there.pl*, another simple-minded example which creates and processes a short fill-out form.

Example 2-4. Processing a Fill-Out Form with Apache::Registry and CGI.pm

```
#!/usr/local/bin/perl

use CGI qw(:standard);
use strict;

my $name = param('name') || 'Anonymous';

print header(),
      start_html(-title=>'Yo!',-bgcolor=>'white'),
      h1("Hello $name"),
      p(
        "To change your name, enter it into the text field below and press",
        em("change name.")
      ),

      start_form(),
      "Name: ",textfield(-name=>'name',-value=>'Anonymous'),
       submit(-value=>'Change Name'),
       end_form(),

      hr(),
      end_html();
```

The script begins by importing CGI.pm's standard group of function definitions.* It then fetches a CGI parameter named *name* and stores it in a local variable, calling CGI.pm's *param()* function to do the dirty work of parsing the CGI query string. The script now calls *CGI::header()* to produce the HTTP header, and builds up an HTML document in one long *print* statement that makes calls to several other CGI functions. Among these calls are ones to produce the fill-out form, a text field, and a submit button.

Figure 2-7 shows a sample page produced by this script.

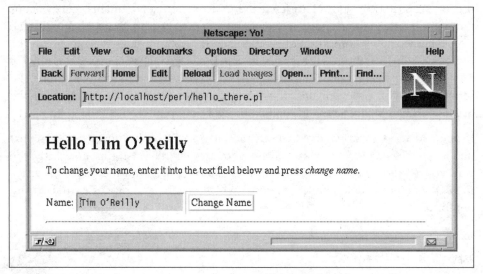

Figure 2-7. The Apache::Registry script generates a fill-out form to accept and process user input.

You'll find that most other CGI scripts will work just fine under *Apache::Registry*. Those that don't are ones that assume that the process will go away after their code exits and don't bother to do any cleanup as a result. For example, scripts that use global variables without initializing them first will be unpleasantly surprised when the global contains leftover data from a previous invocation of the script's code. Scripts that use the process ID to create unique filenames are also in for a shock when they're run again with the same PID.

---

* Although it's handy to import function definitions in this way, there's a significant memory overhead for every symbol you import. If you have a lot of scripts that import from CGI.pm, your *httpd* processes will eventually become too large. You can avoid this by precompiling and importing CGI.pm's function calls from within the Perl startup script by using the command use CGI qw(-compile :all). Alternatively, you can use CGI.pm's object-oriented calling syntax, which does not carry the symbol importation overhead.

The best way to avoid such problems is by writing clean code. Avoid using global variables and always use *use strict* to check for inadvertent typos. While *use strict* may be painful at first, it will save you more time in the long run, along with giving you a warm fuzzy feeling that you are practicing good code hygiene. Be sure to clean up data structures such as open filehandles and database handles before your code exits. The *Apache::register_cleanup()* method is a handy way to arrange to have a cleanup subroutine called before control returns to the server.

In the short term, another approach is to run legacy scripts with *Apache::PerlRun*. Unlike *Apache::Registry*, this module simply runs the script once and forgets about it, just like a conventional CGI script. *Apache::PerlRun* avoids the overhead of launching the Perl interpreter for each request but still suffers the compile-time hit from loading each script. Therefore, it realizes some but not all of the performance increase of *Apache::Registry*.

More information on *Apache::Registry* and *Apache::PerlRun* scripts can be found in Chapters 3 and 4. We discuss *register_cleanup()* and other tricks in Chapter 7.

Troubleshooting Modules

Not every module will work the way you think it will the first time you try it. Because the modules written with the Apache API are by definition embedded in the server, debugging them is not as straightforward as debugging a standalone CGI script. In this section, we cover some general module debugging techniques. You'll find more tips later when we discuss specific issues.

C-Level Debugging

If you are using the C API, you can use standard debuggers to step through your module, examine and change data structures, set watch points, and so forth. Be sure to use a version of *httpd* that has been compiled with debugging symbols and to turn compiler optimizations off. On Unix systems, you can do this by setting the CFLAGS environment variable before running the *configure* script:

```
% CFLAGS=-g ./configure ...
```

Launch your favorite debugger, such as *gdb*, and run *httpd* within it. Be sure to launch *httpd* with the −*X* flag. Ordinarily, Unix versions of *httpd* will prefork many independent processes. This forking will confuse the debugger and will probably confuse you too. −*X* prevents Apache from preforking and keeps the server in the foreground as well. You will also probably want to specify an alternate configuration file with the −*f* switch so that you can use a high numbered port instead of the default port 80.* Be sure to specify different *ErrorLog*, *TransferLog*, *PidFile*, and

ScoreBoardFile directives in the alternate configuration file to avoid conflicts with the live server.

```
% gdb httpd
(gdb) run -X -f ~www/conf/httpd.conf
```

Fetch a few pages from the server to make sure that it is running correctly under the debugger. If there is a problem that triggers a core dump, the (gdb) prompt will return and tell you which function caused the crash. Now that you have an idea of where the problem is coming from, a breakpoint can be set to step through and see exactly what is wrong. If we were debugging *mod_hello* within the *gdb* debugger, the command to use would be this:

```
% gdb httpd
(gdb) b hello_handler
Breakpoint 1 at 0x809cefb: file mod_hello.c, line 82.
(gdb) run -X -f ~www/conf/httpd.conf
```

Now use a browser to fetch a page that will trigger the execution of the break-pointed handler. Control will return to the debugger, allowing you to step through code looking for the problem.

It is also possible to debug *httpd* without running it in −*X* mode. Simply start the server as you normally would, then use the *ps* command to see the process IDs of the servers. Select a PID and start *gdb* with the process ID as an additional argument. The debugger will attach to the process and list all the files it is reading symbols from. It will eventually stop, providing you with a prompt and a chance to set your breakpoints. Be sure to type in the *c* continue command so the child will be able to serve requests again. This approach makes it easy to set breakpoints in dynamically loaded modules, which are not pulled in until the parent server has started. There is a catch though: you might have to request the page you wish to debug a number of times before Apache hands off a request to the process you are attached to. To cut down on the number of servers you must cycle through, simply tune the server's configuration to start only a small number of servers.*

```
% gdb httpd process id number
...
Reading symbols from /usr/local/apache/lib/mod_hello.so...done.
0x400d7a81 in flock ()
(gdb) b hello_handler
Breakpoint 1 at 0x40176c77: file mod_hello.c, line 82.
(gdb) c
Continuing.
```

---

* There are several directives related to managing the number of servers on the farm; these include *Start-Servers, MaxSpareServers, MinSpareServers*, and *MaxClients*.

Perl-Level Debugging

Ironically, debugging misbehaving Apache Perl modules is not as straightforward as debugging C modules. This is because the current version of the Perl source-level debugger can't work when the Perl interpreter is embedded in another program. As of this writing, there is a pre-alpha version of a *mod_perl*-compatible Perl debugger in the works; it could very well be available from the CPAN by the time you read this.

If you are using the *Apache::Registry* CGI emulation layer, then one way to debug your module is to run and debug it as a standalone CGI script. Further, if you use the CGI.pm module in your scripts, you can take advantage of its ability to run CGI scripts from the command line and to seed the script with test parameters. You can then walk through the script with the Perl debugger (`perl -d` *your_script.pl*), examine variables, and execute snippets of Perl code to home in on what your program is doing wrong.

Using Apache::FakeRequest for debugging

If you are using the full *mod_perl* API, or if the bug appears when running under Apache but not when running as a standalone script, then you may be able to track down the problem using *Apache::FakeRequest*, a tiny module that comes with the *mod_perl* distribution. *Apache::FakeRequest* sets up an empty Apache request object that your module can use in lieu of a real request object. *Apache::FakeRequest* methods don't do very much: all they do is get and set internal variables of the same name as the method. However, you can customize the fake request's methods to return test data to your script.

Example 2-5 shows how *Apache::FakeRequest* can be used to debug the *Apache::Hello* module. This example shows the code for a small wrapper script that invokes *Apache::Hello*'s content handler, much as Apache invokes *Apache::Hello::handler()* when a page request comes in. We begin by loading both *Apache::FakeRequest* and *Apache::Hello* (after adjusting the library path so that Perl can find the latter module).

Next, we create a new fake request object. *Apache::FakeRequest::new()* can be called with a series of name=value pairs. Each name corresponds to a method that a real Apache request object would respond to. When your module calls the method without any arguments, *Apache::FakeRequest* just returns the value that you specified. Your module can also call the phony method with an argument, in which case its value will be replaced. Methods that aren't mentioned in *new()* will return *undef*. In our case, we only care about feeding *get_remote_host* to *Apache::Hello*, so we set that method to return *foobar.com*.

Now it's simply a matter of calling our module's handler with the fake request object. If you're using the Perl debugger, you can step into the module's code and watch what it does.

Should you want to customize *Apache::FakeRequest*'s behavior, you can always subclass it and override one or more of its methods.

Example 2-5. This Apache::FakeRequest Wrapper Can Be Used to Debug Apache::Hello

```
#!/usr/local/bin/perl

use lib '/usr/local/apache/lib/perl';
use Apache::FakeRequest ();
use Apache::Hello ();

my $request = Apache::FakeRequest->new('get_remote_host'=>'foobar.com');
Apache::Hello::handler($request);
```

Using Apache::Debug

Another useful debugging tool for Apache Perl modules is *Apache::Debug*. This debugging facility is only available when you use *Apache::Registry*. It's not of use to modules written to use the Apache Perl API directly.

Apache::Debug defines a single subroutine named *dump()*. When *dump()* is called it sends copious debugging information to the remote browser. Hopefully some of the information will help you figure out what's going on.

It's very simple to use *Apache::Debug*. Just add the command `use Apache::Debug()` to the top of your module. Then, when you encounter an unexpected error and want to print out current status information, add a line like the following:

```
Apache::Debug::dump($r, SERVER_ERROR, "Can't find configuration file!");
```

The three arguments to *dump()* are the request object, an error code to return to Apache (usually SERVER_ERROR), and an error message to print at the top of the debugging output.

Apache::Debug also allows you to activate some debugging messages generated by *Apache::Registry*. This can sometimes help you track down obscure problems that relate to the way that *mod_perl* loads and executes your code. To increase the debugging level, add `use Apache::Debug('level' => $level)` to the top of your module, where `$level` is a bit mask generated by ORing together some combination of the following values:

1   Makes a note in the error log whenever your module is recompiled

2   Calls *Apache::Debug::dump()* whenever your module dies or an *eval* fails

4   Turns on verbose tracing

Environment variables for debugging

A pair of environment variables control various aspects of the embedded Perl interpreter's execution and can be used to help debug particularly obstinate problems.

MOD_PERL_TRACE

> When *mod_perl* is built with the *PERL_TRACE* option, a special environment variable, MOD_PERL_TRACE, can be used to enable debugging information. This variable should be set before the server is started and should contain one or more of the letters described below for tracing the various *mod_perl* features. The trace information will be written to the server *ErrorLog*. For example:

```
% setenv MOD_PERL_TRACE dh
% ~www/bin/httpd -X
```

> The first line sets MOD_PERL_TRACE to record trace information during *mod_perl* directive handling (d) and while executing handlers (h). The second line launches Apache in single process mode.

> Here's the complete list of trace options:

> c   Enables tracing during configuration directive handling

> d   Enables tracing during *mod_perl* directive processing during configuration read

> s   Enables tracing during processing of *<Perl>* sections

> h   Enables tracing of Perl handlers during the processing of incoming requests

> g   Enables tracing of global variable handling, such as Perl interpreter construction and execution of *END* blocks

> all   Enables all of the options listed above

PERL_DESTRUCT_LEVEL

> With Apache Versions 1.3 and higher, *mod_perl* will call the *perl_destruct()* Perl API function during the child exit phase. This will cause proper execution of *END* blocks found during server startup, along with invoking the *DESTROY* method on global objects that are still alive. It is possible that this operation may take a long time to finish, causing problems during a restart. The symptom of this is a series of messages that appear in the server log warning that certain child processes did not exit as expected.

> If you are experiencing this problem and your code does not contain any *END* blocks or *DESTROY* methods that need to be run during child server shutdown, you can avoid this problem by setting the PERL_DESTRUCT_LEVEL environment variable to -1:

```
PerlSetEnv PERL_DESTRUCT_LEVEL -1
```

Common Apache Perl module problems

Certain types of problems are common in Apache Perl modules. One common pattern is that the code will seem to fail at random. The first time you fetch a page generated by an Apache Perl module, it will work fine. The second time you fetch it, it won't. If you reload repeatedly, it will sometimes work and sometimes fail, seemingly haphazardly. This pattern is usually due to Apache's preforking behavior. Multiple instances of your module are running, each one in a separate process. In one or more of the processes, the module has crashed because some unexpected sequence of inputs has led it to corrupt a data structure (or something similar). In other processes, the module is still functioning (so far). You'll never be able to figure out what's going on under these circumstances. Kill *httpd* and relaunch it with the *–X* flag. With only one process running, you can more easily figure out what inputs cause the module to misbehave.

Many Apache Perl module bugs are due to a wanton use of global variables. The very first time the module is called, globals are initialized to their undefined states in the way that conventional Perl scripts expect. However, in subsequent calls the globals will contain information left over from previous invocations of the script. This will cause scripts that depend on globals being initially undefined to fail. Suspect this problem if your pages exhibit a pattern of progressive decay in which they seem to work at first and then fail with increasing frequency.

Also be aware that certain actions that are second nature to Perl programmers, such as calling *die()* or *exit()* to abort a script prematurely, may not have quite the result you expect in the context of an Apache Perl module. Under some circumstances a call to *exit()* within a module has been known to make the server misbehave in strange ways. Use *Apache::exit()* instead. *die()* should be reserved for truly unrecoverable errors. *die()* generally causes the browser to display an "Internal Error" message. It's better to replace *die()* with a procedure that displays a helpful error message in the browser window and returns control to Apache. Several techniques for doing this appear in the examples in subsequent chapters.

The next chapter takes you on a tour through the innards of the Apache module API. You'll learn everything you ever wanted to know about request records, connection records, and transaction handlers.

3

The Apache Module Architecture and API

In this chapter we lay out the design of the Apache module architecture and its application programming interface. We describe the phases in which Apache processes each request, list the data types that are available for your use, and go over the directives that control how extension modules can intercede in transaction processing.

This is the broad overview of the API. For a full blow-by-blow description of each function and data structure available to you, see Chapter 9, *Perl API Reference Guide*, and Chapters 10 and 11, *C API Reference Guide, Part I* and *Part II*.

How Apache Works

Much of the Apache API is driven by the simple fact that Apache is a hypertext transfer protocol (HTTP) server that runs in the background as a daemon. Because it is a daemon, it must do all the things that background applications do, namely, read its configuration files, go into the background, shut down when told to, and restart in the case of a configuration change. Because it is an HTTP server, it must be able to listen for incoming TCP/IP connections from web browsers, recognize requests for URIs, parse the URIs and translate them into the names of files or scripts, and return some response to the waiting browser (Figure 3-1). Extension modules play an active role in all these aspects of the Apache server's life.

Like most other servers, Apache multiplexes its operations so that it can start processing a new request before it has finished working on the previous one. On Unix systems, Apache uses a multiprocess model in which it launches a flock of servers: a single parent server is responsible for supervision and one or more children

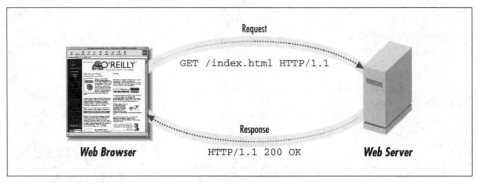

Figure 3-1. The HTTP transaction consists of a URI request from the browser to the server, followed by a document response from the server to the browser.

are actually responsible for serving incoming requests.* The Apache server takes care of the basic process management, but some extension modules need to maintain process-specific data for the lifetime of a process as well. They can do so cleanly and simply via hooks that are called whenever a child is launched or terminated. (The Win32 version of Apache uses multithreading rather than a multi-process model, but as of this writing modules are not given a chance to take action when a new thread is created or destroyed.)

However, what extension modules primarily do is to intercede in the HTTP protocol in order to customize how Apache processes and responds to incoming browser requests. For this reason, we turn now to a quick look at HTTP itself.

The HTTP Protocol

The HTTP protocol was designed to be so simple that anyone with basic programming skills could write an HTTP client or server. In fact, hundreds of people have tried their hands at this, in languages ranging from C to Perl to Lisp. In the basic protocol a browser that wants to fetch a particular document from a server connects to the server via a TCP connection on the port indicated by the URI, usually port 80. The browser then sends the server a series of request lines terminated by a carriage-return/linefeed pair.† At the end of the request, there is an extra blank line to tell the server that the request is finished. The simplest request looks something like this:

```
GET /very/important/document.html HTTP/1.1
Host: www.modperl.com
```

---

* As of this writing, plans are underway for Apache Version 2.0 which will include multithreading support on Unix platforms.

† For various historical and political reasons, different operating systems have differing ideas of what character constitutes the end of a line in text files. The HTTP protocol defines the end of a line to be the character pair represented by ASCII characters 0x0D (carriage return) and 0x0A (newline). In most ASCII environments, these characters are represented by the more familiar "\r" and "\n" escape sequences.

The first line of the request contains three components. The first component is the request method, normally GET, POST, HEAD, PUT, or DELETE. GET is a request to fetch the contents of a document and is the most common. POST is a request which includes a body of data after the headers, normally handled by a dynamic module or an executable of some sort to process the data. It's commonly used to send CGI scripts the contents of fill-out forms. HEAD tells the server to return information about the document but not the document itself. PUT and DELETE are infrequently used: PUT is used to send a new document to the server, creating a new document at the given URI or replacing what was previously there, and DELETE causes the indicated document to be removed. For obvious reasons, PUT and DELETE methods are disabled by default on most servers.

The second component of the request is the URI of the document to be retrieved. It consists of a Unix-style path delimited by slashes. The server often translates the path into an actual file located somewhere on the server's filesystem, but it doesn't have to. In this book, we'll show examples of treating the path as a database query, as a placeholder in a virtual document tree, and other interesting applications.

The third component in the request line is the protocol in use, which in this case is Version 1.1 of the HTTP protocol. HTTP/1.1 is a big improvement over the earlier HTTP/1.0 version because of its support for virtual hosts and its fine-grained control of document caching. However, at the time this book was written most browsers actually implemented a version of HTTP/1.0 with some HTTP/1.1 features grafted on.

Following the first line are a series of HTTP header fields that the browser can send to the server in order to fine-tune the request. Each field consists of a field name, a colon, and then the value of the field, much like an email header. In the HTTP/1.1 protocol, there is only one mandatory header field, a *Host* field indicating which host the request is directed to. The value of this field allows a single server to implement multiple virtual hosts, each with a separate home page and document tree.

Other request header fields are optional. Here's a request sent by a recent version of Netscape Navigator:

```
GET /news.html HTTP/1.1
Connection: Keep-Alive
User-Agent: Mozilla/4.05 [en] (X11; I; Linux 2.0.33 i686)
Host: www.modperl.com
Referer: http://www.modperl.com/index.html
If-Modified-Since: Tue, 24 Feb 1998 11:19:03 GMT
Accept: image/gif, image/x-xbitmap, image/jpeg, image/pjpeg, image/png, */*
Accept-Language: en
Accept-Charset: iso-8859-1,*,utf-8
```

This example shows almost all of the HTTP header fields that you'll ever need to know. The *Connection* field is a suggestion to the server that it should keep the TCP/IP connection open after finishing this request. This is an optimization that improves performance on pages that contain multiple inline images. The *User-Agent* field gives the make and model of the browser. It indicates Netscape Navigator Version 4.05 ("Mozilla" is the code name for Netscape's browsers) running on a Linux system. *Host* is the name of the host given in the URI and is used by the virtual host system to select the right document tree and configuration file. *Referer* (yes, the protocol misspells it) gives the URI of the document that referred the browser to the current document. It's either an HTML file that links to the current page or, if the current document is an image file, the document that contains the image. In this case, the referrer field indicates that the user was viewing file *index.html* on the *www.modperl.com* site before selecting a link to the current document, *news.html*.

If-Modified-Since is another important performance optimization. Many browsers cache retrieved documents locally so that they don't have to go across the network whenever the user revisits a page. However, documents change and a cached document might be out of date. For this reason, some browsers implement a conditional fetch using *If-Modified-Since*. This field indicates the date at which the document was cached. The server is supposed to compare the date to the document's current modification time and only return it to the browser if the document has changed.*

Other fields in a typical request are *Accept, Accept-Language,* and *Accept-Charset.* *Accept* is a list of Multipurpose Internet Mime Extension (MIME) types that the browser will accept. In theory, the information in this field is supposed to be used for content negotiation. The browser tells the server what MIME types it can handle, and the server returns the document in the format that the browser most prefers. In practice, this field has atrophied. In the example above, Netscape sends an anemic list of the image types it can display without the help of plug-ins, followed by a catchall wildcard type of */*.

Accept-Language indicates the language the user prefers, in this case "en" for English. When a document is available in multiple languages, Apache can use the information in this field to return the document in the appropriate language. Lastly, *Accept-Charset* indicates which character sets the browser can display. The iso-8859-1 character set, often known as "Latin-1," contains the characters used in English and most Western European countries. "utf-8" stands for 8-bit Unicode, an

---

* We actually cheated a bit in the preceding example. The version of Netscape that we used for the example generates a version of the *If-Modified-Since* header that is not compliant with the current HTTP specification (among other things, it uses a two-digit year that isn't Y2K-compliant). We edited the field to show the correct HTTP format.

expanded alphabet that accommodates most Western and Asian character sets. In this example, there's also a wildcard that tells the server to send the document even if it isn't written in a character set that the browser knows about specifically.

If the request had been a POST or PUT rather than a GET, there would be one or two additional fields at the bottom of the header. The *Content-Length* field, if present, indicates that the browser will be sending some document data following the header. The value of this field indicates how many bytes of data to expect. The *Content-Type* field, if present, gives the MIME type of the data. The standard MIME type for the contents of fill-out form fields is *application/x-www-form-urlencoded.*

The browser doesn't have to send any of these fields. Just the request line and the *Host* field are sufficient, as you can see for yourself using the *telnet* application:

```
% telnet www.modperl.com 80
Trying 207.198.250.44...
Connected to modperl.com.
Escape character is '^]'.
GET /news.html HTTP/1.1
Host: www.modperl.com

HTTP/1.1 200 OK
Date: Tue, 24 Feb 1998 13:16:02 GMT
Server: Apache/1.3.0 (Unix) mod_perl/1.13
Last-Modified: Wed, 11 Feb 1998 21:05:25 GMT
ETag: "65e5a-37c-35a7d395"
Accept-Ranges: bytes
Content-Length: 892
Connection: close
Content-Type: text/html

<HTML>
<HEAD>
<TITLE>What's New</TITLE>
</HEAD>
<BODY>
  ...
Connection closed by foreign host.
```

The Apache server will handle the request in the manner described later and, if all goes well, return the desired document to the client. The HTTP response is similar to the request. It contains a status line at the top, followed by some optional HTTP header fields, followed by the document itself. The header is separated from the document by a blank line.

The top line of the response starts with the HTTP version number, which in this case is 1.1. This is followed by a numeric status code, and a human-readable status message. As the "OK" message indicates, a response code of 200 means that the request was processed successfully and that the document follows. Other status codes indicate a problem on the user's end, such as the need to authenticate; problems on the server's end, such as a CGI script that has crashed; or a condition that is not an error, such as a notice that the original document has moved to a new location. The list of common status codes can be found later in this chapter.

After the response status line come optional HTTP header fields. *Date* indicates the current time and date and *Server* gives the model and version number of the server. Following this is information about the document itself. *Last-Modified* and *Content-Length* give the document's modification date and total length for use in client-side caching. *Content-Type* gives the document's MIME type, *text/html* in this case.

ETag, or "entity tag" is an HTTP/1.1–specific field that makes document caching more accurate. It identifies the document version uniquely and changes when the document changes. Apache implements this behavior using a combination of the file's last modified time, length, and inode number. *Accept-Ranges* is another HTTP/1.1 extension. It tells the browser that it is all right to request portions of this document. This could be used to retrieve the remainder of a document if the user hit the stop button partway through a long download and then tried to reload the page.

The *Connection* field is set to *close* as a polite way of warning the browser that the TCP connection is about to be shut down. It's an optional field provided for HTTP/1.1 compliance.

There are also a number of HTTP fields that are commonly used for user authentication and authorization. We'll introduce them in Chapter 6, *Authentication and Authorization*.

Following the header comes the document itself, partially shown in the example. The document's length must match the length given in *Content-Length*, and its format must match the MIME type given in the *Content-Type* field.

When you write your own Apache modules, you don't have to worry about all these fields unless you need to customize them. Apache will fill in the fields with reasonable values. Generally you will only need to adjust *Content-Type* to suit the type of document your module creates.

The Apache Life Cycle

Apache's life cycle is straightforward (Figure 3-2). It starts up, initializes, forks off several copies of itself (on Unix systems only), and then enters a loop in which it processes incoming requests. When it is done, Apache exits the loop and shuts itself down. Most of the interesting stuff happens within the request loop, but both

Perl and C-language modules can intervene at other stages as well. They do so by registering short code routines called "handlers" that Apache calls at the appropriate moment.* A phase may have several handlers registered for it, a single handler, or none at all. If multiple modules have registered their interest in handling the same phase, Apache will call them in the reverse order in which they registered. This in turn will depend on the order in which the modules were loaded, either at compile time or at runtime when Apache processes its *LoadModule* directives. If no module handlers are registered for a phase, it will be handled by a default routine in the Apache core.

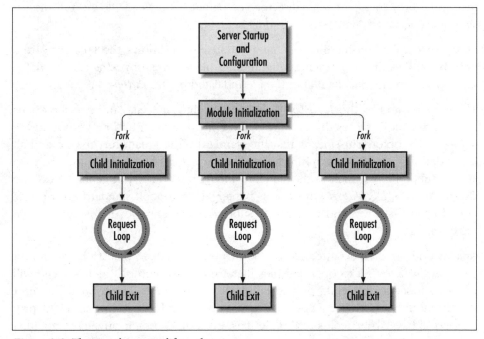

Figure 3-2. The Apache server life cycle

Server Startup and Configuration

When the server is started, Apache initializes globals and other internal resources and parses out its command-line arguments. It then locates and parses its various configuration files.

The configuration files may contain directives that are implemented by external modules. Apache parses each directive according to a prototype found in the

---

* The Apache documentation sometimes refers to handlers as "hooks" or "callbacks," but don't worry, they're all the same thing.

command table that is part of each module and passes the parsed information to the module's configuration-handling routines. Apache processes the configuration directives on a first-come, first-serve basis, so in certain cases, the order in which directives appear is important. For example, before Apache can process a directive that is implemented by a module configured as a dynamically shared object, that module must be pulled in with the *LoadModule* directive.

The process of module configuration is actually somewhat complex because Apache recognizes multiple levels of configuration directives, including global directives, directives that are specific for a particular virtual host, and directives that apply only to a particular directory or partial URI. We defer the full discussion of this topic to Chapters 9, 10, and 11.

Once Apache has processed the configuration files, it knows the location of the various log files. It opens each configured log file, such as *ErrorLog* and *Transfer-Log*. Apache then writes its PID to the file indicated by the *PidFile* directive.

The file indicated by the *ErrorLog* directive is slightly special. After Apache opens the *ErrorLog* file, it closes the existing `stderr` file descriptor and reopens it on the *ErrorLog* descriptor. This means that the standard error stream for Apache and all its loaded modules will be redirected to the error log file. Modules that need to launch subprocesses, such as the standard *mod_cgi* module, will generally call the C API *ap_error_log2stderr()* function (Chapter 11) to rehook standard error to the error log so that the standard error of subprocesses continues to be captured in the error log.

Apache will usually be started as root (on Unix systems), so that it can open port 80. This also allows it to open log files that are owned by root. Later, Apache will normally fork multiple child processes which will run under an unprivileged user ID. By virtue of having a copy of the still-open log file descriptors, child processes will have write access to the log files, even though their privileges wouldn't ordinarily give them this right.

Module Initialization

Next, Apache initializes its modules. Each module has an initialization routine that is passed information about the server in a data structure called a `server_rec`. The `server_rec` contains such information as the configured *ServerName*, the *Port* the server is listening for requests on, and the email address of the *ServerAdmin*. C-language modules are also handed a pointer to a "resource pool" that can be used for memory management. The module initialization routine will do whatever module-specific initialization needs to be done. If something goes wrong, it can log an error message and *exit()* the process to abort Apache's startup entirely.

Perl module authors can step in at the module initialization phase by using the *PerlRequire* and *PerlModule* directives.* These directives both cause a Perl script to be evaluated at *mod_perl* initialization time and are described in more detail later. Note that the server is still running as root during this phase, so any code that gets executed at this point will have superuser powers. This is a good reason to ensure that any scripts called during this period are owned and writable by root only.

When the server is restarted, the configuration and module initialization phases are called again. To ensure that such restarts will be uneventful, Apache actually runs these two phases twice during server startup just to check that all modules can survive a restart.

Child Initialization

On Unix systems Apache now forks itself one or more times to create a set of child processes that will do the actual work of accepting incoming requests. Before accepting any connections, the child processes immediately set their user and group IDs to those of an unprivileged user (such as "nobody" or "guest"). The original parent process (still running as root) hangs around to monitor the status of its children and to launch new ones should the number of child processes drop below a specified level.

Just before each child enters its request loop, each module is given another chance at initialization. Although this would seem redundant with the module initialization phase, it's necessary because some data structures, such as database handles, are not stable across forks. Modules that need to (re)initialize themselves get another chance every time a new child process is created. You might also want to use this phase to perform some action that should be done as an unprivileged user. In the C API, the module's *child_init()* function is called. In the Perl API, you can install a handler for this phase using the *PerlChildInitHandler* directive.

Chapter 7, *Other Request Phases*, discusses the use of child init handlers in more detail.

Child Exit

We'll skip forward now to the child exit phase, leaving the request loop for detailed consideration in the next section. After processing some number of requests, each child process will eventually exit, dying either a natural death when it reaches the limit set by *MaxRequestsPerChild* or because the server as a whole

---

* Older versions of the *mod_perl* package had a *PerlScript* directive, which was later renamed to *PerlRequire*. The *PerlScript* directive has been deprecated, but you might still see references to it in old online archives.

has received a restart or termination request. Under ordinary circumstances, the child will call each module's *child_exit* handler, giving it a chance to clean up after itself before the process disappears. The module can commit database transactions, close files, or do whatever else it needs to. Perl API modules can install a handler for this phase by declaring a *PerlChildExitHandler* in the configuration file. Examples of putting this to use are given in Chapter 7.

The child exit routine is not guaranteed to be called in all cases. If the child exits because of a server crash or other untrappable errors, your routine may never be called.

The Request Loop

Between the initialization/configuration phase and the exit phase is the request loop (shown in Figure 3-3). This is where the server and its modules spend most of their time as they wait for incoming requests. Here's where the fun begins.

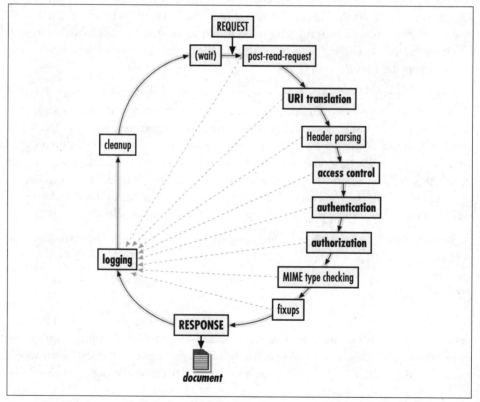

Figure 3-3. The Apache request. The main transaction path is shown in black, and the path taken when a handler returns an error is shown in gray. Phases that you are most likely to write handlers for are shown in bold.

The Apache server core handles the most common aspects of an HTTP conversation: listening for a request, parsing the incoming request line and headers, and composing the outgoing HTTP response message. Each time through the request loop, there are a variety of decisions to make about the incoming request. External modules can define custom handlers to enhance or supersede each decision. If no handler is defined, Apache falls back to its default behavior.

Here are the eight decisions that Apache makes for each request:

1. What is it for? (URI translation phase)

   The requested URI could refer to a physical file, a virtual document produced on the fly by an external script, or a document generated by an internal module. The server needs to have an early idea of what the URI maps to before other questions can be asked and answered. Apache's default translation routines use directives including *Alias, ScriptAlias,* and *DocumentRoot* to translate the URI into a file path. External modules, such as the optional *Rewrite* module, can seize control during this phase to perform more sophisticated translations.

2. Where is it coming from? (access control phase)

3. Who is it coming from? (authentication phase)

4. Who is allowed to perform this particular request? (authorization phase)

   Some documents are restricted by the server's configuration so that not everybody has the right to retrieve them. These three decisions, described in more detail in Chapter 6, determine who can get access to the document.

5. What is the document's type? (MIME type checking phase)

   This step derives a preliminary guess of the requested document's MIME type. Because certain documents (such as CGI scripts and image map files) need to be processed differently than run-of-the-mill static HTML files, the MIME type checking phase must be run before Apache can figure out how to process the document. The server's configuration file determines how it makes this decision. The decision may be based on the document's filename, file extension, or location in the document tree. After type-mapping is done, Apache uses this information to select the "content handler" to generate or transmit the document itself during the response phase.

6. Who will generate the content for this document? (response phase)

   If Apache decides that an extension module should handle the content generation, the document's URI and all the information accumulated about the document so far are passed to the appropriate module. For historical reasons, the handler responsible for the response phase is known as the "content handler."

   The content handler will usually begin by adjusting the HTTP response header to suit its needs. For example, it may change the document's content type from the default value provided by the MIME type checking step. It will then tell Apache to send the (possibly modified) HTTP header to the client. After the header is sent, the module will usually create the content of the document itself and forward it to the client. This may involve reading a static file from disk or creating the document from scratch. Sometimes content handlers will fail for one reason or another, in which case they must return the appropriate error code to Apache so that the server can inform the user.

7. Who's going to log this transaction? (logging phase)

   Whether the content handler's response is a pretty image, a fancy HTML page, or an error of some sort, the outcome should be logged. Apache provides a default logging system that writes to flat files. It is also possible to install a custom log handler to do customized logging, such as writing log entries into a relational database.

8. Who's going to clean up? (cleanup phase)

   Finally, the request is over, and there may be some tidying up left to do. Modules may register cleanup handlers to deallocate resources they allocated earlier, close databases, free memory, and so forth. This phase is distinct from the child exit phase that we described earlier. Whereas the child exit phase happens once per child process, the request cleanup phase happens after each and every transaction.

Internal Requests and Subrequests

Although the majority of transactions will pass through each phase of the request processing cycle from beginning to end, this isn't always the case. An error at any of the phases will terminate processing, causing processing to jump immediately to the logging and cleanup phases.

In addition, there are a variety of conditions that can trigger internal requests. An internal request is just like an ordinary request, except that it is generated by Apache itself. An internal request can be explicitly generated by a handler that has decided to return a document other than the one that the browser requested. By calling the *internal_redirect()* function, the handler tells Apache to stop processing the current request and go process another one.

More commonly, internal requests are generated by Apache's *ErrorDocument* system, when an error returned by a content handler triggers Apache to fetch and display a custom HTML file or CGI script to help explain to the user what went wrong.

A special case of an internal request is a subrequest, which is commonly used by modules to ask "what if" questions. At any stage of the transaction, a handler can pass a file or URI to the *lookup_file()* or *lookup_uri()* functions. Each of these functions creates a request that will appear to handlers just as if it came from a client outside of the server. In the case of *lookup_uri()*, the URI translate handler is the first to be run. The header parser phase is skipped, and then all other handlers down the request chain are run, stopping just before the content response phase. In the case of *lookup_file()*, Apache assumes the given file already exists, so URI translation is skipped and the subrequest starts out with the access checker, continuing along the same road as *lookup_uri()*. After the subrequest is finished, Apache returns the new request record to the caller, which can check for success or failure in the *status* field. The caller may manually run the subrequest's response phase if desired. In any case, the logging phase will never be run for a subrequest, only the main request itself.

For example, the handler responsible for authorization ordinarily does not have access to the MIME type of the requested file because the MIME type checker phase comes after the authorization phase. In order to implement authorization based on the MIME type of the requested document, the authorization handler could generate a subrequest for the requested file in order to run all the phases up to, but not including, the content generation and logging phases. It can then retrieve the file's MIME type from the subrequest result.

The Environment and Subprocesses

Several of Apache's standard modules use environment variables: *mod_cgi* sets a number of environment variables to hold information about the HTTP request prior to launching CGI scripts, *mod_include* uses environment variables in HTML string substitutions, *mod_log_config* can incorporate the values of environment variables into custom log entries, and *mod_access* can base its access restriction decisions on the value of environment variables.

Ordinarily, the environment passed to subprocesses is a strictly limited set of variables that contain information about the server and the current request. You can modify this default list using the *PassEnv*, *SetEnv*, and *UnsetEnv* directives all of which are implemented by the *mod_env* module (compiled in by default). *PassEnv* passes an environment variable from the server's environment into that of the subprocess, while *SetEnv* and *UnsetEnv* allow you to set or unset an environment variable explicitly. Note that *PassEnv* and *SetEnv* are not set until the fixup stage, a rarely used phase that runs just before the response phase. If you need to use such environment variables earlier in the request, the *mod_perl* equivalents, *PerlPassEnv* and *PerlSetEnv*, will set the variables as soon as possible. These work just like the Apache equivalents, except that the two directives can be placed in *<Directory>* and *<Location>* sections, as shown in the following examples:

```
PerlPassEnv     ORGANIZATION
PerlSetEnv      TMPDIR /usr/tmp
```

```
<Location /stage/upload>
PerlSetEnv      TMPDIR /tmp/staging
</Location>
```

The *mod_setenvif* module (compiled in by default) adds the *BrowserMatch* and *SetEnvIf* directives, allowing you to selectively set and unset variables based on attributes of the incoming request.

Apache has a standard way of managing the process environment area. When Apache starts up, it copies certain environment variables from its own environment into an internal table (which variables are inherited in this way can be controlled with the *PassEnv* and *PerlPassEnv* directives). Later, modules that need access to the environment get their information from the table rather than reading it directly from the environment area. Not only is this more efficient, but it gives Apache more control over a potentially security-sensitive domain. If a module such as *mod_cgi* needs to launch a subprocess, it passes the internal environment table to the process rather than using the current system environment.

The Perl and C APIs allow you to examine and set the contents of this environment table. There is also a mechanism for launching and communicating with subprocesses.

We'll now look at the Perl API for installing handlers and manipulating the Apache life cycle.

The Handler API

When Apache calls a handler, it passes information about the current transaction and the server configuration. It's the handler's responsibility to take whatever action is appropriate for this phase and to then return an integer status code to Apache indicating the success or failure of its operation.

Handler Subroutines

In the Perl API, the definition of a handler is short and sweet:

```
sub handler {
    my $r = shift;
    # do something
    return SOME_STATUS_CODE;
}
```

No matter which phase of the Apache life cycle the handler is responsible for, the subroutine structure is always the same. The handler is passed a single argument consisting of a reference to an Apache request object. The request object is an object-oriented version of a central C record structure called the *request record*, and it contains all the information that Apache has collected about the transaction.

By convention, a typical handler will store this object in a lexically scoped variable named $r. The handler retrieves whatever information it needs from the request object, does some processing, and possibly modifies the object to suit its needs. The handler then returns a numeric status code as its function result, informing Apache of the outcome of its work. We discuss the list of status codes and their significance in the next section.

There is one special case, however. If the handler has a function prototype of ($$) indicating that the subroutine takes two scalar arguments, the Perl API treats the handler as an object-oriented method call. In this case, the handler will receive two arguments. The handler's class (package) name or an object reference will be the first argument, and the Apache request object reference will be the second. This allows handlers to take advantage of class inheritance, polymorphism, and other useful object-oriented features. Handlers that use this feature are called "method handlers" and have the following structure:

```
sub handler ($$) {
    my $class = shift;
    my $r = shift;
    # do something
    return SOME_STATUS_CODE;
}
```

We give an example of using a Perl API method handler in the next chapter.

Request handlers declared in the C API are very similar:

```
static int handler (request_rec* r) {
    /* do something */
    return SOME_STATUS_CODE;
}
```

The handler is called with a single argument consisting of a pointer to a **request_rec** request record. The subroutine pulls out whatever information it needs from the request record, modifies it if necessary, and then returns a status code.

However, unlike the Perl API, in which all handlers have the same structure regardless of their phase, the C API handlers that are responsible for the phases of the server life cycle outside the request loop are heterogeneous. For example, a *child_init()* handler in C looks like this:

```
static void child_init (server_rec *s, pool *p) {
    /* do something */
}
```

In this case, there is no request record because there is no request to process at this point. Instead there is a pointer to a server record structure (a **server_rec**) and a memory pool for handling memory allocation issues. We explain the differences fully in Chapter 8, *Customizing the Apache Configuration Process*.

Status Codes

Every handler must return a status code. There are many possible codes, each of which is associated with a symbolic constant. The constants are defined by the *Apache::Constants* module if you are using Perl and the *httpd.h* include file if you are using the C language.

Table 3-1 shows the HTTP status codes, their symbolic constants, and a brief explanation. All constants have a full name that begins with the prefix "HTTP_" as in HTTP_FORBIDDEN. The common ones also have shorter "nicknames" as well, for example, FORBIDDEN.

Table 3-1. Common HTTP Status Codes

Code	Constant (Nickname)	Description
2XX Codes—Success		
200	HTTP_OK (DOCUMENT_FOLLOWS)	The URI was found. Its contents follow.
201	HTTP_CREATED	The URI was created in response to a PUT.
202	HTTP_ACCEPTED	The request was accepted for processing at a later date.
203	HTTP_NON_AUTHORITATIVE	This is nonauthoritative mirrored information.
204	HTTP_NO_CONTENT	The request was successful, but there's no content to display.
206	HTTP_PARTIAL_CONTENT (PARTIAL_CONTENT)	A portion of the document follows.
3XX Codes—Multiple Choices Available		
300	HTTP_MULTIPLE_CHOICES (MULTIPLE_CHOICES)	There are multiple document choices. (Used in content negotiation.)
301	HTTP_MOVED_PERMANENTLY (MOVED)	The document has permanently moved to a new URI.
302	HTTP_MOVED_TEMPORARILY (REDIRECT)	The document has temporarily moved to a new URI.
304	HTTP_NOT_MODIFIED (USE_LOCAL_COPY)	The document has not been modified since it was cached.
4XX Codes—Client-Side Errors		
400	HTTP_BAD_REQUEST (BAD_REQUEST)	The request contains a syntax error.
401	HTTP_UNAUTHORIZED (AUTH_REQUIRED)	The client did not provide correct authorization information.
402	HTTP_PAYMENT_REQUIRED	Payment is required. (Used in charging schemes.)

Table 3-1. Common HTTP Status Codes (continued)

Code	Constant (Nickname)	Description
403	HTTP_FORBIDDEN (FORBIDDEN)	The client is not allowed to access the document.
404	HTTP_NOT_FOUND (NOT_FOUND)	The requested document does not exist.
405	HTTP_METHOD_NOT_ALLOWED (METHOD_NOT_ALLOWED)	The request method (e.g., PUT) is not allowed here.
406	HTTP_NOT_ACCEPTABLE	The request is not acceptable.
407	HTTP_PROXY_AUTHENTICATION_REQUIRED	Proxy server must provide authentication.
408	HTTP_REQUEST_TIME_OUT	The client waited too long to complete the request.
410	HTTP_GONE	The requested document has been permanently removed.
412	HTTP_PRECONDITION_FAILED (PRECONDITION_FAILED)	A conditional retrieval of the document has failed.
413	HTTP_REQUEST_ENTITY_TOO_LARGE	The client tried to PUT or POST data that was too long.
414	HTTP_REQUEST_URI_TOO_LARGE	The client tried to fetch a URI that was too long.
415	HTTP_UNSUPPORTED_MEDIA_TYPE	The client tried to PUT or POST data using an unsupported MIME type.
5XX Codes—Server-Side Errors		
500	HTTP_INTERNAL_SERVER_ERROR (SERVER_ERROR)	The server encountered an unexpected error condition.
501	HTTP_NOT_IMPLEMENTED (NOT_IMPLEMENTED)	An HTTP feature is unimplemented.
502	HTTP_BAD_GATEWAY (BAD_GATEWAY)	An error occurred in a remote server during a proxy request.
503	HTTP_SERVICE_UNAVAILABLE	The server is temporarily down.
504	HTTP_GATEWAY_TIME_OUT	A remote server timed out during a proxy request.
505	HTTP_VERSION_NOT_SUPPORTED	The server doesn't support this version of HTTP.
506	HTTP_VARIANT_ALSO_VARIES (VARIANT_ALSO_VARIES)	A negotiated document has several alternative representations.

Apache::Constants does not export all of the formal HTTP_* names, since only a small handful are used by most modules. However, the constant functions are available for all of these names, should you need them. Chapter 9 gives a complete listing of all the HTTP_* names that are exportable by default. If your module tries to use one of the HTTP_* names and gets an "Undefined subroutine" error, see Chapter 9 for details on accessing it. The nicknames for the common status codes are all exportable by *Apache::Constants.*

The Perl examples throughout this book use the nicknames when available, even though their formal equivalents can be imported using the *Apache::Constants :http* tag. We do this partly because of historical reasons and because the *:common* tag imports a small number of functions—only those we need for the majority of modules. As always with Perl, there's more than one way to do it; the choice is yours.

In addition to the HTTP status codes, Apache defines some return codes of its own which handlers use to send status information to the server.

OK

> This constant indicates that the handler was successful. For most phases Apache will now pass the request on to any other module that has registered its interest in handling the phase. However, for the URI translation, authentication, type-mapping, and response phases, the phase terminates as soon as a handler returns OK. The server behaves this way because it usually makes sense for a single module to handle these phases. However, you can override this behavior using the Perl API's "stacked handlers" mechanism, which we discuss in the next chapter.
>
> The internal Apache OK constant should not be confused with HTTP constant HTTP_OK (known by *Apache::Constants* as DOCUMENT_FOLLOWS).

DECLINED

> The handler has decided it doesn't want to handle the request. Apache will act as if the subroutine were never called and either handle the phase internally or pass the request on to another module that has expressed its interest. Even if all registered modules return DECLINED for a particular phase, it will still be handled by the Apache core, which has default handlers for each phase (even if they do nothing).
>
> It is possible for a module to lie when it declines a transaction. It may actually have done some work but wishes to let another module take the ultimate responsibility for the phase. For example, an authentication handler might manage caching of credential lookups from a database, but not actually make the authentication decision itself.

DONE

> When DONE is returned, Apache immediately jumps out of the request loop, logs the transaction, and closes the client connection. This is one way to halt the transaction without generating an error status.

SERVER_ERROR, UNAUTHORIZED, REDIRECT, BAD_REQUEST, NOT_FOUND ...

> The handler can return any of the HTTP status codes described in Table 3-1. Apache will create the appropriate HTTP header and send it to the browser.

This is the way that handlers can signal that the requested document cannot be found, redirect the browser to another URI, or implement novel authorization schemes. The SERVER_ERROR code is commonly used to signal a fatal error, and it results in the display of the ugly but familiar "internal server error" page.

Apache's response to the status codes can be intercepted and customized with the *ErrorDocument* directive or the *custom_response()* API call. We give examples of using this feature to advantage in Chapter 4, *Content Handlers*, and Chapter 9.

Installing Handlers

The Perl and C APIs use different techniques for installing handlers. In the C API, handlers are specified by placing pointers to the handler subroutines within a static table that is compiled directly into the module code. We discuss this in more detail in Chapter 10. In contrast, Perl API handlers are installed using a series of configuration directives that can be placed in the server's configuration files or even in per-directory *.htaccess* files.

Installing a Perl subroutine as a handler for one of the phases in the Apache life cycle is a matter of writing a *.pm* (Perl module) file to implement the handler, installing it somewhere in the Perl include path, and adding the appropriate *Perl*Handler* directive to one of Apache's configuration files. The term "Perl*Handler," as we use it throughout this book, corresponds to any one of the 15 or so Perl API directives named *PerlTransHandler*, *PerlAccessHandler*, *PerlLogHandler*, and so forth.

If there is only one handler subroutine defined in the *.pm* file, it is convenient to name it *handler()* because the Perl API looks for subroutines with this name by default. Otherwise the subroutine can be named anything you like if you refer to it explicitly in the *Perl*Handler* directive.

Apache Perl modules usually live in the *Apache::* package namespace. This is just a convention, but a good one. It generally indicates that the module is useless outside of the Apache server. That said, the other convention to follow is keeping *Apache::* modules very small, by making good use of the building blocks found on CPAN, putting together new building blocks where appropriate, and simply gluing them together with the Apache API. A typical Apache Perl module file will look like this:

```
package Apache::Foo;
use strict;
use Apache::constants qw(:common);
```

```
sub handler {
    my $r = shift;
    # do something
    return SOME_STATUS_CODE;
}


1;
```

Its declaration in the Apache configuration file will look like this:

```
Perl*Handler Apache::Foo
```

Replace *Perl*Handler* with a legitimate handler directive listed in the next section. When Apache goes to process this directive, it automatically loads and compiles the *Apache::Foo* module if it is not already in memory. It then calls the module's *handler()* subroutine during the appropriate phase of the transaction.

If you want to register several handlers for a particular phase, you can either provide a space-separated list of handlers to install, or repeat the *Perl*Handler* directive on multiple lines. These two techniques can be mixed.

```
Perl*Handler Apache::Foo Apache::Bar Apache::Baz
Perl*Handler Apache::Wiz Apache::Waz
```

If the handler subroutine is not named *handler()*, then you must refer to it explicitly by name. For example, if the handler is named *do_something()*, then the directive should be changed to:

```
Perl*Handler Apache::Foo::do_something
```

Perl*Handler directives that explicitly name the handler subroutines do not cause the module to be automatically loaded. You must do this manually beforehand, either by placing a *PerlModule* directive in the configuration file or indirectly by loading the module in the Perl startup file, if you have one. Here's an example of the first method:

```
PerlModule Apache::Foo
Perl*Handler Apache::Foo::do_something
```

If the module is not already loaded when Apache processes the *Perl*Handler* directive, you will see this confusing message in your server's error log:

```
Undefined subroutine &Apache::Foo::do_something::handler called.
```

It is always a good idea to preload handler modules for better performance either by using the *PerlModule* directive or by pulling in modules with a *PerlRequire* script. The *Perl*Handler* directives offer a shortcut, where a leading + character will tell *mod_perl* to load the handler module at the same time. For example, the following configuraton:

```
Perl*Handler +Apache::Foo
```

is equivalent to this configuration:

```
PerlModule    Apache::Foo
Perl*Handler Apache::Foo
```

Anonymous subroutines can also be used as *Perl*Handlers*, for example:

```
PerlChildInitHandler "sub { warn qq(child $$ starting\n) }"
```

Somewhat surprisingly, although there are 11 phases in the Apache life cycle that affect modules (server initialization, child initialization, child shutdown, and the eight phases of the request loop), there are a few more *Perl*Handler* directives, including ones that don't correspond directly to transaction processing phases, such as *PerlInitHandler*, *PerlDispatchHandler*, and *PerlRestartHandler*. These phases are implemented within the "standard" phases but are given some special treatment by *mod_perl*.

Perl API Configuration Directives

This section lists the configuration directives that the Perl API makes available. Most of these directives install handlers, but there are a few that affect the Perl engine in other ways.

PerlRequire
PerlModule

These directives are used to load Perl modules and files from disk. Both are implemented using the Perl built-in *require* operator. However, there are subtle differences between the two. A *PerlModule* must be a "bareword," that is, a package name without any path information. Perl will search the @INC paths for a *.pm* file that matches the name.

Example:

```
PerlModule Apache::Plotter
```

This will do the same as either of the following Perl language statements:

```
require Apache::Plotter;
use Apache::Plotter ();
```

In contrast, the *PerlRequire* directive expects an absolute or relative path to a file. The Perl API will enclose the path in quotes, then pass it to the *require* function. If you use a relative path, Perl will search through the @INC list for a match.

Examples:

```
PerlRequire /opt/www/lib/directory_colorizer.pl
PerlRequire scripts/delete_temporary_files.pl
```

This will do the same as the following Perl language statement:

```
require '/opt/www/lib/directory_colorizer.pl';
require 'scripts/delete_temporary_files.pl';
```

As with modules and files pulled in directly by the *require* operator, *PerlRequire* and *PerlModule* also require the modules to return a true value (usually 1) to indicate that they were evaluated successfully. Like *require*, these files will be added to the %INC hash so that it will not be evaluated more than once. The *Apache::StatINC* module and the *PerlFreshRestart* directive can alter this behavior so modules can be reloaded.

Both directives will accept any number of modules and files:

```
PerlModule CGI LWP::Simple Apache::Plotter
PerlRequire scripts/startup.pl scripts/config.pl
```

All *PerlModule* and *PerlRequire* files will be loaded during server startup by *mod_perl* during the *module_init* phase. The value of the *ServerRoot* directive is added to the @INC paths by *mod_perl* as an added convenience.

Remember that all the code that is run at server initialization time is run with root privileges when the server is bound to a privileged port, such as the default 80. This means that anyone who has write access to one of the server configuration files, or who has write access to a script or module that is loaded by *PerlModule* or *PerlRequire*, effectively has superuser access to the system. There is a new *PerlOpmask* directive and *PERL_OPMASK_DEFAULT* compile time option, currently in the experimental stages, for disabling possible dangerous operators.

The *PerlModule* and *PerlRequire* directives are also permitted in *.htaccess* files. They will be loaded at request time and be run as the unprivileged web user.

PerlChildInitHandler

This directive installs a handler that is called immediately after a child process is launched. On Unix systems, it is called every time the parent process forks a new child to add to the flock of listening daemons. The handler is called only once in the Win32 version of Apache because that server uses a single-process model.

In contrast to the server initialization phase, the child will be running as an unprivileged user when this handler is called. All *child_init* handlers will be called unless one aborts by logging an error message and calling *exit()* to terminate the process.

Example:

```
PerlChildInitHandler Apache::DBLogin
```

This directive can appear in the main configuration files and within virtual host sections, but not within *<Directory>*, *<Location>*, or *<Files>* sections or within *.htaccess* files.

PerlPostReadRequestHandler

The *post_read_request* handler is called every time an Apache process receives an incoming request, at the point at which the server has read the incoming request's data and parsed the HTTP header fields but before the server has translated the URI to a filename. It is called once per transaction and is intended to allow modules to step in and perform special processing on the incoming data. However, because there's no way for modules to step in and actually contribute to the parsing of the HTTP header, this phase is more often used just as a convenient place to do processing that must occur once per transaction. All *post_read_request* handlers will be called unless one aborts by returning an error code or terminating the phase with DONE.

Example:

```
PerlPostReadRequestHandler Apache::StartTimer
```

This directive can appear in the main configuration files and within virtual host sections but not within *<Directory>*, *<Location>*, or *<Files>* sections or within *.htaccess* files. The reason for this restriction is simply that the request has not yet been associated with a particular filename or directory.

PerlInitHandler

When found at the "top-level" of a configuration file, that is, outside of any *<Location>*, *<Directory>*, or *<Files>* sections, this handler is an alias for *PerlPostReadRequestHandler*. When found inside one of these containers, this handler is an alias for *PerlHeaderParserHandler* described later. Its name makes it easy to remember that this is the first handler invoked when serving an HTTP request.

PerlTransHandler

The *uri_translate* handler is invoked after Apache has parsed out the request. Its job is to take the request, which is in the form of a partial URI, and transform it into a filename.

The handler can also step in to alter the URI itself, to change the request method, or to install new handlers based on the URI. The URI translation phase is often used to recognize and handle proxy requests; we give examples in Chapter 7.

Example:

```
PerlTransHandler Apache::AdBlocker
```

Apache will walk through the registered *uri_translate* handlers until one returns a status other than DECLINED. This is in contrast to most of the other phases, for which Apache will continue to invoke registered handlers even after one has returned OK.

Like *PerlPostReadRequestHandler*, the *PerlTransHandler* directive may appear in the main configuration files and within virtual host sections but not within *<Directory>*, *<Location>*, or *<Files>* sections or within *.htaccess* files. This is because the request has not yet been associated with a particular file or directory.

PerlHeaderParserHandler

After the URI translation phase, Apache again gives you another chance to examine the request headers and to take special action in the *header_parser* phase. Unlike the *post_read_request* phase, at this point the URI has been mapped to a physical pathname. Therefore *PerlHeaderParserHandler* is the first handler directive that can appear within *<Directory>*, *<Location>*, or *<Files>* sections or within *.htaccess* files.

The *header_parser* phase is free to examine and change request fields in the HTTP header, or even to abort the transaction entirely. For this reason, it's common to use this phase to block abusive robots before they start chewing into the resources that may be required in the phases that follow. All registered *header_parser* handlers will be run unless one returns an error code or DONE.

Example:

```
PerlHeaderParserHandler Apache::BlockRobots
```

PerlAccessHandler

The *access_checker* handler is the first of three handlers that are involved in authentication and authorization. We go into this topic in greater depth in Chapter 6.

The *access_checker* handler is designed to do simple access control based on the browser's IP address, hostname, phase of the moon, or other aspects of the transaction that have nothing to do with the remote user's identity. The handler is expected to return OK to allow the transaction to continue, FORBIDDEN to abort the transaction with an unauthorized access error, or DECLINED to punt the decision to the next handler. Apache will continue to step through all registered access handlers until one returns a code other than DECLINED or OK.

Example:

```
PerlAccessHandler Apache::DayLimit
```

The *PerlAccessHandler* directive can occur anywhere, including *<Directory>* sections and *.htaccess* files.

PerlAuthenHandler

The *authentication* handler (sometimes referred to in the Apache documentation as *check_user_id*) is called whenever the requested file or directory is password-protected. This, in turn, requires that the directory be associated with *AuthName, AuthType,* and at least one *require* directive. The interactions among these directives is covered more fully in Chapter 6.

It is the job of the *authentication* handler to check a user's identification credentials, usually by checking the username and password against a database.

If the credentials check out, the handler should return OK. Otherwise the handler returns AUTH_REQUIRED to indicate that the user has not authenticated successfully. When Apache sends the HTTP header with this code, the browser will normally pop up a dialog box that prompts the user for login information.

Apache will call all registered *authentication* handlers, only ending the phase after the last handler has had a chance to weigh in on the decision or when a handler aborts the transaction by returning AUTH_REQUIRED or another error code. As usual, handlers may also return DECLINED to defer the decision to the next handler in line.

Example:

```
PerlAuthenHandler Apache::AuthAnon
```

PerlAuthenHandler can occur anywhere in the server configuration or in *.htaccess* files.

PerlAuthzHandler

Provided that the authentication handler has successfully verified the user's identity, the transaction passes into the *authorization* handler, where the server determines whether the authenticated user is authorized to access the requested URI. This is often used in conjunction with databases to restrict access to a document based on the user's membership in a particular group. However, the authorization handler can base its decision on anything that can be derived from the user's name, such as the user's position in an organizational chart or the user's gender.

Handlers for the authorization phase are only called when the file or directory is password-protected, using the same criteria described earlier for authentication. The handler is expected to return DECLINED to defer the decision, OK to indicate its acceptance of the user's authorization, or AUTH_REQUIRED to indicate that the user is not authorized to access the requested document. Like the authentication handler, Apache will try all the authorization handlers in turn until one returns AUTH_REQUIRED or another error code.

The *authorization* handler interacts with the *require* directive in a way described fully in Chapter 6.

Example:

```
PerlAuthzHandler Apache::AuthzGender
```

The *PerlAuthzHandler* directive can occur anywhere in the server configuration files or in individual *.htaccess* files.

PerlTypeHandler

After the optional access control and authentication phases, Apache enters the *type_checker* phase. It is the responsibility of the *type_checker* handler to assign a provisional MIME type to the requested document. The assigned MIME type will be taken into consideration when Apache decides what content handler to call to generate the body of the document. Because content handlers are free to change the MIME types of the documents they process, the MIME type chosen during the type checking phase is not necessarily the same MIME type that is ultimately sent to the browser. The type checker is also used by Apache's automatic directory indexing routines to decide what icon to display next to the filename.

The default Apache type checker generally just looks up the filename extension in a table of MIME types. By declaring a custom type checker, you can replace this with something more sophisticated, such as looking up the file's MIME type in a document management database.

Because it makes no sense to have multiple handlers trying to set the MIME type of a file according to different sets of rules, the type checker handlers behave like content handlers and URI translation handlers. Apache steps through each registered handler in turn until one returns OK or aborts with an error code. The phase finishes as soon as one module indicates that it has successfully handled the transaction.

Example:

```
PerlTypeHandler Apache::MimeDBI
```

The *PerlTypeHandler* directive can occur anywhere in the server configuration or in *.htaccess* files.

PerlFixupHandler

After the *type_checker* phase but before the content handling phase is an odd beast called the *fixup* phase. This phase is a chance to make any last-minute changes to the transaction before the response is sent. The *fixup* handler's job is like that of the restaurant prep cook who gets all the ingredients cut, sorted, and put in their proper places before the chef goes to work. As an example alluded to earlier, *mod_env* defines a fixup handler to add variables to the environment from configured *SetEnv* and *PassEnv* directives. These variables are put to use by several different modules in the upcoming response phase, including *mod_cgi*, *mod_include*, and *mod_perl*.

All *fixup* handlers are run during an HTTP request, stopping only when a module aborts with an error code.

Example:

```
PerlFixupHandler Apache::HTTP::Equiv
```

The *PerlFixupHandler* directive can occur anywhere in the server configuration files or in *.htaccess* files.

PerlHandler

The next step is the content generation, or *response* phase, installed by the generic-sounding *PerlHandler* directive. Because of its importance, probably 90 percent of the modules you'll write will handle this part of the transaction. The content handler is the master chef of the Apache kitchen, taking all the ingredients assembled by the previous phases—the URI, the translated path-name, the provisional MIME type, and the parsed HTTP headers—whipping them up into a tasty document and serving the result to the browser.

Apache chooses the content handler according to a set of rules governed by the *SetHandler, AddHandler, AddType,* and *ForceType* directives. We go into the details in Chapter 4. For historical reasons as much as anything else, the idiom for installing a Perl content handler uses a combination of the *SetHandler* and *PerlHandler* directives:

```
<Directory /home/http/htdocs/compressed>
   SetHandler  perl-script
   PerlHandler Apache::Uncompress
</Directory>
```

The *SetHandler* directive tells Apache that the Perl interpreter will be the official content handler for all documents in this directory. The *PerlHandler* directive in turn tells Perl to hand off responsibility for the phase to the *handler()* subroutine in the *Apache::Uncompress* package. If no *PerlHandler* directive is specified, Perl will return an empty document.

It is also possible to use the *<Files>* and *<FilesMatch>* directives to assign *mod_perl* content handlers selectively to individual files based on their names. In this example, all files ending with the suffix *.gz* are passed through *Apache::Uncompress*:

```
<FilesMatch "\.gz$">
   SetHandler  perl-script
   PerlHandler Apache::Uncompress
</FilesMatch>
```

There can be only one master chef in a kitchen, and so it is with Apache content handlers. If multiple modules have registered their desire to be the content handler for a request, Apache will try them each in turn until one returns OK or aborts the transaction with an error code. If a handler returns DECLINED, Apache moves on to the next module in the list.

The Perl API relaxes this restriction somewhat, allowing several content handlers to collaborate to build up a composite document using a technique called "chaining." We show you how to take advantage of this feature in the next chapter.

The *PerlHandler* directive can appear anywhere in Apache's configuration files, including virtual host sections, *<Location>* sections, *<Directory>* sections, and *<Files>* sections. It can also appear in *.htaccess* files.

PerlLogHandler

Just before entering the cleanup phase, the log handler will be called in the *logging* phase. This is true regardless of whether the transaction was successfully completed or was aborted somewhere along the way with an error. Everything known about the transaction, including the original request, the translated file name, the MIME type, the number of bytes sent and received, the length of time the transaction took, and the status code returned by the last handler to be called, is passed to the log handler in the request record. The handler typically records the information in some way, either by writing the information to a file, as the standard logging modules do, or by storing the information into a relational database. Log handlers can of course do whatever they like with the information, such as keeping a running total of the number of bytes transferred and throwing out the rest. We show several practical examples of log handlers in Chapter 7.

All registered log handlers are called in turn, even after one of them returns OK. If a log handler returns an HTTP error status, it and all the log handlers that ordinarily follow it, including the built-in ones, will be aborted. This should be avoided unless you really want to prevent some transactions from being logged.

Example:

```
PerlLogHandler  Apache::LogMail
```

The *PerlLogHandler* directive can occur anywhere in the server configuration files or in *.htaccess* files.

PerlCleanupHandler

After each transaction is done, Apache cleans up. During this phase any module that has registered a cleanup handler will be called. This gives the module a chance to deallocate shared memory structures, close databases, clean up temporary files, or do whatever other housekeeping tasks it needs to perform. This phase is always invoked after logging, even if some previous handlers aborted the request handling process by returning some error code.

Internally the cleanup phase is different from the other phases we've discussed. In fact, there isn't really a cleanup phase per se. In the C API, modules that need to perform post-transaction housekeeping tasks register one or more function callbacks with the resource pool that they are passed during initialization. Before the resource pool is deallocated, Apache calls each of the module's callbacks in turn. For this reason, the structure of a cleanup handler routine in the C API is somewhat different from the standard handler. It has this function prototype:

```
void cleanup_handler (void* data);
```

We discuss how to register and use C-language cleanup handlers in Chapter 10.

The Perl API simplifies the situation by making cleanup handlers look and act like other handlers. The *PerlCleanupHandler* directive installs a Perl subroutine as a cleanup handler. Modules may also use the *register_cleanup()* call to install cleanup handlers themselves. Like other handlers in the Perl API, the cleanup subroutine will be called with the Apache request object as its argument. Unlike other handlers, however, a cleanup handler doesn't have to return a function result. If it does return a result code, Apache will ignore the value. An important implication of this is that all registered cleanup functions are always called, despite the status code returned by previous handlers.

Example:

```
PerlCleanupHandler  Apache::Plotter::clean_ink_cartridges
```

The *PerlCleanupHandler* directive can occur anywhere in the server configuration files or in *.htaccess* files.

PerlChildExitHandler

The last handler to be called is the child exit handler. This is called just before the child server process dies. On Unix systems the child exit handler will be called multiple times (but only once per process). On NT systems, the exit handler is called just once before the server itself exits.

Example:

```
PerlChildExitHandler  Apache::Plotter::close_driver
```

PerlFreshRestart

When this directive is set to *On*, mod_perl will reload all the modules found in %INC whenever the server is restarted. This feature is very useful during module development because otherwise, changes to *.pm* files would not take effect until the server was completely stopped and restarted.

The standard *Apache::Registry* module also respects the value of *PerlFreshRestart* by flushing its cache and reloading all scripts when the server is restarted.

This directive can only appear in the main part of the configuration files or in *<VirtualHost>* sections.

PerlDispatchHandler
PerlRestartHandler

These two handlers are not part of the Apache API, but pseudophases added by *mod_perl* to give programmers the ability to fine-tune the Perl API. They are rarely used but handy for certain specialized applications.

The *PerlDispatchHandler* callback, if defined, takes over the process of loading and executing handler code. Instead of processing the *Perl*Handler* directives directly, *mod_perl* will invoke the routine pointed to by *PerlDispatchHandler* and pass it the Apache request object and a second argument indicating the handler that would ordinarily be invoked to process this phase. If the handler has already been compiled, then the second argument is a CODE reference. Otherwise, it is the name of the handler's module or subroutine.

The dispatch handler should handle the request, which it will usually do by running the passed module's *handler()* method. The *Apache::Safe* module, currently under development, takes advantage of *PerlDispatchHandler* to put handlers into a restricted execution space using Malcom Beattie's *Safe* library.

Unlike other *Perl*Handler* directives, *PerlDispatchHandler* must always point to a subroutine name, not to a module name. This means that the dispatch module must be preloaded using *PerlModule*:

```
PerlModule Apache::Safe
<Files *.shtml>
  PerlDispatchHandler Apache::Safe::handler
</Files>
```

PerlRestartHandler points to a routine that is called when the server is restarted. This gives you the chance to step in and perform any cleanup required to tweak the Perl interpreter. For example, you could use this opportunity to trim the global @INC path or collect statistics about the modules that have been loaded.

Perl API Classes and Data Structures

We'll look now at what a handler subroutine sees when it is called. All interaction between the handler and the Apache server is done through the request record. In the Perl API, the request record is encapsulated within a request object, which for historical reasons is blessed into the *Apache::* namespace. The Apache request object contains most of the information about the current transaction. It also contains references to other objects that provide further information about the server and the current transaction. The request object's *server()* method returns an *Apache::Server* object, which contains server configuration information. The *connection()* method returns an *Apache::Connection* object, which contains low-level information about the TCP/IP connection between the browser and the client.

In the C API, information about the request is passed to the handler as a pointer to a request_rec. Included among its various fields are pointers to a server_rec and a conn_rec structure, which correspond to the Perl API's *Apache::Server* and *Apache::Connection* objects. We have much more to say about using the request_rec in Chapters 10 and 11 when we discuss the C-language API in more detail.

The Apache Request Object

The Apache request object (the `request_rec` in C) is the primary conduit for the transfer of information between modules and the server. Handlers can use the request object to perform several types of operations:

Get and set information about the requested document
> The URI of the requested document, its translated file name, its MIME type, and other useful information are available through a set of request object methods. For example, a method named *uri()* returns the requested document's URI, and *content_type()* retrieves the document's MIME type. These methods can also be used to change the values, for example, to set the MIME type of a document generated on the fly.

Get incoming HTTP headers
> All the request headers are available through a method called *header_in()*. From this information you can recover the make and model of the browser, the list of MIME types that the browser can display, any HTTP cookies the server has set, and information about any content the browser wishes to send, such as the contents of a fill-out form.

Get and set outgoing HTTP headers
> The outgoing HTTP headers, which do such things as set HTTP cookies, control browser caching, and provide information about the requested document, can be examined or set via a method called *header_out()*. Certain very common outgoing headers have dedicated methods for setting their values. For example, the outgoing *Content-Type* header is usually set using the *content_type()* method rather than *header_out()*. Once the outgoing header fields are fully set up, the handler can send them to the client with *send_http_header()*.

Read incoming document data
> When the browser sends document information to the server, such as the contents of POSTed forms or uploaded files, the handler can use the request object's *read()* method to read in and manage the submitted information.

Create outgoing document data
> Handlers that are responsible for content generation will use the request object's *print()* method to send document data to the browser. There are also methods for sending whole files in a single step.

Get common per-transaction information
> Commonly needed information, such as the remote browser's hostname and the port at which the server established the connection, is available from the request object through methods with names like *get_remote_host()* and *get_server_port()*. More esoteric information is available through the *Apache::Connection* and *Apache::Server* objects returned by the *connection()* and *server()* methods, respectively.

Log warnings and errors

> The request object provides methods for writing formatted error messages and warnings to the server error log. The simplest and most widely used method is *log_error()*. There is also a fully fledged *Apache::Log* class which gives you access to Apache's more advanced logging API.

Control transaction processing

> By calling the request object's *custom_response()*, *handler()*, or *internal_ redirect()* methods, a handler can control how the transaction is to be processed by setting what modules will handle the content generation phase of the request in the case of success or failure. A handler can also kick off a subrequest using the *lookup_uri()* or *lookup_filename()* methods.

Get module configuration information

> The *PerlSetVar* configuration file directive allows you to pass runtime configuration information to Perl API modules using a simple key/value system. Perl API modules fetch this information with the *dir_config()* method. This eliminates the need to pass runtime information to Perl API modules by making source code modifications. In addition, *mod_perl* supports a more complex configuration API that allows modules to define and use custom configuration directives.

The bulk of this book is devoted to all the many things you can do with the request object.

The Apache::Server Object

The *Apache::Server* class (a `server_rec` in the C API) contains information about the server's configuration. From this object, handlers can recover such things as the email address of the server administrator, the list of virtual hosts that this server supports, and the port number(s) that this server listens to.

The *Apache::Server* object is also where per-server module configuration information is stored and is an integral part of the custom configuration directive API described in Chapter 8.

The Apache::Connection Object

Handlers can use this class to retrieve all sorts of low-level information about the current connection. Among the information stored here are the TCP/IP socket endpoints of the server/browser connection, the remote and local IP addresses, and a flag that indicates when a connection was broken prematurely.

In addition, the *Apache::Connection* object provides information about user authentication. You can recover the type of authentication in use with the *auth_* *type()* method, and the authenticated user's name with the *user()* method. These features are described in more detail in Chapter 6.

Other Core Classes

The Perl API also defines a number of core classes that provide interfaces to other areas of the Apache C API. We'll describe them at length in later chapters when we need to use them. For now, we'll just list them so that you know they're there.

Apache::URI
> Methods for generating and parsing URIs

Apache::Log
> Methods to generate nicely formatted log messages

Apache::File
> Methods to send the contents of static files in an HTTP/1.1–compliant fashion

Apache::Util
> Methods for manipulating HTTP dates and times, and for working with HTML documents

Apache::ModuleConfig and Apache::CmdParms
> Utilities for generating and processing custom configuration directives

Noncore Classes

mod_perl comes with a set of standalone modules that are useful in their own right. The most important of these is *Apache::Registry*, which the next chapter covers in great detail. We list them briefly here just so that you know they exist. See Appendix A, *Standard Noncore Modules*, for a full reference guide to *Apache::Registry* and its kin.

Apache::Registry
> A persistent CGI-like environment for legacy scripts and for writing high-performance modules without using the Apache API.

Apache::PerlRun
> An object-oriented API for running Perl scripts inside of the Apache server. It uses this API within its own handler which provides another CGI emulation environment for running legacy scripts that do not run properly under *Apache::Registry.*

Apache::RegistryLoader
> Speeds up *Apache::Registry* even further by preloading certain CGI scripts.

Apache::Resource
> Controls resource allocation to avoid poorly written scripts from hogging the server.

Apache::PerlSections

> Helper methods for configuring Apache dynamically using Perl embedded in its configuration files.

Apache::StatINC

> Reloads changed modules from disk automatically when they change, rather than the next time the server is restarted.

Apache::Include

> Simple wrappers around the subrequest API and a handler for running within *mod_include*.

Apache::Status

> A Perl runtime browser often helpful when tracking down problems or satisfying curiosities.

The next chapter begins a tutorial that takes you through the API one step at a time, beginning with the all-important response phase. For the definitive reference style listing of classes, methods, functions, and data types, see Chapter 9 for the Perl API and Chapters 10 and 11 for the C API.

4

Content Handlers

This chapter is about writing content handlers for the Apache response phase, when the contents of the page are actually produced. In this chapter you'll learn how to produce dynamic pages from thin air, how to modify real documents on the fly to produce effects like server-side includes, and how Apache interacts with the MIME-typing system to select which handler to invoke.

Starting with this chapter we shift to using the Apache Perl API exclusively for code examples and function prototypes. The Perl API covers the majority of what C programmers need to use the C-language API. What's missing are various memory management functions that are essential to C programmers but irrelevant in Perl. If you are a C programmer, just have patience and the missing pieces will be filled in eventually. In the meantime, follow along with the Perl examples and enjoy yourself. Maybe you'll even become a convert.

Content Handlers as File Processors

Early web servers were designed as engines for transmitting physical files from the host machine to the browser. Even though Apache does much more, the file-oriented legacy still remains. Files can be sent to the browser unmodified or passed through content handlers to transform them in various ways before sending them on to the browser. Even though many of the documents that you produce with modules have no corresponding physical files, some parts of Apache still behave as if they did.

When Apache receives a request, the URI is passed through any URI translation handlers that may be installed (see Chapter 7, *Other Request Phases*, for information on how to roll your own), transforming it into a file path. The *mod_alias* translation handler (compiled in by default) will first process any *Alias*, *ScriptAlias*,

Redirect, or other *mod_alias* directives. If none applies, the *http_core* default translator will simply prepend the *DocumentRoot* directory to the beginning of the URI.

Next, Apache attempts to divide the file path into two parts: a "filename" part which usually (but not always) corresponds to a physical file on the host's filesystem, and an "additional path information" part corresponding to additional stuff that follows the filename. Apache divides the path using a very simple-minded algorithm. It steps through the path components from left to right until it finds something that doesn't correspond to a directory on the host machine. The part of the path up to and including this component becomes the filename, and everything that's left over becomes the additional path information.

Consider a site with a document root of */home/www* that has just received a request for URI */abc/def/ghi.* The way Apache splits the file path into filename and path information parts depends on what directories it finds in the document root:

Physical Directory	Translated Filename	Additional Path Information
/home/www	*/home/www/abc*	*/def/ghi*
/home/www/abc	*/home/www/abc/def*	*/ghi*
/home/www/abc/def	*/home/www/abc/def/ghi*	empty
/home/www/abc/def/ghi	*/home/www/abc/def/ghi*	empty

Note that the presence of any actual files in the path is irrelevant to this process. The division between the filename and the path information depends only on what directories are present.

Once Apache has decided where the file is in the path, it determines what MIME type it might be. This is again one of the places where you can intervene to alter the process with a custom type handler. The default type handler (*mod_mime*) just compares the filename's extension to a table of MIME types. If there's a match, this becomes the MIME type. If no match is found, then the MIME type is undefined. Again, note that this mapping from filename to MIME type occurs even when there's no actual file there.

There are two special cases. If the last component of the filename happens to be a physical directory, then Apache internally assigns it a "magic" MIME type, defined by the DIR_MAGIC_TYPE constant as *httpd/unix-directory.* This is used by the directory module to generate automatic directory listings. The second special case occurs when you have the optional *mod_mime_magic* module installed and the file actually exists. In this case Apache will peek at the first few bytes of the file's contents to determine what type of file it might be. Chapter 7 shows you how to write your own MIME type checker handlers to implement more sophisticated MIME type determination schemes.

After Apache has determined the name and type of the file referenced by the URI, it decides what to do about it. One way is to use information hard-wired into the module's static data structures. The module's `handler_rec` table, which we describe in detail in Chapter 10, *C API Reference Guide, Part I*, declares the module's willingness to handle one or more magic MIME types and associates a content handler with each one. For example, the *mod_cgi* module associates MIME type *application/x-httpd-cgi* with its *cgi_handler()* handler subroutine. When Apache detects that a filename is of type *application/x-httpd-cgi* it invokes *cgi_handler()* and passes it information about the file. A module can also declare its desire to handle an ordinary MIME type, such as *video/quicktime*, or even a wildcard type, such as *video/**. In this case, all requests for URIs with matching MIME types will be passed through the module's content handler unless some other module registers a more specific type.

Newer modules use a more flexible method in which content handlers are associated with files at runtime using explicit names. When this method is used, the module declares one or more content handler names in its `handler_rec` array instead of, or in addition to, MIME types. Some examples of content handler names you might have seen include *cgi-script, server-info, server-parsed, imap-file*, and *perl-script*. Handler names can be associated with files using either *AddHandler* or *SetHandler* directives. *AddHandler* associates a handler with a particular file extension. For example, a typical configuration file will contain this line to associate *.shtml* files with the server-side include handler:

```
AddHandler server-parsed .shtml
```

Now, the *server-parsed* handler defined by *mod_include* will be called on to process all files ending in ".shtml" regardless of their MIME type.

SetHandler is used within *<Directory>*, *<Location>*, and *<Files>* sections to associate a particular handler with an entire section of the site's URI space. In the two examples that follow, the *<Location>* section attaches the *server-parsed* method to all files within the virtual directory */shtml*, while the *<Files>* section attaches *imap-file* to all files that begin with the prefix "map-":

```
<Location /shtml>
  SetHandler server-parsed
</Location>

<Files map-*>
  SetHandler imap-file
</Files>
```

Surprisingly, the *AddHandler* and *SetHandler* directives are not actually implemented in the Apache core. They are implemented by the standard *mod_actions* module, which is compiled into the server by default. In Chapter 7, we show how to reimplement *mod_actions* using the Perl API.

You'll probably want to use explicitly named content handlers in your modules rather than hardcoded MIME types. Explicit handler names make configuration files cleaner and easier to understand. Plus, you don't have to invent a new magic MIME type every time you add a handler.

Things are slightly different for *mod_perl* users because *two* directives are needed to assign a content handler to a directory or file. The reason for this is that the only real content handler defined by *mod_perl* is its internal *perl-script* handler. You use *SetHandler* to assign *perl-script* the responsibility for a directory or partial URI, and then use a *PerlHandler* directive to tell the *perl-script* handler which Perl module to execute. Directories supervised by Perl API content handlers will look something like this:

```
<Location /graph>
    SetHandler   perl-script
    PerlHandler Apache::Graph
</Location>
```

Don't try to assign *perl-script* to a file extension using something like `AddHandler perl-script .pl`; this is generally useless because you'd need to set *PerlHandler* too. If you'd like to associate a Perl content handler with an extension, you should use the *<Files>* directive. Here's an example:

```
<Files ~ "\.graph$">
    SetHandler   perl-script
    PerlHandler Apache::Graph
</Files>
```

There is no *UnSetHandler* directive to undo the effects of *SetHandler*. However, should you ever need to restore a subdirectory's handler to the default, you can do it with the directive `SetHandler default-handler`, as follows:

```
<Location /graph/tutorial>
    SetHandler default-handler
</Location>
```

Adding a Canned Footer to Pages

To show you how content handlers work, we'll develop a module with the Perl API that adds a canned footer to all pages in a particular directory. You could use this, for example, to automatically add copyright information and a link back to the home page. Later on, we'll turn this module into a full-featured navigation bar.

Example 4-1 gives the code for *Apache::Footer*, and Figure 4-1 shows a screenshot of it in action. Since this is our first substantial module, we'll step through the code section by section.

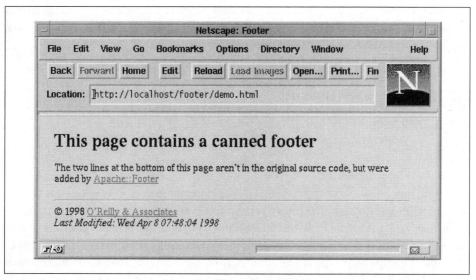

Figure 4-1. The footer on this page was generated automatically by Apache::Footer.

```
package Apache::Footer;

use strict;
use Apache::Constants qw(:common);
use Apache::File ();
```

The code begins by declaring its package name and loading various Perl modules that it depends on. The *use strict* pragma activates Perl checks that prevent us from using global variables before declaring them, disallows the use of function calls without the parentheses, and prevents other unsafe practices. The *Apache::Constants* module defines constants for the various Apache and HTTP result codes; we bring in only those constants that belong to the frequently used *:common* set. *Apache::File* defines methods that are useful for manipulating files.

```
sub handler {
    my $r = shift;
    return DECLINED unless $r->content_type() eq 'text/html';
```

The *handler()* subroutine does all the work of generating the content. It is roughly divided into three parts. In the first part, it fetches information about the requested file and decides whether it wants to handle it. In the second part, it creates the canned footer dynamically from information that it gleans about the file. In the third part, it rewrites the file to include the footer.

In the first part of the process, the handler retrieves the Apache request object and stores it in $r. Next it calls the request's *content_type()* method to retrieve its MIME type. Unless the document is of type *text/html*, the handler stops here and returns a DECLINED result code to the server. This tells Apache to pass the

document on to any other handlers that have declared their willingness to handle
this type of document. In most cases, this means that the document or image will
be passed through to the browser in the usual way.

```
my $file = $r->filename;

unless (-e $r->finfo) {
    $r->log_error("File does not exist: $file");
    return NOT_FOUND;
}
unless (-r _) {
    $r->log_error("File permissions deny access: $file");
    return FORBIDDEN;
}
```

At this point we go ahead and recover the file path, by calling the request object's
filename() method. Just because Apache has assigned the document a MIME type
doesn't mean that it actually exists or, if it exists, that its permissions allow it to be
read by the current process. The next two blocks of code check for these cases.
Using the Perl *–e* file test, we check whether the file exists. If not, we log an error
to the server log using the request object's *log_error()* method and return a result
code of NOT_FOUND. This will cause the server to return a page displaying the
404 "Not Found" error (exactly what's displayed is under the control of the *Error-
Document* directive).

There are several ways to perform file status checks in the Perl API. The simplest
way is to recover the file's pathname using the request object's *filename()* method,
and pass the result to the Perl *–e* file test:

```
unless (-e $r->filename) {
    $r->log_error("File does not exist: $file");
    return NOT_FOUND;
}
```

A more efficient way, however, is to take advantage of the fact that during its path
walking operation Apache already performed a system *stat()* call to collect filesystem information on the file. The resulting status structure is stored in the request
object and can be retrieved with the object's *finfo()* method. So the more efficient
idiom is to use the test `-e $r->finfo`.

Once *finfo()* is called, the *stat()* information is stored into the magic Perl filehandle _ and can be used for subsequent file testing and *stat()* operations, saving
even more CPU time. Using the _ filehandle, we next test that the file is readable
by the current process and return **FORBIDDEN** if this isn't the case. This displays a
403 "Forbidden" error.

```
my $modtime = localtime((stat _)[9]);
```

After performing these tests, we get the file modification time by calling *stat()*. We can use the _ filehandle here too, avoiding the overhead of repeating the *stat()* system call. The modification time is passed to the built-in Perl *localtime()* function to convert it into a human-readable string.

```
my $fh;
unless ($fh = Apache::File->new($file)) {
    $r->log_error("Couldn't open $file for reading: $!");
    return SERVER_ERROR;
}
```

At this point, we attempt to open the file for reading using *Apache::File*'s *new()* method. For the most part, *Apache::File* acts just like Perl's *IO::File* object-oriented I/O package, returning a filehandle on success or *undef* on failure. Since we've already handled the two failure modes that we know how to deal with, we return a result code of SERVER_ERROR if the open is unsuccessful. This immediately aborts all processing of the document and causes Apache to display a 500 "Internal Server Error" message.

```
my $footer = <<END;
<hr>
&copy; 1998 <a href="http://www.ora.com/">O'Reilly &amp; Associates</a><br>
<em>Last Modified: $modtime</em>
END
```

Having successfully opened the file, we build the footer. The footer in this example script is entirely static, except for the document modification date that is computed on the fly.

```
$r->send_http_header;

while (<$fh>) {
    s!(</BODY>)!$footer$1!oi;
} continue {
    $r->print($_);
}
```

The last phase is to rewrite the document. First we tell Apache to send the HTTP header. There's no need to set the content type first because it already has the appropriate value. We then loop through the document looking for the closing </BODY> tag. When we find it, we use a substitution statement to insert the footer in front of it. The possibly modified line is now sent to the browser using the request object's *print()* method.

```
    return OK;
}

1;
```

At the end, we return an OK result code to Apache and end the handler subroutine definition. Like any other *.pm* file, the module itself must end by returning a true value (usually 1) to signal Perl that it compiled correctly.

If all this checking for the existence and readability of the file before processing seems a bit pedantic, don't worry. It's actually unnecessary for you to do this. Instead of explicitly checking the file, we could have simply returned DECLINED if the attempt to open the file failed. Apache would then pass the URI to the default file handler which will perform its own checks and display the appropriate error messages. Therefore we could have replaced the file tests with the single line:

```
my $fh = Apache::File->new($file) || return DECLINED;
```

Doing the tests inside the module this way makes the checks explicit and gives us a chance to intervene to rescue the situation. For example, we might choose to search for a text file of the same name and present it instead. The explicit tests also improve module performance slightly, since the system wastes a small amount of CPU time when it attempts to open a nonexistent file. If most of the files the module serves do exist, however, this penalty won't be significant.

Example 4-1. Adding a Canned Footer to HTML Pages

```
package Apache::Footer;
# file: Apache/Footer.pm

use strict;
use Apache::Constants qw(:common);
use Apache::File ();

sub handler {
    my $r = shift;
    return DECLINED unless $r->content_type() eq 'text/html';

    my $file = $r->filename;

    unless (-e $r->finfo) {
        $r->log_error("File does not exist: $file");
        return NOT_FOUND;
    }
    unless (-r _) {
        $r->log_error("File permissions deny access: $file");
        return FORBIDDEN;
    }

    my $modtime = localtime((stat _)[9]);

    my $fh;
    unless ($fh = Apache::File->new($file)) {
        $r->log_error("Couldn't open $file for reading: $!");
        return SERVER_ERROR;
    }
```

Example 4-1. Adding a Canned Footer to HTML Pages (continued)

```
    my $footer = <<END;
<hr>
&copy; 1998 <a href="">http://www.ora.com/">O'Reilly &amp; Associates</a><br>
<em>Last Modified: $modtime</em>
END

    $r->send_http_header;

    while (<$fh>) {
        s!(</BODY>)!$footer$1!oi;
    } continue {
        $r->print($_);
    }

    return OK;
}

1;
__END__
```

There are several ways to install and use the *Apache::Footer* content handler. If all the files that needed footers were gathered in one place in the directory tree, you would probably want to attach *Apache::Footer* to that location:

```
<Location /footer>
   SetHandler perl-script
   PerlHandler Apache::Footer
</Location>
```

If the files were scattered about the document tree, it might be more convenient to map *Apache::Footer* to a unique filename extension, such as *.footer*. To achieve this, the following directives would suffice:

```
AddType text/html .footer
<Files ~ "\.footer$">
   SetHandler  perl-script
   PerlHandler Apache::Footer
</Files>
```

Note that it's important to associate MIME type *text/html* with the new extension; otherwise, Apache won't be able to determine its content type during the MIME type checking phase.

If your server is set up to allow per-directory access control files to include file information directives, you can place any of these handler directives inside a *.htaccess* file. This allows you to change handlers without restarting the server. For example, you could replace the *<Location>* section shown earlier with a *.htaccess* file in the directory where you want the footer module to be active:

```
SetHandler perl-script
PerlHandler Apache::Footer
```

A Server-Side Include System

The obvious limitation of the *Apache::Footer* example is that the footer text is hardcoded into the code. Changing the footer becomes a nontrivial task, and using different footers for various parts of the site becomes impractical. A much more flexible solution is provided by Vivek Khera's *Apache::Sandwich* module. This module "sandwiches" HTML pages between canned headers and footers that are determined by runtime configuration directives. The *Apache::Sandwich* module also avoids the overhead of parsing the request document; it simply uses the sub-request mechanism to send the header, body, and footer files in sequence.

We can provide more power than *Apache::Sandwich* by using server-side includes. Server-side includes are small snippets of code embedded within HTML comments. For example, in the standard server-side includes that are implemented in Apache, you can insert the current time and date into the page with a comment that looks like this:

```
Today is <!--#echo var="DATE_LOCAL"-->.
```

In this section, we use *mod_perl* to develop our own system of server-side includes, using a simple but extensible scheme that lets you add new types of includes at a moment's whim. The basic idea is that HTML authors will create files that contain comments of this form:

```
<!--#DIRECTIVE PARAM1 PARAM2 PARAM3 PARAM4...-->
```

A directive name consists of any sequence of alphanumeric characters or underscores. This is followed by a series of optional parameters, separated by spaces or commas. Parameters that contain whitespace must be enclosed in single or double quotes in shell command style. Backslash escapes also work in the expected manner.

The directives themselves are not hardcoded into the module but are instead dynamically loaded from one or more configuration files created by the site administrator. This allows the administrator to create a standard menu of includes that are available to the site's HTML authors. Each directive is a short Perl subroutine. A simple directive looks like this one:

```
sub HELLO { "Hello World!"; }
```

This defines a subroutine named *HELLO()* that returns the string "Hello World!" A document can now include the string in its text with a comment formatted like this one:

```
I said <!--#HELLO-->
```

A more complex subroutine will need access to the Apache object and the server-side include parameters. To accommodate this, the Apache object is passed as the first function argument, and the server-side include parameters, if any, follow.

Here's a function definition that returns any field from the incoming request's HTTP header, using the Apache object's *header_in()* method:

```
sub HTTP_HEADER {
  my ($r,$field) = @_;
  $r->header_in($field);
}
```

With this subroutine definition in place, HTML authors can insert the *User-Agent* field into their document using a comment like this one:

```
You are using the browser <!-- #HTTP_HEADER User-Agent -->.
```

Example 4-2 shows an HTML file that uses a few of these includes, and Figure 4-2 shows what the page looks like after processing.

Example 4-2. An HTML File That Uses Extended Server-Side Includes

```
<html> <head> <title>Server-Side Includes</title></head>
<body bgcolor=white>
<h1>Server-Side Includes</h1>
This is some straight text.<p>

This is a "<!-- #HELLO -->" include.<p>

The file size is <strong><!-- #FSIZE --></strong>, and it was
last modified on <!-- #MODTIME %x --><p>

Today is <!-- #DATE "%A, in <em>anno domini</em> %Y"-->.<p>

The user agent is <em><!--#HTTP_HEADER User-Agent--></em>.<p>

Oops: <!--#OOPS 0--><p>

Here is an included file:
<pre>
<!--#INCLUDE /include.txt 1-->
</pre>

<!--#FOOTER-->
</body> </html>
```

Implementing this type of server-side include system might seem to be something of a challenge, but in fact the code is surprisingly compact (Example 4-3). This module is named *Apache::ESSI*, for "extensible server-side includes."

Again, we'll step through the code one section at a time.

```
package Apache::ESSI;

use strict;
use Apache::Constants qw(:common);
use Apache::File ();
use Text::ParseWords qw(quotewords);
my (%MODIFIED, %SUBSTITUTION);
```

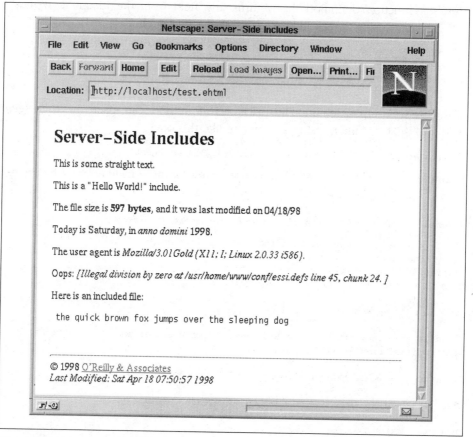

Figure 4-2. A page generated by Apache::ESSI

We start as before by declaring the package name and loading various Perl library modules. In addition to the modules that we loaded in the *Apache::Footer* example, we import the *quotewords()* function from the standard Perl *Text::ParseWords* module. This routine provides command shell–like parsing of strings that contain quote marks and backslash escapes. We also define two lexical variables, %MODIFIED and %SUBSTITUTION, which are global to the package.

```
sub handler {
    my $r = shift;
    $r->content_type() eq 'text/html' || return DECLINED;
    my $fh = Apache::File->new($r->filename) || return DECLINED;
    my $sub = read_definitions($r)      || return SERVER_ERROR;
    $r->send_http_header;
    $r->print($sub->($r, $fh));
    return OK;
}
```

The *handler()* subroutine is quite short. As in the *Apache::Footer* example, *handler()* starts by examining the content type of the document being requested and declines to handle requests for non-HTML documents. The handler recovers the file's physical path by calling the request object's *filename()* method and attempts to open it. If the file open fails, the handler again returns an error code of DECLINED. This avoids *Apache::Footer*'s tedious checking of the file's existence and access permissions, at the cost of some efficiency every time a nonexistent file is requested.

Once the file is opened, we call an internal function named *read_definitions()*. This function reads the server-side includes configuration file and generates an anonymous subroutine to do the actual processing of the document. If an error occurs while processing the configuration file, *read_definitions()* returns *undef* and we return SERVER_ERROR in order to abort the transaction. Otherwise, we send the HTTP header and invoke the anonymous subroutine to perform the substitutions on the contents of the file. The result of invoking the subroutine is sent to the client using the request object's *print()* method, and we return a result code of OK to indicate that everything went smoothly.

```
sub read_definitions {
    my $r = shift;
    my $def = $r->dir_config('ESSIDefs');
    return unless $def;
    return unless -e ($def = $r->server_root_relative($def));
```

Most of the interesting work occurs in *read_definitions()*. The idea here is to read the server-side include definitions, compile them, and then use them to generate an anonymous subroutine that does the actual substitutions. In order to avoid recompiling this subroutine unnecessarily, we cache its code reference in the package variable %SUBSTITUTION and reuse it if we can.

The *read_definitions()* subroutine begins by retrieving the path to the file that contains the server-side include definitions. This information is contained in a per-directory configuration variable named ESSIDefs, which is set in the configuration file using the *PerlSetVar* directive and retrieved within the handler with the request object's *dir_config()* method (see the end of the example for a representative configuration file entry). If, for some reason, this variable isn't present, we return *undef*. Like other Apache configuration files, we allow this file to be specified as either an absolute path or a partial path relative to the server root. We pass the path to the request object's *server_root_relative()* method. This convenient function prepends the server root to relative paths and leaves absolute paths alone. We next check that the file exists using the *–e* file test operator and return *undef* if not.

```
    return $SUBSTITUTION{$def} if $MODIFIED{$def} && $MODIFIED{$def} <= -M _;
```

Having recovered the name of the definitions file, we next check the cache to see whether the subroutine definitions are already cached and, if so, whether the file hasn't changed since the code was compiled and cached. We use two hashes for this purpose. The %SUBSTITUTION array holds the compiled code and %MODIFIED contains the modification date of the definition file the last time it was compiled. Both hashes are indexed by the definition file's path, allowing the module to handle the case in which several server-side include definition files are used for different parts of the document tree. If the modification time listed in %MODIFIED is less than or equal to the definition file's current modification date, we return the cached subroutine.

```
my $package = join "::", __PACKAGE__, $def;
$package =~ tr/a-zA-Z0-9_/_/c;
```

The next two lines are concerned with finding a unique namespace in which to compile the server-side include functions. Putting the functions in their own namespace decreases the chance that function side effects will have unwanted effects elsewhere in the module. We take the easy way out here by using the path to the definition file to synthesize a package name, which we store in a variable named $package.

```
eval "package $package; do '$def'";
if($@) {
    $r->log_error("Eval of $def did not return true: $@");
    return;
}
```

We then invoke *eval()* to compile the subroutine definitions into the newly chosen namespace. We use the *package* declaration to set the namespace and *do* to load and run the definitions file. We use *do* here rather than the more common *require* because *do* unconditionally recompiles code files even if they have been loaded previously. If the *eval* was unsuccessful, we log an error and return *undef.*

```
$SUBSTITUTION{$def} = sub {
    do_substitutions($package, @_);
};
$MODIFIED{$def} = -M $def;   # store modification date
return $SUBSTITUTION{$def};
}
```

Before we exit *read_definitions()*, we create a new anonymous subroutine that invokes the *do_substitutions()* function, store this subroutine in %SUBSTITUTION, and update %MODIFIED with the modification date of the definitions file. We then return the code reference to our caller. We interpose a new anonymous subroutine here so that we can add the contents of the $package variable to the list of variables passed to the *do_substitutions()* function.

```
sub do_substitutions {
    my $package = shift;
```

```
        my($r, $fh) = @_;
        # Make sure that eval() errors aren't trapped.
        local $SIG{__WARN__};
        local $SIG{__DIE__};
        local $/; #slurp $fh
        my $data = <$fh>;
        $data =~ s/<!--\s*\#(\w+)    # start of a function name
                \s*(.*?)            # optional parameters
                \s*-->              # end of comment
               /call_sub($package, $1, $r, $2)/xseg;
        $data;
    }
```

When *handler()* invokes the anonymous subroutine, it calls *do_substitutions()* to do the replacement of the server-side include directives with the output of their corresponding routines. We start off by localizing the `$SIG{__WARN__}` and `$SIG{__DIE__}` handlers and setting them back to the default Perl *CORE::warn()* and *CORE::die()* subroutines. This is a paranoid precaution against the use of *CGI::Carp*, which some *mod_perl* users load into Apache during the startup phase in order to produce nicely formatted server error log messages. The subroutine continues by fetching the lines of the page to be processed and joining them in a single scalar value named `$data`.

We then invoke a string substitution function to replace properly formatted comment strings with the results of invoking the corresponding server-side include function. The substitution uses the *e* flag to treat the replacement part as a Perl expression to be evaluated and the *g* flag to perform the search and replace globally. The search half of the function looks like this:

```
/<!--\s*\#(\w+)\s*(.*?)\s*-->/
```

This detects the server-side include comments while capturing the directive name in $1 and its optional arguments in $2.

The replacement of the function looks like this:

```
/call_sub($package, $1, $r, $2)/
```

This just invokes another utility function, *call_sub()*, passing it the package name, the directive name, the request object, and the list of parameters.

```
sub call_sub {
    my($package, $name, $r, $args) = @_;
    my $sub = \&{join '::', $package, $name};
    $r->chdir_file;
    my $res = eval { $sub->($r, quotewords('[ ,]',0,$args)) };
    return "<em>[$@]</em>" if $@;
    return $res;
}
```

The *call_sub()* routine starts off by obtaining a reference to the subroutine using its fully qualified name. It does this by joining the package name to the subroutine

name and then using the funky Perl \&{...} syntax to turn this string into a subroutine reference. As a convenience to the HTML author, before invoking the subroutine we call the request object's *chdir_file()* method. This simply makes the
current directory the same as the requested file, which in this case is the HTML file
containing the server-side includes.

The server-side include function is now invoked, passing it the request object and
the optional arguments. We call *quotewords()* to split up the arguments on commas or whitespace. In order to trap fatal runtime errors that might occur during the
function's execution, the call is done inside an *eval{}* block. If the call function
fails, we return the error message it died with captured within $@. Otherwise, we
return the value of the call function.

At the bottom of Example 4-3 is an example entry for *perl.conf* (or *httpd.conf* if
you prefer). The idea here is to make *Apache::ESSI* the content handler for all files
ending with the extension *.ehtml*. We do this with a *<Files>* configuration section
that contains the appropriate *SetHandler* and *PerlHandler* directives. We use the
PerlSetVar directive to point the module to the server-relative definitions file,
conf/essi.defs.

In addition to the *<Files>* section, we need to ensure that Apache knows that
.ehtml files are just a special type of HTML file. We use *AddType* to tell Apache to
treat *.ehtml* files as MIME type *text/html*.

You could also use *<Location>* or *<Directory>* to assign the *Apache::ESSI* content
handler to a section of the document tree, or a different *<Files>* directive to make
Apache::ESSI the content handler for all HTML files.

Example 4-3. An Extensible Server-Side Include System

```
package Apache::ESSI;
# file: Apache/ESSI.pm

use strict;
use Apache::Constants qw(:common);
use Apache::File ();
use Text::ParseWords qw(quotewords);
my (%MODIFIED, %SUBSTITUTION);

sub handler {
    my $r = shift;
    $r->content_type() eq 'text/html' || return DECLINED;
    my $fh = Apache::File->new($r->filename) || return DECLINED;
    my $sub = read_definitions($r)      || return SERVER_ERROR;
    $r->send_http_header;
    $r->print($sub->($r, $fh));
    return OK;
}
```

Example 4-3. An Extensible Server-Side Include System (continued)

```perl
sub read_definitions {
    my $r = shift;
    my $def = $r->dir_config('ESSIDefs');
    return unless $def;
    return unless -e ($def = $r->server_root_relative($def));
    return $SUBSTITUTION{$def} if $MODIFIED{$def} && $MODIFIED{$def} <= -M _;

    my $package = join "::", __PACKAGE__, $def;
    $package =~ tr/a-zA-Z0-9_/_/c;

    eval "package $package; do '$def'";

    if($@) {
        $r->log_error("Eval of $def did not return true: $@");
        return;
    }

    $SUBSTITUTION{$def} = sub {
        do_substitutions($package, @_);
    };

    $MODIFIED{$def} = -M $def;   # store modification date
    return $SUBSTITUTION{$def};
}

sub do_substitutions {
    my $package = shift;
    my($r, $fh) = @_;
    # Make sure that eval() errors aren't trapped.
    local $SIG{__WARN__};
    local $SIG{__DIE__};
    local $/; #slurp $fh
    my $data = <$fh>;
    $data =~ s/<!--\s*\#(\w+)   # start of a function name
                \s*(.*?)         # optional parameters
                \s*-->           # end of comment
              /call_sub($package, $1, $r, $2)/xseg;
    $data;
}

sub call_sub {
    my($package, $name, $r, $args) = @_;
    my $sub = \&{join '::', $package, $name};
    $r->chdir_file;
    my $res = eval { $sub->($r, quotewords('[ ,]',0,$args)) };
    return "<em>[$@]</em>" if $@;
    return $res;
}

1;
__END__
```

Here are some *perl.conf* directives to go with *Apache::ESSI*:

```
<Files ~ "\.ehtml$">
  SetHandler  perl-script
  PerlHandler Apache::ESSI
  PerlSetVar  ESSIDefs conf/essi.defs
</Files>
AddType text/html .ehtml
```

At this point you'd probably like a complete server-side include definitions file to go with the module. Example 4-4 gives a short file that defines a core set of functions that you can build on top of. Among the functions defined here are ones for inserting the size and modification date of the current file, the date, fields from the browser's HTTP request header, and a function that acts like the C preprocessor *#include* macro to insert the contents of a file into the current document. There's also an include called *OOPS* which divides the number 10 by the argument you provide. Pass it an argument of zero to see how runtime errors are handled.

The *INCLUDE()* function inserts whole files into the current document. It accepts either a physical pathname or a "virtual" path in URI space. A physical path is only allowed if it lives in or below the current directory. This is to avoid exposing sensitive files such as */etc/passwd*.

If the `$virtual` flag is passed, the function translates from URI space to a physical path name using the *lookup_uri()* and *filename()* methods:

```
$file = $r->lookup_uri($path)->filename;
```

The request object's *lookup_uri()* method creates an Apache subrequest for the specified URI. During the subrequest, Apache does all the processing that it ordinarily would on a real incoming request up to, but not including, activating the content handler. *lookup_uri()* returns an *Apache::SubRequest* object, which inherits all its behavior from the Apache request class. We then call this object's *filename()* method in order to retrieve its translated physical file name.

Example 4-4. Server-Side Include Function Definitions

```
# Definitions for server-side includes.
# This file is require'd, and therefore must end with
# a true value.

use Apache::File ();
use Apache::Util qw(ht_time size_string);

# insert the string "Hello World!"
sub HELLO {
    my $r = shift;
    "Hello World!";
}
```

Example 4-4. Server-Side Include Function Definitions (continued)

```perl
# insert today's date possibly modified by a strftime() format
# string
sub DATE {
    my ($r,$format) = @_;
    return scalar(localtime) unless $format;
    return ht_time(time, $format, 0);
}


# insert the modification time of the document, possibly modified
# by a strftime() format string.
sub MODTIME {
    my ($r,$format) = @_;
    my $mtime = (stat $r->finfo)[9];
    return localtime($mtime) unless $format;
    return ht_time($mtime, $format, 0);
}


# insert the size of the current document
sub FSIZE {
    my $r = shift;
    return size_string -s $r->finfo;
}


# divide 10 by the argument (used to test runtime error trapping)
sub OOPS { 10/$_[1]; }


# insert a canned footer
sub FOOTER {
    my $r = shift;
    my $modtime = MODTIME($r);
    return <<END;
<hr>
&copy; 1998 <a href="http://www.ora.com/">O'Reilly &amp; Associates</a><br>
<em>Last Modified: $modtime</em>
END
}


# insert the named field from the incoming request
sub HTTP_HEADER {
    my ($r,$h) = @_;
    $r->header_in($h);
}


#ensure that path is relative, and does not contain ".."
sub is_below_only { $_[0] !~ m:(^/|(^|/)\.\.(/|$)): }


# Insert the contents of a file.  If the $virtual flag is set
# does a document-root lookup, otherwise treats filename as a
# physical path.
sub INCLUDE {
    my ($r,$path,$virtual) = @_;
    my $file;
```

Example 4-4. Server-Side Include Function Definitions (continued)

```
    if($virtual) {
        $file = $r->lookup_uri($path)->filename;
    }
    else {
        unless(is_below_only($path)) {
            die "Can't include $path\n";
        }
        $file = $path;
    }
    my $fh = Apache::File->new($file) || die "Couldn't open $file: $!\n";
    local $/;
    return <$fh>;
}

1;
```

If you're a fan of server-side includes, you should also check out the Apache *Emb-perl* and *ePerl* packages. Both packages, along with several others available from the CPAN, build on *mod_perl* to create a Perl-like programming language embedded entirely within server-side includes.

Converting Image Formats

Another useful application of Apache content handlers is converting file formats on the fly. For example, with a little help from the Aladdin Ghostscript interpreter, you can dynamically convert Adobe Acrobat (PDF) files into GIF images when dealing with a browser that doesn't have the Acrobat plug-in installed.*

In this section, we show a content handler that converts image files on the fly. It takes advantage of Kyle Shorter's *Image::Magick* package, the Perl interface to John Cristy's ImageMagick library. *Image::Magick* interconverts a large number of image formats, including JPEG, PNG, TIFF, GIF, MPEG, PPM, and even PostScript. It can also transform images in various ways, such as cropping, rotating, solarizing, sharpening, sampling, and blurring.

The *Apache::Magick* content handler accepts URIs in this form:

```
    /path/to/image.ext/Filter1/Filter2?arg=value&arg=value...
```

---

* At least in theory, you can divine what MIME types a browser prefers by examining the contents of the *Accept* header with `$r->header_in('Accept')`. According to the HTTP protocol, this should return a list of MIME types that the browser can handle along with a numeric preference score. The CGI.pm module even has an *accept()* function that leverages this information to choose the best format for a given document type. Unfortunately, this part of the HTTP protocol has atrophied, and neither Netscape's nor Microsoft's browsers give enough information in the *Accept* header to make it useful for content negotiation.

In its simplest form, the handler can be used to perform image format conversions on the fly. For example, if the actual file is named *bluebird.gif* and you request *bluebird.jpg*, the content handler automatically converts the GIF into a JPEG file and returns it. You can also pass arguments to the converter in the query string. For example, to specify a progressive JPEG image (`interlace = "Line"`) with a quality of 50 percent, you can fetch the file by requesting a URI like this one:

```
/images/bluebird.jpg?interlace=Line&quality=50
```

You can also run one or more filters on the image prior to the conversion. For example, to apply the "Charcoal" filter (which makes the image look like a charcoal sketch) and then put a decorative border around it (the "Frame" filter), you can request the image like this:

```
/images/bluebird.jpg/Charcoal/Frame?quality=75
```

Any named arguments that need to be passed to the filter can be appended to the query string, along with the conversion arguments. In the last example, we can specify a gold-colored frame this way:

```
/images/bluebird.jpg/Charcoal/Frame?quality=75&color=gold
```

This API doesn't allow you to direct arguments to specific filters. Fortunately, most of the filters that you might want to apply together don't have overlapping argument names, and filters ignore any arguments that don't apply to them. The full list of filters and conversion operations can be found at the PerlMagick web site, located at *http://www.wizards.dupont.com/cristy/www/perl.html*. You'll find pointers to the latest ImageMagick code library there as well.

One warning before you use this Apache module on your system: some of the operations can be very CPU-intensive, particularly when converting an image with many colors, such as JPEG, to one that has few colors, such as GIF. You should also be prepared for *Image::Magick*'s memory consumption, which is nothing short of voracious.

Example 4-5 shows the code for *Apache::Magick*.

```
package Apache::Magick;

use strict;
use Apache::Constants qw(:common);
use Image::Magick ();
use Apache::File ();
use File::Basename qw(fileparse);
use DirHandle ();
```

We begin as usual by bringing in the modules we need. We bring in *Apache::Constants*, *File::Basename* for its file path parsing utilities, *DirHandle()* for object-oriented interface to directory reading functions, and the *Image::Magick* module itself.

```perl
my %LegalArguments = map { $_ => 1 }
qw (adjoin background bordercolor colormap colorspace
    colors compress density dispose delay dither
    display font format iterations interlace
    loop magick mattecolor monochrome page pointsize
    preview_type quality scene subimage subrange
    size tile texture treedepth undercolor);

my %LegalFilters = map { $_ => 1 }
qw(AddNoise Blur Border Charcoal Chop
    Contrast Crop Colorize Comment CycleColormap
    Despeckle Draw Edge Emboss Enhance Equalize Flip Flop
    Frame Gamma Implode Label Layer Magnify Map Minify
    Modulate Negate Normalize OilPaint Opaque Quantize
    Raise ReduceNoise Rotate Sample Scale Segment Shade
    Sharpen Shear Solarize Spread Swirl Texture Transparent
    Threshold Trim Wave Zoom);
```

We then define two hashes, one for all the filter and conversion arguments recognized by *Image::Magick* and the other for the various filter operations that are available. These lists were cut and pasted from the *Image::Magick* documentation. We tried to exclude the ones that were not relevant to this module, such as ones that create multiframe animations, but a few may have slipped through.

```perl
sub handler {
    my $r = shift;

    # get the name of the requested file
    my $file = $r->filename;

    # If the file exists and there are no transformation arguments
    # just decline the transaction.  It will be handled as usual.
    return DECLINED unless $r->args || $r->path_info || !-r $r->finfo;
```

The *handler()* routine begins as usual by fetching the name of the requested file. We decline to handle the transaction if the file exists, the query string is empty, and the additional path information is empty as well. This is just the common case of the browser trying to fetch an unmodified existing file.

```perl
    my $source;
    my ($base, $directory, $extension) = fileparse($file, '\.\w+');
    if (-r $r->finfo) { # file exists, so it becomes the source
        $source = $file;
      }
    else {              # file doesn't exist, so we search for it
        return DECLINED unless -r $directory;
        $source = find_image($r, $directory, $base);
    }

    unless ($source) {
        $r->log_error("Couldn't find a replacement for $file");
        return NOT_FOUND;
    }
```

We now use *File::Basename*'s *fileparse()* function to parse the requested file into its basename (the filename without the extension), the directory name, and the extension. We check again whether we can read the file, and if so it becomes the source for the conversion. Otherwise, we search the directory for another image file to convert into the format of the requested file. For example, if the URI requested is *bluebird.jpeg* and we find a file named *bluebird.gif*, we invoke *Image::Magick* to do the conversion. The search is done by an internal subroutine named *find_image()*, which we'll examine later. If successful, the name of the source image is stored in `$source`. If unsuccessful, we log the error with the *log_error()* function and return a `NOT_FOUND` result code.

```
$r->send_http_header;
return OK if $r->header_only;
```

At this point, we send the HTTP header using *send_http_header()*. The next line represents an optimization that we haven't seen before. It may be that the client isn't interested in the content of the image file, but just in its meta-information, such as its length and MIME type. In this case, the browser sends an HTTP HEAD request rather than the usual GET. When Apache receives a HEAD request, it sets *header_only()* to true. If we see that this has happened, we return from the handler immediately with an `OK` status code. Although it wouldn't hurt to send the document body anyway, respecting the HEAD request results in a slight savings in processing efficiency and makes the module compliant with the HTTP protocol.

```
my $q = Image::Magick->new;
my $err = $q->Read($source);
```

Otherwise, it's time to read the source image into memory. We create a new *Image::Magick* object, store it in a variable named `$q`, and then load the source image file by calling its *Read()* method. Any error message returned by *Read()* is stored into a variable called `$err`.

```
my %arguments = $r->args;

# Run the filters
for (split '/', $r->path_info) {
   my $filter = ucfirst $_;
   next unless $LegalFilters{$filter};
   $err ||= $q->$filter(%arguments);
}

# Remove invalid arguments before the conversion
for (keys %arguments) {
   delete $arguments{$_} unless $LegalArguments{$_};
}
```

The next phase of the process is to prepare for the image manipulation. The first thing we do is tidy up the input parameters. We retrieve the query string parameters by calling the request object's *args()* method and store them in a hash named `%arguments`.

We then call the request object's *path_info()* method to retrieve the additional path information. We split the path info into a series of filter names and canonicalize them by capitalizing their initial letters using the Perl built-in operator *ucfirst()*. Each of the filters is applied in turn, skipping over any that aren't on the list of filters that *Image::Magick* accepts. We do an OR assignment into $err, so that we maintain the first non-null error message, if any. Having run the files, we remove from the %arguments array any arguments that aren't valid in *Image::Magick*'s file format conversion calls.

```
# Create a temporary file name to use for conversion
my($tmpnam, $fh) = Apache::File->tmpfile;
```

Image::Magick needs to write the image to a temporary file. We call the *Apache::File tmpfile()* method to create a suitable temporary file name. If successful, *tmpfile()* returns the name of the temporary file, which we store in the variable $tmpnam, and a filehandle open for writing into the file, which we store in the variable $fh. The *tmpfile()* method is specially written to avoid a "race condition" in which the temporary file name appears to be unused when the module first checks for it but is created by someone else before it can be opened.

```
# Write out the modified image
open(STDOUT, ">&=" . fileno($fh));
```

The next task is to have *Image::Magick* perform the requested conversion and write it to the temporary file. The safest way to do this would be to pass it the temporary file's already opened filehandle. Unfortunately, *Image::Magick* doesn't accept filehandles; its *Write()* method expects a filename, or the special filename – to write to standard output. However, we can trick it into writing to the filehandle by reopening standard output on the filehandle, which we do by passing the filehandle's numeric file descriptor to *open()* using the rarely seen >&= notation. See the *open()* entry in the *perlfunc* manual page for complete details.

Since STDOUT gets reset before every Perl API transaction, there's no need to save and restore its original value.

```
$extension =~ s/^\.//;
$err ||= $q->Write('filename' => "\U$extension\L:-", %arguments);
if ($err) {
    unlink $tmpnam;
    $r->log_error($err);
    return SERVER_ERROR;
}
close $fh;
```

We now call *Image::Magick*'s *Write()* method with the argument `'filename'=>` *EXTENSION:* – where *EXTENSION* is the uppercased extension of the document that the remote user requested. We also tack on any conversion arguments that were requested. For example, if the remote user requested `bluebird.jpg?quality=75`, the call to *Write()* ends up looking like this:

```
$q->Write('filename'=>'JPG:-','quality'=>75);
```

If any errors occurred during this step or the previous ones, we delete the temporary file, log the errors, and return a SERVER_ERROR status code.

```
    # At this point the conversion is all done!
    # reopen for reading
    $fh = Apache::File->new($tmpnam);
    unless ($fh) {
        $r->log_error("Couldn't open $tmpnam: $!");
        return SERVER_ERROR;
    }

    # send the file
    $r->send_fd($fh);

    # clean up and go
    unlink $tmpnam;
    return OK;
}
```

If the call to *Write()* was successful, we need to send the contents of the temporary file to the waiting browser. We could open the file, read its contents, and send it off using a series of *print()* calls, as we've done previously, but in this case there's a slightly easier way. After reopening the file with *Apache::File*'s *new()* method, we call the request object's *send_fd()* method to transmit the contents of the filehandle in one step. The *send_fd()* method accepts all the same filehandle data types as the Perl built-in I/O operators. After sending off the file, we clean up by unlinking the temporary file and returning an OK status.

We'll now turn our attention to the *find_image()* subroutine, which is responsible for searching the directory for a suitable file to use as the image source if the requested file can't be found:

```
sub find_image {
    my ($r, $directory, $base) = @_;
    my $dh = DirHandle->new($directory) or return;
```

The *find_image()* utility subroutine is straightforward. It takes the request object, the parsed directory name, and the basename of the requested file and attempts to search this directory for an image file that shares the same basename. The routine opens a directory handle with *DirHandle->new()* and iterates over its entries.

```
    my $source;
    for my $entry ($dh->read) {
        my $candidate = fileparse($entry, '\.\w+');
        if ($base eq $candidate) {
```

```
            # determine whether this is an image file
            $source = join '', $directory, $entry;
            my $subr = $r->lookup_file($source);
            last if $subr->content_type =~ m:^image/:;
            undef $source;
         }
      }
```

For each entry in the directory listing, we parse out the basename using
fileparse(). If the basename is identical to the one we're searching for, we call the
request object's *lookup_file()* method to activate an Apache subrequest. *lookup_file()* is similar to *lookup_uri()*, which we saw earlier in the context of server-side
includes, except that it accepts a physical pathname rather than a URI. Because of
this, *lookup_file()* will skip the URI translation phase, but it will still cause Apache
to trigger all the various handlers up to, but not including, the content handler.

In this case, we're using the subrequest for the sole purpose of getting at the
MIME type of the file. If the file is indeed an image of one sort or another, then
we save the request in a lexical variable and exit the loop. Otherwise, we keep
searching.

```
      $dh->close;
      return $source;
   }
```

At the end of the loop, $source will be undefined if no suitable image file was
found, or it will contain the full pathname to the image file if we were successful.
We close the directory handle, and return $source.

Example 4-5. Apache::Magick Converts Image Formats on the Fly

```
package Apache::Magick;
# file: Apache/Magick.pm

use strict;
use Apache::Constants qw(:common);
use Image::Magick ();
use Apache::File ();
use File::Basename qw(fileparse);
use DirHandle ();

my %LegalArguments = map { $_ => 1 }
qw (adjoin background bordercolor colormap colorspace
    colors compress density dispose delay dither
    display font format iterations interlace
    loop magick mattecolor monochrome page pointsize
    preview_type quality scene subimage subrange
    size tile texture treedepth undercolor);

my %LegalFilters = map { $_ => 1 }
qw(AddNoise Blur Border Charcoal Chop
   Contrast Crop Colorize Comment CycleColormap
   Despeckle Draw Edge Emboss Enhance Equalize Flip Flop
```

Example 4-5. Apache::Magick Converts Image Formats on the Fly (continued)

```
    Frame Gamma Implode Label Layer Magnify Map Minify
    Modulate Negate Normalize OilPaint Opaque Quantize
    Raise ReduceNoise Rotate Sample Scale Segment Shade
    Sharpen Shear Solarize Spread Swirl Texture Transparent
    Threshold Trim Wave Zoom);

sub handler {
    my $r = shift;

    # get the name of the requested file
    my $file = $r->filename;

    # If the file exists and there are no transformation arguments
    # just decline the transaction.  It will be handled as usual.
    return DECLINED unless $r->args || $r->path_info || !-r $r->finfo;

    my $source;
    my ($base, $directory, $extension) = fileparse($file, '\.\w+');
    if (-r $r->finfo) { # file exists, so it becomes the source
        $source = $file;
    }
    else {                  # file doesn't exist, so we search for it
        return DECLINED unless -r $directory;
        $source = find_image($r, $directory, $base);
    }

    unless ($source) {
        $r->log_error("Couldn't find a replacement for $file");
        return NOT_FOUND;
    }

    $r->send_http_header;
    return OK if $r->header_only;

    # Read the image
    my $q = Image::Magick->new;
    my $err = $q->Read($source);

    # Conversion arguments are kept in the query string, and the
    # image filter operations are kept in the path info
    my %arguments = $r->args;

    # Run the filters
    for (split '/', $r->path_info) {
        my $filter = ucfirst $_;
        next unless $LegalFilters{$filter};
        $err ||= $q->$filter(%arguments);
    }

    # Remove invalid arguments before the conversion
    for (keys %arguments) {
        delete $arguments{$_} unless $LegalArguments{$_};
    }
```

Example 4-5. Apache::Magick Converts Image Formats on the Fly (continued)

```perl
    # Create a temporary file name to use for conversion
    my($tmpnam, $fh) = Apache::File->tmpfile;

    # Write out the modified image
    open(STDOUT, ">&=" . fileno($fh));
    $extension =~ s/^\.//;
    $err ||= $q->Write('filename' => "\U$extension\L:-", %arguments);
    if ($err) {
        unlink $tmpnam;
        $r->log_error($err);
        return SERVER_ERROR;
    }
    close $fh;

    # At this point the conversion is all done!
    # reopen for reading
    $fh = Apache::File->new($tmpnam);
    unless ($fh) {
        $r->log_error("Couldn't open $tmpnam: $!");
        return SERVER_ERROR;
    }

    # send the file
    $r->send_fd($fh);

    # clean up and go
    unlink $tmpnam;
    return OK;
}

sub find_image {
    my ($r, $directory, $base) = @_;
    my $dh = DirHandle->new($directory) or return;

    my $source;
    for my $entry ($dh->read) {
        my $candidate = fileparse($entry, '\.\w+');
        if ($base eq $candidate) {
            # determine whether this is an image file
            $source = join '', $directory, $entry;
            my $subr = $r->lookup_file($source);
            last if $subr->content_type =~ m:^image/:;
            undef $source;
        }
    }
    $dh->close;
    return $source;
}

1;
__END__
```

Here is a *perl.conf* entry to go with *Apache::Magick*:

```
<Location /images>
  SetHandler perl-script
  PerlHandler Apache::Magick
</Location>
```

A Dynamic Navigation Bar

Many large web sites use a navigation bar to help users find their way around the main subdivisions of the site. Simple navigation bars are composed entirely of link text, while fancier ones use inline images to create the illusion of a series of buttons. Some sites use client-side Java, JavaScript, or frames to achieve special effects like button "rollover," in which the button image changes when the mouse passes over it. Regardless of the technology used to display the navigation bar, they can be troublesome to maintain. Every time you add a new page to the site, you have to remember to insert the correct HTML into the page to display the correct version of the navigation bar. If the structure of the site changes, you might have to manually update dozens or hundreds of HTML files.

Apache content handlers to the rescue. In this section, we develop a navigation bar module called *Apache::NavBar*. When activated, this module automatically adds a navigation bar to the tops and bottoms of all HTML pages on the site. Each major content area of the site is displayed as a hypertext link. When an area is "active" (the user is viewing one of the pages contained within it), its link is replaced with highlighted text (see Figure 4-3).

In this design, the navigation bar is built dynamically from a configuration file. Here's the one that Lincoln uses at his laboratory's site at *http://stein.cshl.org*:

```
# Configuration file for the navigation bar
/index.html          Home
/jade/               Jade
/AcePerl/            AcePerl
/software/boulder/   BoulderIO
/software/WWW/        WWW
/linux/              Linux
```

The right column of this configuration file defines six areas named "Home," "Jade," "AcePerl," "BoulderIO," "WWW," and "Linux" (the odd names correspond to various software packages). The left column defines the URI that each link corresponds to. For example, selecting the "Home" link takes the user to */index.html.* These URIs are also used by the navigation bar generation code to decide when to display an area as active. In the example above, any page that starts with */linux/* is considered to be part of the "Linux" area and its label will be appropriately highlighted. In contrast, since */index.html* refers to a file rather than a partial path, only the home page itself is considered to be contained within the "Home" area.

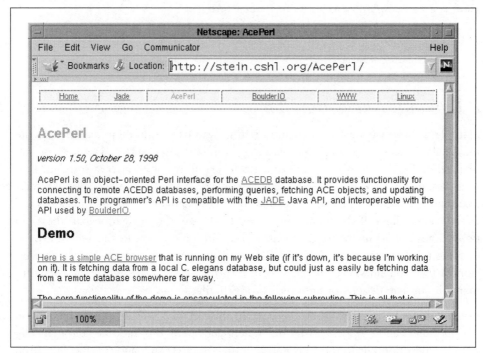

Figure 4-3. The navigation bar at the top of this page was generated dynamically by Apache::NavBar.

Example 4-6 gives the complete code for *Apache::NavBar*. At the end of the example is a sample entry for *perl.conf* (or *httpd.conf* if you prefer) which activates the navigation bar for the entire site.

```
package Apache::NavBar;
# file Apache/NavBar.pm

use strict;
use Apache::Constants qw(:common);
use Apache::File ();

my %BARS = ();
my $TABLEATTS    = 'WIDTH="100%" BORDER=1';
my $TABLECOLOR   = '#C8FFFF';
my $ACTIVECOLOR  = '#FF0000';
```

The preamble brings in the usual modules and defines some constants that will be used later in the code. Among the constants are ones that control the color and size of the navigation bar.

```
sub handler {
    my $r = shift;
    my $bar = read_configuration($r) || return DECLINED;
```

The *handler()* function starts by calling an internal function named *read_configuration()*, which, as its name implies, parses the navigation bar configuration file. If successful, the function returns a custom-designed *NavBar* object that implements the methods we need to build the navigation bar on the fly. As in the server-side includes example, we cache *NavBar* objects in the package global %BARS and only re-create them when the configuration file changes. The cache logic is all handled internally by *read_configuration()*.

If, for some reason, *read_configuration()* returns an undefined value, we decline the transaction by returning DECLINED. Apache will display the page, but the navigation bar will be missing.

```
$r->content_type eq 'text/html'  || return DECLINED;
my $fh = Apache::File->new($r->filename) || return DECLINED;
```

As in the server-side include example, we check the MIME type of the requested file. If it isn't of type *text/html*, then we can't add a navigation bar to it and we return DECLINED to let Apache take its default actions. Otherwise, we attempt to open the file by calling *Apache::File*'s *new()* method. If this fails, we again return DECLINED to let Apache generate the appropriate error message.

```
my $navbar = make_bar($r, $bar);
```

Having successfully processed the configuration file and opened the requested file, we call an internal subroutine named *make_bar()* to create the HTML text for the navigation bar. We'll look at this subroutine momentarily. This fragment of HTML is stored in a variable named $navbar.

```
$r->send_http_header;
return OK if $r->header_only;

local $/ = "";
while (<$fh>) {
    s:(</BODY>):$navbar$1:i;
    s:(<BODY.*?>):$1$navbar:si;
} continue {
    $r->print($_);
}

return OK;
}
```

The remaining code should look familiar. We send the HTTP header and loop through the text in paragraph-style chunks looking for all instances of the <BODY> and </BODY> tags. When we find either tag we insert the navigation bar just below or above it. We use paragraph mode (by setting $/ to the empty string) in order to catch documents that have spread the initial <BODY> tag among multiple lines.

```
sub make_bar {
    my($r, $bar) = @_;
    # create the navigation bar
    my $current_url = $r->uri;
    my @cells;
```

The *make_bar()* function is responsible for generating the navigation bar HTML code. First, it recovers the current document's URI by calling the Apache request object's *uri()* method. Next, it calls *$bar->urls()* to fetch the list of partial URIs for the site's major areas and iterates over the areas in a *for()* loop:

```
for my $url ($bar->urls) {
    my $label = $bar->label($url);
    my $is_current = $current_url =~ /^$url/;
    my $cell = $is_current ?
        qq(<FONT COLOR="$ACTIVECOLOR">$label</FONT>)
            : qq(<A HREF="$url">$label</A>);
    push @cells,
    qq(<TD CLASS="navbar" ALIGN=CENTER BGCOLOR="$TABLECOLOR">$cell</TD>\n);
}
```

For each URI, the code fetches its human-readable label by calling *$bar->label()* and determines whether the current document is part of the area using a pattern match. What happens next depends on whether the current document is part of the area or not. In the former case, the code generates a label enclosed within a <FONT> tag with the COLOR attribute set to red. In the latter case, the code generates a hypertext link. The label or link is then pushed onto a growing array of HTML table cells.

```
    return qq(<TABLE $TABLEATTS><TR>@cells</TR></TABLE>\n);
}
```

At the end of the loop, the code incorporates the table cells into a one-row table and returns the HTML to the caller.

We next look at the *read_configuration()* function:

```
sub read_configuration {
    my $r = shift;
    my $conf_file;
    return unless $conf_file = $r->dir_config('NavConf');
    return unless -e ($conf_file = $r->server_root_relative($conf_file));
```

Potentially there can be several configuration files, each one for a different part of the site. The path to the configuration file is specified by a per-directory Perl configuration variable named *NavConf.* We retrieve the path to the configuration file with *dir_config()*, convert it into an absolute path name with *server_root_relative()*, and test that the file exists with the *-e* operator.

```
    my $mod_time = (stat _)[9];
    return $BARS{$conf_file} if $BARS{$conf_file}
        && $BARS{$conf_file}->modified >= $mod_time;
```

```
        return $BARS{$conf_file} = NavBar->new($conf_file);
    }
```

Because we don't want to reparse the configuration each time we need it, we cache the *NavBar* object in much the same way we did with the server-side include example. Each *NavBar* object has a *modified()* method that returns the time that its configuration file was modified. The *NavBar* objects are held in a global cache named %BARS and indexed by the name of the configuration files. The next bit of code calls *stat()* to return the configuration file's modification time—notice that we can *stat()* the _ filehandle because the foregoing −*e* operation will have cached its results. We then check whether there is already a ready-made *NavBar* object in the cache, and if so, whether its modification date is not older than the configuration file. If both tests are true, we return the cached object; otherwise, we create a new one by calling the *NavBar new()* method.

You'll notice that we use a different technique for finding the modification date here than we did in *Apache::ESSI* (Example 4-3). In the previous example, we used the −*M* file test flag, which returns the relative age of the file in days since the Perl interpreter was launched. In this example, we use *stat()* to determine the absolute age of the file from the filesystem timestamp. The reason for this will become clear later, when we modify the module to handle *If-Modified-Since* caching.

Toward the bottom of the example is the definition for the *NavBar* class. It defines three methods named *new()*, *urls()*, and *label()*:

```
package NavBar;

# create a new NavBar object
sub new {
    my ($class,$conf_file) = @_;
    my (@c,%c);
    my $fh = Apache::File->new($conf_file) || return;
    while (<$fh>) {
        chomp;
        s/^\s+//; s/\s+$//;   # fold leading and trailing whitespace
        next if /^#/ || /^$/; # skip comments and empty lines
        next unless my($url, $label) = /^(\S+)\s+(.+)/;
        push @c, $url;     # keep the url in an ordered array
        $c{$url} = $label; # keep its label in a hash
    }
    return bless {'urls'  => \@c,
                  'labels' => \%c,
                  'modified' => (stat $conf_file)[9]}, $class;
}
```

The *new()* method is called to parse a configuration file and return a new *NavBar* object. It opens up the indicated configuration file, splits each row into the URI and label parts, and stores the two parts into a hash. Since the order in which the various areas appear in the navigation bar is significant, this method also saves the URIs to an ordered array.

```
# return ordered list of all the URIs in the navigation bar
sub urls  { return @{shift->{'urls'}}; }

# return the label for a particular URI in the navigation bar
sub label { return $_[0]->{'labels'}->{$_[1]} || $_[1]; }

# return the modification date of the configuration file
sub modified { return $_[0]->{'modified'}; }

1;
```

The *urls()* method returns the ordered list of areas, and the *label()* method uses the *NavBar* object's hash to return the human-readable label for the given URI. If none is defined, it just returns the URL. *modified()* returns the modification time of the configuration file.

Example 4-6. A Dynamic Navigation Bar

```
package Apache::NavBar;
# file Apache/NavBar.pm

use strict;
use Apache::Constants qw(:common);
use Apache::File ();

my %BARS = ();
my $TABLEATTS   = 'WIDTH="100%" BORDER=1';
my $TABLECOLOR  = '#C8FFFF';
my $ACTIVECOLOR = '#FF0000';

sub handler {
    my $r = shift;
    my $bar = read_configuration($r) || return DECLINED;
    $r->content_type eq 'text/html'  || return DECLINED;
    my $fh = Apache::File->new($r->filename) || return DECLINED;
    my $navbar = make_bar($r, $bar);

    $r->send_http_header;
    return OK if $r->header_only;

    local $/ = "";
    while (<$fh>) {
        s:(</BODY>):$navbar$1:oi;
        s:(<BODY.*?>):$1$navbar:osi;
    } continue {
        $r->print($_);
    }

    return OK;
}
```

Example 4-6. A Dynamic Navigation Bar (continued)

```perl
sub make_bar {
    my($r, $bar) = @_;
    # create the navigation bar
    my $current_url = $r->uri;
    my @cells;
    for my $url ($bar->urls) {
        my $label = $bar->label($url);
        my $is_current = $current_url =~ /^$url/;
        my $cell = $is_current ?
            qq(<FONT COLOR="$ACTIVECOLOR">$label</FONT>)
                : qq(<A HREF="$url">$label</A>);
        push @cells,
        qq(<TD CLASS="navbar" ALIGN=CENTER BGCOLOR="$TABLECOLOR">$cell</TD>\n);
    }
    return qq(<TABLE $TABLEATTS><TR>@cells</TR></TABLE>\n);
}


# read the navigation bar configuration file and return it as a hash.
sub read_configuration {
    my $r = shift;
    my $conf_file;
    return unless $conf_file = $r->dir_config('NavConf');
    return unless -e ($conf_file = $r->server_root_relative($conf_file));
    my $mod_time = (stat _)[9];
    return $BARS{$conf_file} if $BARS{$conf_file}
        && $BARS{$conf_file}->modified >= $mod_time;
    return $BARS{$conf_file} = NavBar->new($conf_file);
}


package NavBar;

# create a new NavBar object
sub new {
    my ($class,$conf_file) = @_;
    my (@c,%c);
    my $fh = Apache::File->new($conf_file) || return;
    while (<$fh>) {
        chomp;
        s/^\s+//; s/\s+$//;    # fold leading and trailing whitespace
        next if /^#/ || /^$/; # skip comments and empty lines
        next unless my($url, $label) = /^(\S+)\s+(.+)/;
        push @c, $url;       # keep the url in an ordered array
        $c{$url} = $label; # keep its label in a hash
    }
    return bless {'urls' => \@c,
                  'labels' => \%c,
                  'modified' => (stat $conf_file)[9]}, $class;
}


# return ordered list of all the URIs in the navigation bar
sub urls  { return @{shift->{'urls'}}; }
```

Example 4-6. A Dynamic Navigation Bar (continued)

```
# return the label for a particular URI in the navigation bar
sub label { return $_[0]->{'labels'}->{$_[1]} || $_[1]; }

# return the modification date of the configuration file
sub modified { return $_[0]->{'modified'}; }

1;
__END__
```

A configuration file section to go with *Apache::NavBar* might read:

```
<Location />
  SetHandler  perl-script
  PerlHandler Apache::NavBar
  PerlSetVar  NavConf conf/navigation.conf
</Location>
```

Because so much of what *Apache::NavBar* and *Apache:ESSI* do is similar, you might want to merge the navigation and server-side include examples. This is just a matter of cutting and pasting the navigation bar code into the server-side function definitions file and then writing a small stub function named *NAVBAR()*. This stub function will call the subroutines that read the configuration file and generate the navigation bar table. You can then incorporate the appropriate navigation bar into your pages anywhere you like with an include like this one:

```
<!--#NAVBAR-->
```

Handling If-Modified-Since

One of us (Lincoln) thought the virtual navigation bar was so neat that he immediately ran out and used it for all documents on his site. Unfortunately, he had some pretty large (>400 MB) files there, and he soon noticed something interesting. Before installing the navigation bar handler, browsers would cache the large HTML files locally and only download them again when they had changed. After installing the handler, however, the files were always downloaded. What happened?

When a browser is asked to display a document that it has cached locally, it sends the remote server a GET request with an additional header field named *If-Modified-Since*. The request looks something like this:

```
GET /index.html HTTP/1.0
If-Modified-Since: Tue, 24 Feb 1998 11:19:03 GMT
User-Agent: (etc. etc. etc.)
```

The server will compare the document's current modification date to the time given in the request. If the document is more recent than that, it will return the whole document. Otherwise, the server will respond with a 304 "not modified" message and the browser will display its cached copy. This reduces network bandwidth usage dramatically.

When you install a custom content handler, the *If-Modified-Since* mechanism no longer works unless *you* implement it. In fact, you can generally ignore *If-Modified-Since* because content handlers usually generate dynamic documents that change from access to access. However, in some cases the content you provide is sufficiently static that it pays to cache the documents. The navigation bar is one such case because even though the bar is generated dynamically, it rarely changes from day to day.

In order to handle *If-Modified-Since* caching, you have to settle on a definition for the document's most recent modification date. In the case of a static document, this is simply the modification time of the file. In the case of composite documents that consist equally of static file content and a dynamically generated navigation bar, the modification date is either the time that the HTML file was last changed or the time that the navigation bar configuration file was changed, whichever happens to be more recent. Fortunately for us, we're already storing the configuration file's modification date in the *NavBar* object, so finding this aggregate modification time is relatively simple.

To use these routines, simply add the following just before the call to $r->send_http_header in the *handler()* subroutine:

```
$r->update_mtime($bar->modified);
$r-.set_last_modified;
my $rc = $r-> meets_conditions
return $rc unless $rc == OK;
```

We first call the *update_mtime()* function with the navigation bar's modification date. This function will compare the specified date with the modification date of the request document and update the request's internal mtime field to the most recent of the two. We then call *set_last_modified()* to copy the mtime field into the outgoing *Last-Modified* header. If a synthesized document depends on several configuration files, you should call *update_mtime()* once for each configuration file, followed by *set_last_modified()* at the very end.

The complete code for the new and improved *Apache::NavBar*, with the *If-Modified-Since* improvements, can be found at this book's companion web site.

If you think carefully about this module, you'll see that it still isn't strictly correct. There's a third modification date that we should take into account, that of the module source code itself. Changes to the source code may affect the appearance of the document without changing the modification date of either the configuration file or the HTML file. We could add a new *update_mtime()* with the modification time of the *Apache::NavBar* module, but then we'd have to worry about modification times of libraries that *Apache::NavBar* depends on, such as *Apache::File*. This gets hairy very quickly, which is why caching becomes a moot issue for any dynamic document much more complicated than this one. See "The

Apache::File Class*" in Chapter 9, *Perl API Reference Guide*, for a complete run-
down of the methods that are available to you for controlling HTTP/1.1 caching.

Sending Static Files

If you want your content handler to send a file through without modifying it, the
easiest way is to let Apache do all the work for you. Simply return DECLINED from
your handler (before you send the HTTP header or the body) and the request will
fall through to Apache's default handler. This is a lot easier, not to mention faster,
than opening up the file, reading it line by line, and transmitting it unchanged. In
addition, Apache will automatically handle a lot of the details for you, first and
foremost of which is handling the *If-Modified-Since* header and other aspects of
client-side caching.

If you have a compelling reason to send static files manually, see *Using
Apache::File to Send Static Files* in Chapter 9 for a full description of the technique. Also see "Redirection," later in this chapter, for details on how to direct the
browser to request a different URI or to make Apache send the browser a different document from the one that was specifically requested.

Virtual Documents

The previous sections of this chapter have been concerned with transforming
existing files. Now we turn our attention to spinning documents out of thin air.
Despite the fact that these two operations seem very different, Apache content
handlers are responsible for them both. A content handler is free to ignore the
translation of the URI that is passed to it. Apache neither knows nor cares that the
document produced by the content handler has no correspondence to a physical
file.

We've already seen an Apache content handler that produces a virtual document.
Chapter 2, *A First Module*, gave the code for *Apache::Hello*, an Apache Perl module that produces a short HTML document. For convenience, we show it again in
Example 4-7. This content handler is essentially identical to the previous content
handlers we've seen. The main difference is that the content handler sets the
MIME content type itself, calling the request object's *content_type()* method to set
the MIME type to type *text/html*. This is in contrast to the idiom we used earlier,
where the handler allowed Apache to choose the content type for it. After this, the
process of emitting the HTTP header and the document itself is the same as we've
seen before.

After setting the content type, the handler calls *send_http_header()* to send the
HTTP header to the browser, and immediately exits with an OK status code if

header_only() returns true (this is a slight improvement over the original Chapter 2 version of the program). We call *get_remote_host()* to get the DNS name of the remote host machine, and incorporate the name into a short HTML document that we transmit using the request object's *print()* method. At the end of the handler, we return OK.

There's no reason to be limited to producing virtual HTML documents. You can just as easily produce images, sounds, and other types of multimedia, provided of course that you know how to produce the file format that goes along with the MIME type.

Example 4-7. "Hello World" Redux

```
package Apache::Hello;
# file: Apache/Hello.pm

use strict;
use Apache::Constants qw(:common);

sub handler {
    my $r = shift;
    $r->content_type('text/html');
    $r->send_http_header;
    return OK unless $r->header_only;
    my $host = $r->get_remote_host;
    $r->print(<<END);
<HTML>
<HEAD>
<TITLE>Hello There</TITLE>
</HEAD>
<BODY>
<H1>Hello $host</H1>
"Hello world" is a terribly overused phrase in programming books,
don't you think?
</BODY>
</HTML>
END
    return OK;
}

1;
```

Redirection

Instead of synthesizing a document, a content handler has the option of redirecting the browser to fetch a different URI using the HTTP redirect mechanism. You can use this facility to randomly select a page or picture to display in response to a URI request (many banner ad generators work this way) or to implement a custom navigation system.

Redirection is extremely simple with the Apache API. You need only add a *Location* field to the HTTP header containing the full or partial URI of the desired destination, and return a REDIRECT result code. A complete functional example using *mod_perl* is only a few lines (Example 4-8). This module, named *Apache::GoHome*, redirects users to the hardcoded URI *http://www.ora.com/*. When the user selects a document or a portion of the document tree that this content handler has been attached to, the browser will immediately jump to that URI.

The module begins by importing the REDIRECT error code from *Apache::Constants* (REDIRECT isn't among the standard set of result codes imported with *:common*). The *handler()* method then adds the desired location to the outgoing headers by calling *Apache::header_out()*. *header_out()* can take one or two arguments. Called with one argument, it returns the current value of the indicated HTTP header field. Called with two arguments, it sets the field indicated by the first argument to the value indicated by the second argument. In this case, we use the two-argument form to set the HTTP *Location* field to the desired URI.

The final step is to return the REDIRECT result code. There's no need to generate an HTML body, since most HTTP-compliant browsers will take you directly to the *Location* URI. However, Apache adds an appropriate body automatically in order to be HTTP-compliant. You can see the header and body message using telnet:

```
% telnet localhost 80
Trying 127.0.0.1...
Connected to localhost.
Escape character is '^]'.
GET /gohome HTTP/1.0

HTTP/1.1 302 Moved Temporarily
Date: Mon, 05 Oct 1998 22:15:17 GMT
Server: Apache/1.3.3-dev (Unix) mod_perl/1.16
Location: http://www.ora.com/
Connection: close
Content-Type: text/html

<!DOCTYPE HTML PUBLIC "-//IETF//DTD HTML 2.0//EN">
<HTML><HEAD>
<TITLE>302 Moved Temporarily</TITLE>
</HEAD><BODY>
<H1>Moved Temporarily</H1>
The document has moved <A HREF="http://www.ora.com/">here</A>.<P>
</BODY></HTML>
Connection closed by foreign host.
```

You'll notice from this example that the REDIRECT status causes a "Moved Temporarily" message to be issued. This is appropriate in most cases because it makes no warrants to the browser that it will be redirected to the same location the next time it tries to fetch the desired URI. If you wish to redirect permanently, you should use the MOVED status code instead, which results in a "301 Moved

Permanently" message. A smart browser might remember the redirected URI and fetch it directly from its new location the next time it's needed.

Example 4-8. Generating a Redirect from a Content Handler

```
package Apache::GoHome;
# file: Apache/GoHome.pm

use strict;
use Apache::Constants qw(REDIRECT);

sub handler {
  my $r = shift;
  $r->content_type('text/html');
  $r->header_out(Location => 'http://www.ora.com/');
  return REDIRECT;
}

1;
__END__
```

As a more substantial example of redirection in action, consider *Apache::RandPicture* (Example 4-9) which randomly selects a different image file to display each time it's called. It works by selecting an image file from among the contents of a designated directory, then redirecting the browser to that file's URI. In addition to demonstrating a useful application of redirection, it again shows off the idiom for interconverting physical file names and URIs.

The handler begins by fetching the name of a directory to fetch the images from, which is specified in the server configuration file by the Perl variable *PictureDir*. Because the selected image has to be directly fetchable by the browser, the image directory must be given as a URI rather than as a physical path.

The next task is to convert the directory URI into a physical directory path. The subroutine adds a / to the end of the URI if there isn't one there already (ensuring that Apache treats the URI as a directory), then calls the request object's *lookup_uri()* and *filename()* methods in order to perform the URI translation steps. The code looks like this:

```
my $subr = $r->lookup_uri($dir_uri);
my $dir = $subr->filename;
```

Now we need to obtain a listing of image files in the directory. The simple way to do this would be to use the Perl glob operator, for instance:

```
chdir $dir;
@files = <*.{jpg,gif}>;
```

However, this technique is flawed. First off, on many systems the glob operation launches a C subshell, which sends performance plummeting and won't even work on systems without the C shell (like Win32 platforms). Second, it makes assumptions about the extension types of image files. Your site may have defined an alternate extension for image files (or may be using a completely different system for keeping track of image types, such as the Apache MIME magic module), in which case this operation will miss some images.

Instead, we create a *DirHandle* object using Perl's directory handle object wrapper. We call the directory handle's *read()* method repeatedly to iterate through the contents of the directory. For each item we ask Apache what it thinks the file's MIME type should be, by calling the *lookup_uri()* method to turn the filename into a subrequest and *content_type()* to fetch the MIME type information from the subrequest. We perform a pattern match on the returned type and, if the file is one of the MIME image types, add it to a growing list of image URIs. The subrequest object's *uri()* method is called to return the absolute URI for the image. The whole process looks like this:

```
my @files;
for my $entry ($dh->read) {
    # get the file's MIME type
    my $rr = $subr->lookup_uri($entry);
    my $type = $rr->content_type;
    next unless $type =~ m:^image/:;
    push @files, $rr->uri;
}
```

Note that we look up the directory entry's filename by calling the *subrequest* object's *lookup_uri()* method rather than using the main request object stored in $r. This takes advantage of the fact that subrequests will look up relative paths relative to their own URI.

The next step is to select a member of this list randomly, which we do using this time-tested Perl idiom:

```
my $lucky_one = $files[rand @files];
```

The last step is to set the *Location* header to point at this file (being sure to express the location as a URI) and to return a **REDIRECT** result code. If you install the module using the sample configuration file and <IMG> tag shown at the bottom of the listing, a different picture will be displayed every time you load the page.

Example 4-9. Redirecting the Browser to a Randomly Chosen Picture

```
package Apache::RandPicture;
# file: Apache/RandPicture.pm

use strict;
use Apache::Constants qw(:common REDIRECT);
use DirHandle ();
```

Example 4-9. Redirecting the Browser to a Randomly Chosen Picture (continued)

```perl
sub handler {
    my $r = shift;
    my $dir_uri = $r->dir_config('PictureDir');
    unless ($dir_uri) {
        $r->log_reason("No PictureDir configured");
        return SERVER_ERROR;
    }
    $dir_uri .= "/" unless $dir_uri =~ m:/$:;

    my $subr = $r->lookup_uri($dir_uri);
    my $dir = $subr->filename;
    # Get list of images in the directory.
    my $dh = DirHandle->new($dir);
    unless ($dh) {
        $r->log_error("Can't read directory $dir: $!");
        return SERVER_ERROR;
    }

    my @files;
    for my $entry ($dh->read) {
        # get the file's MIME type
        my $rr = $subr->lookup_uri($entry);
        my $type = $rr->content_type;
        next unless $type =~ m:^image/:;
        push @files, $rr->uri;
    }
    $dh->close;
    unless (@files) {
        $r->log_error("No image files in directory");
        return SERVER_ERROR;
    }

    my $lucky_one = $files[rand @files];
    $r->header_out(Location => $lucky_one);
    return REDIRECT;
}

1;
__END__
```

A configuration section to go with *Apache::RandPicture* might be:

```
<Location /random/picture>
    SetHandler  perl-script
    PerlHandler Apache::RandPicture
    PerlSetVar  PictureDir  /banners
</Location>
```

And you'd use it in an HTML document like this:

```
<image src="/random/picture" alt="[Our Sponsor]">
```

Although elegant, this technique for selecting a random image file suffers from a bad performance bottleneck. Instead of requiring only a single network operation to get the picture from the server to the browser, it needs two round-trips across the network: one for the browser's initial request and redirect and one to fetch the image itself.

You can eliminate this overhead in several different ways. The more obvious technique is to get rid of the redirection entirely and simply send the image file directly. After selecting the random image and placing it in the variable $lucky_ one, we replace the last two lines of the *handler()* subroutine with code like this:

```
$subr = $r->lookup_uri($lucky_one);
$r->content_type($subr->content_type);
$r->send_http_header;
return OK unless $r->header_only;
my $fh = Apache::File->new($subr->filename) || return FORBIDDEN;
$r->send_fd($fh);
```

We create yet another subrequest, this one for the selected image file, then use information from the subrequest to set the outgoing content type. We then open up the file and send it with the *send_fd()* method.

However, this is still a little wasteful because it requires you to open up the file yourself. A more subtle solution would be to let Apache do the work of sending the file by invoking the subrequest's *run()* method. *run()* invokes the subrequest's content handler to send the body of the document, just as if the browser had made the request itself. The code now looks like this:

```
my $subr = $r->lookup_uri($lucky_one);
unless ($subr->status == DOCUMENT_FOLLOWS) {
    $r->log_error("Can't lookup file $lucky_one}: $!");
    return SERVER_ERROR;
}
$r->content_type($subr->content_type);
$r->send_http_header;
return OK if $r->header_only;
$subr->run;
return OK;
```

We call *lookup_uri()* and check the value returned by its *status()* method in order to make sure that it is DOCUMENT_FOLLOWS (status code 200, the same as HTTP_ OK). This constant is not exported by *Apache::Constants* by default but has to be imported explicitly. We then set the main request's content type to the same as that of the subrequest, and send off the appropriate HTTP header. Finally, we call the subrequest's *run()* method to invoke its content handler and send the contents of the image to the browser.

Internal Redirection

The two *Apache::RandPicture* optimizations that we showed in the previous section involve a lot of typing, and the resulting code is a bit obscure. A far more elegant solution is to let Apache do all the work for you with its internal redirection mechanism. In this scheme, Apache handles the entire redirection internally. It pretends that the web browser made the request for the new URI and sends the contents of the file, without letting the browser in on the secret. It is functionally equivalent to the solution that we showed at the end of the preceding section.

To invoke the Apache internal redirection system, modify the last two lines of *Apache::RandPicture*'s *handler()* subroutine to read like this:

```
$r->internal_redirect($lucky_one);
return OK;
```

The request object's *internal_redirect()* method takes a single argument consisting of an absolute local URI (one starting with a */*). The method does all the work of translating the URI, invoking its content handler, and returning the file contents, if any. Unfortunately *internal_redirect()* returns no result code, so there's no way of knowing whether the redirect was successful (you can't do this from a conventional redirect either). However, the call will return in any case, allowing you to do whatever cleanup is needed. You should exit the handler with a result code of OK.

In informal benchmarks, replacing the basic *Apache::RandPicture* with a version that uses internal redirection increased the throughput by a factor of two, exactly what we'd expect from halving the number of trips through the network. In contrast, replacing all the MIME type lookups with a simpler direct grep for image file extensions had negligible effect on the speed of the module. Apache's subrequest mechanism is very efficient.

If you have very many images in the random pictures directory (more than a few hundred), iterating through the directory listing each time you need to fetch an image will result in a noticeable performance hit. In this case, you'll want to cache the directory listing in a package variable the first time you generate it and only rebuild the listing when the directory's modification time changes (or just wait for a server restart, if the directory doesn't change often). You could adapt the *Apache::ESSI* caching system for this purpose.

Internal redirection is a win for most cases when you want to redirect the browser to a different URI on your own site. Be careful not to use it for external URIs, however. For these, you must either use standard redirection or invoke Apache's proxy API (Chapter 7).

When you use internal redirection to pass control from one module to another, the second module in the chain can retrieve the original query string, the document URI, and other information about the original request by calling the request object's *prev()* method or, in *Apache::Registry* scripts only, by examining certain environment variables. There is also a way, using *Apache::err_header_out()* for the original module to set various HTTP header fields, such as cookies, that will be transferred to the second across the internal redirect. Because internal redirects are most commonly used in error handlers, these techniques are discussed in the section "Handling Errors" later in this chapter.

Processing Input

You can make the virtual documents generated by the Apache API interactive in exactly the way that you would documents generated by CGI scripts. Your module will generate an HTML form for the user to fill out. When the user completes and submits the form, your module will process the parameters and generate a new document, which may contain another fill-out form that prompts the user for additional information. In addition, you can store information inside the URI itself by placing it in the additional path information part.

CGI Parameters

When a fill-out form is submitted, the contents of its fields are turned into a series of name=value parameter pairs that are available for your module's use. Unfortunately, correctly processing these parameter pairs is annoying because, for a number of historical reasons, there are a variety of formats that you must know about and deal with. The first complication is that the form may be submitted using either the HTTP GET or POST method. If the GET method is used, the URI encoded parameter pairs can be found separated by ampersands in the "query string," the part of the URI that follows the ? character:

```
http://your.site/uri/path?name1=val1&name2=val2&name3=val3...
```

To recover the parameters from a GET request, *mod_perl* users should use the request object's *args()* method. In a scalar context this method returns the entire query string, ampersands and all. In an array context, this method returns the parsed name=value pairs; however, you will still have to do further processing in order to correctly handle multivalued parameters. This feature is only found in the Perl API. Programmers who use the C API must recover the query string from the request object's *args* field and do all the parsing manually.

If the client uses the POST method to submit the fill-out form, the parameter pairs can be found in something called the "client block." C API users must call three functions named *setup_client_block()*, *should_client_block()*, and *get_client_block()* in order to retrieve the information.

While these methods are also available in the Perl API, *mod_perl* users have an easier way: they need only call the request object's *content()* method to retrieve the preparsed list of name=value pairs. However, there's a catch: this only works for the older *application/x-www-form-urlencoded* style of parameter encoding. If the browser uses the newer *multipart/form-data* encoding (which is used for file uploads, among other things), then *mod_perl* users will have to read and parse the content information themselves. *read()* will fetch the unparsed content information by looping until the requested number of bytes have been read (or a predetermined timeout has occurred). Fortunately, there are a number of helpful modules that allow *mod_perl* programmers to accept file uploads without parsing the data themselves, including CGI.pm and *Apache::Request*, both of which we describe later.

To show you the general technique for prompting and processing user input, Example 4-10 gives a new version of *Apache::Hello*. It looks for a parameter named *user_name* and displays a customized welcome page, if present. Otherwise, it creates a more generic message. In both cases, it also displays a fill-out form that prompts the user to enter a new value for *user_name*. When the user presses the submission button labeled "Set Name," the information is POSTed to the module and the page is redisplayed (Figure 4-4).

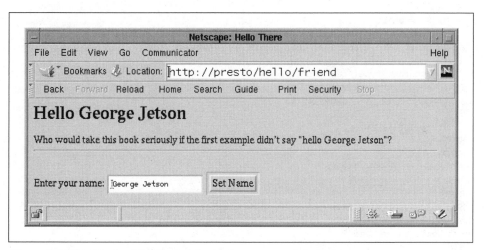

Figure 4-4. The Apache::Hello2 module can process user input.

The code is very simple. On entry to *handler()* the module calls the request object's *method()* method to determine whether the handler was invoked using a POST request, or by some other means (usually GET). If the POST method was used, the handler calls the request object's *content()* method to retrieve the posted parameters. Otherwise, it attempts to retrieve the information from the query string by calling *args()*. The parsed name=value pairs are now stuffed into a hash named %params for convenient access.

Having processed the user input, if any, the handler retrieves the value of the *user_name* parameter from the hash and stores it in a variable. If the parameter is empty, we default to "Unknown User."

The next step is to generate the document. We set the content type to *text/html* as before and emit the HTTP header. We again call the request object's *header_only()* to determine whether the client has requested the entire document or just the HTTP header information.

This is followed by a single long *Apache::print()* statement. We create the HTML header and body, along with a suitable fill-out form. Notice that we use the current value of the user name variable to initialize the appropriate text field. This is a frill that we have always thought was kind of neat.

Example 4-10. Processing User Input with the Apache Perl API

```
package Apache::Hello2;
# file: Apache/Hello2.pm
use strict;
use Apache::Constants qw(:common);

sub handler {
    my $r = shift;
    my %params = $r->method eq 'POST' ? $r->content : $r->args;
    my $user_name = $params{'user_name'} || 'Unknown User';

    $r->content_type('text/html');
    $r->send_http_header;
    return OK if $r->header_only;

    $r->print(<<END);
<HTML>
<HEAD>
<TITLE>Hello There</TITLE>
</HEAD>
<BODY>
<H1>Hello $user_name</H1>
Who would take this book seriously if the first example didn\'t
say "hello $user_name"?
<HR>
<FORM METHOD="POST">
Enter your name: <INPUT TYPE="text" NAME="user_name" VALUE="$user_name">
<INPUT TYPE="submit" VALUE="Set Name">
</FORM>
</BODY>
</HTML>
END
```

Example 4-10. Processing User Input with the Apache Perl API (continued)

```
    return OK;
}

1;
__END__
```

A *perl.conf* entry to go with it might read:

```
<Location /hello/friend>
  SetHandler  perl-script
  PerlHandler Apache::Hello2
</Location>
```

This method of processing user input is only one of several equally valid alternatives. For example, you might want to work with query string and POSTed parameters simultaneously, to accommodate this type of fill-out form:

```
<FORM ACTION="/hello/friend?day=saturday" METHOD="POST">
    <INPUT TYPE="text" NAME="user_name">
    <INPUT TYPE="submit">
</FORM>
```

In this case, you could recover the values of both the *day* and *user_name* parameters using a code fragment like this one:

```
my %params = ($r->args, $r->content);
```

If the same parameter is present in both the query string and the POSTed values, then the latter will override the former. Depending on your application's logic, you might like this behavior. Alternatively, you could store the two types of parameter in different places or take different actions depending on whether the parameters were submitted via GET or POST. For example, you might want to use query string parameters to initialize the default values of the fill-out form and enter the information into a database when a POST request is received.

When you store the parsed parameters into a hash, you lose information about parameters that are present more than once. This can be bad if you are expecting multivalued parameters, such as those generated by a selection list or a series of checkboxes linked by the same name. To keep multivalued information, you need to do something like this:

```
my %params;
my @args = ($r->args, $r->content);
while (my($name,$value) = splice @args,0,2) {
   push @{$params{$name}}, $value;
}
```

This bit of code aggregates the GET and POST parameters into a single array named @args. It then loops through each name=value pair, building up a hash in which the key is the parameter name and the value is an array reference containing all the values for that parameter. This way, if you have a selection list that generates query strings of the form:

```
vegetable=kale&vegetable=broccoli&vegetable=carrots
```

you can recover the complete vegetable list in this manner:

```
@vegetables = @{$params{'vegetable'}};
```

An alternative is to use a module that was still in development at the time this chapter was written. This module, named *Apache::Request*, uses the CGI.pm-style method calls to process user input but does so efficiently by going directly to the request object. With this module, the user input parameters are retrieved by calling *param()*. Call *param()* without any arguments to retrieve a list of all the parameter names. Call *param()* with a parameter name to return a list of the values for that parameter in an array context, and the first member of the list in a scalar context. Unlike the vanilla request object, input of type *multipart/form-data* is handled correctly, and uploaded files can be recovered too (using the same API as CGI.pm).

To take advantage of *Apache::Request* in our "Hello World" module, we modify the top part of the module to read as follows:

```
package Apache::Hello3;
# file: Apache/Hello3.pm

use strict;
use Apache::Constants qw(:common);
use Apache::Request;

sub handler {
    my $r = Apache::Request->new(shift);
    my $user_name = $r->param('user_name') || 'Unknown User';
    $r->content_type('text/html');
    $r->print(<<END);
Who cares if every single example
says "Hello World"???!
END
    ;
    ...
```

The main detail here is that instead of retrieving the request object directly, we wrap it inside an *Apache::Request* object. *Apache::Request* adds *param()* and a few other useful methods and inherits all other method calls from the *Apache* class. More information will be found in the *Apache::Request* manual page when that package is officially released.

Like CGI.pm, *Apache::Request* allows you to handle browser file uploading, although it is somewhat different in detail from the interface provided in CGI.pm versions 2.46 and lower (the two libraries have been brought into harmony in Version 2.47). As in ordinary CGI, you create a file upload field by defining an

<INPUT> element of type "file" within a <FORM> section of type "multipart/form-data". After the form is POSTed, you retrieve the file contents by reading from a filehandle returned by the *Apache::Request upload()* method. This code fragment illustrates the technique:

```
my $r = Apache::Request->new(shift);
my $moose = 0;
my $uploaded_file = $r->upload('uploaded-file');
my $uploaded_name = $r->param('uploaded-file');
while (<$uploaded_file>) {
    $moose++ if /moose/;
}
print "$moose moose(s) found in $uploaded_name\n";
```

Additional Path Information

Recall that after Apache parses an incoming URI to figure out what module to invoke, there may be some extra bits left over. This extra stuff becomes the "additional path information" and is available for your module to use in any way it wishes. Because it is hierarchical, the additional path information part of the URI follows all the same relative path rules as the rest of the URI. For example, .. means to move up one level. For this reason, additional path information is often used to navigate through a virtual document tree that is dynamically created and maintained by a CGI script or module. However, you don't have to take advantage of the hierarchical nature of path information. You can just use it as a handy place to store variables. In the next chapter, we'll use additional path information to stash a session identifier for a long-running web application.

Apache modules fetch additional path information by calling the request object's *path_info()* method. If desired, they can then turn the path information into a physical filename by calling *lookup_uri()*.

An example of how additional path information can be used as a virtual document tree is shown in Example 4-11, which contains the code for *Apache::TreeBrowser*. This module generates a series of documents that are organized in a browseable tree hierarchy that is indistinguishable to the user from a conventional HTML file hierarchy. However, there are no physical files. Instead, the documents are generated from a large treelike Perl data structure that specifies how each "document" should be displayed. Here is an excerpt:

```
'bark'=>{
    -title=>'The Wrong Tree',
    -contents=>'His bark was worse than his bite.',
    'smooth'=>{
        -title=>'Like Butter',
        -contents=>'As smooth as silk.'
        },
    'rough'=>{
```

```
        -title=>'Ruffled',
        -contents=>"Don't get rough with me."
        },
    }...
```

In this bit of the tree, a document named "bark" has the title "The Wrong Tree" and the contents "His bark was worse than his bite." Beneath this document are two subdocuments named "smooth" and "rough." The "smooth" document has the title "Like Butter" and the contents "As smooth as silk." The "rough" document is similarly silly. These subdocuments can be addressed with the additional path information */bark/smooth* and */bark/rough*, respectively. The parent document, naturally enough, is addressed by */bark*. Within the module, we call each chunk of this data structure a "node."

Using the information contained in the data structure, *Apache::TreeBrowser* constructs the document and displays its information along with a browseable set of links organized in hierarchical fashion (see Figure 4-5). As the user moves from document to document, the currently displayed document is highlighted—sort of a hierarchical navigation bar!

The source code listing is long, so we'll run through it a chunk at a time:

```
    package Apache::TreeBrowser;

    use strict;
    use Apache::Constants qw(:common REDIRECT);

    my $TREE = make_tree();

    sub handler {
        my $r = shift;
```

The module starts by importing the usual Apache constants and the **REDIRECT** result code. It then creates the browseable tree by calling an internal subroutine named *make_tree()* and stores the information in a package global named **$TREE**. In a real-life application, this data structure would be created in some interesting way, for example, using a query on a database, but in this case *make_tree()* just returns the hardcoded data structure that follows the **__DATA__** token at the end of the code.

```
        my $path_info = $r->path_info;
        my $path_translated = $r->lookup_uri($path_info)->filename;
        my $current_uri = $r->uri;
```

Now's the time to process the additional path information. The handler fetches the path information by calling the request object's *path_info()* method and fetches the module's base URI by calling *uri()*. Even though we won't be using it, we transform the additional path information into a physical pathname by calling

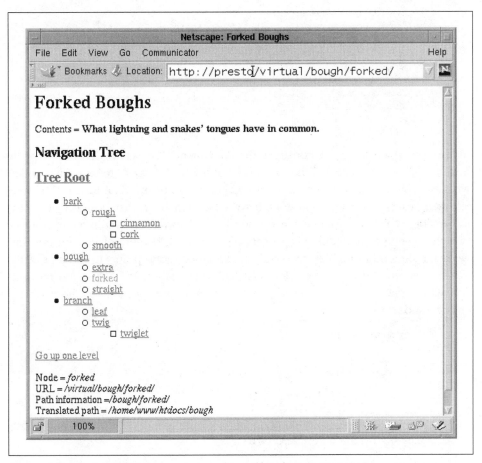

Figure 4-5. Apache::TreeBrowser creates a hierarchical navigation tree.

lookup_uri() and *filename()*. This is useful for seeing how Apache does URI translation.

```
unless ($path_info) {
    $r->header_out(Location => "$current_uri/");
    return REDIRECT;
}
```

For this module to work correctly, some additional path information has to be provided, even if it's only a / character. If we find that the additional path information is empty, we rectify the situation by redirecting the browser to our URI with an additional / appended to the end. This is similar to the way that Apache redirects browsers to directories when the terminal slash is omitted.

```
$r->content_type('text/html');
$r->send_http_header;
```

```
    return OK if $r->header_only;
    my($junk, @components) = split "/", $path_info;

    # follow the components down
    my($node, $name) = ($TREE, '');
    foreach (@components) {
        last unless $node->{$_};
        $name = $_;
        $node = $node->{$_};
    }
```

At this point we begin to construct the document. We set the content type to
text/html, send out the HTTP header, and exit if *header_only()* returns true. Otherwise, we split the path information into its components and then traverse the tree,
following each component name until we either reach the last component on the
list or come to a component that doesn't have a corresponding entry in the tree
(which sometimes happens when users type in the URI themselves). By the time
we reach the end of the tree traversal, the variable $node points to the part of the
tree that is referred to by the additional path information or, if the path information wasn't entirely correct, to the part of the tree corresponding to the last valid
path component.

```
        $r->print(<<END);
    <HTML>
    <HEAD>
    <TITLE>$node->{-title}</TITLE>
    </HEAD>
    <BODY BGCOLOR="white">
    <H1>$node->{-title}</H1>

    Contents = <b>$node->{-contents}</b>

    <H2>Navigation Tree</H2>
    END
        my $prefix = "../" x @components;
        print $prefix ?
            qq(<H3><A HREF="$prefix">Tree Root</A></H3>\n) :
            qq(<H3><FONT COLOR="red">Tree Root</FONT></H3>);
```

We now call *print()* to print out the HTML document. We first display the current
document's title and contents. We then print a hyperlink that points back to the
"root" (really the top level) of the tree. Notice how we construct this link by creating a relative URI based on the number of components in the additional path
information. If the additional path information is currently /bark/rough/cork,
we construct a link whose HREF is ../../../. Through the magic of relative
addressing, this will take us back to the root / document.

```
        print_node('', $TREE, $node, $prefix);
        print qq(<A HREF="../">Go up one level</A><P>) if $name;
```

The next task is to construct the hierarchical navigation system shown in Figure 4-5. We do this by calling *print_node()*, an internal function. This is followed by a link to the next-higher document, which is simply the relative path ` ../`.

```
        $r->print(<<END);
Node = <EM>$name</EM><br>
URI = <EM>$current_uri</EM><br>
Path information =<EM>$path_info</EM><br>
Translated path = <EM>$path_translated</EM>
</BODY>
</HTML>
END


    return OK;
}
```

Last, we print out some more information about the current document, including the internal name of the document, the current URI, the additional path information, and the translated path information.

Let's now look at the *print_node()* subroutine:

```
sub print_node {
    my ($name, $node, $current, $prefix) = @_;
    my (@branches) = grep !/^-/, sort keys %$node;
    if ($name) {
        # print the node itself
        print $node != $current ?
            qq(<LI><A HREF="$prefix$name/">$name</A></LI>\n) :
                qq(<LI><FONT COLOR="red">$name</FONT></LI>\n);
        # print branches underneath it
        $prefix .= "$name/";
    }
    return unless @branches;
    print "<UL>\n";
    foreach (@branches) {
        print_node($_, $node->{$_}, $current, $prefix);
    }
    print "</UL>\n";
}
```

This subroutine is responsible for displaying a tree node as a nested list. It starts by finding all the branches beneath the requested node, which just happens to be all the hash keys that don't begin with a hyphen. It then prints out the name of the node. If the node being displayed corresponds to the current document, the name is surrounded by <FONT> tags to display it in red. Otherwise, the node name is turned into a hyperlink that points to the appropriate document. Then, for each subdocument beneath the current node, it invokes itself recursively to display the subdocument. The most obscure part of this subroutine is the need to append a `$prefix` variable to each URI the routine generates. `$prefix` contains just the right number of `../` sequences to make the URIs point to the root of the virtual document tree. This simplifies the program logic.

The last function in this module is *make_tree()*. It simply reads in the text following the `__DATA__` token and *eval()*s it, turning it into a Perl data structure:

```perl
sub make_tree {
    local $/;
    my $data = <DATA>;
    eval $data;
}


1;
  __DATA__
```

Example 4-11. Using Path Information to Browse a Tree

```perl
package Apache::TreeBrowser;
# file: Apache/TreeBrowser.pm

use strict;
use Apache::Constants qw(:common REDIRECT);

my $TREE = make_tree();

sub handler {
    my $r = shift;
    my $path_info = $r->path_info;
    my $path_translated = $r->lookup_uri($path_info)->filename;
    my $current_uri = $r->uri;
    unless ($path_info) {
        $r->header_out(Location => "$current_uri/");
        return REDIRECT;
    }

    $r->content_type('text/html');
    $r->send_http_header;
    return OK if $r->header_only;
    my($junk, @components) = split "/", $path_info;

    # follow the components down
    my($node, $name) = ($TREE, '');
    foreach (@components) {
        last unless $node->{$_};
        $name = $_;
        $node = $node->{$_};
    }

    $r->print(<<END);
<HTML>
<HEAD>
<TITLE>$node->{-title}</TITLE>
</HEAD>
<BODY BGCOLOR="white">
```

Example 4-11. Using Path Information to Browse a Tree (continued)

```
<H1>$node->{-title}</H1>

Contents = <b>$node->{-contents}</b>

<H2>Navigation Tree</H2>
END

    my $prefix = "../" x @components;
    print $prefix ?
        qq(<H3><A HREF="$prefix">Tree Root</A></H3>\n) :
        qq(<H3><FONT COLOR="red">Tree Root</FONT></H3>);

    print_node('', $TREE, $node, $prefix);
    print qq(<A HREF="../">Go up one level</A><P>) if $name;

    $r->print(<<END);
Node = <EM>$name</EM><br>
URI = <EM>$current_uri</EM><br>
Path information =<EM>$path_info</EM><br>
Translated path = <EM>$path_translated</EM>
</BODY>
</HTML>
END

    return OK;
}

sub print_node {
    my ($name, $node, $current, $prefix) = @_;
    my (@branches) = grep !/^-/, sort keys %$node;
    if ($name) {
        # print the node itself
        print $node != $current ?
            qq(<LI><A HREF="$prefix$name/">$name</A></LI>\n) :
                qq(<LI><FONT COLOR="red">$name</FONT></LI>\n);
        # print branches underneath it
        $prefix .= "$name/";
    }
    return unless @branches;
    print "<UL>\n";
    foreach (@branches) {
        print_node($_, $node->{$_}, $current, $prefix);
    }
    print "</UL>\n";
}

# create a sample tree to browse
sub make_tree {
    local $/;
    my $data = <DATA>;
    eval $data;
}
```

Example 4-11. Using Path Information to Browse a Tree (continued)

```
__DATA__
return {
    -title => 'The Root of All Evil',
    -contents => 'And so it begins...',
    'bark' => {
        -title => 'The Wrong Tree',
        -contents => 'His bark was worse than his bite.',
        'smooth' => {
            -title => 'Like Butter',
            -contents => 'As smooth as silk.',
        },
        'rough' => {
            -title => 'Ruffled',
            -contents => "Don't get rough with me.",
            'cork' => {
                -title => 'Corked',
                -contents => "Corks don't grow on trees...or do they?",
            },
            'cinnamon' => {
                -title => 'The Cinnamon Tree',
                -contents => 'Little bird, little bird in the cinnamon tree...',
            },
        }
    },
    'bough' => {
        -title => 'Stealing a Bough',
        -contents => "I've taken a bough of silence.",
        'forked' => {
            -title => 'Forked Boughs',
            -contents => 'What lightning and snakes\' tongues have in common.',
        },
        'straight' => {
            -title => 'Single Boughs',
            -contents => 'Straight, but not narrow.',
        },
        'extra' => {
            -title => 'Take a Bough',
            -contents => 'Nothing beats that special feeling,
                          when you are stealing that extra bough!',
        },
    },
    'branch' => {
        -title => 'The Branch Not Taken',
        -contents => 'Branch or be branched.',
        'twig' => {
            -title => 'Twiggy',
            -contents => 'Anorexia returns!',
            'twiglet' => {
                -title => 'The Leastest Node',
                -contents => 'Winnie the Pooh, Eeyore, and Twiglet.',
            },
        },
```

Example 4-11. Using Path Information to Browse a Tree (continued)

```
    'leaf' => {
        -title => 'Leaf me Alone!',
        -contents => 'Look back, Leaf Ericksonn.',
    }
  },
}
```

Here is a sample configuration file entry to go with *Apache::TreeBrowser*:

```
<Location /virtual>
SetHandler perl-script
PerlHandler Apache::TreeBrowser
</Location>
```

Apache::Registry

If you are using *mod_perl* to write Apache modules, then you probably want to take advantage of *Apache::Registry*. *Apache::Registry* is a prewritten Apache Perl module that is a content handler for files containing Perl code. In addition to making it unnecessary to restart the server every time you revise a source file, *Apache::Registry* sets up a simulated CGI environment, so that programs that expect to get information about the transaction from environment variables can continue to do so. This allows legacy CGI applications to run under the Apache Perl API, and lets you use server-side code libraries (such as the original CGI.pm) that assume the script is running in a CGI environment.

Apache::Registry is similar in concept to the content filters we created earlier in this chapter, but instead of performing simple string substitutions on the contents of the requested file, *Apache::Registry* compiles and executes the code contained within it. In order to avoid recompiling the script each time it's requested, *Apache::Registry* caches the compiled code and checks the file modification time each time it's requested in order to determine whether it can safely use the cached code or whether it must recompile the file. Should you ever wish to look at its source code, *Apache::Registry* is a good example of a well-written Apache content handler that exercises much of the Perl API.

We created a typical configuration file entry for *Apache::Registry* in Chapter 2. Let's examine it in more detail now.

```
Alias /perl/ /usr/local/apache/perl/
<Location /perl>
    SetHandler     perl-script
    PerlHandler    Apache::Registry
    PerlSendHeader On
    Options        +ExecCGI
</Location>
```

The *Alias* directive simply maps the physical directory */usr/local/apache/perl/* to a virtual directory named */perl.* The *<Location>* section is more interesting. It uses *SetHandler* to make *perl-script* the content handler for this directory and sets *Apache::Registry* to be the module to handle requests for files within this part of the document tree.

The `PerlSendHeader On` line tells *mod_perl* to intercept anything that looks like a header line (such as `Content-Type: text/html`) and to automatically turn it into a correctly formatted HTTP/1.0 header the way that Apache does with CGI scripts. This allows you to write scripts without bothering to call the request object's *send_http_header()* method. Like other *Apache::Registry* features, this option makes it easier to port CGI scripts to the Apache API. If you use CGI.pm's *header()* function to generate HTTP headers, you do not need to activate this directive because CGI.pm detects *mod_perl* and calls *send_http_header()* for you. However, it does not hurt to use this directive anyway.

Option +ExecCGI ordinarily tells Apache that it's all right for the directory to contain CGI scripts. In this case the flag is required by *Apache::Registry* to confirm that you really know what you're doing. In addition, all scripts located in directories handled by *Apache::Registry* must be executable—another check against accidentally leaving wayward nonscript files in the directory.

When you use *Apache::Registry*, you can program in either of two distinct styles. You can choose to ignore the Apache Perl API entirely and act as if your script were executed within a CGI environment, or you can ignore the CGI compatibility features and make Apache API calls. You can also combine both programming styles in a single script, although you run the risk of confusing yourself and anyone else who needs to maintain your code!

A typical example of the first style is the *hello.pl* script (Example 4-12), which you also saw in Chapter 2. The interesting thing about this script is that there's nothing Apache-specific about it. The same script will run as a standard CGI script under Apache or any other web server. Any library modules that rely on the CGI environment will work as well.

Example 4-12. An Apache::Registry Script That Uses CGI-Compatibility Mode

```
#!/usr/local/bin/perl
# file: hello.pl

print "Content-Type: text/html\n\n";

print <<END;
<HTML>
<HEAD>
<TITLE>Hello There</TITLE>
</HEAD>
```

Example 4-12. An Apache::Registry Script That Uses CGI-Compatibility Mode (continued)

```
<BODY>
<H1>Hello $ENV{REMOTE_HOST}</H1>
Who would take this book seriously if the examples
didn't say "hello world" in at least four different ways?
</BODY>
</HTML>
END
```

Example 4-13 shows the same script rewritten more compactly by taking advantage of the various shortcuts provided by the CGI.pm module.

Example 4-13. An Apache::Registry Script That Uses CGI.pm

```
#!/usr/local/bin/perl
# file: hello2.pl

use CGI qw(:standard);
print header,
    start_html('Hello There'),
    h1('Hello',remote_host()),
    'Who would take this book seriously if the examples',
    'didn\'t say "hello world" in at least four different ways?',
    end_html;
```

In contrast, Example 4-14 shows the script written in the Apache Perl API style. If you compare the script to Example 4-7, which used the vanilla API to define its own content handler, you'll see that the contents of this script (with the exception of the #! line at the top) are almost identical to the body of the *handler()* subroutine defined there. The main difference is that instead of retrieving the Apache request object from the subroutine argument list, we get it by calling `Apache->request()`. *request()* is a static (class) method in the Apache package where the current request object can always be found.

There are also some subtle differences between *Apache::Registry* scripts that make Apache API calls and plain content handlers. One thing to notice is that there is no return value from *Apache::Registry* scripts. *Apache::Registry* normally assumes an HTTP status code of 200 (OK). However, you can change the status code manually by calling the request object's *status()* method to change the status code before sending out the header:

```
$r->status(404);  # forbidden
```

Strictly speaking, it isn't necessary to call *send_http_header()* if you have *PerlSendHeader On*. However, it is good practice to do so, and it won't lead to redundant headers being printed.

Alternatively, you can use the CGI compatibility mode to set the status by printing out an HTTP header that contains a *Status:* field:

```
print "Status: 404 Forbidden\n\n";
```

Another subtle difference is that at least one of the command-line switches that may be found on the topmost #! line is significant. The *–w* switch, if present, will signal *Apache::Registry* to turn on Perl warnings by setting the $^W global to a true value. Another common switch used with CGI scripts is *–T*, which turns on taint checking. Currently, taint checking can be activated for the Perl interpreter as a whole only at server startup time by setting the configuration directive *Perl-TaintCheck On*. However, if *Apache::Registry* notices *–T* on the #! line and taint checks are not activated, it will print a warning in the server error log.

Since *Apache::Registry* scripts can do double duty as normal CGI scripts and as *mod_perl* scripts, it's sometimes useful for them to check the environment and behave differently in the two situations. They can do this by checking for the existence of the environment variable MOD_PERL or for the value of GATEWAY_ INTERFACE. When running under *mod_perl*, GATEWAY_INTERFACE will be equal to CGI-Perl/1.1. Under the normal CGI interface, it will be CGI/1.1.

Example 4-14. An Apache::Registry Script That Uses the Apache API

```
#!/usr/local/bin/perl
# file: hello3.pl

use strict;

my $r = Apache->request;
$r->content_type('text/html');
$r->send_http_header;
return OK if $r->header_only;

my $host = $r->get_remote_host;
$r->print(<<END);
<HTML>
<HEAD>
<TITLE>Hello There</TITLE>
</HEAD>
<BODY>
<H1>Hello $host</H1>
Enough with the "Hello worlds" already!
</BODY>
</HTML>
END
```

A Useful Apache::Registry Application

All the *Apache::Registry* examples that we've seen so far have been short and, frankly, silly. Now let's look at an example of a real-world script that actually does something useful. The *guestbook* script (Example 4-15), as its name implies, manages a typical site guestbook, where visitors can enter their names, email addresses, and comments. It works well as both a standalone CGI script and a *mod_perl Apache::Registry* script, automatically detecting when it is running under the Apache Perl API in order to take advantage of *mod_perl*'s features. In addition to showing you how to generate a series of fill-out forms to handle a moderately complex user interaction, this script demonstrates how to read and update a file without the risk of several instances of the script trying to do so simultaneously.

Unlike some other guestbook programs, this one doesn't append users' names to a growing HTML document. Instead, it maintains a flat file in which each user's entry is represented as a single line in the file. Tabs separate the five fields, which are the date of the entry, the user's name, the user's email address, the user's location (e.g., city of residence), and comments. Nonalphanumeric characters are URL-escaped to prevent the format from getting messed up if the user enters newlines or tabs in the fields, giving records that look like:

```
05/07/98  JR  jr_ewing%40dallas.com  Dallas,%20TX  Like%20the%20hat
```

When the script is first called, it presents the user with the option of signing the guestbook file or looking at previous entries (Figure 4-6).

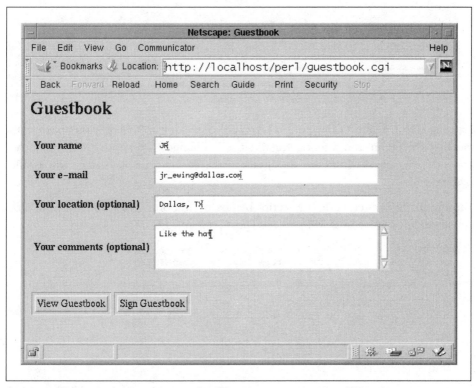

Figure 4-6. The Apache::Registry guestbook script generates its own fill-out form.

If the user presses the button labeled "Sign Guestbook," a confirmation page appears, which echoes the entry and prompts the user to edit or confirm it (Figure 4-7).

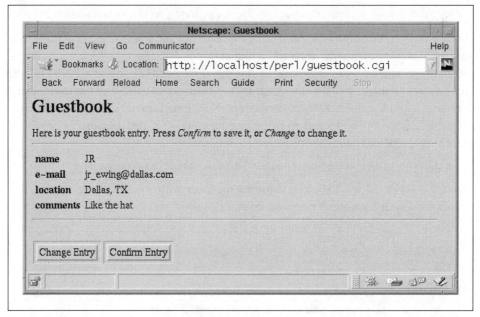

Figure 4-7. The confirmation page generated by guestbook

Pressing the "Change Entry" button takes the user back to the previous page with the fields filled in and waiting for the user's changes. Pressing "Confirm Entry" appends the user's entry to the guestbook file and displays the whole file (Figure 4-8).

Turning to the source code, the script begins by importing functions from a variety of modules, including CGI.pm, *IO::File*, *Fcntl*, and *POSIX*:

```
use strict;
use CGI qw(:standard :html3 escape unescape escapeHTML);
use IO::File ();
use Fcntl qw(:flock);
use POSIX qw(strftime);
use vars qw(@FIELDS %REQUIRED %BIG $GUESTBOOKFILE);

@FIELDS = qw(name e-mail location comments);
%REQUIRED = ('name' => 1, 'e-mail' => 1);
%BIG = ('comments' => 1);
```

The script then defines some constants. @FIELDS is an array of all the fields known to the guestbook. By changing the contents of this array you can generate different fill-out forms. %REQUIRED is a hash that designates certain fields as

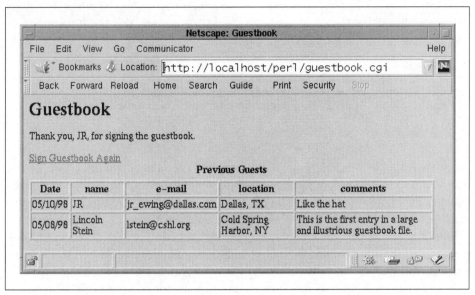

Figure 4-8. The listing of previous guestbook entries generated by guestbook

required, in this case *name* and *e-mail*. The script will refuse to add an entry to the guestbook until these fields are filled out (however, no error checking on the contents of the fields is done). **%BIG** is a hash containing the names of fields that are displayed as large text areas, in this case **comments**. Other fields are displayed as one-line text entries.

```perl
if ($ENV{MOD_PERL}) {
    $GUESTBOOKFILE = Apache->request->dir_config('GuestbookFile');
}
$GUESTBOOKFILE ||= "/usr/tmp/guestbookfile.txt";
```

Next the script checks if it is running under *mod_perl* by checking for the MOD_PERL environment variable. If the script finds that it is running under *mod_perl*, it fetches the Apache request object and queries the object for a per-directory configuration variable named *GuestbookFile*. This contains the physical pathname of the file where the guestbook entries are stored. If the script is a standalone CGI script, or if no *GuestbookFile* configuration variable is defined, the script defaults to a hardcoded file path. In the case of *Apache::Registry* scripts, the *PerlSetVar* directive used to set per-directory configuration variables must be located in a *.htaccess* file in the same directory as the script.

```perl
print header,
    start_html(-title => 'Guestbook', -bgcolor => 'silver'),
    h1("Guestbook");
```

The script now begins to generate the document by calling shortcut functions defined in the CGI module to generate the HTTP header, the HTML header and title, and a level 1 heading of "Guestbook."

```
CASE: {
    $_ = param('action');
    /^sign/i and do    { sign_guestbook(); last CASE; };
    /^confirm/i and do { write_guestbook() and view_guestbook(); last CASE; };
    /^view/i and do    { view_guestbook(1); last CASE; };
    generate_form();
}
```

We now enter the variable part of the script. Depending on what phase of the transaction the user is in, we either want to prompt the user to fill out the guestbook form, confirm an entered entry, or view the entire guestbook. We distinguish between the phases by looking at the contents of a script parameter named *action*. If *action* equals *sign*, we know that the user has just completed the fill-out form and pressed the "Sign Guestbook" button, so we jump to the routine responsible for this part of the transaction. Similarly, we look for *action* values of *confirm* and *view*, and jump to the appropriate routines for these actions. If *action* is missing, or if it has some value we don't expect, we take the default action of generating the fill-out form.

```
print end_html;
exit 0;
```

Having done its work, the script prints out the </HTML> tag and exits.

```
sub generate_form {
    my @rows;
    for my $field (@FIELDS) {
        my $title = "Your $field";
        $title .= " (optional)" if !$REQUIRED{$field};
        my $element = $BIG{$field} ?
            textarea(-name => $field,
                     -rows => 4,
                     -columns => 50,
                     -wrap => 1)
                : textfield(-name => $field, -size => 50);
        push @rows, th($title) . td($element);
    }
    print start_form,
    table(TR{-align => 'LEFT'}, \@rows),
    br,
    submit(-name => 'action', -value => 'View Guestbook'),
    submit(-name => 'action', -value => 'Sign Guestbook'),
    end_form;
}
```

The subroutine responsible for generating the form is named, appropriately enough, *generate_form()*. It iterates over @FIELDS and dynamically generates a text label and a form element for each field, modifying the format somewhat based on whether the field is marked optional or big. Each label/field pair is pushed onto a list named **@rows**. When the loop is finished, **@rows** is turned into a nicely formatted table using CGI.pm's table-generation shortcuts. The "View Guestbook" and "Sign Guestbook" buttons are added to the form, and the routine finishes.

```
sub sign_guestbook {
    my @missing = check_missing(@FIELDS);
    if (@missing) {
        print_warning(@missing);
        generate_form();
        return;
    }
```

sign_guestbook() has a slightly more complex job. Its first task is to check the submitted form for missing required fields by calling the internal subroutine *check_missing()*. If any are missing, it displays the missing fields by calling another internal subroutine, *print_warning()*, and then invokes *generate_form()* to redisplay the form with its current values. No particular hocus-pocus is required to display the partially completed form correctly; this is just one of the beneficial side effects of CGI.pm's "sticky forms" feature.

```
    my @rows;
    foreach (@FIELDS) {
        push @rows, TR(th({-align=>'LEFT'},$_),
                        td(escapeHTML(param($_))));
    }
    print "Here is your guestbook entry.  Press ",
    em('Confirm')," to save it, or ",em('Change'),
    " to change it.",
    hr,
    table(@rows),
    hr;
```

If all the required fields are filled in, *sign_guestbook()* generates an HTML table to display the user's entries. The technique for generating the form is similar to that used in the previous subroutine, except that no special cases are needed for different types of fields. We do, however, have to be careful to call *escapeHTML()* (a function imported from CGI.pm) in order to prevent HTML entities and other funny characters that the user might have entered from messing up the page.

```
    print start_form;
    foreach (@FIELDS) {
        print hidden(-name => $_);
    }
    print submit(-name => 'action',
                    -value => 'Change Entry'),
    submit(-name => 'action',
            -value => 'Confirm Entry'),
    end_form;
}
```

We end the routine by creating a short fill-out form. This form contains the contents of the user's guestbook entry stashed into a series of hidden fields, and push buttons labeled "Change Entry" and "Confirm Entry." We hide the guestbook entry information in this way in order to carry the information forward to the next set of pages.

```
sub check_missing {
    my %p;
    for (@_) { ++$p{$_} if param($_) }
    return grep !$p{$_}, keys %REQUIRED;
}

sub print_warning {
    print font({-color => 'red'},
               'Please fill in the following fields: ',
               em(join ', ', @_),
               '.');
}
```

The *check_missing()* and *print_warning()* subroutines are short and sweet. The first routine uses the Perl *grep()* function to check the list of provided fields against the list of required fields and returns a list of the truants, if any. The second routine accepts a list of missing fields and turns it into a warning of the form, "Please fill in the following fields: *e-mail.*" For emphasis, the message is rendered in a red font (under browsers that understand the <FONT> extension).

The *write_guestbook()* and *view_guestbook()* subroutines are the most complex of the bunch. The main complication is that, on an active site, there's a pretty good chance that a second instance of the script may be invoked by another user before the first instance has completed opening and updating the guestbook file. If the writes overlap, the file could be corrupted and a guestbook entry lost or scrambled. For this reason, it's important for the script to lock the file before working with it.

POSIX-compliant systems (which include both Unix and Windows systems) offer a simple form of advisory file locking through the *flock()* system call. When a process opens a file and *flock()*s it, no other process can *flock()* it until the first process either closes the file or manually relinquishes the lock. There are actually two types of lock. A "shared" lock can be held by many processes simultaneously. An "exclusive" lock can only be held by one process at a time and prevents any other program from locking the file. Typically, a program that wants to read from a file will obtain a shared lock, while a program that wants to write to the file asks the system for an exclusive lock. A shared lock allows multiple programs to read from a file without worrying that some other process will change the file while they are still reading it. A program that wants to write to a file will call *flock()* to obtain an exclusive lock; the call will then block until all other processes have released their locks. After an exclusive lock is granted, no other program can lock the file until the writing process has finished its work and released the lock.

It's important to realize that the *flock()* locking mechanism is advisory. Nothing prevents a program from ignoring the *flock()* call and reading from or writing to a file without seeking to obtain a lock first. However, as long as only the programs you've written yourself attempt to access the file and you're always careful to call *flock()* before working with it, the system works just fine.

```
sub lock {
    my $path = shift;
    my $for_writing = shift;

    my ($lock_type, $path_name, $description);
    if ($for_writing) {
        $lock_type = LOCK_EX;
        $path_name = ">>$path";
        $description = 'writing';
    }
    else {
        $lock_type = LOCK_SH;
        $path_name = $path;
        $description = 'reading';
    }

    my $fh = IO::File->new($path_name) or
        warn "Couldn't open $path for $description: $!", return;

# now try to lock it
    my $success;
    my $tries = 0;
    while ($tries++ < 10) {
        last if $success = flock($fh, $lock_type|LOCK_NB);
        print p("Waiting for $description lock on guestbook file...");
        sleep(1);                    # wait a second
    }
    unless ($success) {
        warn("Couldn't get lock for $description");
        return;
    }
    return $fh;
}
```

To make life a little simpler, the guestbook script defines a utility function named *lock()* that takes care of opening and locking the guestbook file (you'll find the definition at the bottom of the source listing). *lock()* takes two arguments: the name of the file to open and a flag indicating whether the file should be opened for writing. If the write flag is true, the function opens the file in append mode and then attempts to obtain an exclusive lock. Otherwise, it opens the file read only and tries to obtain a shared lock. If successful, the opened filehandle is returned to the caller.

The *flock()* function is used to obtain both types of lock. The first argument is the opened filehandle; the second is a constant indicating the type of lock to obtain. The constants for exclusive and shared locks are LOCK_EX and LOCK_SH,

respectively. Both constants are imported from the *Fcntl* module using the *:flock*
tag. We combine these constants with the LOCK_NB (nonblocking) constant, also
obtained from *Fcntl,* in order to tell *flock()* to return if a lock cannot be obtained
immediately. Otherwise, *flock()* will block indefinitely until the file is available. In
order to avoid a long wait in which the script appears to be hung, we call *flock()*
in a polling loop. If a lock cannot immediately be obtained, we print a warning
message to the browser screen and sleep for 1 second. After 10 consecutive failed
tries, we give up and exit the script. If the lock is successful, we return the filehandle.

```
sub write_guestbook {
    my $fh = lock($GUESTBOOKFILE, 1);
    unless ($fh) {
       print strong('An error occurred: unable to open guestbook file.'),p();
       Delete('action');
       print a({-href => self_url}, 'Try again');
       return;
    }
    seek ($fh,0,2);  # paranoia: seek to end of file
    my $date = strftime('%D',localtime);
    print $fh join("\t", $date, map {escape(param($_))} (@FIELDS)),"\n";
    print "Thank you, ", param('name'),", for signing the guestbook.\n";
    $fh->close;
    1;
}
```

To write a new entry into the guestbook, the *write_guestbook()* function calls
lock() with the path to the guestbook file and a flag indicating we want write
access. If the call fails, we display an appropriate error message and return. Otherwise, we seek to the end of the file, just in case someone else wrote to the file
while we were waiting for the lock. We then join together the current date
(obtained from the POSIX *strftime()* function) with the current values of the guestbook fields and write them out to the guestbook filehandle. To avoid the possibility of the user messing up our tab-delimited field scheme by entering tabs or newlines in the fill-out form, we're careful to escape the fields before writing them to
the file. To do this, we use the *map* operator to pass the fields through CGI.pm's
escape() function. This function is ordinarily used to make text safe for use in
URIs, but it works just as well here.

After writing to the file, we're careful to close the filehandle. This releases the lock
on the file and gives other processes access to it.

```
sub view_guestbook {
    my $show_sign_button = shift;
    print start_form,
    submit(-name => 'Sign Guestbook'),
    end_form
       if $show_sign_button;
    my $fh = lock($GUESTBOOKFILE, 0);
```

```
my @rows;
unless ($fh) {
    print strong('An error occurred: unable to open guestbook file.'),br;
    Delete('action');
    print a({-href => self_url},'Try again');
    return;
}
```

The *view_guestbook()* subroutine looks a lot like the one we just looked at but in reverse. It starts by creating a tiny fill-out form containing a single button labeled "Sign Guestbook." This button is only displayed when someone views the guestbook without signing it first and is controlled by the $show_sign_button flag. Next we obtain a read-only filehandle on the guestbook file by calling *lock()* with a false second argument. If *lock()* returns an undefined result, we print an error message and exit. Otherwise, we read the contents of the guestbook file line by line and split out the fields.

```
while (<$fh>) {
    chomp;
    my @data = map {escapeHTML($_)} map {unescape($_)} split("\t");
    unshift @rows, td(\@data);
}
unshift @rows, th(['Date',@FIELDS]);
print p(
        table({-border => ''},
                caption(strong('Previous Guests')),
                TR(\@rows)));
$fh->close;
print a({-href => '/'}, 'Home');
1;
}
```

The fields are then processed through *map()* twice: once to unescape the URL escape characters using the CGI.pm *unescape()* function and once again to make them safe to display on an HTML page using CGI.pm's *escapeHTML()* function. The second round of escaping is to avoid problems with values that contain the <, >, and & symbols. The processed lines are turned into HTML table cells, and *unshift*ed onto a list named @rows. The purpose of the *unshift* is to reverse the order of the lines, so that more recent guestbook entries appear at the top of the list. We add the headings for the table and turn the whole thing into an HTML table using the appropriate CGI.pm shortcuts. We close the filehandle and exit.

If we were not interested in running this script under standard CGI, we could increase performance slightly and reduce memory consumption substantially by replacing a few functions with their *Apache::* equivalents:

```
IO::File        --> Apache::File
CGI::escape     --> Apache::Util::escape_uri
CGI::unescape   --> Apache::Util::unescape_uri
CGI::escapeHTML --> Apache::Util::escape_html
POSIX::strftime --> Apache::Util::ht_time
```

See the reference listings in Chapter 9 for the proper syntax for these replacements. You'll also find a version of the guestbook script that uses these lightweight replacements on this book's companion web site, *http://www.modperl.com*.

Example 4-15. A Guestbook Script

```perl
#!/usr/local/bin/perl
# guestbook.cgi
use strict;
use CGI qw(:standard :html3 escape unescape escapeHTML);
use IO::File ();
use Fcntl qw(:flock);
use POSIX qw(strftime);
use vars qw(@FIELDS %REQUIRED %BIG $GUESTBOOKFILE);

@FIELDS = qw(name e-mail location comments);
%REQUIRED = ('name' => 1, 'e-mail' => 1);
%BIG = ('comments' => 1);

if ($ENV{MOD_PERL}) {
    $GUESTBOOKFILE = Apache->request->dir_config('GuestbookFile');
}
$GUESTBOOKFILE ||= "/usr/tmp/guestbookfile.txt";

print header,
    start_html(-title => 'Guestbook', -bgcolor => 'silver'),
    h1("Guestbook");

 CASE: {
     $_ = param('action');
     /^sign/i and do    { sign_guestbook(); last CASE; };
     /^confirm/i and do { write_guestbook() and view_guestbook(); last CASE; };
     /^view/i and do    { view_guestbook(1); last CASE; };
     generate_form();
 }

print end_html;
exit 0;

sub generate_form {
    my @rows;
    for my $field (@FIELDS) {
        my $title = "Your $field";
        $title .= " (optional)" if !$REQUIRED{$field};
        my $element = $BIG{$field} ?
            textarea(-name => $field,
                     -rows => 4,
                     -columns => 50,
                     -wrap => 1)
              : textfield(-name => $field, -size => 50);
        push @rows, th($title) . td($element);
    }
    print start_form,
    table(TR{-align => 'LEFT'}, \@rows),
```

Example 4-15. A Guestbook Script (continued)

```
        br,
        submit(-name => 'action', -value => 'View Guestbook'),
        submit(-name => 'action', -value => 'Sign Guestbook'),
        end_form;
}

sub sign_guestbook {
    my @missing = check_missing(@FIELDS);
    if (@missing) {
        print_warning(@missing);
        generate_form();
        return;
    }
    my @rows;
    foreach (@FIELDS) {
        push @rows, TR(th({-align=>'LEFT'},$_),
                        td(escapeHTML(param($_))));
    }
    print "Here is your guestbook entry.  Press ",
    em('Confirm')," to save it, or ",em('Change'),
    " to change it.",
    hr,
    table(@rows),
    hr;

    print start_form;
    foreach (@FIELDS) {
        print hidden(-name => $_);
    }
    print submit(-name => 'action',
                -value => 'Change Entry'),
    submit(-name => 'action',
            -value => 'Confirm Entry'),
    end_form;
}

sub check_missing {
    my %p;
    for (@_) { ++$p{$_} if param($_) }
    return grep !$p{$_}, keys %REQUIRED;
}

sub print_warning {
    print font({-color => 'red'},
                'Please fill in the following fields: ',
                em(join ', ', @_),
                '.');
}

sub write_guestbook {
    my $fh = lock($GUESTBOOKFILE, 1);
    unless ($fh) {
```

Example 4-15. A Guestbook Script (continued)

```perl
        print strong('An error occurred: unable to open guestbook file.'),p();
        Delete('action');
        print a({-href => self_url}, 'Try again');
        return;
    }
    seek ($fh,0,2);  # paranoia: seek to end of file
    my $date = strftime('%D',localtime);
    print $fh join("\t", $date, map {escape(param($_))} (@FIELDS)),"\n";
    print "Thank you, ", param('name'),", for signing the guestbook.\n";
    $fh->close;
    1;
}

sub view_guestbook {
    my $show_sign_button = shift;
    print start_form,
    submit(-name => 'Sign Guestbook'),
    end_form
        if $show_sign_button;
    my $fh = lock($GUESTBOOKFILE, 0);

    my @rows;
    unless ($fh) {
        print strong('An error occurred: unable to open guestbook file.'),br;
        Delete('action');
        print a({-href => self_url},'Try again');
        return;
    }
    while (<$fh>) {
        chomp;
        my @data = map {escapeHTML($_)} map {unescape($_)} split("\t");
        unshift @rows, td(\@data);
    }
    unshift @rows, th(['Date',@FIELDS]);
    print p(
            table({-border => ''},
                caption(strong('Previous Guests')),
                TR(\@rows)));
    $fh->close;
    print a({-href => '/'}, 'Home');
    1;
}

sub lock {
    my $path = shift;
    my $for_writing = shift;

    my ($lock_type, $path_name, $description);
    if ($for_writing) {
        $lock_type = LOCK_EX;
        $path_name = ">>$path";
        $description = 'writing';
```

Example 4-15. A Guestbook Script (continued)

```
    }
    else {
        $lock_type = LOCK_SH;
        $path_name = $path;
        $description = 'reading';
    }

    my $fh = IO::File->new($path_name) or
        warn "Couldn't open $path for $description: $!", return;

# now try to lock it
    my $success;
    my $tries = 0;
    while ($tries++ < 10) {
        last if $success = flock($fh, $lock_type|LOCK_NB);
        print p("Waiting for $description lock on guestbook file...");
        sleep(1);              # wait a second
    }
    unless ($success) {
        warn("Couldn't get lock for $description");
        return;
    }
    return $fh;
}
```

A *.htaccess* file to go with the guestbook script might be:

```
PerlSetVar GuestbookFile /home/www/etc/guests.txt
```

Apache::Registry Traps

There are a number of traps and pitfalls that you can fall into when using *Apache::Registry*. This section warns you about them.

It helps to know how *Apache::Registry* works in order to understand why the traps are there. When the server is asked to return a file that is handled by the *Apache::Registry* content handler (in other words, a script!), *Apache::Registry* first looks in an internal cache of compiled subroutines that it maintains. If it doesn't find a subroutine that corresponds to the script file, it reads the contents of the file and repackages it into a block of code that looks something like this:

```
package $mangled_package_name;
use Apache qw(exit);
sub handler {
    #line 1 $original_filename
    contents of the file
}
```

`$mangled_package_name` is a version of the script's URI which has been modified in such a way as to turn it into a legal Perl package name while keeping it distinct from all other compiled *Apache::Registry* scripts. For example, the *guest-book.cgi* script shown in the last section would be turned into a cached subroutine in the package *Apache::ROOT::perl::guestbook_2ecgi*. The compiled code is then cached for later use.

Before *Apache::Registry* even comes into play, *mod_perl* fiddles with the environment to make it appear as if the script were being called under the CGI protocol. For example, the $ENV{QUERY_STRING} environment variable is initialized with the contents of *Apache::args()*, and $ENV{SERVER_NAME} is filled in from the value returned by *Apache::server_hostname()*. This behavior is controlled by the *PerlSetupEnv* directive, which is *On* by default. If your scripts do not need to use CGI %ENV variables, turning this directive *Off* will reduce memory overhead slightly.

In addition to caching the compiled script, *Apache::Registry* also stores the script's last modification time. It checks the stored time against the current modification time before executing the cached code. If it detects that the script has been modified more recently than the last time it was compiled, it discards the cached code and recompiles the script.

The first and most common pitfall when using *Apache::Registry* is to forget that the code will be persistent across many sessions. Perl CGI programmers commonly make profligate use of globals, allocate mammoth memory structures without disposing of them, and open filehandles and never close them. They get away with this because CGI scripts are short-lived. When the CGI transaction is done, the script exits, and everything is cleaned up automatically.

Not so with *Apache::Registry* scripts (or any other Apache Perl module, for that matter). Globals persist from invocation to invocation, big data structures will remain in memory, and open files will remain open until the Apache child process has exited or the server itself it shut down.

Therefore, it is vital to code cleanly. You should never depend on a global variable being uninitialized in order to determine when a subroutine is being called for the first time. In fact, you should reduce your dependency on globals in general. Close filehandles when you are finished with them, and make sure to kill (or at least wait on) any child processes you may have launched.

Perl provides two useful tools for writing clean code. *use strict* turns on checks that make it harder to use global variables unintentionally. Variables must either be lexically scoped (with *my*) or qualified with their complete package names. The only way around these restrictions is to declare variables you intend to use as globals at the top of the script with *use vars*. This code snippet shows how:

```
use strict;
use vars qw{$INIT $DEBUG @NAMES %HANDLES};
```

We have used *strict* in many of the examples in the preceding sections, and we strongly recommend it for any Perl script you write.

The other tool is Perl runtime warnings, which can be turned on in *Apache::Registry* scripts by including a –*w* switch on the #! line, or within other modules by setting the magic $^W variable to true. You can even enable warnings globally by setting $^W to true inside the server's Perl startup script, if there is one (see Chapter 2).

–*w* will catch a variety of errors, dubious programming constructs, typos, and other sins. Among other things, it will warn when a bareword (a string without surrounding quotation marks) conflicts with a subroutine name, when a variable is used only once, and when a lexical variable is inappropriately shared between an outer and an inner scope (a horrible problem which we expose in all its gory details a few paragraphs later).

–*w* may also generate hundreds of "Use of uninitialized value" messages at run-time, which will fill up your server error log. Many of these warnings can be hard to track down. If there is no line number reported with the warning, or if the reported line number is incorrect,* try using Perl's #line token described in the *perlsyn* manual page and in Chapter 9 under "Special Global Variables, Subroutines, and Literals."

It may also be helpful to see a full stack trace of the code which triggered the warning. The *cluck()* function found in the standard *Carp* module will give you this functionality. Here is an example:

```
use Carp ();
local $SIG{__WARN__} = \&Carp::cluck;
```

Note that –*w* checks are done at runtime, which may slow down script execution time. In production mode, you may wish to turn warnings off altogether or localize warnings using the $^W global variable described in the *perlvar* manpage.

Another subtle *mod_perl* trap that lies in wait for even experienced programmers involves the sharing of lexical variables between outer and inner named subroutines. To understand this problem, consider the following innocent-looking code:

```
#!/usr/local/bin/perl -w

for (0..3) {
    bump_and_print();
}

sub bump_and_print {
    my $a = 1;
```

---

* Certain uses of the *eval* operator and "here" documents are known to throw off Perl's line numbering.

```
sub bump {
    $a++;
    print "In the inner scope, \$a is $a\n";
}
print "In the outer scope, \$a is $a\n";
bump();
}
```

When you run this script, it generates the following inexplicable output:

```
Variable "$a" will not stay shared at ./test.pl line 12.
In the outer scope, $a is 1
In the inner scope, $a is 2
In the outer scope, $a is 1
In the inner scope, $a is 3
In the outer scope, $a is 1
In the inner scope, $a is 4
In the outer scope, $a is 1
In the inner scope, $a is 5
```

For some reason the variable $a has become "unstuck" from its *my()* declaration in *bump_and_print()* and has taken on a life of its own in the inner subroutine *bump()*. Because of the *–w* switch, Perl complains about this problem during the compilation phase, with the terse warning that the variable "will not stay shared." This behavior does not happen if the inner subroutine is made into an anonymous subroutine. It only affects named inner subroutines.

The rationale for the peculiar behavior of lexical variables and ways to avoid it in conventional scripts are explained in the *perldiag* manual page. When using *Apache::Registry* this bug can bite you when you least expect it. Because *Apache::Registry* works by wrapping the contents of a script inside a *handler()* function, inner named subroutines are created whether you want them or not. Hence, this piece of code will *not* do what you expect:

```
#!/usr/local/bin/perl
use CGI qw/param header/;

my $name = param('name');
print header('text/plain');
print_body();
exit 0;

sub print_body {
    print "The contents of \$name is $name.\n";
}
```

The first time you run it, it will run correctly, printing the value of the *name* CGI parameter. However, on subsequent invocations the script will appear to get "stuck" and remember the values of previous invocations. This is because the lexically scoped $name variable is being referenced from within *print_body()*, which, when running under *Apache::Registry*, is a named inner subroutine. Because multi-

ple Apache processes are running, each process will remember a different value of
$name, resulting in bizarre and arbitrary behavior.

Perl may be fixed someday to do the right thing with inner subroutines. In the
meantime, there are several ways to avoid this problem. Instead of making the
outer variable lexically scoped, you can declare it to be a package global, as this
snippet shows:

```
use strict;
use vars '$name';
$name = param('name');
```

Because globals are global, they aren't subject to weird scoping rules.

Alternatively, you can pass the variable to the subroutine as an argument and avoid
sharing variables between scopes altogether. This example shows that variant:

```
my $name = param('name');
print_body($name);

sub print_body {
    my $name = shift;
    print "The contents of \$name is $name.\n";
}
```

Finally, you can put the guts of your application into a library and *use* or *require*
it. The *Apache::Registry* then becomes only a hook that invokes the library:

```
#!/usr/local/bin/perl
require "my_application_guts";
do_everything();
```

The shared lexical variable problem is a good reason to use the *–w* switch during
Apache::Registry script development and debugging. If you see warnings about a
variable not remaining shared, you have a problem, even if the ill effects don't
immediately manifest themselves.

Another problem that you will certainly run into involves the use of custom libraries by *Apache::Registry* scripts. When you make an editing change to a script, the
Apache::Registry notices the recent modification time and reloads the script. However, the same isn't true of any library file that you load into the script with *use* or
require. If you make a change to a *require*d file, the script will continue to run the
old version of the file until the script itself is recompiled for some reason. This can
lead to confusion and much hair-tearing during development!

You can avoid going bald by using *Apache::StatINC*, a standard part of the *mod_*
perl distribution. It watches over the contents of the internal Perl %INC array and
reloads any files that have changed since the last time it was invoked. Installing
Apache::StatINC is easy. Simply install it as the *PerlInitHandler* for any directory

that is managed by *Apache::Registry*. For example, here is an *access.conf* entry that installs both *Apache::Registry* and *Apache::StatINC*:

```
Alias /perl/ /usr/local/apache/perl/
<Location /perl>
  SetHandler      perl-script
  PerlHandler     Apache::Registry
  PerlInitHandler Apache::StatINC
  PerlSendHeader  On
  Options         +ExecCGI
</Location>
```

Because *Apache::StatINC* operates at a level above the level of individual scripts, any nonstandard library locations added by the script with *use lib* or by directly manipulating the contents of @INC will be ignored. If you want these locations to be monitored by *Apache::StatINC*, you should make sure that they are added to the library search path before invoking the script. You can do this either by setting the PERL5LIB environment variable before starting up the Apache server (for instance, in the server startup script), or by placing a *use lib* line in your Perl startup file, as described in Chapter 2.

When you use *Apache::StatINC*, there is a slight overhead for performing a *stat* on each included file every time a script is run. This overhead is usually immeasurable, but it will become noticeable on a heavily loaded server. In this case, you may want to forego it and instead manually force the embedded Perl interpreter to reload *all* its compiled scripts by restarting the server with *apachectl*. In order for this to work, the *PerlFreshRestart* directive must be turned on in the Apache configuration file. If you haven't done so already, add this line to *perl.conf* or one of the other configuration files:

```
PerlFreshRestart On
```

You can try reloading compiled scripts in this way whenever things seem to have gotten themselves into a weird state. This will reset all scripts to known initial settings and allow you to investigate problems systematically. You might also want to stop the server completely and restart it using the *–X* switch. This forces the server to run as a single process in the foreground. Interacting with a single process rather than multiple ones makes it easier to debug misbehaving scripts. In a production environment, you'll want to do this on a test server in order to avoid disrupting web services.

Handling Errors

Errors in Apache modules do occur, and tracking them down is significantly trickier than in standalone Perl or C programs. Some errors are due to bugs in your code, while others are due to the unavoidable hazards of running in a networked environment. The remote user might cancel a form submission before it is entirely done, the connection might drop while you're updating a database, or a file that you're trying to access might not exist.

A virtuous Apache module must let at least two people know when a problem has occurred: you, the module's author, and the remote user. You can communicate errors and other exception conditions to yourself by writing out entries to the server log. For alerting the user when a problem has occurred, you can take advantage of the simple but flexible Apache ErrorDocument system, use *CGI::Carp*, or roll your own error handler.

Error Logging

We talked about tracking down code bugs in Chapter 2 and will talk more about C-language specific debugging in Chapter 10. This section focuses on defensive coding techniques for intercepting and handling other types of runtime errors.

The most important rule is to *log everything*. Log anything unexpected, whether it is a fatal error or a condition that you can work around. Log expected but unusual conditions too, and generate routine logging messages that can help you trace the execution of your module under normal conditions.

Apache versions 1.3 and higher offer *syslog*-like log levels ranging in severity from *debug*, for low-priority messages, through *warn*, for noncritical errors, to *emerg*, for fatal errors that make the module unusable. By setting the *LogLevel* directive in the server configuration file, you can adjust the level of messages that are written to the server error log. For example, by setting *LogLevel* to *warn*, messages with a priority level of *warn* and higher are displayed in the log; lower-priority messages are ignored.

To use this adjustable logging API, you must load the standard *Apache::Log* module. This adds a *log()* method to the Apache request object, which will return an *Apache::Log* object. You can then invoke this object's methods in order to write nicely formatted log entries to the server's error log at the priority level you desire. Here's a short example:

```
use Apache::Log ();

my $log = $r->log;
$log->debug("Trying to lock guestbook file now");
unless (lock($GUESTBOOKFILE,1)) {
    $log->emerg("Can't get lock!");
    return SERVER_ERROR;
}
$log->debug("Got lock");
```

In this example, we first obtain a log object by calling the request object's *log()* method. We call the log object's *debug()* method to send a debug message to the error log and then try to perform a locking operation. If the operation fails, we log an error message at the *emerg* priority level using the log object's *emerg()* method and exit. Otherwise, we log another debugging message.

You'll find the full list of method calls made available by *Apache::Log* in Chapter 9, in the subsection "Logging Methods" under "The Apache Request Object." In addition, the Apache Perl API offers three simpler methods for entering messages into the log file. You don't have to import the *Apache::Log* module to use these methods, and they're appropriate for smaller projects (such as most of the examples in this book).

$r->log_error($message)

> *log_error()* writes out a time-stamped message into the server error log using a facility of *error*. Use it for critical errors that make further normal execution of the module impossible. This method predates the 1.3 LogLevel API but still exists for backward compatibility and as a shortcut to *$r->log->error*.

$r->warn($message)

> *warn()* will log an error message with a severity level of *warn*. You can use this for noncritical errors or unexpected conditions that you can work around. This method predates the 1.3 LogLevel API but still exists for backward compatibility and as a shortcut to *$r->log->warn*.

$r->log_reason($message, $file)

> This is a special-purpose log message used for errors that occur when a content handler tries to process a file. It results in a message that looks something like this:

```
access to /usr/local/apache/htdocs/index.html failed for ppp12.yahoo.com,
    reason: user phyllis not authorized
```

You might also choose to include a $DEBUG global in your modules, either hard-coding it directly into the source, or by pulling its value out of the configuration file with *Apache::dir_config()*. Your module can then check this global every time it does something significant. If set to a true value, your script should send verbose informational messages to the Apache error log (or to an alternative log file of your choice).

The ErrorDocument System

Apache provides a handy *ErrorDocument* directive that can be used to display a custom page when a handler returns a non-OK status code. The custom page can be any URI, including a remote web page, a local static page, a local server-side include document, or a CGI script or module. In the last three cases, the server generates an internal redirect, making the redirection very efficient.

For example, the configuration file for Lincoln's laboratory site contains this directive:

```
ErrorDocument 404 /perl/missing.cgi
```

When the server encounters a 404 "Not Found" status code, whether generated by a custom module or by the default content handler, it will generate an internal redirect to a *mod_perl* script named *missing.cgi*. Before calling the script, Apache sets some useful environment variables including the following:

REDIRECT_URL

The URL of the document that the user was originally trying to fetch.

REDIRECT_STATUS

The status code that caused the redirection to occur.

REDIRECT_REQUEST_METHOD

The method (GET or POST) that caused the redirection.

REDIRECT_QUERY_STRING

The original query string, if any.

REDIRECT_ERROR_NOTES

The logged error message, if any.

A slightly simplified version of *missing.cgi* that works with *Apache::Registry* (as well as a standalone CGI script) is shown in Example 4-16. For a screenshot of what the user gets when requesting a nonexistent URI, see Figure 4-9.

Example 4-16. A Simple Apache::Registry ErrorDocument Handler

```
#!/usr/local/bin/perl
# file: missing.cgi
use CGI qw(:standard);
use strict;

print header,
      start_html(-title => 'Missing Document', -bgcolor => 'white'),
      h1(img({-src => '/icons/unknown.gif'}),
      'Document Not Found'),
      p("I'm sorry, but the document you requested,",
        strong($ENV{REDIRECT_URL}),
        "is not available.  Please try the",
        a({-href => "/search.html"}, "search page"),
        "for help locating the document."),
      hr,
      address(a({-href => "mailto:$ENV{SERVER_ADMIN}"}, 'webmaster')),
      end_html;
```

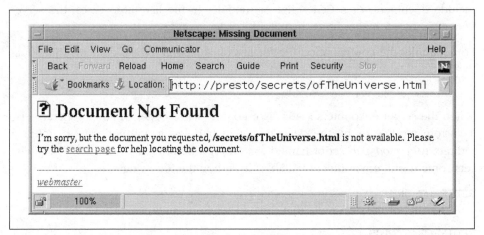

Figure 4-9. The missing.cgi script generates a custom page to display when a URI is not found.

If you want to implement the *ErrorDocument* handler as a vanilla Apache Perl API script, the various *REDIRECT_* environment variables will not be available to you. However, you can get the same information by calling the request object's *prev()* method. This returns the request object from the original request. You can then query this object to recover the requested URI, the request method, and so forth.

Example 4-17 shows a rewritten version of *missing.cgi* that uses *prev()* to recover the URI of the missing document. The feature to note in this code is the call to *$r->prev* on the fifth line of the *handler()* subroutine. If the handler was invoked as the result of an internal redirection, this call will return the original request object, which we then query for the requested document by calling its *uri()* method. If the handler was invoked directly (perhaps by the user requesting its URI), the original request will be undefined and we use an empty string for the document URI.

Example 4-17. An ErrorDocument Handler Using the Vanilla Apache API

```
package Apache::Missing;
# File: Apache/Missing.pm

use strict;
use Apache::Constants qw(:common);
use CGI qw(:html);

sub handler {
    my $r = shift;
    $r->content_type('text/html');
    $r->send_http_header;
    return OK if $r->header_only;

    my $original_request = $r->prev;
    my $original_uri = $original_request ? $original_request->uri : '';
```

Example 4-17. An ErrorDocument Handler Using the Vanilla Apache API (continued)

```
    my $admin = $r->server->server_admin;

    $r->print(
            start_html(-title => 'Missing Document',
                        -bgcolor => 'white'),
            h1(img({-src => '/icons/unknown.gif'}),
                'Document Not Found'),
            p(
              "I'm sorry, but the document you requested,",
              strong($original_uri),
              ", is not available.  Please try the",
              a({-href => "/search.html"}, "search page"),
              "for help locating the document."
              ),
            hr,
            address(a({-href => "mailto:$admin"}, 'webmaster')),
            end_html
            );

    return OK;
}

1;
__END__
```

Here's an example using *Apache::Missing* in the configuration file:

```
    <Location /Missing>
        SetHandler   perl-script
        PerlHandler Apache::Missing
    </Location>
```

If the static nature of the Apache *ErrorDocument* directive is inadequate for your needs, you can set the error document dynamically from within a handler by calling the request object's *custom_response()* method. This method takes two arguments: the status code of the response you want to handle and the URI of the document or module that you want to pass control to. This error document setting will persist for the lifetime of the current request only. After the handler exits, the setting returns to its default.

For example, the following code snippet sets up a custom error handler for the SERVER_ERROR error code (a generic error that covers a variety of sins). If the *things_are_ok()* subroutine (not implemented here) returns a true value, we do our work and return an OK status. Otherwise, we set the error document to point to a URI named */Carp* and return a SERVER_ERROR status.

```
    package Apache::GoFish;
    # file: Apache/GoFish.pm

    use strict;
    use Apache::Constants qw(:common);
```

```
sub handler {
    my $r = shift;
    if (things_are_ok($r)) {
      do_something();
      return OK;
    }
    $r->custom_response(SERVER_ERROR, "/Carp");
    return SERVER_ERROR;
}

1;
__END__
```

HTTP Headers and Error Handling

You already know about using *header_out()* to set HTTP header fields. A properly formatted HTTP header is sent to the browser when your module explicitly calls *send_http_header()*, or it is sent for you automatically if you are using *Apache::Registry*, the *PerlSendHeader* directive is set to *On*, and your script prints some text that looks like an HTTP header.

You have to be careful, however, if your module ever returns non-OK status codes. Apache wants to assume control over the header generation process in the case of errors; if your module has already sent the header, then Apache will send a redundant set of headers with unattractive results. This applies both to real HTTP errors, like BAD_REQUEST and NOT_FOUND, as well as to nonfatal conditions like REDIRECT and AUTH_REQUIRED.

Consider the following fishy example:

```
package Apache::Crash;
# File: Apache/Crash.pm

use strict;
use Apache::Constants qw(:common);
use constant CRASH => 1;

sub handler {
    my $r = shift;
    $r->content_type('text/plain');
    $r->send_http_header;
    return OK if $r->header_only;
    return SERVER_ERROR if CRASH;
    $r->print('Half a haddock is better than none.');
    return OK;
}

1;
__END__
```

After setting the document MIME type, this module sends off the HTTP header. It then checks a constant named CRASH and if true, which it always is, returns a status code of SERVER_ERROR. Apache would ordinarily send a custom HTTP header in response to this status code, but because the module has already emitted a header, it's too late. Confusion results. If we map this module to the URI */Crash*, we can telnet directly to the server to demonstrate the problem:

```
% telnet www.modperl.com 80
Trying 192.168.2.5...
Connected to modperl.com.
Escape character is '^]'.
GET /Crash HTTP/1.0

HTTP/1.1 200 OK
Date: Thu, 21 May 1998 11:31:40 GMT
Server: Apache/1.3b6
Connection: close
Content-Type: text/plain

HTTP/1.1 200 OK
Date: Thu, 21 May 1998 11:31:40 GMT
Server: Apache/1.3b6
Connection: close
Content-Type: text/html

<HTML><HEAD>
<TITLE>500 Internal Server Error</TITLE>
</HEAD><BODY>
<H1>Internal Server Error</H1>
The server encountered an internal error or
misconfiguration and was unable to complete
your request.<P>
</BODY></HTML>
Connection closed by foreign host.
```

Not only are there two HTTP headers here, but both of them indicate a status code of 200 OK, which is definitely not right. When displayed in the browser, the page will be marred by extraneous header lines at the top of the screen.

The cardinal rule is that you should never call *Apache::send_http_header()* until your module has completed all its error checking and has decided to return an OK status code. Here's a better version of *Apache::Crash* that avoids the problem:

```
package Apache::Crash;
# File: Apache/Crash.pm

use strict;
use Apache::Constants qw(:common);
use constant CRASH => 1;

sub handler {
    my $r = shift;
    return SERVER_ERROR if CRASH;
    $r->content_type('text/plain');
    $r->send_http_header;
```

```
        return OK if $r->header_only;
        $r->print('Half a haddock is better than none.');
        return OK;
}


1;
__END__
```

Now when we telnet to the server, the server response looks the way it should:

```
(~) 103% telnet www.modperl.com 80
Trying 192.168.2.5...
Connected to modperl.com.
Escape character is '^]'.
GET /Crash HTTP/1.0

HTTP/1.1 500 Internal Server Error
Date: Thu, 21 May 1998 11:40:56 GMT
Server: Apache/1.3b6
Connection: close
Content-Type: text/html

<HTML><HEAD>
<TITLE>500 Internal Server Error</TITLE>
</HEAD><BODY>
<H1>Internal Server Error</H1>
The server encountered an internal error or
misconfiguration and was unable to complete
your request.<P>
</BODY></HTML>
```

Another important detail about error handling is that Apache ignores the fields that you set with *header_out()* when your module generates an error status or invokes an internal redirect. This is usually not a problem, but there are some cases in which this restriction can be problematic. The most typical case is the one in which you want a module to give the browser a cookie and immediately redirect to a different URI. Or you might want to assign an error document to the **UNAUTHORIZED** status code so that a custom login screen appears when the user tries to access a restricted page. In both cases you need to manipulate the HTTP header fields prior to the redirect.

For these cases, call the request object's *err_header_out()* method. It has identical syntax to *header_out()*, but the fields that you set with it are sent to the browser only when an error has occurred. Unlike ordinary headers, the fields set with *err_header_out()* persist across internal redirections, and so they are passed to Apache *ErrorDocument* handlers and other local URIs.

This provides you with a simple way to pass information between modules across internal redirects. Combining the example from this section with the example from the previous section gives the modules shown in Example 4-18. *Apache::GoFish* generates a **SERVER_ERROR**, which is intercepted and handled by the custom ErrorDocument handler named *Apache::Carp* (Example 4-19). Before relinquishing control, however, *Apache::GoFish* creates a custom HTTP field named *X-Odor* which gives the error handler something substantial to complain about. The end result is shown in Figure 4-10.

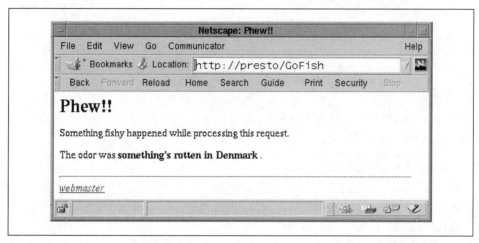

Figure 4-10. When Apache::GoFish generates a custom error document, it displays the contents of the custom X-Odor header.

The code should be fairly self-explanatory. The main point to notice is *Apache::GoFish*'s use of *err_header_out()* to set the value of the *X-Odor* field, and *Apache::Carp*'s use of the same function to retrieve it. Like *header_out()*, when you call *err_header_out()* with a single argument, it returns the current value of the field and does not otherwise alter the header. When you call it with two arguments, it sets the indicated field.

An interesting side effect of this technique is that the *X-Odor* field is also returned to the browser in the HTTP header. This could be construed as a feature. If you wished to pass information between the content handler and the error handler without leaving tracks in the HTTP header, you could instead use the request object's "notes" table to pass messages from one module to another. Chapter 9 covers how to use this facility (see the description of the *notes()* method under "Server Core Functions").

Example 4-18. Invoking a Custom Error Handler Document

```
package Apache::GoFish;
# File: Apache/GoFish.pm

use Apache::Constants qw(:common :response);
use constant CRASH=>1;

sub handler {
    my $r = shift;
    $r->err_header_out('X-Odor'=>"something's rotten in Denmark");
```

Example 4-18. Invoking a Custom Error Handler Document (continued)

```
    $r->custom_response(SERVER_ERROR, "/Carp");
    return SERVER_ERROR if CRASH;
    $r->content_type('text/plain');
    $r->send_http_header;
    return OK if $r->header_only;
    $r->print('Half a haddock is better than none.');
    return OK;
}
1;
__END__
```

Here is a sample configuration entry:

```
    <Location /GoFish>
        SetHandler perl-script
        PerlHandler Apache::GoFish
    </Location>
```

Example 4-19. An Error Handler to Complement the Previous Example

```
package Apache::Carp;
# File: Apache/Carp.pm
use strict;
use Apache::Constants qw(:common);
use CGI qw(:html);

sub handler {
    my $r = shift;
    my $odor = $r->err_header_out('X-Odor');
    $odor ||= 'unspecified odor';
    $r->content_type('text/html');
    $r->send_http_header;
    return OK if $r->header_only;

    my $original_request = $r->prev;
    my $original_uri = $original_request ? $original_request->uri : '';
    my $admin = $r->server->server_admin;

    $r->print(
            start_html(-title => 'Phew!!', -bgcolor => 'white'),
            h1('Phew!!'),
            p("Something fishy happened while processing this request."),
            p("The odor was ", strong($odor), '.'),
            hr,
            address(a({-href => "mailto:$admin"}, 'webmaster')),
            end_html
            );

    return OK;
}

1;
__END__
```

Here is a sample configuration entry:

```
<Location /Carp>
    SetHandler  perl-script
    PerlHandler Apache::Carp
</Location>
```

Chaining Content Handlers

The C-language Apache API only allows a single content handler to completely process a request. Several handlers may be given a shot at it, but the first one to return an OK status will terminate the content handling phase of the transaction.

There are times when it would be nice to chain handlers into a pipeline. For example, one handler could add canned headers and footers to the page, another could correct spelling errors, while a third could add trademark symbols to all proprietary names. Although the native C API can't do this yet,* the Perl API can, using a technique called "stacked handlers."

It is actually quite simple to stack handlers. Instead of declaring a single module or subroutine in the *PerlHandler* directive, you declare several. Each handler will be called in turn in the order in which it was declared. The exception to this rule is if one of the handlers in the series returns an error code (anything other than OK, DECLINED, or DONE). Handlers can adjust the stacking order themselves, or even arrange to process each other's output.

Simple Case of Stacked Handlers

Example 4-20 gives a very simple example of a stack of three content handlers. It's adapted slightly from the *mod_perl* manual page. For simplicity, all three handlers are defined in the same file, and are subroutines named *header()*, *body()*, and *footer()*. As the names imply, the first handler is responsible for the top of the page (including the HTTP header), the second is responsible for the middle, and the third for the bottom.

A suitable configuration section looks like this:

```
PerlModule My
<Location /My>
  SetHandler perl-script
  PerlHandler My::header My::body My::footer
</Location>
```

---

* At the time this was written, the Apache developers were discussing a layered I/O system which will be part of the Apache 2.0 API.

We first load the whole module into memory using the *PerlModule* directive. We then declare a URI location */My* and assign the *perl-script* handler to it. Perl in turn is configured to run the *My::header*, *My::body*, and *My::footer* subroutines by passing them as arguments to a *PerlHandler* directive. In this case, the */My* location has no corresponding physical directory, but there's no reason that it couldn't.

After bringing in the OK constant from *Apache::Constants*, we define the subroutines *header()*, *body()*, and *footer()*. *header()* sets the document's content type to plain text, sends the HTTP header, and prints out a line at the top of the document. *body()* and *footer()* both print out a line of text to identify themselves. The resulting page looks like this:

```
header text
body text
footer text
```

Example 4-20. A Simple Stacked Handler

```perl
package My;

use strict;
use Apache::Constants 'OK';

sub header {
    my $r = shift;
    $r->content_type('text/plain');
    $r->send_http_header;
    $r->print("header text\n");
    OK;
}
sub body {
    my $r = shift;
    $r->print("body text\n");
    OK;
}
sub footer {
    my $r = shift;
    $r->print("footer text\n");
    OK;
}
1;
```

Coordinating Stacked Handlers

Stacked handlers often have to coordinate their activities. In the example of the previous section, the *header()* handler must be run before either of the other two in order for the HTTP header to come out correctly. Sometimes it's useful to make the first handler responsible for coordinating the other routines rather than relying on the configuration file. The request object's *push_handlers()* method will help you do this.

push_handlers() takes two arguments: a string representing the phase to handle, and a reference to a subroutine to handle that phase. For example, this code fragment will arrange for the *footer()* subroutine to be the next content handler invoked:

```
$r->push_handlers(PerlHandler => \&footer);
```

With this technique, we can rewrite the previous example along the lines shown in Example 4-21. In the revised module, we declare a subroutine named *handler()* that calls *push_handlers()* three times, once each for the header, body, and footer of the document. It then exits. The other routines are unchanged.

The revised configuration file entry looks like this:

```
<Location /MyChain>
  SetHandler perl-script
  PerlHandler My::Chain
</Location>
```

Because we followed the *mod_perl* convention of naming the first handler subroutine *handler()*, there's now no need for a *PerlModule* statement to load the module into memory.

Example 4-21. Coordinated Stacked Handlers

```
package My::Chain;

use strict;
use Apache::Constants 'OK';

sub handler {
    my $r = shift;
    for my $cv (\&header, \&body, \&footer) {
        $r->push_handlers(PerlHandler => $cv);
    }
    OK;
}

sub header {
    my $r = shift;
    $r->content_type('text/plain');
    $r->send_http_header;
    $r->print("header text\n");
    OK;
}

sub body {
    my $r = shift;
    $r->print("body text\n");
    OK;
}

sub footer {
    my $r = shift;
```

Example 4-21. Coordinated Stacked Handlers (continued)

```
    $r->print("footer text\n");
    OK;
}


1;
__END__
```

Stacked Handler Pipelining

The stacked handlers we looked at in the previous example didn't interact. When one was finished processing, the next took over. A more sophisticated set of handlers might want to pipeline their results in such a way that the output of one handler becomes the input to the next. This would allow the handlers to modify each other's output in classic Unix filter fashion. This sounds difficult, but in fact it's pretty simple. This section will show you how to set up a filter pipeline. As an aside, it will also introduce you to the concept of Apache Perl API method handlers.

The trick to achieving a handler pipeline is to use "tied" filehandles to connect the neighbors together. In the event that you've never worked with a tied filehandle before, it's a way of giving a filehandle seemingly magic behavior. When you *print()* to a tied filehandle, the data is redirected to a method in a user-defined class rather than going through the usual filesystem routines. To create a tied filehandle, you simply declare a class that defines a method named *TIEHANDLE()* and various methods to handle the sorts of things one does with a filehandle, such as *PRINT()* and *READ()*.

Here's a concrete example of a tied filehandle class that interfaces to an antique daisywheel printer of some sort:

```
    package DaisyWheel;

    sub TIEHANDLE {
      my($class, $printer_name) = @_;
      open_daisywheel($printer_name);
      bless { 'printer' => $printer_name }, $class;
    }

    sub PRINT {
      my $self = shift;
      send_to_daisywheel($self->{'printer'}, @_);
    }

    sub DESTROY {
      my $self = shift;
      close_daisywheel($self->{'printer'});
    }

    1;
    __END__
```

The *TIEHANDLE()* method gets called first. It is responsible for opening the daisy-wheel printer driver (routine not shown here!) and returning a blessed object containing its instance variables. The *PRINT()* method is called whenever the main program prints to the tied filehandle. Its arguments are the blessed object and a list containing the arguments to *print()*. It recovers the printer name from its instance variables and then passes it, and the items to print, to an internal routine that does the actual work. *DESTROY()* is called when the filehandle is *untie()*d or closed. It calls an internal routine that closes the printer driver.

To use this class, a program just has to call *tie()* with the name of an appropriate printer:

```
use DaisyWheel ();
tie *DAISY, 'DaisyWheel', 'dwj002';
print DAISY "Daisy... Daisy... Daisy the Kangaroo.\n";
print DAISY "She wanted to live in a private home,\n";
print DAISY "So she ran away from the zoo!\n";
close DAISY;
```

A more complete tied filehandle class might include a *PRINTF()* method, a *READ()* method, a *READLINE()* method, and a *GETC()* method, but for output-only file-handles *PRINT()* is usually enough.

Now back to Apache. The strategy will be for each filter in the pipeline, including the very first and last ones, to print to STDOUT, rather than directly invoking the *Apache::print()* method via the request object. We will arrange for STDOUT to be *tied()* in each case to a *PRINT()* method defined in the next filter down the chain. The whole scheme looks something like this:

```
filter1 -> filter2::PRINT()    [STDOUT tied to filter2]
filter2 -> filter3::PRINT()    [STDOUT tied to filter3]
filter3 -> filter4::PRINT()    [STDOUT tied to filter4]
                .
                .
                .
filterN -> Apache::PRINT()     [STDOUT tied to Apache]
```

Interestingly enough, the last filter in the chain doesn't have to get special treatment. Internally, the Apache request ties STDOUT to *Apache::PRINT()*, which in turn calls *Apache::print()*. This is why handlers can use `$r->print('something')` and `print('something')` interchangeably.

To simplify setting up these pipelines, we'll define a utility class called *Apache::Forward.** *Apache::Forward* is a null filter that passes its input through to the next filter in the chain unmodified. Modules that inherit from this class override its *PRINT()* method to do something interesting with the data.

---

* The more obvious name, *Apache::Filter*, is already taken by a third-party module that does output chaining in a slightly different manner.

Example 4-22 gives the source code for *Apache::Forward*. We'll discuss the code one section at a time.

```
package Apache::Forward;

use strict;
use Apache::Constants qw(OK SERVER_ERROR);
use vars qw($VERSION);
$VERSION = '1.00';

sub handler ($$) {
    my($class, $r) = @_;
    my $next = tied *STDOUT || return SERVER_ERROR;
    tie *STDOUT, $class, $r, $next or return SERVER_ERROR;
    $r->register_cleanup(sub { untie *STDOUT });
    OK;
}
```

Most of the work is done in the *handler()* subroutine, which is responsible for correctly tying the STDOUT filehandle. Notice that the function prototype for *handler()* is ($$), or two scalar arguments. This is a special signal to Apache to activate its method handler behavior. Instead of calling *handler()* like an ordinary subroutine, Apache calls *handler()* like this:

```
Apache::Forward->handler($r);
```

The result is that the *handler()* receives the class name as its first argument, and the request object as the second argument. This object-oriented calling style allows *Apache::Forward* to be subclassed.

The *handler()* subroutine begins by recovering the identity of the *next* handler in the pipeline. It does this by calling *tied()* on the STDOUT filehandle. *tied()* returns a reference to whatever object a filehandle is tied to. It will always return a valid object, even when the current package is the last filter in the pipeline. This is because Apache ties STDOUT to itself, so the last filter will get a reference to the Apache object. Nevertheless, we do check that *tied()* returns an object and error out if not—just in case.

Next the subroutine reties STDOUT to itself, passing *tie()* the request object and the reference to the next filter in the pipeline. This call shouldn't fail, but if it does, we return a server error at this point.

Before finishing up, the *handler()* method needs to ensure that the filehandle will be untied before the transaction terminates. We do this by registering a handler for the cleanup phase. This is the last handler to be called before a transaction terminates and is traditionally reserved for this kind of garbage collection. We use *register_cleanup()* to push an anonymous subroutine that unties STDOUT. When the time comes, the filehandle will be untied, automatically invoking the class's *DESTROY()* method. This gives the object a chance to clean up, if it needs to.

Note that the client connection will be closed before registered cleanups are run, so class *DESTROY()* methods should not attempt to send any data to the client.

```
sub TIEHANDLE {
    my($class, $r, $next) = @_;
    bless { 'r' => $r,          # request object
            'next' => $next     # next in the chain
          }, $class;
}
```

The next routine to consider is *TIEHANDLE()*, whose job is to return a new blessed object. It creates a blessed hash containing the keys **r** and **next**. **r** points to the request object, and **next** points to the next filter in the pipeline. Both of these arguments were passed to us by *handler()*.

```
sub PRINT {
    my $self = shift;
    # Subclasses should do something interesting here
    $self->forward(@_);
}
```

The *PRINT()* method is invoked whenever the caller wants to print something to the tied filehandle. The arguments consist of the blessed object and a list of data items to be processed. Subclasses will want to modify the data items in some way, but we just forward them unmodified to the next filter in line by calling an internal routine named *forward()*.

```
#sub DESTROY {
#    my $self = shift;
#    # maybe clean up here
#}
```

DESTROY() is normally responsible for cleaning up. There's nothing to do in the general case, so we comment out the definition to avoid being called, saving a bit of overhead.

```
sub forward {
    shift()->{'next'}->PRINT(@_);
}
```

forward() is called by *PRINT()* to forward the modified data items to the next filter in line. We shift the blessed object off the argument stack, find the next filter in line, and invoke its *PRINT()* method.

Example 4-22. A Chained Content Handler

```
package Apache::Forward;

use strict;
use Apache::Constants qw(OK SERVER_ERROR);
use vars qw($VERSION);
$VERSION = '1.00';
```

Example 4-22. A Chained Content Handler (continued)

```
sub handler ($$) {
    my($class, $r) = @_;
    my $next = tied *STDOUT || return SERVER_ERROR;
    tie *STDOUT, $class, $r, $next or return SERVER_ERROR;
    $r->register_cleanup(sub { untie *STDOUT });
    OK;
}

sub TIEHANDLE {
    my($class, $r, $next) = @_;
    bless { 'r' => $r,           # request object
            'next' => $next      # next in the chain
          }, $class;
}

sub PRINT {
    my $self = shift;
    # Subclasses should do something interesting here
    $self->forward(@_);
}

#sub DESTROY {
#    my $self = shift;
#    # maybe clean up here
#}

sub forward {
    shift()->{'next'}->PRINT(@_);
}

1;
__END__
```

Having defined the filter base class, we can now define filters that actually do
something. We'll show a couple of simple ones to give you the idea first, then create a larger module that does something useful.

Apache::Upcase (Example 4-23) transforms everything it receives into uppercase
letters. It inherits from *Apache::Forward* and then overrides the *PRINT()* method.
PRINT() loops through the list of data items, calling *uc()* on each. It then forwards the modified data to the next filter in line by calling its *forward()* method
(which we do not need to override).

Example 4-23. Apache::Upcase Transforms Its Input into Uppercase

```
package Apache::Upcase;

use strict;
use Apache::Forward ();
use vars qw(@ISA $VERSION);
@ISA = qw(Apache::Forward);
$VERSION = '1.00';
```

Example 4-23. Apache::Upcase Transforms Its Input into Uppercase (continued)

```
sub PRINT {
    my $self = shift;
    $self->forward(map { uc $_ } @_);
}


1;
__END__
```

Along the same lines, *Apache::Censor* (Example 4-24) filters its input data to replace four-letter words with starred versions. It takes the definition of "four-letter word" a little liberally, transforming "sent" into "s**t." It is identical in every way to *Apache::Upcase*, except that *PRINT()* performs a global regular expression substitution on the input data. The transformed data is then forwarded to the next filter as before.

Example 4-24. A Handler that Removes Four-Letter Words

```
package Apache::Censor;

use strict;
use Apache::Forward ();
use vars qw(@ISA $VERSION);
@ISA = qw(Apache::Forward);
$VERSION = '1.00';

sub PRINT {
    my($self, @data) = @_;
    foreach (@data) { s/\b(\w)\w{2}(\w)\b/$1**$2/g; }
    $self->forward(@data);
}


1;
__END__
```

To watch these filters in action, we need a data source. Here's a very simple content handler that emits a constant string. It is very important that the content be sent with a regular *print()* statement rather than the specialized *$r->print()* method. If you call *Apache::print()* directly, rather than through the tied STDOUT filehandle, you short-circuit the whole chain!

```
package Apache::TestFilter;

use strict;
use Apache::Constants 'OK';

sub handler {
    my $r = shift;
    $r->content_type('text/plain');
    $r->send_http_header;
    print(<<END);
This is some text that is being sent out with a print()
statement to STDOUT.  We do not know whether STDOUT is tied
```

```
    to Apache or to some other source, and in fact it does not
    really matter.  We are just the content source.  The filters
    come later.
END
    OK;
}


1;
__END__
```

The last step is to provide a suitable entry in the configuration file. The *PerlHandler* directive should declare the components of the pipeline in *reverse* order. As Apache works its way forward from the last handler in the pipeline to the first, each of the handlers unties and reties STDOUT. The last handler in the series is the one that creates the actual content. It emits its data using *print()* and the chained handlers do all the rest. Here's a sample entry:

```
<Location /Filter>
   SetHandler  perl-script
   PerlHandler Apache::Upcase Apache::Censor Apache::TestFilter
</Location>
```

Figure 4-11 shows the page that appears when the pipeline runs.

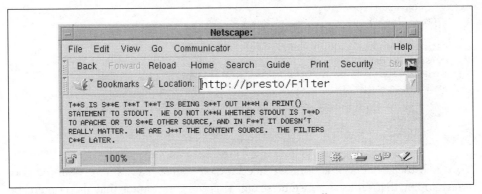

Figure 4-11. The final output from three chained content handlers

The last filter we'll show you is actually useful in its own right. When inserted into a filter pipeline, it compresses the data stream using the GZip protocol, and flags the browser that the data has been GZip-encoded by adding a *Content-Encoding* field to the HTTP header. Browsers that support on-the-fly decompression of GZip data will display the original document without any user intervention.*

---

* For historical reasons this facility is limited to Unix versions of Netscape Navigator, to PowerPC versions of Navigator on the Macintosh, and to some other Unix-based browsers such as W3-Emacs. However, now that Navigator's source code has been released to the developer community, we hope to see a more widespread implementation of this useful feature.

This filter requires the *zlib* compression library and its Perl interface, Paul Marquess' *Compress::Zlib*. *zlib*, along with instructions on installing it, can be found at *ftp://ftp.uu.net/pub/archiving/zip/zlib**. As usual, you can find *Compress::Zlib* at CPAN. Together these libraries provide both stream-based and in-memory compression/decompression services, as well as a high-level interface for creating and reading *gzip* files.

The filter is a little more complicated than the previous ones because GZip works best when the entire document is compressed in a single large segment. However, the filter will be processing a series of *print()* statements on data that is often as short as a single line. Although we could compress each line as a single segment, compression efficiency suffers dramatically. So instead we buffer the output, using *zlib*'s stream-oriented compression routines to emit the encoded data whenever *zlib* thinks enough data has been received to compress efficiently. We also have to take care of the details of creating a valid GZip header and footer. The header consists of the current date, information about the operating system, and some flags. The footer contains a CRC redundancy check and the size of the uncompressed file.

Example 4-25 gives the complete code for *Apache::GZip*. Although it inherits its core functionality from *Apache::Forward*, each subroutine has to be tweaked a bit to support the unique requirements of GZip compression.

```perl
package Apache::GZip;

use strict;
use Apache::Constants qw(:common);
use Compress::Zlib qw(deflateInit crc32 MAX_WBITS Z_DEFLATED);
use Apache::Forward ();
use vars qw($VERSION @ISA);

use constant GZIP_MAGIC => 0x1f8b;
use constant OS_MAGIC => 0x03;

$VERSION = '1.00';
@ISA = qw(Apache::Forward);
```

After the usual preamble, we import the compression routines from *Compress::Zlib*, and bring in the *Apache::Forward* class. We then define a couple of constants needed for the GZip header (in case you're wondering, we got these constants by looking at the *zlib* C code).

```perl
sub handler ($$) {
    my($class, $r) = @_;
    #return DECLINED unless $r->header_in("Accept-Encoding") =~ /gzip/;
    $r->content_encoding('gzip');
    $class->SUPER::handler($r);
}
```

In order for the browser to automatically decompress the data, it needs to see a *Content-Encoding* field with the value `gzip` in the HTTP header. In order to insert this field, we override the parent class's *handler()* subroutine and set the field using the request object's *content_encoding()* method. We then call our superclass's *handler()* method to do the rest of the work.

The commented line that comes before the call to *content_encoding()* is an attempt to "do the right thing." Browsers are supposed to send a header named *Accept-Encoding* if they can accept compressed or otherwise encoded data formats. This line tests whether the browser can accept the GZip format and declines the transaction if it can't. Unfortunately, it turns out that many Netscape browsers don't transmit this essential header, so we skip the test.[*]

```
sub TIEHANDLE {
    my $class = shift;
    my $r = shift;
    my $self = $class->SUPER::TIEHANDLE($r, @_);
    my $d = deflateInit(-WindowBits => -MAX_WBITS()) || return;
    @{$self}{'crc','d','l','h'} = (crc32(undef),$d,0,0);
    $r->push_handlers(PerlHandler => sub { $self->flush });
    return $self;
}
```

All the compression work is done in *TIEHANDLE()*, *PRINT()*, and *flush()*. *TIEHANDLE()* begins by invoking the superclass's *handler()* method to create an object blessed into the current class. The method then creates a new *Compress::Zlib* deflation object by calling *deflateInit()*, using an argument of `-WindowBits` that is appropriate for GZip files (again, we got this by reading the *zlib* C source code). Finally we add a few new instance variables to the object and return it to the caller. The instance variables include *crc*, for the cyclic redundancy check, *d* for the deflation object, *l* for the total length of the uncompressed data, and *h* for a flag that indicates whether the header has been printed.[†] Finally, *TIEHANDLE()* will call the *push_handlers()* method, installing our *flush()* method at the end of the output chain.

```
sub gzheader {
    pack("nccVcc", GZIP_MAGIC, Z_DEFLATED, 0,time,0, OS_MAGIC)
}

sub PRINT {
    my $self = shift;
    $self->forward(gzheader()) unless $self->{'h'}++;
```

---

[*] Andreas Koenig's *Apache::GzipChain* module, which does much the same thing as this one, contains a hardcoded pattern match for the browser type contained in the *User-Agent* field. You can add this sort of test yourself if you wish, or wait for the browser developers to implement *Accept-Encoding* correctly.

[†] At the time this chapter was being prepared, the author of *Compress::Zlib*, Paul Marquess, was enhancing his library to make this manual manipulation of the compressed output stream unnecessary.

```
        foreach (@_) {
          my $data = $self->{d}->deflate($_);
          $self->{l} += length($_);
          $self->{crc} = crc32($_, $self->{crc});
          $self->forward($data);
        }
    }
```

The *PRINT()* method is called once each time the previous filter in the pipeline calls *print()*. It first checks whether the GZip header has already been sent, and sends it if not. The GZip header is created by the *gzheader()* routine and consists of a number of constants packed into a 10-byte string. It then passes each of its arguments to the deflation object's *deflate()* method to compress the information, then forwards whatever compressed data is returned to the next filter in the chain (or Apache, if this is the last filter). The subroutine also updates the running total of bytes compressed and calculates the CRC, using *Compress::Zlib*'s *crc32()* subroutine.

```
    sub flush {
        my $self = shift;
        my $data = $self->{d}->flush;
        return unless $self->{'h'};
        $self->forward($data);
        $self->forward(pack("V V", $self->{'crc'}, $self->{'l'}));
    }
```

The *flush()* routine is called when the last of our chained handlers is run. Because *zlib* buffers its compressed data, there is usually some data left in its internal buffers that hasn't yet been printed. We call the deflation object's *flush()* method to obtain whatever is left and forward it onward. Lastly we forward the CRC and the total length of the uncompressed file, creating the obligatory GZip footer.

Apache::GZip will usually go last in the filter chain, like this:

```
    <Location /Compressed>
      SetHandler  perl-script
      PerlHandler Apache::GZip OneFilter AnotherFilter
    </Location>
```

You can use *Apache::GZip* with any content handler that prints directly to STDOUT. Most of the modules given in this chapter send data via *$r->print()*. Simply delete the *$r->* part to make them compatible with *Apache::GZip* and other chained content handlers.

Example 4-25. A Handler That Compresses Its Input Before Forwarding It

```
package Apache::GZip;

use strict;
use Apache::Constants qw(:common);
```

Example 4-25. A Handler That Compresses Its Input Before Forwarding It (continued)

```perl
use Compress::Zlib qw(deflateInit crc32 MAX_WBITS Z_DEFLATED);
use Apache::Forward ();
use vars qw($VERSION @ISA);

use constant GZIP_MAGIC => 0x1f8b;
use constant OS_MAGIC => 0x03;

$VERSION = '1.00';
@ISA = qw(Apache::Forward);

sub handler ($$) {
    my($class, $r) = @_;
    #return DECLINED unless $r->header_in("Accept-Encoding") =~ /gzip/;
    $r->content_encoding('gzip');
    $class->SUPER::handler($r);
}

sub TIEHANDLE {
    my $class = shift;
    my $r = shift;
    my $self = $class->SUPER::TIEHANDLE($r, @_);
    my $d = deflateInit(-WindowBits => -MAX_WBITS()) || return;
    @{$self}{'crc','d','l','h'} = (crc32(undef),$d,0,0);
    $r->push_handlers(PerlHandler => sub { $self->flush });
    return $self;
}

sub gzheader {
    pack("nccVcc", GZIP_MAGIC, Z_DEFLATED, 0,time,0, OS_MAGIC)
}

sub PRINT {
    my $self = shift;
    $self->forward(gzheader()) unless $self->{'h'}++;
    foreach (@_) {
        my $data = $self->{d}->deflate($_);
        $self->{l} += length($_);
        $self->{crc} = crc32($_, $self->{crc});
        $self->forward($data);
    }
}

sub flush {
    my $self = shift;
    my $data = $self->{d}->flush;
    return unless $self->{'h'};
    $self->forward($data);
    $self->forward(pack("V V", $self->{'crc'}, $self->{'l'}));
}

1;
__END__
```

Readers who are interested in content handler pipelines should be aware of Jan Pazdziora's *Apache::OutputChain* module. It accomplishes the same thing as *Apache::Forward* but uses an object model that is less transparent than this one (among other things, the *Apache::OutputChain* module must always appear first on the *PerlHandler* list). You should also have a look at Andreas Koenig's *Apache::PassFile* and *Apache::GZipChain* modules. The former injects a file into an OutputChain and is an excellent way of providing the input to a set of filters. The latter implements compression just as *Apache::GZip* does but doesn't buffer the compression stream, losing efficiency when *print()* is called for multiple small data segments.

Just as this book was going to press, Ken Williams announced *Apache::Filter*, a chained content handler system that uses a more devious scheme than that described here. Among the advantages of this system is that you do not have to list the components of the pipeline in reverse order.

Other Types of Stacked Handlers

Content handlers aren't the only type of Apache Perl API handler that can be stacked. Translation handlers, type handlers, authorization handlers, and in fact all types of handlers can be chained using exactly the same techniques we used for the content phase.

A particularly useful phase for stacking is the cleanup handler. Your code can use this to register any subroutines that should be called at the very end of the transaction. You can deallocate resources, unlock files, decrement reference counts, or clear globals. For example, the CGI.pm module maintains a number of package globals controlling various programmer preferences. In order to continue to work correctly in the persistent environment of *mod_perl*, CGI.pm has to clear these globals after each transaction. It does this by arranging for an internal routine named *_reset_globals()* to be called at the end of each transaction using this line of code:

```
$r->push_handlers('PerlCleanupHandler',\&CGI::_reset_globals);
```

Your program can push as many handlers as it likes, but you should remember that despite its name, the handler stack doesn't act like the classic LIFO (last-in/first-out) stack. Instead it acts like a FIFO (first-in/first-out) queue. Also remember that if the same handler is pushed twice, it will be invoked twice.

Method Handlers

It should come as no surprise that between the Apache distribution and third-party modules, there exist dozens of authentication modules, several directory indexing modules, and a couple of extended server-side include modules. All of these modules contain code that was copied and pasted from each other. In some cases all but a minuscule portion of the module consists of duplicated code.

Code duplication is not bad in and of itself, but it is wasteful of memory resources and, more important, of developers' time. It would be much better if code could be *reused* rather than duplicated, by using a form of object-oriented subclassing. For the C-language API there's not much hope of this. Vanilla C doesn't provide object-oriented features, while C++ would require both the Apache core and every extension module to adopt the same class hierarchy—and it's a little late in the game for this to happen.

Fortunately, the Perl language does support a simple object-oriented model that doesn't require that everyone buy into the same class hierarchy. This section describes how these object-oriented features can be used by Perl API modules to reuse code instead of duplicating it.

We've already looked at piecing together documents in various ways. Here we will explore an implementation using method handlers. There are two classes involved with this example: *My::PageBase* and *My::Page.*

Example 4-26 shows the *My::PageBase* class, which provides the base functionality for the family of documents derived from this class. *My::PageBase* stitches together a document by calling four methods: the *header()* method sends the HTTP headers, the *top()* method emits the beginning of an HTML document, including the title, the *body()* method emits the main contents of the page, and the *bottom()* method adds a common footer. *My::PageBase* includes generic definitions for *header()*, *top()*, *body()*, and *bottom()*, each of which can be overridden by its subclasses. These are all very simple methods. See Example 4-26 for the definitions.

The *My::PageBase handler()* method looks like this:

```
sub handler ($$) {
    my($self, $r) = @_;
    unless (ref($self)) {
        $self = $self->new;
    }
    for my $meth (qw(header top body bottom)) {
        $self->$meth($r);
    }
    return OK;
}
```

The key to using *My::PageBase* in an object-oriented way is the *handler()* subroutine's use of the ($$) function prototype. This tells *mod_perl* that the handler wants two arguments: the static class name or object, followed by the Apache request object that is normally passed to handlers. When the handler is called, it retrieves its class name or object reference and stores it in the lexical variable $self. It checks whether $self is an object reference, and if not, it calls its own *new()* method to create a new object. It then invokes the *header()*, *top()*, *body()*, and *bottom()* methods in turn.

The *My::PageBase new()* method turn the arguments passed to it into a blessed hash in the *My::PageBase* package. Each key in the hash is an attribute that can be used to construct the page. We do not define any default attributes:

```
sub new {
    my $class = shift;
    bless {@_}, $class;
}
```

We will see later why this method is useful.

As we saw in the section on the *Apache::Forward* module, method handlers are configured just like any other:

```
<Location /my>
  PerlHandler My::PageBase
  SetHandler perl-script
</Location>
```

However, for clarity's sake, or if you use a handler method named something other than *handler()*, you can use Perl's standard -> method-calling notation. You will have to load the module first with the *PerlModule* directive:

```
PerlModule My::PageBase
<Location /my>
  PerlHandler My::PageBase->handler
  SetHandler perl-script
</Location>
```

When *My::PageBase* is installed in this way and you request URI */my*, you will see the exciting screen shown in Figure 4-12.

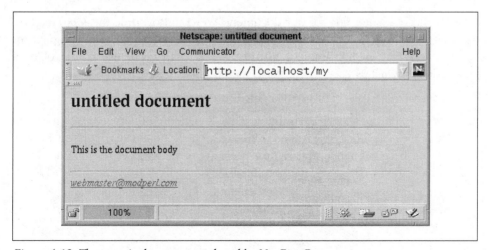

Figure 4-12. The generic document produced by My::PageBase

Naturally, we'll want to add a bit more spice to this page. Because the page is modularized, we can do so one step at a time by subclassing *Apache::PageBase*'s methods. The *My::Page* class does so by inheriting from the *My::PageBase* class and simply overriding the *body()* method.

```
package My::Page;
# file: My/Page.pm

use strict;
use vars qw(@ISA);
use My::PageBase ();
@ISA = qw(My::PageBase);

sub body {
    my($self, $r) = @_;
    $r->print(<<END);
<p><img src="/icons/cover.gif" align=CENTER>
This is My homepage</p>
<br clear=all>
END
}

1;
__END__
```

Then change the configuration to invoke the *handler()* method via *My::Page* rather than *My::PageBase*:

```
PerlModule My::Page
<Location /my>
  PerlHandler My::Page->handler
  SetHandler perl-script
</Location>
```

Things look almost the same, but the body text has changed (Figure 4-13).

Now we need a better title for our document. We could override the *top()* method as we did for *body()*, but that would involve cutting and pasting a significant amount of HTML (see Example 4-26). Instead, we can make use of the object's *title* attribute, which is used by the *top()* method in this way:

```
my $title = $self->{title} || "untitled document";
```

So how do we set the *title* attribute? This is where the *My::PageBase new()* method comes in. When it is called with a set of attribute=value pairs, it blesses them into a hash reference and returns the new object. To set the title attribute, we just have to call the *new()* method like this:

```
use My::Page ();
$My::Homepage = My::Page->new(title => 'My Homepage');
```

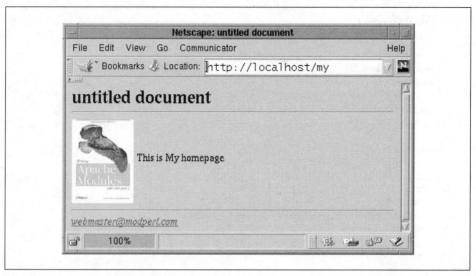

Figure 4-13. My::Page overrides the body() method of My::PageBase, creating a more interesting document.

This will create a global scalar variable in the *My* namespace named `$My::Homepage`. It's most convenient to do this during server startup—for instance, in the Perl startup file.

Now we just change the configuration section to use the *object* as the handler rather than the class name:

```
<Location /my>
    PerlHandler $My::Homepage->handler
    SetHandler perl-script
</Location>
```

The object will be retrieved by *mod_perl* and used to invoke the handler, which will lead to the creation of the page shown in Figure 4-14.

Example 4-26. Using a Method Handler for Object-Oriented Programming Techniques

```
package My::PageBase;
# file: My/PageBase.pm

use strict;
use Apache::Constants qw(:common);

sub new {
    my $class = shift;
    bless {@_}, $class;
}
```

Example 4-26. Using a Method Handler for Object-Oriented Programming Techniques (continued)

```perl
sub handler ($$) {
    my($self, $r) = @_;
    unless (ref($self)) {
        $self = $self->new;
    }
    for my $meth (qw(header top body bottom)) {
        $self->$meth($r);
    }
    return OK;
}

sub header {
    my($self, $r) = @_;
    $r->content_type($self->{type} || "text/html");
    $r->send_http_header;
}

sub top {
    my($self, $r) = @_;
    my $title = $self->{title} || "untitled document";
    $r->print(<<EOF);
<html>
<head>
<title>$title</title>
</head>
<body>
<h1>$title</h1>
<hr>
EOF
}

sub bottom {
    my($self, $r) = @_;
    my $admin = $r->server->server_admin;
    $r->print(<<EOF);
<hr>
<i><a href="mailto:$admin">$admin</a></i>
</body>
</html>
EOF
}

sub body {
    my($self, $r) = @_;
    $r->print("<p>This is the document body<p>");
}

1;
__END__
```

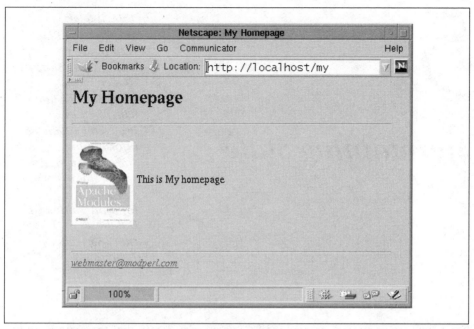

Figure 4-14. After creating a My::Page object with a title attribute defined, the page displays a custom title and level 1 header.

This wraps up our discussion of the basic techniques for generating page content, filtering files, and processing user input. The next chapter ventures into the perilous domain of imposing state on the stateless HTTP protocol. You'll learn techniques for setting up user sessions, interacting with databases, and managing long-term relationships with users.

5

Maintaining State

If you've ever written a complicated CGI script, you know that the main inconvenience of the HTTP architecture is its stateless nature. Once an HTTP transaction is finished, the server forgets all about it. Even if the same remote user connects a few seconds later, from the server's point of view it's a completely new interaction and the script has to reconstruct the previous interaction's state. This makes even simple applications like shopping carts and multipage questionnaires a challenge to write.

CGI script developers have come up with a standard bag of tricks for overcoming this restriction. You can save state information inside the fields of fill-out forms, stuff it into the URI as additional path information, save it in a cookie, ferret it away in a server-side database, or rewrite the URI to include a session ID. In addition to these techniques, the Apache API allows you to maintain state by taking advantage of the persistence of the Apache process itself.

This chapter takes you on a tour of various techniques for maintaining state with the Apache API. In the process, it also shows you how to hook your pages up to relational databases using the Perl DBI library.

Choosing the Right Technique

The main issue in preserving state information is where to store it. Six frequently used places are shown in the following list. They can be broadly broken down into client-side techniques (items 1 through 3) and server-side techniques (items 4 through 6).

1. Store state in hidden fields

2. Store state in cookies

3. Store state in the URI

4. Store state in web server process memory

5. Store state in a file

6. Store state in a database

In client-side techniques the bulk of the state information is saved on the browser's side of the connection. Client-side techniques include those that store information in HTTP cookies and those that put state information in the hidden fields of a fill-out form. In contrast, server-side techniques keep all the state information on the web server host. Server-side techniques include any method for tracking a user session with a session ID.

Each technique for maintaining state has unique advantages and disadvantages. You need to choose the one that best fits your application. The main advantage of the client-side techniques is that they require very little overhead for the web server: no data structures to maintain in memory, no database lookups, and no complex computations. The disadvantage is that client-side techniques require the cooperation of remote users and their browser software. If you store state information in the hidden fields of an HTML form, users are free to peek at the information (using the browser's "View Source" command) or even to try to trick your application by sending a modified version of the form back to you.* If you use HTTP cookies to store state information, you have to worry about older browsers that don't support the HTTP cookie protocol and the large number of users (estimated at up to 20 percent) who disable cookies out of privacy concerns. If the amount of state information you need to save is large, you may also run into bandwidth problems when transmitting the information back and forth.

Server-side techniques solve some of the problems of client-side methods but introduce their own issues. Typically you'll create a "session object" somewhere on the web server system. This object contains all the state information associated with the user session. For example, if the user has completed several pages of a multipage questionnaire, the session will hold the current page number and the responses to previous pages' questions. If the amount of state information is small, and you don't need to hold onto it for an extended period of time, you can keep

---

* Some sites that use the hidden fields technique in their shopping carts script report upward of 30 attempts per month by users to submit fraudulently modified forms in an attempt to obtain merchandise they didn't pay for.

it in the web server's process memory. Otherwise, you'll have to stash it in some long-term storage, such as a file or database. Because the information is maintained on the server's side of the connection, you don't have to worry about the user peeking or modifying it inappropriately.

However, server-side techniques are more complex than client-side ones. First, because these techniques must manage the information from multiple sessions simultaneously, you must worry about such things as database and file locking. Otherwise, you face the possibility of leaving the session storage in an inconsistent state when two HTTP processes try to update it simultaneously. Second, you have to decide when to expire old sessions that are no longer needed. Finally, you need a way to associate a particular session object with a particular browser. Nothing about a browser is guaranteed to be unique: not its software version number, nor its IP address, nor its DNS name. The browser has to be coerced into identifying itself with a unique session ID, either with one of the client-side techniques or by requiring users to authenticate themselves with usernames and passwords.

A last important consideration is the length of time you need to remember state. If you only need to save state across a single user session and don't mind losing the state information when the user quits the browser or leaves your site, then hidden fields and URI-based storage will work well. If you need state storage that will survive the remote user quitting the browser but don't mind if state is lost when you reboot the web server, then storing state in web server process memory is appropriate. However, for long-term storage, such as saving a user's preferences over a period of months, you'll need to use persistent cookies on the client side or store the state information in a file or database on the server side.

Maintaining State in Hidden Fields

Figure 5-1 shows the main example used in this chapter, an online hangman game. When the user first accesses the program, it chooses a random word from a dictionary of words and displays a series of underscores for each of the word's letters. The game prompts the user to type in a single letter guess or, if he thinks he knows it, the whole word. Each time the user presses return (or the "Guess" button), the game adds the guess to the list of letters already guessed and updates the display. Each time the user makes a wrong guess, the program updates the image to show a little bit more of the stick figure, up to six wrong guesses total. When the game is over, the user is prompted to start a new game. A status area at the top of the screen keeps track of the number of words the user has tried, the number of games he's won, and the current and overall averages (number of letters guessed per session).*

---

* Lincoln was very gratified when he tested the first working version of the game on his wife. She took over the computer and refused to give it back for hours!

This hangman game is a classic case of a web application that needs to maintain state across an extended period of time. It has to keep track of several pieces of information, including the unknown word, the letters that the user has already guessed, the number of wins, and a running average of guesses. In this section, we implement the game using hidden fields to record the persistent information. In later sections, we'll reimplement it using other techniques to maintain state.

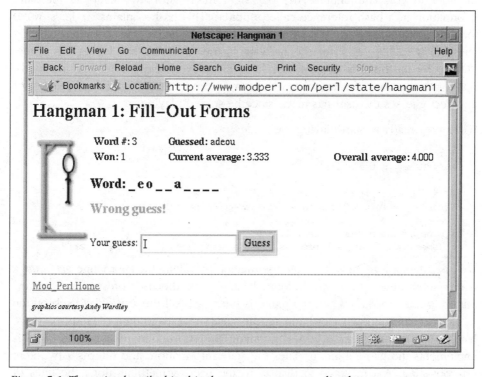

Figure 5-1. The script described in this chapter generates an online hangman game.

The complete code for the first version of the hangman game is given in Example 5-1. It is an *Apache::Registry* script and therefore runs equally well as a vanilla CGI script as under *mod_perl* (except for being much faster under *mod_perl*, of course). Much of the code is devoted to the program logic of choosing a new word from a random list of words, processing the user's guesses, generating the HTML to display the status information, and creating the fill-out form that prompts the user for input.

This is a long script, so we'll step through the parts that are relevant to saving and retrieving state a section at a time:

```
# file: hangman1.cgi
# hangman game using hidden form fields to maintain state
```

```
use IO::File ();
use CGI qw(:standard);

use strict;
use constant WORDS => '/usr/games/lib/hangman-words';
use constant ICONS => '/icons/hangman';
use constant TRIES => 6;
```

In order to compartmentalize the persistent information, we keep all the state information in a hash reference called $state. This hash contains six keys: WORD for the unknown word, GUESSED for the list of letters the user has already guessed, GUESSES_LEFT for the number of tries the user has left in this game, GAMENO for the number of games the user has played (the current one included), WON for the number of games the user has won, and TOTAL for the total number of incorrect guesses the user has made since he started playing.

We're now ready to start playing the game:

```
# retrieve the state
my $state = get_state();

# reinitialize if we need to
$state    = initialize($state) if !$state or param('restart');

# process the current guess, if any
my($message, $status) = process_guess(param('guess') || '', $state);
```

We first attempt to retrieve the state information by calling the subroutine *get_state()*. If this subroutine returns an undefined value or if the user presses the "restart" button, which appears when the game is over, we call the *initialize()* subroutine to pick a new unknown word and set the state variables to their defaults. Next we handle the user's guess, if any, by calling the subroutine *process_guess()*. This implements the game logic, updates the state information, and returns a two-item list consisting of a message to display to the user (something along the lines of "Good guess!") and a status code consisting of one of the words "won", "lost", "continue", or "error."

The main task now is to generate the HTML page:

```
# start the page
print header,
    start_html(-Title   => 'Hangman 1',
               -bgcolor => 'white',
               -onLoad  => 'if (document.gf) document.gf.guess.focus()'),
    h1('Hangman 1: Fill-Out Forms');

# draw the picture
picture($state);

# draw the statistics
status($message, $state);
```

```
# Prompt the user to restart or to enter the next guess.
if ($status =~ /^(won|lost)$/) {
    show_restart_form($state);
}
else {
    show_guess_form($state);
}
print hr,
    a({-href => '/'}, "Home"),
    p(cite({-style => "fontsize: 10pt"}, 'graphics courtesy Andy Wardley')),
    end_html();
```

Using CGI.pm functions, we generate the HTTP header and the beginning of the HTML code. We then generate an <IMG> tag using the state information to select which "hanged man" picture to show and display the status bar. If the status code returned by *process_guess()* indicates that the user has completed the game, we display the fill-out form that prompts the user to start a new game. Otherwise, we generate the form that prompts the user for a new guess. Finally we end the HTML page and exit.

Let's look at the relevant subroutines now, starting with the *initialize()* function:

```
sub initialize {
    my $state = shift;
    $state = {} unless $state;
    $state->{WORD}         = pick_random_word();
    $state->{GUESSES_LEFT} = TRIES;
    $state->{GUESSED}      = '';
    $state->{GAMENO}      += 1;
    $state->{WON}         += 0;
    $state->{TOTAL}       += 0;
    return $state;
}
```

All the state maintenance is performed in the subroutines *initialize()*, *get_state()*, and *set_state()*. *initialize()* creates a new empty state variable if one doesn't already exist, or resets just the per-game fields if one does. The per-game fields that always get reset are WORD, GUESSES_LEFT, and GUESSED. The first field is set to a new randomly chosen word, the second to the total number of tries that the user is allowed, and the third to an empty hash reference. GAMENO and TOTAL need to persist across user games. GAMENO is bumped up by one each time *initialize()* is called. TOTAL is set to zero only if it is not already defined. The (re)initialized state variable is now returned to the caller.

```
sub save_state {
    my $state = shift;
    foreach (qw(WORD GAMENO GUESSES_LEFT WON TOTAL GUESSED)) {
        print hidden(-name => $_, -value => $state->{$_}, -override => 1);
    }
}
```

The *save_state()* routine is where we store the state information. Because it stashes the information in hidden fields, this subroutine must be called within a <FORM> section. Using CGI.pm's *hidden()* HTML shortcut, we produce a series of hidden tags whose names correspond to each of the fields in the state hash. For the variables WORD, GAMENO, GUESSES_LEFT, and so on, we just call *hidden()* with the name and current value of the variable. The output of this subroutine looks something like the following HTML:

```
<INPUT TYPE="hidden" NAME="WORD" VALUE="tourists">
<INPUT TYPE="hidden" NAME="GAMENO" VALUE="2">
<INPUT TYPE="hidden" NAME="GUESSES_LEFT" VALUE="5">
<INPUT TYPE="hidden" NAME="WON" VALUE="0">
<INPUT TYPE="hidden" NAME="TOTAL" VALUE="7">
<INPUT TYPE="hidden" NAME="GUESSED" VALUE="eiotu">
```

get_state() reverses this process, reconstructing the hash of state information from the hidden form fields:

```
sub get_state {
    return undef unless param();
    my $state = {};
    foreach (qw(WORD GAMENO GUESSES_LEFT WON TOTAL GUESSED)) {
        $state->{$_} = param($_);
    }
    return $state;
}
```

This subroutine loops through each of the scalar variables, calls *param()* to retrieve its value from the query string, and assigns the value to the appropriate field of the state variable.

The rest of the script is equally straightforward. The *process_guess()* subroutine (too long to reproduce inline here; see Example 5-1) first maps the unknown word and the previously guessed letters into hashes for easier comparison later. Then it does a check to see if the user has already won the game but hasn't moved on to a new game (which can happen if the user reloads the page).

The subroutine now begins to process the guess. It does some error checking on the user's guess to make sure that it is a valid series of lowercase letters and that the user hasn't already guessed it. The routine then checks to see whether the user has guessed a whole word or a single letter. In the latter case, the program fails the user immediately if the guess isn't an identical match to the unknown word. Otherwise, the program adds the letter to the list of guesses and checks to see whether the word has been entirely filled in. If so, the user wins. If the user has guessed incorrectly, we decrement the number of turns left. If the user is out of turns, he loses. Otherwise, we continue.

The *picture()* routine generates an <IMG> tag pointing to an appropriate picture. There are six static pictures named *h0.gif* through *h5.gif*. This routine generates the right filename by subtracting the total number of tries the user is allowed from the number of turns he has left.

The *status()* subroutine is responsible for printing out the game statistics and the word itself. The most interesting part of the routine is toward the end, where it uses *map()* to replace the not-yet-guessed letters of the unknown word with underscores.

pick_random_word() is the routine that chooses a random word from a file of words. Many Linux systems happen to have a convenient list of about 38,000 words located in */usr/games/lib* (it is used by the Berkeley ASCII terminal hangman game). (If you don't have such a file on your system, check for */usr/dict/ words*, */usr/share/words*, */usr/words/dictionary*, and other variants.) Each word appears on a separate line. We work our way through each line, using a clever algorithm that gives each word an equal chance of being chosen without knowing the length of the list in advance. For a full explanation of how and why this algorithm works, see Chapter 8 of *Perl Cookbook*, by Tom Christiansen and Nathan Torkington (O'Reilly & Associates, 1998).

Because the state information is saved in the document body, the *save_state()* function has to be called from the part of the code that generates the fill-out forms. The two places where this happens are the routines *show_guess_form()* and *show_restart_form()*:

```
sub show_guess_form {
    my $state = shift;
    print start_form(-name => 'gf'),
        "Your guess: ",
        textfield(-name => 'guess', -value => '', -override => 1),
        submit(-value => 'Guess');
    save_state($state);
    print end_form;
}
```

show_guess_form() produces the fill-out form that prompts the user for his guess. It calls *save_state()* after opening a <FORM> section and before closing it.

```
sub show_restart_form {
    my $state = shift;
    print start_form,
        "Do you want to play again?",
        submit(-name => 'restart', -value => 'Another game');
    delete $state->{WORD};
    save_state($state);
    print end_form;
}
```

show_restart_form() is called after the user has either won or lost a game. It creates a single button that prompts the user to restart. Because the game statistics have to be saved across games, we call *save_state()* here too. The only difference from *show_guess_form()* is that we explicitly delete the WORD field from the state variable. This signals the script to generate a new unknown word on its next invocation.

Astute readers may wonder at the *−onLoad* argument that gets passed to the *start_html()* function toward the beginning of the code. This argument points to a fragment of JavaScript code to be executed when the page is first displayed. In this case, we're asking the keyboard focus to be placed in the text field that's used for the player's guess, avoiding the annoyance of having to click in the text field before typing into it. We promise we won't use JavaScript anywhere else in this book!

Example 5-1. A Hangman Game Using Fill-out Forms to Save State

```perl
# file: hangman1.cgi
# hangman game using hidden form fields to maintain state

use IO::File ();
use CGI qw(:standard);

use strict;
use constant WORDS => '/usr/games/lib/hangman-words';
use constant ICONS => '/icons/hangman';
use constant TRIES => 6;

# retrieve the state
my $state = get_state();

# reinitialize if we need to
$state    = initialize($state) if !$state or param('restart');

# process the current guess, if any
my($message, $status) = process_guess(param('guess') || '', $state);

# start the page
print header,
    start_html(-Title  => 'Hangman 1',
               -bgcolor => 'white',
               -onLoad  => 'if (document.gf) document.gf.guess.focus()'),
    h1('Hangman 1: Fill-Out Forms');

# draw the picture
picture($state);

# draw the statistics
status($message, $state);

# Prompt the user to restart or for his next guess.
if ($status =~ /^(won|lost)$/) {
    show_restart_form($state);
}
else {
    show_guess_form($state);
}
```

Example 5-1. A Hangman Game Using Fill-out Forms to Save State (continued)

```perl
print hr,
    a({-href => '/'}, "Home"),
    p(cite({-style => "fontsize: 10pt"}, 'graphics courtesy Andy Wardley')),
    end_html();

########## subroutines #############
# This is called to process the user's guess
sub process_guess {
    my($guess, $state) = @_;

    # lose immediately if user has no more guesses left
    return ('', 'lost') unless $state->{GUESSES_LEFT} > 0;

    my %guessed = map { $_ => 1 } $state->{GUESSED} =~ /(.)/g;
    my %letters = map { $_ => 1 } $state->{WORD} =~ /(.)/g;

    # return immediately if user has already guessed the word
    return ('', 'won') unless grep(!$guessed{$_}, keys %letters);

    # do nothing more if no guess
    return ('', 'continue') unless $guess;

    # This section processes individual letter guesses
    $guess = lc $guess;
    return ("Not a valid letter or word!", 'error')
        unless $guess =~ /^[a-z]+$/;
    return ("You already guessed that letter!", 'error')
        if $guessed{$guess};

    # This section is called when the user guesses the whole word
    if (length($guess) > 1 and $guess ne $state->{WORD}) {
        $state->{TOTAL} += $state->{GUESSES_LEFT};
        return (qq{You lose.  The word was "$state->{WORD}."}, 'lost')
    }

    # update the list of guesses
    foreach ($guess =~ /(.)/g) { $guessed{$_}++; }
    $state->{GUESSED} = join '', sort keys %guessed;

    # correct guess -- word completely filled in
    unless (grep(!$guessed{$_}, keys %letters)) {
        $state->{WON}++;
        return (qq{You got it!  The word was "$state->{WORD}."}, 'won');
    }

    # incorrect guess
    if (!$letters{$guess}) {
        $state->{TOTAL}++;
        $state->{GUESSES_LEFT}--;
        # user out of turns
        return (qq{The jig is up.  The word was "$state->{WORD}".}, 'lost')
            if $state->{GUESSES_LEFT} <= 0;
```

Example 5-1. A Hangman Game Using Fill-out Forms to Save State (continued)

```perl
        # user still has some turns
        return ('Wrong guess!', 'continue');
    }

    # correct guess but word still incomplete
    return (qq{Good guess!}, 'continue');
}

# create the cute hangman picture
sub picture {
    my $tries_left = shift->{GUESSES_LEFT};
    my $picture = sprintf("%s/h%d.gif", ICONS, TRIES-$tries_left);
    print img({-src   => $picture,
               -align => 'LEFT',
               -alt   => "[$tries_left tries left]"});
}

# print the status
sub status {
    my($message, $state) = @_;
    # print the word with underscores replacing unguessed letters
    print table({-width => '100%'},
            TR(
                td(b('Word #:'), $state->{GAMENO}),
                td(b('Guessed:'), $state->{GUESSED})
                ),
            TR(
                td(b('Won:'), $state->{WON}),
                td(b('Current average:'),
                    sprintf("%2.3f", $state->{TOTAL}/$state->{GAMENO})),
                td(b('Overall average:'),
                    $state->{GAMENO} > 1 ?
                       sprintf("%2.3f",
                           ($state->{TOTAL}-(TRIES-$state->{GUESSES_LEFT}))/
                                    ($state->{GAMENO}-1))
                       : '0.000')
                )
            );
    my %guessed = map { $_ => 1 } $state->{GUESSED} =~ /(.)/g;
    print h2("Word:",
            map {$guessed{$_} ? $_ : '_'}
            $state->{WORD} =~ /(.)/g);
    print h2(font({-color => 'red'}, $message)) if $message;
}

# print the fill-out form for requesting input
sub show_guess_form {
    my $state = shift;
    print start_form(-name => 'gf'),
          "Your guess: ",
          textfield(-name => 'guess', -value => '', -override => 1),
          submit(-value => 'Guess');
```

Example 5-1. A Hangman Game Using Fill-out Forms to Save State (continued)

```perl
    save_state($state);
    print end_form;
}


# ask the user if he wants to start over
sub show_restart_form {
    my $state = shift;
    print start_form,
          "Do you want to play again?",
          submit(-name => 'restart', -value => 'Another game');
    delete $state->{WORD};
    save_state($state);
    print end_form;
}


# pick a word, any word
sub pick_random_word {
    my $list = IO::File->new(WORDS)
        || die "Couldn't open ${\WORDS}: $!\n";
    my $word;
    rand($.) < 1 && ($word = $_) while <$list>;
    chomp $word;
    $word;
}


################## state maintenance ##############
# This is called to initialize a whole new state object
# or to create a new game.
sub initialize {
    my $state = shift;
    $state = {} unless $state;
    $state->{WORD}         = pick_random_word();
    $state->{GUESSES_LEFT}     = TRIES;
    $state->{GUESSED}   = '';
    $state->{GAMENO}    += 1;
    $state->{WON}       += 0;
    $state->{TOTAL}     += 0;
    return $state;
}


# Retrieve an existing state
sub get_state {
    return undef unless param();
    my $state = {};
    foreach (qw(WORD GAMENO GUESSES_LEFT WON TOTAL GUESSED)) {
        $state->{$_} = param($_);
    }
    return $state;
}


# Save the current state
sub save_state {
```

Example 5-1. A Hangman Game Using Fill-out Forms to Save State (continued)

```
my $state = shift;
foreach (qw(WORD GAMENO GUESSES_LEFT WON TOTAL GUESSED)) {
    print hidden(-name => $_, -value => $state->{$_}, -override => 1);
}
}
```

Although this method of maintaining the hangman game's state works great, it has certain obvious limitations. The most severe of these is that it's easy for the user to cheat. All he has to do is to choose the "View Source" command from his browser's menu bar and there's the secret word in full view, along with all other state information. The user can use his knowledge of the word to win the game, or he can save the form to disk, change the values of the fields that keep track of his wins and losses, and resubmit the doctored form in order to artificially inflate his statistics.

These considerations are not too important for the hangman game, but they become real issues in applications in which money is at stake. Even with the hangman game we might worry about the user tampering with the state information if we were contemplating turning the game into an Internet tournament. Techniques for preventing user tampering are discussed later in this chapter.

Maintaining State with Cookies

The other main client-side technique we'll consider uses HTTP cookies to store state information. HTTP cookies are named bits of information that are transmitted between the server and browser within the HTTP header. Ordinarily the server creates a cookie by including a *Set-Cookie* field in the HTTP header. The browser then stashes away the cookie information in a small in-memory or on-disk database. The next time the browser makes a request from that particular server, it returns that cookie in a *Cookie* field.

Cookies are relatively flexible. You can create cookies that will be returned to only one specific server or to any server in your domain. You can set them up so that they're returned only when users access a particular part of the document tree or any URI in the document hierarchy. They can be set to expire immediately when the user exits the browser, or they can be made to persist on the user's disk database for an extended period of time. You can also create secure cookies that are only returned to the server when a secure protocol, such as SSL, is in effect. This prevents cookies from being intercepted in transit by network eavesdroppers.

The exact format of HTTP cookies is somewhat involved and is described in the HTTP specification at *http://www.w3.org/Protocols*. Fortunately it's easy to make cookies in the right format using the *CGI::Cookie* module. To create a cookie with the name `Hangman`, a value equal to the hangman state variable `$state`, and an expiration time one month from now, you would call *CGI::Cookie::new()* in this way:

```
$cookie = CGI::Cookie->new(-name    => 'Hangman',
                           -value   => {WORD => 'terpitude',
                                        GAMENO => 1},
                           -expires => '+1M');
```

You can now send the cookie to the browser among the HTTP header fields using the *–cookie* argument to CGI.pm's *header()* method as shown here:

```
print header(-cookie => $cookie);
```

On subsequent invocations of the program you can retrieve named cookies sent by the browser with CGI.pm's *cookie()* method:

```
%cookie = cookie('Hangman');
```

Note that CGI.pm allows you to set and retrieve cookies that consist of entire hashes.

If you want to bypass CGI.pm and do the cookie management yourself within the Perl Apache API, you can use *CGI::Cookie* to create and parse the cookie format and then get the cookies in and out of the HTTP header using the Apache *header_in()* and *header_out()* methods. The experimental *Apache::Request* module also has cookie-handling functions.

Using the Perl Apache API, here's how to add a cookie to the HTTP header:

```
$r->header_out('Set-Cookie' => $cookie);
```

Here's how to retrieve and parse the cookies from the HTTP header and then find the one named `Hangman`:

```
%cookies = CGI::Cookie->parse($r->header_in('Cookie'));
$cookie = $cookies{'Hangman'};
```

Because we already require it for the hangman game, we'll use the CGI.pm short-cuts for cookie management. We only need to make a few changes to reimplement the hangman game to use cookies for state maintenance. The updated subroutines are shown in Example 5-2.

```
use CGI::Cookie ();
# retrieve the state
my $state = get_state() unless param('clear');
```

At the top of the file, in addition to importing functions from CGI.pm, we bring in the *CGI::Cookie* module. This isn't strictly necessary, since CGI.pm will do it for us, but it makes the code clearer. We retrieve the state as before by calling *get_state()*, but now we do it only if the CGI parameter `clear` is *not* defined. We'll see why we made this change later.

```
$state   = initialize($state) if !$state or param('restart');
my($message, $status) = process_guess(param('guess') || '', $state);
print header(-cookie => save_state($state)),
    start_html(-Title   => 'Hangman 2',
               -bgcolor => 'white',
               -onLoad  => 'if (document.gf) document.gf.guess.focus()'),
    h1('Hangman 2');
```

Next, having retrieved the state, we (re)initialize it if necessary in order to choose a fresh word at the beginning of a new game. We process the user's guess by calling *process_guess()* and then print out the HTTP header. Here's where we find the first big difference. Instead of sending the state information to the browser within the HTML body, we need to save it in the HTTP header. We call *save_state()* in order to create a correctly formatted cookie, then send it down the wire to the browser by passing it to CGI.pm's *header()* method as the value of the *–cookie* argument.

```
sub get_state {
    my %cookie = cookie(COOKIE_NAME);
    return undef unless %cookie;
    return \%cookie;
}

sub save_state {
    my $state = shift;
    return CGI::Cookie->new(-name => COOKIE_NAME,
                            -value => $state,
                            -expires => '+1M');
}
```

Turning our attention to the pivotal *get_state()* and *save_state()* functions, we see that *get_state()* calls CGI.pm's *cookie()* method to retrieve the value of the cookie named **Hangman** (stored in the constant **COOKIE_NAME**). *cookie()* takes care of flattening and expanding arrays and hashes for us (but not more complex structures, unfortunately), so we don't need to copy any fields to a separate **$state** variable, we just return a reference to the cookie hash itself! Similarly, in *save_state()*, we just turn the entire state structure into a cookie by passing it to *CGI::Cookie::new()*. We specify an expiration time of one month in the future (**+1M**). This allows the cookie to persist between browser sessions.

Because we don't have to mess around with hidden fields in this example, the *show_guess_form()* subroutine doesn't need to call *save_state()*. Likewise, we can remove the call to *save_state()* from *show_restart_form()*. The latter subroutine has an additional modification, the addition of a checkbox labeled "Clear scores" (see Figure 5-2). If the user selects this checkbox before pressing the new game button, the program clears out the state entirely, treating *get_state()* as if it returned an undefined value.

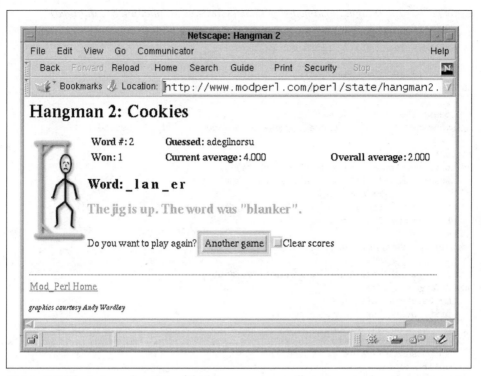

Figure 5-2. The improved version of the hangman game allows users to clear their aggregate scores and start over.

The rationale for this feature is to capitalize on a bonus that you get when you use persistent cookies. Because the cookie is stored on the user's disk until it expires, the user can quit the browser completely and come back to the game some days later to find it in exactly the state he left it. It's eerie and wonderful at the same time. Of course, the user might want to start out fresh, particularly if he hasn't been doing so well. The "Clear scores" checkbox lets him wipe the slate clean.

Example 5-2. The Hangman Game Using Cookies for State Maintenance

```
# file: hangman2.cgi
# hangman game using cookies to save state

use IO::File ();
use CGI qw(:standard);
use CGI::Cookie ();

use strict;
use constant WORDS => '/usr/games/lib/hangman-words';
use constant ICONS => '/icons/hangman';
use constant COOKIE_NAME => 'Hangman';
use constant TRIES => 6;
```

Example 5-2. The Hangman Game Using Cookies for State Maintenance (continued)

```perl
# retrieve the state
my $state = get_state() unless param('clear');

# reinitialize if we need to
$state    = initialize($state) if !$state or param('restart');

# process the current guess, if any
my($message, $status) = process_guess(param('guess') || '', $state);

# start the page
print header(-cookie => save_state($state)),
    start_html(-Title   => 'Hangman 2',
               -bgcolor => 'white',
               -onLoad  => 'if (document.gf) document.gf.guess.focus()'),
    h1('Hangman 2: Cookies');
```

. . . nothing in the middle is different . . .

```perl
# print the fill-out form for requesting input
sub show_guess_form {
    my $state = shift;
    print start_form(-name => 'gf'),
          "Your guess: ",
          textfield(-name => 'guess', -value => '', -override => 1),
          submit(-value => 'Guess');
    print end_form;
}


# ask the user if he wants to start over
sub show_restart_form {
    my $state = shift;
    print start_form,
          "Do you want to play again?",
          submit(-name => 'restart', -value => 'Another game'),
          checkbox(-name => 'clear', -label => 'Clear scores');
    delete $state->{WORD};
    print end_form;
}


# Retrieve an existing state
sub get_state {
    my %cookie = cookie(COOKIE_NAME);
    return undef unless %cookie;
    return \%cookie;
}


# Save the current state
sub save_state {
    my $state = shift;
    return CGI::Cookie->new(-name => COOKIE_NAME,
                            -value => $state,
                            -expires => '+1M');
}
```

Protecting Client-Side Information

The cookie-based implementation of the hangman game is a lot classier than the first implementation. Not only does it have the advantage of maintaining state across browser sessions, but the game is also somewhat harder to cheat. While the user is actively playing the game, the cookie is kept in memory where it is difficult to read without the benefit of a debugger. However, after the user quits the browsing session, the cookie is written out to disk; determined cheaters could still find and edit the cookie database file if they wanted to make their statistics look better.

When you store information on the client side of the connection, peeking and tampering is a general problem. Fortunately, the cure is relatively simple. To prevent tampering, you can use a message authentication check (MAC)—a form of checksum that will detect if the user has altered the information in any way. To prevent peeking, you can encrypt the information using an encryption key that is known to you but not to the user.

Message Authentication Checks

Let's add a MAC to the cookie used in the last section's example. There are many ways to compute a checksum, but the most reliable use a class of algorithms known as message digests. A message digest algorithm takes a large amount of data (usually called the "message") and crunches it through a complex series of bit shifts, rotates, and other bitwise operations until it has been reduced to a smallish number known as a hash. The widely used MD5 message digest algorithm produces a 128-bit hash.

Because information is lost during the message digest operation, it is a one-way affair: given a hash, you can't reconstruct the original message. Because of the complexity of the digest operation, it is extremely difficult to deliberately create a message that will digest to a particular hash. Changing just one bit anywhere in a message will result in a hash that is utterly unlike the previous one. However, you can confirm that a particular message was likely to have produced a particular hash simply by running the message through the digest algorithm again and comparing the result to the hash.

To create a MAC, follow this general recipe:

1. Choose a secret key. The key can be any combination of characters of any length. Long keys that don't spell out words or phrases are preferred. Keep the secret key well guarded.

2. Select the fields that will be used for the MAC. You should include any field that you don't want the user to alter. You can also add consistency-checking

fields such as the remote browser's IP address and an expiration date. This helps protect against the information being intercepted en route by some unscrupulous eavesdropper and used later to impersonate the user.

3. Compute the MAC by concatenating the fields and the secret key and running them through the digest algorithm. You actually need to concatenate the key and run the digest algorithm twice. Otherwise a technically savvy user could take advantage of one of the mathematical properties of the algorithm to append his own data to the end of the fields. Assuming you're using the MD5 algorithm, the formula looks like this:*

```
$MAC = MD5->hexhash($secret .
    MD5->hexhash(join '', $secret, @fields));
```

The MAC is now sent to the user along with the other state information.

4. When the state information is returned by the user, retrieve the various fields and the MAC. Repeat the digest process and compare it to the retrieved MAC. If they match, you know that the user hasn't modified or deleted any of the fields.

Example 5-3 shows the changes needed to add a MAC to the cookie-based hangman system.

```
use MD5 ();
use constant COOKIE_NAME => 'Hangman3';
use constant SECRET => 'Omn1um ex Ovum';
```

At the top of the script, we add a line to bring in functions from the MD5 package. This module isn't a standard part of Perl, but you can easily obtain it at CPAN. You'll find it easy to compile and install. The only other change we need to make to the top of the script is to add a new constant: the secret key (an obscure Latin phrase with some of the letters replaced with numbers). In this case we hard-code the secret key. You might prefer to read it from a file, caching the information in memory until the file modification date changes.

We now define a function named *MAC()* whose job is to generate a MAC from the state information and, optionally, to compare the new MAC to the MAC already stored in the state information:

```
# Check or generate the MAC authentication information
sub MAC {
    my($state, $action) = @_;
    return undef unless ref($state);
    my(@fields) = @{$state}{qw(WORD GUESSES_LEFT GUESSED GAMENO WON TOTAL)};
```

---

* As this book was going to press, Gisle Aas had released a *Digest::HMAC* module which implements a more sophisticated version of this algorithm. You should consider using it for highly sensitive applications.

```
        my $newmac = MD5->hexhash(SECRET .
                        MD5->hexhash(join '', SECRET, @fields));
        return $state->{MAC} = $newmac if $action eq 'generate';
        return $newmac eq $state->{MAC} if $action eq 'check';
        return undef;
    }
```

MAC() takes two arguments: the $state hash reference and an $action variable that indicates whether we want to generate a new MAC or check an old one. As described in the MAC recipe, we fetch the various fields from $state, concatenate them with the secret key, and then take the MD5 digest. If $action indicates that we are to generate the MAC, we now save the digest into a new state variable field called MAC. If, on the other hand, $action indicates that we are to check the MAC, we compare the new MAC against the contents of this field and return a true value if the old field both exists and is identical to the newly calculated digest. Otherwise we return false.

We now modify *get_state()* and *save_state()* to take advantage of the MAC information:

```
    # Retrieve an existing state
    sub get_state {
        my %cookie = cookie(COOKIE_NAME);
        return undef unless %cookie;
        authentication_error() unless MAC(\%cookie, 'check');
        return \%cookie;
    }
```

get_state() retrieves the cookie as before, but before returning it to the main part of the program, it passes the cookie to *MAC()* with an action code of check. If *MAC()* returns a true result, we return the cookie to the caller. Otherwise, we call a new function, *authentication_error()*, which displays an error message and exits immediately.

```
    # Save the current state
    sub save_state {
        my $state = shift;
        MAC($state, 'generate');  # add MAC to the state
        return CGI::Cookie->new(-name => COOKIE_NAME,
                                -value => $state,
                                -expires => '+1M');
    }
```

Before *save_state()* turns the state variable into a cookie, it calls *MAC()* with an action code of generate to add the MAC stamp to the state information. It then calls *CGI::Cookie::new()* as before in order to create a cookie that contains both the state information and the MAC code. You may notice that we've changed the cookie name from Hangman to Hangman3. This is in order to allow both versions of this script to coexist peacefully on the same server.

The *authentication_error()* subroutine is called if the MAC check fails:

```
# Authentication error page
sub authentication_error {
    my $cookie = CGI::Cookie->new(-name => COOKIE_NAME, -expires => '-1d');
    print header(-cookie => $cookie),
          start_html(-title => 'Authentication Error',
                     -bgcolor =>'white'),
          img({-src => sprintf("%s/h%d.gif",ICONS,TRIES),
              -align => 'LEFT'}),
          h1(font({-color => 'red'}, 'Authentication Error')),
          p('This application was unable to confirm the integrity of the',
           'cookie that holds your current score.',
           'Please reload the page to start a fresh session.'),
          p('If the problem persists, contact the webmaster.');
    exit 0;
}
```

This routine displays a little HTML page advising the user of the problem (Figure 5-3) and exits. Before it does so, however, it sends the user a new empty cookie named **Hangman3** with the expiration time set to a negative number. This causes the browser to discard the cookie and effectively clears the session. This is necessary in order to allow the user to continue to play. Otherwise the browser would continue to display this error whenever the user tried to access the page.

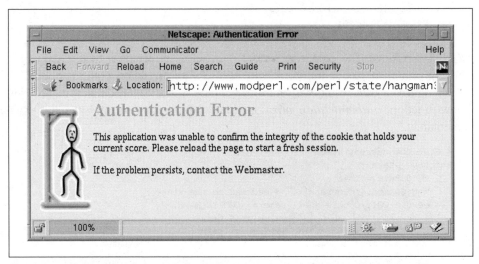

Figure 5-3. If the cookie fails to verify, the hangman3 script generates this error page.

If you are following along with the working demo at *www.modperl.com*, you might want to try quitting your browser, opening up the cookie database file with a text editor, and making some changes to the cookie (try increasing your number of wins by a few notches). When you try to open the hangman script again, the program should bring you up short.

With minor changes, you can easily adapt this technique for use with the hidden field version of the hangman script.

There are a number of ways of calculating MACs; some are more suitable than others for particular applications. For a very good review of MAC functions, see *Applied Cryptography*, by Bruce Schneir (John Wiley & Sons, 1996). In addition, the *Cryptobytes* newsletter has published several excellent articles on MAC functions. Back issues are available online at *http://www.rsa.com/rsalabs/pubs/ cryptobytes/*.

Example 5-3. The Cookie-Based Hangman Game with a Message Authentication Check

```
# file: hangman3.cgi
# hangman game using cookies and a MAC to save state

use IO::File ();
use CGI qw(:standard);
use CGI::Cookie ();
use MD5 ();

use strict;
use constant WORDS => '/usr/games/lib/hangman-words';
use constant ICONS => '/icons/hangman';
use constant TRIES => 6;
use constant COOKIE_NAME => 'Hangman3';
use constant SECRET => 'Omn1um ex Ovum';

... everything in the middle remains the same ...

# Check or generate the MAC authentication information
sub MAC {
    my($state, $action) = @_;
    return undef unless ref($state);
    my(@fields) = @{$state}{qw(WORD GUESSES_LEFT GUESSED GAMENO WON TOTAL)};
    my($newmac) = MD5->hexhash(SECRET .
                             MD5->hexhash(join '', SECRET, @fields));
    return $newmac eq $state->{MAC} if $action eq 'check';
    return $state->{MAC} = $newmac if $action eq 'generate';
    undef;
}

# Retrieve an existing state
sub get_state {
    my %cookie = cookie(COOKIE_NAME);
    return undef unless %cookie;
    authentication_error() unless MAC(\%cookie, 'check');
    return \%cookie;
}

# Save the current state
sub save_state {
```

*Example 5-3. The Cookie-Based Hangman Game with a Message Authentication
Check (continued)*

```perl
    my $state = shift;
    MAC($state, 'generate');  # add MAC to the state
    return CGI::Cookie->new(-name => COOKIE_NAME,
                            -value => $state,
                            -expires => '+1M');
}

# Authentication error page
sub authentication_error {
    my $cookie = CGI::Cookie->new(-name => COOKIE_NAME, -expires => '-1d');
    print header(-cookie => $cookie),
          start_html(-title => 'Authentication Error',
                     -bgcolor =>'#f5deb3'),
          img({-src => sprintf("%s/h%d.gif", ICONS, TRIES),
               -align => 'LEFT'}),
          h1(font({-color => 'red'}, 'Authentication Error')),
          p('This application was unable to confirm the integrity of the',
            'cookie that holds your current score.',
            'Please reload the page to start a fresh session.'),
          p('If the problem persists, contact the webmaster.');
    exit 0;
}
```

Encrypting Client-Side State Information

Message authentication checks implement a "look but don't touch" policy. Users
can't modify the state information, but they can still see what's there. In many web
applications, there's no harm in this, but with the hangman game it has the
unwanted consequence that the user can peek at the unknown word, either by
viewing the page source in the fill-out form version or by quitting the browser and
viewing the cookie database file.

To prevent this from happening without abandoning client-side storage entirely,
you can encrypt the state information. Your application will have the secret key
necessary to decrypt the information, but without launching an expensive
cryptanalysis project (and maybe not even then) the user won't be able to get at
the data. Encryption can be combined with a MAC in order to obtain truly bullet-
proof client-side authentication.

Example 5-4 shows the hangman game code modified to save its state using
encrypted cookies. It takes advantage of a recently introduced Perl module called
Crypt::CBC. This implements the Cipher Block Chaining encryption mode and
allows the encryption of messages of arbitrary length (previously only block-mode
ciphers were available for Perl, which force you to encrypt the message in rigid 8-
byte units). *Crypt::CBC* must be used in conjunction with a block-mode cipher,
either *Crypt::DES* or *Crypt::IDEA*. The former implements the popular U.S. Data
Encryption Standard encryption algorithm, while the latter implements the newer

and stronger International Data Encryption Algorithm. You can download these modules from CPAN.*

To save space, we again show just the changes to the basic hangman script that are needed to encrypted state information.

```
use MD5 ();
use Crypt::CBC ();

# retrieve the state
$CIPHER ||= Crypt::CBC->new(SECRET, 'IDEA');
my $state = get_state() unless param('clear');
```

At the top of the script we now bring in the *Crypt::CBC* module, as well as *MD5*. We then create a *Crypt::CBC* object and store it in a new global variable called $CIPHER. The *Crypt::CBC::new()* method takes two arguments: our secret key and the name of the block algorithm to use for encryption. We use the IDEA algorithm here because it is much harder to crack than the older DES. When we initialize the $CIPHER variable we take advantage of the persistence of Apache API scripts. The ||= assignment guarantees that a new *Crypt::CBC* object will be created only if $CIPHER does not previously exist. This reduces the amount of computation the script has to do at startup time.

The actual encryption and decryption is performed in *save_state()* and *get_state()*.

```
# Save the current state
sub save_state {
    my $state = shift;
    MAC($state, 'generate');  # add MAC to the state
    # encrypt the cookie
    my $encrypted = $CIPHER->encrypt_hex(join ':', %{$state});
    return CGI::Cookie->new(-name => COOKIE_NAME,
                            -value => $encrypted,
                            -expires => '+1M');
}
```

In *save_state()*, we generate the MAC as before but add an additional step. We first serialize the state hash reference by joining its keys and values with the : character (we chose this character because we know that it never occurs in the state information). We next call the $CIPHER object's *encrypt_hex()* method to encrypt the serialized information and store it in a variable named $encrypted. *encrypt_hex()* first performs the encryption and then converts the encrypted information into a printable hexadecimal string. This encrypted string is then turned into an HTTP cookie named Hangman4.

---

* Be aware that some countries regulate the use of cryptography. For example, cryptography is illegal in France, while the United States forbids the export of cryptographic software beyond its territorial borders. If you are living outside the U.S., don't download *Crypt::DES* or *Crypt::IDEA* from an American CPAN site. Use one of the European or Asian mirrors instead ;-). At the time this was written, the *Crypt::DES* and *Crypt::IDEA* modules required the *gcc* compiler to build correctly. Hopefully, this will have changed by the time you read this.

```
# Retrieve an existing state
sub get_state {
    my $cookie = cookie(COOKIE_NAME);
    return undef unless $cookie;
    # decrypt the cookie
    my %state = split ':', $CIPHER->decrypt_hex($cookie);
    authentication_error() unless MAC(\%state, 'check');
    return \%state;
}
```

The *get_state()* subroutine performs the corresponding decryption of the data. It retrieves the cookie, decrypts it by calling the $CIPHER object's *decrypt_hex()* method, and turns it back into a hash by splitting on the : character. We then check the MAC as before and return the state information to the caller.

If the user were to peek at his cookies file, he'd see something like this (some of the fields have been removed for the sake of simplicity):

```
www.modperl.com /perl/state/ Hangman4 5e650600dc0fac462d0d86adf3c
5d7e5fc46a5b2991b10093b548fafacc7d50c48923cdcb375a703f1e3224dfa98455
360f2423a0e6a95ccf791731e2946faef347c0b1f4ef6e5893cab190a2b0772c40bf
ce32d7a5ce8a74e2fc65cdc7d5b5a
```

The long hexadecimal string following the cookie's name is the encrypted information. The user cannot access the data contained in this string, nor can he make any changes to it. Any change to the string will cause a section of the data to decrypt incorrectly, making the MAC check fail.

Note that you can use this technique to encrypt the contents of fill-out fields as well, allowing you to store client-side information securely even when the user has set the browser to refuse cookies.

The amount of state information stored by the hangman script is relatively modest. Therefore, there isn't significant overhead either from the encryption/decryption process or from the transmission of the encrypted information across the network. The *Hangman4* script has the same subjective response rate as the unencrypted scripts. If the amount of state information were to grow quite large, however, the encryption overhead might become noticeable. Another thing to watch out for is the size of the cookie; the maximum size a browser can store is about 4 KB. With large amounts of state information, you might consider compressing the state data before encrypting it. The *Compress::Zlib* module, which we used in the previous chapter, makes this convenient. Be sure to compress the data *before* you encrypt it. Encrypted data is notoriously uncompressable.

Example 5-4. The Hangman Game with Encryption of Client-Side Data

```
#!/usr/local/bin/perl

# file: hangman4.pl
# hangman game using encrypted cookies to save state
```

Example 5-4. The Hangman Game with Encryption of Client-Side Data (continued)

```perl
use IO::File ();
use CGI qw(:standard);
use CGI::Cookie ();
use MD5 ();
use Crypt::CBC ();

use strict;
use vars '$CIPHER';
use constant WORDS => '/usr/games/lib/hangman-words';
use constant ICONS => '/icons/hangman';
use constant TRIES => 6;
use constant COOKIE_NAME => 'Hangman4';
use constant SECRET => 'Omn1um ex Ovum';

# retrieve the state
$CIPHER ||= CBC->new(SECRET,'IDEA');
my $state = get_state() unless param('clear');
```

. . . everything in the middle remains the same . . .

```perl
# Save the current state
sub save_state {
    my $state = shift;
    MAC($state,'generate');  # add MAC to the state
    # encrypt the cookie
    my $encrypted = $CIPHER->encrypt_hex(join(':',%{$state}));
    return CGI::Cookie->new(-name=>COOKIE_NAME,
                            -value=>$encrypted,
                            -expires=>'+1M');
}

# Retrieve an existing state
sub get_state {
    my $cookie = cookie(COOKIE_NAME);
    return undef unless $cookie;
    # decrypt the cookie
    my %state = split ':', $CIPHER->decrypt_hex($cookie);
    authentication_error() unless MAC(\%state, 'check');
    return \%state;
}
```

Storing State at the Server Side

Client-side storage of state information works well when each of the user sessions is independent of the others. But what if we wanted to combine the information from users, for example, to display a list of the top-scoring players in an Internet-wide tournament?

This is where server-side state storage comes in. When you store the user information at the server side rather than the client side, you have full access to the list of all users and to the record of what they've done and what they're doing. You can crunch, tally, tabulate, and cross-reference this information to your heart's content. Server-side storage also has the advantage of being more secure, since the information never leaves the server, and it is more resilient to failure. If the user's browser crashes in the midst of accepting or updating a cookie, that information isn't lost because it's stored safely on the server. The downside is scalability and performance. Each user session that you store on the server side consumes some amount of memory, disk, and CPU cycles. When you store state information on the server side, you have to be careful to conserve these resources, for example, by deleting user sessions that are no longer in use.

We will consider two types of server-side techniques in this section: storing the information transiently in main memory and storing it in a SQL database.

Storing State Information in Main Memory

Because Apache server processes are persistent across multiple accesses, you can store small amounts of state information in main memory. When the user first runs your application, it generates a random unique session identifier (session ID) and stores the state information in a data structure, for instance, a hash table keyed by the session ID. The application then sends the session ID back to the user in the form of a cookie, a hidden field, or a component of the URI. When the same user connects again, your application recovers the session ID and retrieves the state information from its data structure.

Sounds simple, but there are some catches. On Win32 systems this scheme works flawlessly because there is only one server process and one single-threaded Perl interpreter. However, on Unix systems there are multiple Apache processes running simultaneously, each with its own memory space. When a user fetches a page, there's no guarantee that he will connect to the same server process as before. What's more, server processes do die from time to time when they reach the limit specified by Apache's *MaxRequestsPerChild* directive.

If you are using *mod_perl* on a Unix system, you can work around these problems by using Benjamin Sugars' *IPC::Shareable* module. It ties Perl data structures (scalars and hashes, but not arrays) to shared memory segments, allowing multiple processes to access the same data structures. The tying process invokes shared memory calls whenever you store data to or fetch values from the tied variable, causing the information to be maintained in a shared memory segment.

As a bonus, the shared data structures persist even when the processes using it go away, so the state information will survive even a complete server shutdown and restart (but not a system reboot). The downside is that working with the shared data structures is not entirely transparent. You have to lock the tied variables prior to updating them and use them in a way that doesn't cause excessive consumption of system resources.

IPC::Shareable is available on CPAN. It requires Raphael Manfredi's *Storable* module as well.

Here's the idiom for placing a hash in shared memory:

```
tie %H, 'IPC::Shareable', 'Test', {create => 1, mode => 0666};
```

The first argument gives the name of the variable to tie, in this case %H. The second is the name of the *IPC::Shareable* module. The third argument is a "glue" ID that will be used to identify this variable to the processes that will be sharing it. It can be an integer or any string of up to four letters. In the example above we use a glue of Test. The last argument is a hash reference containing the options to pass to *IPC::Shareable*. There are a variety of options, but the ones you will be using most frequently are *create*, which if true causes the shared memory segment to spring into existence if it doesn't exist already, and *mode*, which specifies an octal access mode for the segment. The default mode of 0666 makes the memory segment world-readable and writable. This is useful during debugging so that you can spy on what your module is doing. For production, you will want to make the mode more restrictive, such as 0600 to restrict access to the Apache server only.*

If successful, *tie()* will tie %H to the shared memory segment and return a reference to the tied object (which you can ignore). Other processes can now attach to this segment by calling *tie()* with the same glue ID. When one process gets or sets a key in %H, all the other processes see the change. When a process is finished with the tied variable, it should *untie()* it. Scalar variables can be tied in a similar way.

Shared hashes work a lot like ordinary hashes. You can store scalar variables or complex data structures into its keys. Any of these code fragments is legal:

```
$H{'fee'}            = 'I smell the blood';
$H{'fie'}            = ['of', 'an', 'englishman'];
$H{'foe'}            = {'and' => 'it', 'makes' => 'me', 'very' => 'hungry'};
$H{'fum'}{'later'}   = 'Do you have any after dinner mints?';
```

You can also store blessed objects into shared variables but not into filehandles or globs.

It's important to realize what is and what is not tied when you use *IPC::Shareable*. In the first example we copy a simple scalar value into shared memory space. Any changes that we make to the value, such as a string substitution, are immediately visible to all processes that share the variable.

In the second example, we construct an anonymous array and copy it into the shared variable. Internally *IPC::Shareable* uses the *Storable freeze()* function to serialize the structure into a binary representation and then place it in shared

---

* The octal modes used in *IPC::Shareable* are similar to file modes and have the same effect on other processes' ability to access the data. Do not confuse them with *umask*, which has no effect on shared memory.

memory. As a consequence, changing an individual array element will *not* propagate correctly to other processes:

```
$H{'fie'}[2] = 'frenchman';  # this change will NOT propagate
```

Instead, you must copy the array into ordinary memory, make the changes, and copy it back:

```
my $temp = $H{'fie'};
$temp->[2] = 'frenchman';
$H{'fie'} = $temp;
```

For similar reasons we must also use this workaround to change elements in the third example, where the value is an anonymous hash.

Oddly enough, the fourth example behaves differently. In this case, we assign a value to an "automatic" anonymous hash. The hash is automatic because before the assignment, the key fum didn't even exist. After the assignment, not only does fum exist, but it points to an anonymous hash with the single key `later`. Behind the scenes, *IPC::Shareable* creates a new tied hash and stores it at $H{'fum'}. We can now read and write to this tied hash directly and the changes will be visible to all processes. The same thing will happen if you first assign an empty hash reference to a key and then start filling in the hash values one by one:

```
$H{'fum'} = {};
$H{'fum'}{'later'}  = 'Do you have any after dinner mints?';
```

Although this sounds like a neat feature, it can be a programming trap. Each tied hash that is created by this method occupies its own shared memory segment. If you use this feature too liberally, you'll end up exhausting your system's shared memory segments and subsequent attempts to tie variables will fail.

Another trap involves updating shared variables. Many update operations aren't atomic, even simple ones like $a++. If multiple processes try to update the same shared variable simultaneously, the results can be unpredictable. If you need to perform a nonatomic operation, or if you need a variable to be in a known state across several statements, you should lock before updating it and unlock it when you're through. The *shlock()* and *shunlock()* methods allow you to do this. You'll need to call *tied()* on the variable in order to obtain the underlying tied *IPC::Shareable* object and then invoke the object's *shlock()* or *shunlock()* method:

```
tied(%H)->shlock;
$H{'englishmen eaten'}++;
tied(%H)->shunlock;
```

Example 5-5 shows the code for *Hangman5*. The top of the file now loads the *IPC::Shareable* module and defines a shared global named %SESSIONS:

```
use IPC::Shareable ();
use constant SIGNATURE   => 'HANG';
```

```
use constant COOKIE_NAME  => 'SessionID5';
use constant MAX_SESSIONS => 100;
use vars qw(%SESSIONS);
```

%SESSIONS will be tied to shared memory, and it will contain multiple session keys, each one identified by a unique eight-digit numeric session ID. The value of each session will be the familiar $state anonymous hash reference.

```
# bind session structure to shared memory
bind_sessions() unless defined(%SESSIONS) && tied(%SESSIONS);

# fetch or generate the session id
my $session_id = get_session_id();
```

The first step in the revised script is to call a new subroutine named *bind_sessions()* to tie the %SESSIONS global to shared memory. It does this only if %SESSIONS hasn't previously been tied, which will be the case whenever this script is called for the first time in a new child process. After this we call another new subroutine named *get_session_id()* either to retrieve the old session ID for this user or to generate a new one if this is a new user.

```
# get rid of old sessions to avoid consuming resources
expire_old_sessions($session_id);
```

Next comes a call to *expire_old_sessions()* with the current session ID as the argument. Because we're keeping the session information in a limited resource, we must be careful to remove old sessions when they're no longer in use. We accomplish this by maintaining a rolling list of active sessions. The current session is moved to the top of the list while older sessions drift downward to the bottom. When the list exceeds a preset limit of simultaneous sessions (MAX_SESSIONS => 100 in this example), the oldest session is deleted.

The remainder of the body of the script should look very familiar. It's modified only very slightly from the examples we've seen before:

```
# retrieve the state
my $state = get_state($session_id) unless param('clear');

# reinitialize if we need to
$state    = initialize($state) if !$state or param('restart');

# process the current guess, if any
my($message, $status) = process_guess(param('guess') || '', $state);

# save the modified state
save_state($state, $session_id);
```

The *get_state()* function now takes the session ID as its argument. It retrieves the state from the %SESSIONS variable and copies it into $state, which we process as before. We then write the modified state information back into shared memory by calling *save_state()* with the state variable and the session ID.

```
# start the page
print header(-Cookie => => cookie(-name => COOKIE_NAME,
                                   -value => $session_id,
                                   -expires => '+1h'));
```

The last task is to associate the session ID with the user. We do this by handing the remote browser a cookie containing the ID. Unlike the previous example, this cookie is set to expire after an hour of idle time. We expect the sessions to turn over rapidly, so it doesn't make sense to save the session ID for any longer than that. Although this might seem similar to the previous cookie examples, the big difference is that the cookie doesn't hold any state information itself. It's just a tag for the information stored at the server side.

Let's now turn to the new subroutines:

```
# Bind the session variables to shared memory using IPC::Shareable
sub bind_sessions {
    die "Couldn't bind shared memory"
        unless tie %SESSIONS, 'IPC::Shareable', SIGNATURE,
                {create => 1, mode => 0644};
}
```

The *bind_sessions()* function calls *tie()* to bind %SESSIONS to shared memory. The signature is defined in a constant, and we call *IPC::Shareable* with options that cause the shared memory segment to be created with mode 0644 (world readable) if it doesn't already exist. This will allow you to peak at (but not modify) the variable while the server is running.

The *get_session_id()* method is responsible for choosing a unique ID for new sessions, or recovering the old ID from ongoing sessions:

```
sub get_session_id {
    my $id = cookie(COOKIE_NAME);
    return $id if defined($id) and exists $SESSIONS{$id};
    # Otherwise we have to generate an id.
    # Use the random number generator to find an unused key.
    tied(%SESSIONS)->shlock;
    do {
        $id = sprintf("%8d", 1E8*rand());
    } until !exists($SESSIONS{$id});
    # must avoid assigning an empty hash to IPC::Shareable
    $SESSIONS{$id} = {WORD => ''};
    tied(%SESSIONS)->shunlock;
    $id;
}
```

get_session_id() first attempts to recover a previously assigned session ID from the browser cookie. If the cookie does exist, and the session ID is still valid (it's a valid key for %SESSIONS), we return it. Otherwise we need to generate a new key that is not already in use. To do this we lock %SESSIONS so that it doesn't change underneath us, then enter a small loop that calls the random number generator repeatedly to generate eight-digit session IDs.* For each ID, we check whether it exists in %SESSIONS and exit the loop when we find one that doesn't. Having found a good ID, we reserve a slot for it by assigning a small anonymous hash to %SESSIONS. Notice that we do not use an empty hash for this purpose, as this would cause *IPC::Shareable* to create a new unwanted tied variable. We unlock the variable and return the ID.

The *expire_old_sessions()* subroutine is responsible for garbage-collecting old session information that is no longer in use:

```
sub expire_old_sessions {
    my $id = shift;
    tied(%SESSIONS)->shlock;
    my @sessions = grep($id ne $_, @{$SESSIONS{'QUEUE'}});
    unshift @sessions, $id;
    if (@sessions > MAX_SESSIONS) {
        my $to_delete = pop @sessions;
        delete $SESSIONS{$to_delete};
    }
    $SESSIONS{'QUEUE'} = \@sessions;
    tied(%SESSIONS)->shunlock;
}
```

This subroutine works by maintaining a sorted list of sessions in an anonymous array located at the special key $SESSIONS{'QUEUE'}. The subroutine begins by locking %SESSIONS so that it doesn't change during the update process. It recovers the sorted list, removes the current session for the list using the *grep()* operator, and *unshift()*s the current session ID to the top of the list. It then looks at the size of the list, and if there are more sessions than allowed by MAX_SESSIONS, it *pop()*s a session ID from the bottom of the list and deletes that session from the %SESSIONS array. The modified list is copied back into %SESSIONS, which is then unlocked.

```
sub get_state {
    my $id = shift;
    return undef unless $SESSIONS{$id} and $SESSIONS{$id}{'WORD'};
    $SESSIONS{$id};
}

sub save_state {
    my($state, $id) = @_;
    $SESSIONS{$id} = $state;
}
```

get_state() and *save_state()* are trivial in this implementation. *get_state()* looks up the state information in %SESSIONS using the session ID as its key. *save_state()*

---

* Using *rand()* is not the best way to create unique IDs, because it makes them easy to guess. However, it's simple and fast. The section on DBI databases presents a way to generate hard-to-guess IDs using the MD5 digest function.

saves the state into %SESSIONS at the indicated ID. Since the assignment is atomic, we don't need to lock the hash for either operation.

Example 5-5. The Hangman Game with Server-Side State in Shared Memory

```
# file: hangman5.cgi
# hangman game using IPC::Shareable and cookies

use IO::File ();
use CGI qw(:standard);
use CGI::Cookie ();
use IPC::Shareable ();

use strict;
use constant WORDS => '/usr/games/lib/hangman-words';
use constant ICONS => '/icons/hangman';
use constant TRIES => 6;
use constant SIGNATURE    => 'HANG';
use constant COOKIE_NAME  => 'SessionID5';
use constant MAX_SESSIONS => 100;
use vars qw(%SESSIONS);

# bind session structure to shared memory
bind_sessions() unless defined(%SESSIONS) && tied(%SESSIONS);

# fetch or generate the session id
my $session_id = get_session_id();

# get rid of old sessions to avoid consuming resources
expire_old_sessions($session_id);

# retrieve the state
my $state = get_state($session_id) unless param('clear');

# reinitialize if we need to
$state    = initialize($state) if !$state or param('restart');

# process the current guess, if any
my($message, $status) = process_guess(param('guess') || '', $state);

# save the modified state
save_state($state, $session_id);

# start the page
print header(-Cookie    => cookie(-name => COOKIE_NAME,
                                  -value => $session_id,
                                  -expires => '+5d')),
```

. . . everything in the middle remains the same . . .

```
# Bind the session variables to shared memory using IPC::Shareable
sub bind_sessions {
    die "Couldn't bind shared memory"
        unless tie %SESSIONS, 'IPC::Shareable', SIGNATURE,
                {create => 1, mode => 0666};
```

Example 5-5. The Hangman Game with Server-Side State in Shared Memory (continued)

```perl
}

# Fetch or generate the session ID.
# It's simply a key into the %SESSIONS variable
sub get_session_id {
    my $id = cookie(COOKIE_NAME);
    return $id if defined($id) and exists $SESSIONS{$id};
    # Otherwise we have to generate an id.
    # Use the random number generator to find an unused key.
    tied(%SESSIONS)->shlock;
    do {
        $id = sprintf("%8d", 1E8*rand());
    } until !exists($SESSIONS{$id});
    # must avoid assigning an empty hash to IPC::Shareable's tied arrays
    $SESSIONS{$id} = {WORD => ''};
    tied(%SESSIONS)->shunlock;
    $id;
}

# bring the current session to the front and
# get rid of any that haven't been used recently
sub expire_old_sessions {
    my $id = shift;
    tied(%SESSIONS)->shlock;
    my @sessions = grep($id ne $_, @{$SESSIONS{'QUEUE'}});
    unshift @sessions, $id;
    if (@sessions > MAX_SESSIONS) {
        my $to_delete = pop @sessions;
        delete $SESSIONS{$to_delete};
    }
    $SESSIONS{'QUEUE'} = [@sessions];
    tied(%SESSIONS)->shunlock;
}

# Retrieve an existing state
sub get_state {
    my $id = shift;
    my $s = $SESSIONS{$id};
    return undef unless $s and $s->{WORD};
    return $SESSIONS{$id};
}

# Save the current state
sub save_state {
    my($state, $id) = @_;
    $SESSIONS{$id} = $state;
}
```

The main problem with this technique is that the amount of state information that you can store in shared memory is very limited, making it unsuitable for high-volume or high-reliability applications. A better server-side solution involves using database management systems, which we turn to in the next section.

Storing State Information in SQL Databases

Persistent memory is only suitable for storing small amounts of state information for relatively short periods of time. If you need to reliably store lots of information for a long time, you need a server-side database.

The DBI library, designed by Tim Bunce and others, is a generic Perl interface to relational database management systems (DBMSs) that speak SQL (Standard Query Language). The DBI library speaks to specific databases by way of DBD (Database Driver) modules. You can make queries on any database that has a DBD module available for it. These modules are sometimes provided by the database vendor and sometimes by third parties. DBD modules for Oracle, Sybase, Illustra, mSQL, MySQL, and others can be found at CPAN.

Full information on using DBI can be found in its manual pages and in *Advanced Perl Programming* by Sriram Srinivasan (O'Reilly & Associates, 1997). We'll summarize just enough here so that you can follow the examples if you're not already familiar with DBI.

Before you can work with the DBI interface, you must select and install a relational database. If you have access to a Unix system and do not already have such a database installed, a good one to start with is MySQL, a popular database management system that you can freely download from *http://www.tcx.se/*.[*]

In relational databases, all information is organized in tables. Each row of the table is a data record, and each column is a field of the record. For example, here is one way to represent the hangman data:

```
table: hangman
+----------+--------+-------+------+---+------------+-----+-------------+
|session_id|  WORD  |GUESSED|GAMENO|WON|GUESSES_LEFT|TOTAL|     modified|
+----------+--------+-------+------+---+------------+-----+-------------+
|fd2c95dd1 |entice  |e      |   10|  6|           6|   34|19980623195601|
|97aff0de2 |bifocals|aeilort|    4|  2|           3|   20|19980623221335|
+----------+--------+-------+------+---+------------+-----+-------------+
```

Most of the columns in the table above directly correspond to the fields in the now-familiar hangman state object. In addition to these fields we add two more columns. *session_id* is a string that uniquely identifies each user session and is used as a key into the table for fast record lookup. For reasons that will become apparent soon, we use a short hexadecimal string as the session ID. We also add a timestamp field named *modified* which holds the date and time at which the

---

[*] MySQL can be used freely for some purposes but must be licensed (for a reasonable price) for others. Please see the licensing terms for full details.

record was last changed. If you look carefully, you'll see that the column consists of the four-digit year and two digits each for the month, day, hour, minute, and second. This timestamp will come in handy for detecting old unused sessions and clearing them out periodically.

In SQL databases, each table column has a defined data type and a maximum field length. Available data types include integers, floating point numbers, character strings, date/time types, and sometimes more esoteric types. Unfortunately the data types supported by database management systems vary considerably, limiting the portability of applications among different vendors' products. In this and the next chapter, our examples use MySQL data types and functions. You may have to make some modifications in order to support another database system.

The most basic way to communicate with a SQL database is via a text monitor—a small terminal-like application in which you type SQL queries to the database and view the results. To create the definition for the table shown above, you could issue the SQL CREATE command:

```
mysql> CREATE TABLE hangman (
          session_id       char(8) primary key,
          WORD             char(30),
          GUESSED          char(26),
          GAMENO           int,
          WON              int,
          GUESSES_LEFT     int,
          TOTAL            int,
          modified         timestamp
       );
```

This declares a table named *hangman* using the MySQL syntax. The *session_id* column is declared to be a string of at most eight characters, and it is also declared to be the primary key for the table. This ensures that a given session ID is unique, and speeds up table lookups considerably. The *WORD* and *GUESSED* columns are declared to be strings of at most 30 and 26 characters, respectively, and *GAMENO, WON, GUESSES_LEFT,* and *TOTAL* are declared to be integers (using the default length). We declare the column named *modified* to be a timestamp, taking advantage of a MySQL-specific feature that updates the field automatically whenever the record that contains it is changed.

You can then load some sample data into the database using a SQL INSERT statement:

```
mysql> INSERT INTO hangman (session_id,WORD,GUESSED,GAMENO,WON,
                            GUESSES_LEFT,TOTAL)
          VALUES ('a0000001', 'spruce', '',1,0,6,0);
```

This inserts the indicated values for the columns *session_id* through *TOTAL.* We don't explicitly set the value of the *modified* column because MySQL takes care of that for us.

We can now perform some queries over the database using the SQL SELECT statement.

To see everything in the hangman table:

```
mysql> SELECT * FROM hangman;
+----------+--------+-------+------+---+------------+-----+--------------+
|session_id|  WORD  |GUESSED|GAMENO|WON|GUESSES_LEFT|TOTAL|    modified  |
+----------+--------+-------+------+---+------------+-----+--------------+
|fd2c95dd1 |entice  |e      |   10 |  6|           6|   34|19980623195601|
|a0000001  |spruce  |       |    1 |  0|           6|    0|19980625101526|
|97aff0de2 |bifocals|aeilort|    4 |  2|           3|   20|19980623221335|
+----------+--------+-------+------+---+------------+-----+--------------+
```

The part of the query following the SELECT command chooses which columns to display. In this case we use * to indicate all columns. The FROM keyword names the table to select the data from.

If we wished to look at just the *session_id*, *WORD*, and *GAMENO* fields from the table, we could use this query:

```
mysql> SELECT session_id,WORD,GAMENO FROM hangman;
+------------+----------+--------+
| session_id | WORD     | GAMENO |
+------------+----------+--------+
| fd2c95dd   | entice   |     10 |
| a0000001   | spruce   |      1 |
| 97aff0de   | bifocals |      4 |
+------------+----------+--------+
```

An optional WHERE clause allows us to filter the records so that only records matching a set of criteria are displayed. For example, this query shows only session records from players who have played five games or more:

```
mysql> SELECT session_id,WORD,GAMENO FROM hangman WHERE GAMENO >= 5;
+------------+--------+--------+
| session_id | WORD   | GAMENO |
+------------+--------+--------+
| fd2c95dd   | entice |     10 |
+------------+--------+--------+
```

This query retrieves the session with the ID **a0000001**:

```
mysql> SELECT session_id,WORD,GAMENO FROM hangman WHERE session_id='a0000001';
+------------+--------+--------+
| session_id | WORD   | GAMENO |
+------------+--------+--------+
| a0000001   | spruce |      1 |
+------------+--------+--------+
```

Finally, this query retrieves all sessions that were modified within the past 24 hours:

```
mysql> SELECT session_id,WORD,GAMENO FROM hangman
       WHERE unix_timestamp()-unix_timestamp(modified) < 60*60*24;
```

```
+------------+--------+--------+
| session_id | WORD   | GAMENO |
+------------+--------+--------+
| a0000001   | spruce |      1 |
+------------+--------+--------+
```

The last example shows the use of the MySQL-specific *unix_timestamp()* function. Called without arguments, *unix_timestamp()* returns the current time and date as the number of seconds since the start of the Unix epoch. The function can also be called with a timestamp field as the argument, in which case it operates on the timestamp rather than the current time. The effect of the query above is to subtract the modified field from the current time and compare the difference to one day. The SQL language allows you to form queries that are substantially more complex than these, including ones that combine the results of multiple tables. We won't delve into the full SQL syntax, but you'll find the definitive reference in *A Guide to the SQL Standard* by C. J. Date with Hugh Darwen (Addison-Wesley, 1997), and plenty of practical examples in *Advanced Perl Programming* by Sriram Srinivasan.

The INSERT statement can only be used to create a new record (or row) of the table. If we were to try to execute the insertion statement shown earlier a second time, the attempt would fail because any given session ID can only occur once in the table. This feature guarantees the uniqueness of session IDs. To change the values in an existing record, we would use an UPDATE statement instead. A typical UPDATE statement looks like this:

```
mysql> UPDATE hangman SET GAMENO=GAMENO+1
       WHERE session_id='a0000001';
Query OK, 1 row affected (0.09 sec)
```

Like the SELECT statement, UPDATE can have a WHERE clause which limits what records it affects. For each selected record, columns are updated according to one or more column=newvalue pairs. In the example shown above, we're incrementing the *GAMENO* column by one. A SELECT statement shows that the update worked.

```
mysql> SELECT session_id,WORD,GAMENO FROM hangman
       WHERE session_id='a0000001';
+------------+--------+--------+
| session_id | WORD   | GAMENO |
+------------+--------+--------+
| a0000001   | spruce |      2 |
+------------+--------+--------+
```

Lastly, the DELETE statement can be used to delete all records that satisfy the criteria set out in the WHERE clause. This query deletes all sessions older than a day:

```
mysql> DELETE FROM hangman
       WHERE unix_timestamp()-unix_timestamp(modified)>60*60*24;
Query OK, 2 rows affected (0.00 sec)
```

If you forget to include a WHERE clause in the UPDATE and DELETE statements, every record in the database will be affected by the operation. This is generally to be avoided.

Using DBI

The DBI interface provides methods for opening SQL databases, sending queries to the opened database, and reading the answers returned by those queries.

To open a database, you call *DBI->connect()* with the "data source name," a string that tells the database driver where the database is located. If the database requires a username and password for access, you can pass that information in the *connect()* call as well. The format of the data source name is DBMS-specific. For a MySQL database, it looks like this:

```
"dbi:mysql:$database:$hostname:$port"
```

All MySQL data sources begin with "dbi:mysql". They are followed by the name of the database, and, optionally, by the name and port of the remote host on which the DBMS is running. If the hostname and port are omitted, the driver defaults to using a standard port on the local host. To connect to a database named *www* on the local host using the username *games* and the password *grok*, you'd make this call:

```
$dbh = DBI->connect('dbi:mysql:www', 'games', 'grok');
```

If successful, *connect()* returns a database handle, $dbh, which is used for subsequent communication with the database. The *connect()* method also accepts an optional fourth argument which consists of a hash reference of parameter name=value pairs. These control a variety of database options, such as whether to automatically commit all changes made to the database. The only option that we'll use in the examples that follow is *PrintError*, which when set to false, suppresses the printing of unwanted database warnings to the server error log.

The database handle has several methods, the most important of which are *do()*, *prepare()*, and *errstr()*. *do()* is used to execute SQL statements which do not return a list of records, such as INSERT, DELETE, UPDATE, or CREATE. If the operation is successful, *do()* returns a count of the number of rows modified. For example, the following query sets the *GAMENO* field of all sessions to 1 and returns the number of rows affected:

```
$count = $dbh->do('UPDATE hangman SET GAMENO=1');
die $dbh->errstr unless defined $count;
```

If the database encountered an error while processing the statement (for example, the SQL contained a syntax error), it will return *undef*. The *errstr()* method can be used to retrieve an informative error message from the driver.

SELECT queries can return a potentially large number of records, often more than will fit into memory at once. For this reason, the results from SELECT queries are returned in the form of statement handle objects. You then call the statement handle's *fetch()* method repeatedly to retrieve each row of the result.

Here's an example of retrieving the *session_id* and *WORD* fields from each session in the hangman database:

```
$sth = $dbh->prepare('SELECT session_id,WORD FROM hangman')
      || die $dbh->errstr;
$sth->execute() || die $sth->errstr;
while (my $row = $sth->fetch) {
   my($session, $word) = @$row;
   print "session => $session, word => $word\n";
}
$sth->finish;
```

The example starts with a call to the database handle's *prepare()* method with the text of the SQL SELECT statement. *prepare()* parses the SQL and checks it for syntactic correctness but does not actually execute it. The query is returned as a statement handler which we store into the variable `$sth`. If some error occurred while preparing the statement, *prepare()* returns *undef*, in which case we return the *errstr()* error text.

Next we call the statement handler's *execute()* method. This performs the query and returns either the number of rows retrieved or *undef* if an error occurred. In the case of a syntactically correct query that happens to return no rows (because the table is empty or because no records satisfied the criteria in the WHERE clause), *execute()* returns the value `0E0` which Perl regards as true in a logical context, but as zero in a numeric one.

Now we enter a loop in which we call the statement handler's *fetch()* method. Each time it's called, *fetch()* returns the requested columns in the form of an array *reference*. To retrieve the values themselves, we just dereference the value into a list. Because we requested the columns *session_id* and *WORD*, we get a reference to a two-item array back from *fetch()*. When there are no more rows left, *fetch()* returns *undef*.

DBI actually offers a family of fetch functions. *fetchrow_array()* is like *fetch()*, but it dereferences the row first and returns an array corresponding to the list of requested columns. Another function, *fetchrow_hashref()*, turns the current row into a hash of the column names and their values and returns the hash's reference to the caller. This allows us to make the example above more readable at the cost of making it somewhat less efficient:

```
$sth = $dbh->prepare('SELECT session_id,WORD FROM hangman')
      || die $dbh->errstr;
$sth->execute || die $sth->errstr;
```

```
while (my $row = $sth->fetchrow_hashref) {
    print "session => $row->{session_id}, word => $row->{WORD}\n";
}
$sth->finish;
```

DBI also provides a *fetchrow_arrayref()* method for fetching the row as an array reference. It is identical in every respect to *fetch()*.

When you are finished with a statement handler, you should call its *finish()* method in order to free up the resources it uses.

The last thing you need to know about statement handlers is that many DBI drivers allow you to put placeholders, indicated by the ? character, inside SQL statements. *prepare()* compiles the statement and returns a statement handler as before, but when you later call *execute()* you pass in the values to be substituted into the placeholders. This allows you to treat statement handlers much as you would a subroutine by calling it repeatedly with different runtime arguments. For example, we can create a statement handler for returning the entire row of a given session with this bit of code:

```
$sth = $dbh->prepare('SELECT * FROM hangman WHERE session_id=?');
```

Now we can fetch information on session **fd2c95dd**, by calling the statement handler's *execute()* method this way:

```
$sth->execute('fd2c95dd');
```

The same statement handler can later be used to fetch information from other named sessions. You should still call *finish()* at the end of each series of fetches, even though you are going to reuse the statement handler. Failure to do so can lead to memory leaks.

When you are completely finished with a database handle, you should call its *disconnect()* method in order to sever the connection and clean up.

Apache::DBI and mod_perl

One of the problems with using DBI databases from conventional CGI scripts is that there's often a significant amount of overhead associated with opening a database connection. When you run a *mod_perl*-enabled version of Apache, you can take advantage of persistent database connections. Instead of creating a new database handle each time your Apache Perl module or *Apache::Registry* script runs, you check a global variable for a previously opened handle. If the global is empty, you open a new database connection. Otherwise, you use the contents of the global. A concise way of expressing this logic is with this snippet of code:

```
$DBH ||= DBI->connect($data_source, $user, $password);
```

Apache::DBI, a module written by Edmund Mergl, makes handling persistent database connections even easier. It replaces DBI's *connect()* and *disconnect()* methods with versions that handle persistent connections behind the scenes. *connect()* maintains a cache of database handles and returns one of them in response to attempts to open the same database multiple times. It also checks that the database handle is still "live" (some databases have a nasty habit of timing out inactive sessions) and reconnects if necessary. *disconnect()* is replaced by a no-op so that database handles are not inadvertently closed.

To activate *Apache::DBI*, you need only use it some time before loading the module or modules that need DBI services. One convenient place to load *Apache::DBI* is in the Perl startup file:

```
# perl startup file
use Apache::DBI ();
use Apache::Registry ();
use CGI::Cookie ();
... etc.
```

If you don't have a Perl startup file, you can also load the module at server startup time by adding this directive to one of the server configuration files:

```
PerlModule Apache::DBI
```

You will now have persistent database connections when using *mod_perl*, and conventional use-once-and-throw-away connections when using standard CGI.

A DBI Backend for Hangman

Like the persistent memory version of the hangman game, the DBI implementation has to have code to open the database, to set and fetch session records from the database, to generate unique session IDs for each incoming connection, and to expire old sessions that we're no longer interested in. Example 5-6 shows what's new and different on the server side. There are no visible changes in the user interface.

This script assumes a database has already been set up that contains a table named *hangman* with this structure:[*]

```
CREATE TABLE hangman (
      session_id      char(8) primary key,
      WORD            char(30),
      GUESSED         char(26),
      GAMENO          int,
      WON             int,
      GUESSES_LEFT    int,
```

---

[*] The *modified* field is a MySQL-specific data type, and later we will take advantage of other MySQL features involving the handling of dates. SQL databases vary widely in their handling of dates and times, and we prefer to show you an efficient implementation of the application on a specific database than an inefficient implementation that might work more generically. To port this code to the database of your choice, you will need to change the data type of the modified column to a date/time type that your database understands and modify the *expires()* subroutine to work with this changed type.

```
    TOTAL            int,
    modified         timestamp,
    KEY(modified)
)
```

Before stepping through the script, let's first look at *get_state()* and *save_state()*:

```
sub get_state {
    my $id = shift;
    my $sth = $DBH->prepare(<<END) || die "Prepare: ", $DBH->errstr;
SELECT * FROM $DB_TABLE WHERE session_id='$id'
END
    $sth->execute || die "Execute: ", $sth->errstr;
    my $state = $sth->fetchrow_hashref;
    $sth->finish;
    return $state;
}
```

get_state() is responsible for recovering the state information as a hash reference, given the ID of an existing session. At its core is this SQL statement:

```
SELECT * FROM hangman WHERE session_id='$id'
```

This selects all columns from the record named by the session ID. We then call DBI's *fetchrow_hashref()* to retrieve the record in the form as a hash reference in which the keys (WORD, GUESSED, GAMENO, and so on) correspond to the columns of the selected record. As it happens, this hashref is identical to the state variable that the higher levels of the script operate on, so all we have to do is to return it.

The *save_state()* subroutine is almost as simple:

```
sub save_state {
    my($state, $id) = @_;
    my $sth = $DBH->prepare(<<END) || die "prepare: ", $DBH->errstr;
UPDATE $DB_TABLE
    SET WORD=?,GUESSED=?,GAMENO=?,WON=?,TOTAL=?,GUESSES_LEFT=?
    WHERE session_id='$id'
END
    $sth->execute(@{$state}{qw(WORD GUESSED GAMENO WON TOTAL GUESSES_LEFT)})
        || die "execute: ", $DBH->errstr;
    $sth->finish;
}
```

This subroutine constructs a DBI statement handler containing placeholders for the six keys in $state. It then calls the statement handler's *execute()* statement to write the values from $state into the database.

The remainder of the code is concerned with the generation and maintenance of session IDs. Although most of the state information is stored on the server's side of the connection, there's more to the story. There will always have to be some information stored by the client because otherwise, there would be no way for the server to distinguish one client from another and, hence, no way to retrieve the correct session record. Some of the obvious ways of distinguishing one client from another, such as recording their IP addresses, do not work well in practice (a dial-in user may have several IP addresses, and conversely, all America Online users share the IP address of a few large proxy servers). The general technique for identifying clients is to generate a session ID for them when they first connect to your application and then arrange for them to return the session ID to you on subsequent requests. A session ID can be anything you like. In the hangman game we use an eight-digit hexadecimal number, which is sufficient for about four billion active sessions.

We've already seen two techniques that can be adapted to this purpose: HTTP cookies and fill-out forms. Because the session ID is a relatively small amount of information, there's also a third option available to us. We can store the session ID in the URI itself as additional path information. When a connection comes in from a new client we assign it a randomly generated ID, append it to our URI as additional path information, and send the client an HTTP *redirect()* directive to make it fetch this new URI. On subsequent requests, we recover the session ID from the additional path information. This technique has an advantage over cookies in that it is compatible with all browsers, including those for which the user has disabled cookies. It has the disadvantage that the session ID is visible to the user. The URI displayed by the browser will look something like this:

```
http://www.modperl.com/perl/hangman5.cgi/fd2c95dd
```

A side benefit of this technique is that the user can bookmark this URI, session ID and all, and come back to a game later.

Beginning our walkthrough of the script, we bring in the DBI library and define a few new constants:

```
use DBI ();

use strict;
use vars qw($DBH $DB_TABLE $ID_LENGTH);
use constant EXPIRE => 60*60*24*30;  # allow 30 days before expiration
use constant DB     => 'dbi:mysql:www';
use constant DBAUTH => 'nobody:';
use constant SECRET => 'modperl reigns';
use constant MAX_TRIES => 10;
$DB_TABLE           = "hangman6";
$ID_LENGTH          = 8;  # length of the session ID
```

EXPIRE is the length of time to keep sessions around before expiring them from the database. Unlike the shared-memory version of the script, the session data is stored on disk. This means that we can be less draconian in our expiration policy. An unused session is allowed 30 days before being recycled. DB is the DBI data source name for the database, and DBAUTH is the database authentication information, in the format *username:password.* SECRET and MAX_TRIES are used in the generation of new session keys. $DB_TABLE is the database table name to use and $ID_LENGTH is the length of the session key in characters.

```
$DBH = DBI->connect(DB, split(':', DBAUTH, 2), {PrintError => 0})
    || die "Couldn't open database: ", $DBI::errstr;
my($session_id, $note) = get_session_id();
```

The script begins by opening the database and saving its database handle in a global named $DBH. Next, we retrieve the session ID (or generate a new one) by calling a subroutine named *get_session_id()*. *get_session_id()* returns a two-element list: the session ID and a note that can be used to alert the user to exceptional conditions. In this script, the only exceptional condition that occurs is when the user tries to use a session ID that has expired.

```
my $state = get_state($session_id) unless param('clear');
$state    = initialize($state) if !$state or param('restart');
my($message, $status) = process_guess(param('guess') || '', $state);
save_state($state, $session_id);
```

With the session ID in hand, we retrieve the state by calling the *get_state()* subroutine that we looked at earlier. We then (re)initialize the state variable as before if need be, process the user's guess if any, and call *save_state()* to write the modified session back to the database. The remainder of the script is unchanged from previous versions, except that we display the note returned by *get_session_id()* at the top of the page if it's nonempty.

We'll look at the *get_session_id()* subroutine now, which is responsible for retrieving an existing session ID or generating a new one:

```
sub get_session_id {
    my(@result);
    expire_old_sessions();
    my($id) = path_info() =~ m:^/([a-h0-9]{$ID_LENGTH}):o;
    return @result if $id and @result = check_id($id);

    # If we get here, there's not already an ID in the path info.
    my $session_id = generate_id();
    die "Couldn't make a new session id" unless $session_id;
    print redirect(script_name() . "/$session_id");
    exit 0;
}
```

This subroutine first expires all out-of-date sessions by calling *expire_old_sessions()*.* Next, it calls CGI.pm's *path_info()* function to return the additional path information and attempt to match it against the expected session ID pattern.

---

* If there are many session records, *expire_old_sessions()* will rapidly become a performance drain on the script. In high-volume applications, you will want to move session expiration into a separate standalone process that runs at regular intervals under the Unix *cron* or NT *at* utilities. For the hangman application, a nightly expiration is more than sufficient.

If a likely looking session ID is found, we call *check_id()* to ensure that the session ID actually corresponds to a database record. Otherwise, we call *generate_id()* to create a new session ID. We append the ID to our URI (using CGI.pm's *script_name()* function), incorporate it into a call to *redirect()*, and exit. In this case the subroutine never returns to the caller, but the redirected browser immediately generates a second call to the script, this time with the session ID appended to the URI.

The *expire_old_sessions()* subroutine is simple:

```
sub expire_old_sessions {
    $DBH->do(<<END);
DELETE FROM $DB_TABLE
    WHERE (unix_timestamp()-unix_timestamp(modified))>${\EXPIRE}
END
}
```

The subroutine consists of a single DBI call that sends a SQL DELETE statement to the database. The effect of the call is to delete all session records that are older than the time limit set by the EXPIRE constant.

generate_id(), which chooses new session IDs, is slightly more complex:

```
sub generate_id {
    # Create a new session id
    my $tries = 0;
    my $id = hash(SECRET . rand());
    while ($tries++ < MAX_TRIES) {
        last if $DBH->do("INSERT INTO $DB_TABLE (session_id) VALUES ('$id')");
        $id = hash(SECRET . $id);
    }
    return undef if $tries >= MAX_TRIES;  # we failed
    return $id;
}
```

The reason for this complexity is that it is important to generate a unique session ID in such a way that valid session IDs cannot be trivially guessed. Otherwise it would be possible for a malicious person to hijack another user's session by misappropriating that user's session ID. This is not important in the hangman game, but becomes an issue in transactions in which things of value (money, merchandise, confidential information) are changing hands. A simple sequence of session IDs, such as choosing one higher than the previous highest, is too obvious. IDs generated from the *rand()* call are unreliable as well because once you know where you are in the series, you can generate all the subsequent values.

Instead, we use a combination of *rand()* and the MD5 message digest algorithm. We begin by computing the MD5 hash of the value of *rand()* concatenated with a secret phrase. This extra concatenation step makes it impossible to derive the value of the next session ID from the previous one. Instead of calling MD5 directly, we call a small internal subroutine, *hash()*, to compute the MD5 hash and then truncate it to eight characters. This reduces the size of the session ID at the cost of making the ID somewhat easier to guess.* We then enter a loop in which we repeatedly attempt to insert the current session ID into the database. If a record with that session ID does not already exist in the database, the insertion statement returns a true result code and we immediately return the ID. Otherwise we generate a new trial ID by hashing the current ID concatenated with the secret, and try again. We do this up to **MAX_TRIES** times, at which point we give up. This allows us to fill up the space of possible session IDs to approximately 90 percent, or around 3 billion.

The *check_id()* subroutine is called by *get_session_id()* when the browser provides a previous session ID. Its job is to check that the session ID still corresponds to a database record. If not, it attempts to insert a record with that session ID into the database and delivers a warning to the user that his game session may have expired.

```
sub check_id {
    my $id = shift;
    return ($id, '')
        if $DBH->do("SELECT 1 FROM $DB_TABLE WHERE session_id='$id'") > 0;
    return ($id, 'The record of your game may have expired.  Restarting.')
        if $DBH->do("INSERT INTO $DB_TABLE (session_id) VALUES ('$id')");
    return ();
}
```

The reason we try to reuse old session IDs is that the user may have bookmarked the URI of the game, session ID and all. We honor the bookmark so that the user doesn't have to discard it and enter a new one after his session has expired. *check_id()* consists of two DBI calls. In the first, it makes a SQL SELECT query looking for a record matching the provided session ID. Since we're only interested in whether the query succeeds or fails, we select a constant 1 instead of a named set of columns. If the query fails, then the database does not already contain the session ID. We call DBI again to insert the session ID into the database. If this fails (which it might in the unusual case of another instance of this script picking the same session ID from within *generate_id()*) we return an empty list. Otherwise we return the ID and the warning message. Although the user has lost the record of his old set of games, his bookmarked URI will still be valid and can now be used to return to the new set.

---

* The size of the session ID determines the number of guesses a would-be hijacker has to make before getting a correct one. There are about 4.3 billion eight-digit session IDs. If you have 10,000 active sessions, this means that the hijacker has to guess (and try) 430,000 IDs before getting lucky. You'll probably notice this number of hits on your server long before anything untoward happens. If you have 100,000 active sessions, however, only 43,000 guesses are required, and you might want to use a longer session ID. In practice, it's almost always easier for a hijacker to recover a session ID by some other method (such as packet-sniffing) than by guessing.

The last new routine defined in this version of the game is *hash()*, which simply computes the MD5 digest of the value passed to it, then truncates it to $ID_LENGTH characters:

```
sub hash {
    my $value = shift;
    return substr(MD5->hexhash($value), 0, $ID_LENGTH);
}
```

Example 5-6. The Hangman Game with a DBI Backend

```perl
#!/usr/local/bin/perl

# file: hangman6.pl
# hangman game using DBI

use IO::File ();
use CGI qw(:standard);
use DBI ();
use MD5 ();

use strict;
use vars qw($DBH $ID_LENGTH);
use constant WORDS => '/usr/games/lib/hangman-words';
use constant ICONS => '/icons/hangman';
use constant TRIES => 6;

# session settings
use constant EXPIRE => 60*60*24*30;  # allow 30 days before expiration
use constant DB     => 'dbi:mysql:www';
use constant DBAUTH => 'nobody:';
use constant SECRET => 'modperl reigns';
use constant MAX_TRIES => 10;
$ID_LENGTH          = 8;  # length of the session ID

# Open the database
$DBH = DBI->connect(DB,split(':',DBAUTH,2),{PrintError=>0})
    || die "Couldn't open database: ",$DBI::errstr;

# get the current session ID, or make one
my ($session_id,$note) = get_session_id();

# retrieve the state
my $state      = get_state($session_id) unless param('clear');

# reinitialize if we need to
$state     = initialize($state) if !$state or param('restart');

# process the current guess, if any
my ($message,$status) = process_guess(param('guess') || '',$state);

# save the modified state
save_state($state,$session_id);
```

Example 5-6. The Hangman Game with a DBI Backend (continued)

```perl
# start the page
print header(),
    start_html(-Title   => 'Hangman 5',
               -bgcolor => 'white',
               -onLoad  => 'if (document.gf) document.gf.guess.focus()'),
    h1('Hangman 5: Database Sessions with URL rewriting');

print p(font({-color=>'red'},$note)) if $note;
```

. . . everything in the middle is the same . . .

```perl
# Retrieve the session ID from the path info.  If it's not
# already there, add it to the path info with a redirect.
sub get_session_id {
    my(@result);
    expire_old_sessions();
    my($id) = path_info() =~ m:^/([a-h0-9]{$ID_LENGTH}):o;
    return @result if $id and @result = check_id($id);

    # If we get here, there's not already an ID in the path info.
    my $session_id = generate_id();
    die "Couldn't make a new session id" unless $session_id;
    print redirect(script_name() . "/$session_id");
    exit 0;
}

# Find a new unique ID and insert it into the database
sub generate_id {
    # Create a new session id
    my $tries = 0;
    my $id = hash(SECRET . rand());
    while ($tries++ < MAX_TRIES) {
        last if $DBH->do("INSERT INTO $DB_TABLE (session_id) VALUES ('$id')");
        $id = hash(SECRET . $id);
    }
    return undef if $tries >= MAX_TRIES;  # we failed
    return $id;
}

# check to see that an old ID is valid
sub check_id {
    my $id = shift;
    return ($id, '')
        if $DBH->do("SELECT 1 FROM $DB_TABLE WHERE session_id='$id'") > 0;
    return ($id, 'The record of your game may have expired.  Restarting.')
        if $DBH->do("INSERT INTO $DB_TABLE (session_id) VALUES ('$id')");
    return ();
}

# generate a hash value
sub hash {
    my $value = shift;
    return substr(MD5->hexhash($value), 0, $ID_LENGTH);
}
```

Example 5-6. The Hangman Game with a DBI Backend (continued)

```
sub expire_old_sessions {
    $DBH->do(<<END);
DELETE FROM $DB_TABLE
    WHERE (unix_timestamp()-unix_timestamp(modified))>${\EXPIRE}
END
}

# get the state from the database
sub get_state {
    my $id = shift;
    my $sth = $DBH->prepare("SELECT * FROM $DB_TABLE WHERE session_id='$id'
    AND WORD<>NULL")
        || die "Prepare: ", $DBH->errstr;
    $sth->execute || die "Execute: ", $sth->errstr;
    my $state = $sth->fetchrow_hashref;
    $sth->finish;
    return $state;
}

# save the state in the database
sub save_state {
    my($state, $id) = @_;
    my $sth = $DBH->prepare(<<END) || die "prepare: ", $DBH->errstr;
UPDATE $DB_TABLE
    SET WORD=?,GUESSED=?,GAMENO=?,WON=?,TOTAL=?,GUESSES_LEFT=?
    WHERE session_id='$id'
END
    $sth->execute(@{$state}{qw(WORD GUESSED GAMENO WON TOTAL GUESSES_LEFT)})
        || die "execute: ", $DBH->errstr;
    $sth->finish;
}
```

URI-Based Session ID Problems and Solutions

There are a couple of problems with URI-based session IDs. One is that because the session ID is tacked onto the end of the URI, relative URIs will no longer work correctly. For example, a reference to another *Apache::Registry* script named *high_scores.pl* located in the same directory will be resolved by the browser to something like this:

```
http://your.site/perl/hangman.pl/high_scores.pl
```

This is obviously *not* what you want, because the session ID has been replaced by the name of the script you want to run! Fortunately, the Apache API provides a simple fix for this. Store the session ID to the left of the script name rather than the right, like this:

```
http://your.site/fd2c95dd/perl/hangman6.cgi
```

To handle URIs like this, you can write a custom URI translation handler to modify the URI before it gets to the script. The full details of writing translation handlers are discussed in Chapter 7, *Other Request Phases*, but a simple module to accomplish this named *Apache::StripSession* is shown in Example 5-7. Briefly, the module checks whether the requested URI begins with something that looks like a session ID (eight hexadecimal digits). If it does, the handler strips out the session ID and uses *subprocess_env()* to place the ID in an environment variable named SESSION_ID. The handler replaces the request's original URI with the altered one and then returns DECLINED, telling Apache to pass the request onward to the standard translation handlers that will do the work of turning the new URI into a physical file path.

Example 5-7. A Translation Handler for Stripping Session IDs from URIs

```
package Apache::StripSession;
# file: Apache/StripSession.pm
use strict;
use Apache::Constants qw(:common);

sub handler {
    my $r = shift;
    my($junk, $session, @rest) = split '/', $r->uri;
    return DECLINED unless $session =~ /^[0-9a-h]{8}$/;
    $r->subprocess_env('SESSION_ID' => $session);
    my $new_uri = join "/", "", @rest;
    $r->uri($new_uri);
    return DECLINED;
}

1;
__END__
```

Add this directive to *srm.conf* to activate *Apache::StripSession*:

```
PerlTransHandler Apache::StripSession
```

With this translation handler in place, the *get_session_id()* no longer has to play games with the additional path information in order to recover the session ID. It can just read it from the environment. The other change to the subroutine is that the call to *redirect()* now places the session ID in front of the script name rather than after it:

```
sub get_session_id {
    expire_old_sessions();
    return check_id($ENV{SESSION_ID}) if $ENV{SESSION_ID};

    my $session_id = generate_id();
    die "Couldn't make a new session id" unless $session_id;
    print redirect("/$session_id" . script_name());
    exit 0;
}
```

A more serious potential problem with URI-based session IDs is that under some circumstances it is possible for the session ID to "leak" to other sites via the HTTP referrer header (which, for historical reasons, is spelled "Referer"). If a page that has a session ID in its URI contains a hypertext link to another site, or even an image whose source is at another site, the page's URI, session ID included, will show up in the remote site's referrer log. Therefore, you must be careful not to include pointers to other sites in pages that use this method for storing session IDs. To get around this problem, you can put the session ID in a cookie, as the next section demonstrates.

Using DBI to Its Full Advantage

Once you keep session information stored in a database, there are all sorts of interesting things you can do with it. For example, you can easily compute statistics, such as the average number of games that users have played or how many guesses they have to make on average to arrive at the correct answer.

In this section we take advantage of this ability to create a "top winners" list. Whenever the user finishes a game, or any time he presses the "Show High Scores" button, he is presented with a list of the 15 top-scoring players. If the user is one of the winners, his entry is boldfaced. At the end of each game, the top winners list is displayed again, and the user is given a chance to add his name to the database. The new screen is shown in Figure 5-4.

For variety, this version of hangman stores its session ID in a client-side cookie rather than in the URI.

Because this is the final and most feature-rich version of hangman, we give the code in its entirety in Example 5-8. A variety of things have changed. Let's start with the table definition:

```
CREATE TABLE hangman (
        session_id      char(8)  primary key,
        username        char(40) default 'anonymous',
        WORD            char(30),
        GUESSED         char(26),
        GAMENO          int,
        WON             int,
        GUESSES_LEFT    int,
        TOTAL           int,
        modified        timestamp,
        KEY(modified)
    )
```

In addition to the state variables that we've used before, we've added a new column named *username* with a default value of **anonymous**. When a new user starts playing the game, he is initially anonymous. Whenever he wins a game, he gets the right to enter his name or handle into the database. Subsequently, his name is displayed on the hangman page in nice bold red letters, and it also appears on the top winners list, provided the user can score high enough to get there. Even

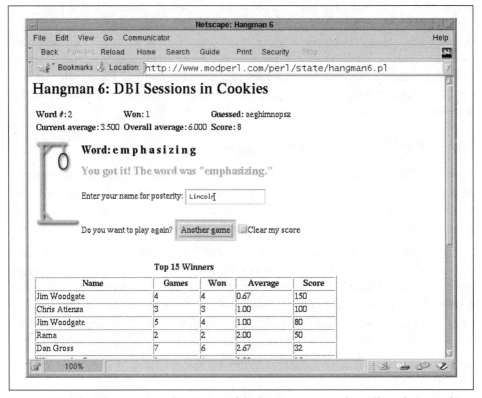

Figure 5-4. When the user wins this version of the hangman game, he's allowed to enter his name. The top 15 winners are displayed in a hall of fame list.

though the table definition has changed, the *get_state()* and *set_state()* subroutines used in the previous version of the game are sufficiently generic that they don't need alteration.

The other change is that the session ID is now stored in a cookie, rather than in a URI. The code required to store the session ID in a cookie is similar to what we used earlier for the shared memory example (Example 5-5):

```
sub get_session_id {
    my(@result);
    expire_old_sessions();
    my $id = cookie('sessionID');
    return @result if defined($id) and
        $id =~ m/^([a-h0-9]{$ID_LENGTH})$/o and
            @result = check_id($id);
    # If we get here, there's not already a valid cookie
    my $session_id = generate_id();
    die "Couldn't make a new session id" unless $session_id;
    return $session_id;
}
```

get_session_id() attempts to retrieve a cookie named *sessionID*. If it finds such a cookie, it first checks that the session ID looks right and then passes it to *check_id()* to confirm that the session is in the database. If there's no session cookie, it calls *generate_id()* to create a new ID and return it. Later when we generate the HTTP header we will incorporate this session ID into a cookie that is sent to the client.

The biggest change relative to the previous version of the script is the addition of a new subroutine called *show_scores()*, which displays an HTML table of the top 15 winners, the number of games they've won and lost, the average number of letters guessed per word, and an aggregate score. This subroutine is called at the end of each game by *show_restart_form()*, and is also called whenever the user presses the new "Show High Scores" button (CGI parameter *show_scores*).

The top of the *show_scores()* routine looks like this:

```
sub show_scores {
    my($current_session, $count) = @_;
    my $tries = TRIES;
    my $sth = $DBH->prepare(<<END) || die "prepare: ", $DBH->errstr;
SELECT session_id,username,
       GAMENO,WON,(TOTAL+GUESSES_LEFT-$tries)/(GAMENO-1) as AVG,
       round(100*WON/(GAMENO*(TOTAL+GUESSES_LEFT-$tries)/(GAMENO-1)))
       as SCORE
FROM $DB_TABLE
WHERE GAMENO > 1 and TOTAL+GUESSES_LEFT > $tries and WON > 0
ORDER BY SCORE DESC
LIMIT $count
END
```

The core of *show_scores()* is a big SQL SELECT statement that retrieves the top-scoring players based on a formula that divides the percentage of games won by the average number of guesses per game. The SQL statement sorts the returned list in descending order by score, then skims off the top records and returns them. The remainder of the routine calls *execute()* followed by a *fetchrow_array()* loop. Each retrieved record is turned into a row of an HTML table and printed out. The code is straightforward; see the listing for the details.

Another significant change is in the *show_guess_form()* routine:

```
sub show_guess_form {
    my $state = shift;
    print start_form(-name => 'gf'),
        "Your guess: ",
        textfield(-name => 'guess', -value => '', -override => 1),
        submit(-value => 'Guess'),
        br({-clear => 'ALL'}),
        submit(-name => 'show_scores', -value => 'Show High Scores'),
    submit(-Style => 'color: red', -name => 'abort', -value => 'Give Up');
    print end_form;
}
```

This version of *show_guess_form()* adds a new button labeled "Give Up," which allows the user to give up and move on to the next word. *process_guess()* is modified to recognize this condition and treat it as an incorrect attempt to guess the whole word.

Other changes to the hangman script allow the user to enter and edit his name. *show_restart_form()* has been modified to include an HTML text field that prompts the user to type in his name. The routine now looks like this:

```
sub show_restart_form {
    my($state, $status, $session_id) = @_;
    print start_form;
    print p("Enter your name for posterity: ",
            textfield(-name => 'change_name', -value => $state->{'username'}))
        if $status eq 'won';
    print
        p("Do you want to play again?",
          submit(-name => 'restart', -value => 'Another game'),
          checkbox(-name => 'clear', -label => 'Clear my score'));
    print end_form;
    show_scores($session_id, TOP_COUNT);
}
```

When the restart form is submitted, the script checks for the *change_name* parameter and calls a new subroutine named *set_username()* if present:

```
set_username($session_id, param('change_name')) if param('change_name');
```

set_username(), in turn, issues the appropriate SQL UPDATE command to insert the user's name into the database:

```
sub set_username {
    my($session, $newname) = @_;
    $newname = $DBH->quote($newname);
    $DBH->do("UPDATE $DB_TABLE SET username=$newname
              WHERE session_id='$session'")
        || die "update: ", $DBH->errstr;
}
```

This subroutine uses a trick that we haven't seen before. Because the username is typed in by the user, there's no guarantee that it doesn't contain funny characters, such as quotation marks, which will throw off the SQL parser. To avoid this, we pass the username through the DBI *quote()* function. This escapes funny characters and puts quotes around the string, making it safe to use in SQL.

The final frill on this script is an odd little subroutine defined at the bottom of the code named *Apache::DBI:db::ping()*:

```
sub Apache::DBI::db::ping {
    my $dbh = shift;
    return $dbh->do('select 1');
}
```

MySQL, like some other networked databases, will time out if a client has been idle for some period of time. If this happens, the hangman script will fail with a fatal database error the next time it tries to make a query. To avoid this eventuality, the *Apache::DBI* module attempts to reconnect to the database if it notices that the database has gone silent. However, *Apache::DBI* does this checking by calling the database driver's *ping()* method, and the MySQL DBI driver doesn't implement *ping()* (at least, not at the time that this was written). To avoid the embarrassment of having our hangman game get hung, we define our own version of *ping()*. It simply calls a SQL SELECT statement that's guaranteed to be true. If the database is still up, the call succeeds. If the database has timed out, the subroutine returns false and *Apache::DBI* reestablishes the connection behind the scenes.

Example 5-8. Hangman with All the Trimmings

```
# file: hangman7.cgi
# hangman game with all the trimmings

use IO::File ();
use CGI qw(:standard);
use DBI ();
use MD5 ();

use strict;
use vars qw($DBH $DB_TABLE $ID_LENGTH);
use constant WORDS => '/usr/games/lib/hangman-words';
use constant ICONS => '/icons/hangman';
use constant TRIES => 6;
use constant TOP_COUNT => 15; # how many top scores to show

# session settings
use constant EXPIRE => 60*60*24*30;  # allow 30 days before expiration
use constant DB     => 'dbi:mysql:www';
use constant DBAUTH => 'nobody:';
use constant SECRET => "something obscure";
use constant COOKIE_NAME => 'hangman7';
use constant MAX_TRIES => 10;
$DB_TABLE              = "hangman7";
$ID_LENGTH            = 8;

# Open the database
$DBH = DBI->connect(DB, split(':', DBAUTH, 2), {PrintError => 0})
    || die "Couldn't open database: ", $DBI::errstr;

# get the current session ID, or make one
my($session_id, $note) = get_session_id();

# retrieve the state
my $state      = get_state($session_id) unless param('clear');

# reinitialize if we need to -- we need to check for "change_name"
# because it's possible for the user to hit return in the change name field!
```

Example 5-8. Hangman with All the Trimmings (continued)

```perl
$state    = initialize($state) if !$state or param('restart')
    or param('change_name');

# process the current guess, if any
set_username($session_id, param('change_name')) if param('change_name');

my($message, $status) = process_guess(param('guess') || '', $state)
    unless param('show_scores');

# start the page
print header(-Cookie  => cookie(-name    => COOKIE_NAME,
                                -value   => $session_id,
                                -expires => '+' . EXPIRE . 'd')
            ),
    start_html(-Title   => 'Hangman 7',
               -bgcolor => 'white',
               -onLoad  => 'if (document.gf) document.gf.guess.focus()'),
    h1('Hangman 7: DBI Sessions in Cookies');

if (param() and !cookie(COOKIE_NAME)) {
    print h2(font({-color => 'red'},
    "You need to activate cookies to play this game"));
    footer();
    exit 0;
}
print h2(font({-color => 'red'}, "Player: $state->{username}")) if
    $state->{username} and $state->{username} ne 'anonymous';


print p(font({-color => 'red'}, $note)) if $note;

# save the modified state
save_state($state, $session_id);

# draw the statistics
show_status($state);

# Prompt the user to restart or for his next guess.
if (param('show_scores')) {
    show_scores($session_id, TOP_COUNT);
    print start_form, submit(-name => 'play', -value => 'Play'), end_form;
}
else {
    # draw the picture
    show_picture($state);
    show_word($state);
    print h2(font({-color => 'red'}, $message)) if $message;
    if ($status =~ /^(won|lost)$/) {
       show_restart_form($state, $status, $session_id);
    }
    else {
       show_guess_form($state);
    }
}
```

Example 5-8. Hangman with All the Trimmings (continued)

```perl
footer();

$DBH->disconnect;

########## subroutines #############
# This is called to process the user's guess
sub process_guess {
    my($guess, $state) = @_;

    # lose immediately if user has no more guesses left
    return ('', 'lost') unless $state->{GUESSES_LEFT} > 0;

    # lose immediately if user aborted
    if (param('abort')) {
        $state->{TOTAL} += $state->{GUESSES_LEFT};
        $state->{GUESSES_LEFT} = 0;
        return (qq{Chicken! The word was "$state->{WORD}."}, 'lost') ;
    }

    # break the word and guess into individual letters
    my %guessed = map { $_ => 1 } $state->{GUESSED} =~ /(.)/g;
    my %letters = map { $_ => 1 } $state->{WORD} =~ /(.)/g;

    # return immediately if user has already guessed the word
    return ('', 'won') unless grep(!$guessed{$_}, keys %letters);

    # do nothing more if no guess
    return ('', 'continue') unless $guess;

    # This section processes individual letter guesses
    $guess = lc $guess;
    return ("Not a valid letter or word!", 'error')
        unless $guess =~ /^[a-z]+$/;
    return ("You already guessed that letter!", 'error')
        if $guessed{$guess};

    # This section is called when the user guesses the whole word
    if (length($guess) > 1 and $guess ne $state->{WORD}) {
        $state->{TOTAL} += $state->{GUESSES_LEFT};
        $state->{GUESSES_LEFT} = 0;
        return (qq{You lose.  The word was "$state->{WORD}."}, 'lost')
    }

    # update the list of guesses
    foreach ($guess =~ /(.)/g) { $guessed{$_}++; }
    $state->{GUESSED} = join '', sort keys %guessed;

    # correct guess -- word completely filled in
    unless (grep(!$guessed{$_}, keys %letters)) {
        $state->{WON}++;
        return (qq{You got it!  The word was "$state->{WORD}."}, 'won');
    }
```

Example 5-8. Hangman with All the Trimmings (continued)

```perl
    # incorrect guess
    if (!$letters{$guess}) {
        $state->{TOTAL}++;
        $state->{GUESSES_LEFT}--;
        # user out of turns
        return (qq{The jig is up.  The word was "$state->{WORD}".}, 'lost')
            if $state->{GUESSES_LEFT} <= 0;
        # user still has some turns
        return ('Wrong guess!', 'continue');
    }

    # correct guess but word still incomplete
    return (qq{Good guess!}, 'continue');
}

# create the cute hangman picture
sub show_picture {
    my $tries_left = shift->{GUESSES_LEFT};
    my $picture = sprintf("%s/h%d.gif", ICONS, TRIES-$tries_left);
    print img({-src => $picture,
               -align => 'LEFT',
               -alt => "[$tries_left tries left]"});
}

# print the status
sub show_status {
    my $state = shift;
    my $current_average = $state->{TOTAL}/$state->{GAMENO};
    my $overall_average = $state->{GAMENO}>1 ?
        ($state->{TOTAL}-(TRIES-$state->{GUESSES_LEFT}))/($state->{GAMENO}-1) : 0;
    my $score = $overall_average > 0 ?
        (100*$state{WON}/($state->{GAMENO}*$overall_average)) : 0;

    # print the word with underscores replacing unguessed letters
    print table(TR({-width => '90%'},
                   td(b('Word #:'), $state->{GAMENO}),
                   td(b('Won:'), $state->{WON}),
                   td(b('Guessed:'), $state->{GUESSED}),
                   ),
                TR(
                   td(b('Current average:'), sprintf("%2.3f", $current_average)),
                   td(b('Overall average:'), sprintf("%2.3f", $overall_average)),
                   td(b('Score:'), sprintf("%3.0f", $score))
                   )
                );
}

sub show_word {
    my $state = shift;
    my %guessed = map { $_ => 1 } $state->{GUESSED} =~ /(.)/g;
    print h2("Word:",
             map {$guessed{$_} ? $_ : '_'}
             $state->{WORD} =~ /(.)/g);
}
```

Example 5-8. Hangman with All the Trimmings (continued)

```perl
# print the fill-out form for requesting input
sub show_guess_form {
    my $state = shift;
    print start_form(-name => 'gf'),
          "Your guess: ",
          textfield(-name => 'guess', -value => '', -override => 1),
          submit(-value => 'Guess'),
          br({-clear => 'ALL'}),
          submit(-name => 'show_scores', -value => 'Show High Scores'),
      submit(-Style => 'color: red', -name => 'abort', -value => 'Give Up');
    print end_form;
}


# ask the user if he wants to start over
sub show_restart_form {
    my($state, $status, $session_id) = @_;
    print start_form;
    print p("Enter your name for posterity: ",
            textfield(-name => 'change_name', -value => $state->{'username'}))
        if $status eq 'won';
    print
      p("Do you want to play again?",
        submit(-name => 'restart', -value => 'Another game'),
        checkbox(-name => 'clear', -label => 'Clear my score'));
    print end_form;
    show_scores($session_id, TOP_COUNT);
}


# pick a word, any word
sub pick_random_word {
    my $list = IO::File->new(WORDS)
        || die "Couldn't open ${\WORDS}: $!\n";
    my $word;
    rand($.) < 1 && ($word = $_) while <$list>;
    chomp $word;
    $word;
}


################## state maintenance ##############
# This is called to initialize a whole new state object
# or to create a new game.
sub initialize {
    my $state = shift;
    $state = {} unless $state;
    $state->{WORD}        = pick_random_word();
    $state->{GUESSES_LEFT}    = TRIES;
    $state->{TOTAL}     += 0;
    $state->{GUESSED}   = '';
    $state->{GAMENO}    += 1;
    $state->{WON}       += 0;
    $state->{username} = param('change_name') if param('change_name');
    return $state;
}
```

Example 5-8. Hangman with All the Trimmings (continued)

```perl
# Retrieve the session ID from the path info.  If it's not
# already there, add it to the path info with a redirect.
sub get_session_id {
    my(@result);
    expire_old_sessions();
    my $id = cookie(COOKIE_NAME);
    return @result if defined($id) and
        $id =~ m/^([a-h0-9]{$ID_LENGTH})$/o and
            @result = check_id($id);
    # If we get here, there's not already a valid cookie
    my $session_id = generate_id();
    die "Couldn't make a new session id" unless $session_id;
    return $session_id;
}


# Find a new unique ID and insert it into the database
sub generate_id {
    # Create a new session id
    my $tries = 0;
    my $id = hash(SECRET . rand());
    while ($tries++ < MAX_TRIES) {
        last if $DBH->do("INSERT INTO $DB_TABLE (session_id) VALUES ('$id')");
        $id = hash($id);
    }
    return undef if $tries >= MAX_TRIES;   # we failed
    return $id;
}


# check to see that an old ID is valid
sub check_id {
    my $id = shift;
    return ($id, '')
        if $DBH->do("SELECT 1 FROM $DB_TABLE WHERE session_id='$id'") > 0;
    return ($id, 'The record of your game may have expired.  Restarting.')
        if $DBH->do("INSERT INTO $DB_TABLE (session_id) VALUES ('$id')");
    return ();
}


# generate a hash value
sub hash {
    my $value = shift;
    return substr(MD5->hexhash($value), 0, $ID_LENGTH);
}

sub expire_old_sessions {
    $DBH->do(<<END);
DELETE FROM $DB_TABLE
    WHERE (unix_timestamp()-unix_timestamp(modified))>${\EXPIRE}
END
}
```

Example 5-8. Hangman with All the Trimmings (continued)

```
# get the state from the database
sub get_state {
    my $id = shift;
    my $sth = $DBH->prepare("SELECT * FROM $DB_TABLE WHERE session_id='$id'
        AND WORD<>NULL")
        || die "Prepare: ", $DBH->errstr;
    $sth->execute || die "Execute: ", $sth->errstr;
    my $state = $sth->fetchrow_hashref;
    $sth->finish;
    return $state;
}


# save the state in the database
sub save_state {
    my($state, $id) = @_;
    my $sth = $DBH->prepare(<<END) || die "prepare: ", $DBH->errstr;
UPDATE $DB_TABLE
    SET WORD=?,GUESSED=?,GAMENO=?,WON=?,TOTAL=?,GUESSES_LEFT=?
    WHERE session_id='$id'
END
    $sth->execute(@{$state}{qw(WORD GUESSED GAMENO WON TOTAL GUESSES_LEFT)})
        || die "execute: ", $sth->errstr;
    $sth->finish;
}


# Return true if the current session is one of the top ten
# Overall score is the percentage of games won weighted by the average
# number of guesses taken.
sub show_scores {
    my($current_session, $count) = @_;
    my $tries = TRIES;
    my $sth = $DBH->prepare(<<END) || die "prepare: ", $DBH->errstr;
SELECT session_id,username,
       GAMENO,WON,(TOTAL+GUESSES_LEFT-$tries)/(GAMENO-1) as AVG,
       round(100*WON/(GAMENO*(TOTAL+GUESSES_LEFT-$tries)/(GAMENO-1))) as SCORE
FROM $DB_TABLE
WHERE GAMENO > 1 and TOTAL+GUESSES_LEFT > $tries and WON > 0
ORDER BY SCORE DESC
LIMIT $count
END
    ;
    $sth->execute || die "execute: ", $sth->errstr;
    my @rows = th([qw(Name Games Won Average Score)]);
    while (my(@rec) = $sth->fetchrow_array) {
        my $id = shift @rec;
        push @rows, $id eq $current_session ?
                th({-align => 'LEFT'}, \@rec) : td(\@rec);
    }
    print br({-clear => 'ALL'}),
            table({-border => 'undef', -width => '75%'},
                caption(b("Top $count Winners")),
              TR(\@rows));
```

Example 5-8. Hangman with All the Trimmings (continued)

```
    $sth->finish;
}

# change the username in the database
sub set_username {
    my($session, $newname) = @_;
    $newname = $DBH->quote($newname);
    $DBH->do("UPDATE $DB_TABLE SET username=$newname
    WHERE session_id='$session'")
        || die "update: ", $DBH->errstr;
}

# fix the absence of ping() in the mysql interface.
sub Apache::DBI::db::ping {
    my $dbh = shift;
    return $dbh->do('select 1');
}

# print bottom of page
sub footer {
    print hr,
    a({-href => '/'}, "Home"),
    p(cite({-Style => "fontsize: 10pt"}, 'graphics courtesy Andy Wardley')),
    end_html();
}
```

Other Server-Side Techniques

Before we finish up this chapter, we touch on a couple of other techniques for storing state information on the server side of the connection.

Non-DBI Databases

Because of its portability, the DBI database interface is probably the right choice for most server-side database applications. However, any database system that was designed to support multiple write access will work for this application. For example, the object-oriented ACEDB system that Lincoln works with is well suited to applications that require complex, richly interlinked information to be stored. The database is freeware; you can find out more about it at *http://stein.cshl.org/AcePerl/*.

You might be tempted to try to store session information using a Unix NDBM, GDBM, or DB_FILE database. If you try this, you may be in for an unpleasant surprise. These databases were designed for good multiuser read performance but not for transactions in which several processes are reading and writing simultaneously. They keep an in-memory cache of a portion of the database and don't immediately know when another process has updated a portion that's cached. As a result, the database can easily become corrupt if multiple Apache daemons open it for writing.

You can work around this problem by carefully locking the files, flushing after each write, and closing and reopening the file at strategic points, but believe us, it isn't worth it. Version 2 of the Berkeley DB library does support transactions, however, and Paul Marquess's experimental *Berkeley_DB* module provides an interface to it. We have not experimented with this database yet, but it looks like it might provide a lightweight solution for storing web session information in situations where a DBI database would be overkill.

Using Authentication to Provide Session IDs

Because the techniques for storing state information on the server side all require some sort of session ID to be maintained by the browser, they share a drawback. Regardless of whether the session ID is stored in a cookie or inside the URI, it sticks to the browser, not to the user. When the reigning hangman champ moves from his home computer to his office computer, he loses access to his current score information. Of course you could instruct users to write down their session IDs and type them back into the URI or cookie file when they move to a new machine, but this is awkward and inconvenient. You could try to recover session IDs from usernames, but this makes it too easy for people to steal each other's sessions.

In some applications, it makes sense to give each user a unique username/password pair and ask users to log in to your application. You can then use the username as the session key and be guaranteed that no sessions will conflict. Users can't steal each others' sessions without guessing the password, which is sufficient security for most applications.

The simplest way to do this is to use Apache's built-in authentication modules for password-protecting your script's URI. When the user tries to access the script, he is presented with a dialog box prompting him for his username and password. Apache verifies the information he provides against a file of stored usernames and passwords and allows access to the script if the information checks out. Before calling your script, Apache places the username into the request object. If you are using *Apache::Registry*, this information can be recovered from the CGI environment variable $ENV{REMOTE_USER}. From within an Apache Perl module, you can recover the username from the connection object in this way:

```
$username = $r->connection->user;
```

With this technique we can write a concise replacement for the *get_session_id()* subroutine in the server-side hangman scripts:

```
sub get_session_id {
   return $ENV{REMOTE_USER};
}
```

The Apache distribution comes with a variety of authentication modules that use text files or Unix DBM files as their password databases. These may be adequate for your needs, or you might want to integrate the database of usernames and passwords with the database you use to store session information. The next chapter shows you how to do this and much more.

Apache::Session

After this chapter was written, Jeffrey Baker released an *Apache::Session* module that implements many of the techniques described in this chapter. This module had undergone several revisions, including contributions from many *mod_perl* developers that have stabilized and enhanced *Apache::Session*, making it fit for a production environment across all platforms. We strongly recommend taking a look at this module when considering application state management implementation.

6

Authentication and Authorization

In previous chapters we've seen how to create dynamic pages, interact with the remote user, and maintain state across sessions. We haven't worried much about issues of user authorization: the web server and all its modules were assumed to be accessible by all.

In the real world, access to the web server is not always unrestricted. The module you're working on may provide access to a database of proprietary information, may tunnel through a firewall system, or may control a hardware device that can be damaged if used improperly. Under circumstances like these you'll need to take care that the module can be run only by authorized users.

In this chapter, we step back to an earlier phase of the HTTP transaction, one in which Apache attempts to determine the identity of the person at the other end of the connection and whether he or she is authorized to access the resource. Apache's APIs for authentication and authorization are straightforward yet powerful. You can implement simple password-based checking in just a few lines of code. With somewhat more effort, you can implement more sophisticated authentication systems, such as ones based on hardware tokens.

Access Control, Authentication, and Authorization

When a remote user comes knocking at Apache's door to request a document, Apache acts like the bouncer standing at the entrance to a bar. It asks three questions:

- Is the bar open for business?

  If the bar's closed, no one can come in. The patron is brusquely turned away, regardless of who he or she may be.

- Is the patron who he or she claims to be?

  The bouncer demands to see some identification and scrutinizes it for authenticity. If the ID is forged, the bouncer hustles the patron away.

- Is this patron authorized to enter?

  Based on the patron's confirmed identity, the bouncer decides whether this person is allowed in. The patron must be of legal drinking age and, in the case of a private club, must be listed in the membership roster. Or there may be arbitrary restrictions, such as "Ladies' Night."

In the context of the HTTP protocol, the first decision is known as "access control," the second as "authentication," and the third as "authorization." Each is the responsibility of a separate Apache handler which decides who can access the site and what they are allowed to see when they enter. Unlike the case of the bouncer at the bar, Apache access control and authentication can be as fine-grained as you need it to be. In addition to controlling who is allowed to enter the bar (web site), you can control what parts of the bar (partial URI paths) they're allowed to sit in, and even what drinks (individual URIs) they can order. You can control access to real files and directories as easily as virtual ones created on the fly.

How Access Control Works

Access control is any type of restriction that doesn't require you to determine the identity of the remote user. Common examples of access control are those based on the IP address of the remote user's computer, on the time of day of the request, or on certain attributes of the requested document (for example, the remote user tries to fetch a directory listing when automatic directory indexing has been disabled).

Access control uses the HTTP FORBIDDEN status code (403). When a user attempts to fetch a URI that is restricted in this way, the server returns this status code to tell the user's browser that access is forbidden and no amount of authentication will change that fact. The easiest way to understand this interaction is to see it in action. If you have access to a command-line telnet program, you can talk directly to a server to see its responses. Try this (the URI is live):

```
% telnet www.modperl.com 80
Connected to www.modperl.com.
Escape character is '^]'.
GET /articles/ HTTP/1.0

HTTP/1.1 403 Forbidden
Date: Mon, 10 Nov 1998 12:43:08 GMT
```

```
Server: Apache/1.3.3 mod_perl/1.16
Connection: close
Content-Type: text/html

<HTML><HEAD>
<TITLE>403 Forbidden</TITLE>
</HEAD><BODY>
<H1>Forbidden</H1>
You don't have permission to access /articles/
on this server.<P>
</BODY></HTML>
Connection closed by foreign host.
```

In this example, after connecting to the web server's port, we typed in a GET request to fetch the URI */articles/*. However, access to this URI has been turned off at the server side using the following configuration file directives:

```
<Location /articles>
  deny from all
</Location>
```

Because access is denied to everyone, the server returns an HTTP header indicating the 403 status code. This is followed by a short explanatory HTML message for the browser to display. Since there's nothing more that the user can do to gain access to this document, the browser displays this message and takes no further action.

Apache's standard modules allow you to restrict access to a file or directory by the IP address or domain name of the remote host. By writing your own access control handler, you can take complete control of this process to grant or deny access based on any arbitrary criteria you choose. The examples given later in this chapter show you how to limit access based on the day of the week and on the user agent, but you can base the check on anything that doesn't require user interaction. For example, you might insist that the remote host has a reverse domain name system mapping or limit access to hosts that make too many requests over a short period of time.

How Authentication and Authorization Work

In contrast to access control, the process of authenticating a remote user is more involved. The question "is the user who he or she claims to be?" sounds simple, but the steps for verifying the answer can be simple or complex, depending on the level of assurance you desire. The HTTP protocol does not provide a way to answer the question of authenticity, only a method of asking it. It's up to the web server itself to decide when a user is or is not authenticated.

When a web server needs to know who a user is, it issues a challenge using the HTTP 401 "Authorization Required" code (Figure 6-1). In addition to this code, the HTTP header includes one or more fields called *WWW-Authenticate*, indicating the type (or types) of authentication that the server considers acceptable. *WWW-Authenticate* may also provide other information, such as a challenge string to use in cryptographic authentication protocols.

When a client sees the 401 response code, it studies the *WWW-Authenticate* header and fetches the requested authentication information if it can. If need be, the client requests some information from the user, such as prompting for an account name and password or requiring the user to insert a smart token containing a cryptographic signature.

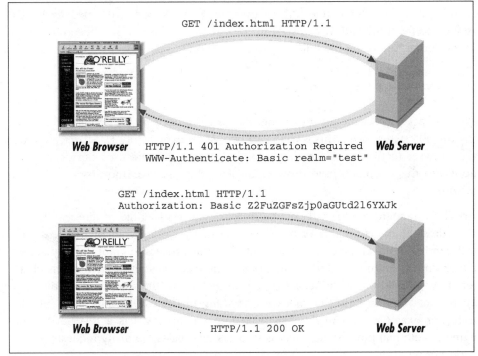

Figure 6-1. During web authentication, the server challenges the browser to provide authentication information, and the browser reissues the request with an Authorization header.

Armed with this information, the browser now issues a second request for the URI, but this time it adds an *Authorization* field containing the information necessary to establish the user's credentials. (Notice that this field is misnamed since it provides authentication information, not authorization information.) The server checks the contents of *Authorization*, and if it passes muster, the request is passed on to the authorization phase of the transaction, where the server will decide whether the authenticated user has access to the requested URI.

On subsequent requests to this URI, the browser remembers the user's authentication information and automatically provides it in the *Authorization* field. This way the user doesn't have to provide his credentials each time he fetches a page. The browser also provides the same information for URIs at the same level or beneath the current one, anticipating the common situation in which an entire directory tree is placed under access control. If the authentication information becomes invalid (for example, in a scheme in which authentication expires after a period of time), the server can again issue a 401 response, forcing the browser to request the user's credentials all over again.

The contents of *WWW-Authenticate* and *Authorization* are specific to the particular authentication scheme. Fortunately, only three authentication schemes are in general use, and just one dominates the current generation of browsers and servers.* This is the Basic authentication scheme, the first authentication scheme defined in the HTTP protocol. Basic authentication is, well, basic! It is the standard account name/password scheme that we all know and love.

Here's what an unauthorized response looks like. Feel free to try it for yourself.

```
% telnet www.modperl.com 80
Connected to www.modperl.com.
Escape character is '^]'.
GET /private/ HTTP/1.0

HTTP/1.1 401 Authorization Required
Date: Mon, 10 Nov 1998 1:01:17 GMT
Server: Apache/1.3.3 mod_perl/1.16
WWW-Authenticate: Basic realm="Test"
Connection: close
Content-Type: text/html

<HTML><HEAD>
<TITLE>Authorization Required</TITLE>
</HEAD><BODY>
<H1>Authorization Required</H1>
This server could not verify that you
are authorized to access the document you
requested.  Either you supplied the wrong
credentials (e.g., bad password), or your
browser doesn't understand how to supply
the credentials required.<P>
</BODY></HTML>
Connection closed by foreign host.
```

In this example, we requested the URI */private/*, which has been placed under Basic authentication. The returned HTTP 401 status code indicates that some sort of authentication is required, and the *WWW-Authenticate* field tells the browser to use Basic authentication. The *WWW-Authenticate* field also contains scheme-specific information following the name of the scheme. In the case of Basic

---

* The three authentication schemes in general use are Basic, Digest, and Microsoft's proprietary NTLM protocol used by its MSIE and IIS products.

authentication, this information consists of the authorization "realm," a short label that the browser will display in the password prompt box. One purpose of the realm is to hint to the user which password he should provide on systems that maintain more than one set of accounts. Another purpose is to allow the browser to automatically provide the same authentication information if it later encounters a discontiguous part of the site that uses the same realm name. However, we have found that not all browsers implement this feature.

Following the HTTP header is some HTML for the browser to display. Unlike the situation with the 403 status, however, the browser doesn't immediately display this page. Instead it pops up a dialog box to request the user's account name and password. The HTML is only displayed if the user presses "Cancel", or in the rare case of browsers that don't understand Basic authentication.

After the user enters his credentials, the browser attempts to fetch the URI once again, this time providing the credential information in the *Authorization* field. The request (which you can try yourself) will look something like this:

```
% telnet www.modperl.com 80
Connected to www.modperl.com.
Escape character is '^]'.
GET /private/ HTTP/1.0
Authorization: Basic Z2FuZGFsZjp0aGUtd216YXJk

HTTP/1.1 200 OK
Date: Mon, 10 Nov 1998 1:43:56 GMT
Server: Apache/1.3.3 mod_perl/1.16
Last-Modified: Thu, 29 Jan 1998 11:44:21 GMT
ETag: "1612a-18-34d06b95"
Content-Length: 24
Accept-Ranges: bytes
Connection: close
Content-Type: text/plain

Hi there.

How are you?
Connection closed by foreign host.
```

The contents of the *Authorization* field are the security scheme, "Basic" in this case, and scheme-specific information. For Basic authentication, this consists of the user's name and password, concatenated together and encoded with base64. Although the example makes it look like the password is encrypted in some clever way, it's not—a fact that you can readily prove to yourself if you have the *MIME::Base64* module installed:[*]

```
% perl -MMIME::Base64 -le 'print decode_base64 "Z2FuZGFsZjp0aGUtd216YXJk"'
gandalf:the-wizard
```

---

[*] *MIME::Base64* is available from CPAN.

Standard Apache offers two types of authentication: the Basic authentication shown above, and a more secure method known as Digest. Digest authentication, which became standard with HTTP/1.1, is safer than Basic because passwords are never transmitted in the clear. In Digest authentication, the server generates a random "challenge" string and sends it to the browser. The browser encrypts the challenge with the user's password and returns it to the server. The server also encrypts the challenge with the user's stored password and compares its result to the one returned by the browser.* If the two match, the server knows that the user knows the correct password. Unfortunately, the commercial browser vendors haven't been as quick to innovate as Apache, so Digest authentication isn't widely implemented on the browser side. At the same time, some might argue that using Basic authentication over the encrypted Secure Sockets Layer (SSL) protocol is simpler, provided that the browser and server both implement SSL. We discuss SSL authentication techniques at the end of this chapter.

Because authentication requires the cooperation of the browser, your options for customizing how authentication works are somewhat limited. You are essentially limited to authenticating based on information that the user provides in the standard password dialog box. However, even within these bounds, there are some interesting things you can do. For example, you can implement an anonymous login system that gives the user a chance to provide contact information without requiring vigorous authentication.

After successfully authenticating a user, Apache enters its authorization phase. Just because a user can prove that he is who he claims to be doesn't mean he has unrestricted access to the site! During this phase Apache applies any number of arbitrary tests to the authenticated username. Apache's default handlers allow you to grant access to users based on their account names or their membership in named groups, using a variety of flat file and hashed lookup table formats.

By writing custom authorization handlers, you can do much more than this. You can perform a SQL query on an enterprise database, consult the company's current organizational chart to implement role-based authorization, or apply ad hoc rules like allowing users named "Fred" access on alternate Tuesdays. Or how about something completely different from the usual web access model, such as a system in which the user purchases a certain number of "pay per view" accesses in advance? Each time he accesses a page, the system decrements a counter in a database. When the user's access count hits zero, the server denies him access.

---

* Actually, the user's plain-text password is not stored on the server side. Instead, the server stores an MD5 hash of the user's password and the hash, not the password itself, are used on the server and browser side to encrypt the challenge. Because users tend to use the same password for multiple services, this prevents the compromise of passwords by unscrupulous webmasters.

Access Control with mod_perl

This section shows you how to write a simple access control handler in *mod_perl*.

A Simple Access Control Module

To create an access control module, you'll install a handler for the access control phase by adding a *PerlAccessHandler* directive to one of Apache's configuration files or to a per-directory *.htaccess* file. The access control handler has the job of giving thumbs up or down for each attempted access to the URI. The handler indicates its decision in the result code it returns to the server. OK will allow the user in, FORBIDDEN will forbid access by issuing a 403 status code, and DECLINED will defer the decision to any other access control handlers that may be installed.

We begin with the simplest type of access control, a stern module called *Apache::GateKeeper* (Example 6-1). *Apache::GateKeeper* recognizes a single configuration variable named *Gate*. If the value of *Gate* is open, the module allows access to the URI under its control. If the value of *Gate* is closed, the module forbids access. Any other value results in an "internal server error" message.

The code is straightforward. It begins in the usual way by importing the common Apache and HTTP constants from *Apache::Constants*:

```
package Apache::GateKeeper;
# file: Apache/GateKeeper.pm
use strict;
use Apache::Constants qw(:common);

sub handler {
    my $r = shift;
    my $gate = $r->dir_config("Gate");
    return DECLINED unless defined $gate;
    return OK if lc($gate) eq 'open';
```

When the handler is executed, it fetches the value of the *Gate* configuration variable. If the variable is absent, the handler declines to handle the transaction, deferring the decision to other handlers that may be installed. If the variable is present, the handler checks its value, and returns a value of OK if *Gate* is open.

```
    if (lc $gate eq 'closed') {
        $r->log_reason("Access forbidden unless the gate is open",
        $r->filename);
        return FORBIDDEN;
    }

    $r->log_error($r->uri, ": Invalid value for Gate ($gate)");
    return SERVER_ERROR;
}
```

On the other hand, if the value of *Gate* is "closed" the handler returns a FORBIDDEN error code. In the latter case, the subroutine also writes a message to the log file using the *log_reason()* logging method (see "Error Logging," in Chapter 4, *Content Handlers*). Any other value for *Gate* is a configuration error, which we check for, log, and handle by returning SERVER_ERROR.

Example 6-1. Simple Access Control

```
package Apache::GateKeeper;
# file: Apache/GateKeeper.pm
use strict;
use Apache::Constants qw(:common);

sub handler {
    my $r = shift;
    my $gate = $r->dir_config("Gate");
    return DECLINED unless defined $gate;
    return OK if lc $gate eq 'open';

    if (lc $gate eq 'closed') {
        $r->log_reason("Access forbidden unless the gate is open", $r->filename);
        return FORBIDDEN;
    }

    $r->log_error($r->uri, ": Invalid value for Gate ($gate)");
    return SERVER_ERROR;
}

1;
__END__

# .htaccess file entry
PerlAccessHandler Apache::GateKeeper
PerlSetVar Gate closed
```

The bottom of the listing shows the two-line *.htaccess* entry required to turn on *Apache::GateKeeper* for a particular directory (you could also use a *<Location>* or *<Directory>* entry for this purpose). It uses the *PerlAccessHandler* directive to install *Apache::GateKeeper* as the access handler for this directory, then calls *PerlSetVar* to set the Perl configuration variable *Gate* to closed.

How does the GateKeeper access control handler interact with other aspects of Apache access control, authentication, and authorization? If an authentication handler is also installed—for example, by including a *require valid-user* directive in the *.htaccess* file—then *Apache::GateKeeper* is called as only the first step in the process. If *Apache::GateKeeper* returns OK, then Apache will go on to the authentication phase and the user will be asked to provide his name and password.

However, this behavior can be modified by placing the line *Satisfy any* in the *.htaccess* file or directory configuration section. When this directive is in effect, Apache will try access control first and then try authentication/authorization. If

either returns OK, then the request will be satisfied. This lets certain privileged
users get into the directory even when *Gate* is closed. (The bouncer steps aside
when he recognizes his boss!)

Now consider a *.htaccess* file like this one:

```
PerlAccessHandler Apache::GateKeeper
PerlSetVar Gate open

order deny,allow
deny from all
allow from 192.168.2
```

This configuration installs two access control handlers: one implemented by the
standard *mod_access* module (which defines the *order, allow,* and *deny* directives) and *Apache::GateKeeper.* The two handlers are potentially in conflict. The
IP-based restrictions implemented by *mod_access* forbid access from any address
but those in a privileged 192.168.2 subnet. *Apache::GateKeeper,* in contrast, is set
to allow access to the subdirectory from anyone. Who wins?

The Apache server's method for resolving these situations is to call each handler in
turn in the reverse order of installation. If the handler returns FORBIDDEN, then
Apache immediately refuses access. If the handler returns OK or DECLINED, however, Apache passes the request to the next handler in the chain. In the example
given above, *Apache::GateKeeper* gets first shot at approving the request because it
was installed last (*mod_access* is usually installed at compile time). If
Apache::GateKeeper approves or declines the request, then the request will be
passed on to *mod_access.* However, if *Apache::GateKeeper* returns FORBIDDEN,
then the request is immediately refused and *mod_access* isn't even invoked at all.
The system is not unlike the UN Security Council: for a resolution to pass, all members must either vote "yes" or abstain. Any single "no" (or "nyet") acts as a veto.

The *Satisfy any* directive has no effect on this situation.

Time-Based Access Control

For a slightly more interesting access handler, consider Example 6-2, which implements access control based on the day of the week. URIs protected by this handler will only be accessible on the days listed in a variable named *ReqDay.* This
could be useful for a web site that observes the Sabbath, or, more plausibly, it
might form the basis for a generic module that implements time-based access control. Many sites perform routine maintenance at scheduled times of the day, and
it's often helpful to keep visitors out of directories while they're being updated.

The handler, *Apache::DayLimit,* begins by fetching the *ReqDay* configuration variable. If not present, it declines the transaction and gives some other handler a
chance to consider it. Otherwise, the handler splits out the day names, which are
assumed to be contained in a space- or comma-delimited list, and compares them

to the current day obtained from the *localtime()* function. If there's a match, the handler allows the access by returning OK. Otherwise, it returns the FORBIDDEN HTTP error code as before, and access is denied.

Example 6-2. Access Control by the Day of Week

```
package Apache::DayLimit;

use strict;
use Apache::Constants qw(:common);
use Time::localtime;

my @wday = qw(sunday monday tuesday wednesday thursday friday saturday);

sub handler {
    my $r = shift;
    my $requires = $r->dir_config("ReqDay");
    return DECLINED unless $requires;

    my $day = $wday[localtime->wday];
    return OK if $requires =~ /$day([,\s]+|$)/i;

    $r->log_reason(qq{Access forbidden on weekday "$day"}, $r->uri);
    return FORBIDDEN;
}

1;
__END__
```

A *<Location>* section to go with *Apache::DayLimit*:

```
<Location /weekends_only>
    PerlSetVar ReqDay saturday,sunday
    PerlAccessHandler Apache::DayLimit
</Location>
```

Browser-Based Access Control

Web-crawling robots are an increasing problem for webmasters. Robots are supposed to abide by an informal agreement known as the robot exclusion standard (RES), in which the robot checks a file named *robots.txt* that tells it what parts of the site it is allowed to crawl through. Many rude robots, however, ignore the RES or, worse, exploit *robots.txt* to guide them to the "interesting" parts. The next example (Example 6-3) gives the outline of a robot exclusion module called *Apache::BlockAgent*. With it you can block the access of certain web clients based on their *User-Agent* field (which frequently, although not invariably, identifies robots).

The module is configured with a "bad agents" text file. This file contains a series of pattern matches, one per line. The incoming request's *User-Agent* field will be compared to each of these patterns in a case-insensitive manner. If any of the patterns hit, the request will be refused. Here's a small sample file that contains pattern matches for a few robots that have been reported to behave rudely:

```
^teleport pro\/1\.28
^nicerspro
^mozilla\/3\.0 \(http engine\)
^netattache
^crescent internet toolpak http ole control v\.1\.0
^go-ahead-got-it
^wget
^devsoft's http component v1\.0
^www\.pl
^digout4uagent
```

Rather than hardcode the location of the bad agents file, we set its path using a configuration variable named *BlockAgentFile*. A directory configuration section like this sample *perl.conf* entry will apply the *Apache::BlockAgent* handler to the entire site:

```
<Location />
   PerlAccessHandler Apache::BlockAgent
   PerlSetVar BlockAgentFile conf/bad_agents.txt
</Location>
```

Apache::BlockAgent is a long module, so we'll step through the code a section at a time.

```
package Apache::BlockAgent;

use strict;
use Apache::Constants qw(:common);
use Apache::File ();
use Apache::Log ();
use Safe ();

my $Safe = Safe->new;
my %MATCH_CACHE;
```

The module brings in the common Apache constants and loads file-handling code from *Apache::File*. It also brings in the *Apache::Log* module, which makes the logging API available. The standard *Safe* module is pulled in next, and a new compartment is created where code will be compiled. We'll see later how the %MATCH_ CACHE package variable is used to cache the code routines that detect undesirable user agents. Most of *Apache::BlockAgent*'s logic is contained in the short *handler()* subroutine:

```
sub handler {
    my $r = shift;
    my($patfile, $agent, $sub);
    return DECLINED unless $patfile = $r->dir_config('BlockAgentFile');
    return FORBIDDEN unless $agent = $r->header_in('User-Agent');
    return SERVER_ERROR unless $sub = get_match_sub($r, $patfile);
```

```
        return OK if $sub->($agent);
        $r->log_reason("Access forbidden to agent $agent", $r->filename);
        return FORBIDDEN;
    }
```

The code first checks that the *BlockAgentFile* configuration variable is present. If not, it declines to handle the transaction. It then attempts to fetch the *User-Agent* field from the HTTP header, by calling the request object's *header_in()* method. If no value is returned by this call (which might happen if a sneaky robot declines to identify itself), we return FORBIDDEN from the subroutine, blocking access.

Otherwise, we call an internal function named *get_match_sub()* with the request object and the path to the bad agent file. *get_match_sub()* uses the information contained within the file to compile an anonymous subroutine which, when called with the user agent identification, returns a true value if the client is accepted, or false if it matches one of the forbidden patterns. If *get_match_sub()* returns an undefined value, it indicates that one or more of the patterns didn't compile correctly and we return a server error. Otherwise, we call the returned subroutine with the agent name and return OK or FORBIDDEN, depending on the outcome.

The remainder of the module is taken up by the definition of *get_match_sub()*. This subroutine is interesting because it illustrates the advantage of a persistent module over a transient CGI script:

```
    sub get_match_sub {
        my($r, $filename) = @_;
        $filename = $r->server_root_relative($filename);
        my $mtime = (stat $filename)[9];

        # try to return the sub from cache
        return $MATCH_CACHE{$filename}->{'sub'} if
            $MATCH_CACHE{$filename} &&
                $MATCH_CACHE{$filename}->{'mod'} >= $mtime;
```

Rather than tediously read in the bad agents file each time we're called, compile each of the patterns, and test them, we compile the pattern match tests into an anonymous subroutine and store it in the %MATCH_CACHE package variable, along with the name of the pattern file and its modification date. Each time the subroutine is called, the subroutine checks %MATCH_CACHE to see whether this particular pattern file has been processed before. If the file has been seen before, the routine then compares the file's modification time against the date stored in the cache. If the file is not more recent than the cached version, then we return the cached subroutine. Otherwise, we compile it again.

Next we open up the bad agents file, fetch the patterns, and build up a subroutine line by line using a series of string concatenations:

```
        my($fh, @pats);
        return undef unless $fh = Apache::File->new($filename);
        chomp(@pats = <$fh>); # get the patterns into an array
```

```
my $code = "sub { local \$_ = shift;\n";
foreach (@pats) {
   next if /^#/;
   $code .= "return if /$_/i;\n";
}
$code .= "1; }\n";
$r->server->log->debug("compiled $filename into:\n $code");
```

Note the use of *$r->server->log->debug()* to send a debugging message to the server log file. This message will only appear in the error log if the *LogLevel* is set to *debug*. If all goes well, the synthesized subroutine stored in $code will end up looking something like this:

```
sub {
  $_ = shift;
  return if /^teleport pro\/1\.28/i;
  return if /^nicerspro/i;
  return if /^mozilla\/3\.0 \(http engine\)/i;
     ...
  1;
}
```

After building up the subroutine, we run a match-all regular expression over the code in order to untaint what was read from disk. In most cases, blindly untainting data is a bad idea, rendering the taint check mechanism useless. To mitigate this we use a *Safe* compartment and the *reval()* method, disabling potentially dangerous operations such as *system()*.

```
# create the sub, cache and return it
($code) = $code =~ /^(.*)$/s; #untaint
my $sub = $Safe->reval($code);
unless ($sub) {
    $r->log_error($r->uri, ": ", $@);
    return;
}
```

The untainting step is required only if taint checks are turned on with the *Perl-TaintCheck on* directive (see Appendix A, *Standard Noncore Modules*). The result of *reval()*ing the string is a CODE reference to an anonymous subroutine or *undef* if something went wrong during the compilation. In the latter case, we log the error and return.

The final step is to store the compiled subroutine and the bad agent file's modification time into %MATCH_CACHE:

```
@{ $MATCH_CACHE{$filename} }{'sub','mod'} = ($sub, $mtime);
return $MATCH_CACHE{$filename}->{'sub'};
}
```

Because there may be several pattern files applicable to different parts of the site, we key %MATCH_CACHE by the path to the file. We then return the compiled subroutine to the caller.

As we saw in Chapter 4, *Content Handlers*, this technique of compiling and caching a dynamically evaluated subroutine is a powerful optimization that allows *Apache::BlockAgent* to keep up with even very busy sites. Going one step further, the *Apache::BlockAgent* module could avoid parsing the pattern file entirely by defining its own custom configuration directives. The technique for doing this is described in Chapter 7, *Other Request Phases.**

Example 6-3. Blocking Rude Robots with Apache::BlockAgent

```perl
package Apache::BlockAgent;

use strict;
use Apache::Constants qw(:common);
use Apache::File ();
use Apache::Log ();
use Safe ();

my $Safe = Safe->new;
my %MATCH_CACHE;

sub handler {
    my $r = shift;
    my($patfile, $agent, $sub);
    return DECLINED unless $patfile = $r->dir_config('BlockAgentFile');
    return FORBIDDEN unless $agent = $r->header_in('User-Agent');
    return SERVER_ERROR unless $sub = get_match_sub($r, $patfile);
    return OK if $sub->($agent);
    $r->log_reason("Access forbidden to agent $agent", $r->filename);
    return FORBIDDEN;
}

# This routine creates a pattern matching subroutine from a
# list of pattern matches stored in a file.
sub get_match_sub {
    my($r, $filename) = @_;
    $filename = $r->server_root_relative($filename);
    my $mtime = (stat $filename)[9];

    # try to return the sub from cache
    return $MATCH_CACHE{$filename}->{'sub'} if
        $MATCH_CACHE{$filename} &&
            $MATCH_CACHE{$filename}->{'mod'} >= $mtime;

    # if we get here, then we need to create the sub
    my($fh, @pats);
    return unless $fh = Apache::File->new($filename);
    chomp(@pats = <$fh>); # get the patterns into an array
    my $code = "sub { local \$_ = shift;\n";
    foreach (@pats) {
```

---

* The *mod_rewrite* module may also be worth perusing. Its rewrite rules can be based on the *User-Agent* field, time of day, and other variables.

Example 6-3. Blocking Rude Robots with Apache::BlockAgent (continued)

```
        next if /^#/;
        $code .= "return if /$_/i;\n";
    }
    $code .= "1; }\n";
    $r->server->log->debug("compiled $filename into:\n $code");

    # create the sub, cache and return it
    ($code) = $code =~ /^(.*)$/s; #untaint
    my $sub = $Safe->reval($code);
    unless ($sub) {
        $r->log_error($r->uri, ": ", $@);
        return;
    }
    @{ $MATCH_CACHE{$filename} }{'sub','mod'} = ($sub, $mtime);
    return $MATCH_CACHE{$filename}->{'sub'};
}

1;
__END__
```

Blocking Greedy Clients

A limitation of using pattern matching to identify robots is that it only catches the robots that you know about and that identify themselves by name. A few devious robots masquerade as users by using user agent strings that identify themselves as conventional browsers. To catch such robots, you'll have to be more sophisticated.

A trick that some *mod_perl* developers have used to catch devious robots is to block access to things that *act* like robots by requesting URIs at a rate faster than even the twitchiest of humans can click a mouse. The strategy is to record the time of the initial access by the remote agent and to count the number of requests it makes over a period of time. If it exceeds the speed limit, it gets locked out. *Apache::SpeedLimit* (Example 6-4) shows one way to write such a module.

The module starts out much like the previous examples:

```
    package Apache::SpeedLimit;

    use strict;
    use Apache::Constants qw(:common);
    use Apache::Log ();
    use IPC::Shareable ();
    use vars qw(%DB);
```

Because it needs to track the number of hits each client makes on the site, *Apache::SpeedLimit* faces the problem of maintaining a persistent variable across multiple processes. Here, because performance is an issue in a script that will be called for every URI on the site, we solve the problem by tying a hash to shared memory using *IPC::Shareable*. The tied variable, %DB, is keyed to the name of the remote client. Each entry in the hash holds four values: the time of the client's first access to the site, the time of the most recent access, the number of hits the client has made on the site, and whether the client has been locked out for exceeding the speed limit.*

```
sub handler {
    my $r = shift;
    return DECLINED unless $r->is_main;  # don't handle sub-requests

    my $speed_limit = $r->dir_config('SpeedLimit')  || 10;
    # Accesses per minute
    my $samples = $r->dir_config('SpeedSamples')    || 10;
    # Sampling threshold (hits)
    my $forgive = $r->dir_config('SpeedForgive')    || 20;
    # Forgive after this period
```

The *handler()* subroutine first fetches some configuration variables. The recognized directives include *SpeedLimit*, the number of accesses per minute that any client is allowed to make; *SpeedSamples*, the number of hits that the client must make before the module starts calculating statistics, and *SpeedForgive*, a "statute of limitations" on breaking the speed limit. If the client pauses for *SpeedForgive* minutes before trying again, the module will forgive it and treat the access as if it were the very first one.

A small but important detail is the second line in the handler, where the subroutine declines the transaction unless *is_main()* returns true. It is possible for this handler to be invoked as the result of an internal subrequest, for example, when Apache is rapidly iterating through the contents of an automatically indexed directory to determine the MIME types of each of the directory's files. We do not want such subrequests to count against the user's speed limit totals, so we ignore any request that isn't the main one. *is_main()* returns true for the main request, false for subrequests.

In addition to this, there's an even better reason for the *is_main()* check because the very next thing the handler routine does is to call *lookup_uri()* to look up the requested file's content type and to ignore requests for image files. Without the check, the handler would recurse infinitely:

```
my $content_type = $r->lookup_uri($r->uri)->content_type;
return OK if $content_type =~ m:^image/:i; # ignore images
```

The rationale for the check for image files is that when a browser renders a graphics-intensive page, it generates a flurry of requests for inline images that can easily exceed the speed limit. We don't want to penalize users for this, so we ignore

---

* On systems that don't have *IPC::Shareable* available, a tied DBM file might also work, but you'd have to open and close it each time the module is called. This would have performance implications. A better solution would be to store the information in a DBI database, as described in Chapter 5, *Maintaining State*. Windows systems use a single-process server, and don't have to worry about this issue.

requests for inline images. It's necessary to make a subrequest to fetch the requested file's MIME type because access control handlers ordinarily run before the MIME type checker phase.

If we are dealing with a nonimage document, then it should be counted against the client's total. In the next section of the module, we tie a hash named %DB to shared memory using the *IPC::Shareable* module. We're careful only to tie the variable the first time the handler is called. If %DB is already defined, we don't tie it again:[*]

```
tie %DB, 'IPC::Shareable', 'SPLM', {create => 1, mode => 0644}
  unless defined %DB;
```

The next task is to create a unique ID for the client to use as a key into the hash:

```
my($ip, $agent) = ($r->connection->remote_ip,
                   $r->header_in ('User-Agent'));
my $id = "$ip:$agent";
my $now = time()/60; # minutes since the epoch
```

The client's IP address alone would be adequate in a world of one desktop PC per user, but the existence of multiuser systems, firewalls, and web proxies complicates the issue, making it possible for multiple users to appear to originate at the same IP address. This module's solution is to create an ID that consists of the IP address concatenated with the *User-Agent* field. As long as Microsoft and Netscape release new browsers every few weeks, this combination will spread clients out sufficiently for this to be a practical solution. A more robust solution could make use of the optional cookie generated by Apache's *mod_usertrack* module, but we didn't want to make this example overly complex. A final preparatory task is to fetch the current time and scale it to minute units.

```
tied(%DB)->shlock;
my($first, $last, $hits, $locked) = split ' ', $DB{$id};
```

Now we update the user's statistics and calculate his current fetch speed. In preparation for working with the shared data we call the tied hash's *shlock()* method, locking the data structure for writing. Next, we look up the user's statistics and split them into individual fields.

At this point in the code, we enter a block named **CASE** in which we take a variety of actions depending on the current field values:

```
my $result = OK;
my $l = $r->server->log;
CASE:
  {
```

---

[*] An alternative approach would be to use a *PerlChildInitHandler* to tie the %DB. This technique is described in more detail in Chapter 7, *Other Request Phases.*

Just before entering the block, we set a variable named $result to a default of OK. We also retrieve an *Apache::Log* object to use for logging debugging messages.

The first case we consider is when the $first access time is blank:

```
unless ($first) { # we're seeing this client for the first time
    $l->debug("First request from $ip.  Initializing speed counter.");
    $first = $last = $now;
    $hits = $locked = 0;
    last CASE;
}
```

In this case, we can safely assume that this is the first time we're seeing this client. Our action is to initialize the fields and exit the block.

The second case occurs when the interval between the client's current and last accesses is longer than the grace period:

```
if ($now - $last > $forgive) {
    # beyond the grace period.  Treat like first
    $l->debug("$ip beyond grace period.Reinitializing speed counter.");
    $last = $first = $now;
    $hits = $locked = 0;
    last CASE;
}
```

In this case, we treat this access as a whole new session and reinitialize all the fields to their starting values. This "forgives" the client, even if it previously was locked out.

At this point, we can bump up the number of hits and update the last access time. If the number of hits is too small to make decent statistics, we just exit the block at this point:

```
$last = $now; $hits++;
if ($hits < $samples) {
    $l->debug("$ip not enough samples to calculate speed.");
    last CASE;
}
```

Otherwise, if the user is already locked out, we set the result code to FORBIDDEN and immediately exit the block. Once a client is locked out of the site, we don't unlock it until the grace period has passed:

```
if ($locked) { # already locked out, so forbid access
    $l->debug("$ip locked");
    $result = FORBIDDEN;
    last CASE;
}
```

If the client isn't yet locked out, then we calculate its average fetch speed by dividing the number of accesses it has made by the time interval between now and its

first access. If this value exceeds the speed limit, we set the `$locked` variable to
true and set the result code to FORBIDDEN:

```
my $interval = $now - $first;
$l->debug("$ip speed = ", $hits/$interval);
if ($hits/$interval > $speed_limit) {
    $l->debug("$ip exceeded speed limit.  Blocking.");
    $locked = 1;
    $result = FORBIDDEN;
    last CASE;
}
}
```

At the end of the module, we check the result code. If it's FORBIDDEN we emit a
log entry to explain the situation. We now update %DB with new values for the
access times, number of hits, and lock status and unlock the shared memory.
Lastly, we return the result code to Apache:

```
$r->log_reason("Client exceeded speed limit.", $r->filename)
    if $result == FORBIDDEN;
$DB{$id} = join " ", $first, $now, $hits, $locked;
tied(%DB)->shunlock;

return $result;
}
```

To apply the *Apache::SpeedLimit* module to your entire site, you would create a
configuration file entry like the following:

```
<Location />
  PerlAccessHandler Apache::SpeedLimit
  PerlSetVar        SpeedLimit   20   # max 20 accesses/minute
  PerlSetVar        SpeedSamples 5    # 5 hits before doing statistics
  PerlSetVar        SpeedForgive 30   # amnesty after 30 minutes
</Location>
```

Example 6-4. Blocking Greedy Clients

```
package Apache::SpeedLimit;
# file: Apache/SpeedLimit.pm

use strict;
use Apache::Constants qw(:common);
use Apache::Log ();
use IPC::Shareable ();
use vars qw(%DB);

sub handler {
    my $r = shift;
    return DECLINED unless $r->is_main;  # don't handle sub-requests

    my $speed_limit = $r->dir_config('SpeedLimit') || 10;
    # Accesses per minute
    my $samples = $r->dir_config('SpeedSamples')   || 10;(hits)
```

Example 6-4. Blocking Greedy Clients (continued)

```
    # Sampling threshold (hits)
    my $forgive = $r->dir_config('SpeedForgive')    || 20;
    # Forgive after this period (minutes)
  # Forgive after this period (minutes)

    my $content_type = $r->lookup_uri($r->uri)->content_type;
    return OK if $content_type =~ m:^image/:i; # ignore images
    tie %DB, 'IPC::Shareable', 'SPLM', {create => 1, mode => 0644}
      unless defined %DB;

    my($ip, $agent) = ($r->connection->remote_ip,
                       $r->header_in('User-Agent'));
    my $id = "$ip:$agent";
    my $now = time()/60; # minutes since the epoch

    # lock the shared memory while we work with it
    tied(%DB)->shlock;
    my($first, $last, $hits, $locked) = split ' ', $DB{$id};
    my $result = OK;
    my $l = $r->server->log;
  CASE:
    {
        unless ($first) { # we're seeing this client for the first time
            $l->debug("First request from $ip.  Initializing speed counter.");
            $first = $last = $now;
            $hits = $locked = 0;
            last CASE;
        }

        if ($now - $last > $forgive) {
            # beyond the grace period.  Treat like first
            $l->debug("$ip beyond grace period.Reinitializing speed counter.");
            $last = $first = $now;
            $hits = $locked = 0;
            last CASE;
        }

        # update the values now
        $last = $now; $hits++;
        if ($hits < $samples) {
            $l->debug("$ip not enough samples to calculate speed.");
            last CASE;
        }

        if ($locked) { # already locked out, so forbid access
            $l->debug("$ip locked");
            $result = FORBIDDEN;
            last CASE;
        }

        my $interval = $now - $first;
        $l->debug("$ip speed = ", $hits/$interval);
```

Example 6-4. Blocking Greedy Clients (continued)

```
        if ($hits/$interval > $speed_limit) {
            $l->debug("$ip exceeded speed limit.  Blocking.");
            $locked = 1;
            $result = FORBIDDEN;
            last CASE;
        }
    }

    $r->log_reason("Client exceeded speed limit.", $r->filename)
        if $result == FORBIDDEN;
    $DB{$id} = join " ", $first, $now, $hits, $locked;
    tied(%DB)->shunlock;

    return $result;
}

1;
__END__
```

Authentication Handlers

Let's look at authentication handlers now. The authentication handler's job is to determine whether the user is who he or she claims to be, using whatever standards of proof your module chooses to apply. There are many exotic authentication technologies lurking in the wings, including smart cards, digital certificates, one-time passwords, and challenge/response authentication, but at the moment the types of authentication available to modules are limited at the browser side. Most browsers only know about the username and password system used by Basic authentication. You can design any authentication system you like, but it must ultimately rely on the user typing some information into the password dialog box. Fortunately there's a lot you can do within this restriction, as this section will show.

A Simple Authentication Handler

Example 6-5 implements *Apache::AuthAny*, a module that allows users to authenticate with any username and password at all. The purpose of this module is just to show the API for a Basic authentication handler.

Example 6-5. A Skeleton Authentication Handler

```
package Apache::AuthAny;
# file: Apache/AuthAny.pm

use strict;
use Apache::Constants qw(:common);
```

Example 6-5. A Skeleton Authentication Handler (continued)

```perl
sub handler {
    my $r = shift;

    my($res, $sent_pw) = $r->get_basic_auth_pw;
    return $res if $res != OK;

    my $user = $r->connection->user;
    unless($user and $sent_pw) {
        $r->note_basic_auth_failure;
        $r->log_reason("Both a username and password must be provided",
                       $r->filename);
        return AUTH_REQUIRED;
    }

    return OK;
}

1;
__END__
```

The configuration file entry that goes with it might be:

```
<Location /protected>
  AuthName Test
  AuthType Basic
  PerlAuthenHandler Apache::AuthAny
  require valid-user
</Location>
```

For Basic authentication to work, protected locations must define a realm name
with *AuthName* and specify an *AuthType* of *Basic*. In addition, in order to trigger
Apache's authentication system, at least one *require* directive must be present. In
this example, we specify a requirement of *valid-user*, which is usually used to
indicate that any registered user is allowed access. Last but not least, the *PerlAuthenHandler* directive tells *mod_perl* which handler to call during the authentication phase, in this case *Apache::AuthAny*.

By the time the handler is called, Apache will have done most of the work in
negotiating the HTTP Basic authentication protocol. It will have alerted the
browser that authentication is required to access the page, and the browser will
have prompted the user to enter his name and password. The handler needs only
to recover these values and validate them.

It won't take long to walk through this short module:

```perl
package Apache::AuthAny;
# file: Apache/AuthAny.pm

use strict;
use Apache::Constants qw(:common);
```

```
sub handler {
    my $r = shift;
    my($res, $sent_pw) = $r->get_basic_auth_pw;
```

Apache::AuthAny starts off by importing the common result code constants. Upon entry its *handler()* subroutine immediately calls the Apache method *get_basic_ auth_pw()*. This method returns two values: a result code and the password sent by the client. The result code will be one of the following:

OK

The browser agreed to authenticate using Basic authentication.

DECLINED

The requested URI is protected by a scheme other than Basic authentication, as defined by the *AuthType* configuration directive. In this case, the password field is invalid.

SERVER_ERROR

No realm is defined for the protected URI by the *AuthName* configuration directive.

AUTH_REQUIRED

The browser did not send any *Authorization* header at all, or the browser sent an *Authorization* header with a scheme other than Basic. In either of these cases, the *get_basic_auth_pw()* method will also invoke the *note_basic_auth_ failure()* method described later in this section.

The password returned by *get_basic_auth_pw()* is only valid when the result code is OK. Under all other circumstances you should ignore it. If the result code is anything other than OK the appropriate action is to exit, passing the result code back to Apache:

```
    return $res if $res != OK;
```

If *get_basic_auth_pw()* returns OK, we continue our work. Now we need to find the username to complement the password. Because the username may be needed by later handlers, such as the authorization and logging modules, it's stored in a stable location inside the request object's connection record. The username can be retrieved by calling the request object's *connection()* method to return the current *Apache::Connection* object and then calling the connection object's *user()* method:

```
    my $user = $r->connection->user;
```

The values we retrieve contain exactly what the user typed into the name and password fields of the dialog box. If the user has not yet authenticated, or pressed the submit button without filling out the dialog completely, one or both of these fields may be empty. In this case, we have to force the user to (re)authenticate:

```
    unless($user and $sent_pw) {
        $r->note_basic_auth_failure;
```

```
        $r->log_reason("Both a username and password must be provided",
                    $r->filename);
        return AUTH_REQUIRED;
    }
```

To do this, we call the request object's *note_basic_auth_failure()* method to add the *WWW-Authenticate* field to the outgoing HTTP headers. Without this call, the browser would know it had to authenticate but would not know what authentication method and realm to use. We then log a message to the server error log using the *log_reason()* method and return an AUTH_REQUIRED result code to Apache.

The resulting log entry will look something like this:

```
[Sun Jan 11 16:36:31 1998] [error] access to /protected/index.html
    failed for wallace.telebusiness.co.nz, reason: Both a username and
    password must be provided
```

If, on the other hand, both a username and password are present, then the user has authenticated properly. In this case we can return a result code of OK and end the handler:

```
        return OK;
    }
```

The username will now be available to other handlers and CGI scripts. In particular, the username will be available to any authorization handler further down the handler chain. Other handlers can simply retrieve the username from the connection object just as we did.

Notice that the *Apache::AuthAny* module never actually checks what is inside the username and password. Most authentication modules will compare the username and password to a pair looked up in a database of some sort. However, the *Apache::AuthAny* module is handy for developing and testing applications that require user authentication before the real authentication module has been implemented.

An Anonymous Authentication Handler

Now we'll look at a slightly more sophisticated authentication module, *Apache::AuthAnon*. This module takes the basics of *Apache::AuthAny* and adds logic to perform some consistency checks on the username and password. This module implements anonymous authentication according to FTP conventions. The username must be "anonymous" or "anybody," and the password must look like a valid email address.

Example 6-6 gives the source code for the module. Here is a typical configuration file entry:

```
    <Location /protected>
        AuthName Anonymous
        AuthType Basic
```

```
    PerlAuthenHandler Apache::AuthAnon
    require valid-user

    PerlSetVar Anonymous anonymous|anybody
</Location>
```

Notice that the *<Location>* section has been changed to make *Apache::AuthAnon* the *PerlAuthenHandler* for the */protected* subdirectory and that the realm name has been changed to *Anonymous*. The *AuthType* and *require* directives have not changed. Even though we're not performing real username checking, the *require* directive still needs to be there in order to trigger Apache's authentication handling. A new *PerlSetVar* directive sets the configuration directive *Anonymous* to a case-insensitive pattern match to perform on the provided username. In this case, we're accepting either of the usernames *anonymous* or *anybody*.

Turning to the code listing, you'll see that we use the same basic outline of *Apache::AuthAny*. We fetch the provided password by calling the request object's *get_basic_auth_pw()* method and the username by calling the connection object's *user()* method. We now perform our consistency checks on the return values. First, we check for the presence of a pattern match string in the *Anonymous* configuration variable. If not present, we use a hardcoded default of **anonymous**. Next, we attempt to match the password against an email address pattern. While not RFC-compliant, the $email_pat pattern given here will work in most cases. If either of these tests fails, we log the reason why and reissue a Basic authentication challenge by calling *note_basic_auth_failure()*. If we succeed, we store the provided email password in the request notes table for use by modules further down the request chain.

While this example is not much more complicated than *Apache::AuthAny* and certainly no more secure, it does pretty much everything that a real authentication module will do.

A useful enhancement to this module would be to check that the email address provided by the user corresponds to a real Internet host. One way to do this is by making a call to the Perl *Net::DNS* module to look up the host's IP address and its mail exchanger (an MX record). If neither one nor the other is found, then it is unlikely that the email address is correct.

Example 6-6. Anonymous Authentication

```
package Apache::AuthAnon;
# file: Apathe/AuthAnon.pm

use strict;
use Apache::Constants qw(:common);

my $email_pat = '[.\w-]+\@\w+\.[.\w]*[^.]';
my $anon_id  = "anonymous";
```

Example 6-6. Anonymous Authentication (continued)

```
sub handler {
    my $r = shift;

    my($res, $sent_pwd) = $r->get_basic_auth_pw;
    return $res if $res != OK;

    my $user = lc $r->connection->user;
    my $reason = "";

    my $check_id = $r->dir_config("Anonymous") || $anon_id;

    $reason = "user did not enter a valid anonymous username "
        unless $user =~ /^$check_id$/i;

    $reason .= "user did not enter an email address password "
        unless $sent_pwd =~ /^$email_pat$/o;

    if($reason) {
        $r->note_basic_auth_failure;
        $r->log_reason($reason,$r->filename);
        return AUTH_REQUIRED;
    }

    $r->notes(AuthAnonPassword => $sent_pwd);

    return OK;
}

1;
__END__
```

Authenticating Against a Database

Let's turn to systems that check the user's identity against a database. We debated a bit about what type of authentication database to use for these examples. Candidates included the Unix password file, the Network Information System (NIS), and Bellcore's S/Key one-time password system, but we decided that these were all too Unix-specific. So we turned back to the DBI abstract database interface, which at least is portable across Windows and Unix systems.

Chapter 5, *Maintaining State*, talked about how the DBI interface works, and showed how to use *Apache::DBI* to avoid opening and closing database sessions with each connection. For a little variety, we'll use *Tie::DBI* in this chapter. It's a simple interface to DBI database tables that makes them look like hashes. For example, here's how to tie variable %h to a MySQL database named *test_www*:

```
tie %h, 'Tie::DBI', {
    db    => 'mysql:test_www',
    table => 'user_info',
    key   => 'user_name',
};
```

The options that can be passed to *tie()* include *db* for the database source string or a previously opened database handle, *table* for the name of the table to bind to (in this case, *user_info*), and *key* for the field to use as the hash key (in this case, *user_name*). Other options include authentication information for logging into the database. After successfully tying the hash, you can now access the entire row keyed by username *fred* like this:

```
$record = $h{'fred'}
```

and the *passwd* column of the row like this:

```
$password = $h{'fred'}{'passwd'};
```

Because %h is tied to the *Tie::DBI* class, all stores and retrievals are passed to *Tie::DBI* methods which are responsible for translating the requested operations into the appropriate SQL queries.

In our examples we will be using a MySQL database named *test_www*. It contains a table named *user_info* with the following structure:

```
+-----------+---------------+-------+--------------------+
| user_name | passwd        | level | groups             |
+-----------+---------------+-------+--------------------+
| fred      | 8uUnFnRlW18qQ |     2 | users,devel        |
| andrew    | No9eULpnXZAjY |     2 | users              |
| george    | V8R6zaQuOAWQU |     3 | users              |
| winnie    | L1PKv.rN0UmsQ |     3 | users,authors,devel|
| root      | UOY3rvTFXJAh2 |     5 | users,authors,admin|
| morgana   | 93EhPjGSTjjqY |     1 | users              |
+-----------+---------------+-------+--------------------+
```

The password field is encrypted with the Unix *crypt()* call, which conveniently enough is available to Perl scripts as a built-in function call. The *level* column indicates the user's level of access to the site (higher levels indicate more access). The *groups* field provides a comma-delimited list of groups that the user belongs to, providing another axis along which we can perform authorization. These will be used in later examples.

Tie::DBI is not a standard part of Perl. If you don't have it, you can find it at CPAN in the *modules* subdirectory. You'll also need the *DBI* (database interface) module and a *DBD* (Database Driver) module for the database of your choice.

For the curious, the script used to create this table and its test data are given in Example 6-7. We won't discuss it further here.

Example 6-7. Creating the Test DBI Table

```
#!/usr/local/bin/perl

use strict;
use Tie::DBI ();
```

Example 6-7. Creating the Test DBI Table (continued)

```perl
my $DB_NAME = 'test_www';
my $DB_HOST = 'localhost';

my %test_users = (
                #user_name        groups           level    passwd
                'root'    => [qw(users,authors,admin  5      superman)],
                'george'  => [qw(users                3      jetson)],
                'winnie'  => [qw(users,authors,devel  3      thepooh)],
                'andrew'  => [qw(users                2      llama23)],
                'fred'    => [qw(users,devel          2      bisquet)],
                'morgana' => [qw(users                1      lafey)]
                );

# Sometimes it's easier to invoke a subshell for simple things
# than to use the DBI interface.
open MYSQL, "|mysql -h $DB_HOST -f $DB_NAME" or die $!;
print MYSQL <<END;
    DROP TABLE user_info;
CREATE TABLE user_info (
                    user_name   CHAR(20) primary key,
                    passwd      CHAR(13) not null,
                    level       TINYINT  not null,
                    groups      CHAR(100)
                    );
END

close MYSQL;

tie my %db, 'Tie::DBI', {
    db => "mysql:$DB_NAME:$DB_HOST",
    table => 'user_info',
    key   => 'user_name',
    CLOBBER=>1,
} or die "Couldn't tie to $DB_NAME:$DB_HOST";

my $updated = 0;
for my $id (keys %test_users) {
    my($groups, $level, $passwd) = @{$test_users{$id}};
    $db{$id} = {
        passwd  => crypt($passwd, salt()),
        level   => $level,
        groups  => $groups,
    };
    $updated++;
}
untie %db;
print STDERR "$updated records entered.\n";

# Possible BUG: Assume that this system uses two character
# salts for its crypt().
```

Example 6-7. Creating the Test DBI Table (continued)

```perl
sub salt {
    my @saltset = (0..9, 'A'..'Z', 'a'..'z', '.', '/');
    return join '', @saltset[rand @saltset, rand @saltset];
}
```

To use the database for user authentication, we take the skeleton from *Apache::AuthAny* and flesh it out so that it checks the provided username and password against the corresponding fields in the database. The complete code for *Apache::AuthTieDBI* and a typical configuration file entry are given in Example 6-8.

The *handler()* subroutine is succinct:

```perl
sub handler {
    my $r = shift;

    # get user's authentication credentials
    my($res, $sent_pw) = $r->get_basic_auth_pw;
    return $res if $res != OK;
    my $user = $r->connection->user;

    my $reason = authenticate($r, $user, $sent_pw);

    if($reason) {
        $r->note_basic_auth_failure;
        $r->log_reason($reason, $r->filename);
        return AUTH_REQUIRED;
    }
    return OK;
}
```

The routine begins like the previous authentication modules by fetching the user's password from *get_basic_auth_pw()* and username from *$r->connection->user*. If successful, it calls an internal subroutine named *authenticate()* with the request object, username, and password. *authenticate()* returns *undef* on success or an error message on failure. If an error message is returned, we log the error and return AUTH_REQUIRED. Otherwise, we return OK.

Most of the interesting stuff happens in the *authenticate()* subroutine:

```perl
sub authenticate {
    my($r, $user, $sent_pw) = @_;

    # get configuration information
    my $dsn        = $r->dir_config('TieDatabase') || 'mysql:test_www';
    my $table_data = $r->dir_config('TieTable')    || 'users:user:passwd';
    my($table, $userfield, $passfield) = split ':', $table_data;

    $user && $sent_pw or return 'empty user names and passwords disallowed';
```

Apache::AuthTieDBI relies on two configuration variables to tell it where to look for authentication information: *TieDatabase* indicates what database to use in standard DBI Data Source Notation. *TieTable* indicates what database table and fields to use, in the form `table:username_column:password_column`. If these configuration variables aren't present, the module uses various hardcoded defaults. At this point the routine tries to establish contact with the database by calling *tie()*:

```
tie my %DB, 'Tie::DBI', {
    db => $dsn, table => $table, key => $userfield,
} or return "couldn't open database";
```

Provided that the *Apache::DBI* module was previously loaded (see the section "Storing State Information in SQL Databases" in Chapter 5), the database handle will be cached behind the scenes and there will be no significant overhead for calling *tie()* once per transaction. Otherwise it would be a good idea to cache the tied %DB variable and reuse it as we've done in other modules. We've assumed in this example that the database itself doesn't require authentication. If this isn't the case on your system, modify the call to *tie()* to include the *user* and *password* options:

```
tie my %DB, 'Tie::DBI', {
  db => $dsn, table => $table, key => $userfield,
  user => 'aladdin', password => 'opensesame'
} or return "couldn't open database";
```

Replace the username and password shown here with values that are valid for your database.

The final steps are to check whether the provided user and password are valid:

```
$DB{$user} or return "invalid account";
my $saved_pw = $DB{$user}{$passfield};
$saved_pw eq crypt($sent_pw, $saved_pw) or return "password mismatch";

# if we get here, all is well
return "";
}
```

The first line of this chunk checks whether $user is listed in the database at all. The second line recovers the password from the tied hash, and the third line calls *crypt()* to compare the current password to the stored one.

In case you haven't used *crypt()* before, it takes two arguments, the plain text password and a two- or four-character "salt" used to seed the encryption algorithm. Different salts yield different encrypted passwords.* The returned value is

---

* The salt is designed to make life a bit harder for password-cracking programs that use a dictionary to guess the original plain-text password from the encrypted password. Because there are 4,096 different two-character salts, this increases the amount of disk storage the cracking program needs to store its dictionary by three orders of magnitude. Unfortunately, now that high-capacity disk drives are cheap, this is no longer as much an obstacle as it used to be.

the encrypted password with the salt appended at the beginning. When checking a plain-text password for correctness, it's easiest to use the encrypted password itself as the salt. *crypt()* will use the first few characters as the salt and ignore the rest. If the newly encrypted value matches the stored one, then the user provided the correct plain-text password.

If the encrypted password matches the saved password, we return an empty string to indicate that the checks passed. Otherwise, we return an error message.

Example 6-8. Apache::AuthTieDBI authenticates against a DBI database

```perl
package Apache::AuthTieDBI;

use strict;
use Apache::Constants qw(:common);
use Tie::DBI ();

sub handler {
    my $r = shift;

    # get user's authentication credentials
    my($res, $sent_pw) = $r->get_basic_auth_pw;
    return $res if $res != OK;
    my $user = $r->connection->user;

    my $reason = authenticate($r, $user, $sent_pw);

    if($reason) {
        $r->note_basic_auth_failure;
        $r->log_reason($reason, $r->filename);
        return AUTH_REQUIRED;
    }
    return OK;
}

sub authenticate {
    my($r, $user, $sent_pw) = @_;

    # get configuration information
    my $dsn        = $r->dir_config('TieDatabase') || 'mysql:test_www';
    my $table_data = $r->dir_config('TieTable')    || 'users:user:passwd';
    my($table, $userfield, $passfield) = split ':', $table_data;

    $user && $sent_pw or return 'empty user names and passwords disallowed';

    tie my %DB, 'Tie::DBI', {
        db => $dsn, table => $table, key => $userfield,
    } or return "couldn't open database";

    $DB{$user} or return "invalid account";

    my $saved_pw = $DB{$user}{$passfield};
    $saved_pw eq crypt($sent_pw, $saved_pw) or return "password mismatch";
```

Example 6-8. Apache::AuthTieDBI authenticates against a DBI database (continued)

```
    # if we get here, all is well
    return "";
}

1;
__END__
```

A configuration file entry to go along with *Apache::AuthTieDBI*:

```
<Location /registered_users>
    AuthName "Registered Users"
    AuthType Basic
    PerlAuthenHandler Apache::AuthTieDBI

    PerlSetVar      TieDatabase   mysql:test_www
    PerlSetVar      TieTable      user_info:user_name:passwd

    require valid-user
</Location>
```

The next section builds on this example to show how the other fields in the tied database can be used to implement a customizable authorization scheme.

Authorization Handlers

Sometimes it's sufficient to know that a user can prove his or her identity, but more often that's just the beginning of the story. After authentication comes the optional authorization phase of the transaction, in which your handler gets a chance to determine whether *this* user can fetch *that* URI.

If you felt constrained by HTTP's obsession with conventional password checking, you can now breathe a sigh of relief. Authorization schemes, as opposed to authentication, form no part of the HTTP standard. You are free to implement any scheme you can dream up. In practice, most authentication schemes are based on the user's account name, since this is the piece of information that you've just gone to some effort to confirm. What you do with that datum, however, is entirely up to you. You may look up the user in a database to determine his or her access privileges, or you may grant or deny access based on the name itself. We'll show a useful example of this in the next section.

A Gender-Based Authorization Module

Remember the bar that lets only women through the door on Ladies' Night? Here's a little module that enforces that restriction. *Apache::AuthzGender* enforces gender-based restrictions using Jon Orwant's *Text::GenderFromName*, a port of an *awk* script originally published by Scott Pakin in the December 1991 issue of *Computer Language Monthly. Text::GenderFromName* uses a set of pattern-matching rules to guess people's genders from their first names, returning "m", "f", or *undef* for male names, female names, and names that it can't guess.

Example 6-9 gives the code and a configuration file section to go with it. In order to have a username to operate on, authentication has to be active. This means there must be *AuthName* and *AuthType* directives, as well as a *require* statement. You can use any authentication method you choose, including the standard text, DBM, and DB modules. In this case, we use *Apache::AuthAny* from the example earlier in this chapter because it provides a way of passing in arbitrary usernames.

In addition to the standard directives, *Apache::AuthzGender* accepts a configuration variable named *Gender*. *Gender* can be either of the characters *M* or *F*, to allow access by people of the male and female persuasions, respectively.

Turning to the code (Example 6-9), the *handler()* subroutine begins by retrieving the username by calling the connection object's *user()* method. We know this value is defined because it was set during authentication. Next we recover the value of the *Gender* configuration variable.

We now apply the *Text::GenderFromName* module's *gender()* function to the username and compare the result to the desired value. There are a couple of details to worry about. First, *gender()* is case-sensitive. Unless presented with a name that begins with an initial capital, it doesn't work right. Second, the original *awk* script defaulted to male when it hadn't a clue, but Jon removed this default in order to "contribute to the destruction of the oppressive Patriarchy." A brief test convinced us that the module misses male names far more often than female ones, so the original male default was restored (during our test, the module recognized neither of the author's first names as male!). A few lines are devoted to normalizing the capitalization of usernames, changing the default gender to male, and to uppercasing *gender()*'s return value so that it can be compared to the *Gender* configuration variable.

If there's a mismatch, authorization has failed. We indicate this in exactly the way we do in authorization modules, by calling the request object's *note_basic_auth_failure()* method, writing a line to the log, and returning a status code of AUTH_REQUIRED. If the test succeeds, we return OK.

Example 6-9. Apache::AuthzGender Implements Gender-Based Authorization

```
package Apache::AuthzGender;

use strict;
use Text::GenderFromName qw(gender);
use Apache::Constants qw(:common);

sub handler {
    my $r = shift;

    my $user = ucfirst lc $r->connection->user;
```

Example 6-9. Apache::AuthzGender Implements Gender-Based Authorization (continued)

```
    my $gender = uc($r->dir_config('Gender')) || 'F';

    my $guessed_gender = uc(gender($user)) || 'M';

    unless ($guessed_gender eq $gender) {
        $r->note_basic_auth_failure;
        $r->log_reason("$user is of wrong apparent gender", $r->filename);
        return AUTH_REQUIRED;
    }

    return OK;
}

1;
__END__
```

Example *access.conf*:

```
    <Location /ladies_only>
      AuthName Restricted
      AuthType Basic
      PerlAuthenHandler Apache::AuthAny
      PerlAuthzHandler  Apache::AuthzGender
      PerlSetVar Gender F
      require valid-user
    </Location>
```

Advanced Gender-Based Authorization

A dissatisfying feature of *Apache::AuthzGender* is that when an unauthorized user finally gives up and presses the cancel button, Apache displays the generic "Unauthorized" error page without providing any indication of why the user was refused access. Fortunately this is easy to fix with a custom error response. We can call the request object's *custom_response()* method to display a custom error message, an HTML page, or the output of a CGI script when the **AUTH_REQUIRED** error occurs.

Another problem with *Apache::AuthzGender* is that it uses a nonstandard way to configure the authorization scheme. The standard authorization schemes use a *require* directive as in:

```
    require group authors
```

At the cost of making our module slightly more complicated, we can accommodate this too, allowing access to the protected directory to be adjusted by any of the following directives:

```
    require gender F          # allow females
    require user Webmaster Jeff # allow Webmaster or Jeff
    require valid-user         # allow any valid user
```

Example 6-10 shows an improved *Apache::AuthzGender* that implements these changes. The big task is to recover and process the list of *require* directives. To retrieve the directives, we call the request object's *requires()* method. This method returns an array reference corresponding to all of the *require* directives in the current directory and its parents. Rather than being a simple string, however, each member of this array is actually a hash reference containing two keys: *method_mask* and *requirement*. The *requirement* key is easy to understand. It's simply all the text to the right of the *require* directive (excluding comments). You'll process this text according to your own rules. There's nothing magical about the keywords *user*, *group*, or *valid-user*.

The *method_mask* key is harder to explain. It consists of a bit mask indicating what methods the *require* statement should be applied to. This mask is set when there are one or more *<LIMIT>* sections in the directory's configuration. The GET, PUT, POST, and DELETE methods correspond to the first through fourth bits of the mask (counting from the right). For example, a require directive contained within a *<LIMIT GET POST>* section will have a method mask equal to binary 0101, or decimal 5. If no *<LIMIT>* section is present, the method mask will be -1 (all bits set, all methods restricted). You can test for particular bits using the method *number* constants defined in the *:methods* section of *Apache::Constants*. For example, to test whether the current mask applies to POST requests, you could write a piece of code like this one (assuming that the current *requires()* is in $_):

```
if ($_->{method_mask} & (1 << M_POST)) {
  warn "Current requirements apply to POST";
}
```

In practice, you rarely have to worry about the method mask within your own authorization modules because *mod_perl* automatically filters out any *require* statement that wouldn't apply to the current transaction.

In the example given earlier, the array reference returned by *requires()* would look like this:

```
[
  {
    requirement => 'gender F',
    method_mask => -1
  },
  {
    requirement => 'user Webmaster Jeff',
    method_mask => -1
  },
  {
    requirement => 'valid-user',
    method_mask => -1
  }
]
```

The revised module begins by calling the request object's *requires()* method and storing it in a lexical variable $requires:

```
my $r = shift;
my $requires = $r->requires;
return DECLINED unless $requires;
```

If *requires()* returns *undef*, it means that no require statements were present, so we decline to handle the transaction. (This shouldn't actually happen, but it doesn't hurt to make sure.) The script then recovers the user's name and guesses his or her gender, as before.

Next we begin our custom error message:

```
my $explanation = <<END;
<TITLE>Unauthorized</TITLE>
<H1>You Are Not Authorized to Access This Page</H1>
Access to this page is limited to:
<OL>
END
```

The message will be in a *text/html* page, so we're free to use HTML formatting. The error warns that the user is unauthorized, followed by a numbered list of the requirements that the user must meet in order to gain access to the page (Figure 6-2). This will help us confirm that the requirement processing is working correctly.

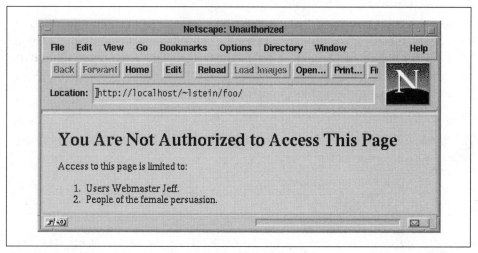

Figure 6-2. The custom error message generated by Apache::AuthzGender specifically lists the requirements that the user has failed to satisfy.

Now we process the requirements one by one by looping over the array contained in $requires:

```
for my $entry (@$requires) {
    my($requirement, @rest) = split /\s+/, $entry->{requirement};
```

For each requirement, we extract the text of the *require* directive and split it on whitespace into the requirement type and its arguments. For example, the line **require gender M** would result in a requirement type of *gender* and an argument of *M*. We act on any of three different requirement types. If the requirement equals *user*, we loop through its arguments seeing if the current user matches any of the indicated usernames. If a match is found, we exit with an OK result code:

```
if (lc $requirement eq 'user') {
    foreach (@rest) { return OK if $user eq $_; }
    $explanation .= "<LI>Users @rest.\n";
}
```

If the requirement equals *gender*, we loop through its arguments looking to see whether the user's gender is correct and again return OK if a match is found:[*]

```
elsif (lc $requirement eq 'gender') {
    foreach (@rest) { return OK if $guessed_gender eq uc $_; }
    $explanation .= "<LI>People of the @G{@rest} persuasion.\n";
}
```

Otherwise, if the requirement equals *valid-user,* then we simply return OK because the authentication module has already made sure of this for us:

```
elsif (lc $requirement eq 'valid-user') {
    return OK;
}
}
$explanation .= "</OL>";
```

As we process each *require* directive, we add a line of explanation to the custom error string. We never use this error string if any of the requirements are satisfied, but if we fall through to the end of the loop, we complete the ordered list and set the explanation as the response for AUTH_REQUIRED errors by passing the explanation string to the request object's *custom_response()* method:

```
$r->custom_response(AUTH_REQUIRED, $explanation);
```

The module ends by noting and logging the failure, and returning an AUTH_REQUIRED status code as before:

```
$r->note_basic_auth_failure;
$r->log_reason("user $user: not authorized", $r->filename);
return AUTH_REQUIRED;
}
```

The logic of this module places a logical OR between the requirements. The user is allowed access to the site if any of the *require* statements is satisfied, which is consistent with the way Apache handles authorization in its standard modules.

---

[*] Because there are only two genders, looping through all the *require* directive's arguments is overkill, but we do it anyway to guard against radical future changes in biology.

However, you can easily modify the logic so that all requirements must be met in order to allow the user access.

Example 6-10. An Improved Apache::AuthzGender

```perl
package Apache::AuthzGender2;

use strict;
use Text::GenderFromName qw(gender);
use Apache::Constants qw(:common);

my %G = ('M' => "male", 'F' => "female");

sub handler {
    my $r = shift;
    my $requires = $r->requires;
    return DECLINED unless $requires;
    my $user = ucfirst lc $r->connection->user;
    my $guessed_gender = uc(gender($user)) || 'M';

    my $explanation = <<END;
<TITLE>Unauthorized</TITLE>
<H1>You Are Not Authorized to Access This Page</H1>
Access to this page is limited to:
<OL>
END

    for my $entry (@$requires) {
        my($requirement, @rest) = split /\s+/, $entry->{requirement};
        if (lc $requirement eq 'user') {
            foreach (@rest) { return OK if $user eq $_; }
            $explanation .= "<LI>Users @rest.\n";
        }
        elsif (lc $requirement eq 'gender') {
            foreach (@rest) { return OK if $guessed_gender eq uc $_; }
            $explanation .= "<LI>People of the @G{@rest} persuasion.\n";
        }
        elsif (lc $requirement eq 'valid-user') {
            return OK;
        }
    }

    $explanation .= "</OL>";

    $r->custom_response(AUTH_REQUIRED, $explanation);
    $r->note_basic_auth_failure;
    $r->log_reason("user $user: not authorized", $r->filename);
    return AUTH_REQUIRED;
}

1;
__END__
```

Authorizing Against a Database

In most real applications you'll be authorizing users against a database of some sort. This section will show you a simple scheme for doing this that works hand-in-glove with the *Apache::AuthTieDBI* database authentication system that we set up in the *"Authenticating Against a Database"* section earlier in this chapter. To avoid making you page backward, we repeat the contents of the test database here:

```
+-----------+---------------+-------+--------------------+
| user_name | passwd        | level | groups             |
+-----------+---------------+-------+--------------------+
|   fred    | 8uUnFnRlW18qQ |     2 | users,devel        |
|   andrew  | No9eULpnXZAjY |     2 | users              |
|   george  | V8R6zaQuOAWQU |     3 | users              |
|   winnie  | L1PKv.rN0UmsQ |     3 | users,authors,devel|
|   root    | UOY3rvTFXJAh2 |     5 | users,authors,admin|
|  morgana  | 93EhPjGSTjjqY |     1 | users              |
+-----------+---------------+-------+--------------------+
```

The module is called *Apache::AuthzTieDBI*, and the idea is to allow for *require* statements like these:

```
require $user_name eq 'fred'
require $level >=2 && $groups =~ /\bauthors\b/;
require $groups =~/\b(users|admin)\b/
```

Each *require* directive consists of an arbitrary Perl expression. During evaluation, variable names are replaced by the name of the corresponding column in the database. In the first example above, we require the username to be exactly *fred*. In the second case, we allow access by any user whose level is greater than or equal to 2 and who belongs to the *authors* group. In the third case, anyone whose groups field contains either of the strings *users* or *admin* is allowed in. As in the previous examples, the require statements are ORed with each other. If multiple *require* statements are present, the user has to satisfy only one of them in order to be granted access. The directive *require valid-user* is treated as a special case and not evaluated as a Perl expression.

Example 6-11 shows the code to accomplish this. Much of it is stolen directly out of *Apache::AuthTieDBI*, so we won't review how the database is opened and tied to the %DB hash. The interesting part begins about midway down the *handler()* method:

```
    if ($DB{$user}) {  # evaluate each requirement
        for my $entry (@$requires) {
            my $op = $entry->{requirement};
            return OK if $op eq 'valid-user';
            $op =~ s/\$\{?(\w+)\}?/\$DB{'$user'}{$1}/g;
            return OK if eval $op;
            $r->log_error($@) if $@;
        }
    }
```

After making sure that the user actually exists in the database, we loop through each of the *require* statements and recover its raw text. We then construct a short string to evaluate, replacing anything that looks like a variable with the appropriate reference to the tied database hash. We next call *eval()* and return OK if a true value is returned. If none of the *require* statements evaluates to true, we log the problem, note the authentication failure, and return AUTH_REQUIRED. That's all there is to it!

Although this scheme works well and is actually quite flexible in practice, you should be aware of one small problem before you rush off and implement it on your server. Because the module is calling *eval()* on Perl code read in from the configuration file, anyone who has write access to the file or to any of the per-directory *.htaccess* files can make this module execute Perl instructions with the server's privileges. If you have any authors at your site whom you don't fully trust, you might think twice about making this facility available to them.

A good precaution would be to modify this module to use the *Safe* module. Add the following to the top of the module:

```
use Safe ();

sub safe_eval {
    package main;
    my($db, $code) = @_;
    my $cpt = Safe->new;
    local *DB = $db;
    $cpt->share('%DB', '%Tie::DBI::', '%DBI::', '%DBD::');
    return $cpt->reval($code);
}
```

The *safe_eval()* subroutine creates a safe compartment and shares the %DB, %Tie::DBI::, %DBI::, and %DBD:: namespaces with it (the list of namespaces to share was identified by trial and error). It then evaluates the *require* code in the safe compartment using *Safe::reval()*.

To use this routine, modify the call to *eval()* in the inner loop to call *save_eval()*:

```
return OK if safe_eval(\%DB, $op);
```

The code will now be executed in a compartment in which dangerous calls like *system()* and *unlink()* have been disabled. With suitable modifications to the shared namespaces, this routine can also be used in other places where you might be tempted to run *eval()*.

Example 6-11. Authorization Against a Database with Apache::AuthzTieDBI

```
package Apache::AuthzTieDBI;
# file: Apache/AuthTieDBI.pm

use strict;
use Apache::Constants qw(:common);
```

Example 6-11. Authorization Against a Database with Apache::AuthzTieDBI (continued)

```perl
use Tie::DBI ();

sub handler {
    my $r = shift;
    my $requires = $r->requires;

    return DECLINED unless $requires;
    my $user = $r->connection->user;

    # get configuration information
    my $dsn        = $r->dir_config('TieDatabase') || 'mysql:test_www';
    my $table_data = $r->dir_config('TieTable')    || 'users:user:passwd';
    my($table, $userfield, $passfield) = split ':', $table_data;

    tie my %DB, 'Tie::DBI', {
        db => $dsn, table => $table, key => $userfield,
    } or die "couldn't open database";

    if ($DB{$user}) {  # evaluate each requirement
        for my $entry (@$requires) {
            my $op = $entry->{requirement};
            return OK if $op eq 'valid-user';
            $op =~ s/\$\{?(\w+)\}?/\$DB{'$user'}{$1}/g;
            return OK if eval $op;
            $r->log_error($@) if $@;
        }
    }

    $r->note_basic_auth_failure;
    $r->log_reason("user $user: not authorized", $r->filename);
    return AUTH_REQUIRED;
}

1;
__END__
```

An *access.conf* entry to go along with this module might look like this:

```
<Location /registered_users>
  AuthName Enlightenment
  AuthType Basic
  PerlAuthenHandler Apache::AuthTieDBI
  PerlSetVar        TieDatabase mysql:test_www
  PerlSetVar        TieTable    user_info:user_name:passwd

  PerlAuthzHandler  Apache::AuthzTieDBI
  require $user_name eq 'fred'
  require $level >=2 && $groups =~ /authors/;
</Location>
```

Before going off and building a 500,000 member authentication database around this module, please realize that it was developed to show the flexibility of using Perl expressions for authentication rather than as an example of the best way to design group membership databases. If you are going to use group membership as

your primary authorization criterion, you would want to normalize the schema so
that the user's groups occupied their own table:

```
+-----------+------------+
| user_name | user_group |
+-----------+------------+
| fred      | users      |
| fred      | devel      |
| andrew    | users      |
| george    | users      |
| winnie    | users      |
| winnie    | authors    |
| winnie    | devel      |
+-----------+------------+
```

You could then test for group membership using a SQL query and the full DBI
API.

Authentication and Authorization's Relationship with Subrequests

If you have been trying out the examples so far, you may notice that the authentication and authorization handlers are called more than once for certain requests.
Chances are, these requests have been for a / directory, where the actual file sent
back is one configured with the *DirectoryIndex* directive, such as *index.html* or
index.cgi. For each file listed in the *DirectoryIndex* configuration, Apache will run
a subrequest to determine if the file exists and has suffecient permissions to use in
the response. As we learned in Chapter 3, *The Apache Module Architecture and
API*, a subrequest will trigger the various request phase handlers, including
authentication and authorization. Depending on the resources required to provide
these services, it may not be desirable for the handlers to run more than once for a
given HTTP request. Auth handlers can avoid being called more than once by
using the *is_initial_req()* method, for example:

```
sub handler {
    my $r = shift;
    return OK unless $r->is_initial_req;
    ...
```

With this test in place, the main body of the handler will only be run once per
HTTP request, during the very first internal request. Note that this approach should
be used with caution, taking your server access configuration into consideration.

Binding Authentication to Authorization

Authorization and authentication work together. Often, as we saw in the previous
example, you find *PerlAuthenHandler* and *PerlAuthzHandlers* side by side in the
same access control section. If you have a pair of handlers that were designed to

work together, and only together, you simplify the directory configuration some-what by binding the two together so that you need only specify the authentica-tion handler.

To accomplish this trick, have the authentication handler call *push_handlers()* with a reference to the authorization handler code before it exits. Because the authentication handler is always called before the authorization handler, this will temporarily place your code on the handler list. After processing the transaction, the authorization handler is set back to its default.

In the case of *Apache::AuthTieDBI* and *Apache::AuthzTieDBI*, the only change we need to make is to place the following line of code in *Apache::AuthTieDBI* some-where toward the top of the handler subroutine:

```
$r->push_handlers(PerlAuthzHandler => \&Apache::AuthzTieDBI::handler);
```

We now need to bring in *Apache::AuthTieDBI* only. The authorization handler will automatically come along for the ride:

```
<Location /registered_users>
  AuthName Enlightenment
  AuthType Basic
  PerlAuthenHandler Apache::AuthTieDBI
  PerlSetVar        TieDatabase mysql:test_www
  PerlSetVar        TieTable    user_info:user_name:passwd
  require $user_name eq 'fred'
  require $level >=2 && $groups =~ /authors/;
</Location>
```

Since the authentication and authorization modules usually share common code, it might make sense to merge the authorization and authentication handlers into the same *.pm* file. This scheme allows you to do that. Just rename the authorization subroutine to something like *authorize()* and keep *handler()* as the entry point for the authentication code. Then at the top of *handler()* include a line like this:

```
$r->push_handlers(PerlAuthzHandler => \&authorize);
```

We can now remove redundant code from the two handlers. For example, in the *Apache::AuthTieDBI* modules, there is common code that retrieves the per-direc-tory configuration variables and opens the database. This can now be merged into a single initialization subroutine.

Cookie-Based Access Control

The next example is a long one. To understand its motivation, consider a large site that runs not one but multiple web servers. Perhaps each server mirrors the others in order to spread out and reduce the load, or maybe each server is responsible for a different part of the site.

Such a site might very well want to have each of the servers perform authentication and access control against a shared database, but if it does so in the obvious way, it faces some potential problems. In order for each of the servers to authenticate against a common database, they will have to connect to it via the network. But this is less than ideal because connecting to a network database is not nearly so fast as connecting to a local one. Furthermore, the database network connections generate a lot of network overhead and compete with the web server for a limited pool of operating-system file descriptors. The performance problem is aggravated if authentication requires the evaluation of a complex SQL statement rather than a simple record lookup.

There are also security issues to consider when using a common authentication database. If the database holds confidential information, such as customer account information, it wouldn't do to give all the web servers free access to the database. A break-in on any of the web servers could compromise the confidentiality of the information.

Apache::TicketAccess was designed to handle these and other situations in which user authentication is expensive. Instead of performing a full authentication each time the user requests a page, the module only authenticates against a relational database the very first time the user connects (see Figure 6-3). After successfully validating the user's identity, the module issues the user a "ticket" to use for subsequent accesses. This ticket, which is no more than an HTTP cookie, carries the user's name, IP address, an expiration date, and a cryptographic signature. Until it expires, the ticket can be used to gain entry to any of the servers at the site. Once a ticket is issued, validating it is fast; the servers merely check the signature against the other information on the ticket to make sure that it hasn't been tampered with. No further database accesses are necessary. In fact, only the machine that actually issues the tickets, the so-called ticket master, requires database connectivity.

The scheme is reasonably secure because the cryptographic signature and the incorporation of the user's IP address make the cookies difficult to forge and intercept, and even if they are intercepted, they are only valid for a short period of time, preventing replay attacks. The scheme is more secure than plain Basic authentication because it greatly reduces the number of times the clear text password passes over the network. In fact, you can move the database authentication functions off the individual web servers entirely and onto a central server whose only job is to check users' credentials and issue tickets. This reduces the exposure of sensitive database information to one machine only.

Another use for a system like this is to implement nonstandard authentication schemes, such as a one-time password or a challenge-response system. The server that issues tickets doesn't need to use Basic authentication. Instead, it can verify the identity of the user in any way that it sees fit. It can ask the user for his

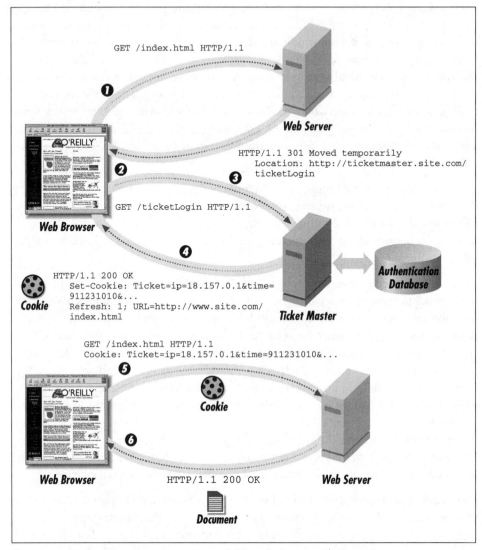

Figure 6-3. In Apache::TicketAccess, the "ticket master" gives browsers an access ticket in the form of a cookie. The ticket is then used for access to other web servers.

mother's maiden name, or enter the value that appears on a SecureID card. Once the ticket is issued, no further user interaction is required.

The key to the ticket system is the MD5 hash algorithm, which we previously used in Chapter 5 to create message authentication checks (MACs). As in that chapter, we will use MD5 here to create authenticated cookies that cannot be tampered with or forged. If you don't already have it, MD5 can be found in CPAN under the *modules* directory.

The tickets used in this system have a structure that looks something like this:

```
IP=$IP time=$time expires=$expires user=$user_name hash=$hash
```

The hash is an MD5 digest that is calculated according to this formula:

```
my $hash=MD5->hexhash($secret .
        MD5->hexhash(join ":", $secret, $IP, $time, $expires, $user_name)
        );
```

The other fields are explained below:

`$secret`

> This is a secret key known only to the servers. The key is any arbitrary string containing ASCII and 8-bit characters. A long set of random characters is best. This key is shared among all the servers in some secure way and updated frequently (once a day or more). It is the only part of the ticket that doesn't appear as plain text.

`$IP`

> The user's IP address. This makes it harder for the ticket to be intercepted and used by outside parties because they would also have to commandeer the user's IP address at the same time.[*]

`$time`

> This is the time and date that the ticket was issued, for use in expiring old tickets.

`$expires`

> This is the number of minutes for which a ticket is valid. After this period of time, the user will be forced to reauthenticate. The longer a ticket is valid, the more convenient it is for the user, but the easier it is for an interloper to intercept the ticket. Shorter expiration times are more secure.

`$user_name`

> This is the user's name, saved from the authentication process. It can be used by the web servers for authorization purposes.

By recovering the individual fields of the ticket, recalculating the hash, and comparing the new hash to the transmitted one, the receiving server can verify that the ticket hasn't been tampered with in transit. The scheme can easily be extended to

---

[*] The incorporation of the IP address into the ticket can be problematic if many of your users are connected to the web through a proxy server (America Online for instance!). Proxy servers make multiple browsers all seem to be coming from the same IP address, defeating this check. Worse, some networks are configured to use multiple proxy servers on a round-robin basis, so the same user may not keep the same apparent IP address within a single session! If this presents a problem for you, you can do one of three things: (1) remove the IP address from the ticket entirely; (2) use just the first three numbers in the IP address (the network part of a class C address); or (3) detect and replace the IP address with one of the fields that proxy servers sometimes use to identify the browser, such as *X-Forwarded-For* (see the description of *remote_ip()* in "The Apache::Connection Class," in Chapter 9, *Perl API Reference Guide*.

encode the user's access privileges, the range of URIs he has access to, or any other information that the servers need to share without going back to a database.

We use two rounds of MD5 digestion to compute the hash rather than one. This prevents a malicious user from appending extra information to the end of the ticket by exploiting one of the mathematical properties of the MD5 algorithm. Although it is unlikely that this would present a problem here, it is always a good idea to plug this known vulnerability.

The secret key is the linchpin of the whole scheme. Because the secret key is known only to the servers and not to the rest of the world, only a trusted web server can issue and validate the ticket. However, there is the technical problem of sharing the secret key among the servers in a secure manner. If the key were intercepted, the interloper could write his own tickets. In this module, we use either of two methods for sharing the secret key. The secret key may be stored in a file located on the filesystem, in which case it is the responsibility of the system administrator to distribute it among the various servers that use it (NFS is one option, *rdist*, FTP, or secure shell are others). Alternatively, the module also allows the secret key to be fetched from a central web server via a URI. The system administrator must configure the configuration files so that only internal hosts are allowed to access it.

We'll take a top-down approach to the module starting with the access control handler implemented by the machines that accept tickets. Example 6-12 gives the code for *Apache::TicketAccess* and a typical entry in the configuration file. The relevant configuration directives look like this:

```
<Location /protected>
  PerlAccessHandler Apache::TicketAccess
  PerlSetVar        TicketDomain   .capricorn.org
  PerlSetVar        TicketSecret  http://master.capricorn.org/secrets/key.txt
  ErrorDocument     403 http://master.capricorn.org/ticketLogin
</Location>
```

These directives set the access control handler to use *Apache::TicketAccess*, and set two per-directory configuration variables using *PerlSetVar*. *TicketDomain* is the DNS domain over which issued tickets are valid. If not specified, the module will attempt to guess it from the server hostname, but it's best to specify that information explicitly. *TicketSecret* is the URI where the shared secret key can be found. It can be on the same server or a different one. Instead of giving a URI, you may specify a physical path to a file on the local system. The contents of the file will be used as the secret.

The last line is an *ErrorDocument* directive that redirects 403 ("Forbidden") errors to a URI on the ticket master machine. If a client fails to produce a valid ticket—or has no ticket at all—the web server it tried to access will reject the request, causing Apache to redirect the client to the ticket master URI. The ticket master will handle the details of authentication and authorization, give the client a ticket, and then redirect it back to the original server.

Turning to the code for *Apache::TicketAccess*, you'll find that it's extremely short because all the dirty work is done in a common utility library named *Apache::TicketTool*. The handler fetches the request object and uses it to create a new *TicketTool* object. The *TicketTool* is responsible for fetching the per-directory configuration options, recovering the ticket from the HTTP headers, and fetching the secret key. Next we call the *TicketTool*'s *verify_ticket()* method to return a result code and an error message. If the result code is true, we return OK.

If *verify_ticket()* returns false, we do something a bit more interesting. We're going to set in motion a chain of events that leads to the client being redirected to the server responsible for issuing tickets. However, after it issues the ticket, we want the ticket master to redirect the browser back to the original page it tried to access. If the ticket issuer happens to be the same as the current server, we can (and do) recover this information from the Apache subrequest record. However, in the general case the server that issues the ticket is not the same as the current one, so we have to cajole the browser into transmitting the URI of the current request to the issuer.

To do this, we invoke the *TicketTool* object's *make_return_address()* method to create a temporary cookie that contains the current request's URI. We then add this cookie to the error headers by calling the request object's *err_header_out()* method. Lastly, we return a FORBIDDEN status code, triggering the *ErrorDocument* directive and causing Apache to redirect the request to the ticket master.

Example 6-12. Ticket-Based Access Control

```
package Apache::TicketAccess;

use strict;
use Apache::Constants qw(:common);
use Apache::TicketTool ();

sub handler {
    my $r = shift;
    my $ticketTool = Apache::TicketTool->new($r);
    my($result, $msg) = $ticketTool->verify_ticket($r);
    unless ($result) {
        $r->log_reason($msg, $r->filename);
        my $cookie = $ticketTool->make_return_address($r);
        $r->err_headers_out->add('Set-Cookie' => $cookie);
        return FORBIDDEN;
    }
    return OK;
}

1;
__END__
```

Now let's have a look at the code to authenticate users and issue tickets. Example 6-13 shows *Apache::TicketMaster*, the module that runs on the central authentication server, along with a sample configuration file entry.

For the ticket issuer, the configuration is somewhat longer than the previous one, reflecting its more complex role:

```
<Location /ticketLogin>
   SetHandler   perl-script
   PerlHandler Apache::TicketMaster
   PerlSetVar   TicketDomain    .capricorn.org
   PerlSetVar   TicketSecret    http://master.capricorn.org/secrets/key.txt
   PerlSetVar   TicketDatabase mysql:test_www
   PerlSetVar   TicketTable     user_info:user_name:passwd
   PerlSetVar   TicketExpires   10
</Location>
```

We define a URI called */ticketLogin*. The name of this URI is arbitrary, but it must match the URI given in protected directories' *ErrorDocument* directive. This module is a standard content handler rather than an authentication handler. Not only does this design allow us to create a custom login screen (Figure 6-4), but we can design our own authentication system, such as one based on answering a series of questions correctly. Therefore, we set the Apache handler to *perl-script* and use a *PerlHandler* directive to set the content handler to *Apache::TicketMaster*.

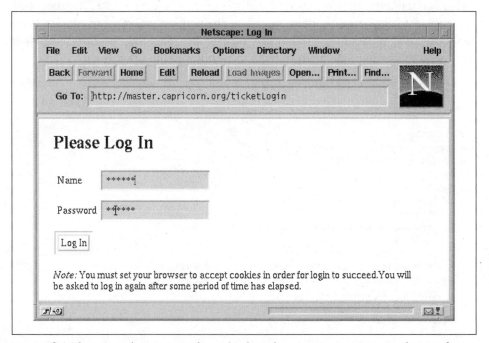

Figure 6-4. The custom login screen shown by the ticket master server prompts the user for a username and password.

Five *PerlSetVar* directives set some per-directory configuration variables. Two of them we've already seen. *TicketDomain* and *TicketSecret* are the same as the corresponding variables on the servers that use *Apache::TicketAccess*, and should be set to the same values throughout the site.

The last three per-directory configuration variables are specific to the ticket issuer. *TicketDatabase* indicates the relational database to use for authentication. It consists of the DBI driver and the database name separated by colons. *TicketTable* tells the module where it can find usernames and passwords within the database. It consists of the table name, the username column and the password column, all separated by colons. The last configuration variable, *TicketExpires*, contains the time (expressed in minutes) for which the issued ticket is valid. After this period of time the ticket expires and the user has to reauthenticate. In this system we measure the ticket expiration time from the time that it was issued. If you wish, you could modify the logic so that the ticket expires only after a certain period of inactivity.

The code is a little longer than *Apache::TicketAccess*. We'll walk through the relevant parts.

```
package Apache::TicketMaster;

use strict;
use Apache::Constants qw(:common);
use Apache::TicketTool ();
use CGI qw(:standard);
```

Apache::TicketMaster loads *Apache::Constants*, the *Apache::TicketTool* module, and CGI.pm, which will be used for its HTML shortcuts.

```
sub handler {
    my $r = shift;
    my($user, $pass) = map { param($_) } qw(user password);
```

Using the reverse logic typical of CGI scripts, the *handler()* subroutine first checks to see whether script parameters named *user* and *password* are already defined, indicating that the user has submitted the fill-out form.

```
    my $request_uri = param('request_uri') ||
        ($r->prev ? $r->prev->uri : cookie('request_uri'));

    unless ($request_uri) {
        no_cookie_error();
        return OK;
    }
```

The subroutine then attempts to recover the URI of the page that the user attempted to fetch before being bumped here. The logic is only a bit twisted. First, we look for a hidden CGI parameter named *request_uri*. This might be present if the user failed to authenticate the first time and resubmits the form. If this parameter isn't present, we check the request object to see whether this request is the result of an internal redirect, which will happen when the same server both accepts and issues tickets. If there is a previous request, we recover its URI. Otherwise, the client may have been referred to us via an external redirect. Using CGI.pm's *cookie()* method, we check the request for a cookie named *request_uri* and recover its value. If we've looked in all these diverse locations and still don't have a location, something's wrong. The most probable. explanation is that the user's browser doesn't accept cookies or the user has turned cookies off. Since the whole security scheme depends on cookies being active, we call an error routine named *no_cookie_error()* that gripes at the user for failing to configure his browser correctly.

```
my $ticketTool = Apache::TicketTool->new($r);
my($result, $msg);
if ($user and $pass) {
    ($result, $msg) = $ticketTool->authenticate($user, $pass);
    if ($result) {
        my $ticket = $ticketTool->make_ticket($r, $user);
        unless ($ticket) {
            $r->log_error("Couldn't make ticket -- missing secret?");
            return SERVER_ERROR;
        }
        go_to_uri($r, $request_uri, $ticket);
        return OK;
    }
}
make_login_screen($msg, $request_uri);
return OK;
}
```

We now go on to authenticate the user. We create a new *TicketTool* from the request object. If both the username and password fields are filled in, we call on *TicketTool's* *authenticate()* method to confirm the user's ID against the database. If this is successful, we call *make_ticket()* to create a cookie containing the ticket information and invoke our *go_to_uri()* subroutine to redirect the user back to the original URI.

If authentication fails, we display an error message and prompt the user to try the login again. If the authentication succeeds, but *TicketTool* fails to return a ticket for some reason, we exit with a server error. This scenario only happens if the secret key cannot be read. Finally, if either the username or the password are missing, or if the authentication attempt failed, we call *make_login_screen()* to display the sign-in page.

The *make_login_screen()* and *no_cookie_error()* subroutines are straightforward, so we won't go over them. However, *go_to_uri()* is more interesting:

```
sub go_to_uri {
    my($r, $requested_uri, $ticket) = @_;
    print header(-refresh => "1; URL=$requested_uri", -cookie => $ticket),
        start_html(-title => 'Successfully Authenticated', -bgcolor => 'white'),
```

```
      h1('Congratulations'),
      h2('You have successfully authenticated'),
      h3("Please stand by..."),
      end_html();
}
```

This subroutine uses CGI.pm methods to create an HTML page that briefly displays a message that the user has successfully authenticated, and then automatically loads the page that the user tried to access in the first place. This magic is accomplished by adding a *Refresh* field to the HTTP header, with a refresh time of one second and a refresh URI of the original page. At the same time, we issue an HTTP cookie containing the ticket created during the authentication process.

Example 6-13. The Ticket Master

```
package Apache::TicketMaster;

use strict;
use Apache::Constants qw(:common);
use Apache::TicketTool ();
use CGI qw(:standard);

# This is the log-in screen that provides authentication cookies.
# There should already be a cookie named "request_uri" that tells
# the login screen where the original request came from.
sub handler {
    my $r = shift;
    my($user, $pass) = map { param($_) } qw(user password);
    my $request_uri = param('request_uri') ||
        ($r->prev ? $r->prev->uri : cookie('request_uri'));

    unless ($request_uri) {
        no_cookie_error();
        return OK;
    }

    my $ticketTool = Apache::TicketTool->new($r);
    my($result, $msg);
    if ($user and $pass) {
        ($result, $msg) = $ticketTool->authenticate($user, $pass);
        if ($result) {
            my $ticket = $ticketTool->make_ticket($r, $user);
            unless ($ticket) {
                $r->log_error("Couldn't make ticket -- missing secret?");
                return SERVER_ERROR;
            }
            go_to_uri($r, $request_uri, $ticket);
            return OK;
        }
    }
    make_login_screen($msg, $request_uri);
    return OK;
}
```

Example 6-13. The Ticket Master (continued)

```perl
sub go_to_uri {
    my($r, $requested_uri, $ticket) = @_;
    print header(-refresh => "1; URL=$requested_uri", -cookie => $ticket),
    start_html(-title => 'Successfully Authenticated', -bgcolor => 'white'),
    h1('Congratulations'),
    h2('You have successfully authenticated'),
    h3("Please stand by..."),
    end_html();
}

sub make_login_screen {
    my($msg, $request_uri) = @_;
    print header(),
    start_html(-title => 'Log In', -bgcolor => 'white'),
    h1('Please Log In');
    print h2(font({color => 'red'}, "Error: $msg")) if $msg;
    print start_form(-action => script_name()),
    table(
        Tr(td(['Name',     textfield(-name => 'user')])),
        Tr(td(['Password', password_field(-name => 'password')]))
        ),
            hidden(-name => 'request_uri', -value => $request_uri),
            submit('Log In'), p(),
            end_form(),
            em('Note: '),
            "Set your browser to accept cookies in order for login to succeed.",
            "You will be asked to log in again after some period of time.";
}

# called when the user tries to log in without a cookie
sub no_cookie_error {
    print header(),
    start_html(-title => 'Unable to Log In', -bgcolor => 'white'),
    h1('Unable to Log In'),
    "This site uses cookies for its own security.  Your browser must be capable ",
    "of processing cookies ", em('and'), " cookies must be activated. ",
    "Please set your browser to accept cookies, then press the ",
    strong('reload'), " button.", hr();
}

1;
__END__
```

By now you're probably curious to see how *Apache::TicketTool* works, so let's have a look at it (Example 6-14).

```perl
package Apache::TicketTool;

use strict;
use Tie::DBI ();
use CGI::Cookie ();
use MD5 ();
use LWP::Simple ();
```

```
use Apache::File ();
use Apache::URI ();
```

We start by importing the modules we need, including *Tie::DBI*, *CGI::Cookie*, and the MD5 module.

```
my $ServerName = Apache->server->server_hostname;

my %DEFAULTS = (
    'TicketDatabase' => 'mysql:test_www',
    'TicketTable'    => 'user_info:user_name:passwd',
    'TicketExpires'  => 30,
    'TicketSecret'   => 'http://$ServerName/secret_key.txt',
    'TicketDomain'   => undef,
);

my %CACHE;  # cache objects by their parameters to minimize time-consuming
operations
```

Next we define some default variables that were used during testing and development of the code and an object cache named %CACHE. %CACHE holds a pool of TicketTool objects and was designed to increase the performance of the module. Rather than reading the secret key each time the module is used, the key is cached in memory. This cache is flushed every time there is a ticket mismatch, allowing the key to be changed frequently without causing widespread problems. Similarly, we cache the name of the name of the server, by calling *Apache->server->server_hostname* (see "The Apache::Server Class" in Chapter 9 for information on retrieving other server configuration values).

```
sub new {
    my($class, $r) = @_;
    my %self = ();
    foreach (keys %DEFAULTS) {
        $self{$_} = $r->dir_config($_) || $DEFAULTS{$_};
    }
    # post-process TicketDatabase and TicketDomain
    ($self{TicketDomain} = $ServerName) =~ s/^[^.]+//
        unless $self{TicketDomain};

    # try to return from cache
    my $id = join '', sort values %self;
    return $CACHE{$id} if $CACHE{$id};

    # otherwise create new object
    return $CACHE{$id} = bless \%self, $class;
}
```

The *TicketTool new()* method is responsible for initializing a new *TicketTool* object or fetching an appropriate old one from the cache. It reads the per-directory configuration variables from the passed request object and merges them with the defaults. If no *TicketDomain* variable is present, it attempts to guess one from the server hostname. The code that manages the cache indexes the cache array with the values of the per-directory variables so that several different configurations can coexist peacefully.

```
sub authenticate {
    my($self, $user, $passwd) = @_;
    my($table, $userfield, $passwdfield) = split ':', $self->{TicketTable};

    tie my %DB, 'Tie::DBI', {
        'db'    => $self->{TicketDatabase},
        'table' => $table, 'key' => $userfield,
    } or return (undef, "couldn't open database");

    return (undef, "invalid account")
        unless $DB{$user};

    my $saved_passwd = $DB{$user}->{$passwdfield};
    return (undef, "password mismatch")
        unless $saved_passwd eq crypt($passwd, $saved_passwd);

    return (1, '');
}
```

The *authenticate()* method is called by the ticket issuer to authenticate a username and password against a relational database. This method is just a rehash of the *Tie::DBI* database authentication code that we have seen in previous sections.

```
sub fetch_secret {
    my $self = shift;
    unless ($self->{SECRET_KEY}) {
        if ($self->{TicketSecret} =~ /^http:/) {
            $self->{SECRET_KEY} = LWP::Simple::get($self->{TicketSecret});
        } else {
            my $fh = Apache::File->new($self->{TicketSecret}) || return undef;
            $self->{SECRET_KEY} = <$fh>;
        }
    }
    $self->{SECRET_KEY};
}
```

The *fetch_secret()* method is responsible for fetching the secret key from disk or via the web. The subroutine first checks to see whether there is already a secret key cached in memory and returns that if present. Otherwise it examines the value of the *TicketSecret* variable. If it looks like a URI, we load the LWP *Simple* module and use it to fetch the contents of the URI.* If *TicketSecret* doesn't look like a URI, we attempt to open it as a physical pathname using *Apache::File* methods and read its contents. We cache the result and return it.

---

* The LWP library (Library for Web Access in Perl) is available at any CPAN site and is highly recommended for web client programming. We use it again in Chapter 7 when we develop a banner-ad blocking proxy.

```
sub invalidate_secret { undef shift->{SECRET_KEY}; }
```

The *invalidate_secret()* method is called whenever there seems to be a mismatch between the current secret and the cached one. This method deletes the cached secret, forcing the secret to be reloaded the next time it's needed.

The *make_ticket()* and *verify_ticket()* methods are responsible for issuing and checking tickets:

```
sub make_ticket {
    my($self, $r, $user_name) = @_;
    my $ip_address = $r->connection->remote_ip;
    my $expires = $self->{TicketExpires};
    my $now = time;
    my $secret = $self->fetch_secret() or return undef;
    my $hash = MD5->hexhash($secret .
                MD5->hexhash(join ':', $secret, $ip_address, $now,
                            $expires, $user_name)
            );
    return CGI::Cookie->new(-name => 'Ticket',
                            -path => '/',
                            -domain => $self->{TicketDomain},
                            -value => {
                              'ip' => $ip_address,
                              'time' => $now,
                              'user' => $user_name,
                              'hash' => $hash,
                              'expires' => $expires,
                            });
}
```

make_ticket() gets the user's name from the caller, the browser's IP address from the request object, the expiration time from the value of the *TicketExpires* configuration variable, and the secret key from the *fetch_secret()* method. It then concatenates these values along with the current system time and calls MD5's *hexhash()* method to turn them into an MD5 digest.

The routine now incorporates this digest into an HTTP cookie named *Ticket* by calling *CGI::Cookie->new()*. The cookie contains the hashed information, along with plain text versions of everything except for the secret key. A cute feature of *CGI::Cookie* is that it serializes simple data structures, allowing you to turn hashes into cookies and later recover them. The cookie's domain is set to the value of *TicketDomain*, ensuring that the cookie will be sent to all servers in the indicated domain. Note that the cookie itself has no expiration date. This tells the browser to keep the cookie in memory only until the user quits the application. The cookie is never written to disk.

```
sub verify_ticket {
    my($self, $r) = @_;
    my %cookies = CGI::Cookie->parse($r->header_in('Cookie'));
```

```
        return (0, 'user has no cookies') unless %cookies;
        return (0, 'user has no ticket') unless $cookies{'Ticket'};
        my %ticket = $cookies{'Ticket'}->value;
        return (0, 'malformed ticket')
            unless $ticket{'hash'} && $ticket{'user'} &&
                $ticket{'time'} && $ticket{'expires'};
        return (0, 'IP address mismatch in ticket')
            unless $ticket{'ip'} eq $r->connection->remote_ip;
        return (0, 'ticket has expired')
            unless (time - $ticket{'time'})/60 < $ticket{'expires'};
        my $secret;
        return (0, "can't retrieve secret")
            unless $secret = $self->fetch_secret;
        my $newhash = MD5->hexhash($secret .
                        MD5->hexhash(join ':', $secret,
                            @ticket{qw(ip time expires user)})
                );
        unless ($newhash eq $ticket{'hash'}) {
            $self->invalidate_secret;   #maybe it's changed?
            return (0, 'ticket mismatch');
        }
        $r->connection->user($ticket{'user'});
         return (1, 'ok');
    }
```

verify_ticket() does the same thing but in reverse. It calls *CGI::Cookie->parse()* to parse all cookies passed in the HTTP header and stow them into a hash. The method then looks for a cookie named *Ticket*. If one is found, it recovers each of the ticket's fields and does some consistency checks. The method returns an error if any of the ticket fields are missing, if the request's IP address doesn't match the ticket's IP address, or if the ticket has expired.

verify_ticket() then calls *secret_key()* to get the current value of the secret key and recomputes the hash. If the new hash doesn't match the old one, then either the secret key has changed since the ticket was issued or the ticket is a forgery. In either case, we invalidate the cached secret and return false, forcing the user to repeat the formal authentication process with the central server. Otherwise the function saves the username in the connection object by calling `$r->connection->user($ticket{'user'})` and returns true result code. The username is saved into the connection object at this point so that authorization and logging handlers will have access to it. It also makes the username available to CGI scripts via the `REMOTE_USER` environment variable.

```
    sub make_return_address {
        my($self, $r) = @_;
        my $uri = Apache::URI->parse($r, $r->uri);
        $uri->scheme("http");
        $uri->hostname($r->get_server_name);
        $uri->port($r->get_server_port);
        $uri->query(scalar $r->args);
```

```
        return CGI::Cookie->new(-name => 'request_uri',
                                -value => $uri->unparse,
                                -domain => $self->{TicketDomain},
                                -path => '/');
    }
```

The last method, *make_return_address()*, is responsible for creating a cookie to transmit the URI of the current request to the central authentication server. It recovers the server hostname, port, path, and CGI variables from the request object and turns it into a full URI. It then calls *CGI::Cookie->new()* to incorporate this URI into a cookie named *request_uri*, which it returns to the caller. *scheme()*, *hostname()*, and the other URI processing calls are explained in detail in Chapter 9, under "The Apache::URI Class."

Example 6-14. The Ticket Issuer

```
package Apache::TicketTool;

use strict;
use Tie::DBI ();
use CGI::Cookie ();
use MD5 ();
use LWP::Simple ();
use Apache::File ();
use Apache::URI ();

my $ServerName = Apache->server->server_hostname;

my %DEFAULTS = (
   'TicketDatabase' => 'mysql:test_www',
   'TicketTable'    => 'user_info:user_name:passwd',
   'TicketExpires'  => 30,
   'TicketSecret'   => 'http://$ServerName/secret_key.txt',
   'TicketDomain'   => undef,
);

my %CACHE;  # cache objects by their parameters to minimize time-consuming
operations

# Set up default parameters by passing in a request object
sub new {
    my($class, $r) = @_;
    my %self = ();
    foreach (keys %DEFAULTS) {
       $self{$_} = $r->dir_config($_) || $DEFAULTS{$_};
    }
    # post-process TicketDatabase and TicketDomain
    ($self{TicketDomain} = $ServerName) =~ s/^[^.]+//
       unless $self{TicketDomain};

    # try to return from cache
    my $id = join '', sort values %self;
    return $CACHE{$id} if $CACHE{$id};
```

Example 6-14. The Ticket Issuer (continued)

```perl
    # otherwise create new object
    return $CACHE{$id} = bless \%self, $class;
}


# TicketTool::authenticate()
# Call as:
# ($result,$explanation) = $ticketTool->authenticate($user,$passwd)
sub authenticate {
    my($self, $user, $passwd) = @_;
    my($table, $userfield, $passwdfield) = split ':', $self->{TicketTable};

    tie my %DB, 'Tie::DBI', {
        'db'    => $self->{TicketDatabase},
        'table' => $table, 'key' => $userfield,
    } or return (undef, "couldn't open database");

    return (undef, "invalid account")
        unless $DB{$user};

    my $saved_passwd = $DB{$user}->{$passwdfield};
    return (undef, "password mismatch")
        unless $saved_passwd eq crypt($passwd, $saved_passwd);

    return (1, '');
}


# TicketTool::fetch_secret()
# Call as:
# $ticketTool->fetch_secret();
sub fetch_secret {
    my $self = shift;
    unless ($self->{SECRET_KEY}) {
        if ($self->{TicketSecret} =~ /^http:/) {
            $self->{SECRET_KEY} = LWP::Simple::get($self->{TicketSecret});
        } else {
            my $fh = Apache::File->new($self->{TicketSecret}) || return undef;
            $self->{SECRET_KEY} = <$fh>;
        }
    }
    $self->{SECRET_KEY};
}


# invalidate the cached secret
sub invalidate_secret { undef shift->{SECRET_KEY}; }


# TicketTool::make_ticket()
# Call as:
# $cookie = $ticketTool->make_ticket($r,$username);
#
sub make_ticket {
    my($self, $r, $user_name) = @_;
    my $ip_address = $r->connection->remote_ip;
    my $expires = $self->{TicketExpires};
    my $now = time;
```

Example 6-14. The Ticket Issuer (continued)

```perl
    my $secret = $self->fetch_secret() or return undef;
    my $hash = MD5->hexhash($secret .
                 MD5->hexhash(join ':', $secret, $ip_address, $now,
                               $expires, $user_name)
               );
    return CGI::Cookie->new(-name => 'Ticket',
                            -path => '/',
                            -domain => $self->{TicketDomain},
                            -value => {
                               'ip' => $ip_address,
                               'time' => $now,
                               'user' => $user_name,
                               'hash' => $hash,
                               'expires' => $expires,
                            });
}


# TicketTool::verify_ticket()
# Call as:
# ($result,$msg) = $ticketTool->verify_ticket($r)
sub verify_ticket {
    my($self, $r) = @_;
    my %cookies = CGI::Cookie->parse($r->header_in('Cookie'));
    return (0, 'user has no cookies') unless %cookies;
    return (0, 'user has no ticket') unless $cookies{'Ticket'};
    my %ticket = $cookies{'Ticket'}->value;
    return (0, 'malformed ticket')
        unless $ticket{'hash'} && $ticket{'user'} &&
            $ticket{'time'} && $ticket{'expires'};
    return (0, 'IP address mismatch in ticket')
        unless $ticket{'ip'} eq $r->connection->remote_ip;
    return (0, 'ticket has expired')
        unless (time - $ticket{'time'})/60 < $ticket{'expires'};
    my $secret;
    return (0, "can't retrieve secret")
        unless $secret = $self->fetch_secret;
    my $newhash = MD5->hexhash($secret .
                    MD5->hexhash(join ':', $secret,
                            @ticket{qw(ip time expires user)})
                 );
    unless ($newhash eq $ticket{'hash'}) {
        $self->invalidate_secret;   #maybe it's changed?
        return (0, 'ticket mismatch');
    }
    $r->connection->user($ticket{'user'});
    return (1, 'ok');
}


# Call as:
# $cookie = $ticketTool->make_return_address($r)
sub make_return_address {
    my($self, $r) = @_;
    my $uri = Apache::URI->parse($r, $r->uri);
```

Example 6-14. The Ticket Issuer (continued)

```
    $uri->scheme("http");
    $uri->hostname($r->get_server_name);
    $uri->port($r->get_server_port);
    $uri->query(scalar $r->args);

    return CGI::Cookie->new(-name => 'request_uri',
                            -value => $uri->unparse,
                            -domain => $self->{TicketDomain},
                            -path => '/');
}

1;
__END__
```

Authentication with the Secure Sockets Layer

The Secure Sockets Layer (SSL) is a widely used protocol for encrypting Internet transmissions. It was originally introduced by Netscape for use with its browser and server products and has been adapted by the Internet Engineering Task Force (IETF) for use in its standard Transport Layer Security (TLS) protocol.

When an SSL-enabled browser talks to an SSL-enabled server, they exchange cryptographic certificates and authenticate each other using secure credentials known as digital certificates. They then set up an encrypted channel with which to exchange information. Everything that the browser sends to the server is encrypted, including the requested URI, cookies, and the contents of fill-out forms, and everything that the server returns to the browser is encrypted as well.

For the purposes of authentication and authorization, SSL can be used in two ways. One option is to combine SSL encryption with Basic authentication. The Basic authentication protocol continues to work exactly as described in the previous section, but now the user's password is protected from interception because it is part of the encrypted data stream. This option is simple and doesn't require any code changes.

The other option is to use the browser's digital certificate for authorization. The server automatically attempts to authenticate the browser's digital certificate when it first sets up the SSL connection. If it can't, the SSL connection is refused. If you wish, you can use the information provided in the browser's certificate to decide whether this user is authorized to access the requested URI. In addition to the user's name, digital certificates contain a variety of standard fields and any number of optional ones; your code is free to use any of these fields to decide whether the user is authorized.

The main advantage of the digital certificate solution is that it eliminates the problems associated with passwords—users forgetting them or, conversely, choosing ones that are too easy to guess. The main disadvantage is that most users don't use digital certificates. On most of the public Web, authentication is one-way only. The server authenticates itself to the browser, but not vice-versa. Therefore, authentication by digital certificate is only suitable in intranet environments where the company issues certificates to its employees as a condition of their accessing internal web servers.

There are several SSL-enabled versions of Apache, and there will probably be more in the future. Each offers a different combination of price, features, and support. The current list follows:

Open-source (free) versions:

* Ben Laurie's Apache SSL at *http://www.apache-ssl.org/*
* Ralf S. Engelschall's *mod_ssl* at *http://www.engelschall.com/sw/mod_ssl/*

Commercial versions:

* C2Net Stronghold at *http://www.c2.net/*
* Covalent Raven SSL Module at *http://raven.covalent.net/*
* Red Hat Secure Server at *http://www.redhat.com/products/*

Using Digital Certificates for Authorization

The SSL protocol does most of its work at a level beneath the workings of the HTTP protocol. The exchange and verificaton of digital certificates and the establishment of the encrypted channel all occur before any of Apache's handlers run. For this reason, authorization based on the contents of a digital certificate looks quite different from the other examples we've seen in this chapter. Furthermore, the details of authorization vary slightly among the different implementations of ApacheSSL. This section describes the way it works in Ralf S. Engelschall's *mod_ ssl*. If you are using a different version of ApacheSSL, you should check your vendor's documentation for differences.

The text representation of a typical client certificate is shown in Example 6-15. It consists of a "Subject" section, which gives information on the person to whom the certificate is issued, and a "Certificate" section, which gives information about the certificate itself. Within the Subject section are a series of tag=value pairs. There can be an arbitrary number of such pairs, but several are standard and can be found in any certificate:

CN   User's common name

EMail   User's email address

O   User's organization (employer)

OU   Organizational unit (e.g., department)

L   User's locality, usually a city or town

SP   User's state or province

C   User's country code

The user's distinguished name (DN) is a long string consisting of the concatenation of each of these fields in the following format:

```
/C=US/SP=MA/L=Boston/O=Capricorn Organization/OU=Sales/CN=Wanda/
Email=wanda@capricorn.com
```

European users will recognize the footprints of the OSI standards committee here. The DN is guaranteed to be unique among all the certificates issued by a particular certificate-granting authority.

The Certificate section contains the certificate's unique serial number and other data, followed by more tag=value pairs giving information about the organization issuing the certificate. The standard fields are the same as those described for the Subject. This is followed by a Validity period, which gives the span of time that the certificate should be considered valid.

You are free to use any of these fields for authorization. You can authorize based on the user's CN field, on the certificate's serial number, on the Validity period, on the DN, or on any of the Subject or Issuer tags.

The certificate information is actually stored in a compact binary form rather than the text form shown here. When the connection is established, the SSL library parses out the certificate fields and stores them in a private data structure. During the *fixup* phase, these fields are turned into various environment variables with names like `SSL_CLIENT_S_DN_CN` (to be read as "the common name subfield of the distinguished name of the subject section of the client's certificate"). However, the mappings between certificate field and environment variable differ from version to version of ApacheSSL, and you will have to check your vendor's documentation for the details.

Example 6-15. An Example Client Certificate

```
Subject:
    C=US
    SP=MA
    L=Boston
    O=Capricorn Organization
    OU=Sales
    CN=Wanda
    Email=wanda@capricorn.com

Certificate:
    Data:
        Version: 1 (0x0)
```

Example 6-15. An Example Client Certificate (continued)

```
      Serial Number: 866229881 (0x33a19e79)
      Signature Algorithm: md5WithRSAEncryption
   Issuer:
      C=US
      SP=MA
      L=Boston
      O=Capricorn Consulting
      OU=Security Services
      CN=Capricorn Signing Services Root CA
      Email=lstein@capricorn.com
   Validity:
          Not Before: Jun 13 19:24:41 1998 GMT
          Not After : Jun 13 19:24:41 1999 GMT
```

The most straightforward way to authenticate based on certificate information is to take advantage of the *SSLRequire* access control directive. In *mod_ssl*, such a directive might look like this:

```
<Location /certified>
    SSLRequire  %{SSL_CLIENT_S_DN_CN} in ("Wanda Henderson","Joe Bloe") \
                and %{REMOTE_ADDR} =~ m/^192\.128\.3\.[0-9]+$/
</Location>
```

This requires that the CN tag of the DN field of the *S*ubject section of the certificate match either "Wanda Henderson" or "Joe Bloe", and that the browser's IP address satisfy a pattern match placing it within the 192.128.3 subnetwork. *mod_ssl* has a rich language for querying the contents of the client certificate. See its documentation for the details. Other ApacheSSL implementations also support operations similar to *SSLRequire*, but they differ somewhat in detail.

Note that to Apache, *SSLRequire* is an access control operation rather than an authentication/authorization operation. This is because no action on the part of the user is needed to gain access—his browser either has the right certificate, or it doesn't.

A slightly more involved technique for combining certificate information with user authorization is to take advantage of the *FakeBasicAuth* option of the *SSLOptions* directive. When this option is enabled, *mod_ssl* installs an authentication handler that retrieves the DN from the certificate. The handler base64-encodes the DN and a hardcoded password (consisting of the string "password"), stuffs them into the incoming *Authorization* header field, and returns DECLINED. In effect, this fakes the ordinary Basic authentication process by making it seem as if the user provided a username and password pair. The DN is now available for use by downstream authentication and authorization modules, where it appears as the username.

However, using *FakeBasicAuth* means that *mod_ssl* must be the first authentication handler run for the request and that an authentication handler further down the chain must be able to authenticate using the client's DN. It is much simpler to bypass all authentication handlers and obtain of the DN by using a subrequest. This takes advantage of the fact that during the fixup phase, *mod_ssl* places parsed copies of the certificate fields into the subprocess environment table, preparatory to copying them into a CGI script's environment.

As an example, we'll show a simple authorization module named *Apache::AuthzSSL* which checks that a named field of the DN name matches that given in one or more *require* directives. A typical configuration section will look like this:

```
SSLVerifyClient require
SSLVerifyDepth 2
SSLCACertificateFile  conf/ssl.crt/ca-bundle.crt
<Directory /usr/local/apache/htdocs/ID/please>
    SSLRequireSSL
    AuthName SSL
    AuthType Basic
    PerlAuthenHandler Apache::OK
    PerlAuthzHandler  Apache::AuthzSSL
    require  C US
    require  O "Capricorn Organization"
    require OU Sales Marketing
</Directory>
```

The *SSLVerifyClient* directive, which must be present in the main part of the configuration file, requires that browsers present client certificates. The *SSLVerify-Depth* and *SSLCACertificateFile* directives are used to configure how deeply *mod_ssl* should verify client certificates (see the *mod_ssl* documentation for details). The *SSLRequireSSL* directive requires that SSL be active in order to access the contents of this directory.

AuthName and *AuthType* are not required, since we are not performing Basic authentication, but we put them in place just in case some module downstream is expecting them. Since the password is invariant when client certificate verification is in use, we bypass password checking by installing *Apache::OK* as the authentication handler for this directory.* *Apache::OK* is a ring module that exits with an OK result code. We then install *Apache::AuthzSSL* as the authorization handler and give it three different *require* statements to satisfy. We require that the country field equal "US," the organization field equal "Capricorn Organization," and the organizational unit be one of "Sales" or "Marketing."

Example 6-16 gives the code for *Apache::AuthzSSL*. It brings in *Apache::Constants* and the *quotewords()* text parsing function from the standard *Text::ParseWords*

---

* *Apache::OK* is always available, along with *Apache::DECLINED*, since they are imported from *Apache::Constants* by *Apache.pm* at server startup time.

module. It recovers the request object and calls its *requires()* method to retrieve the list of authorization requirements that are in effect.

The handler then issues a subrequest and retrieves the value of SSL_CLIENT_DN from the subrequest's environment table. The subrequest is necessary because the parsed certificate fields aren't placed into the table until the fixup stage, which ordinarily occurs after the authorization phase. Notice that the handler returns OK if *is_main()* returns false, avoiding infinite recursion during the subrequest. Once the DN is recovered, it is split into its individual fields using a pattern match operation.

Now the routine loops through each of the requirements, breaking them into a DN field name and a list of possible values, each of which it checks in turn. If none of the specified values matches the DN, we log an error and return a FORBIDDEN (not an AUTH_REQUIRED) status code. If we satisfy all the requirements and fall through to the bottom of the loop, we return an OK result code.

Example 6-16. Authorizing Clients Based On Their Digital Certificate's DN

```
package Apache::AuthzSSL;

use strict;
use Apache::Constants qw(:common);
use Text::ParseWords  qw(quotewords);

sub handler {
    my $r = shift;
    return OK unless $r->is_main;

    my $requires = $r->requires;
    return DECLINED unless $requires;

    my $subr = $r->lookup_uri($r->uri);
    my $dn = $subr->subprocess_env('SSL_CLIENT_S_DN');
    return DECLINED unless $dn;
    my(%dn) = $dn =~ m{/([^=]+)=([^/]+)}g;

  REQUIRES:
    for my $entry (@$requires) {
        my($field, @values) = quotewords('\s+', 0, $entry->{requirement});
        foreach (@values) {
            next REQUIRES if $dn{$field} eq $_;
        }
        $r->log_reason("user $dn{CN}: not authorized", $r->filename);
        return FORBIDDEN;
    }
    # if we get here, then we passed all the requirements
    return OK;
}

1;
__END__
```

The only subtlety in this module is the rationale for returning FORBIDDEN in an authorization module rather than in the more typical *note_basic_auth_failure()* call followed by AUTH_REQUIRED. The reason for this is that returning AUTH_REQUIRED will set in motion a chain of events that will ultimately result in the user being prompted for a username and password. But there's nothing the user can type in to satisfy this module's requirements, so this is just a tease. Returning FORBIDDEN, in contrast, will display a more accurate message denying the user permission to view the page.

A more advanced certificate authorization module would probably go to a database to determine whether the incoming certificate satisfied the requirements.

As another example, Example 6-17 shows a small access handler that rejects all certificates issued by out-of-state issuers. It does so by looking at the value of the subprocess variable SSL_CLIENT_I_DN_SP, which returns the issuer's state or province code. This handler can be installed with a configuration section like this one:

```
SSLVerifyClient require
 <Location /government/local>
    SSLRequireSSL
    PerlAccessHandler Apache::CheckCertState
    PerlSetVar  IssuerState Maryland
 </Location>
```

The code simply retrieves the contents of the *IssuerState* configuration variable and the SSL_CLIENT_I_DN_SP subprocess environment variable. If either is undefined, the handler returns DECLINED. Next the handler checks whether the two variables are equal, and if so, returns OK. Otherwise the routine returns FORBIDDEN, displaying the "access denied" message on the user's browser.

Example 6-17. Apache::CheckCertState Checks the SP (State/Province) Field of the Certificate Issuer

```
package Apache::CheckCertState;
# file: Apache/CheckCertState.pm
use Apache::Constants qw(:common);

sub handler {
    my $r = shift;
    return DECLINED unless $r->is_main;
    my $state = $r->dir_config('IssuerState');
    return DECLINED unless defined $state;
    my $subr = $r->lookup_uri($r->uri);
    my $client_state = $subr->subprocess_env('SSL_CLIENT_I_DN_SP') || "";
    return OK if $client_state eq $state;
    return FORBIDDEN;
}

1;
__END__
```

We hope this chapter has given you some idea of the range and versatility of Apache modules for controlling who can gain access to your site and what they do once they've connected. With the tools and examples presented in this chapter as a starting point, you should be able to implement almost any access control system you can imagine.

The next chapter turns to some of the more esoteric handlers and module functionality, showing you a variety of techniques for simplifying Apache administration and customizing the server's behavior.

7

Other Request Phases

The previous chapters have taken you on a wide-ranging tour of the most popular and useful areas of the Apache API. But we're not done yet! The Apache API allows you to customize URI translation, logging, the handling of proxy transactions, and the manner in which HTTP headers are parsed. There's even a way to incorporate snippets of Perl code directly into HTML pages that use server-side includes.

We've already shown you how to customize the response, authentication, authorization, and access control phases of the Apache request cycle. Now we'll fill in the cracks. At the end of the chapter, we show you the Perl server-side include system, and demonstrate a technique for extending the Apache Perl API by subclassing the Apache request object itself.

The Child Initialization and Exit Phases

Apache provides hooks into the child process initialization and exit handling. The child process initialization handler, installed with *PerlChildInitHandler,* is called just after the main server forks off a child but before the child has processed any incoming requests. The child exit handler, installed with *PerlChildExitHandler*, is called just before the child process is destroyed.

You might need to install handlers for these phases in order to perform some sort of module initialization that won't survive a fork. For example, the *Apache::DBI* module has a child init handler that initializes a cache of per-child database connections, and the *Apache::Resource* module steps in during this phase to set up resource limits on the child processes. The latter is configured in this way:

```
PerlChildInitHandler Apache::Resource
```

Like other handlers, you can install a child init handler programmatically using *Apache::push_handlers()*. However, because the child init phase comes so early, the only practical place to do this is from within the parent process, in either a Perl startup file configured with a *PerlModule* or *PerlRequire* directive. For example, here's how to install an anonymous subroutine that will execute during child initialization to choose a truly random seed value for Perl's random number generator (using the *Math::TrulyRandom* module):

```
use Math::TrulyRandom ();
Apache->push_handlers(PerlChildInitHandler => sub {
    srand Math::TrulyRandom::truly_random_value();
});
```

Install this piece of code in the Perl startup file. By changing the value of the random number seed on a per-child basis, it ensures that each child process produces a different sequence of random numbers when the built-in *rand()* function is called.

The child exit phase complements the child initialization phase. Child processes may exit for various reasons: the *MaxRequestsPerChild* limit may have been reached, the parent server was shut down, or a fatal error occurred. This phase gives modules a chance to tidy up after themselves before the process exits.

The most straightforward way to install a child exit handler is with the explicit *PerlChildExitHandler* directive, as in:

```
PerlChildExitHandler Apache::Guillotine
```

During the child exit phase, *mod_perl* invokes the Perl API function *perl_destruct()* to run the contents of END blocks and to invoke the DESTROY method for any global objects that have not gone out of scope already.* Refer to the section "Special Global Variables, Subroutines, and Literals" in Chapter 9, *Perl API Reference Guide*, for details.

---

* *perl_destruct()* is an internal Perl subroutine that is normally called just once by the Perl executable after a script is run.

Note that neither child initialization nor exit hooks are available on Win32 platforms since the Win32 port of Apache uses a single process.

The Post Read Request Phase

When a listening server receives an incoming request, it reads the HTTP request line and parses any HTTP headers sent along with it. Provided that what's been read is valid HTTP, Apache gives modules an early chance to step in during the *post_read_request* phase, known to the Perl API world as the *PerlPostReadRequest-Handler*. This is the very first callback that Apache makes when serving an HTTP request, and it happens even before URI translation turns the requested URI into a physical pathname.

The *post_read_request* phase is a handy place to initialize per-request data that will be available to other handlers in the request chain. Because of its usefulness as an initialization routine, *mod_perl* provides the directive *PerlInitHandler* as a more readable alias to *PerlPostReadRequestHandler*.

Since the *post_read_request* phase happens before URI translation, *PerlPost-ReadRequestHandler* cannot appear in *<Location>*, *<Directory>*, or *<Files>* sections. However, the *PerlInitHandler* directive is actually a bit special. When it appears outside a *<Directory>* section, it acts as an alias for *PerlPostReadRequest-Handler* as just described. However, when it appears within a *<Directory>* section, it acts as an alias for *PerlHeaderParserHandler* (discussed later in this chapter), allowing for per-directory initialization. In other words, wherever you put *Perl-InitHandler*, it will act the way you expect.

Several optional Apache modules install handlers for the *post_read_request* phase. For example, the *mod_unique_id* module steps in here to create the UNIQUE_ID environment variable. When the module is activated, this variable is unique to each request over an extended period of time and so is useful for logging and the generation of session IDs (see Chapter 5, *Maintaining State*). Perl scripts can get at the value of this variable by reading $ENV{UNIQUE_ID} or by calling $r-> subprocess_env('UNIQUE_ID').

mod_setenvif also steps in during this phase to allow you to set environment variables based on the incoming client headers. For example, this directive will set the environment variable LOCAL_REFERRAL to true if the *Referer* header matches a certain regular expression:

```
SetEnvIf Referer \.acme\.com LOCAL_REFERRAL
```

mod_perl itself uses the *post_read_request* phase to process the *PerlPassEnv* and *PerlSetEnv* directives, allowing environment variables to be passed to modules that execute early in the request cycle. The built-in Apache equivalents, *PassEnv* and

SetEnv, don't get processed until the fixup phase, which may be too late. The *Apache::StatINC* module, which watches *.pm* files for changes and reloads them if necessary, is also usually installed into this phase:

```
PerlPostReadRequestHandler Apache::StatINC
PerlInitHandler Apache::StatINC  # same thing, but easier to type
```

The URI Translation Phase

One of the web's virtues is its Uniform Resource Identifier (URI) and Uniform Resource Locator (URL) standards. End users never know for sure what is sitting behind a URI. It could be a static file, a dynamic script, a proxied request, or something even more esoteric. The file or program behind a URI may change over time, but this too is transparent to the end user.

Much of Apache's power and flexibility comes from its highly configurable URI translation phase, which comes relatively early in the request cycle, after the *post_read_request* and before the *header_parser phases*. During this phase, the URI requested by the remote browser is translated into a physical filename, which may in turn be returned directly to the browser as a static document or passed on to a CGI script or Apache API module for processing. During URI translation, each module that has declared its interest in handling this phase is given a chance to modify the URI. The first module to handle the phase (i.e., return something other than a status of DECLINED) terminates the phase. This prevents several URI translators from interfering with one another by trying to map the same URI onto several different file paths.

By default, two URI translation handlers are installed in stock Apache distributions. The *mod_alias* module looks for the existence of several directives that may apply to the current URI. These include *Alias, ScriptAlias, Redirect, AliasMatch,* and other directives. If it finds one, it uses the directive's value to map the URI to a file or directory somewhere on the server's physical filesystem. Otherwise, the request falls through to the default URI translation handler, which simply appends the URI to the value of the *DocumentRoot* configuration directive, forming a file path relative to the document root.

The optional *mod_rewrite* module implements a much more comprehensive URI translator that allows you to slice and dice URIs in various interesting ways. It is extremely powerful but uses a series of pattern matching conditions and substitution rules that can be difficult to get right.

Once a translation handler has done its work, Apache walks along the returned filename path in the manner described in Chapter 4, *Content Handlers,* finding where the path part of the URI ends and the additional path information begins.

This phase of processing is performed internally and cannot be modified by the module API.

In addition to their intended role in transforming URIs, translation handlers are sometimes used to associate certain types of URIs with specific upstream handlers. We'll see examples of this later in the chapter when we discuss creating custom proxy services in the section "Handling Proxy Requests."

A Very Simple Translation Handler

Let's look at an example. Many of the documents browsed on a web site are files that are located under the configured *DocumentRoot*. That is, the requested URI is a filename relative to a directory on the hard disk. Just so you can see how simple a translation handler's job can be, we present a Perl version of Apache's default translation handler found in the *http_core* module.

```perl
package Apache::DefaultTrans;

use Apache::Constants qw(:common BAD_REQUEST);
use Apache::Log ();

sub handler {
    my $r = shift;
    my $uri = $r->uri;

    if($uri !~ m:^/: or index($uri, '*')) {
        $r->log->error("Invalid URI in request ", $r->the_request);
        return BAD_REQUEST;
    }

    $r->filename($r->document_root . $r->uri);

    return OK;
}

1;
__END__
```

The handler begins by subjecting the requested URI to a few sanity checks, making sure that it begins with a slash and doesn't contain any * characters. If the URI fails these tests, we log an error message and return **BAD_REQUEST**. Otherwise, all is well and we join together the value of the *DocumentRoot* directive (retrieved by calling the request object's *document_root()* method) and the URI to create the complete file path. The file path is now written into the request object by passing it to the *filename()* method.

We don't check at this point whether the file exists or can be opened. This is the job of handlers further down the request chain.

To install this handler, just add the following directive to the main part of your *perl.conf* configuration file (or any other Apache configuration file, if you prefer):

```
PerlTransHandler Apache::DefaultTrans
```

Beware. You probably won't want to keep this handler installed for long. Because it overrides other translation handlers, you'll lose the use of *Alias*, *ScriptAlias*, and other standard directives.

A Practical Translation Handler

Here's a slightly more complex example. Consider a web-based system for archiving software binaries and source code. On a nightly basis an automated system will copy changed and new files from a master repository to multiple mirror sites. Because of the vagaries of the Internet, it's important to confirm that the entire file, and not just a fragment of it, is copied from one mirror site to the other.

One technique for solving this problem would be to create an MD5 checksum for each file and store the information on the repository. After the mirror site copies the file, it checksums the file and compares it against the master checksum retrieved from the repository. If the two values match, then the integrity of the copied file is confirmed.

In this section, we'll begin a simple system to retrieve precomputed MD5 checksums from an archive of files. To retrieve the checksum for a file, you simply append the extension *.cksm* to the end of its URI. For example, if the archived file you wish to retrieve is:

```
/archive/software/cookie_cutter.tar.gz
```

then you can retrieve a text file containing its MD5 checksum by fetching this URI:

```
/archive/software/cookie_cutter.tar.gz.cksm
```

The checksum files will be precomputed and stored in a physical directory tree that parallels the document hierarchy. For example, if the document itself is physically stored in:

```
/home/httpd/htdocs/archive/software/cookie_cutter.tar.gz
```

then its checksum will be stored in a parallel tree in this file:

```
/home/httpd/checksums/archive/software/cookie_cutter.tar.gz
```

The job of the URI translation handler is to map requests for */file/path/file-name.cksm* files into the physical file */home/httpd/checksums/file/path/filename*. When called from a browser, the results look something like the screenshot in Figure 7-1.

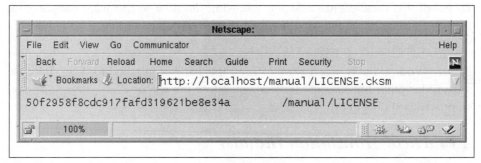

Figure 7-1. A checksum file retrieved by Apache::Checksum1

As often happens with Perl programs, the problem takes longer to state than to
solve. Example 7-1 shows a translation handler, *Apache::Checksum1*, that accomplishes this task. The structure is similar to other Apache Perl modules. After the
usual preamble, the *handler()* subroutine shifts the Apache request object off the
call stack and uses it to recover the URI of the current request, which is stashed in
the local variable `$uri`. The subroutine next looks for a configuration directive
named *ChecksumDir* which defines the top of the tree where the checksums are
to be found. If defined, *handler()* stores the value in a local variable named
`$cksumdir`. Otherwise, it assumes a default value defined in `DEFAULT_CHECKSUM_
DIR`.

Now the subroutine checks whether this URI needs special handling. It does this
by attempting a string substitution which will replace the *.cksm* URI with a physical path to the corresponding file in the checksums directory tree. If the substitution returns a false value, then the requested URI does not end with the *.cksm*
extension and we return `DECLINED`. This leaves the requested URI unchanged and
allows Apache's other translation handlers to work on it. If, on the other hand, the
substitution returns a true result, then `$uri` holds the correct physical pathname to
the checksum file. We call the request object's *filename()* method to set the physical path returned to Apache and return `OK`. This tells Apache that the URI was successfully translated and prevents any other translation handlers from being called.

Example 7-1. A URI Translator for Checksum Files

```
package Apache::Checksum1;
# file: Apache/Checksum1.pm
use strict;
use Apache::Constants qw(:common);
use constant DEFAULT_CHECKSUM_DIR => '/usr/tmp/checksums';

sub handler {
    my $r = shift;
    my $uri = $r->uri;
    my $cksumdir = $r->dir_config('ChecksumDir') || DEFAULT_CHECKSUM_DIR;
    $cksumdir = $r->server_root_relative($cksumdir);
```

Example 7-1. A URI Translator for Checksum Files (continued)

```
    return DECLINED unless $uri =~ s!^(.+)\.cksm$!$cksumdir$1!;
    $r->filename($uri);
    return OK;
}


1;
__END__
```

The configuration for this translation handler should look something like this:

```
# checksum translation handler directives
PerlTransHandler  Apache::Checksum1
PerlSetVar        ChecksumDir /home/httpd/checksums
<Directory /home/httpd/checksums>
  ForceType text/plain
</Directory>
```

This configuration declares a URI translation handler with the *PerlTransHandler* directive and sets the Perl configuration variable *ChecksumDir* to */home/httpd/ checksums*, the top of the checksum tree. We also need a *<Directory>* section to force all files in the checksums directory to be of type *text/plain*. Otherwise, the default MIME type checker will try to use each checksum file's extension to determine its MIME type.

There are a couple of important points about this configuration section. First, the *PerlTransHandler* and *PerlSetVar* directives are located in the main section of the configuration file, not in a *<Directory>*, *<Location>*, or *<Files>* section. This is because the URI translation phase runs very early in the request processing cycle, before Apache has a definite URI or file path to use in selecting an appropriate *<Directory>*, *<Location>*, or *<Files>* section to take its configuration from. For the same reason, *PerlTransHandler* is not allowed in *.htaccess* files, although you can use it in virtual host sections.

The second point is that the *ForceType* directive is located in a *<Directory>* section rather than in a *<Location>* block. The reason for this is that the *<Location>* section refers to the requested URI, which is not changed by this particular translation handler. To apply access control rules and other options to the physical file path returned by the translation handler, you must use *<Directory>* or *<Files>*.

To set up the checksum tree, you'll have to write a script that will recurse through the web document hierarchy (or a portion of it) and create a mirror directory of checksum files. In case you're interested in implementing a system like this one, Example 7-2 gives a short script named *checksum.pl* that does this. It uses the *File::Find* module to walk the tree of source files, the *MD5* module to generate MD5 checksums, and *File::Path* and *File::Basename* for filename manipulations. New checksum files are only created if the checksum file doesn't exist or the modification time of the source file is more recent than that of an existing checksum file.

You call the script like this:

```
% checksum.pl -source ~www/htdocs -dest ~www/checksums
```

Replace *~www/htdocs* and *~www/checksums* with the paths to the web document tree and the checksums directory on your system.

Example 7-2. checksum.pl Creates a Parallel Tree of Checksum Files

```perl
#!/usr/local/bin/perl

use File::Find;
use File::Path;
use File::Basename;
use IO::File;
use MD5;
use Getopt::Long;
use strict;
use vars qw($SOURCE $DESTINATION $MD5);

GetOptions('source=s'      =>  \$SOURCE,
           'destination=s' =>  \$DESTINATION)  || die <<USAGE;
Usage: $0
       Create a checksum tree.
Options:
     -source        <path>  File tree to traverse [.]
     -destination   <path>  Destination for checksum tree [TMPDIR]
Option names may be abbreviated.
USAGE

$SOURCE       ||= '.';
$DESTINATION ||= $ENV{TMPDIR} || '/tmp';
die "Must specify absolute destination directory" unless $DESTINATION=~m!^/!;
$MD5 = new MD5;

find(\&wanted,$SOURCE);

# This routine is called for each node (directory or file) in the
# source tree.  On entry, $_ contains the filename,
# and $File::Find::name contains its full path.
sub wanted {
    return unless -f $_ && -r _;
    my $modtime = (stat _)[9];
    my ($source,$dest,$url);
    $source = $File::Find::name;
    ($dest = $source)=~s/^$SOURCE/$DESTINATION/o;
    return if -e $dest && $modtime <= (stat $dest)[9];
    ($url = $source) =~s/^$SOURCE//o;
    make_checksum($_,$dest,$url);
}

# This routine is called with the source file, the destination in which
# to write the checksum, and a URL to attach as a comment to the checksum.
sub make_checksum {
```

Example 7-2. checksum.pl Creates a Parallel Tree of Checksum Files (continued)

```
    my ($source,$dest,$url) = @_;
    my $sfile = IO::File->new($source) || die "Couldn't open $source: $!\n";
    mkpath dirname($dest);  # create the intermediate directories
    my $dfile = IO::File->new(">$dest") || die "Couldn't open $dest: $!\n";
    $MD5->reset;
    $MD5->addfile($sfile);
    print $dfile $MD5->hexdigest(),"\t$url\n"; # write the checksum
}
__END__
```

Using a Translation Handler to Change the URI

Instead of completely translating a URI into a filename, a translation handler can modify the URI itself and let other handlers do the work of completing the translation into a physical path. This is very useful because it allows the handler to interoperate with other URI translation directives such as *Alias* and *UserDir*.

To change the URI, your translation handler should set it with the Apache request object's *uri()* method instead of (or in addition to) the *filename()* method $r->uri($new_uri);.

After changing the URI, your handler should then return DECLINED, *not* OK. This may seem counter-intuitive. However, by returning DECLINED, your translation handler is telling Apache that it has declined to do the actual work of matching the URI to a filename and is asking Apache to pass the modified request on to other registered translation handlers.

Example 7-3 shows a reworked version of the checksum translation handler that alters the URI rather than sets the filename directly. The code is nearly identical to the first version of this module, but instead of retrieving a physical directory path from a *PerlSetVar* configuration variable named *ChecksumDir*, the handler looks for a variable named *ChecksumPath* which is expected to contain the virtual (URI space) directory in which the checksums can be found. If the variable isn't defined, then */checksums* is assumed. We perform the string substitution on the requested URI as before. If the substitution succeeds, we write the modified URI back into the request record by calling the request object's *uri()* method. We then return DECLINED so that Apache will pass the altered request on to other translation handlers.

Example 7-3. A Translation Handler That Changes the URI

```
package Apache::Checksum2;
# file: Apache/Checksum2.pm
use strict;
use Apache::Constants qw(:common);
use constant DEFAULT_CHECKSUM_PATH => '/checksums';
```

Example 7-3. A Translation Handler That Changes the URI (continued)

```
sub handler {
    my $r = shift;
    my $uri = $r->uri;
    my $cksumpath = $r->dir_config('ChecksumPath') || DEFAULT_CHECKSUM_PATH;
    return DECLINED unless $uri =~ s!^(.+)\.cksm$!$cksumpath$1!;
    $r->uri($uri);
    return DECLINED;
}


1;
__END__
```

The configuration file entries needed to work with *Apache::Checksum2* are shown below. Instead of passing the translation handler a physical path in the *Checksum-Dir* variable, we use *ChecksumPath* to pass a virtual URI path. The actual translation from a URI to a physical path is done by the standard *mod_alias* module from information provided by an *Alias* directive. Another point to notice is that because the translation handler changed the URI, we can now use a *<Location>* section to force the type of the checksum files to *text/plain*.

```
PerlTransHandler   Apache::Checksum2
PerlSetVar         ChecksumPath /checksums
Alias              /checksums/ /home/www/checksums/
<Location /checksums>
  ForceType text/plain
</Location>
```

In addition to interoperating well with other translation directives, this version of the checksum translation handler deals correctly with the implicit retrieval of *index.html* files when the URI ends in a directory name. For example, retrieving the partial URI */archive/software/.cksm* will be correctly transformed into a request for */home/httpd/checksums/archive/software/index.html*.

On the downside, this version of the translation module may issue potentially confusing error messages if a checksum file is missing. For example, if the user requests URI */archive/software/index.html.cksm* and the checksum file is not present, Apache's default "Not Found" error message will read, "The requested URL /checksums/archive/software/index.html was not found on this server." The user may be confused to see an error message that refers to a URI other than the one he requested.

Another example of altering the URI on the fly can be found in Chapter 5, where we used a translation handler to manage session IDs embedded in URIs. This handler copies the session ID from the URI into an environment variable for later use by the content handler, then strips the session ID from the URI and writes it back into the request record.

Installing a Custom Response Handler in the URI Translation Phase

In addition to its official use as the place to modify the URI and filename of the requested document, the translation phase is also a convenient place to set up custom content handlers for particular URIs. To continue with our checksum example, let's generate the checksum from the requested file on the fly rather than using a precomputed value. This eliminates the need to maintain a parallel directory of checksum files but adds the cost of additional CPU cycles every time a checksum is requested.

Example 7-4 shows *Apache::Checksum3*. It's a little longer than the previous examples, so we'll step through it a chunk at a time.

```
package Apache::Checksum3;
# file: Apache/Checksum3.pm
use strict;
use Apache::Constants qw(:common);
use Apache::File ();
use MD5 ();

my $MD5 = MD5->new;
```

Because this module is going to produce the MD5 checksum itself, we bring in the *Apache::File* and MD5 modules. We then create a file-scoped lexical MD5 object that will be used within the package to generate the MD5 checksums of requested files.

```
sub handler {
    my $r = shift;
    my $uri = $r->uri;
    return DECLINED unless $uri =~ s/\.cksm$//;
    $r->uri($uri);
```

We define two subroutines. The first, named *handler()*, is responsible for the translation phase of the request. Like its predecessors, this subroutine recovers the URI from the request object and looks for the telltale *.cksm* extension. However, instead of constructing a new path that points into the checksums directory, we simply strip off the extension and write the modified path back into the request record.

```
    $r->handler("perl-script");
    $r->push_handlers(PerlHandler => \&checksum_handler);
    return DECLINED;
}
```

Now the interesting part begins. We set the request's content handler to point to the second subroutine in the module, *checksum_handler()*. This is done in two phases. First we call `$r->handler("perl-script")` to tell Apache to invoke the Perl interpreter for the content phase of the request. Next we call *push_handlers()*

to tell Perl to call our *checksum_handler()* method when the time comes. Together, these routines have the same effect as the configuration directives *SetHandler* and *PerlHandler*. Our work done, we return a result code of DECLINED in order to let the other translation handlers do their job.

Apache will now proceed as usual through the authorization, authentication, MIME type checking, and fixup phases until it gets to the content phase, at which point *Apache::Checksum3* will be reentered through the *checksum_handler()* routine:

```
sub checksum_handler {
    my $r = shift;
    my $file = $r->filename;
    my $sfile = Apache::File->new($file) || return DECLINED;
    $r->content_type('text/plain');
    $r->send_http_header;
    return OK if $r->header_only;
    $MD5->reset;
    $MD5->addfile($sfile);
    $r->print($MD5->hexdigest(),"\t",$r->uri,"\n");
    return OK;
}
```

Like the various content handlers we saw in Chapter 4, *checksum_handler()* calls the request object's *filename()* method to retrieve the physical filename and attempts to open it, returning DECLINED in case of an error. The subroutine sets the content type to *text/plain* and sends the HTTP header. If this is a HEAD request, we return. Otherwise, we invoke the MD5 module's *reset()* method to clear the checksum algorithm, call *addfile()* to process the contents of the file, and then *hexdigest()* to emit the checksum.

Because this module is entirely self-contained, it has the simplest configuration of them all:

```
PerlTransHandler Apache::Checksum3
```

Like other *PerlTransHandler* directives, this one must be located in the main part of the configuration file or in a virtual host section.

Example 7-4. Calculating Checksums on the Fly

```
package Apache::Checksum3;
# file: Apache/Checksum3.pm
use strict;
use Apache::Constants qw(:common);
use Apache::File ();
use MD5 ();

my $MD5 = MD5->new;

sub handler {
    my $r = shift;
    my $uri = $r->uri;
    return DECLINED unless $uri =~ s/\.cksm$//;
```

Example 7-4. Calculating Checksums on the Fly (continued)

```
    $r->uri($uri);
    $r->handler("perl-script");
    $r->push_handlers(PerlHandler => \&checksum_handler);
    return DECLINED;
}

sub checksum_handler {
    my $r = shift;
    my $file = $r->filename;
    my $sfile = Apache::File->new($file) || return DECLINED;
    $r->content_type('text/plain');
    $r->send_http_header;
    return OK if $r->header_only;
    $MD5->reset;
    $MD5->addfile($sfile);
    $r->print($MD5->hexdigest(),"\t",$r->uri,"\n");
    return OK;
}

1;
__END__
```

Don't think that you must always write a custom translation handler in order to gain control over the URI translation phase. The powerful *mod_rewrite* module gives you great power to customize this phase. For example, by adding a *mod_ rewrite RewriteRule* directive, you can define a substitution rule that transforms requests for *.cksm* URIs into requests for files in the checksum directory, doing in a single line what our first example of a translation handler did in 17.

The Header Parser Phase

After Apache has translated the URI into a filename, it enters the *header parser* phase. This phase gives handlers a chance to examine the incoming request header and to take special action, perhaps altering the headers on the fly (as we will do below to create an anonymous proxy server) or blocking unwanted transactions at an early stage. For example, the header parser phase is commonly used to block unwanted robots before they consume the server resources during the later phases. You could use the *Apache::BlockAgent* module, implemented as an access handler in the last chapter, to block robots during this earlier phase.

Header parser handlers are installed with the *PerlHeaderParserHandler*. Because the URI has been mapped to a filename at this point, the directive is allowed in *.htaccess* files and directory configuration sections, as well as in the main body of the configuration files. All registered header parser handlers will be run unless one returns an error code or DONE.

When *PerlInitHandler* is used within a directory section or a *.htaccess* file, it acts as an alias for *PerlHeaderParserHeader*.

Implementing an Unsupported HTTP Method

One nontrivial use for the header parser phase is to implement an unsupported HTTP request method. The Apache server handles the most common HTTP methods, such as GET, HEAD, and POST. Apache also provides hooks for managing the less commonly used PUT and DELETE methods, but the work of processing the method is left to third-party modules to implement. In addition to these methods, there are certain methods that are part of the HTTP/1.1 draft that are not supported by Apache at this time. One such method is PATCH, which is used to change the contents of a document on the server side by applying a "diff" file provided by the client.[*]

This section will show how to extend the Apache server to support the PATCH method. The same techniques can be used to experiment with other parts of HTTP drafts or customize the HTTP protocol for special applications.

If you've never worked with patch files, you'll be surprised at how insanely useful they are. Say you have two versions of a large file, an older version named *file.1.html* and a newer version named *file.2.html*. You can use the Unix *diff* command to compute the difference between the two, like this:

```
% diff file.1.html file.2.html > file.diff
```

When *diff* is finished, the output file, *file.diff*, will contain only the lines that have changed between the two files, along with information indicating the positions of the changed lines in the files. You can examine a diff file in a text editor to see how the two files differ. More interestingly, however, you can use Larry Wall's *patch* program to apply the diff to *file.1.html*, transforming it into a new file identical to *file.2.html*. *patch* is simple to use:

```
% patch file.1.html < file.diff
```

Because two versions of the same file tend to be more similar than they are different, diff files are usually short, making it much more efficient to send the diff file around than the entire new version. This is the rationale for the HTTP/1.1 PATCH method. It complements PUT, which is used to transmit a whole new document to the server, by sending what should be changed between an existing document and a new one. When a client requests a document with the PATCH method, the URI it provides corresponds to the file to be patched, and the request's content is the diff file to be applied.

---

[*] Just two weeks prior to the production stage of this book, *Script* support for the PATCH method was added in Apache 1.3.4-dev.

Example 7-5 gives the code for the PATCH handler, appropriately named *Apache::PATCH*. It defines both the server-side routines for accepting PATCH documents, and a small client-side program to use for submitting patch files to the server.

```
package Apache::PATCH;
# file: Apache/PATCH.pm

use strict;
use vars qw($VERSION @EXPORT @ISA);
use Apache::Constants qw(:common BAD_REQUEST);
use Apache::File ();
use File::Basename 'dirname';

@ISA = qw(Exporter);
@EXPORT = qw(PATCH);
$VERSION = '1.00';

use constant PATCH_TYPE => 'application/diff';
my $PATCH_CMD = "/usr/local/bin/patch";
```

We begin by pulling in required modules, including *Apache::File* and *File::Basename*. We also bring in the *Exporter* module. This is not used by the server-side routines but is needed by the client-side library to export the *PATCH()* subroutine. We now declare some constants, including a MIME type for the submitted patch files, the location of the *patch* program on our system, and two constants that will be used to create temporary scratch files.

The main entry point to server-side routines is through a header parsing phase handler named *handler()*. It detects whether the request uses the PATCH method and, if so, installs a custom response handler to deal with it. This means we install the patch routines with this configuration directive:

```
PerlHeaderParserHandler Apache::PATCH
```

The rationale for installing the patch handler with the *PerlHeaderParserHandler* directive rather than *PerlTransHandler* is that we can use the former directive within directory sections and *.htaccess* files, allowing us to make the PATCH method active only for certain parts of the document tree.

The definition of *handler()* is simple:

```
sub handler {
    my $r = shift;
    return DECLINED unless $r->method eq 'PATCH';
    unless ($r->some_auth_required) {
        $r->log_reason("Apache::PATCH requires access control");
        return FORBIDDEN;
    }
    $r->handler("perl-script");
    $r->push_handlers(PerlHandler => \&patch_handler);
    return OK;
}
```

We recover the request object and call *method()* to determine whether the request method equals PATCH. If not, we decline the transaction. Next we perform a simple but important security check. We call *some_auth_required()* to determine whether the requested URI is under password protection. If the document is *not* protected, we log an error and return a result code of FORBIDDEN. This is a hard-wired insurance that the file to be patched is protected in some way using any of the many authentication modules available to Apache (see Chapter 6, *Authentication and Authorization*, for a few).

If the request passes the checks, we adjust the content handler to be the *patch_handler()* subroutine by calling the request object's *handler()* and *push_handlers()* methods. This done, we return OK, allowing other installed header parsers to process the request.

The true work of the module is done in the *patch_handler()* subroutine, which is called during the response phase:

```
sub patch_handler {
    my $r = shift;

    return BAD_REQUEST
        unless lc($r->header_in("Content-type")) eq PATCH_TYPE;
```

This subroutine recovers the request object and immediately checks the content type of the submitted data. Unless the submitted data has MIME type *application/diff*, indicating a diff file, we return a result code of BAD_REQUEST.

```
    # get file to patch
    my $filename = $r->filename;
    my $dirname = dirname($filename);
    my $reason;
    do {
        -e $r->finfo or $reason = "$filename does not exist", last;
        -w _        or $reason = "$filename is not writable", last;
        -w $dirname  or $reason = "$filename directory is not writable", last;
    };
    if ($reason) {
        $r->log_reason($reason);
        return FORBIDDEN;
    }
```

Next we check whether the patch operation is likely to succeed. In order for the *patch* program to work properly, both the file to be patched and the directory that contains it must be writable by the current process.[*] This is because *patch* creates

---

[*] In order for the PATCH method to work you will have to make the files and directories to be patched writable by the web server process. You can do this either by making the directories world-writable, or by changing their user or group ownerships so that the web server has write permission. This has security implications, as it allows buggy CGI scripts and other web server security holes to alter the document tree. A more secure solution would be to implement PATCH using a conventional CGI script running under the standard Apache *suexec* extension, or the *sbox* CGI wrapper (*http://stein.cshl.org/WWW/software/sbox*).

a temporary file while processing the diff and renames it when it has successfully completed its task. We recover the filename corresponding to the request and the name of the directory that contains it. We then subject the two to a series of file tests. If any of the tests fails, we log the error and return FORBIDDEN.

```
# get patch data
my $patch;
$r->read($patch, $r->header_in("Content-length"));

# new temporary file to hold output of patch command
my($tmpname, $patch_out) = Apache::File->tmpfile;
unless($patch_out) {
    $r->log_reason("can't create temporary output file: $!");
    return FORBIDDEN;
}
```

The next job is to retrieve the patch data from the request. We do this using the request object's *read()* method to copy *Content-length* bytes of patch data from the request to a local variable named $patch. We are about to call the *patch* command, but before we do so we must arrange for its output (both standard output and standard error) to be saved to a temporary file so that we can relay the output to the user. We call the *Apache::File* method *tmpfile()* to return a unique temporary filename. We store the temporary file's name and handle into variables named $tmpname and $patch_out, respectively. If for some reason *tmpfile()* is unable to open a temporary file, it will return an empty list. We log the error and return FORBIDDEN.

```
# redirect child processes stdout and stderr to temporary file
open STDOUT, ">&=" . fileno($patch_out);
```

We want the output from *patch* to go to the temporary file rather than to standard output (which was closed by the parent server long, long ago). So we reopen STDOUT, using the >&= notation to open it on the same file descriptor as $patch_out.* See the description of *open()* in the *perlfunc* manual page for a more detailed description of this facility.

```
# open a pipe to the patch command
local $ENV{PATH}; #keep -T happy
my $patch_in = Apache::File->new("| $PATCH_CMD $filename 2>&1");
unless ($patch_in) {
    $r->log_reason("can't open pipe to $PATCH_CMD: $!");
    return FORBIDDEN;
}
```

At this point we open up a pipe to the patch command and store the pipe in a new filehandle named $patch_in. We call *patch* with a single command-line

---

* Why not just redirect the output of *patch* to the temporary file by invoking *patch* with the >$tmpname notation? Because this leaves us exposed to a race condition in which some other process replaces the temporary file with a link to a more important file. When *patch* writes to this file, it inadvertently clobbers it. Arranging for *patch* to write directly to the filehandle returned by *tmpfile()* avoids this trap.

argument, the name of the file to change stored in `$filename`. The piped open command also uses the 2>&1 notation, which is the Bourne shell's arcane way of indicating that standard error should be redirected to the same place that standard output is directed, which in this case is to the temporary file. If we can't open the pipe for some reason, we log the error and exit.

```
# write data to the patch command
print $patch_in $patch;
close $patch_in;
close $patch_out;
```

We now print the diff file to the *patch* pipe. *patch* will process the diff file and write its output to the temporary file. After printing, we close the command pipe and the temporary filehandle.

```
$patch_out = Apache::File->new($tmpname);

# send the result to the user
$r->send_http_header("text/plain");
$r->send_fd($patch_out);
close $patch_out;

return OK;
}
```

The last task is to send the *patch* output back to the client. We send the HTTP header, using the convenient form that allows us to set the MIME type in a single step. We now send the contents of the temporary file using the request method's *send_fd()* method. Our work done, we close the temporary filehandle and return OK.*

Example 7-5. Implementing the PATCH Method

```
package Apache::PATCH;
# file: Apache/PATCH.pm

use strict;
use vars qw($VERSION @EXPORT @ISA);
use Apache::Constants qw(:common BAD_REQUEST);
use Apache::File ();
use File::Basename 'dirname';

@ISA = qw(Exporter);
@EXPORT = qw(PATCH);
$VERSION = '1.00';
```

---

* Users interested in the HTTP PATCH method should also be aware of the IETF WebDAV (Distributed Authoring and Versioning) standard at *http://www.ics.uci.edu/pub/ietf/webdav/* and Greg Stein's Apache module implementation of these protocol extensions at *http://www.lyra.org/greg/mod_dav/*.

Example 7-5. Implementing the PATCH Method (continued)

```perl
use constant PATCH_TYPE => 'application/diff';
my $PATCH_CMD = "/usr/local/bin/patch";

sub handler {
    my $r = shift;
    return DECLINED unless $r->method eq 'PATCH';
    unless ($r->some_auth_required) {
        $r->log_reason("Apache::PATCH requires access control");
        return FORBIDDEN;
    }
    $r->handler("perl-script");
    $r->push_handlers(PerlHandler => \&patch_handler);
    return OK;
}

sub patch_handler {
    my $r = shift;

    return BAD_REQUEST
        unless lc($r->header_in("Content-type")) eq PATCH_TYPE;

    # get file to patch
    my $filename = $r->filename;
    my $dirname = dirname($filename);
    my $reason;
    do {
        -e $r->finfo or $reason = "$filename does not exist", last;
        -w _        or $reason = "$filename is not writable", last;
        -w $dirname or $reason = "$filename directory is not writable", last;
    };
    if ($reason) {
        $r->log_reason($reason);
        return FORBIDDEN;
    }

    # get patch data
    my $patch;
    $r->read($patch, $r->header_in("Content-length"));

    # new temporary file to hold output of patch command
    my($tmpname, $patch_out) = Apache::File->tmpfile;
    unless($patch_out) {
        $r->log_reason("can't create temporary output file: $!");
        return FORBIDDEN;
    }

    # redirect child processes stdout and stderr to temporary file
    open STDOUT, ">&=" . fileno($patch_out);

    # open a pipe to the patch command
    local $ENV{PATH}; #keep -T happy
```

Example 7-5. Implementing the PATCH Method (continued)

```perl
    my $patch_in = Apache::File->new("| $PATCH_CMD $filename 2>&1");
    unless ($patch_in) {
        $r->log_reason("can't open pipe to $PATCH_CMD: $!");
        return FORBIDDEN;
    }
    # write data to the patch command
    print $patch_in $patch;
    close $patch_in;
    close $patch_out;

    $patch_out = Apache::File->new($tmpname);

    # send the result to the user
    $r->send_http_header("text/plain");
    $r->send_fd($patch_out);
    close $patch_out;

    return OK;
}

# This part is for command-line invocation only.
my $opt_C;

sub PATCH {
    require LWP::UserAgent;
    @Apache::PATCH::ISA = qw(LWP::UserAgent);

    my $ua = __PACKAGE__->new;
    my $url;
    my $args = @_ ? \@_ : \@ARGV;

    while (my $arg = shift @$args) {
        $opt_C = shift @$args, next if $arg eq "-C";
        $url = $arg;
    }

    my $req = HTTP::Request->new('PATCH' => $url);

    my $patch = join '', <STDIN>;
    $req->content(\$patch);
    $req->header('Content-length' => length $patch);
    $req->header('Content-type'   => PATCH_TYPE);
    my $res = $ua->request($req);

    if($res->is_success) {
        print $res->content;
    }
    else {
        print $res->as_string;
    }
}
```

Example 7-5. Implementing the PATCH Method (continued)

```
sub get_basic_credentials {
    my($self, $realm, $uri) = @_;
    return split ':', $opt_C, 2;
}

1;
__END__
```

At the time this chapter was written, no web browser or publishing system had actually implemented the PATCH method. The remainder of the listing contains code for implementing a PATCH client. You can use this code from the command line to send patch files to servers that have the PATCH handler installed and watch the documents change in front of your eyes.

The PATCH client is simple, thanks to the LWP library. Its main entry point is an exported subroutine named *PATCH()*:

```
sub PATCH {
    require LWP::UserAgent;
    @Apache::PATCH::ISA = qw(LWP::UserAgent);

    my $ua = __PACKAGE__->new;
    my $url;
    my $args = @_ ? \@_ : \@ARGV;

    while (my $arg = shift @$args) {
        $opt_C = shift @$args, next if $arg eq "-C";
        $url = $arg;
    }
```

PATCH() starts by creating a new LWP user agent using the subclassing technique discussed later in the *Apache::AdBlocker* module (see "Handling Proxy Requests" in this chapter). It recovers the authentication username and password from the command line by looking for a −*C* (credentials) switch, which is then stored into a package lexical named `$opt_C`. The subroutine shifts the URL of the document to patch off the command line and store it in `$url`.

```
    my $req = HTTP::Request->new('PATCH' => $url);

    my $patch = join '', <STDIN>;
    $req->content(\$patch);
    $req->header('Content-length' => length $patch);
    $req->header('Content-type'   => PATCH_TYPE);
    my $res = $ua->request($req);
```

The subroutine now creates a new *HTTP::Request* object that specifies PATCH as its request method and sets its content to the diff file read in from STDIN. It also sets the *Content-length* and *Content-type* HTTP headers to the length of the diff file and *application/diff*, respectively. Having set up the request, the subroutine sends the request to the remote server by calling the user agent's *request()* method.

```
if($res->is_success) {
    print $res->content;
}
else {
    print $res->as_string;
}
}
```

If the response indicates success (*is_success()* returns true) then we print out the text of the server's response. Otherwise, the routine prints the error message contained in the response object's *as_string()* method.

```
sub get_basic_credentials {
    my($self, $realm, $uri) = @_;
    return split ':', $opt_C, 2;
}
```

The *get_basic_credentials()* method, defined at the bottom of the source listing, is actually an override of an *LWP::UserAgent* method. When *LWP::UserAgent* tries to access a document that is password-protected, it invokes this method to return the username and password required to fetch the resource. By subclassing *LWP::User-Agent* into our own package and then defining a *get_basic_credentials()* method, we're able to provide our parent class with the contents of the $opt_C command-line switch.

To run the client from the command line, invoke it like this:

```
% perl -MApache::PATCH -e PATCH -- -C username:password \
    http://www.modperl.com/index.html < index.html.diff

Hmm... Looks like a new-style context diff to me...
The text leading up to this was:
--------------------------
|*** index.html.new    Mon Aug 24 21:52:29 1998
|--- index.html        Mon Aug 24 21:51:06 1998
--------------------------
Patching file /home/httpd/htdocs/index.html using Plan A...
Hunk #1 succeeded at 8.
done
```

A tiny script named *PATCH* that uses the module can save some typing:

```
#!/usr/local/bin/perl

use Apache::PATCH;
PATCH;

__END__
```

Now the command looks like this:

```
% PATCH -C username:password \
    http://www.modperl.com/index.html < index.html.diff
```

Customizing the Type Checking Phase

Following the successful completion of the access control and authentication steps (if configured), Apache tries to determine the MIME type (e.g., *image/gif*) and encoding type (e.g., *x-gzip*) of the requested document. The types and encodings are usually determined by filename extensions. (The term "suffix" is used interchangeably with "extension" in the Apache source code and documentation.) Table 7-1 lists a few common examples.

Table 7-1. MIME Types and Encodings for Common File Extensions

MIME types

extension	type
.txt	text/plain
.html, .htm	text/html
.gif	image/gif
.jpg, .jpeg	image/jpeg
.mpeg, .mpg	video/mpeg
pdf	application/pdf

Encodings

extension	encoding
.gz	x-gzip
.Z	x-compress

By default, Apache's type checking phase is handled by the standard *mod_mime* module, which combines the information stored in the server's *conf/mime.types* file with *AddType* and *AddEncoding* directives to map file extensions onto MIME types and encodings.

The contents of the request record's *content_type* field are used to set the default outgoing *Content-Type* header, which the client uses to decide how to render the document. However, as we've seen, content handlers can, and often do, change the content type during the later response phase.

In addition to its responsibility for choosing MIME and encoding types for the requested document, the type checking phase handler also performs the crucial task of selecting the content handler for the document. *mod_mime* looks first for a *SetHandler* directive in the current directory or location. If one is set, it uses that handler for the requested document. Otherwise, it dispatches the request based on the MIME type of the document. This process was described in more detail at the beginning of Chapter 4. Also see "Reimplementing mod_mime in Perl," in Chapter 8, *Customizing the Apache Configuration Process*, where we reproduce all of *mod_mime*'s functionality with a Perl module.

A DBI-Based Type Checker

In this section, we'll show you a simple type checking handler that determines the MIME type of the document on the basis of a DBI database lookup. Each record of the database table will contain the name of the file, its MIME type, and its encoding.* If no type is registered in the database, we fall through to the default *mod_mime* handler.

This module, *Apache::MimeDBI*, makes use of the simple *Tie::DBI* class that was introduced in the previous chapter. Briefly, this class lets you tie a hash to a relational database table. The tied variable appears as a hash of hashes in which the outer hash is a list of table records indexed by the table's primary key and the inner hash contains the columns of that record, indexed by column name. To give a concrete example, for the purposes of this module we'll set up a database table named *doc_types* having this structure:

```
+----------+-----------+------------+
| filename | mime_type | encoding   |
+----------+-----------+------------+
| test1    | text/plain | NULL      |
| test2    | text/html  | NULL      |
| test3    | text/html  | x-compress |
| test4    | text/html  | x-gzip     |
| test5    | image/gif  | NULL      |
+----------+-----------+------------+
```

Assuming that a hash named %DB is tied to this table, we'll be able to access its columns in this way:

```
$type     = $DB{'test2'}{'mime_type'};
$encoding = $DB{'test2'}{'encoding'};
```

Example 7-6 gives the source for *Apache::MimeDBI*.

```
package Apache::MimeDBI;
# file Apache/MimeDBI.pm

use strict;
use Apache::Constants qw(:common);
```

---

* An obvious limitation of this module is that it can't distinguish between similarly named files in different directories.

```
use Tie::DBI ();
use File::Basename qw(basename);

use constant DEFAULT_DSN    => 'mysql:test_www';
use constant DEFAULT_LOGIN  => ':';
use constant DEFAULT_TABLE  => 'doc_types';
use constant DEFAULT_FIELDS => 'filename:mime_type:encoding';
```

The module starts by pulling in necessary Perl libraries, including *Tie::DBI* and the *File::Basename* filename parser. It also defines a series of default configuration constants. DEFAULT_DSN is the default DBI data source to use, in the format *driver:database:host:port*. DEFAULT_LOGIN is the username and password for the web server to use to log into the database, separated by a : character. Both fields are blank by default, indicating no password needs to be provided. DEFAULT_TABLE is the name of the table in which to look for the MIME type and encoding information. DEFAULT_FIELDS are the names of the filename, MIME type, and encoding columns, again separated by the : character. These default values can be overridden with the per-directory Perl configuration variables *MIME-Database, MIME-Login, MIMETable,* and *MIMEFields.*

```
sub handler {
    my $r = shift;

    # get filename
    my $file = basename $r->filename;

    # get configuration information
    my $dsn       = $r->dir_config('MIMEDatabase') || DEFAULT_DSN;
    my $table     = $r->dir_config('MIMETable')    || DEFAULT_TABLE;
    my($filefield, $mimefield, $encodingfield) =
        split ':',$r->dir_config('MIMEFields') || DEFAULT_FIELDS;
    my($user, $pass) =
        split ':', $r->dir_config('MIMELogin') || DEFAULT_LOGIN;
```

The *handler()* subroutine begins by shifting the request object off the subroutine call stack and using it to recover the requested document's filename. The directory part of the filename is then stripped away using the *basename()* routine imported from *File::Basename.* Next, we fetch the values of our four configuration variables. If any are undefined, we default to the values defined by the previously declared constants.

```
tie my %DB, 'Tie::DBI', {
    'db' => $dsn, 'table' => $table, 'key' => $filefield,
    'user' => $user, 'password' => $pass,
};
my $record;
```

We now tie a hash named %DB to the indicated database by calling the *tie()* operator. If the hash is successfully tied to the database, this routine will return a true value (actually, an object reference to the underlying *Tie::DBI* object itself).

Otherwise, we return a value of DECLINED and allow other modules their chance at the MIME checking phase.

```
return DECLINED unless tied %DB and $record = $DB{$file};
```

The next step is to check the tied hash to see if there is a record corresponding to the current filename. If there is, we store the record in a variable named $record. Otherwise, we again return DECLINED. This allows files that are not specifically named in the database to fall through to the standard file extension–based MIME type determination.

```
$r->content_type($record->{$mimefield});
$r->content_encoding($record->{$encodingfield})
        if $record->{$encodingfield};
```

Since the file is listed in the database, we fetch the values of the MIME type and encoding columns and write them into the request record by calling the request object's *content_type()* and *content_encoding()*, respectively. Since most documents do not have an encoding type, we only call *content_encoding()* if the column is defined.

```
    return OK;
}
```

Our work is done, so we exit the handler subroutine with an OK status code.

At the end of the code listing is a short shell script which you can use to initialize a test database named *test_www*. It will create the table shown in this example.

To install this module, add a *PerlTypeHandler* directive like this one to one of the configuration files or a *.htaccess file*:

```
<Location /mimedbi>
  PerlTypeHandler Apache::MimeDBI
</Location>
```

If you need to change the name of the database, the login information, or the table structure, be sure to include the appropriate *PerlSetVar* directives as well.

Figure 7-2 shows the automatic listing of a directory under the control of *Apache::MimeDBI*. The directory contains several files. *test1* through *test5* are listed in the database with the MIME types and encodings shown in the previous table. Their icons reflect the MIME types and encodings returned by the handler subroutine. This MIME type will also be passed to the browser when it loads and renders the document. *test6.html* doesn't have an entry in the database, so it falls through to the standard MIME checking module, which figures out its type through its file extension. *test7* has neither an entry in the database nor a recognized file extension, so it is displayed with the "unknown document" icon. Without help from *Apache::MimeDBI*, all the files without extensions would end up as unknown MIME types.

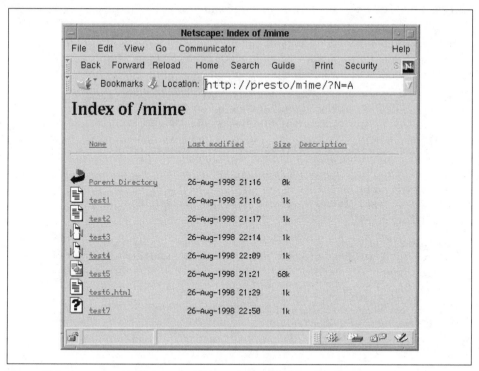

Figure 7-2. An automatic listing of a directory controlled by Apache::MimeDBI

If you use this module, you should be sure to install and load *Apache::DBI* during the server startup phase, as described in Chapter 5. This will make the underlying database connections persistent, dramatically decreasing the time necessary for the handler to do its work.

Example 7-6. A DBI-Based MIME Type Checker

```
package Apache::MimeDBI;
# file Apache/MimeDBI.pm

use strict;
use Apache::Constants qw(:common);
use Tie::DBI ();
use File::Basename qw(basename);

use constant DEFAULT_DSN    => 'mysql:test_www';
use constant DEFAULT_LOGIN  => ':';
use constant DEFAULT_TABLE  => 'doc_types';
use constant DEFAULT_FIELDS => 'filename:mime_type:encoding';

sub handler {
    my $r = shift;
```

Example 7-6. A DBI-Based MIME Type Checker (continued)

```
    # get filename
    my $file = basename $r->filename;

    # get configuration information
    my $dsn       = $r->dir_config('MIMEDatabase') || DEFAULT_DSN;
    my $table     = $r->dir_config('MIMETable')    || DEFAULT_TABLE;
    my($filefield, $mimefield, $encodingfield) =
        split ':', $r->dir_config('MIMEFields') || DEFAULT_FIELDS;
    my($user, $pass) =
        split ':', $r->dir_config('MIMELogin') || DEFAULT_LOGIN;

    # pull information out of the database
    tie my %DB, 'Tie::DBI', {
        'db' => $dsn, 'table' => $table, 'key' => $filefield,
        'user' => $user, 'password' => $pass,
    };
    my $record;
    return DECLINED unless tied %DB and $record = $DB{$file};

    # set the content type and encoding
    $r->content_type($record->{$mimefield});
    $r->content_encoding($record->{$encodingfield})
        if $record->{$encodingfield};

    return OK;
}

1;
__END__

# Here's a shell script to add the test data:
#!/bin/sh
mysql test_www <<END
DROP TABLE doc_types;
CREATE TABLE doc_types (
        filename        char(127) primary key,
        mime_type       char(30)  not null,
        encoding        char(30)
);
INSERT into doc_types values ('test1','text/plain',null);
INSERT into doc_types values ('test2','text/html',null);
INSERT into doc_types values ('test3','text/html','x-compress');
INSERT into doc_types values ('test4','text/html','x-gzip');
INSERT into doc_types values ('test5','image/gif',null);
END
```

Customizing the Fixup Phase

The *fixup* phase is sandwiched between the type checking phase and the response phase. It gives modules a last-minute chance to add information to the environment or to modify the request record before the content handler is invoked. For instance, the standard *mod_usertrack* module implements the *Cookie-Tracking* directive in this phase, adding a user-tracking cookie to the outgoing HTTP headers and recording a copy of the incoming cookie to the notes table for logging purposes.

As an example of a useful Perl-based fixup handler, we'll look at *Apache::HttpEquiv*, a module written by Rob Hartill and used here with his permission. The idea of *Apache::HttpEquiv* is simple. The module scans the requested HTML file for any <META> tags containing the HTTP-EQUIV and CONTENT attributes. The information is then added to the outgoing HTTP headers.

For example, if the requested file contains this HTML:

```
<HTML>
<HEAD><TITLE>My Page</TITLE>
<META HTTP-EQUIV="Expires" CONTENT="Wed, 31 Jul 1998 16:40:00 GMT">
<META HTTP-EQUIV="Set-Cookie" CONTENT="open=sesame">
```

the handler will convert the <META> tags into these response headers:

```
Expires: Wed, 31 Jul 1998 16:40:00 GMT
Set-Cookie: open=sesame
```

Example 7-7 gives the succinct code for *Apache::HttpEquiv*. The *handler()* routine begins by testing the current request for suitability. It returns with a status code of **DECLINED** if any of the following are true:

- The request is a subrequest.

- The requested document's MIME type is something other than *text/html*.

- The requested file cannot be opened.

The second item is the main reason that this module has to be run as a fixup handler. Prior to this phase, the MIME type of the document is not known because the MIME type checker hasn't yet run.

Next the handler scans through the requested file, line by line, looking for suitable <META> tags. If any are found, the request object's *header_out()* method is called to set the indicated header. To gain a little bit of efficiency, the subroutine aborts the search early when a <BODY> or </HEAD> tag is encountered.

Once the file is completely scanned, the subroutine closes and return an OK status code.

To configure *Apache::HttpEquiv*, add the following line to your configuration file:

```
<Location /httpequiv>
 PerlFixupHandler Apache::HttpEquiv
 </Location>
```

Example 7-7. Apache::HttpEquiv Turns <META> Tags into HTTP Headers

```
package Apache::HttpEquiv;
# file: Apache/HttpEquiv.pm
use strict;
use Apache::Constants qw(:common);

sub handler {
    my $r = shift;
    local(*FILE);

    return DECLINED if # don't scan the file if..
        !$r->is_main # a subrequest
            || $r->content_type ne "text/html" # it isn't HTML
                || !open(FILE, $r->filename); # we can't open it

    while(<FILE>) {
        last if m!<BODY>|</HEAD>!i; # exit early if in BODY
        if (m/META HTTP-EQUIV="([^"]+)"\s+CONTENT="([^"]+)"/i) {
            $r->header_out($1 => $2);
        }
    }
    close(FILE);
    return OK;
}

1;
__END__
```

The Logging Phase

The very last phase of the transaction before the cleanup at the end is the logging phase. At this point, the request record contains everything there is to know about the transaction, including the content handler's final status code and the number of bytes transferred from the server to the client.

Apache's built-in logging module *mod_log_config* ordinarily handles this phase by writing a line of summary information to the transfer log. As its name implies, this module is highly configurable. You can give it *printf()*-like format strings to customize the appearance of the transfer log to your requirements, have it open multiple log files, or even have it pipe the log information to an external process for special processing.

By handling the logging phase yourself, you can perform special processing at the end of each transaction. For example, you can update a database of cumulative hits, bump up a set of hit count files, or notify the owner of a document that his page has been viewed. There are a number of log handlers on CPAN, including *Apache::DBILogger*, which sends log information to a relational database, and *Apache::Traffic*, which keeps summaries of bytes transferred on a per-user basis.

Sending Email When a Page Is Hit

The first example of a log handler that we'll show is *Apache::LogMail*. It sends email to a designated address whenever a particular page is hit and can be used in low-volume applications, such as the vanity home pages of ISP customers. A typical configuration directive would look like this:

```
<Location /~kryan>
    PerlLogHandler Apache::LogMail
    PerlSetVar     LogMailto  kryan@public.com
    PerlSetVar     LogPattern \.(html|txt)$
</Location>
```

With this configuration in place, hits on pages in the */~kryan* directory will generate email messages. The *LogMailto* Perl configuration variable specifies *kryan@public.com* as the lucky recipient of these messages, and *LogPattern* specifies that only files ending with *.html* or *.txt* will generate messages (thus eliminating noise caused by hits on inline images).

Example 7-8 shows the code. After the usual preliminaries, we define the logging phase's *handler()* routine:

```
sub handler {
    my $r = shift;

    my $mailto = $r->dir_config('LogMailto');
    return DECLINED unless $mailto;
    my $filepattern = $r->dir_config('LogPattern');
    return DECLINED if $filepattern
        && $r->filename !~ /$filepattern/;
```

The subroutine begins by fetching the contents of the *LogMailto* configuration variable. If none is defined, it declines the transaction. Next it fetches the contents of *LogPattern*. If it finds a pattern, it compares it to the requested document's filename and again declines the transaction if no match is found.

```
    my $request = $r->the_request;
    my $uri     = $r->uri;
    my $agent   = $r->header_in("User-agent");
    my $bytes   = $r->bytes_sent;
    my $remote  = $r->get_remote_host;
    my $status  = $r->status_line;
    my $date    = localtime;
```

Now the subroutine gathers up various fields of interest from the request object, including the requested URI, the *User-Agent* header, the name of the remote host, and the number of bytes sent (method *bytes_sent()*).

```
    local $ENV{PATH}; #keep -T happy
    unless (open MAIL, "|/usr/lib/sendmail -oi -t") {
        $r->log_error("Couldn't open mail: $!");
        return DECLINED;
    }
```

We open a pipe to the *sendmail* program and use it to send a message to the designated user with the information we've gathered.* The flags used to open up the *sendmail* pipe instruct it to take the recipient's address from the header rather than the command line and prevent it from terminating prematurely if it sees a line consisting of a dot.

```
    print MAIL <<END;
To: $mailto
From: mod_perl httpd <$from>
Subject: Somebody looked at $uri

At $date, a user at $remote looked at
$uri using the $agent browser.

The request was $request,
which resulted returned a code of $status.

$bytes bytes were transferred.
END
    close MAIL;
      return OK;
}
```

All text that we print to the **MAIL** pipe is transferred to *sendmail*'s standard input. The only trick here is to start the message with a properly formatted mail header with the *To:*, *From:*, and *Subject:* fields followed by a blank line. When we close the pipe, the mail is bundled up and sent off for delivery.

The final email message will look something like this:

```
From: Mod Perl <webmaster@public.com>
To: kryan@public.com
Subject: Somebody looked at /~kryan/guestbook.txt
Date: Thu, 27 Aug 1998 08:14:23 -0400

At Thu Aug 27 08:14:23 1998, a user at 192.168.2.1 looked at
/~kryan/guestbook.txt using the Mozilla/4.04 [en] (X11; I; Linux
2.0.33 i686) browser.

The request was GET /~kryan/guestbook.txt HTTP/1.0,
which resulted returned a code of 200 OK.

462 bytes were transferred.
```

---

* *sendmail* is only available on Unix systems. If you are using Windows or Windows NT, you would be best served by replacing the piped open with the appropriate calls to the Perl *Net::SMTP* module. You can find this module on CPAN.

Example 7-8. A Logging Module to Notify of Hits via Email

```perl
package Apache::LogMail;
# File: Apache/LogMail.pm

use strict;
use Apache::Constants qw(:common);

sub handler {
    my $r = shift;

    my $mailto = $r->dir_config('LogMailto');
    return DECLINED unless $mailto;

    my $filepattern = $r->dir_config('LogPattern');
    return DECLINED if $filepattern
        && $r->filename !~ /$filepattern/;

    my $request = $r->the_request;
    my $uri     = $r->uri;
    my $agent   = $r->header_in("User-agent");
    my $bytes   = $r->bytes_sent;
    my $remote  = $r->get_remote_host;
    my $status  = $r->status_line;
    my $date    = localtime;

    my $from = $r->server->server_admin || "webmaster";
    local $ENV{PATH}; #keep -T happy
    unless (open MAIL, "|/usr/lib/sendmail -oi -t") {
        $r->log_error("Couldn't open mail: $!");
        return DECLINED;
    }

    print MAIL <<END;
To: $mailto
From: mod_perl httpd <$from>
Subject: Somebody looked at $uri

At $date, a user at $remote looked at
$uri using the $agent browser.

The request was $request,
which resulted returned a code of $status.

$bytes bytes were transferred.
END

    close MAIL;
    return OK;
}

1;
__END__
```

A DBI Database Logger

The second example of a log phase handler is a DBI database logger. The information from the transaction is sent to a relational database using the DBI interface. The record of each transaction is appended to the end of a relational table, which can be queried and summarized in a myriad of ways using SQL.

This is a skeletal version of the much more complete *Apache::DBILog* and *Apache::DBILogConfig* modules, which you should consult before rolling your own.

In preparation to use this module you'll need to set up a database with the appropriate table definition. A suitable MySQL table named *access_log* is shown here:

```
+---------+--------------+------+-----+---------------------+-------+
| Field   | Type         | Null | Key | Default             | Extra |
+---------+--------------+------+-----+---------------------+-------+
| when    | datetime     |      |     | 0000-00-00 00:00:00 |       |
| host    | char(255)    |      |     |                     |       |
| method  | char(4)      |      |     |                     |       |
| url     | char(255)    |      |     |                     |       |
| auth    | char(50)     | YES  |     | NULL                |       |
| browser | char(50)     | YES  |     | NULL                |       |
| referer | char(255)    | YES  |     | NULL                |       |
| status  | int(3)       |      |     | 0                   |       |
| bytes   | int(8)       | YES  |     | 0                   |       |
+---------+--------------+------+-----+---------------------+-------+
```

This table can be created with the following script:

```
#!/bin/sh

mysql -B test_www <<END
create table access_log (
           when     datetime not null,
           host     varchar(255) not null,
           method   varchar(4)   not null,
           url      varchar(255) not null,
           auth     varchar(50),
           browser  varchar(50),
           referer  varchar(255),
           status   smallint(3) default 0,
           bytes    int(8)
);
END
```

The database must be writable by the web server, which should be provided with the appropriate username and password to log in.

The code (Example 7-9) is short and very similar to the previous example, so we won't reproduce it inline.

We begin by bringing in modules that we need, including DBI and the *ht_time()* function from *Apache::Util*. Next we declare some constants defining the database, table, and database login information. Since this is just a skeleton of a module, we have hardcoded these values instead of taking them from *PerlSetVar* configuration directives. You can follow the model of *Apache::MimeDBI* if you wish to make this module more configurable.

The *handler()* subroutine recovers the request object and uses it to fetch all the information we're interested in recording, which we store in locals. We also call *ht_time()* to produce a nicely formatted representation of the *request_time()* in a format that SQL accepts. We connect to the database and create a statement handle containing a SQL INSERT statement. We invoke the statement handler's *execute()* statement to write the information into the database, and return with a status code of OK.

The only trick to this handler, which we left out of *Apache::LogMail*, is the use of the *last()* to recover the request object. *last()* returns the final request object in a chain of internal redirects and other subrequests. Usually there are no subrequests, and *last()* just returns the main (first) request object, in which case the $orig and $r objects in *Apache::LogDBI* would point to the same request record. In the event that a subrequest did occur, for example, if a request for / was resolved to */index.html*, we want to log the *request_time*, *uri*, and *status* from the ultimate request.

Example 7-9. A DBI Database Log Handler

```
package Apache::LogDBI;
# file: Apache/LogDBI.pm
use Apache::Constants qw(:common);

use strict;
use DBI ();
use Apache::Util qw(ht_time);

use constant DSN       => 'dbi:mysql:test_www';
use constant DB_TABLE  => 'access_log';
use constant DB_AUTH   => ':';

sub handler {
    my $orig = shift;
    my $r = $orig->last;
    my $date    = ht_time($orig->request_time, '%Y-%m-%d %H:%M:%S', 0);
    my $host    = $r->get_remote_host;
    my $method  = $r->method;
    my $url     = $orig->uri;
    my $user    = $r->connection->user;
    my $referer = $r->header_in('Referer');
    my $browser = $r->header_in('User-agent');
```

Example 7-9. A DBI Database Log Handler (continued)

```
    my $status  = $orig->status;
    my $bytes   = $r->bytes_sent;

    my $dbh = DBI->connect(DSN, split ':', DB_AUTH) || die $DBI::errstr;
    my $sth = $dbh->prepare("INSERT INTO ${\DB_TABLE} VALUES(?,?,?,?,?,?,?,?,?)")
                || die $dbh->errstr;

    $sth->execute($date,$host,$method,$url,$user,
                $browser,$referer,$status,$bytes) || die $dbh->errstr;
    $sth->finish;
    return OK;
}

1;
__END__
```

This handler can be installed with the following configuration file directive:

```
    PerlLogHandler Apache::LogDBI
```

You can place this directive in the main part of the configuration file in order to log all accesses, or place it in a directory section if you're interested in logging a particular section of the site only. An alternative is to install *Apache::LogDBI* as a cleanup handler, as described in the next section.

Having web transactions logged to a relational database gives you the ability to pose questions of great complexity. Just to give you a taste of what's possible, here are a few useful SQL queries to try:

- How many hits have I had to date, and how many total bytes transferred?

    ```
    SELECT count(*),sum(bytes) FROM access_log;
    ```

- How many hits did I have the day before yesterday?

    ```
    SELECT count(*) FROM access_log
        WHERE to_days(when)=to_days(now())-2;
    ```

- How many hits have I had, grouped by hour of access?

    ```
    SELECT date_format(when,'H') as hour,count(*) FROM access_log
        GROUP BY hour;
    ```

- What URLs may be broken, and who is pointing at them?

    ```
    SELECT url,referer,count(url) FROM access_log
        WHERE status=404
        GROUP BY url;
    ```

- What are the top 10 most popular URLs on my site?

    ```
    SELECT url,count(*) as count FROM access_log
        GROUP BY url
        ORDER BY count desc
        LIMIT 10;
    ```

- What is my site's transfer rate, sorted by the hour of day?

```
SELECT date_format(when,'H') as hour,
    sum(bytes)/(60*60) as bytes_per_min
  FROM access_log
  GROUP BY hour;
```

Registered Cleanups

Although the logging phase is the last official phase of the request cycle, there is one last place where modules can do work. This is the cleanup phase, during which any code registered as a cleanup handler is called to perform any per-transaction tidying up that the module may need to do.

Cleanup handlers can be installed in either of two ways. They can be installed by calling the request object's *register_cleanup()* method with a reference to a subroutine or method to invoke, or by using the *PerlCleanupHandler* directive to register a subroutine from within the server configuration file. Here are some examples:

```
# within a module file
$r->register_cleanup(sub { warn "server $$ done serving request\n" });

# within a configuration file
PerlModule         Apache::Guillotine  # make sure it's loaded
PerlCleanupHandler Apache::Guillotine::mopup()
```

There is not actually a cleanup phase per se. Instead, the C API provides a call-back mechanism for functions that are invoked just before their memory pool is destroyed. A handful of Apache API methods use this mechanism underneath for simple but important tasks, such as ensuring that files, directory handles, and sockets are closed. In Chapter 10, *C API Reference Guide, Part I*, you will see that the C version expects a few more arguments, including a **pool** pointer.

There are actually two *register_cleanup()* methods: one associated with the *Apache* request object and the other associated with the *Apache::Server* object. The difference between the two is that handlers installed with the request object's method will be run when the request is done, while handlers installed with the server object's method will be run only when the server shuts down or restarts:

```
$r->register_cleanup(sub { "child $$ served another request" })
Apache->server->register_cleanup(sub { warn "server $$ restarting\n" });
```

We've already been using *register_cleanup()* indirectly with the *Apache::File tmpfile()* method, where it is used to unlink a temporary file at the end of the transaction even if the handler aborts prematurely. Another example can be found in CGI.pm, where a cleanup handler resets that module's package globals to a known state after each transaction. Here's the relevant code fragment:

```
Apache->request->register_cleanup(\&CGI::_reset_globals);
```

A more subtle use of registered cleanups is to perform delayed processing on requests. For example, certain contributed *mod_perl* logging modules, like *Apache::DBILogger* and *Apache::Traffic*, take a bit more time to do their work than the standard logging modules do. Although the overhead is small, it does lengthen the amount of time the user has to wait before the browser's progress monitor indicates that the page is fully loaded. In order to squeeze out the last ounce of performance, these modules defer the real work to the cleanup phase. Because cleanups occur after the response is finished, the user will not have to wait for the logging module to complete its work.[*]

To take advantage of delayed processing, we can run the previous section's *Apache::LogDBI* module during the cleanup phase rather than the log phase. The change is simple. Just replace the *PerlLogHandler* directive with *PerlCleanupHandler*:

```
PerlCleanupHandler Apache::LogDBI
```

Because the cleanup handler can be used for post-transactional processing, the Perl API provides *post_connection()* as an alias for *register_cleanup()*. This can improve code readability somewhat:

```
sub handler {
    shift->post_connection(\&logger);
}
```

Cleanup handlers follow the same calling conventions as other handlers. On entry, they receive a reference to an Apache object containing all the accumulated request and response information. They can return a status code if they wish to, but Apache will ignore it.

We've finally run out of transaction phases to talk about, so we turn our attention to a more esoteric aspect of Apache, the proxy server API.

Handling Proxy Requests

The HTTP proxy protocol was originally designed to allow users unfortunate enough to be stuck behind a firewall to access external web sites. Instead of connecting to the remote server directly, an action forbidden by the firewall, users point their browsers at a proxy server located on the firewall machine itself. The proxy goes out and fetches the requested document from the remote site and forwards the retrieved document to the user.

---

[*] Of course, moving the work out of the transaction and into the cleanup phase just means that the child server or thread cannot serve another request until this work is done. This only becomes a problem if the number of concurrent requests exceeds the level that your server can handle. In this case, the next incoming request may have to wait a little longer for the connection to be established. You can decide if the subjective tradeoff is worth it.

Nowadays most firewall systems have a web proxy built right in so there's no need for dedicated proxying servers. However, proxy servers are still useful for a variety of purposes. For example, a caching proxy (of which Apache is one example) will store frequently requested remote documents in a disk directory and return the cached documents directly to the browser instead of fetching them anew. Anonymizing proxies take the outgoing request and strip out all the headers that can be used to identify the user or his browser. By writing Apache API modules that participate in the proxy process, you can achieve your own special processing of proxy requests.

The proxy request/response protocol is nearly the same as vanilla HTTP. The major difference is that instead of requesting a server-relative URI in the request line, the client asks for a full URL, complete with scheme and host. In addition, a few optional HTTP headers beginning with *Proxy-* may be added to the request. For example, a normal (nonproxy) HTTP request sent by a browser might look like this:

```
GET /foo/index.html HTTP/1.0
Accept: image/gif, image/x-xbitmap, image/jpeg, image/pjpeg, */*
Pragma: no-cache
Connection: Keep-Alive
User-Agent: Mozilla/2.01 (WinNT; I)
Host: www.modperl.com:80
```

In contrast, the corresponding HTTP proxy request will look like this:

```
GET http://www.modperl.com/foo/index.html HTTP/1.0
Accept: image/gif, image/x-xbitmap, image/jpeg, image/pjpeg, */*
Pragma: no-cache
User-Agent: Mozilla/2.01 (WinNT; I)
Host: www.modperl.com:80
Proxy-Connection: Keep-Alive
```

Notice that the URL in the request line of an HTTP proxy request includes the scheme and hostname. This information enables the proxy server to initiate a connection to the distant server. To generate this type of request, the user must configure his browser so that HTTP and, optionally, FTP requests are proxied to the server. This usually involves setting values in the browser's preference screens. An Apache server will be able to respond to this type of request if it has been compiled with the *mod_proxy* module. This module is part of the core Apache distribution but is not compiled in by default.

You can interact with Apache's proxy mechanism at the translation handler phase. There are two types of interventions you can make. You can take an ordinary (nonproxy) request and change it into one so that it will be handled by Apache's standard proxy module, or you can take an incoming proxy request and install your own content handler for it so that you can examine and possibly modify the response from the remote server.

Invoking mod_proxy for Nonproxy Requests

We'll look first at *Apache::PassThru*, an example of how to turn an ordinary request into a proxy request.* Because this technique uses Apache's *mod_proxy* module, this module will have to be compiled and installed in order for this example to run on your system.

The idea behind the example is simple. Requests for URIs beginning with a certain path will be dynamically transformed into a proxy request. For example, we might transform requests for URLs beginning with */CPAN/* into a request for *http://www.perl.com/CPAN/*. The request to *www.perl.com* will be done completely behind the scenes; nothing will reveal to the user that the directory hierarchy is being served from a third-party server rather than our own. This functionality is the same as the *ProxyPass* directive provided by *mod_proxy* itself. You can also achieve the same effect by providing an appropriate rewrite rule to *mod_rewrite*.

The configuration for this example uses a *PerlSetVar* to set a variable named *Perl-PassThru*. A typical entry in the configuration directive will look like this:

```
PerlTransHandler Apache::PassThru
PerlSetVar PerlPassThru '/CPAN/   => http://www.perl.com/,\
                         /search/ => http://www.altavista.digital.com/'
```

The *PerlPassThru* variable contains a string representing a series of *URI=>proxy* pairs, separated by commas. A backslash at the end of a line can be used to split the string over several lines, improving readability (the ability to use backslash as a continuation character is actually an Apache configuration file feature but not a well-publicized one). In this example, we map the URI */CPAN/* to *http://www.perl.com/* and */search/* to *http://www.altavista.digital.com/*. For the mapping to work correctly, local directory names should end with a slash in the manner shown in the example.

The code for *Apache::PassThru* is given in Example 7-10. The *handler()* subroutine begins by retrieving the request object and calling its *proxyreq()* method to determine whether the current request is a proxy request:

```
sub handler {
    my $r = shift;
    return DECLINED if $r->proxyreq;
```

If this is already a proxy request, we don't want to alter it in any way, so we decline the transaction. Otherwise, we retrieve the value of *PerlPassThru*, split it

---

* There are several third-party Perl API modules on CPAN that handle proxy requests, including one named *Apache::ProxyPass* and another named *Apache::ProxyPassThru*. If you are looking for the functionality of *Apache::PassThru*, you should examine one of these more finished products before using this one as the basis for your own module.

into its key/value components with a pattern match, and store the result in a hash named %mappings:

```
my $uri = $r->uri;
my %mappings = split /\s*(?:,|=>)\s*/, $r->dir_config('PerlPassThru');
```

We now loop through each of the local paths, looking for a match with the current request's URI. If a match is found, we perform a string substitution to replace the local path with the corresponding proxy URI. Otherwise, we continue to loop:

```
for my $src (keys %mappings) {
    next unless $uri =~ s/^$src/$mappings{$src}/;
    $r->proxyreq(1);
    $r->uri($uri);
    $r->filename("proxy:$uri");
    $r->handler('proxy-server');
    return OK;
    }
    return DECLINED;
}
```

If the URI substitution succeeds, there are four steps we need to take to transform this request into something that *mod_proxy* will handle. The first two are obvious, but the others are less so. First, we need to set the proxy request flag to a true value by calling `$r->proxyreq(1)`. Next, we change the requested URI to the proxied URI by calling the request object's *uri()* method. In the third step, we set the request filename to the string **proxy:** followed by the URI, as in *proxy:http:// www.perl.com/CPAN/*. This is a special filename format recognized by *mod_proxy*, and as such is somewhat arbitrary. The last step is to set the content handler to **proxy-server**, so that the request is passed to *mod_proxy* to handle the response phase.

If we turned the local path into a proxy request, we return OK from the translation handler. Otherwise, we return DECLINED.

Example 7-10. Invoking Apache's Proxy Request Mechanism from Within a Translation Handler

```
package Apache::PassThru;
# file: Apache/PassThru.pm;
use strict;
use Apache::Constants qw(:common);

sub handler {
    my $r = shift;
    return DECLINED if $r->proxyreq;
    my $uri = $r->uri;
    my %mappings = split /\s*(?:,|=>)\s*/, $r->dir_config('PerlPassThru');
    for my $src (keys %mappings) {
        next unless $uri =~ s/^$src/$mappings{$src}/;
        $r->proxyreq(1);
        $r->uri($uri);
        $r->filename("proxy:$uri");
```

Example 7-10. Invoking Apache's Proxy Request Mechanism from Within a Translation Handler (continued)

```
        $r->handler('proxy-server');
        return OK;
    }
    return DECLINED;
}
1;
__END__
```

An Anonymizing Proxy

As public concern about the ability of web servers to track people's surfing sessions grows, anonymizing proxies are becoming more popular. An anonymizing proxy is similar to an ordinary web proxy, except that certain HTTP headers that provide identifying information such as the *Referer, Cookie, User-Agent,* and *From* fields are quietly stripped from the request before forwarding it on to the remote server. Not only is this identifying information removed, but the identity of the requesting host is obscured. The remote server knows only the hostname and IP address of the proxy machine, not the identity of the machine the user is browsing from.

You can write a simple anonymizing proxy in the Apache Perl API in all of 18 lines (including comments). The source code listing is shown in Example 7-11. Like the previous example, it uses Apache's *mod_proxy,* so that module must be installed before this example will run correctly.

The module defines a package global named @Remove containing the names of all the request headers to be stripped from the request. In this example, we remove *User-Agent, Cookie, Referer,* and the infrequently used *From* field. The *handler()* subroutine begins by fetching the Apache request object and checking whether the current request uses the proxy protocol. However, unlike the previous example where we wanted the existence of the proxy to be secret, here we expect the user to explicitly configure his browser to use our anonymizing proxy. So here we return DECLINED if *proxyreq()* returns false.

If *proxyreq()* returns true, we know that we are in the midst of a proxy request. We loop through each of the fields to be stripped and delete them from the incoming headers table by using the request object's *header_in()* method to set the field to *undef.* We then return OK to signal Apache to continue processing the request. That's all there is to it.

To activate the anonymizing proxy, install it as a URI translation handler as before:

```
PerlTransHandler Apache::AnonProxy
```

An alternative that works just as well is to call the module during the header parsing phase (see the discussion of this phase earlier). In some ways, this makes more sense because we aren't doing any actual URI translation, but we are modifying the HTTP header. Here is the appropriate directive:

```
PerlHeaderParserHandler Apache::AnonProxy
```

The drawback to using *PerlHeaderParserHandler* like this is that, unlike *PerlTransHandler*, the directive is allowed in directory configuration sections and *.htaccess* files. But directory configuration sections are irrelevant in proxy requests, so the directive will silently fail if placed in one of these sections. The directive should go in the main part of one of the configuration files or in a virtual host section.

Example 7-11. A Simple Anonymizing Proxy

```
package Apache::AnonProxy;
# file: Apache/AnonProxy.pm
use strict;
use Apache::Constants qw(:common);

my @Remove = qw(user-agent cookie from referer);

sub handler {
    my $r = shift;
    return DECLINED unless $r->proxyreq;
    foreach (@Remove) {
        $r->header_in($_ => undef);
    }
    return OK;
}

1;
__END__
```

In order to test that this handler was actually working, we set up a test Apache server as the target of the proxy requests and added the following entry to its configuration file:

```
CustomLog logs/nosy_log "%h %{Referer}i %{User-Agent}i %{Cookie}i %U"
```

This created a "nosy" log that contains entries for the *Referer, User-Agent*, and *Cookie* fields. Before installing the anonymous proxy module, entries in this log looked like this (the lines have been wrapped to fit on the page):

```
192.168.2.5 http://prego/ Mozilla/4.04 [en] (X11; I; Linux 2.0.33 i686)
    - /tkdocs/tk_toc.ht
192.168.2.5 http://prego/ Mozilla/4.04 [en] (X11; I; Linux 2.0.33 i686)
    POMIS=10074 /perl/hangman1.pl
```

In contrast, after installing the anonymizing proxy module, all the identifying information was stripped out, leaving only the IP address of the proxy machine:

```
192.168.2.5 - - - /perl/hangman1.pl
192.168.2.5 - - - /icons/hangman/h0.gif
192.168.2.5 - - - /cgi-bin/info2www
```

Handling the Proxy Process on Your Own

As long as you only need to monitor or modify the request half of a proxy transaction, you can use Apache's *mod_proxy* module directly as we did in the previous two examples. However, if you also want to intercept the response so as to modify the information returned from the remote server, then you'll need to handle the proxy request on your own.

In this section, we present *Apache::AdBlocker*. This module replaces Apache's *mod_proxy* with a specialized proxy that filters the content of certain URLs. Specifically, it looks for URLs that are likely to be banner advertisements and replaces their content with a transparent GIF image that says "Blocked Ad." This can be used to "lower the volume" of commercial sites by removing distracting animated GIFs and brightly colored banners. Figure 7-3 shows what the AltaVista search site looks like when fetched through the *Apache::AdBlocker* proxy.

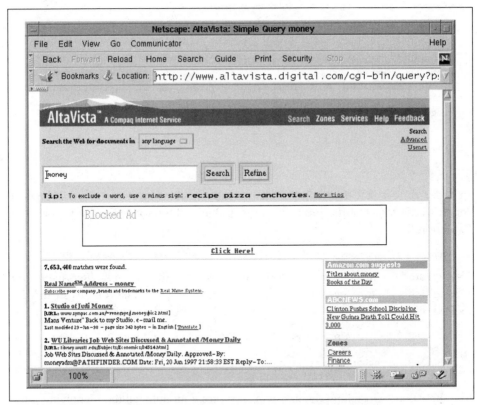

Figure 7-3. The AltaVista search engine after filtering by Apache::AdBlocker

The code for *Apache::AdBlocker* is given in Example 7-12. It is a bit more complicated than the other modules we've worked with in this chapter but not much more. The basic strategy is to install two handlers. The first handler is activated during the URI translation phase. It doesn't actually alter the URI or filename in any way, but it does inspect the transaction to see if it is a proxy request. If this is the case, the handler installs a custom content handler to actually go out and do the request. In this respect, the translation handler is similar to *Apache::Checksum3*, which also installs a custom content handler for certain URIs.

Later on, when its content handler is called, the module uses the Perl LWP library to fetch the remote document. If the document does not appear to be a banner ad, the content handler forwards it on to the waiting client. Otherwise, the handler does a little switcheroo, replacing the advertisement with a custom GIF image of exactly the same size and shape as the ad. This bit of legerdemain is completely invisible to the browser, which goes ahead and renders the image as if it were the original banner ad.

In addition to the LWP library, this module requires the *GD* and *Image::Size* libraries for creating and manipulating images. They are available on CPAN if you do not already have them installed.

Turning to the code, after the familiar preamble we create a new *LWP::UserAgent* object that we will use to make all our requests for documents from remote servers:

```
@ISA = qw(LWP::UserAgent);
$VERSION = '1.00';

my $UA = __PACKAGE__->new;
$UA->agent(join "/", __PACKAGE__, $VERSION);
```

We actually subclass *LWP::UserAgent*, using the `@ISA` global to create an inheritance relationship between *LWP::UserAgent* and our own package. Although we don't override any of *LWP::UserAgent*'s methods, making our module a subclass of *LWP::UserAgent* allows us to cleanly customize these methods at a later date should we need to.

We now create a new instance of the *LWP::UserAgent* subclass, using the special token `__PACKAGE__` which evaluates at compile time to the name of the current package. In this case, `__PACKAGE__->new` is equivalent to `Apache::AdBlocker->new` (or `new Apache::AdBlocker` if you prefer Smalltalk syntax). Immediately afterward we call the object's *agent()* method with a string composed of the package name and version number. This is the calling card that LWP sends to the remote hosts' web servers as the HTTP *User-Agent* field. The method we use for constructing the *User-Agent* field creates the string `Apache::AdBlocker/1.00`.

```
my $Ad = join "|", qw{ads? advertisements? banners? adv promotions?};
```

The last initialization step is to define a package global named `$Ad` that defines a pattern match that picks up many (but certainly not all) banner advertisement

URIs. Most ads contain variants on the words "ad," "advertisement," "banner," or "promotion" somewhere in the URI, although this may have changed by the time you read this!

```
sub handler {
    my $r = shift;
    return DECLINED unless $r->proxyreq;
    $r->handler("perl-script"); #ok, let's do it
    $r->push_handlers(PerlHandler => \&proxy_handler);
    return OK;
}
```

The next part of the module is the definition of the *handler()* subroutine, which in this case will be run during the URI translation phase. It simply checks whether the current transaction is a proxy request and declines the transaction if not. Otherwise, it calls the request object's *handler()* method to set the content handler to *perl-script* and calls *push_handlers()* to make the module's *proxy_handler()* subroutine the callback for the response phase of the transaction. *handler()* then returns OK to flag that it has handled the URI translation phase.

Most of the work is done in *proxy_handler()*. Its job is to use LWP's object-oriented methods to create an *HTTP::Request* object. The *HTTP::Request* is then forwarded to the remote host by the *LWP::UserAgent*, returning an *HTTP::Response*. The response must then be returned to the waiting browser, possibly after replacing the content. The only subtlety here is the need to copy the request headers from the incoming Apache request's *headers_in()* table to the *HTTP::Request* and, in turn, to copy the response headers from the *HTTP::Response* into the Apache request *headers_out()* table. If this copying back and forth isn't performed, then documents that rely on the exact values of certain HTTP fields, such as CGI scripts, will fail to work correctly across the proxy.

```
sub proxy_handler {
    my $r = shift;

    my $request = HTTP::Request->new($r->method, $r->uri);
```

proxy_handler() starts by recovering the Apache request object. It then uses the request object's *method()* and *uri()* methods to fetch the request method and the URI. These are used to create and initialize a new *HTTP::Request*. We now feed the incoming header fields from the Apache request object into the corresponding fields in the outgoing *HTTP::Request*:

```
$r->headers_in->do(sub {
    $request->header(@_);
});
```

We use a little trick to accomplish the copy. The *headers_in()* method (as opposed to the *header_in()* method that we have seen before) returns an instance of the *Apache::Table* class. This class, described in more detail in Chapter 9 (see "The Apache::Table Class"), implements methods for manipulating Apache's various table-like structures, including the incoming and outgoing HTTP header fields. One of these methods is *do()*, which when passed a CODE reference invokes the code once for each header field, passing to the routine the header's name and value each time. In this case, we call *do()* with an anonymous subroutine that passes the header keys and values on to the *HTTP::Request* object's *header()* method. It is important to use *headers->do()* here rather than copying the headers into a hash because certain headers, particularly *Cookie*, can be multivalued.

```
# copy POST data, if any
if($r->method eq 'POST') {
    my $len = $r->header_in('Content-length');
    my $buf;
    $r->read($buf, $len);
    $request->content($buf);
}
```

The next block of code checks whether the request method is POST. If so, we must copy the POSTed data from the incoming request to the *HTTP::Request* object. We do this by calling the request object's *read()* method to read the POST data into a temporary buffer. The data is then copied into the *HTTP::Request* by calling its *content()* method. Request methods other than POST may include a request body, but this example does not cope with these rare cases.

The *HTTP::Request* object is now complete, so we can actually issue the request:

```
my $response = $UA->request($request);
```

We pass the *HTTP::Request* object to the user agent's *request()* method. After a delay for the network fetch, the call returns an *HTTP::Response* object, which we copy into a variable named **$response**.

```
$r->content_type($response->header('Content-type'));
$r->status($response->code);
$r->status_line(join " ", $response->code, $response->message);
```

Now the process of copying the headers is reversed. Every header in the LWP *HTTP::Response* object must be copied to the Apache request object. First, we handle a few special cases. We call the *HTTP::Response* object's *header()* method to fetch the content type of the returned document and immediately pass the result to the Apache request object's *content_type()* method. Next, we set the numeric HTTP status code and the human-readable HTTP status line. We call the *HTTP::Response* object's *code()* and *message()* methods to return the numeric code and human-readable messages, respectively, and copy them to the Apache request object, using the *status()* and *status_line()* methods to set the values.

When the special case headers are done, we copy all the other header fields, using the *HTTP::Response* object's *scan()* method:

```
$response->scan(sub {
    $r->header_out(@_);
});
```

scan() is similar to the *Apache::Table do()* method: it loops through each of the header fields, invoking an anonymous callback routine for each one. The callback sets the corresponding field in the Apache request object using the *header_out()* method.

```
if ($r->header_only) {
    $r->send_http_header();
    return OK;
}
```

The outgoing header is complete at this point, so we check whether the current transaction is a HEAD request. If so, we emit the HTTP header and exit with an OK status code.

```
my $content = \$response->content;
if($r->content_type =~ /^image/ and $r->uri =~ /\b($Ad)\b/i) {
    block_ad($content);
    $r->content_type("image/gif");
}
```

Otherwise, the time has come to deal with potential banner ads. To identify likely ads, we require that the document be an image and that its URI satisfy the regular expression match defined at the top of the module. We retrieve the document contents by calling the *HTTP::Response* object's *content()* method, and store a reference to the contents in a local variable named $content.* We now check whether the document's MIME type is one of the image variants and that the URI satisfies the advertisement pattern match. If both of these are true, we call *block_ad()* to replace the content with a customized image. We also set the document's content type to *image/gif,* since this is what *block_ad()* produces.

```
$r->content_type('text/html') unless $$content;
$r->send_http_header;
$r->print($$content || $response->error_as_HTML);
```

We send the HTTP header, then print the document contents. Notice that the document content may be empty, which can happen when LWP connects to a server that is down or busy. In this case, instead of printing an empty document, we return the nicely formatted error message returned by the *HTTP::Response* object's *error_as_HTML()* method.

---

* In this example, we call the response object's *content()* method to slurp the document content into a scalar. However, it can be more efficient to use the three-argument form of *LWP::UserAgent's response()* method to read the content in fixed-size chunks. See the *LWP::UserAgent* manual page for details.

```
        return OK;
    }
```

Our work is done, so we return an OK status code.

The *block_ad()* subroutine is short and sweet. Its job is to take an image in any of several possible formats and replace it with a custom GIF of exactly the same dimensions. The GIF will be transparent, allowing the page background color to show through, and will have the words "Blocked Ad" printed in large friendly letters in the upper lefthand corner.

```
sub block_ad {
    my $data = shift;
    my($x, $y) = imgsize($data);

    my $im = GD::Image->new($x,$y);
```

To get the width and height of the image, we call *imgsize()*, a function imported from the *Image::Size* module. *imgsize()* recognizes most web image formats, including GIF, JPEG, XBM, and PNG. Using these values, we create a new blank *GD::Image* object and store it in a variable named $im.

```
    my $white = $im->colorAllocate(255,255,255);
    my $black = $im->colorAllocate(0,0,0);
    my $red = $im->colorAllocate(255,0,0);
```

We call the image object's *colorAllocate()* method three times to allocate color table entries for white, black, and red. Then we declare that the white color is transparent, using the *transparent()* method:

```
    $im->transparent($white);
    $im->string(GD::gdLargeFont(),5,5,"Blocked Ad",$red);
    $im->rectangle(0,0,$x-1,$y-1,$black);

    $$data = $im->gif;
    }
```

The routine calls the *string()* method to draw the message starting at coordinates (5,5) and finally frames the whole image with a black rectangle. The custom image is now converted into GIF format with the *gif()* method and copied into $$data, overwriting whatever was there before.

```
    sub redirect_ok {return undef;}
```

The last detail is to define a *redirect_ok()* method to override the default *LWP::UserAgent* method. By returning *undef* this method tells LWP not to handle redirects internally but to pass them on to the browser to handle. This is the correct behavior for a proxy server.

Activating this module is just a matter of adding the following line to one of the configuration files:

```
    PerlTransHandler Apache::AdBlocker
```

Users who wish to make use of this filtering service should configure their browsers to proxy their requests through your server.

Example 7-12. A Banner Ad Blocking Proxy

```
package Apache::AdBlocker;
# file: Apache/AdBlocker.pm

use strict;
use vars qw(@ISA $VERSION);
use Apache::Constants qw(:common);
use GD ();
use Image::Size qw(imgsize);
use LWP::UserAgent ();

@ISA = qw(LWP::UserAgent);
$VERSION = '1.00';

my $UA = __PACKAGE__->new;
$UA->agent(join "/", __PACKAGE__, $VERSION);

my $Ad = join "|", qw{ads? advertisements? banners? adv promotions?};

sub handler {
    my $r = shift;
    return DECLINED unless $r->proxyreq;
    $r->handler("perl-script"); #ok, let's do it
    $r->push_handlers(PerlHandler => \&proxy_handler);
    return OK;
}

sub proxy_handler {
    my $r = shift;

    my $request = HTTP::Request->new($r->method, $r->uri);

    $r->headers_in->do(sub {
        $request->header(@_);
    });

    # copy POST data, if any
    if($r->method eq 'POST') {
        my $len = $r->header_in('Content-length');
        my $buf;
        $r->read($buf, $len);
        $request->content($buf);
    }

    my $response = $UA->request($request);
    $r->content_type($response->header('Content-type'));

    #feed response back into our request_rec*
    $r->status($response->code);
    $r->status_line(join " ", $response->code, $response->message);
```

Example 7-12. A Banner Ad Blocking Proxy (continued)

```perl
    $response->scan(sub {
        $r->header_out(@_);
    });

    if ($r->header_only) {
        $r->send_http_header();
        return OK;
    }

    my $content = \$response->content;
    if($r->content_type =~ /^image/ and $r->uri =~ /\b($Ad)\b/i) {
        block_ad($content);
        $r->content_type("image/gif");
    }

    $r->content_type('text/html') unless $$content;
    $r->send_http_header;
    $r->print($$content || $response->error_as_HTML);

    return OK;
}

sub block_ad {
    my $data = shift;
    my($x, $y) = imgsize($data);

    my $im = GD::Image->new($x,$y);

    my $white = $im->colorAllocate(255,255,255);
    my $black = $im->colorAllocate(0,0,0);
    my $red   = $im->colorAllocate(255,0,0);

    $im->transparent($white);
    $im->string(GD::gdLargeFont(),5,5,"Blocked Ad",$red);
    $im->rectangle(0,0,$x-1,$y-1,$black);

    $$data = $im->gif;
}

sub redirect_ok {return undef;}

1;
__END__
```

Perl Server-Side Includes

Another feature of *mod_perl* is that it integrates with the Apache *mod_include* server-side include (SSI) system. Provided that *mod_perl* was built with the *PERL_SSI* option (or with the recommended setting of *EVERYTHING=1*), the Perl API adds a new *#perl* element to the standard *mod_include* server-side include system, allowing server-side includes to call Perl subroutines directly.

The syntax for calling Perl from SSI documents looks like this:

```
<!--#perl sub="subroutine" args="arguments"-->
```

The tag looks like other server-side include tags but contains the embedded element *#perl*. The *#perl* element recognizes two attributes, *sub* and *args*. The required *sub* attribute specifies the subroutine to be invoked. This attribute must occur only once in the tag. It can be the name of any subroutine already loaded into the server (with a *PerlModule* directive, for instance) or an anonymous subroutine created on the fly. When this subroutine is invoked, it is passed a blessed *Apache* request object just as if it were a handler for the response phase. Any text that the subroutine prints will appear on the HTML page.

The optional *args* attribute can occur once or several times in the tag. If present, *args* attributes specify additional arguments to be passed to the subroutine. They will be presented to the subroutine in the same order in which they occur in the tag.

Example 7-13 shows a simple server-side include page that uses *#perl* elements. It has two Perl includes. The simpler of the two is just a call to a routine named *MySSI::remote_host()*. When executed, it calls the request object's *get_remote_host()* method to fetch the DNS name of the remote host machine:

```
<!--#perl sub="MySSI::remote_host" -->
```

MySSI::remote_host() must be preloaded in order for this include to succeed. One way to do this is inside the Perl startup file. Alternatively, it could be defined in a module named *MySSI.pm* and loaded with the directive *PerlModule MySSI*. In either case, the definition of *remote_host()* looks like this:

```
package MySSI;
sub remote_host {
    my $r = shift;
    print $r->get_remote_host;
}
```

You could also define the routine to call the request object's *print()* method, as in `$r->print($r->get_remote_host)`. It's your call.

The more complex of the two includes defined in this example calls a Perl subroutine that it creates on the fly. It looks like this:

```
<!--#perl arg="Hello" arg="SSI" arg="World"
        sub="sub {
                my($r, @args) = @_;
                print qq(@args);
            }"
-->
```

In this case the *sub* attribute points to an anonymous subroutine defined using the **sub** {} notation. This subroutine retrieves the request object and a list of arguments, which it simply prints out. Because double quotes are already used to surround the attribute, we use Perl's *qq* operator to surround the arguments. An equally valid alternative would be to backslash the quotes, as in `print \"@args\"`.

This tag also has three *arg* attributes, which are passed, in order of appearance, to the subroutine. The effect is to print the string "Hello SSI World".

In order to try this example out, you'll have to have server-side includes activated. This can be done by uncommenting the following two lines in the standard *srm.conf* server configuration file:

```
AddType    text/html    .shtml
AddHandler server-parsed .shtml
```

You'll also have to activate the *Includes* option in the directory in which the document is located. The final result is shown in Figure 7-4.

Example 7-13. A Server-Side Include Document Using #perl Elements

```
<html>
<!-- file: perl_include.shtml -->
<head>
<title> mod_include #perl example </title>
</head>
<body>
<h1>mod_include #perl example</h1>

This document uses the <i>mod_include</i> <b>perl</b> command to
invoke Perl subroutines.

<h3>Here is an Anonymous Subroutine</h3>

Message =

<!--#perl arg="Hello" arg="SSI" arg="World"
        sub="sub {
                my($r, @args) = @_;
                print qq(@args);
            }"
-->

<h3>Here is a Predefined Subroutine</h3>

Remote host = <!--#perl sub="MySSI::remote_host" -->

<hr>
</body>
</html>
```

That's all there is to it. You can mix and match any of the standard *mod_include* commands in your document along with any Perl code that you see fit. There's also an *Apache::Include* module included with the *mod_perl* distribution that

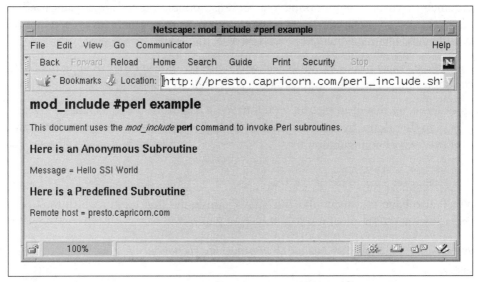

Figure 7-4. The page displayed by the example server-side include document

allows you to invoke *Apache::Registry* scripts directly from within server-side includes. See Appendix A, *Standard Noncore Modules,* for details.

While this approach is simple, it is not particularly powerful. If you wish to produce complex server-side include documents with conditional sections and content derived from databases, we recommend that you explore *HTML::Embperl, Apache::ePerl, HTML::Mason,* and other template-based systems that can be found on CPAN. Also see Appendix F, *HTML::Embperl—Embedding Perl Code in HTML,* which contains an abbreviated version of the *HTML::Embperl* manual page, courtesy of Gerald Richter.

Subclassing the Apache Class

It's appropriate that the last topic we discuss in this chapter is the technique for extending the *Apache* class itself with Perl's subclassing mechanism. Because the Perl API is object-oriented, you are free to subclass the *Apache* class should you wish to override its behavior in any way.

To be successful, the new subclass must add *Apache* (or another *Apache* subclass) to its @ISA array. In addition, the subclass's *new()* method must return a blessed hash reference which contains either an r or _r key. This key must point to a bona fide *Apache* object.

Example 7-14 subclasses *Apache,* overriding the *print()* and *rflush()* methods. The *Apache::MyRequest::print* method does not send data directly to the client. Instead, it pushes all data into an array reference inside the *Apache::MyRequest* object. When the *rflush()* method is called, the *SUPER* class methods, *print* and *rflush,* are called to actually send the data to the client.

Example 7-14. Apache::MyRequest Is a Subclass of Apache

```
package Apache::MyRequest;
use strict;

use Apache ();
use vars qw(@ISA);
@ISA = qw(Apache);

sub new {
    my($class, $r) = @_;
    $r ||= Apache->request;
    return bless {
        '_r' => $r,
        'data' => [],
    }, $class;
}

sub print {
    my $self = shift;
    push @{$self->{data}}, @_;
}

sub rflush {
    my $self = shift;
    $self->SUPER::print("MyDATA:\n", join "\n", @{$self->{data}});
    $self->SUPER::rflush;
    @{$self->{data}} = ();
}

1;
__END__
```

Here is an example of an *Apache::Registry* script that uses *Apache::MyRequest.* The *send_http_header()* method is inherited from the *Apache* class, while the *print()* and *rflush()* methods invoke those in the *Apache::MyRequest* class:

```
use Apache::MyRequest ();
sub handler {
    my $r = Apache::MyRequest->new(shift);
    $r->send_http_header('text/plain');
    $r->print(qw(one two three));
    $r->rflush;
    ...
}
```

The next chapter covers another important topic in the Apache Perl API: how to control and customize the Apache configuration process so that modules can implement first-class configuration directives of their own.

8

Customizing the Apache Configuration Process

This chapter covers an important but complex aspect of the Apache Perl API—the process of controlling and customizing the Apache configuration process itself. Using the techniques shown in this chapter, you will be able to define new configuration file directives that provide runtime configuration information to your modules. You will also be able to take over all or part of the Apache configuration process and write Perl code to dynamically configure the server at startup time.

Simple Configuration with the PerlSetVar Directive

The Apache Perl API provides a simple mechanism for passing information from configuration files to Perl modules using the *PerlSetVar* directive. As we've seen, the directive takes two arguments, the name of a variable and its value:

```
PerlSetVar FoodForThought apples
```

Because Perl is such a whiz at parsing text, it's trivial to pass an array or even a hash in this way. For example, here's one way (out of a great many) to pass an array:

```
# in configuration file
PerlSetVar FoodForThought apples:oranges:kiwis:mangos

# in Perl module
@foodForThought = split ":", $r->dir_config('FoodForThought');
```

And here's a way to pass a hash:

```
# in configuration file
PerlSetVar FoodForThought apples=>23,kiwis=>12
```

```
# in Perl module
%foodForThought = split /\s*(?:=>|,)\s*/, $r->dir_config('FoodForThought);
```

Notice that the pattern match allows whitespace to come before or after the comma or arrow operators, just as Perl does.

By modifying the pattern match appropriately, you can pass more complex configuration information. The only trick is to remember to put double quotes around the configuration value if it contains whitespace and not to allow your text editor to wrap it to another line. You can use backslash as a continuation character if you find long lines a pain to read:

```
PerlSetVar FoodForThought "apples    => 23,\
                           kiwis     => 12,\
                           rutabagas => 0"
```

If you have a *really* complex configuration, then you are probably better off using a separate configuration file and pointing to it using a single *PerlSetVar* directive. The *server_root_relative()* method is useful for specifying configuration files that are relative to the server root:

```
# in server configuration file
PerlSetVar  FoodConfig conf/food.conf

# in Perl module
$conf_file = $r->server_root_relative($r->dir_config('FoodConfig'));
```

Despite the simplicity of this approach, there are times when you may prefer to create your own "first-class" configuration directives. This becomes particularly desirable when you have many different directives, when the exact syntax of the directives is important and you want Apache to check the syntax at startup time, or when you are planning to distribute your module and want it to appear polished. There is also a performance penalty associated with parsing *PerlSetVar* configuration at request time, which you avoid using first-class configuration directives because they are parsed once at server startup time.

The Apache Configuration Directive API

Apache provides an API for defining configuration directives. You provide the directive's name, syntax, and a string briefly summarizing the directive's intended usage. You may also limit the applicability of the directive to certain parts of the configuration files. Apache parses the directive and passes the parsed structure to your module for processing. Your module will then use this information to set up global variables or initialize whatever it needs.

The process of defining new configuration directives is not as simple as other parts of the Perl API. This is because configuration directives are defined in a compiled

C structure that cannot be built dynamically at runtime. In order to work with this restriction, *mod_perl* requires you to take the following roundabout route:

1. Create an empty module directory with *h2xs*.

2. Modify the newly created *Makefile.PL* file to declare an array containing the definitions for the new configuration directives and to invoke the *command_table()* function from a helper module named *Apache::ExtUtils*.

3. Write a *.pm* file containing Perl handlers for each of the configuration directives you define.

4. Run *perl Makefile.PL* to autogenerate a *.xs* file.

5. Run *make* and *make install* to create the loadable module and move it into place.

6. Add a *PerlModule* directive to the server configuration file to load the module at server startup time.

We'll take you through a short example first to show you the whole process and then get into the details later. Our candidate for adding configuration directives is the *Apache::PassThru* module (Example 7-10), which transparently maps portions of the server's document tree onto remote servers using Apache's proxy mechanism.

As you may recall, *Apache::PassThru* used a single *PerlSetVar* variable named *PerlPassThru*, which contained a series of *URI=>proxy* pairs stored in one long string. Although this strategy is adequate, it's not particularly elegant. Our goal here is to create a new first-class configuration directive named *PerlPassThru*. *PerlPassThru* will take two arguments: a local URI and a remote URI to map it to. You'll be able to repeat the directive to map several local URIs to remote servers. Because it makes no sense for the directory to appear in directory sections or *.htaccess* files, *PerlPassThru* will be limited to the main parts of the *httpd.conf*, *srm.conf*, and *access.conf* files, as well as to *<VirtualHost>* sections.

First we'll need something to start with, so we use *h2xs* to create a skeletal module directory:

```
% h2xs -Af -n Apache::PassThru
Writing Apache/PassThru/PassThru.pm
Writing Apache/PassThru/PassThru.xs
Writing Apache/PassThru/Makefile.PL
Writing Apache/PassThru/test.pl
Writing Apache/PassThru/Changes
Writing Apache/PassThru/MANIFEST
```

The *−A* and *−f* command-line switches turn off the generation of autoloader stubs and the C header file conversion steps, respectively. *−n* gives the module a name. We'll be editing the files *Makefile.PL* and *PassThru.pm*. *PassThru.xs* will be overwritten when we go to make the module, so there's no need to worry about it.

The next step is to edit the *Makefile.PL* script to add the declaration of the *PerlPassThru* directive and to arrange for *Apache::ExtUtils'* *command_table()* function to be executed at the appropriate moment. Example 8-1 shows a suitable version of the file.

Example 8-1. Makefile.PL for the Improved Apache::PassThru

```
package Apache::PassThru;
# File: Apache/PassThru/Makefile.PL

use ExtUtils::MakeMaker;

use Apache::ExtUtils qw(command_table);
use Apache::src ();

my @directives = (
                 { name       => 'PerlPassThru',
                   errmsg     => 'a local path and a remote URI to pass through to',
                   args_how => 'TAKE2',
                   req_override => 'RSRC_CONF'
                 }
                 );

command_table(\@directives);

WriteMakefile(
    'NAME'         => __PACKAGE__,
    'VERSION_FROM' => 'PassThru.pm',
    'INC'          => Apache::src->new->inc,
    'INSTALLSITEARCH' => '/usr/local/apache/lib/perl',
    'INSTALLSITELIB'  => '/usr/local/apache/lib/perl',
);
__END__
```

We've made multiple modifications to the *Makefile.PL* originally produced by *h2xs*. First, we've placed a *package* declaration at the top, putting the whole script in the *Apache::PassThru* namespace. Then, after the original use ExtUtils::Make-Maker line, we load two *mod_perl*-specific modules: *Apache::ExtUtils*, which defines the *command_table()* function, and *Apache::src*, a small utility class that can be used to find the location of the Apache header files. These will be needed during the make.

Next, we define the new configuration directives themselves. We create a list named @directives, each element of which corresponds to a different directive. In this case, we only have one directive to declare, so @directives is one element long.

Each element of the list is an anonymous hash containing one or more of the keys name, errmsg, args_how, and req_override (we'll see later how to implement the most common type of directive using a succinct anonymous array form). name corresponds to the name of the directive, *PerlPassThru* in this case, and errmsg corresponds to a short message that will be displayed in the event of a configuration syntax error. `args_how` tells Apache how to parse the directive's arguments. In this case we specify `TAKE2`, which tells Apache that the directive takes two (and only two) arguments. We'll go over the complete list of parsing options later and also show you a shortcut for specifying parsing options using Perl prototypes.

The last key, `req_override`, tells Apache what configuration file contexts the directive is allowed in. In this case we specify the most restrictive context, `RSRC_CONF`, which limits the directive to appearing in the main part of the configuration files or in virtual host sections. Notice that `RSRC_CONF` is an ordinary string, *not* a bareword function call!

Having defined our configuration directive array, we pass a reference to it to the *command_table()* function. When run, this routine writes out a file named *PassThru.xs* to the current directory. *command_table()* uses the package information returned by the Perl *caller()* function to figure out the name of the file to write. This is why it was important to include a package declaration at the top of the script.

The last part of *Makefile.PL* is the call *WriteMakefile()*, a routine provided by *ExtUtils::MakeMaker* and automatically placed in *Makefile.PL* by *h2xs*. However, we've modified the autogenerated call in three small but important ways. The `INC` key, which *MakeMaker* uses to generate include file switches, has been modified to use the value returned by `Apache::src->new->inc` (a shorthand way of creating a new *Apache::src* object and immediately calling its *inc()* method). This call will return a list of directories that contain various header files needed to build Apache C-language modules. We've also added the keys `INSTALLSITEARCH` and `INSTALLSITELIB` to the parameters passed to *WriteMakeFile()*, in each case specifying the path we use for Apache Perl API modules on our system (you'll have to modify this for your setup). This ensures that when we run *make install* the module file and its loadable object will be moved to the location of Apache-specific modules rather than the default Perl library directory.

The next step is to modify *PassThru.pm* to accommodate the new configuration directive. We start with the file from Example 7-10 and add the following lines to the top:

```
use Apache::ModuleConfig ();
use DynaLoader ();
use vars qw($VERSION);

$VERSION = '1.00';

if($ENV{MOD_PERL}) {
    no strict;
    @ISA = qw(DynaLoader);
    __PACKAGE__->bootstrap($VERSION);
}
```

This brings in code for fetching and modifying the current configuration settings and loads the *DynaLoader* module, which provides the *bootstrap()* routine for loading shared library code. We test the MOD_PERL environment variable to find out if we are running inside *httpd* and, if so, invoke *bootstrap()* to load the object file that contains the compiled directory configuration record.

Next, we add the following configuration processing callback routine to the file:

```
sub PerlPassThru ($$$$) {
   my($cfg, $parms, $local, $remote) = @_;
   $cfg->{PassThru}{$local} = $remote;
}
```

The callback (also known as the "directive handler") is a subroutine that will be called each time Apache processes a *PerlPassThru* directive. It is responsible for stashing the information into a configuration record where it can be retrieved later by the *handler()* subroutine. The name of the subroutine must exactly match the name of the configuration directive, capitalization included. It should also have a prototype that correctly matches the syntax of the configuration directive. All configuration callbacks are called with at least two scalar arguments, indicated by the function prototype ($$). The first argument, $cfg, is the per-directory or per-server object where the configuration data will be stashed. As we will explain shortly, your handlers will recover this object and retrieve the values of the configuration directives it needs. The second argument, $parms, is an *Apache::Cmd-Parms* object from which you can retrieve various other information about the configuration.

Callbacks may be passed other parameters as well, corresponding to the arguments of the configuration directive that the callback is responsible for. Because *PerlPassThru* is a TAKE2 directive, we expect two additional arguments, so the complete function prototype is ($$$$).

The body of the subroutine is trivial. For all intents and purposes, the configuration object is a hash reference in which you can store arbitrary key/value pairs. The convention is to choose a key with the same name as the configuration directive. In this case, we use an anonymous hash to store the current local and remote URIs into the configuration object at a key named *PassThru*. This allows us to have multiple mappings while guaranteeing that each local URI is unique.

The *Apache::PassThru handler()* subroutine needs a slight modification as well. We remove this line:

```
my %mappings = split /\s*(?:,|=>)\s*/, $r->dir_config('PerlPassThru');
```

and substitute the following:

```
my %mappings = ();
if(my $cfg = Apache::ModuleConfig->get($r)) {
    %mappings = %{ $cfg->{PassThru} } if $cfg->{PassThru};
}
```

We call the *Apache::ModuleConfig* class method *get()*, passing it the request object. This retrieves the same configuration object that was previously processed by *PerlPassThru()*. We then fetch the value of the configuration object's *PassThru* key. If the key is present, we dereference it and store it into **%mappings**. We then proceed as before. Example 8-2 gives the complete code for the modified module.

The last step is to arrange for *Apache::PassThru* to be loaded at server startup time. The easiest way to do this is to load the module with a *PerlModule* directive:

```
PerlModule Apache::PassThru
```

The only trick to this is that you must be careful that the *PerlModule* directive is called before any *PerlPassThru* directives appear. Otherwise, Apache won't recognize the new directive and will abort with a configuration file syntax error. The other caveat is that *PerlModule* only works to bootstrap configuration directives in *mod_perl* Versions 1.17 and higher. If you are using an earlier version, use this configuration section instead:

```
<Perl>
  use Apache::PassThru ();
</Perl>
```

<Perl> sections are described in detail toward the end of this chapter.

Now change the old *Apache::PassThru* configuration to use the first-class *Perl-PassThru* directive:

```
PerlModule Apache::PassThru
PerlTransHandler Apache::PassThru

PerlPassThru /CPAN   http://www.perl.com/CPAN
PerlPassThru /search http://www.altavista.com
```

After restarting the server, you should now be able to test the *Apache::PassThru* handler to confirm that it correctly proxies the */CPAN* and */search* URIs.

If your server has the *mod_info* module configured, you should be able to view the entry for the *Apache::PassThru* module. It will look something like this:

```
Module Name: Apache::PassThru

Content handlers: none

Configuration Phase Participation: Create Directory Config, Create
      Server Config

Request Phase Participation: none

Module Directives:
      PerlPassThru - a local path and a remote URI to pass through
      to
```

```
Current Configuration:
httpd.conf
        PerlPassThru /CPAN http://www.perl.com/CPAN
        PerlPassThru /search http://www.altavista.com
```

Now try changing the syntax of the *PerlPassThru* directive. Create a directive that has too many arguments or one that has too few. Try putting the directive inside a *<Directory>* section or *.htaccess* file. Any attempt to violate the syntax restrictions we specified in *Makefile.PL* with the *args_how* and *req_override* keys should cause a syntax error at server startup time.

Example 8-2. Apache::PassThru with a Custom Configuration Directive

```perl
package Apache::PassThru;
# file: Apache/PassThru.pm;
use strict;
use vars qw($VERSION);
use Apache::Constants qw(:common);
use Apache::ModuleConfig ();
use DynaLoader ();

$VERSION = '1.00';

if($ENV{MOD_PERL}) {
    no strict;
    @ISA = qw(DynaLoader);
    __PACKAGE__->bootstrap($VERSION);
}

sub handler {
    my $r = shift;
    return DECLINED if $r->proxyreq;
    my $uri = $r->uri;
    my %mappings = ();

    if(my $cfg = Apache::ModuleConfig->get($r)) {
        %mappings = %{ $cfg->{PassThru} } if $cfg->{PassThru};
    }

    foreach my $src (keys %mappings) {
        next unless $uri =~ s/^$src/$mappings{$src}/;
        $r->proxyreq(1);
        $r->uri($uri);
        $r->filename("proxy:$uri");
        $r->handler('proxy-server');
        return OK;
    }
    return DECLINED;
}

sub PerlPassThru ($$$$) {
    my($cfg, $parms, $local, $remote) = @_;
```

Example 8-2. Apache::PassThru with a Custom Configuration Directive (continued)

```
    unless ($remote =~ /^http:/) {
        die "Argument '$remote' is not a URL\n";
    }
    $cfg->{PassThru}{$local} = $remote;
}

1;
__END__
```

Designing Configuration Directives

We'll now look in more detail at how you can precisely control the behavior of configuration directives.

As you recall, a module's configuration directives are declared in an array of hashes passed to the *command_table()* function. Each hash contains the required keys, `name` and `errmsg`. In addition, there may be any of four optional keys: `func`, `args_how`, `req_override`, and `cmd_data`.

For example, this code fragment defines two configuration directives named *TrafficCopSpeedLimit* and *TrafficCopRightOfWay*:

```
    @directives = (
            {
              name    => 'TrafficCopSpeedLimit',
              errmsg  => 'an integer specifying the maximum allowable
                          kilobytes per second',
              func    => 'right_of_way',
              args_how => 'TAKE1',
              req_override => 'OR_ALL',
            },
            {
              name    => 'TrafficCopRightOfWay',
              errmsg  => 'list of domains that can go as fast as they
                          want',
              args_how => 'ITERATE',
              req_override => 'OR_ALL',
              cmd_data => '[A-Z_]+',
            },
          );
    command_table(\@directives);
```

The required `name` key points to the name of the directive. It should have exactly the same spelling and capitalization as the directive you want to implement (Apache doesn't actually care about the capitalization of directives, but Perl does when it goes to call your configuration processing callbacks). Alternatively, you can use the optional `func` key to specify a subroutine with a different name than the configuration directive.

The mandatory `errmsg` key should be a short but succinct usage statement that summarizes the arguments that the directive takes.

The optional **args_how** key tells Apache how to parse the directive. There are 11 (!) possibilities corresponding to different numbers of mandatory and optional arguments. Because the number of arguments passed to the Perl callback function for processing depends on the value of **args_how**, the callback function must know in advance how many arguments to expect. The various **args_how** options are described in the next section.

The optional **cmd_data** key is used to pass arbitrary information to the directive handler. The handler can retrieve this information by calling the *info()* method of the *Apache::CmdParms* object that is passed to the directive callback. In our example, we use this information to pass a pattern match expression to the callback. This is how it might be used:

```
sub TrafficCopRightOfWay ($$@) {
    my($cfg, $parms, $domain) = @_;
    my $pat = $parms->info;
    unless ($domain =~ /^$pat$/i) {
        die "Invalid domain: $domain\n";
    }
    $cfg->{RightOfWay}{$domain}++;
}
```

req_override, another optional key, is used to restrict the directive so that it can only legally appear in certain sections of the configuration files.

Specifying Configuration Directive Syntax

Most configuration-processing callbacks will declare function prototypes that describe how they are intended to be called. Although in the current implementation Perl does not check callbacks' prototypes at runtime, they serve a very useful function nevertheless. The *command_table()* function can use callback prototypes to choose the correct syntax for the directive on its own. If no **args_how** key is present in the definition of the directive, *command_table()* will pull in the *.pm* file containing the callback definitions and attempt to autogenerate the *args_how* field on its own, using the Perl *prototype()* built-in function. By specifying the correct prototype, you can forget about **args_how** entirely and let *command_table()* take care of choosing the correct directive parsing method for you.

If both an **args_how** and a function prototype are provided, *command_table()* will use the value of **args_how** in case of a disagreement. If neither an **args_how** nor a function prototype is present, *command_table()* will choose a value of **TAKE123**, which is a relatively permissive parsing rule.

Apache supports a total of 11 different directive parsing methods. This section lists their symbolic constants and the Perl prototypes to use if you wish to take advantage of configuration definition shortcuts.

NO_ARGS ($$) *or no prototype at all*

The directive takes no arguments. The callback will be invoked once each time the directive is encountered.

```
sub TrafficCopOn ($$) {
  shift->{On}++;
}
```

TAKE1 ($$$)

The directive takes a single argument. The callback will be invoked once each time the directive is encountered, and the argument of the directive will be passed to the callback as the third argument.

```
sub TrafficCopActiveSergeant ($$$) {
  my($cfg, $parms, $arg) = @_;
  $cfg->{Sergeant} = $arg;
}
```

TAKE2 ($$$$)

The directive takes two arguments. They are passed to the callback as the third and fourth arguments.

```
sub TrafficCopLimits ($$$$) {
  my($cfg, $parms, $minspeed, $maxspeed) = @_;
  $cfg->{Min} = $minspeed;
  $cfg->{Max} = $maxspeed;
}
```

TAKE3 ($$$$$)

This is like **TAKE1** and **TAKE2**, but the directive takes three mandatory arguments.

TAKE12 ($$$;$)

In this interesting variant, the directive takes one mandatory argument and a second optional one. This can be used when the second argument has a default value that the user may want to override.

```
sub TrafficCopWarningLevel ($$$;$) {
  my($cfg, $parms, $severity_level, $msg) = @_;
  $cfg->{severity} = $severity_level;
  $cfg->{msg} = $msg || "You have exceeded the speed limit. Your
                         license please?"
}
```

TAKE23 ($$$$;$)

TAKE23 is just like **TAKE12**, except now there are two mandatory arguments and an optional third one.

TAKE123 ($$$;$$)

In the **TAKE123** variant, the first argument is mandatory and the other two are optional. This is useful for providing defaults for two arguments.

ITERATE ($$@)

ITERATE is used when a directive can take an unlimited number of arguments. For example, the *mod_autoindex IndexIgnore* directive specifies a list of one or more file extensions to ignore in directory listings:

```
IndexIgnore .bak .sav .hide .conf
```

Although the function prototype suggests that the callback's third argument will be a list, this is not the case. In fact, the callback is invoked repeatedly with a single argument, once for each argument in the list. It's done this way for interoperability with the C API.

The callback should be prepared to be called once for each argument in the directive argument list, and to be called again each time the directive is repeated. For example:

```
sub TrafficCopRightOfWay ($$@) {
  my($cfg, $parms, $domain) = @_;
  $cfg->{RightOfWay}{$domain}++;
}
```

ITERATE2 ($$@;@)

ITERATE2 is an interesting twist on the **ITERATE** theme. It is used for directives that take a mandatory first argument followed by a list of arguments to be applied to the first. A familiar example is the *AddType* directive, in which a series of file extensions are applied to a single MIME type:

```
AddType image/jpeg JPG JPEG JFIF jfif
```

As with **ITERATE**, the callback function prototype for **ITERATE2** is there primarily to provide a unique signature that can be recognized by *command_table()*. Apache will invoke your callback once for each item in the list. Each time Apache runs your callback, it passes the routine the constant first argument (*image/jpeg* in the example) and the current item in the list (JPG the first time around, JPEG the second time, and so on). In the example above, the configuration processing routine will be run a total of four times.

Let's say *Apache::TrafficCop* needs to ticket cars parked on only the days when it is illegal, such as street sweeping day:

```
TrafficCopTicket street_sweeping monday wednesday friday
```

The **ITERATE2** callback to handle this directive would look like:

```
sub TrafficCopTicket ($$@;@) {
   my($cfg, $parms, $violation, $day) = @_;
   push @{ $cfg->{Ticket}{$violation} }, $day;
}
```

RAW_ARGS ($$$;*)

An *args_how* of RAW_ARGS instructs Apache to turn off parsing altogether. Instead, it simply passes your callback function the line of text following the directive. Leading and trailing whitespace is stripped from the text, but it is not otherwise processed. Your callback can then do whatever processing it wishes to perform.

This callback receives four arguments, the third of which is a string-valued scalar containing the text following the directive. The last argument is a file-handle tied to the configuration file. This filehandle can be used to read data from the configuration file starting on the line following the configuration directive. It is most common to use a RAW_ARGS prototype when processing a "container" directive. For example, let's say our TrafficCop needs to build a table of speed limits for a given district:

```
<TrafficCopSpeedLimits charlestown>
   Elm St.      20
   Payson Ave. 15
   Main St.     25
</TrafficCopSpeedLimits>
```

By using the RAW_ARGS prototype, the third argument passed in will be charlestown>; it's up to the handler to strip the trailing >. Now the handler can use the tied filehandle to read the following configuration lines, until it hits the container end token, </TrafficCopSpeedLimits>. For each configuration line that is read in, leading and trailing whitespace is stripped, as is the trailing newline. The handler can then apply any parsing rules it wishes to the line of data:

```
my $EndToken = "</TrafficCopSpeedLimits>";

sub TrafficCopSpeedLimits ($$$;*) {
   my($cfg, $parms, $district, $cfg_fh) = @_;
   $district =~ s/>$//;
   while((my $line = <$cfg_fh>) !~ m:^$EndToken:o) {
       my($road, $limit) = ($line =~ /(.*)\s+(\S+)$/);
       $cfg->{SpeedLimits}{$district}{$road} = $limit;
   }
}
```

There is a trick to making configuration containers work. In order to be recognized as a valid directive, the *name* entry passed to *command_table()* must contain the leading <. This token will be stripped by *Apache::ExtUtils* when it maps the directive to the corresponding subroutine callback.

```
my @directives = (
               { name     => '<TrafficCopSpeedLimits',
                 errmsg   => 'a district speed limit container',
                 args_how => 'RAW_ARGS',
                 req_override => 'OR_ALL'
               },
             );
```

One other trick, which is not required but can provide some more user friend-liness, is to provide a handler for the container end token. In our example, the

Apache configuration gears will never see the `</TrafficCopSpeedLimits>` token, as our `RAW_ARGS` handler will read in that line and stop reading when it is seen. However, in order to catch cases in which the `</TrafficCop-SpeedLimits>` text appears without a preceding `<TrafficCopSpeed-Limits>` opening section, we need to turn the end token into a directive that simply reports an error and exits.

command_table() includes special tests for directives whose names begin with `</`. When it encounters a directive like this, it strips the leading `</` and trailing `>` characters from the name and tacks **_END** onto the end. This allows us to declare an end token callback like this one:

```
my $EndToken = "</TrafficCopSpeedLimits>";
sub TrafficCopSpeedLimits_END () {
    die "$EndToken outside a <TrafficCopSpeedLimits> container\n";
}
```

which corresponds to a directive definition like this one:

```
my @directives = (
                ...
            { name => '</TrafficCopSpeedLimits>',
              errmsg => 'end of speed limit container',
              args_how => 'NO_ARGS',
              req_override => 'OR_ALL',
            },
            );
```

Now, should the server admin misplace the container end token, the server will not start, complaining with this error message:

```
Syntax error on line 89 of httpd.conf:
</TrafficCopSpeedLimits> outside a <TrafficCopSpeedLimits> container
```

FLAG ($$$)

When the **FLAG** prototype is used, Apache will only allow the argument to be one of two values, *On* or *Off.* This string value will be converted into an integer: 1 if the flag is *On,* 0 if it is *Off.* If the configuration argument is anything other than *On* or *Off,* Apache will complain:

```
Syntax error on line 90 of httpd.conf:
TrafficCopRoadBlock must be On or Off
```

Here's an example:

```
# Makefile.PL
my @directives = (
                ...
            { name => 'TrafficCopRoadBlock',
              errmsg => 'On or Off',
              args_how => 'FLAG',
              req_override => 'OR_ALL',
            },
```

```
# TrafficCop.pm
sub TrafficCopRoadBlock ($$$) {
    my($cfg, $parms, $arg) = @_;
    $cfg->{RoadBlock} = $arg;
}
```

On successfully processing a directive, its handler should simply return. If an error occurs while processing the directive, the routine should *die()* with a string describing the source of the error. There is also a third possibility. The configuration directive handler can return DECLINE_CMD, a constant that must be explicitly imported from *Apache::Constants*. This is used in the rare circumstance in which a module redeclares another module's directive in order to override it. The directive handler can then return DECLINE_CMD when it wishes the directive to fall through to the original module's handler.

Restricting Configuration Directive Usage

In addition to specifying the syntax of your custom configuration directives, you can establish limits on how they can be used by specifying the req_override key in the data passed to *command_table()*. This option controls which parts of the configuration files the directives can appear in, called the directive's "context" in the Apache manual pages. This key should point to a bitmap formed by combining the values of several C-language constants:

RSRC_CONF

> The directive can appear in any *.conf* file outside a directory section (*<Directory>*, *<Location>*, or *<Files>*; also *<FilesMatch>* and kin). The directive is not allowed in *.htaccess* files.

ACCESS_CONF

> The directive can appear within directory sections. The directive is not allowed in *.htaccess* files.

OR_AUTHCFG

> The directive can appear within directory sections but not outside them. It is also allowed within *.htaccess* files, provided that the directive *AllowOverride AuthConfig* is set for the current directory.

OR_LIMIT

> The directive can appear within directory sections but not outside them. It is also allowed within *.htaccess* files, provided that the directive *AllowOverride Limit* is set for the current directory.

OR_OPTIONS

> The directive can appear anywhere within the *.conf* files as well as within *.htaccess* files provided that *AllowOverride Options* is set for the current directory.

OR_FILEINFO

> The directive can appear anywhere within the *.conf* files as well as within *.htaccess* files provided that *AllowOverride FileInfo* is set for the current directory.

OR_INDEXES

> The directive can appear anywhere within the *.conf* files as well as within *.htaccess* files provided that *AllowOverride Indexes* is set for the current directory.

OR_ALL

> The directive can appear anywhere. It is not limited in any way.

OR_NONE

> The directive cannot be overridden by any of the *AllowOverride* options.

The value of **req_override** is actually a bit mask. Apache derives the directive context by taking the union of all the set bits. This allows you to combine contexts by combining them with logical ORs and ANDs. For example, the following combination of constants will allow the directive to appear anywhere in a *.conf* file but forbid it from ever being used in a *.htaccess* file:

```
'req_override' => 'RSRC_CONF | ACCESS_CONF'
```

As in the case of **args_how**, the value of the **req_override** key is not evaluated by Perl. It is simply a string that is written into the *.xs* file and eventually passed to the C compiler. This means that any errors in the string you provide for **req_override** will not be caught until the compilation phase.

Directive Definition Shortcuts

We've already seen how to simplify your configuration directives by allowing *command_table()* to deduce the correct **args_how** from the callback's function prototype. One other shortcut is available to you as well.

If you pass *command_table()* a list of array references rather than hash references, then it will take the first item in each array ref to be the name of the configuration directive, and the second item to be the error/usage message. **req_override** will default to OR_ALL (allowing the directive to appear anywhere), and **args_how** will be derived from the callback prototype, if present, or TAKE123 if not.

By taking advantage of this shortcut, we can rewrite the list of configuration directives at the beginning of this section more succinctly:

```
@directives = (
        [
        'TrafficCopSpeedLimit',
        'an integer specifying the maximum allowable bytes per second',
        ],
```

```
           [
            'TrafficCopRightOfWay',
             'list of domains that can go as fast as they want',
           ],
          );
       command_table(\@directives);
```

You can also mix and match the two configuration styles. The **@directives** list can contain a mixture of array refs and hash refs. *command_table()* will do the right thing.

Configuration Creation and Merging

Digging deeper, the process of module configuration is more complex than you'd expect because Apache recognizes multiple levels of configuration directives. There are global directives contained within the main *httpd.conf* file, per-server directives specific to virtual hosts contained within *<VirtualHost>* sections, and per-directory configuration directives contained within *<Directory>* sections and *.htaccess* files.

To understand why this issue is important, consider this series of directives:

```
TrafficCopSpeedLimit 55

<Location /I-95>
    TrafficCopRightOfWay .mil .gov
    TrafficCopSpeedLimit 65
</Location>

<Location /I-95/exit-13>
    TrafficCopSpeedLimit 30
</Location>
```

When processing URLs in */I-95/exit13*, there's a potential source of conflict because the *TrafficCopSpeedLimit* directive appears in several places. Intuitively, the more specific directive should take precedence over the one in its parent directory, but what about *TrafficCopRightOfWay*? Should */I-95/exit13* inherit the value of *TrafficCopRightOfWay* or ignore it?

On top of this, there is the issue of per-server and per-directory configuration information. Some directives, such as *HostName*, clearly apply to the server as a whole and have no reason to change on a per-directory basis. Other directives, such as *Options*, apply to individual directories or URIs. Per-server and per-directory configuration information should be handled separately from each other.

To handle these issues, modules may declare as many as four subroutines to set configuration policy: *SERVER_CREATE()*, *DIR_CREATE()*, *SERVER_MERGE()*, and *DIR_MERGE()*.

The *SERVER_CREATE()* and *DIR_CREATE()* routines are responsible for creating per-server and per-directory configuration objects. If present, they are invoked *before* Apache has processed any of the module's configuration directives in order to create a default per-server or per-directory configuration. Provided that at least one of the module's configuration directives appears in the main part of the configuration file, *SERVER_CREATE()* will be called once for the main server host and once for each virtual host. Similarly, *DIR_CREATE()* will be called once for each directory section (including *<Location>* and *.htaccess* files) in which at least one of the module's configuration directives appears.

As Apache parses and processes the module's custom directives, it invokes the directive callbacks to add information to the per-server and per-directory configuration records. Since the vast majority of modules act at a per-directory level, Apache passes the per-directory configuration object to the callbacks as the first argument. This is the $cfg argument that we saw in the previous examples. A callback that is concerned with processing per-server directives will simply ignore this argument and use the *Apache::ModuleConfig* class to retrieve the per-server configuration record manually. We'll see how to do this later.

Later in the configuration process, one or both of the *SERVER_MERGE()* and *DIR_MERGE()* subroutines may be called. These routines are responsible for merging a parent per-server or per-directory configuration record with a configuration that is lower in the hierarchy. For example, merging will be required when one or more of a module's configuration directives appear in both a *<Location /images>* section and a *<Location /images/PNG>* section. In this case, *DIR_CREATE()* will be called to create default configuration records for each of the */images* and */images/PNG* directories, and the configuration directives' callbacks will be called to set up the appropriate fields in these newly created configurations. After this, the *DIR_MERGE()* subroutine is called once to merge the two configuration objects together. The merged configuration now becomes the per-directory configuration for */images/PNG*.

This merging process is repeated as many times as needed. If a directory or virtual host section contains none of a particular module's configuration directives, then the configuration handlers are skipped and the configuration for the closest ancestor of the directory is used instead.

In addition to being called at server startup time, the *DIR_CREATE()* function may be invoked again at request time, for example, whenever Apache processes a *.htaccess* file. The *DIR_MERGE()* functions are always invoked at request time in order to merge the current directory's configuration with its parents.

When C modules implement configuration directive handlers they must, at the very least, define a per-directory or per-server constructor for their configuration data. However, if a Perl module does not implement a constructor, *mod_perl* uses a default per-directory constructor that creates a hash reference blessed into the current package's class. Later Apache calls your module's directive callbacks to fill in this empty hash, which is, as usual, passed in as the $cfg argument. No per-server configuration object is created by default.

Neither C nor Perl modules are required to implement merging routines. If they do not, merging simply does not happen and Apache uses the most specific configuration record. In the example at the top of this section, the configuration record for the URI location */I-95/exit-13* would contain the current value of *TrafficCop-SpeedLimit* but no specific value for *TrafficCopRightOfWay*.

Depending on your module's configuration system, you may wish to implement one or more of the configuration creation and merging methods described in the following list. The method names use the all-uppercase naming convention because they are never called by any other user code.

DIR_CREATE()

If the directive handler's class defines or inherits a *DIR_CREATE()* method, it will be invoked to create per-directory configuration objects. This object is the second argument passed to all directive handlers, which is normally used to store the configuration arguments. When no *DIR_CREATE()* method is found, *mod_perl* will construct the configuration object for you like this:

```
bless {}, $Class;
```

You might use a *DIR_CREATE()* method to define various defaults or to use something other than a hash reference to store the configuration values. This example uses a blessed hash reference and sets the value of *TopLimit* to a default value:

```
package Apache::TrafficCop;

sub new {
    return bless {}, shift;
}

sub DIR_CREATE {
    my $class = shift;
    my $self = $class->new;
    $self->{TopLimit} ||= 65;
    return $self;
}
```

DIR_MERGE()

When the *<Directory>* or *<Location>* hierarchy contains configuration entries at multiple levels, the directory merger routine will be called on to merge all the directives into the current, bottom-most level.

When defining a *DIR_MERGE()* method, the parent configuration object is passed as the first argument, and the current object as the second. In the example *DIR_MERGE()* routine shown below, the keys of the current configuration will override any like-named keys in the parent. The return value should be a merged configuration object blessed into the module's class:

```
sub DIR_MERGE {
    my($parent, $current) = @_;
    my %new = (%$parent, %$current);
    return bless \%new, ref($parent);
}
```

SERVER_CREATE()
SERVER_MERGE()

The *SERVER_CREATE()* and *SERVER_MERGE()* methods work just like *DIR_CREATE()* and *DIR_MERGE()*. The difference is simply in the scope and timing in which they are created and merged. The *SERVER_CREATE()* method is only called once per configured virtual server. The *SERVER_MERGE()* method is invoked during server startup time, rather than at request time like *DIR_MERGE()*.

The Apache::CmdParms and Apache::ModuleConfig Classes

The configuration mechanism uses two auxiliary classes, *Apache::CmdParms* and *Apache::ModuleConfig*, to pass information between Apache and your module.

Apache::ModuleConfig is the simpler of the two. It provides just a single method, *get()*, which retrieves a module's current configuration information. The return value is the object created by the *DIR_CREATE()* or *SERVER_CREATE()* methods.

The *get()* method is called with the current request object or server object and an optional additional argument indicating which module to retrieve the configuration from. In the typical case, you'll omit this additional argument to indicate that you want to fetch the configuration information for the current module. For example, we saw this in the *Apache::PassThru handler()* routine:

```
my $cfg = Apache::ModuleConfig->get($r);
```

This call returns the per-directory configuration object because the argument to *get()* is the current request. To obtain the per-server configuration object, provided that you defined a *SERVER_CREATE()* routine, pass the request's server object instead:

```
my $cfg = Apache::ModuleConfig->get($r->server);
```

As a convenience, the per-directory configuration object for the current module is always the first argument passed to any configuration processing callback routine.

Directives processing callbacks that need to operate on server-specific configuration data should ignore this hash and fetch the configuration data themselves using a technique we will discuss shortly.

It is also possible for one module to peek at another module's configuration data by naming its package as the second argument to *get()*:

```
my $friends_cfg = Apache::ModuleConfig->get($r, 'Apache::TrafficCop');
```

You can now read and write the other module's configuration information!

Apache::CmdParms is a helpful class that Apache uses to pass a variety of configuration information to modules. An *Apache::CmdParms* object is the second argument passed to directive handler routines.

The various methods available from *Apache::CmdParms* are listed fully in Chapter 9, *Perl API Reference Guide*. The two you are most likely to use in your modules are *server()* and *path()*. *server()* returns the *Apache::Server* object corresponding to the current configuration. From this object you can retrieve the virtual host's name, its configured port, the document root, and other core configuration information. For example, this code retrieves the administrator's name from within a configuration callback and adds it to the module's configuration table:

```
sub TrafficCopActiveSergeant ($$$) {
    my($cfg, $parms, $arg) = @_;
    $cfg->{Sergeant} = $arg;
    my $chief_of_police = $parms->server->server_admin;
    $cfg->{ChiefOfPolice} = $chief_of_police;
}
```

The *server()* method is also vital when directive processing callbacks need to set server-specific configuration information. In this case, the per-directory configuration passed as the first callback argument must be ignored, and the per-server configuration must be fetched by calling the *Apache::ModuleConfig get()* with the server object as its argument.

Here's an example:

```
sub TrafficCopDispatcher ($$$) {
    my($cfg, $parms, $arg) = @_;
    my $scfg = Apache::ModuleConfig->get($parms->server)
    $scfg->{Dispatcher} = $arg;
}
```

If the configuration-processing routine is being called to process a container directive such as *<Location>* or *<Directory>*, the *Apache::CmdParms path()* method will return the directive's argument. Depending on the context this might be a URI, a directory path, a virtual host address, or a filename pattern.

See Chapter 9 for details on other methods that *Apache::ModuleConfig* and *Apache::CmdParms* makes available.

Reimplementing mod_mime in Perl

As a full example of creating custom configuration directives, we're going to reimplement the standard *mod_mime* module in Perl. It has a total of seven different directives, each with a different argument syntax. In addition to showing you how to handle a complex configuration setup, this example will show you in detail what goes on behind the scenes as *mod_mime* associates a content handler with each URI request.

This module replaces the standard *mod_mime* module. You do not have to remove *mod_mime* from the standard compiled-in modules in order to test this module. However, if you wish to remove *mod_mime* anyway in order to convince yourself that the replacement actually works, the easiest way to do this is to compile *mod_mime* as a dynamically loaded module and then comment out the lines in *httpd.conf* that load it. In either case, install *Apache::MIME* as the default MIME-checking phase handler by putting this line in *perl.conf* or one of the other configuration files:

```
PerlTypeHandler Apache::MIME
```

Like the previous example, the configuration information is contained in two files. *Makefile.PL* (Example 8-3) describes the directives, and *Apache/MIME.pm* (Example 8-4) defines the callbacks for processing the directives at runtime. In order to reimplement *mod_mime*, we need to reimplement a total of seven directives, including *SetHandler*, *AddHandler*, *AddType*, and *AddEncoding*.

Makefile.PL defines the seven directives using the anonymous hash method. All but one of the directives is set to use the OR_FILEINFO context, which allows the directives to appear anywhere in the main configuration files, as well as in *.htaccess* files, provided that *Override FileInfo* is also set. The exception, *TypesConfig*, is the directive that indicates where the default table of MIME types is to be found. It only makes sense to process this directive during server startup, so its context is given as RSRC_CONF, limiting the directive to the body of any of the *.conf* files. We don't specify the args_how key for the directives; instead, we allow *command_table()* to figure out the syntax for us by looking at the function prototypes in *MIME.pm*.

Running *perl Makefile.PL* will now create a *.xs* file, which will be compiled into a loadable object file during *make*.

Example 8-3. Makefile.PL for Apache::MIME

```
package Apache::MIME;
# File: Makefile.PL

use ExtUtils::MakeMaker;
# See lib/ExtUtils/MakeMaker.pm for details of how to influence
# the contents of the Makefile that is written.
```

Example 8-3. Makefile.PL for Apache::MIME (continued)

```perl
use Apache::src ();
use Apache::ExtUtils qw(command_table);

my @directives = (
    { name         => 'SetHandler',
      errmsg       => 'a handler name',
      req_override => 'OR_FILEINFO' },
    { name         => 'AddHandler',
      errmsg       => 'a handler name followed by one or more file extensions',
      req_override => 'OR_FILEINFO' },
    { name         => 'ForceType',
      errmsg       => 'a handler name',
      req_override => 'OR_FILEINFO' },
    { name         => 'AddType',
      errmsg       => 'a mime type followed by one or more file extensions',
      req_override => 'OR_FILEINFO' },
    { name         => 'AddLanguage',
      errmsg       => 'a language (e.g., fr), followed by one or more file
extensions',
      req_override => 'OR_FILEINFO' },
    { name         => 'AddEncoding',
      errmsg       => 'an encoding (e.g., gzip), followed by one or more file
extensions',
      req_override => 'OR_FILEINFO' },
    { name         => 'TypesConfig',
      errmsg       => 'the MIME types config file',
      req_override => 'RSRC_CONF'
    },
);

command_table \@directives;

WriteMakefile(
    'NAME'         => __PACKAGE__,
    'VERSION_FROM' => 'MIME.pm',
    'INC'          => Apache::src->new->inc,
);
__END__
```

Turning to Example 8-4, we start by bringing in the *DynaLoader* and *Apache::ModuleConfig* modules as we did in the overview example at the beginning of this section:

```perl
package Apache::MIME;
# File: Apache/MIME.pm

use strict;
use vars qw($VERSION @ISA);
use LWP::MediaTypes qw(read_media_types guess_media_type add_type add_
encoding);
use DynaLoader ();
use Apache ();
```

```
use Apache::ModuleConfig ();
use Apache::Constants qw(:common DIR_MAGIC_TYPE DECLINE_CMD);

@ISA = qw(DynaLoader);

$VERSION = '0.01';

if($ENV{MOD_PERL}) {
    no strict;
    @ISA = qw(DynaLoader);
    __PACKAGE__->bootstrap($VERSION);
}
```

We also bring in *Apache, Apache::Constants,* and an LWP library called *LWP::MediaTypes*. The *Apache* and *Apache::Constants* libraries will be used within the *handler()* subroutine, while the LWP library provides utilities for guessing MIME types, languages, and encodings from file extensions. As before, *Apache::MIME* needs to call *bootstrap()* immediately after loading other modules in order to bring in its compiled *.xs* half. Notice that we have to explicitly import the DIR_MAGIC_TYPE and DECLINE_CMD constants from *Apache::Constants*, as these are not exported by default.

Let's skip over *handler()* for the moment and look at the seven configuration callbacks: *TypesConfig(), AddType(), AddEncoding(),* and so on.

```
sub TypesConfig ($$$) {
    my($cfg, $parms, $file) = @_;
    my $types_config = Apache->server_root_relative($file);
    read_media_types($types_config);
    #to co-exist with mod_mime.c
    return DECLINE_CMD if Apache->module("mod_mime.c");
}
```

TypesConfig() has a function prototype of ($$$), indicating a directive syntax of TAKE1. It will be called with the name of the file holding the MIME types table as its third argument. The callback retrieves the filename, turns it into a server-relative path, and stores the path into a lexical variable. The callback then calls the LWP function *read_media_types()* to parse the file and add the MIME types found there to an internal table maintained by *LWP::MediaTypes*. When the *LWP::MediaTypes* function *guess_media_type()* is called subsequently, this table will be consulted. Note that there is no need, in this case, to store the configuration information into the $cfg hash reference because the information is only needed at the time the configuration directive is processed.

Another important detail is that the *TypesConfig* handler will return DECLINE_CMD if the *mod_mime* module is installed. This gives *mod_mime* a chance to also read the *TypesConfig* file. If *mod_mime* isn't given this opportunity, it will complain bitterly and abort server startup. However, we don't allow any of the other directive handlers to fall through to *mod_mime* in this way, effectively cutting *mod_mime* out of the loop.

```
sub AddType ($$@;@) {
    my($cfg, $parms, $type, $ext) = @_;
    add_type($type, $ext);
}
```

The *AddType()* directive callback is even shorter. Its function prototype is (`$$@;@`), indicating an `ITERATE2` syntax. This means that if the *AddType* directive looks like this:

```
AddType application/x-chicken-feed .corn .barley .oats
```

the function will be called three times. Each time the callback is invoked its third argument will be *application/x-chicken-feed* and the fourth argument will be successively set to *.corn*, *.barley*, and *.oats*. The function recovers the third and fourth parameters and passes them to the *LWP::MediaTypes* function *add_type()*. This simply adds the file type and extension to LWP's internal table.

```
sub AddEncoding ($$@;@) {
    my($cfg, $parms, $enc, $ext) = @_;
    add_encoding($enc, $ext);
}
```

AddEncoding() is similar to *AddType()* but uses the *LWP::MediaTypes add_encoding()* function to associate a series of file extensions with a MIME encoding.

More interesting are the *SetHandler()* and *AddHandler()* callbacks:

```
sub SetHandler ($$$) {
    my($cfg, $parms, $handler) = @_;
    $cfg->{'handler'} = $handler;
}

sub AddHandler ($$@;@) {
    my($cfg, $parms, $handler, $ext) = @_;
    $cfg->{'handlers'}->{$ext} = $handler;
}
```

The job of the *SetHandler* directive is to force requests for the specified path to be passed to the indicated content handler, no questions asked. *AddHandler()*, in contrast, adds a series of file extensions to the table consulted by the MIME type checker when it attempts to choose the proper content handler for the request. In both cases, the configuration information is needed again at request time, so we have to keep it in long-term storage within the `$cfg` hash.

SetHandler() is again a `TAKE1` type of callback. It recovers the content handler name from its third argument and stores it in the `$cfg` data structure under the key `handler`. *AddHandler()* is an `ITERATE2` callback which receives the name of a content handler and a file extension as its third and fourth arguments. The callback stuffs this information into an anonymous hash maintained in `$cfg` under the `handlers` key.

```
sub ForceType ($$$) {
    my($cfg, $parms, $type) = @_;
    $cfg->{'type'} = $type;
}
```

The *ForceType* directive is used to force all documents in a path to be a particular MIME type, regardless of their file extensions. It's often used within a *<Directory>* section to force the type of all documents contained within and is helpful for dealing with legacy documents that don't have informative file extensions. The *ForceType()* callback uses a `TAKE1` syntax in which the required argument is a MIME type. The callback recovers the MIME type and stores it in the `$cfg` hash reference under the key `type`.

```
sub AddLanguage ($$@;@) {
    my($cfg, $parms, $language, $ext) = @_;
    $ext =~ s/^\.//;
    $cfg->{'language_types'}->{$ext} = lc $language;
}
```

The last directive handler, *AddLanguage()*, implements the *AddLanguage* directive, in which a series of file extensions are associated with a language code (e.g., "fr" for French, "en" for English). It is an `ITERATE2` callback and works just like *AddHandler()*, except that the dot is stripped off the file extension before storing it into the `$cfg hash`. This is because of an old inconsistency in the way that *mod_mime* works, in which the *AddLanguage* directive expects dots in front of the file extensions, while the *AddType* and *AddHandler* directives do not.

Now we turn our attention to the *handler()* subroutine itself. This code will be called at request time during the MIME type checking phase. It has five responsibilities:

1. Guess the MIME content type for the requested document.

2. Guess the content encoding for the requested document.

3. Guess the content language for the requested document.

4. Set the content handler for the request.

5. If the requested document is a directory, initiate special directory processing.

Items 1 through 3 are important but not critical. The content type, encoding, and language may well be changed during the response phase by the content handler. In particular, the MIME type is very frequently changed (e.g., by CGI scripts). Item 4, however, is crucial since it determines what code will be invoked to respond to the request. It is also necessary to detect and treat requests for directory names specially, using a pseudo-MIME type to initiate Apache's directory handling.

```
sub handler {
    my $r = shift;

    if(-d $r->finfo) {
        $r->content_type(DIR_MAGIC_TYPE);
        return OK;
    }
}
```

handler() begins by shifting the Apache request object off the subroutine stack. The subroutine now does a series of checks on the requested document. First, it checks whether *$r->finfo()* refers to a directory. If so, then *handler()* sets the request content type to a pseudo-MIME type defined by the constant DIR_MAGIC_ TYPE and exits. Returning DIR_MAGIC_TYPE signals Apache that the user requested a directory, causing the server to pass control to any content handlers that list this constant among the MIME types they handle. *mod_dir* and *mod_auto-index* are two of the standard modules that are capable of generating directory listings.

```
my($type, @encoding) = guess_media_type($r->filename);
$r->content_type($type) if $type;
unshift @encoding, $r->content_encoding if $r->content_encoding;
$r->content_encoding(join ", ", @encoding) if @encoding;
```

If the file is not a directory, then we try to guess its MIME type and encoding. We call on the *LWP::MediaTypes* function *guess_media_type()* to do the work, passing it the filename and receiving a MIME type and list of encodings in return. Although unusual, it is theoretically possible for a file to have multiple encodings, and *LWP::MediaTypes* allows this. The returned type is immediately used to set the MIME type of the requested document by calling the request object's *content_ type()* method. Likewise, the list of encodings is added to the request using *content_encoding()* after joining them together into a comma-delimited string. The only subtlety here is that we honor any previously defined encoding for the requested document by adding it to the list of encodings returned by *guess_ media_type()*. This is in case the handler for a previous phase happened to add some content encoding.

Now comes some processing that depends on the values in the configuration hash, so we recover the $cfg variable by calling *Apache::ModuleConfig*'s *get()* method:

```
my $cfg = Apache::ModuleConfig->get($r);
```

The next task is to parse out the requested file's extensions and use them to set the file's MIME type and/or language.

```
for my $ext (LWP::MediaTypes::file_exts($r->filename)) {
    if(my $type = $cfg->{'language_types'}->{$ext}) {
        my $ltypes = $r->content_languages;
        push @$ltypes, $type;
        $r->content_languages($ltypes);
    }
```

Using the *LWP::MediaTypes* function *file_exts()*, we split out all the extensions in the requested document's filename and loop through them. This allows a file named *travel.html.fr* to be recognized and dealt with appropriately.

We first check whether the extension matches one of the extensions in the configuration object's *language_types* key. If so, we use the extension to set the language code for the document. Although it is somewhat unusual, the HTTP specification allows a document to specify multiple languages in its *Content-Language* field, so we go to some lengths to merge multiple language codes into one long list which we then set with the request object's *content_languages()* method.

```
if(my $type = $cfg->{'handlers'}->{$ext} and !$r->proxyreq) {
    $r->handler($type);
}

}
```

While still in the loop, we deal with the content handler for the request. We check whether the extension is among the ones defined in the configuration variable's **handlers** hash. If so, we call the request object's *handler()* method to set the content handler to the indicated value. The only catch is that if the current transaction is a proxy request, we do not want to alter the content handler because another module may have set the content handler during the URI translation phase.

```
$r->content_type($cfg->{'type'}) if $cfg->{'type'};
$r->handler($cfg->{'handler'}) if $cfg->{'handler'};
```

After looping through the file extensions, we handle the *ForceType* and *SetHandler* directives, which have the effect of overriding file extensions. If the configuration key **type** is nonempty, we use it to force the MIME type to the specified value. Likewise, if *handler* is nonempty, we again call *handler()*, replacing whatever content handler was there before.

```
return OK;
}
```

At the end of *handler()*, we return OK to tell Apache that the MIME type checking phase has been handled successfully.

Although this module was presented mainly as an exercise, with minimal work it can be used to improve on *mod_mime*. For example, you might have noticed that the standard *mod_mime* has no *ForceEncoding* or *ForceLanguage* directives that allow you to override the file extension mappings in the way that you can with *ForceType*. This is easy enough to fix in *Apache::MIME* by adding the appropriate directive definitions and callbacks.

Example 8-4. Apache::MIME Reimplements the Standard mod_mime Module

```perl
package Apache::MIME;
# File: Apache/MIME.pm

use strict;
use vars qw($VERSION @ISA);
use LWP::MediaTypes qw(read_media_types guess_media_type add_type add_encoding);
use DynaLoader ();
use Apache ();
use Apache::ModuleConfig ();
use Apache::Constants qw(:common DIR_MAGIC_TYPE DECLINE_CMD);

@ISA = qw(DynaLoader);

$VERSION = '0.01';

if($ENV{MOD_PERL}) {
    no strict;
    @ISA = qw(DynaLoader);
    __PACKAGE__->bootstrap($VERSION);
}

sub handler {
    my $r = shift;

    if(-d $r->finfo) {
        $r->content_type(DIR_MAGIC_TYPE);
        return OK;
    }

    my($type, @encoding) = guess_media_type($r->filename);
    $r->content_type($type) if $type;
    unshift @encoding, $r->content_encoding if $r->content_encoding;
    $r->content_encoding(join ", ", @encoding) if @encoding;

    my $cfg = Apache::ModuleConfig->get($r);

    for my $ext (LWP::MediaTypes::file_exts($r->filename)) {
        if(my $type = $cfg->{'language_types'}->{$ext}) {
            my $ltypes = $r->content_languages;
            push @$ltypes, $type;
            $r->content_languages($ltypes);
        }

        if(my $type = $cfg->{'handlers'}->{$ext} and !$r->proxyreq) {
            $r->handler($type);
        }

    }

    $r->content_type($cfg->{'type'}) if $cfg->{'type'};
    $r->handler($cfg->{'handler'}) if $cfg->{'handler'};

    return OK;
}
```

Example 8-4. Apache::MIME Reimplements the Standard mod_mime Module (continued)

```perl
sub TypesConfig ($$$) {
    my($cfg, $parms, $file) = @_;
    my $types_config = Apache->server_root_relative($file);
    read_media_types($types_config);
    #to co-exist with mod_mime.c
    return DECLINE_CMD if Apache->module("mod_mime.c");
}

sub AddType ($$@;@) {
    my($cfg, $parms, $type, $ext) = @_;
    add_type($type, $ext);
}

sub AddEncoding ($$@;@) {
    my($cfg, $parms, $enc, $ext) = @_;
    add_encoding($enc, $ext);
}

sub SetHandler ($$$) {
    my($cfg, $parms, $handler) = @_;
    $cfg->{'handler'} = $handler;
}

sub AddHandler ($$@;@) {
    my($cfg, $parms, $handler, $ext) = @_;
    $cfg->{'handlers'}->{$ext} = $handler;
}

sub ForceType ($$$) {
    my($cfg, $parms, $type) = @_;
    $cfg->{'type'} = $type;
}

sub AddLanguage ($$@;@) {
    my($cfg, $parms, $language, $ext) = @_;
    $ext =~ s/^\.//;
    $cfg->{'language_types'}->{$ext} = lc $language;
}

1;
__END__
```

Configuring Apache with Perl

We've just seen how you can configure Perl modules using the Apache configuration mechanism. Now we turn it around to show you how to configure Apache from within Perl. Instead of configuring Apache by hand (editing a set of configuration files), the Perl API allows you to write a set of Perl statements to dynamically configure Apache at runtime. This gives you limitless flexibility. For example, you can create complex configurations involving hundreds of virtual hosts without manually typing hundreds of *<VirtualHost>* sections into *httpd.conf.* Or you can write a master configuration file that will work without modification on any machine in a "server farm." You could even look up configuration information at runtime from a relational database.

The key to Perl-based server configuration is the *<Perl>* directive. Unlike the other directives defined by *mod_perl*, this directive is paired to a corresponding *</Perl>* directive, forming a Perl section.

When Apache hits a Perl section during startup time, it passes everything within the section to *mod_perl. mod_perl*, in turn, compiles the contents of the section by evaluating it inside the *Apache::ReadConfig* package. After compilation is finished, *mod_perl* walks the *Apache::ReadConfig* symbol table looking for global variables with the same names as Apache's configuration directives. The values of those globals are then fed into Apache's normal configuration mechanism as if they'd been typed directly into the configuration file. The upshot of all this is that instead of setting the account under which the server runs with the *User* directive:

```
User www
```

you can write this:

```
<Perl>
  $User = 'www';
</Perl>
```

This doesn't look like much of a win until you consider that you can set this global using any arbitrary Perl expression, for example:

```
<Perl>
  my $hostname = `hostname`;
  $User = 'www'     if $hostname =~ /^papa-bear/;
  $User = 'httpd'   if $hostname =~ /^momma-bear/;
  $User = 'nobody'  if $hostname =~ /^goldilocks/;
</Perl>
```

The Perl global that you set must match the spelling of the corresponding Apache directive. Globals that do not match known Apache directives are silently ignored. Capitalization is not currently significant.

In addition to single-valued directives such as *User, Group,* and *ServerRoot,* you can use *<Perl>* sections to set multivalued directives such as *DirectoryIndex* and *AddType.* You can also configure multipart sections such as *<Directory>* and *<VirtualHost>*. Depending on the directive, the Perl global you need to set may be a scalar, an array, or a hash. To figure out what type of Perl variable to use, follow these rules:

Directive takes no arguments

There are few examples of configuration directives that take no arguments. The only one that occurs in the standard Apache modules is *CacheNegotiatedDocs,* which is part of *mod_negotiation*. To create a nonargument directive, set the corresponding scalar variable to the empty string ' ':

```
$CacheNegotiatedDocs = '';
```

Directive takes one argument

This is probably the most common case. Set the corresponding global to the value of your choice.

```
$Port = 8080;
```

Directive takes multiple arguments

These include directives such as *DirectoryIndex* and *AddType*. Create a global array with the name of the directive and set it to the list of desired arguments.

```
@DirectoryIndex = map { "index.$_" } qw(html htm shtml cgi);
```

An alternative to this is to create a scalar variable containing the usual value of the directive as a string, for example:

```
$DirectoryIndex = "index.html index.htm index.shtml index.cgi";
```

Directive is repeated multiple times

If a directive is repeated multiple times with different arguments each time, you can represent it as an array of arrays. This example using the *AddIcon* directive shows how:

```
@AddIcon = (
          [ '/icons/compressed.gif' => qw(.Z .z .gz .tgz .zip) ],
          [ '/icons/layout.gif'     => qw(.html .shtml .htm .pdf) ],
);
```

Directive is a block section with begin and end tags

Configuration sections like *<VirtualHost>* and *<Directory>* are mapped onto Perl hashes. Use the directive's argument (the hostname, directory, or URI) as the hash key, and make the value stored at this key an anonymous hash containing the desired directive/value pairs. This is easier to see than to describe. Consider the following virtual host section:

```
<VirtualHost 192.168.2.5:80>
    ServerName    www.fishfries.org
    DocumentRoot  /home/httpd/fishfries/htdocs
    ErrorLog      /home/httpd/fishfries/logs/error.log
    TransferLog   /home/httpd/fishfries/logs/access.log
    ServerAdmin   webmaster@fishfries.org
</Virtual>
```

You can represent this in a *<Perl>* section by the following code:

```
$VirtualHost{'192.168.2.5:80'} = {
    ServerName    => 'www.fishfries.org',
    DocumentRoot  => '/home/httpd/fishfries/htdocs',
    ErrorLog      => '/home/httpd/fishfries/logs/error.log',
    TransferLog   => '/home/httpd/fishfries/logs/access.log',
    ServerAdmin   => 'webmaster@fishfries.org',
};
```

There is no special Perl variable which maps to the *<IfModule>* directive container; however, the *Apache module* method will provide you with this functionality.

```
if(Apache->module("mod_ssl.c")) {
    push @Include, "ssl.conf";
}
```

The *Apache define()* method can be used to implement an *<IfDefine>* container, as follows:

```
if(Apache->define("MOD_SSL")) {
    push @Include, "ssl.conf";
}
```

Certain configuration blocks may require directives to be in a particular order. As you probably know, Perl does not maintain hash values in any predictable order. Should you need to preserve order with hashes inside *<Perl>* sections, simply install Gurusamy Sarathy's *Tie::IxHash* module from CPAN. Once installed, *mod_perl* will tie %VirtualHost, %Directory, %Location, and %Files hashes to this class, preserving their order when the Apache configuration is generated.

Directive is a block section with multiple same-value keys

The Apache named virtual host mechanism provides a way to configure virtual hosts using the same IP address.

```
NameVirtualHost 192.168.2.5

<VirtualHost 192.168.2.5>
  ServerName one.fish.net
  ServerAdmin webmaster@one.fish.net
</VirtualHost>

<VirtualHost 192.168.2.5>
  ServerName red.fish.net
  ServerAdmin webmaster@red.fish.net
</VirtualHost>
```

In this case, the %VirtualHost syntax from the previous section would not work, since assigning a hash reference for the given IP address will overwrite the original entry. The solution is to use an array reference whose values are hash references, one for each virtual host entry. Example:

```
$VirtualHost{'192.168.2.5'} = [
    {
        ServerName   => 'one.fish.net',
        ...
        ServerAdmin  => 'webmaster@one.fish.net',
    },
    {
        ServerName   => 'red.fish.net',
        ...
```

```
            ServerAdmin => 'webmaster@red.fish.net',
        },
    ];
```

Directive is a nested block

Nested block sections are mapped onto anonymous hashes, much like main sections. For example, to put two *<Directory>* sections inside the virtual host of the previous example, you can use this code:

```
<Perl>
my $root = '/home/httpd/fishfries';
$VirtualHost{'192.168.2.5:80'} = {
    ServerName    => 'www.fishfries.org',
    DocumentRoot  => "$root/htdocs",
    ErrorLog      => "$root/logs/error.log",
    TransferLog   => "$root/logs/access.log",
    ServerAdmin   => 'webmaster@fishfries.org',
    Directory     => {
        "$root/htdocs"  => {
            Options => 'Indexes FollowSymlinks',
            AllowOverride => 'Options Indexes Limit FileInfo',
            Order   => 'deny,allow',
            Deny    => 'from all',
            Allow   => 'from fishfries.org',
        },
        "$root/cgi-bin" => {
            AllowOverride => 'None',
            Options       => 'ExecCGI',
            SetHandler    => 'cgi-script',
        },
    },
};
</Perl>
```

Notice that all the usual Perlisms, such as interpolation of the $root variable into the double-quoted strings, still work here. Another thing to see in this example is that in this case we've chosen to write the multivalued *Options* directive as a single string:

```
Options => 'Indexes FollowSymlinks',
```

The alternative would be to use an anonymous array for the directive's arguments, as in:

```
Options => ['Indexes','FollowSymlinks'],
```

Both methods work. The only gotcha is that you must always be sure of what is an argument list and what isn't. In the *Options* directive, "Indexes" and "FollowSymlinks" are distinct arguments and can be represented as an anonymous array. In the *Order* directive, the string deny,allow is a single argument, and representing it as the array ['deny','allow'] will *not* work, even though it looks like it should (use the string deny,allow instead).

<Perl> sections are available if you built and installed *mod_perl* with the PERL_
SECTIONS configuration variable set (Appendix B, *Building and Installing mod_
perl*). They are evaluated in the order in which they appear in *httpd.conf,
srm.conf*, and *access.conf*. This allows you to use later *<Perl>* sections to override
values declared in earlier parts of the configuration files.

Debugging *<Perl>* Sections

If there is a syntax error in the Perl code causing it to fail during compilation,
Apache will report the problem and the server will not start.

One way to catch Perl syntax errors ahead of time is to structure your *<Perl>* sections like this:

```
<Perl>
#!perl

... code here ...

__END__
</Perl>
```

You can now directly syntax-check the configuration file using the Perl interpreter's *−cx* switches. *−c* makes Perl perform a syntax check, and *−x* tells the
interpreter to ignore all junk prior to the #!perl line:

```
% perl -cx httpd.conf
httpd.conf syntax OK
```

If the Perl code is syntactically correct, but the Apache configuration generated
from it contains an error, an error message will be sent to the server error log, but
the server will still start. In general, it is always a good to look at the error log after
starting the server to make sure startup went smoothly. If you have not picked up
this good habit already, we strongly recommend you do so when working with
<Perl> configuration sections.

Another helpful trick is to build *mod_perl* with the PERL_TRACE configuration
option set to *true*. Then, when the environment variable MOD_PERL_TRACE is set
to *s*, *httpd* will output diagnostics showing how the *<Perl>* section globals are converted into directive string values.

Another tool that is occasionally useful is the *Apache::PerlSections* module. It
defines two public routines named *dump()* and *store()*. *dump()* dumps out the
current contents of the *<Perl>* section as a pretty-printed string. *<Perl>* does the
same but writes the contents to the file of your choice. Both methods are useful
for making sure that the configuration you are getting is what you expect.

Apache::PerlSections requires the Perl *Devel::SymDump* and *Data::Dumper* modules, both available on CPAN. Here is a simple example of its use:

```
<Perl>
#!perl
use Apache::PerlSections();
$User = 'nobody';
$VirtualHost{'192.168.2.5:80'} = {
    ServerName   => 'www.fishfries.org',
    DocumentRoot => '/home/httpd/fishfries/htdocs',
    ErrorLog     => '/home/httpd/fishfries/logs/error.log',
    TransferLog  => '/home/httpd/fishfries/logs/access.log',
    ServerAdmin  => 'webmaster@fishfries.org',
};
print STDERR Apache::PerlSections->dump();
__END__
</Perl>
```

This will cause the following to appear on the command line at server startup time:

```
package Apache::ReadConfig;
#scalars:

$User = 'nobody';

#arrays:

#hashes:

%VirtualHost = (
  '192.168.2.5:80' => {
    'ServerAdmin' => 'webmaster@fishfries.org',
    'ServerName' => 'www.fishfries.org',
    'DocumentRoot' => '/home/httpd/fishfries/htdocs',
    'ErrorLog' => '/home/httpd/fishfries/logs/error.log',
    'TransferLog' => '/home/httpd/fishfries/logs/access.log'
  }
);

1;
__END__
```

The output from *dump()* and *store()* can be stored to a file and reloaded with a *require* statement. This allows you to create your configuration in a modular fashion:

```
<Perl>
  require "standard_configuration.pl";
  require "virtual_hosts.pl";
  require "access_control.pl";
</Perl>
```

More information about *Apache::PerlSections* can be found in Appendix A, *Standard Noncore Modules.*

Simple Dynamic Configuration

If the Perl configuration syntax seems a bit complex for your needs, there is a simple alternative. The special variables `$PerlConfig` and `@PerlConfig` are treated as raw Apache configuration data. Their values are fed directly to the Apache configuration engine and treated just as if they were lines of text from a conventional file:

```
<Perl>
$PerlConfig  = "User $ENV{USER}\n";
$PerlConfig .= "ServerAdmin $ENV{USER}\@$hostname\n";
</Perl>

<Perl>
for my $host (qw(one red two blue)) {
    $host = "$host.fish.net";
    push @PerlConfig, <<EOF;

  Listen $host

  <VirtualHost $host>

  ServerAdmin webmaster\@$host
  ServerName $host
  # ... more config here ...
  </VirtualHost>

EOF
}
</Perl>
```

One more utility method is available: *Apache->httpd_conf*, which simply pushes each argument into the **@PerlConfig** array and tacks a newline onto the end of each.

```
Apache->httpd_conf(
    "User $ENV{USER}",
    "ServerAdmin $ENV{USER}\@$hostname",
);
```

A Real-Life Example

For a complete example of an Apache configuration constructed with *<Perl>* sections, we'll look at Doug's setup. As a freelance contractor, Doug must often configure his development server in a brand-new environment. Rather than creating a customized server configuration file each time, Doug uses a generic configuration that can be brought up anywhere, simply by running:

```
% httpd -f $HOME/httpd.conf
```

This one step automatically creates the server and document roots if they don't exist, as well as the log and configuration directories. It also detects the user that it is being run as, and configures the *User* and *Group* directives to match.

Example 8-5 shows a slightly simplified version of Doug's *httpd.conf.* It contains only two hard-coded Apache directives:

```
# file: httpd.conf
PerlPassEnv HOME
Port 9008
```

There's a *PerlPassEnv* directive with the value of HOME, required in order to make the value of this environment variable visible to the code contained within the *<Perl>* section, and there's a *Port* directive set to Doug's favorite port number.

The rest of the configuration file is written entirely in Perl:

```
<Perl>
#!perl

$ServerRoot = "$ENV{HOME}/www";
```

The *<Perl>* section begins by choosing a path for the server root. Doug likes to have his test environment set up under his home directory in *~/www*, so the variable $ServerRoot is set to $ENV{HOME}/www. The server root will now be correctly configured regardless of whether users' directories are stored under */home*, */users*, or */var/users*.

```
unless (-d "$ServerRoot/logs") {
    for my $dir ("", qw(logs conf htdocs perl)) {
        mkdir "$ServerRoot/$dir", 0755;
    }
    require File::Copy;
    File::Copy::cp($0, "$ServerRoot/conf");
}
```

Next, the code detects whether the server root has been properly initialized and, if not, creates the requisite directories and subdirectories. It looks to see whether *$ServerRoot/logs* exists and is a directory. If not, the code proceeds to create the directories, calling *mkdir()* repeatedly to create first the server root and subsequently *logs, conf, htdocs,* and *perl* subdirectories beneath it. The code then copies the generic *httpd.conf* file that is currently running into the newly created *conf* subdirectory, using the *File::Copy* module's *cp()* routine. Somewhat magically, *mod_perl* arranges for the Perl global variable $0 to hold the path of the *.conf* file that is currently being processed.

```
if(-e "$ServerRoot/startup.pl") {
    $PerlRequire = "startup.pl";
}
```

Next, the code checks whether there is a *startup.pl* present in the configuration directory. If this is the first time the server is being run, the file won't be present, but there may well be one there later. If the file exists, the code sets the `$PerlRequire` global to load it.

```
$User  = getpwuid($>) || $>;
$Group = getgrgid($)) || $);

$ServerAdmin = $User;
```

The code sets the *User*, *Group*, and *ServerAdmin* directives next. The user and group are taken from the Perl magic variables `$>` and `$)`, corresponding to the user and group IDs of the person who launched the server. Since this is the default when Apache is run from a nonroot shell, this has no effect now but will be of use if the server is run as root at a later date. Likewise, `$ServerAdmin` is set to the name of the current user.

```
$ServerName = `hostname`;
$DocumentRoot = "$ServerRoot/htdocs";

my $types = "$ServerRoot/conf/mime.types";
$TypesConfig = -e $types ? $types : "/dev/null";
```

The server name is set to the current host's name by setting the `$ServerName` global, and the document root is set to *$ServerRoot/htdocs*. We look to see whether the configuration file *mime.types* is present and, if so, use it to set `$TypesConfig` to this value. Otherwise, we use */dev/null*.

```
push @Alias,
        ["/perl"  => "$ServerRoot/perl"],
        ["/icons" => "$ServerRoot/icons"];
```

Next, the *<Perl>* section declares some directory aliases. The URI */perl* is aliased to *$ServerRoot/perl*, and */icons* is aliased to *$ServerRoot/icons*. Notice how the `@Alias` global is set to an array of arrays in order to express that it contains multiple *Alias* directives.

```
my $servers = 3;

for my $s (qw(MinSpareServers MaxSpareServers StartServers MaxClients)) {
    $$s = $servers;
}
```

Following this, the code sets the various parameters controlling Apache's preforking. The server doesn't need to handle much load, since it's just Doug's development server, so `MaxSpareServers` and friends are all set to a low value of three. We use "symbolic" or "soft" references here to set the globals indirectly. We loop through a set of strings containing the names of the globals we wish to set, and assign values to them as if they were scalar references rather than plain strings. Perl automatically updates the symbol table for us, avoiding the much more convoluted code that would be required to create the global using globs or by accessing the symbol table directly. Note that this technique will be blocked if strict reference checking is turned on with **use strict 'refs'**.

```
for my $l (qw(LockFile ErrorLog TransferLog PidFile ScoreBoardFile)) {
    $$l = "logs/$l";

    #clean out the logs
    local *FH;
    open FH, ">$ServerRoot/$$l";
    close FH;
}
```

We use a similar trick to configure the *LockFile, ErrorLog, TransferLog,* and other log file–related directives. A few additional lines of code truncate the various log files to zero length if they already exist. Doug likes to start with a clean slate every time he reconfigures and restarts a server.

```
my @mod_perl_cfg = qw{
   SetHandler perl-script
   Options    +ExecCGI
};

$Location{"/perl-status"} = {
    @mod_perl_cfg,
    PerlHandler => "Apache::Status",
};

$Location{"/perl"} = {
    @mod_perl_cfg,
    PerlHandler => "Apache::Registry",
};
```

The remainder of the configuration file sets up some directories for running and debugging Perl API modules. We create a lexical variable named **@mod_perl_cfg** that contains some common options, and then use it to configure the */perl-status* and */perl <Location>* sections. The */perl-status* URI is set up so that it runs *Apache::Status* when retrieved, and */perl* is put under the control of *Apache::Registry* for use with registry scripts.

```
use Apache::PerlSections ();
Apache::PerlSections->store("$ServerRoot/ServerConfig.pm");
```

The very last thing that the *<Perl>* section does is to write out the current configuration into the file *$ServerRoot/ServerConfig.pm*. This snapshots the current configuration in a form that Doug can review and edit, if necessary. Just the configuration variables set within the *<Perl>* section are snapshot. The *PerlPassEnv* and *Port* directives, which are outside the section, are not captured and will have to be added manually.

This technique makes possible the following interesting trick:

```
% httpd -C "PerlModule ServerConfig"
```

The −*C* switch tells *httpd* to process the directive *PerlModule*, which in turn loads the module file *ServerConfig.pm*. Provided that Perl's PERL5LIB environment variable is set up in such a way that Perl will be able to find the module, this has the effect of reloading the previously saved configuration and setting Apache to exactly the same state it had before.

Example 8-5. Doug's Generic httpd.conf

```perl
# file: httpd.conf
PerlPassEnv HOME
Port 9008

<Perl>
#!perl

$ServerRoot = "$ENV{HOME}/www";

unless (-d "$ServerRoot/logs") {
    for my $dir ("", qw(logs conf htdocs perl)) {
        mkdir "$ServerRoot/$dir", 0755;
    }
    require File::Copy;
    File::Copy::cp($0, "$ServerRoot/conf");
}

if(-e "$ServerRoot/startup.pl") {
    $PerlRequire = "startup.pl";
}

$User  = getpwuid($>) || $>;
$Group = getgrgid($)) || $);

$ServerAdmin = $User;

$ServerName = `hostname`;
$DocumentRoot = "$ServerRoot/htdocs";

my $types = "$ServerRoot/conf/mime.types";
$TypesConfig = -e $types ? $types : "/dev/null";

push @Alias,
        ["/perl"  => "$ServerRoot/perl"],
        ["/icons" => "$ServerRoot/icons"];

my $servers = 3;

for my $s (qw(MinSpareServers MaxSpareServers StartServers MaxClients)) {
    $$s = $servers;
}

for my $l (qw(LockFile ErrorLog TransferLog PidFile ScoreBoardFile)) {
    $$l = "logs/$l";
```

Example 8-5. Doug's Generic httpd.conf (continued)

```
    #clean out the logs
    local *FH;
    open FH, ">$ServerRoot/$$l";
    close FH;
}

my @mod_perl_cfg = qw{
  SetHandler perl-script
  Options    +ExecCGI
};

$Location{"/perl-status"} = {
    @mod_perl_cfg,
    PerlHandler => "Apache::Status",
};

$Location{"/perl"} = {
    @mod_perl_cfg,
    PerlHandler => "Apache::Registry",
};

use Apache::PerlSections ();
Apache::PerlSections->store("$ServerRoot/ServerConfig.pm");

__END__
</Perl>
```

Documenting Configuration Files

When *mod_perl* is configured with the server, configuration files can be documented with POD (Perl's "plain old documentation" system). There are only a handful of POD directives that *mod_perl* recognizes but enough to mix POD with an actual server configuration. The recognized directives are as follows:

=pod

> When a =pod token is found in the configuration file, *mod_perl* will soak up the file line-by-line, until a =cut token or a special =over token is reached.

=cut

> When a =cut token is found, *mod_perl* will turn the configuration processing back over to Apache.

=over

> The =over directive can be used in conjunction with the =back directive to hand sections back to Apache for processing. This allows the *pod2** converters to include the actual configuration sections in its output. In order to allow for =over to be used elsewhere, *mod_perl* will hand these sections back to Apache only if the line contains the string *apache*.

> =over to apache

=back

> When *mod_perl* is inside a special **=over** section as described above, it will go back to POD-soaking mode once it sees a **=back** directive.
>
> ```
> =back to pod
> ```

__END__

> Although **__END__** is not a POD directive, *mod_perl* recognizes this token when present in a server configuration file. It will simply read in the rest of the configuration file, ignoring each line until there is nothing left to read.

Here is a complete example:

```
=pod

=head1 NAME

httpd.conf - The main server configuration file

=head2 Standard Module Configuration

=over 4

=item mod_status

=over to apache

 #Apache will process directives in this section
 <Location /server-status>
    SetHandler server-status
    ...
 </Location>

=back to pod

=item ...

...

=back

=cut

__END__
The server will not try to process anything here
```

We've now covered the entire Apache module API, at least as far as Perl is concerned. The next chapter presents a complete reference guide to the Perl API, organized by topic. This is followed in Chapters 10 and 11, *C API Reference Guide*, by a reference guide to the C-language API, which fills in the details that C programmers need to know about.

9

Perl API Reference Guide

This chapter gives the definitive list of all the Perl API classes and method calls. They are organized functionally by class, starting with the *Apache* request object and moving onward through *Apache::SubRequest, Apache::Server, Apache::Connection, Apache::URI, Apache::Util, Apache::Log,* and other classes.

At the end of this chapter we discuss the *Apache::File* class, which provides advanced functionality for HTTP/1.1 requests, and a discussion of the various magic globals, subroutines, and literals that *mod_perl* recognizes.

The Apache Request Object

The Apache request object implements a huge number of methods. To help you find the method you're looking for, we've broken them down into eight broad categories:

Client request methods

Methods that have to do with retrieving information about the current request, such as fetching the requested URI, learning the request document's filename, or reading incoming HTTP headers.

Server response methods

Methods that are concerned with setting outgoing information, such as setting outgoing headers and controlling the document language and compression.

Sending data to the client

Methods for sending document content data to the client.

Server core functions

Methods that control key aspects of transaction processing but are not directly related to processing browser data input or output. For example, the subrequest API is covered in this section.

Server configuration methods

Methods for retrieving configuration information about the server.

Logging

Methods for logging error messages and warnings to the server error log.

Access control methods

Methods for controlling access to restricted documents and for authenticating remote users.

mod_perl-specific methods

Methods that use special features of *mod_perl* which have no counterpart in the C API. They include such things as the *gensym()* method for generating anonymous filehandles and *set_handlers()* for altering the list of subroutines that will handle the current request.

Should you wish to subclass the *Apache* object in order to add application-specific features, you'll be pleased to find that it's easy to do so. Please see "Subclassing the Apache Class," in Chapter 7, *Other Request Phases,* for instructions.

Client Request Methods

This section covers the request object methods that are used to query or modify the incoming client request. These methods allow you to retrieve such information as the URI the client has requested, the request method in use, the content of any submitted HTML forms, and various items of information about the remote host.

args()

The *args()* method returns the contents of the URI query string (that part of the request URI that follows the ? character, if any). When called in a scalar context, *args()* returns the entire string. When called in a list context, the method returns a list of parsed key/value pairs:

```
my $query = $r->args;
my %in    = $r->args;
```

One trap to be wary of: if the same argument name is present several times (as can happen with a selection list in a fill-out form), assignment of *args()* to a hash will discard all but the last argument. To avoid this, you'll need to use the more complex argument processing scheme described in Chapter 4, *Content Handlers.*

connection()

This method returns an object blessed into the *Apache::Connection* class. See "The Apache::Connection Class" later in this chapter for information on what you can do with this object once you get it.

```
my $c = $r->connection;
```

content()

> When the client request method is POST, which generally occurs when the remote client is submitting the contents of a fill-out form, the *$r->content* method returns the submitted information but only if the request content type is *application/x-www-form-urlencoded*. When called in a scalar context, the entire string is returned. When called in a list context, a list of parsed name=value pairs is returned.
>
> To handle other types of PUT or POSTed content, you'll need to use a module such as CGI.pm or *Apache::Request* or use the *read()* method and parse the data yourself.
>
> Note that you can only call *content()* once. If you call the method more than once, it will return *undef* (or an empty list) after the first try.

filename()

> The *filename()* method sets or returns the result of the URI translation phase. During the URI translation phase, your handler will call this method with the physical path to a file in order to set the filename. During later phases of the transaction, calling this method with no arguments returns its current value.
>
> Examples:

```
my $fname = $r->filename;
unless (open(FH, $fname)) {
    die "can't open $fname $!";
}

my $fname = do_translation($r->uri);
$r->filename($fname);
```

finfo()

> Immediately following the translation phase, Apache walks along the components of the requested URI trying to determine where the physical file path ends and the additional path information begins (this is described at greater length at the beginning of Chapter 4). In the course of this walk, Apache makes the system *stat()* call one or more times to read the directory information along the path. When the walk is finished, the *stat()* information for the translated filename is cached in the request record, where it can be recovered using the *finfo()* method. If you need to *stat()* the file, you can take advantage of this cached stat structure rather than repeating the system call.
>
> When *finfo()* is called, it moves the cached stat information into the special filehandle _ that Perl uses to cache its own stat operations. You can then perform file test operations directly on this filehandle rather than on the file itself, which would incur the penalty of another *stat()* system call. For convenience, *finfo()* returns a reference to the _ filehandle, so file tests can be done directly on the return value of *finfo()*.

The following three examples all result with the same value for `$size`. However, the first two avoid the overhead of the implicit *stat()* performed by the last.

```
my $size = -s $r->finfo;

$r->finfo;
my $size = -s _;

my $size = -s $r->filename; # slower
```

It is possible for a module to be called upon to process a URL that does not correspond to a physical file. In this case, the *stat()* structure will contain the result of testing for a nonexistent file, and Perl's various file test operations will all return false.

The *Apache::Util* package contains a number of routines that are useful for manipulating the contents of the stat structure. For example, the *ht_time()* routine turns Unix timestamps into HTTP-compatible human readable strings. See the *Apache::Util* manpage and the section "The Apache::URI Class" later in this chapter for more details.

```
use Apache::Util qw(ht_time);

if(-d $r->finfo) {
    printf "%s is a directory\n", $r->filename;
}
else {
    printf "Last Modified: %s\n", ht_time((stat _)[9]);
}
```

get_client_block()
setup_client_block()
should_client_block()

The *get_*, *setup_*, and *should_client_block* methods are lower-level ways to read the data sent by the client in POST and PUT requests. This protocol exactly mirrors the C-language API described in Chapter 10, *C API Reference Guide, Part I*, and provides for timeouts and other niceties. Although the Perl API supports them, Perl programmers should generally use the simpler *read()* method instead.

get_remote_host()

This method can be used to look up the remote client's DNS hostname or simply return its IP address. When a DNS lookup is successful, its result is cached and returned on subsequent calls to *get_remote_host()* to avoid costly multiple lookups. This cached value can also be retrieved with the *Apache::Connection* object's *remote_host()* method.

This method takes an optional argument. The type of lookup performed by this method is affected by this argument, as well as the value of the

HostNameLookups directive. Possible arguments to this method, whose symbolic names can be imported from the *Apache::Constants* module using the *:remotehost* import tag, are the following:

REMOTE_HOST

> If this argument is specified, Apache will try to look up the DNS name of the remote host. This lookup will fail if the Apache configuration directive *HostNameLookups* is set to *Off* or if the hostname cannot be determined by a DNS lookup, in which case the function will return *undef*.

REMOTE_NAME

> When called with this argument, the method will return the DNS name of the remote host if possible, or the dotted decimal representation of the client's IP address otherwise. This is the default lookup type when no argument is specified.

REMOTE_NOLOOKUP

> When this argument is specified, *get_remote_host()* will not perform a new DNS lookup (even if the *HostNameLookups* directive says so). If a successful lookup was done earlier in the request, the cached hostname will be returned. Otherwise, the method returns the dotted decimal representation of the client's IP address.

REMOTE_DOUBLE_REV

> This argument will trigger a double-reverse DNS lookup regardless of the setting of the *HostNameLookups* directive. Apache will first call the DNS to return the hostname that maps to the IP number of the remote host. It will then make another call to map the returned hostname back to an IP address. If the returned IP address matches the original one, then the method returns the hostname. Otherwise, it returns *undef*. The reason for this baroque procedure is that standard DNS lookups are susceptible to DNS spoofing in which a remote machine temporarily assumes the apparent identity of a trusted host. Double-reverse DNS lookups make spoofing much harder and are recommended if you are using the hostname to distinguish between trusted clients and untrusted ones. However, double reverse DNS lookups are also twice as expensive.

In recent versions of Apache, double-reverse name lookups are always performed for the name-based access checking implemented by *mod_access*.

Here are some examples:

```
my $remote_host = $r->get_remote_host;

# same as above
use Apache::Constants qw(:remotehost);
my $remote_host = $r->get_remote_host(REMOTE_NAME);
```

```
# double-reverse DNS lookup
use Apache::Constants qw(:remotehost);
my $remote_host = $r->get_remote_host(REMOTE_DOUBLE_REV) || "nohost";
```

get_remote_logname()

This method returns the login name of the remote user or *undef* if the user's login could not be determined. Generally, this only works if the remote user is logged into a Unix or VMS host and that machine is running the *identd* daemon (which implements a protocol known as RFC 1413).

The success of the call also depends on the *IdentityCheck* configuration directive being turned on. Since identity checks can adversely impact Apache's performance, this directive is off by default.

```
my $remote_logname = $r->get_remote_logname;
```

headers_in()

When called in a list context, the *headers_in()* method returns a list of key/value pairs corresponding to the client request headers. When called in a scalar context, it returns a hash reference tied to the *Apache::Table* class. This class provides methods for manipulating several of Apache's internal key/value table structures and, for all intents and purposes, acts just like an ordinary hash table. However, it also provides object methods for dealing correctly with multivalued entries. See "The Apache::Table Class" later in this chapter for details.

```
my %headers_in = $r->headers_in;
my $headers_in = $r->headers_in;
```

Once you have copied the headers to a hash, you can refer to them by name. See Table 9-1 for a list of incoming headers that you may need to use. For example, you can view the length of the data that the client is sending by retrieving the key *Content-length*:

```
%headers_in = $r->headers_in;
my $cl = $headers_in{'Content-length'};
```

You'll need to be aware that browsers are not required to be consistent in their capitalization of header field names. For example, some may refer to *Content-Type* and others to *Content-type*. The Perl API copies the field names into the hash as is, and like any other Perl hash, the keys are case-sensitive. This is a potential trap.

For these reasons it's better to call *headers_in()* in a scalar context and use the returned tied hash. Since *Apache::Table* sits on top of the C table API, lookup comparisons are performed in a case-insensitive manner. The tied interface also allows you to add or change the value of a header field, in case you want to modify the request headers seen by handlers downstream. This code fragment shows the tied hash being used to get and set fields:

```
my $headers_in = $r->headers_in;
my $ct = $headers_in->{'Content-Length'};
$headers_in->{'User-Agent'} = 'Block this robot';
```

It is often convenient to refer to header fields without creating an intermediate hash or assigning a variable to the *Apache::Table* reference. This is the usual idiom:

```
my $cl = $r->headers_in->{'Content-Length'};
```

Certain request header fields such as *Accept*, *Cookie*, and several other request fields are multivalued. When you retrieve their values, they will be packed together into one long string separated by commas. You will need to parse the individual values out yourself. Individual values can include parameters which will be separated by semicolons. Cookies are common examples of this:

```
Set-Cookie: SESSION=1A91933A; domain=acme.com; expires=Wed, 21-Oct-1998
20:46:07 GMT
```

A few clients send headers with the same key on multiple lines. In this case, you can use the *Apache::Table::get()* method to retrieve all of the values at once.

For full details on the various incoming headers, see the documents at *http://www.w3.org/Protocols*. Nonstandard headers, such as those transmitted by experimental browsers, can also be retrieved with this method call.

Table 9-1. Incoming HTTP Request Headers

Field	Description
Accept	MIME types that the client accepts
Accept-encoding	Compression methods that the client accepts
Accept-language	Languages that the client accepts
Authorization	Used by various authorization/authentication schemes
Connection	Connection options, such as *Keep-alive*
Content-length	Length, in bytes, of data to follow
Content-type	MIME type of data to follow
Cookie	Client-side data
From	Email address of the requesting user (deprecated)
Host	Virtual host to retrieve data from
If-modified-since	Return document only if modified since the date specified
If-none-match	Return document if it has changed
Referer	URL of document that linked to the requested one
User-agent	Name and version of the client software

header_in()

> The *header_in()* method (singular, not plural) is used to get or set the value
> of a client incoming request field. If the given value is *undef*, the header will
> be removed from the list of header fields:
>
> ```
> my $cl = $r->header_in('Content-length');
> $r->header_in($key, $val); #set the value of header '$key'
> $r->header_in('Content-length' => undef); #remove the header
> ```
>
> The key lookup is done in a case-insensitive manner. The *header_in()*
> method predates the *Apache::Table* class but remains for backward compatibil-
> ity and as a bit of a shortcut to using the *headers_in()* method.

header_only()

> If the client issues a HEAD request, it wants to receive the HTTP response
> headers only. Content handlers should check for this by calling *header_only()*
> before generating the document body. The method will return true in the case
> of a HEAD request and false in the case of other requests. Alternatively, you
> could examine the string value returned by *method()* directly, although this
> would be less portable if the HTTP protocol were some day expanded to sup-
> port more than one header-only request method.
>
> ```
> # generate the header & send it
> $r->send_http_header;
> return OK if $r->header_only;
>
> # now generate the document...
> ```
>
> Do *not* try to check numeric value returned by *method_number()* to identify a
> header request. Internally, Apache uses the M_GET number for both HEAD and
> GET methods.

method()

> This method will return the string version of the request method, such as GET,
> HEAD, or POST. Passing an argument will change the method, which is occa-
> sionally useful for internal redirects (Chapter 4) and for testing authorization
> restriction masks (Chapter 6, *Authentication and Authorization*).
>
> ```
> my $method = $r->method;
> $r->method('GET');
> ```
>
> If you update the method, you probably want to update the method number
> accordingly as well.

method_number()

> This method will return the request method number, which refers to internal
> constants defined by the Apache API. The method numbers are available to
> Perl programmers from the *Apache::Constants* module by importing the *:meth-
> ods* set. The relevant constants include M_GET, M_POST, M_PUT, and M_DELETE.
> Passing an argument will set this value, mainly used for internal redirects and

for testing authorization restriction masks. If you update the method number, you probably want to update the method accordingly as well.

Note that there isn't an **M_HEAD** constant. This is because when Apache receives a HEAD request, it sets the method number to **M_GET** and sets *header_only()* to return true.

```
use Apache::Constants qw(:methods);

if ($r->method_number == M_POST) {
    # change the request method
    $r->method_number(M_GET);
    $r->method("GET");
    $r->internal_redirect('/new/place');
}
```

There is no particular advantage of using *method_number()* over *method()* for Perl programmers, other than being only slightly more efficient.

parsed_uri()

When Apache parses the incoming request, it will turn the request URI into a predigested **uri_components** structure. The *parsed_uri()* method will return an object blessed into the *Apache::URI* class, which provides methods for fetching and setting various parts of the URI. See "The Apache::Util Class" later in this chapter for details.

```
use Apache::URI ();
my $uri = $r->parsed_uri;
my $host = $uri->hostname;
```

path_info()

The *path_info()* method will return what is left in the path after the URI translation phase. Apache's default translation method, described at the beginning of Chapter 4, uses a simple directory-walking algorithm to decide what part of the URI is the file and what part is the additional path information.

You can provide an argument to *path_info()* in order to change its value:

```
my $path_info = $r->path_info;
$r->path_info("/some/additional/information");
```

Note that in most cases, changing the *path_info()* requires you to sync the *uri()* with the update. In the following example, we calculate the original URI minus any path info, change the existing path info, then properly update the URI:

```
my $path_info = $r->path_info;
my $uri = $r->uri;
my $orig_uri = substr $uri, 0, length($uri) - length($path_info);
$r->path_info($new_path_info);
$r->uri($orig_uri . $r->path_info);
```

protocol

> The *$r->protocol* method will return a string identifying the protocol that the
> client speaks. Typical values will be `HTTP/1.0` or `HTTP/1.1`.
>
> ```
> my $protocol = $r->protocol;
> ```
>
> This method is read-only.

proxyreq()

> The *proxyreq()* method returns true if the current HTTP request is for a proxy
> URI—that is, if the actual document resides on a foreign server somewhere
> and the client wishes Apache to fetch the document on its behalf. This method
> is mainly intended for use during the filename translation phase of the
> request.
>
> ```
> sub handler {
>     my $r = shift;
>     return DECLINED unless $r->proxyreq;
>     # do something interesting...
> }
> ```
>
> See Chapter 7 for examples.

read()

> The *read()* method provides Perl API programmers with a simple way to get
> at the data submitted by the browser in POST and PUT requests. It should be
> used when the information submitted by the browser is not in the *application/
> x-www-form-urlencoded* format that the *content()* method knows how to
> handle.
>
> Call *read()* with a scalar variable to hold the read data and the length of the
> data to read. Generally, you will want to ask for the entire data sent by the cli-
> ent, which can be recovered from the incoming *Content-length* field:[*]
>
> ```
> my $buff;
> $r->read($buff, $r->header_in('Content-length'));
> ```
>
> Internally, Perl sets up a timeout in case the client breaks the connection pre-
> maturely. The exact value of the timeout is set by the *Timeout* directive in the
> server configuration file. If a timeout does occur, the script will be aborted.
>
> Within a handler you may also recover client data by simply reading from
> STDIN using Perl's *read()*, *getc()*, and readline (`<>`) functions. This works
> because the Perl API ties STDIN to *Apache::read()* before entering handlers.

---

[*] As of this writing, HTTP/1.1 requests that do not have a *Content-length* header, such as those that use
chunked encoding, are not properly handled by this API.

server()

> This method returns a reference to an *Apache::Server* object, from which you can retrieve all sorts of information about low-level aspects of the server's configuration. See "The Apache::Server Class" for details.

```
my $s = $r->server;
```

the_request()

> This method returns the unparsed request line sent by the client. *the_request()* is primarily used by log handlers, since other handlers will find it more convenient to use methods that return the information in preparsed form. This method is read-only.

```
my $request_line = $r->the_request;
print LOGFILE $request_line;
```

> Note that *the_request()* is functionally equivalent to this code fragment:

```
my $request_line = join ' ', $r->method, $r->uri, $r->protocol;
```

uri()

> The *uri()* method returns the URI requested by the browser. You may also pass this method a string argument in order to set the URI seen by handlers further down the line, which is something that a translation handler might want to do.

```
my $uri = $r->uri;
$r->uri("/something/else");
```

Server Response Methods

This section covers the API methods used to build and query the outgoing server response message. These methods allow you to set the type and length of the outgoing document, set HTTP cookies, assign the document a language or compression method, and set up authorization and authentication schemes.

Most of the methods in this section are concerned with setting the values of the outgoing HTTP response header fields. We give a list of all of the fields you are likely to use in Table 9-2. For a comprehensive list, see the HTTP/1.0 and HTTP/1.1 specifications found at *http://www.w3.org/Protocols*.

Table 9-2. Response Header Fields

Field	Description
Allowed	The methods allowed by this URI, such as POST
Content-encoding	The compression method of this data
Content-language	The language in which this document is written
Content-length	Length, in bytes, of data to follow
Content-type	MIME type of this data
Date	The current date in GMT (Greenwich Mean Time)

Table 9-2. Response Header Fields (continued)

Field	Description
Expires	The date the document expires
Last-modified	The date the document was last modified
Link	The URL of this document's "parent," if any
Location	The location of the document in redirection responses
ETag	The opaque ID for this version of the document
Message-id	The ID of this document, if any
MIME-version	The version of MIME used (currently 1.0)
Pragma	Hints to the browser, such as "no-cache"
Public	The requests that this URL responds to (rarely used)
Server	The name and version of the server software
Set-cookie	The client-side cookie to give to a browser
WWW-authenticate	Used in the various authorization schemes
Vary	Criteria that can be used to select this document

bytes_sent()

> This method will retrieve the number of bytes of information sent by the server to the client, excluding the length of the HTTP headers. It is only useful after the *send_http_header()* method (described later) has been called. This method is normally used by log handlers to record and summarize network usage. See Chapter 7 for examples.

```
my $bytes_sent = $r->bytes_sent;
```

cgi_header_out()

> This method is similar to the *header_out()* function. Given a key/value pair, it sets the corresponding outgoing HTTP response header field to the indicated value, replacing whatever was there before. However, unlike *header_out()*, which blindly sets the field to whatever you tell it, *cgi_header_out()* recognizes certain special keys and takes the appropriate action. This is used to emulate the magic fields recognized by Apache's own *mod_cgi* CGI-handling routines.

> Table 9-3 lists the headers that trigger special actions by *cgi_header_out()*.

Table 9-3. Special Actions Triggered by cgi_header_out()

Header	Actions
Content-type	Sets `$r->content_type` to the given value
Status	Sets `$r->status` to the integer value in the string Sets `$r->status_line` to the given value
Location	Sets *Location* in the `headers_out` table to the given value and performs an internal redirect if URI is relative

Table 9-3. Special Actions Triggered by cgi_header_out() (continued)

Header	Actions
Content-length	Sets *Content-length* in the `headers_out` table to the given value
Transfer-encoding	Sets *Transfer-encoding* in the `headers_out` table to the given value
Last-modified	Parses the string date, feeding the time value to *ap_update_ mtime()* and invoking *ap_set_last_modified()*
Set-cookie	Calls *ap_table_add()* to support multiple *Set-cookie* headers
Other	Calls a*p_table_merge()* with given key and value

You generally can use the *Apache::Table* or *header_out()* methods to achieve the results you want. *cgi_header_out()* is provided for those who wish to create a CGI emulation layer, such as *Apache::Registry*. Those who are designing such a system should also look at *send_cgi_header()*, described in "Sending Data to the Client" later in this chapter.

content_encoding()

This method gets or sets the document encoding. Content encoding fields are strings like `gzip` or `compress`, and indicate that the document has been compressed or otherwise encoded. Browsers that handle the particular encoding scheme can decode or decompress the document on the fly.

Getting or setting *content_encoding()* is equivalent to using *headers_out()* or *header_out()* to change the value of the *Content-encoding* header. Chapters 4 and 7 give examples of querying and manipulating the content encoding field.

```
my $enc = $r->content_encoding;
if($r->filename =~ /\.gz$/) {
   $r->content_encoding("gzip");
}
```

content_languages()

The *content_languages()* method gets or sets the *Content-language* HTTP header field. Called without arguments, it returns an array reference consisting of two-letter language identifiers, for example, "en" for English and "no" for Norwegian. You can also pass it an array reference to set the list of languages to a new value. This method can be used to implement support for multilanguage documents. See the *Apache::MIME* module in Chapter 7 for an example.

content_languages() is a convenient interface to the lower-level *header_out()* and *headers_out()* methods.

```
my $languages = $r->content_languages;
$r->content_languages(['en']);
```

content_type()

> This method corresponds to the *Content-type* header field, which tells the browser the MIME type of the returned document. Common MIME types include *text/plain, text/html,* and *image/gif. content_type()* can be used either to get or set the current value of this field. It is important to use *content_type()* to set the content type rather than calling *headers_out()* or *header_out()* to change the outgoing HTTP header directly. This is because a copy of the content type is kept in the request record, and other modules and core protocol components will consult this value rather than the outgoing headers table.

```
my $ct = $r->content_type;
$r->content_type('text/plain');
```

custom_response()

> When a handler returns a code other than OK, DECLINED, or DONE, Apache aborts processing and throws an error. When an error is thrown, application programs can catch it and replace Apache's default processing with their own custom error handling routines by using the *ErrorDocument* configuration directive. The arguments to *ErrorDocument* are the status code to catch and a custom string, static document, or CGI script to invoke when the error occurs.

> The module-level interface to Apache's error handling system is *custom_response()*. Like the directive, the method call takes two arguments. The first argument is a valid response code from Table 3.1. The second is either a string to return in response to the error, or a URI to invoke to handle the request. This URI can be a static document, a CGI script, or even a content handler in an Apache module. Chapters 4 and 6 have more extensive coverage of the error handling system.

```
use Apache::Constants qw(:common);
$r->custom_response(AUTH_REQUIRED, "sorry, I don't know you.");
$r->custom_response(SERVER_ERROR, "/perl/server_error_handler.pl");
```

err_headers_out()

> Apache actually keeps two sets of outgoing response headers: one set to use when the transaction is successful and another to use in the case of a module returning an error code. Although maintaining a dual set of headers may seem redundant, it makes custom error handlers much easier to write, as we saw in Chapter 4. *err_headers_out()* is equivalent to *headers_out()*, but it gets and sets values in the table of HTTP header response fields that are sent in the case of an error.

> Unlike ordinary header fields, error fields are sent to the browser even when the module aborts or returns an error status code. This allows modules to do such things as set cookies when errors occur or implement custom authorization schemes. Error fields also persist across internal redirects when one

content handler passes the buck to another. This feature is necessary to support the *ErrorDocument* mechanism.

```
my %err_headers_out = $r->err_headers_out;
my $err_headers_out = $r->err_headers_out;
$r->err_headers_out->{'X-Odor'} = "Something's rotten in Denmark";
```

err_header_out()

Like the *header_in()* and *header_out()* methods, *err_header_out()* predates the *Apache::Table* class. It can be used to get or set a single field in the error headers table. As with the other header methods, the key lookups are done in a case-insensitive manner. Its syntax is identical to *header_out()*:

```
my $loc = $r->err_header_out('Location');
$r->err_header_out(Location => 'http://www.modperl.com/');
$r->err_header_out(Location => undef);
```

headers_out()

headers_out() provides modules with the ability to get or set any of the outgoing HTTP response header fields. When called in a list context, *headers_out()* returns a list of key/value pairs corresponding to the current server response headers. The capitalization of the field names is not canonicalized prior to copying them into the list.

When called in a scalar context, this method returns a hash reference tied to the *Apache::Table* class. This class provides an interface to the underlying **headers_out** data structure. Fetching a key from the tied hash will retrieve the corresponding HTTP field in a case-insensitive fashion, and assigning to the hash will change the value of the header so that it is seen by other handlers further down the line, ultimately affecting the header that is sent to the browser.

The headers that are set with *headers_out()* are cleared when an error occurs, and do not persist across internal redirects. To create headers that persist across errors and internal redirects, use *err_headers_out()*, described earlier.

```
my %headers_out = $r->headers_out;
my $headers_out = $r->headers_out;
$headers_out->{Set-cookie} = 'SESSION_ID=3918823';
```

The *Content-type*, *Content-encoding*, and *Content-language* response fields have special meaning to the Apache server and its modules. These fields occupy their own slots of the request record itself and should always be accessed using their dedicated methods rather than the generic *headers_out()* method. If you forget and use *headers_out()* instead, Apache and other modules may not recognize your changes, leading to confusing results. In addition, the *Pragma: no-cache* idiom, used to tell browsers not to cache the document, should be set indirectly using the *no_cache()* method.

The many features of the *Apache::Table* class are described in more detail in its own section.

header_out()

Before the *Apache::Table* class was written, *header_out()* was used to get or set the value of an individual HTTP field. Like the *header_in()* method, *header_out()* predates the *Apache::Table* class but remains for backwards compatibility and as a bit of a shortcut to using the *headers_in* method.

If passed a single argument, *header_out()* returns the value of the corresponding field from the outgoing HTTP response header. If passed a key/value pair, *header_out()* stably changes the value of the corresponding header field. A field can be removed entirely by passing *undef* as its value. The key lookups are done in a case-insensitive manner.

```
my $loc = $r->header_out('Location');
$r->header_out(Location => 'http://www.modperl.com/');
$r->header_out(Location => undef);
```

handler()

The *handler* method gets or sets the name of the module that is responsible for the content generation phase of the current request. For example, for requests to run CGI scripts, this will be the value **cgi-script**. Ordinarily this value is set in the configuration file using the *SetHandler* or *AddHandler* directives. However, your handlers can set this value during earlier phases of the transaction, typically the MIME type checking or fixup phases.

Chapter 7 gives examples of how to use *handler()* to create a handler that dispatches to other modules based on the document's type.

```
my $handler = $r->handler;
if($handler eq "cgi-script") {
    warn "shame on you.  Fixing.\n"
    $r->handler('perl-script');
}
```

handler() cannot be used to set handlers for anything but the response phase. Use *set_handlers()* or *push_handlers()* to change the handlers for other phases (see "mod_perl-Specific Methods" later in this chapter).

no_cache()

The *no_cache()* method gets or sets a boolean flag that indicates that the data being returned is volatile. Browsers that respect this flag will avoid writing the document out to the client-side cache. Setting this flag to true will cause Apache to emit an *Expires* field with the same date and time as the original request.

```
$current_flag = $r->no_cache();
$r->no_cache(1);    # set no-cache to true
```

request_time()

> This method returns the time at which the request started, expressed as a Unix timestamp in seconds since the start of an arbitrary period called the "epoch."* You can pass this to Perl's *localtime()* function to get a human-readable string or to any of the available time- and date-handling Perl modules to manipulate it in various ways. Unlike most of the other methods, this one is read-only.

```
my $date = scalar localtime $r->request_time;
warn "request started at $date";
```

status()

> The *status()* method allows you to get or set the status code of the outgoing HTTP response. Usually you will set this value indirectly by returning the status code as the handler's function result. However, there are rare instances when you want to trick Apache into thinking that the module returned an OK status code but actually send the browser a non-OK status.

> Call the method with no arguments to retrieve the current status code. Call it with a numeric value to set the status. Constants for all the standard status codes can be found in *Apache::Constants*.

```
use Apache::Constants qw(:common);

my $rc = $r->status;
$r->status(SERVER_ERROR);
```

status_line()

> *status_line()* is used to get or set the error code and the human-readable status message that gets sent to the browser. Ordinarily you should use *status()* to set the numeric code and let Apache worry about translating this into a human readable string. However, if you want to generate an unusual response line, you can use this method to set the line. To be successful, the response line *must* begin with one of the valid HTTP status codes.

```
my $status_line = $r->status_line;
$r->status_line("200 Bottles of Beer on the Wall");
```

> If you update the status line, you probably want to update *status()* accordingly as well.

Sending Data to the Client

The methods in this section are invoked by content handlers to send header and document body data to the waiting browser. Noncontent handlers should not call these methods.

---

* In case you were wondering, the epoch began at 00:00:00 GMT on January 1, 1970, and is due to end in 2038. There's probably a good explanation for this choice.

print()

The Apache C API provides several functions for sending formatted data to the client. However, Perl is more flexible in its string handling functions, so only one method, *print()*, is needed.

The *print()* method is similar to Perl's built-in *print()* function, except that all the data you print eventually winds up being displayed on the user's browser. Like the built-in *print()*, this method will accept a variable number of strings to print out. However, the Apache *print()* method does not accept a filehandle argument for obvious reasons.

Like the *read()* method, *print()* sets a timeout so that if the client connection is broken, the handler won't hang around indefinitely trying to send data. If a timeout does occur, the script will be aborted.

The method also checks the Perl autoflush global $|. If the variable is non-zero, *print()* will flush the buffer after every command, rather than after every line. This is consistent with the way the built-in *print()* works.

```
$r->print("hello" , " ", "world!");
```

An interesting feature of the Apache Perl API is that the STDOUT filehandle is tied to *Apache* so that if you use the built-in *print()* to print to standard output, the data will be redirected to the request object's *print()* method. This allows CGI scripts to run unmodified under *Apache::Registry*, and also allows one content handler's output to be transparently chained to another handler's input. The section "The Apache TIEHANDLE Interface" later in this chapter goes into more detail on tying filehandles to the Perl API, and Chapter 4 has more to say about chained handlers.

```
print "hello world!";  # automatically invokes Apache::print()
```

There is also an optimization built into *print()*. If any of the arguments to the method are scalar references to strings, they are automatically dereferenced for you. This avoids needless copying of large strings when passing them to subroutines.

```
$a_large_string = join '', <GETTYSBURG_ADDRESS>;
$r->print(\$a_large_string);
```

printf()

The *printf()* method works just like the built-in function of the same name, except that the data is sent to the client. Calling the built-in *printf()* on STDOUT will indirectly invoke this method because STDOUT is tied.

```
$r->printf("Hello %s", $r->connection->user);
```

rflush()

For efficiency's sake, Apache usually buffers the data printed by the handler and sends it to the client only when its internal buffers fill (or the handler is done). The *rflush()* method causes Apache to flush and send its buffered out-going data immediately. You may wish to do this if you have a long-running content handler and you wish the client to begin to see the data sooner.

Don't call *rflush()* if you don't need to, because it causes a performance hit.* This method is also called automatically after each *print()* if the Perl global variable $| is nonzero.

```
$r->rflush;
```

send_cgi_header()

As we mentioned in the section on *cgi_header_out()*, the *mod_cgi* module scans for and takes special action on certain header fields emitted by CGI scripts. Developers who wish to develop a CGI emulation layer can take advantage of *send_cgi_header()*. It accepts a single string argument formatted like a CGI header, parses it into fields, and passes the parsed fields to *cgi_header_out()*. *cgi_header_out()* then calls *send_http_header()* to send the completed header to the browser.

Don't forget to put a blank line at the end of the headers, just as a CGI script would:

```
$r->send_cgi_header(<<EOF);
Status: 200 Just Fine
Content-type: text/html
Set-cookie: open=sesame

EOF
```

You're welcome to use this method even if you aren't emulating the CGI envi-ronment, since it provides a convenient one-shot way to set and send the entire HTTP header; however, there is a performance hit associated with pars-ing the header string.

As an aside, this method is used to implement the behavior of the *PerlSend-Header* directive. When this directive is set to *On*, *mod_perl* scans the first lines of text printed by the content handler until it finds a blank line. Every-thing above the blank line is then sent to *send_cgi_header()*.

send_fd()

Given an open filehandle, filehandle glob, or glob reference as argument, this method sends the contents of the file to the client. Internally, the Perl inter-face extracts the file descriptor from the filehandle and uses that directly, which is generally faster than calling the higher-level Perl methods. The

---

* If you are wondering why this method has an *r* prefix, it is carried over from the C API I/O methods (described in Chapter 10), all of which have an *ap_r* prefix. This is the only I/O method from the group for which there is a direct Perl interface. If you find that the *r* prefix is not pleasing to the eye, this is no accident. It is intended to discourage the use of *rflush()* due to the performance implications.

confusing naming of this method (it takes a filehandle, not a file descriptor) is for consistency with the naming of the corresponding C API function call.

This method is generally used by content handlers that wish to send the browser the unmodified contents of a file.

```
my $fh = Apache::gensym();  # generate a new filehandle name
open($fh, $r->filename) || return NOT_FOUND;
$r->send_fd($fh);
close($fh);
```

send_http_header()

This method formats the outgoing response data into a proper HTTP response and sends it to the client. The header is constructed from values previously set by calls to *content_type()*, *content_encoding()*, *content_language()*, *status_line()*, and *headers_out()*. Naturally, this method should be called before any other methods for sending data to the client.

Because setting the document's MIME type is such a common operation, the Perl version of this API call allows you to save a few keystrokes by specifying the content type as an optional argument to *send_http_header()*. This is exactly equivalent to calling *content_type()* followed by *send_http_header()*.

```
$r->send_http_header;
$r->send_http_header('text/plain');
```

A content type passed to *send_http_header()* will override any previous calls to *content_type()*.

Server Core Functions

This section covers the API methods that are available for your use during the processing of a request but are not directly related to incoming or outgoing data.

chdir_file()

Given a filename as argument, change from the current directory to the directory in which the file is contained. This is a convenience routine for modules that implement scripting engines, since it is common to run the script from the directory in which it lives. The current directory will remain here, unless your module changes back to the previous directory. As there is significant overhead associated with determining the current directory, we suggest using the `$Apache::Server::CWD` variable or the *server_root_relative()* method if you wish to return to the previous directory afterward.

```
$r->chdir_file($r->filename);
```

child_terminate()

Calling this method will cause the current child process to shutdown gracefully after the current transaction is completed and the logging and cleanup phases are done. This method is not available on Win32 systems.

```
$r->child_terminate;
```

hard_timeout()
kill_timeout()
reset_timeout()
soft_timeout()

The timeout API governs the interaction of Apache with the client. At various points during the request/response cycle, a browser that is no longer responding can be timed out so that it doesn't continue to hold the connection open. Timeouts are primarily of concern to C API programmers, as *mod_perl* handles the details of timeouts internally for read and write methods. However, these calls are included in the Perl API for completeness.

The *hard_timeout()* method initiates a "hard" timeout. If the client read or write operation takes longer than the time specified by Apache's *Timeout* directive, then the current handler will be aborted immediately and Apache will immediately enter the logging phase. *hard_timeout()* takes a single string argument which should contain the name of your module or some other identification. This identification will be incorporated into the error message that is written to the server error log when the timeout occurs.

soft_timeout(), in contrast, does not immediately abort the current handler. Instead, when a timeout occurs control returns to the handler, but all read and write operations are replaced with no-ops so that no further data can be sent or received to the client. In addition, the *Apache::Connection* object's *aborted()* method will return true. Like *hard_timeout()*, you should pass this method the name of your module in order to be able to identify the source of the timeout in the error log.

The *reset_timeout()* method can be called to set a previously initiated timer back to zero. It is usually used between a series of read or write operations in order to restart the timer.

Finally, the *kill_timeout()* method is called to cancel a previously initiated timeout. It is generally called when a series of I/O operations are completely done.

The following examples will give you the general idea of how these four methods are used. Remember, however, that in the Perl API these methods are not really necessary because they are called internally by the *read()* and *print()* methods.

```
# typical hard_timeout() usage
$r->hard_timeout("Apache::Example while reading data");
while (... read data loop ...) {
    ...
    $r->reset_timeout;
}
$r->kill_timeout;
```

```
# typical soft_timeout() usage
$r->soft_timeout("Apache::Example while reading data");
while (... read data loop ...) {
    ...
    $r->reset_timeout;
}
$r->kill_timeout;
```

internal_redirect()

Unlike a full HTTP redirect in which the server tells the browser to look somewhere else for the requested document, the *internal_redirect()* method tells Apache to return a different URI without telling the client. This is a lot faster than a full redirect.

The required argument is an absolute URI path on the current server. The server will process the URI as if it were a whole new request, running the URI translation, MIME type checking, and other phases before invoking the appropriate content handler for the new URI. The content handler that eventually runs is not necessarily the same as the one that invoked *internal_redirect()*. This method should only be called within a content handler.

Do *not* use *internal_redirect()* to redirect to a different server. You'll need to do a full redirect for that. Both redirection techniques are described in more detail in Chapter 4.

```
$r->internal_redirect("/new/place");
```

Apache implements its *ErrorDocument* feature as an internal redirect, so many of the techniques that apply to internal redirects also apply to custom error handling.

internal_redirect_handler()

This method does the same thing as *internal_redirect()* but arranges for the content handler used to process the redirected URI to be the same as the current content handler.

```
$r->internal_redirect_handler("/new/place");
```

is_initial_req()

There are several instances in which an incoming URI request can trigger one or more secondary internal requests. An internal request is triggered when *internal_redirect()* is called explicitly, and it also happens behind the scenes when *lookup_file()* and *lookup_uri()* are called.

With the exception of the logging phase, which is run just once for the primary request, secondary requests are run through each of the transaction processing phases, and the appropriate handlers are called each time. There may be times when you don't want a particular handler running on a subrequest or internal redirect, either to avoid performance overhead or to avoid infinite recursion. The *is_initial_req()* method will return a true value if the current request is the primary one and false if the request is the result of a subrequest or an internal redirect.

```
return DECLINED unless $r->is_initial_req;
```

is_main()

This method can be used to distinguish between subrequests triggered by handlers and the "main" request triggered by a browser's request for a URI or an internal redirect. *is_main()* returns a true value for the primary request and for internal redirects and false for subrequests. Notice that this is slightly different from *is_initial_req()*, which returns false for internal redirects as well as subrequests.

is_main() is commonly used to prevent infinite recursion when a handler gets reinvoked after it has made a subrequest.

```
return DECLINED unless $r->is_main;
```

Like *is_initial_req()*, this is a read-only method.

last()
main()
next()
prev()

When a handler is called in response to a series of internal redirects, *Error-Documents*, or subrequests, it is passed an ordinary-looking request object and can usually proceed as if it were processing a normal request. However, if a module has special needs, it can use these methods to walk the chain to examine the request objects passed to other requests in the series.

main() will return the request object of the parent request, the top of the chain. *last()* will return the last request in the chain. *prev()* and *next()* will return the previous and next requests in the chain, respectively. Each of these methods will return a reference to an object belonging to the *Apache* class or *undef* if the request doesn't exist.

The *prev()* method is handy inside an *ErrorDocument* handler to get at the information from the request that triggered the error. For example, this code fragment will find the URI of the failed request:

```
my $failed_uri = $r->prev->uri;
```

The *last()* method is mainly used by logging modules. Since Apache may have performed several subrequests while attempting to resolve the request, the *last* object will always point to the final result.

```
my $bytes_sent = $r->last->bytes_sent;
```

Should your module wish to log all internal requests, the *next()* method will come in handy.

```
sub My::logger {
    my $r = shift;
```

```
my $first = $r->uri;
my $last = $r->last->uri;
warn "first: $first, last: $last\n";

for (my $rr = $r; $rr; $rr = $rr->next) {
    my $uri = $rr->uri;
    my $status = $rr->status;
    warn "request: $uri, status: $status\n";
}

return OK;
}
```

Assuming the requested URI was */*, which was mapped to */index.html* by the *DirectoryIndex* configuration, the example above would output these messages to the *ErrorLog*:

```
first: /, last: /index.html
request: /, status: 200
request: /index.html, status: 200
```

The *next()* and *main()* methods are rarely used, but they are included for completeness. Handlers that need to determine whether they are in the main request should call `$r->is_main()` rather than `!$r->main()`, as the former is marginally more efficient.

location()

If the current handler was triggered by a *Perl*Handler* directive within a *<Location>* section, this method will return the path indicated by the *<Location>* directive.

For example, given this *<Location>* section:

```
<Location /images/dynamic_icons>
    SetHandler perl-script
    PerlHandler Apache::Icon
</Location>
```

location() will return */images/dynamic_icons*.

This method is handy for converting the current document's URI into a relative path.

```
my $base = $r->location;
(my $relative = $r->uri) =~ s/^$base//;
```

lookup_file()
lookup_uri()

lookup_file() and *lookup_uri()* invoke Apache subrequests. A subrequest is treated exactly like an ordinary request, except that the post read request, header parser, response generation, and logging phases are not run. This allows modules to pose "what-if" questions to the server. Subrequests can be used to learn the MIME type mapping of an arbitrary file, map a URI to a filename, or find out whether a file is under access control. After a successful lookup, the response phase of the request can optionally be invoked.

Both methods take a single argument corresponding to an absolute filename or a URI path, respectively. *lookup_uri()* performs the URI translation on the provided URI, passing the request to the access control and authorization handlers, if any, and then proceeds to the MIME type checking phase. *lookup_file()* behaves similarly but bypasses the initial URI translation phase and treats its argument as a physical file path.

Both methods return an *Apache::SubRequest* object, which is identical for all intents and purposes to a plain old *Apache* request object, as it inherits all methods from the *Apache* class. You can call the returned object's *content_type()*, *filename()*, and other methods to retrieve the information left there during subrequest processing.

The subrequest mechanism is extremely useful, and there are many practical examples of using it in Chapters 4, 5, and 6. The following code snippets show how to use subrequests to look up first the MIME type of a file and then a URI:

```
my $subr = $r->lookup_file('/home/http/htdocs/images/logo.tif');
my $ct = $subr->content_type;
```

```
my $ct = $r->lookup_uri('/images/logo.tif')->content_type;
```

In the *lookup_uri()* example, */images/logo.tif* will be passed through the same series of *Alias*, *ServerRoot*, and URI rewriting translations that the URI would be subjected to if it were requested by a browser.

If you need to pass certain HTTP header fields to the subrequest, such as a particular value of *Accept*, you can do so by calling *headers_in()* before invoking *lookup_uri()* or *lookup_file()*.

It is often a good idea to check the status of a subrequest in case something went wrong. If the subrequest was successful, the **status** value will be that of **HTTP_OK**.

```
use Apache::Constants qw(:common HTTP_OK);
my $subr = $r->lookup_uri("/path/file.html");
my $status = $subr->status;

unless ($status == HTTP_OK) {
    die "subrequest failed with status: $status";
}
```

notes()

There are times when handlers need to communicate among themselves in a way that goes beyond setting the values of HTTP header fields. To accommodate this, Apache maintains a "notes" table in the request record. This table is simply a list of key/value pairs. One handler can add its own key/value entry to the notes table, and later the handler for a subsequent phase can retrieve the note. Notes are maintained for the life of the current request and are deleted when the transaction is finished.

When called with two arguments, this method sets a note. When called with a single argument, it retrieves the value of that note. Both the keys and the values must be simple strings.

```
$r->notes('CALENDAR' => 'Julian');
my $cal = $r->notes('CALENDAR');
```

When called in a scalar context with no arguments, a hash reference tied to the *Apache::Table* class will be returned.

```
my $notes = $r->notes;
my $cal = $notes->{CALENDAR};
```

This method comes in handy for communication between a module written in Perl and one written in C. For example, the logging API saves error messages under a key named **error-notes**, which could be used by *ErrorDocuments* to provide a more informative error message.

The *LogFormat* directive, part of the standard *mod_log_config* module, can incorporate notes into log messages using the formatting character **%n**. See the Apache documentation for details.

subprocess_env()

The *subprocess_env()* method is used to examine and change the Apache environment table. Like other table-manipulation functions, this method has a variety of behaviors depending on the number of arguments it is called with and the context in which it is called. Call the method with no arguments in a scalar context to return a hash reference tied to the *Apache::Table* class:

```
my $env = $r->subprocess_env;
my $docroot = $env->{'DOCUMENT_ROOT'};
```

Call the method with a single argument to retrieve the current value of the corresponding entry in the environment table, or *undef* if no entry by that name exists:

```
my $doc_root = $r->subprocess_env("DOCUMENT_ROOT");
```

You may also call the method with a key/value pair to set the value of an entry in the table:

```
$r->subprocess_env(DOOR => "open");
```

Finally, if you call *subprocess_env()* in a void context with no arguments, it will reinitialize the table to contain the standard variables that Apache adds to the environment before invoking CGI scripts and server-side include files:

```
$r->subprocess_env;
```

Changes made to the environment table only persist for the length of the request. The table is cleared out and reinitialized at the beginning of every new transaction.

In the Perl API, the primary use for this method is to set environment variables for other modules to see and use. For example, a fixup handler could use this call to set up environment variables that are later recognized by *mod_include* and incorporated into server-side include pages. You do not ordinarily need to call *subprocess_env()* to read environment variables because *mod_perl* automatically copies the environment table into the Perl %ENV array before entering the response handler phase.

A potential confusion arises when a Perl API handler needs to launch a subprocess itself using *system()*, backticks, or a piped open. If you need to pass environment variables to the subprocess, set the appropriate keys in %ENV just as you would in an ordinary Perl script. *subprocess_env()* is only required if you need to change the environment in a subprocess launched by a *different* handler or module.

register_cleanup()

The *register_cleanup()* method registers a subroutine that will be called after the logging stage of a request. This is much the same as installing a cleanup handler with the *PerlCleanupHandler* directive. See Chapter 7 for some practical examples of using *register_cleanup()*.

The method expects a code reference argument:

```
sub callback {
    my $r = shift;
    my $uri = $r->uri;
    warn "process $$ all done with $uri\n";
}
$r->register_cleanup(\&callback);
```

Server Configuration Methods

Several methods give you access to the Apache server's configuration settings. You can inspect the configuration and, in many cases, change it dynamically. The most commonly needed configuration information can be obtained directly from the methods given in this section. More esoteric information can be obtained via the *Apache::Server* object returned by the request object's *server()* method. See the section "The Apache::Server Class" for details.

dir_config()

The *dir_config()* method and the *PerlSetVar* configuration directive together form the primary way of passing configuration information to Apache Perl modules.

The *PerlSetVar* directive can occur in the main part of a configuration file, in a *<VirtualHost>*, *<Directory>*, *<Location>*, or *<Files>* section, or in a *.htaccess* file. It takes a key/value pair separated by whitespace.

In the following two examples, the first directive sets a key named `Gate` to a value of `open`. The second sets the same key to a value of `wide open and beckoning`. Notice how quotes are used to protect arguments that contain whitespace:

```
PerlSetVar Gate open
PerlSetVar Gate "wide open and beckoning"
```

Configuration files can contain any number of *PerlSetVar* directives. If multiple directives try to set the same key, the usual rules of directive precedence apply. A key defined in a *.htaccess* file has precedence over a key defined in a *<Directory>*, *<Location>*, or *<Files>* section, which in turn has precedence over a key defined in a *<VirtualHost>* section. Keys defined in the main body of the configuration file have the lowest precedence of all.

Configuration keys set with *PerlSetVar* can be recovered within Perl handlers using *dir_config()*. The interface is simple. Called with the name of a key, *dir_config()* looks up the key and returns its value if found or *undef* otherwise.

```
my $value = $r->dir_config('Gate');
```

If called in a scalar context with no arguments, *dir_config()* returns a hash reference tied to the *Apache::Table* class. See "The Apache::Table Class" for details.

```
my $dir_config = $r->dir_config;
my $value = $dir_config->{'Gate'};
```

Only scalar values are allowed in configuration variables set by *PerlSetVar*. If you want to pass an array or hash, separate the items by a character that doesn't appear elsewhere in the string and call *split()* to break the retrieved variable into its components.

document_root()

The *document_root()* method returns the value of the document root directory. The value of the document root is set by the server configuration directive *DocumentRoot* and usually varies between different virtual hosts. Apache uses the document root to translate the URI into a physical pathname unless a more specific translation rule, such as *Alias*, applies.

```
my $doc_root = $r->document_root;
```

If you are used to using the environment variable `DOCUMENT_ROOT` within your CGI scripts in order to resolve URIs into physical pathnames, be aware that there's a much better way to do this in the Apache API. Perform a subrequest with the URI you want to resolve, and then call the returned object's *filename()* method. This works correctly even when the URI is affected by *Alias* directives or refers to user-maintained virtual directories:

```
my $image = $r->lookup_uri('/~fred/images/cookbook.gif')->filename;
```

If you're interested in fetching the physical file corresponding to the current request, call the current request object's *filename()* method:

```
my $file = $r->filename;
```

get_server_port()

This method returns the port number on which the server is listening.

```
my $port = $r->get_server_port;
```

If *UseCanonicalName* is configured to be *On* (the default), this method will return the value of the *Port* configuration directive. If no *Port* directive is present, the default port 80 is returned. If *UseCanonicalName* is *Off* and the client sent a *Host* header, then the method returns the actual port specified here, regardless of the value of the *Port* directive.

get_server_name()

This read-only method returns the name of the server handling the request.

```
my $name = $r->get_server_name;
```

This method is sensitive to the value of the *UseCanonicalName* configuration directive. If *UseCanonicalName* is *On* (the default), the method will always return the value of the current *ServerName* configuration directive. If *UseCanonicalName* is *Off*, then this method will return the value of the incoming request's *Host* header if present, or the value of the *ServerName* directive otherwise. These values can be different if the server has several different DNS names.

The lower-level *server_name()* method in the *Apache::Server* class always acts as if *UseCanonicalName* were on.

server_root_relative()

Called without any arguments, the *server_root_relative()* method returns the currently configured *ServerRoot* directory (in which Apache's binaries, configuration files, and logs commonly reside). If you pass this method a relative pathname, it will resolve the relative pathname to an absolute one based on the value of the server root. This is the preferred way to locate configuration and log files that are stored beneath the server root.

```
# return ServerRoot
my $ServerRoot = $r->server_root_relative;

# return $ServerRoot/logs/my.log
my $log = $r->server_root_relative("logs/my.log");
```

The *server_root_relative* method can also be invoked without a request object by calling it directly from the Apache class. The following example, which might be found at the beginning of a Perl startup file, first imports the Apache module and then uses *server_root_relative()* to add a site-specific library directory to the search path. It does this in a *BEGIN {}* block to ensure that this code is evaluated first. It then loads a local module named *My::App*, which presumably will be found in the site-specific directory.

```
#!/usr/bin/perl
# modify the search path
BEGIN {
   use Apache():
   use lib Apache->server_root_relative("lib/my_app");
}
use My::App ();
```

Logging Methods

This section covers request object methods that generate entries in the server error log. They are handy for debugging and error reporting. Prior to Apache 1.3, the error-logging API was a very simple one that didn't distinguish between different levels of severity. Apache now has a more versatile logging API similar to the Unix *syslog* system.* Each entry is associated with a severity level from low (*debug*) to high (*critical*). By adjusting the value of the *LogLevel* directive, the webmaster can control which error messages are recorded to the error log file.

First we cover the interface to the earlier API. Then we discuss the *Apache::Log* class, which implements the 1.3 interface.

Pre-1.3 API methods

log_error()

> The *log_error()* method writes a nicely timestamped error message to the server error log. It takes one or more string arguments, concatenates them into a line, and writes out the result. This method logs at the "error" log level according to the newer API.
>
> For example, this code:
>
> ```
> $r->log_error("Can't open index.html $!");
> ```
>
> results in the following *ErrorLog* entry:
>
> ```
> [Tue Jul 21 16:28:51 1998] [error] Can't open index.html No such file or
> directory
> ```

---

* In fact, the log-level API now provides direct *syslog* support. See the Apache documentation for the *ErrorLog* directive, which explains how to enable logging via *syslog*.

log_reason()

The *log_reason()* method behaves like *log_error()* but generates additional information about the request that can help with the postmortem. Here is the format of the entries produced by this method:

```
[$DATE] [error] access to $URI failed for $HOST, reason: $MESSAGE
```

where $DATE is the time and date of the request, $URI is the requested URI, $HOST is the remote host, and $MESSAGE is a message that you provide. For example, this code fragment:

```
$r->log_reason("Can't open index.html $!");
```

might generate the following entry in the error log:

```
[Tue Jul 21 16:30:47 1998] [error] access to /perl/index.pl
 failed for w15.yahoo.com, reason: Can't open index.html No such file
 or directory
```

The argument to *log_reason()* is the message you wish to display in the error log. If you provide an additional second argument, it will be displayed rather than the URI of the request. This is usually used to display the physical path of the requested file:

```
$r->log_reason("Can't open file $!", $r->filename);
```

This type of log message is most often used by content handlers that need to open and process the requested file before transmitting it to the browser, such as server-side include systems.

warn()

warn() is similar to *log_error()*, but on post-1.3.0 versions of Apache it will result in the logging of a message only when *LogLevel* is set to *warn* or higher.

Example:

```
$r->warn("Attempting to open index.html");
```

as_string()

The *as_string()* method is a handy debugging aid for working out obscure problems with HTTP headers. It formats the current client request and server response fields into an HTTP header and returns it as a multiline string. The request headers will come first, followed by a blank line, followed by the response. Here is an example of using *as_string()* within a call to *warn()* and the output it might produce:

```
$r->warn("HTTP dump:\n", $r->as_string);

[Tue Jul 21 16:51:51 1998] [warn] HTTP dump:
GET /perl/index.pl HTTP/1.0
User-Agent: lwp-request/1.32
Host: localhost:9008

200 OK
Connection: close
Content-Type: text/plain
```

The Apache::Log class

Apache version 1.3 introduced the notion of a log level. There are eight log levels, ranging in severity from *emerg* to *debug*. When modules call the new API logging routines, they provide the severity level of the message. You can control which messages appear in the server error logging by adjusting a new *LogLevel* directive. Messages greater than or equal to the severity level given by *LogLevel* appear in the error log. Messages below the cutoff are discarded.

The *Apache::Log* API provides eight methods named for each of the severity levels. Each acts like the request object's *error_log()* method, except that it logs the provided message using the corresponding severity level.

In order to use the new logging methods, you must **use Apache::Log** in the Perl startup file or within your module. You must then fetch an *Apache::Log* object by calling the *log()* method of either an *Apache* (`$r->log()`) or an *Apache::Server* object (`$r->server->log()`). Both objects have access to the same methods described below. However, the object returned from the `$r->log()` provides some additional functionality. It will include the client IP address, in dotted decimal form, with the log message. In addition, the message will be saved in the request's *notes* table, under a key named **error-notes**. It is the equivalent of the C-language API's a*p_log_rerror()* function (Chapter 10).

The methods described in this section can be called with one or more string arguments or a subroutine reference. If a subroutine reference is used, it is expected to return a string which will be used in the log message. The subroutine will only be invoked if the *LogLevel* is set to the given level or higher. This is most useful to provide verbose debugging information during development while saving CPU cycles during production.

log()

> The *log()* method returns an object blessed into the *Apache::Log* class. *log()* is implemented both for the *Apache* class and for the *Apache::Server* class.
>
> ```
> use Apache::Log ();
> my $log = $r->log;        # messages will include client ip address
> my $log = $r->server->log; # message will not include client ip address
> ```

emerg()

> This logs the provided message at the *emergency* log level, a level ordinarily reserved for problems that render the server unusable.
>
> ```
> $log->emerg("Cannot open lock file!");
> ```

alert()

> This logs the message using the *alert* level, which is intended for problems that require immediate attention.
>
> ```
> $log->alert("getpwuid: couldn't determine user name from uid");
> ```

crit()

This logs the message at the *critical* level, intended for severe conditions.

```
$log->crit("Cannot open configuration database!");
```

error()

This logs the message at the *error* level, a catchall for noncritical error conditions.

```
$log->error("Parse of script failed: $@");
```

warn()

The *warn* level is intended for warnings that may or may not require someone's attention.

```
$log->warn("No database host specified, using default");
```

notice()

notice() is used for normal but significant conditions.

```
$log->notice("Cannot connect to master database, trying slave $host");
```

info()

This method is used for informational messages.

```
$log->info("CGI.pm version is old, consider upgrading") if
    $CGI::VERSION < 2.42;
```

debug()

This logs messages at the *debug* level, the lowest of them all. It is used for messages you wish to print during development and debugging. The *debug* level will also include the filename and line number of the caller in the log message.

```
$log->debug("Reading configuration from file $fname");
```

```
$log->debug(sub {
    "The request: " . $r->as_string;
});
```

Access Control Methods

The Apache API provides several methods that are used for access control, authentication, and authorization. We gave complete examples of using these methods in Chapter 6.

allow_options()

The *allow_options()* method gives module writers access to the per-directory *Options* configuration. It returns a bitmap in which a bit is set to 1 if the corresponding option is enabled. The *Apache::Constants* module provides symbolic constants for the various options when you import the tab *:options*. You will typically perform a bitwise AND (&) on the options bitmap to check which ones are enabled.

For example, a script engine such as *Apache::Registry* or *Apache::SSI* might want to check if it's allowed to execute a script in the current location using this code:

```
use Apache::Constants qw(:common :options);

unless($r->allow_options & OPT_EXECCGI) {
    $r->log_reason("Options ExecCGI is off in this directory",
                   $r->filename);
    return FORBIDDEN;
}
```

A full list of option constants can be found in the *Apache::Constants* manual page.

auth_name()

This method will return the current value of the per-directory configuration directive *AuthName*, which is used in conjunction with password-protected directories. *AuthName* declares an authorization "realm," which is intended as a high-level grouping of an authentication scheme and a URI tree to which it applies.

If the requested file or directory is password-protected, *auth_name()* will return the realm name. An authentication module can then use this realm name to determine which database to authenticate the user against. This method can also be used to set the value of the realm for use by later handlers.

```
my $auth_name = $r->auth_name();
$r->auth_name("Protected Area");
```

auth_type()

Password-protected files and directories will also have an authorization type, which is usually one of "Basic" or "Digest." The authorization type is set with the configuration directive *AuthType* and retrieved with the API method *auth_type()*. Here's an example from a hypothetical authentication handler that can only authenticate using the Basic method:

```
my $auth_type = $r->auth_type;
unless (lc($auth_type) eq "basic") {
    $r->warn(__PACKAGE__, " can't handle AuthType $auth_type");
    return DECLINED;
}
```

The differences between Basic and Digest authentication are discussed in Chapter 6.

get_basic_auth_pw()

The *get_basic_auth_pw()* method returns a two-element list. If the current request is protected with Basic authentication, the first element of the returned list will be OK and the second will be the plaintext password entered by the user. Other possible return codes include `DECLINED`, `SERVER_ERROR`, and `AUTH_REQUIRED`, which are described in Chapter 6.

```
my($ret, $sent_pw) = $r->get_basic_auth_pw;
```

You can get the username part of the pair by calling `$r->connection->user` as described in the section "The Apache::Connection Class."

note_basic_auth_failure()

If a URI is protected by Basic authentication and the browser fails to provide a valid username/password combination (or none at all), authentication handlers are expected to call the *note_basic_auth_failure()* method. This sets up the outgoing HTTP headers in such a way that users will be (re)challenged to provide their usernames and passwords for the current security realm.

```
my($ret, $sent_pw) = $r->get_basic_auth_pw;
unless($r->connection->user and $sent_pw) {
    $r->note_basic_auth_failure;
    $r->log_reason("Both a username and password must be provided");
    return AUTH_REQUIRED;
}
```

Although it would make sense for *note_basic_auth_failure()* to return a status code of `AUTH_REQUIRED`, it actually returns no value.

requires()

This method returns information about each of the *require* directives currently in force for the requested URI. Since there may be many *require* directives, this method returns an array reference. Each item in the array is a hash that contains information about a different *require* directive. The format of this data structure is described in detail in Chapter 6, under "A Gender-Based Authorization Module."

satisfies()

Documents can be under access control (e.g., access limited by hostname or password) and authentication/authorization control (password protection) simultaneously. The *Satisfy* directive determines how Apache combines the two types of restriction. If *Satisfy All* is specified, Apache will not grant access to the requested document unless both the access control and authentication/ authorization rules are satisfied. If *Satisfy Any* is specified, remote users are allowed to retrieve the document if they meet the requirements of either one of the restrictions.

Authorization and access control modules gain access to this configuration variable through the *satisfies()* method. It will return one of the three constants `SATISFY_ALL`, `SATISFY_ANY`, or `SATISFY_NOSPEC`. The latter is returned when there is no applicable *satisfy* directive at all. These constants can be imported by requesting the *:satisfy* tag from *Apache::Constants*.

The following code fragment illustrates an access control handler that checks the status of the *satisfy* directive. If the current document is forbidden by access control rules, the code checks whether SATISFY_ANY is in effect and, if so, whether authentication is also required (using the *some_auth_required()* method call described next). Unless both of these conditions are true, the handler logs an error message. Otherwise, it just returns the result code, knowing that any error logging will be performed by the authentication handler.

```
use Apache::Constants qw(:common :satisfy);

if ($ret == FORBIDDEN) {
    $r->log_reason("Client access denied by server configuration")
        unless $r->satisfies == SATISFY_ANY && $r->some_auth_required;
    return $ret;
}
```

some_auth_required()

If the configuration for the current request requires some form of authentication or authorization, this method returns true. Otherwise, it returns an *undef* value.

```
unless ($r->some_auth_required) {
    $r->log_reason("I won't go further unless the user is authenticated");
    return FORBIDDEN;
}
```

mod_perl-Specific Methods

There are a handful of Perl API methods for which there is no C-language counterpart. Those who are only interested in learning the C API can skip this section.

exit()

It is common to come across Perl CGI scripts that use the Perl built-in *exit()* function to leave the script prematurely. Calling *exit()* from within a CGI script, which owns its process, is harmless, but calling *exit()* from within *mod_perl* would have the unfortunate effect of making the entire child process exit unceremoniously, in most cases before completing the request or logging the transaction. On Win32 systems, calling *exit()* will make the whole server quit. Oops!

For this reason *mod_perl*'s version of this function call, *Apache::exit()*, does not cause the process to exit. Instead, it calls Perl's *croak()* function to halt script execution but does not log a message to the *ErrorLog*. If you really want the child server process to exit, call *Apache::exit()* with an optional status argument of DONE (available in *Apache::Constants*). The child process will be shut down but only after it has had a chance to properly finish handling the current requests.

In scripts running under *Apache::Registry*, Perl's built-in *exit()* is overridden by *Apache::exit()* so that legacy CGI scripts don't inadvertently shoot themselves in the foot. In Perl Versions 5.005 and higher, *exit()* is overridden everywhere, including within handlers. In versions of *mod_perl* built with Perl 5.004, however, handlers can still inadvertently invoke the built-in *exit()*, so you should be on the watch for this mistake. One way to avoid it is to explicitly import the `exit` symbol when you load the Apache module.

Here are various examples of *exit()*:

```
$r->exit;
Apache->exit;
$r->exit(0);
$r->exit(DONE);

use Apache 'exit';   #this override's Perl's builtin
exit;
```

If a handler needs direct access to the Perl built-in version of *exit()* after it has imported Apache's version, it should call *CORE::exit()*.

gensym()

This function creates an anonymous glob and returns a reference to it for use as a safe file or directory handle. Ordinary bareword filehandles are prone to namespace clashes. The *IO::File* class avoids this, but some users have found that the *IO::File* carries too much overhead. *Apache::gensym* avoids this overhead and still avoids namespace clashes.

```
my $fh = Apache->gensym;
open $fh, $r->filename or die $!;
$r->send_fd($fh);
close $fh;
```

Because of its cleanliness, most of the examples in this book use the *Apache::File* interface for reading and writing files (see "The Apache::File Class"). If you wish to squeeze out a bit of overhead, you may wish to use *Apache::gensym()* with Perl's built-in *open()* function instead.

current_callback()

If a module wishes to know what handler is currently being run, it can find out with the *current_callback()* method. This method is most useful to *PerlDispatchHandlers* who wish to only take action for certain phases.

```
if($r->current_callback eq "PerlLogHandler") {
    $r->warn("Logging request");
}
```

get_handlers()

The *get_handlers()* method will return an array reference containing the list of all handlers that are configured to handle the current request. This method takes a single argument specifying which handlers to return.

```
my $handlers = $r->get_handlers('PerlAuthenHandler');
```

set_handlers()

If you would like to change the list of Perl handlers configured for the current request, you can change it with *set_handlers()*. This method takes two arguments; the name of the handler you wish to change and an array reference pointing to one or more references to the handler subroutines you want to run for that phase. If any handlers were previously defined, such as with a *Perl*Handler* directive, they are replaced by this call. Provide a second argument of *undef* to remove all handlers for that phase.

```
$r->set_handlers(PerlAuthenHandler => [\&auth_one, \&auth_two]);
$r->set_handlers(PerlAuthenHandler => undef);
```

push_handlers()

The *push_handlers()* method is used to add a new Perl handler routine to the current request's handler "stack". Instead of replacing the list of handlers, it just appends a new handler to the list. Each handler is run in turn until one returns an error code. You'll find more information about using stacked handlers and examples in Chapters 4, 6, and 7.

This method takes two arguments: the name of the phase you want to manipulate and a reference to the subroutine you want to handle that phase.

Example:

```
$r->push_handlers(PerlLogHandler => \&my_logger);
```

module()

If you need to find out if a Perl module has already been loaded, the *module()* method will tell you. Pass it the package name of the module you're interested in. It will return a true value if the module is loaded.

```
do { #something } if Apache->module('My::Module');
```

This method can also be used to test if a C module is loaded. In this case, pass it the filename of the module, just as you would use with the *IfModule* directive. It will return a true value if the module is loaded.

```
do { #something } if Apache->module('mod_proxy.c');
```

define()

Apache Version 1.3.1 added a *−D* command-line switch that can be used to pass the server parameter names for conditional configuration with the *IfDefine* directive. These names exist for the lifetime of the server and can be accessed at any time by Perl modules using the *define()* method.

```
if(Apache->define("SSL")) {
    #the server was started with -DSSL
}
```

post_connection()

This method is simply an alias for the *register_cleanup()* method described in the "Server Core Functions" section.

request()

> The *Apache->request()* class method returns a reference to the current request object, if any. Handlers that use the vanilla Perl API will not need to call this method because the request object is passed to them in their argument list. However, *Apache::Registry* scripts and plain Perl modules do not have a subroutine entry point and therefore need a way to gain access to the request object. For example, CGI.pm uses this method to provide proper *mod_perl* support.
>
> Called with no arguments, *request()* returns the stored *Apache* request object. It may also be called with a single argument to set the stored request object. This is what *Apache::Registry* does before invoking a script.
>
> ```
> my $r = Apache->request;   # get the request
> Apache->request($r);       # set the request
> ```
>
> Actually, it's a little known fact that *Apache::Registry* scripts can access the request object directly via @_. This is slightly faster than using *Apache->request()* but has the disadvantage of being obscure. This technique is demonstrated in "Subclassing the Apache Class" in Chapter 7.

httpd_conf()

> The *httpd_conf()* method allows you to pass new directives to Apache at startup time. Pass it a multiline string containing the configuration directives that you wish Apache to process. Using string interpolation, you can use this method to dynamically configure Apache according to arbitrarily complex rules.
>
> *httpd_conf()* can only be called during server startup, usually from within a Perl startup file. Because there is no request method at this time, you must invoke *httpd_conf()* directly through the *Apache* class.
>
> ```
> my $ServerRoot = '/local/web';
> Apache->httpd_conf(<<EOF);
> Alias /perl $ServerRoot/perl
> Alias /cgi-bin $ServerRoot/cgi-bin
> EOF
> ```
>
> Should a syntax error occur, Apache will log an error and the server will exit, just as it would if the error was present in the *httpd.conf* configuration file. A more sophisticated way of configuring Apache at startup time via *<Perl>* sections is discussed in Chapter 8, *Customizing the Apache Configuration Process*.

Other Core Perl API Classes

The vast bulk of the functionality of the Perl API is contained in the *Apache* object. However, a number of auxiliary classes, including *Apache::Table*, *Apache::Connection*, and *Apache::Server*, provide additional methods for accessing and manipulating the state of the server. This section discusses these classes.

The Apache TIEHANDLE Interface

In the CGI environment, the standard input and standard output file descriptors are redirected so that data read and written is passed through Apache for processing. In the Apache module API, handlers ordinarily use the Apache *read()* and *print()* methods to communicate with the client. However, as a convenience, *mod_perl* ties the STDIN and STDOUT filehandles to the *Apache* class prior to invoking Perl API modules. This allows handlers to read from standard input and write to standard output exactly as if they were in the CGI environment.

The *Apache* class supports the full TIEHANDLE interface, as described in *perltie(1)*. STDIN and STDOUT are already tied to *Apache* by the time your handler is called. If you wish to tie your own input or output filehandle, you may do so by calling *tie()* with the request object as the function's third parameter:

```
tie *BROWSER, 'Apache', $r;
print BROWSER 'Come out, come out, wherever you are!';
```

Of course, it is better not to hardcode the *Apache* class name, as $r might be blessed into a subclass:

```
tie *BROWSER, ref $r, $r;
```

The Apache::SubRequest Class

The Apache methods *lookup_uri()* and *lookup_file()* return a request record object blessed into the *Apache::SubRequest* class. The *Apache::SubRequest* class is a subclass of *Apache* and inherits most of its methods from there. Here are two examples of fetching subrequest objects:

```
my $subr = $r->lookup_file($filename);
my $subr = $r->lookup_uri($uri);
```

The *Apache::SubRequest* class adds a single new method, *run()*.

run()

> When a subrequest is created, the URI translation, access checks, and MIME checking phases are run, but unlike a real request, the content handler for the response phase is not actually run. If you would like to invoke the content handler, the *run()* method will do it:

```
my $status = $subr->run;
```

> When you invoke the subrequest's response handler in this way, it will do everything a response handler is supposed to, including sending the HTTP headers and the document body. *run()* returns the content handler's status code as its function result. If you are invoking the subrequest *run()* method from within your own content handler, you must not send the HTTP header and document body yourself, as this would be appended to the bottom of the information that has already been sent. Most handlers that invoke *run()* will

immediately return its status code, pretending to Apache that they handled the request themselves:

```
my $status = $subr->run;
return $status;
```

The Apache::Server Class

The *Apache::Server* class provides the Perl interface to the C API **server_rec** data structure, which contains lots of low-level information about the server configuration. Within a handler, the current *Apache::Server* object can be obtained by calling the Apache request object's *server()* method. At Perl startup time (such as within a startup script or a module loaded with *PerlModule*), you can fetch the server object by invoking *Apache->server* directly. By convention, we use the variable $s for server objects.

```
#at request time
sub handler {
    my $r = shift;
    my $s = $r->server;
    ....
}

#at server startup time, e.g., PerlModule or PerlRequire
my $s = Apache->server;
```

This section discusses the various methods that are available to you via the server object. They correspond closely to the fields of the **server_rec** structure, which we revisit in Chapter 10.

is_virtual()

This method returns true if the current request is being applied to a virtual server. This is a read-only method.

```
my $is_virtual = $s->is_virtual;
```

log()

The *log()* method retrieves an object blessed into the *Apache::Log* class. You can then use this object to access the full-featured logging API. See "The Apache::Log class" for details.

```
use Apache::Log ();
my $log = $s->log;
```

The *Apache::Server::log()* method is identical in most respects to the *Apache::log()* method discussed earlier. The difference is that messages logged with *Apache::log()* will include the IP address of the browser and add the messages to the *notes* table under a key named **error-notes**. See the description of *notes()* under "Server Core Functions."

port()

> This method returns the port on which this (virtual) server is listening. If no
> port is explicitly listed in the server configuration file (that is, the server is lis-
> tening on the default port 80), this method will return 0. Use the higher-level
> *Apache::get_server_port()* method if you wish to avoid this pitfall.

```
my $port = $r->server->port || 80;
```

> This method is read-only.

server_admin()

> This method returns the email address of the person responsible for this server
> as configured by the *ServerAdmin* directive.

```
my $admin = $s->server_admin;
```

> This method is read-only.

server_hostname()

> This method returns the (virtual) hostname used by this server, as set by the
> *ServerName* directive.

```
my $hostname = $s->server_hostname;
```

> This method is read-only.

names()

> If this server is configured to use virtual hosts, the *names()* method will return
> the names by which the current virtual host is recognized as specified by the
> *ServerAlias* directives (including wildcarded names). The function result is an
> array reference containing the hostnames. If no alias names are present or the
> server is not using virtual hosts, this will return a reference to an empty list.

```
my $s = $r->server;
my $names = $s->names;
print "Names = @$names\n";
```

next()

> Apache maintains a linked list of all configured virtual servers, which can be
> accessed with the *next()* method.

```
for(my $s = Apache->server; $s; $s = $s->next) {
    printf "Contact %s regarding problems with the %s site\n",
            $s->server_admin, $s->server_hostname;
}
```

log_error()

> This method is the same as the *Apache::log_error()* method, except that it's
> available through the *Apache::Server* object. This allows you to use it in Perl
> startup files and other places where the request object isn't available.

```
my $s = Apache->server;
$s->log_error("Can't open config file $!");
```

warn()

> This method is the same as the *Apache::warn()* method, but it's available through the *Apache::Server* object. This allows you to use it in Perl startup files and other places where the request object isn't available.

```
my $s = Apache->server;
$s->warn("Can't preload script $file $!");
```

The Apache::Connection Class

The *Apache::Connection* class provides a Perl interface to the C-language `conn_rec` data structure, which provides various low-level details about the network connection back to the client. Within a handler, the connection object can be obtained by calling the Apache request object's *connection()* method. The connection object is not available outside of handlers for the various request phases because there is no connection established in those cases. By convention, we use the variable `$c` for connection objects.

```
sub handler {
  my $r = shift;
  my $c = $r->connection;
  ...
}
```

In this section we discuss the various methods made available by the connection object. They correspond closely to the fields of the C API `conn_rec` structure discussed in Chapter 10.

aborted()

> This method returns true if the client has broken the connection prematurely. This can happen if the remote user's computer has crashed, a network error has occurred, or, more trivially, the user pressed the stop button before the request or response was fully transmitted. However, this value is only set if a soft timeout occurred.

```
if($c->aborted) {
   warn "uh,oh, the client has gone away!";
}
```

> See the description of *soft_timeout()* earlier.

auth_type()

> If authentication was used to access a password protected document, this method returns the type of authentication that was used, currently either Basic or Digest. This method is different from the request object's *auth_type()* method, which we discussed earlier, because the request object's method returns the value of the *AuthType* configuration directive; in other words, the type of authentication the server would *like* to use. The connection object's

auth_type() method returns a value only when authentication was success-fully completed and returns *undef* otherwise.

```
if($c->auth_type ne 'Basic') {
    warn "phew, I feel a bit better";
}
```

This method is read-only.

local_addr()

This method returns a packed SOCKADDR_IN structure in the same format as returned by the Perl *Socket* module's *pack_sockaddr_in()* function. This packed structure contains the port and IP address at the server's side of the connection. This is set by the server when the connection record is created, so it is always defined.

```
use Socket ();

sub handler {
    my $r = shift;
    my $local_add = $r->connection->local_addr;
    my($port, $ip) = Socket::unpack_sockaddr_in($local_add);
    ...
}
```

For obvious reasons, this method is read-only.

remote_addr()

This method returns a packed SOCKADDR_IN structure for the port and IP address at the client's side of the connection. This is set by the server when the connection record is created, so it is always defined.

Among other things, the information returned by this method and *local_addr()* can be used to perform RFC 1413 ident lookups on the remote client, even when the configuration directive *IdentityCheck* is turned off. Here is an example using Jan-Pieter Cornet's *Net::Ident* module:

```
use Net::Ident qw(lookupFromInAddr);

my $remoteuser = lookupFromInAddr ($c->local_addr,
                                   $c->remote_addr, 2);
```

remote_host()

This method returns the hostname of the remote client. It only returns the name if the *HostNameLookups* directive is set to *On* and the DNS lookup was successful—that is, the DNS contains a reverse name entry for the remote host. If hostname-based access control is in use for the given request, a double-reverse lookup will occur regardless of the *HostNameLookups* setting, in which case, the cached hostname will be returned. If unsuccessful, the method returns *undef.*

It is almost always better to use the high-level *get_remote_host()* method available from the Apache request object (discussed earlier). The high-level method returns the dotted IP address of the remote host if its DNS name isn't available, and it caches the results of previous lookups, avoiding overhead when you call the method multiple times.

```
my $remote_host = $c->remote_host || "nohost";
my $remote_host = $r->get_remote_host(REMOTE_HOST); # better
```

This method is read-only.

remote_ip()

This method returns the dotted decimal representation of the remote client's IP address. It is set by the server when the connection record is created and is always defined.

```
my $remote_ip = $c->remote_ip;
```

The *remote_ip()* can also be changed, which is helpful if your server is behind a proxy such as the squid accelerator. By using the *X-Forwarded-For* header sent by the proxy, the *remote_ip* can be set to this value so logging modules include the address of the real client. The only subtle point is that *X-Forwarded-For* may be multivalued in the case of a single request that has been forwarded across multiple proxies. It's safest to choose the last IP address in the list since this corresponds to the original client.

```
my $header = $r->headers_in->{'X-Forwarded-For'};
if( my $ip = (split /,\s*/, $header)[-1] ) {
   $r->connection->remote_ip($ip);
}
```

remote_logname()

This method returns the login name of the remote user, provided that the configuration directive *IdentityCheck* is set to *On* and the remote user's machine is running an *identd* daemon. If one or both of these conditions is false, the method returns *undef.*

It is better to use the high-level *get_remote_logname()* method which is provided by the request object. When the high-level method is called, the result is cached and reused if called again. This is not true of *remote_logname().*

```
my $remote_logname = $c->remote_logname || "nobody";
my $remote_logname = $r->get_remote_logname;  # better
```

user()

When Basic authentication is in effect, *user()* returns the name that the remote user provided when prompted for his username and password. The password itself can be recovered from the request object by calling *get_basic_auth_pw().*

```
my $username = $c->user;
```

The Apache::Table Class

The HTTP message protocol is simple largely because of its consistent use of the
key/value paradigm in its request and response header fields. Because much of an
external module's work is getting and setting these header fields, Apache provides
a simple yet powerful interface called the **table** structure. Apache tables are
keyed case-insensitive lookup tables. API function calls allow you to obtain the list
of defined keys, iterate through them, get the value of a key, and set key values.
Since many HTTP header fields are potentially multivalued, Apache also provides
functionality for getting, setting, and merging the contents of multivalued fields.

The following five C data structures are implemented as tables. This list is likely to
grow in the future.

- headers_in
- headers_out
- err_headers_out
- notes
- subprocess_env

As discussed in "The Apache Request Object," the Perl API provides five method
calls, named *headers_in()*, *headers_out()*, *err_headers_out()*, *notes()*, and
subprocess_env(), that retrieve these tables. The Perl manifestation of the Apache
table API is the *Apache::Table* class. It provides a TIEHASH interface that allows
transparent access to its methods via a tied hash reference, as well as API methods that can be called directly.

The TIEHASH interface is easy to use. Simply call one of the methods listed earlier in a scalar context to return a tied hash reference. For example:

```
my $table = $r->headers_in;
```

The returned object can now be used to get and set values in the *headers_in* table
by treating it as an ordinary hash reference, but the keys are looked up case-insen-
sitively. Examples:

```
my $type = $table->{'Content-type'};
my $type = $table->{'CONTENT-TYPE'};  # same thing
$table->{'Expires'} = 'Sat, 08 Aug 1998 01:39:20 GMT';
```

If the field you are trying to access is multivalued, then the tied hash interface suffers the limitation that fetching the key will only return the *first* defined value of
the field. You can get around this by using the object-oriented interface to access
the table (we show an example of this later) or by using the *each* operator to
access each key and value sequentially. The following code snippet shows one
way to fetch all the *Set-cookie* fields in the outgoing HTTP header:

```
while (my($key, $value) = each %{$r->headers_out}) {
    push @cookies, $value if lc($key) eq 'set-cookie';
}
```

When you treat an *Apache::Table* object as a hash reference, you are accessing its internal *get()* and *set()* methods (among others) indirectly. To gain access to the full power of the table API, you can invoke these methods directly by using the method call syntax.

Here is the list of publicly available methods in *Apache::Table*, along with brief examples of usage:

add()

The *add()* method will add a key/value pair to the table. Because Apache tables can contain multiple instances of a key, you may call *add()* multiple times with different values for the same key. Instead of the new value of the key replacing the previous one, it will simply be appended to the list. This is useful for multivalued HTTP header fields such as *Set-Cookie*. The outgoing HTTP header will contain multiple instances of the field.

```
my $out = $r->headers_out;
for my $cookie (@cookies) {
    $out->add("Set-cookie" => $cookie);
}
```

Another way to add multiple values is to pass an array reference as the second argument. This code has the same effect as the previous example:

```
my $out = $r->headers_out;
$out->add("Set-cookie" => \@cookies);
```

clear()

This method wipes the current table clean, discarding its current contents. It's unlikely that you would want to perform this on a public table, but here's an example that clears the notes table:

```
$r->notes->clear;
```

do()

This method provides a way to iterate through an entire table item by item. Pass it a reference to a code subroutine to be called once for each table entry. The subroutine should accept two arguments corresponding to the key and value, respectively, and should return a true value. The routine can return a false value to terminate the iteration prematurely.

This example dumps the contents of the *headers_in* field to the browser:

```
$r->headers_in->do(sub {
                my($key, $value) = @_;
                $r->print("$key => $value\n");
                1;
            });
```

For another example of *do()*, see Example 7-12, where we use it to transfer the incoming headers from the incoming Apache request to an outgoing LWP *HTTP::Request* object.

get()

Probably the most frequently called method, the *get()* function returns the table value at the given key. For multivalued keys, *get()* implements a little syntactic sugar. Called in a scalar context, it returns the first value in the list. Called in an array context, it returns all values of the multivalued key.

```
my $ua      = $r->headers_in->get('User-agent');
my @cookies = $r->headers_in->get('Cookie');
```

get() is the underlying method that is called when you use the tied hash interface to retrieve a key. However, the ability to fetch a multivalued key as an array is only available when you call *get()* directly using the object-oriented interface.

merge()

merge() behaves like *add()*, except that each time it is called the new value is merged into the previous one, creating a single HTTP header field containing multiple comma-delimited values.

In the HTTP protocol, a comma-separated list of header values is equivalent to the same values specified by repeated header lines. Some buggy clients may not accept merged headers, however. In this case, it is worthwhile to control the merging explicitly and avoid merging headers that cause trouble (like *Set-cookie*).

merge() works like *add()*. You can either merge a series of entries one at a time:

```
my @languages = qw(en fr de);
foreach (@languages) {
  $r->headers_out->merge("Content-language" => $_);
}
```

or merge a bunch of entries in a single step by passing an array reference:

```
$r->headers_out->merge("Content-language" => \@languages);
```

new()

The *new()* method is available to create an *Apache::Table* object from scratch. It requires an *Apache* object to allocate the table and, optionally, the number of entries to initially allocate. Note that just like the other *Apache::Table* objects returned by API methods, references cannot be used as values, only strings.

```
my $tab = Apache::Table->new($r); #default, allocates 10 entries

my $tab = Apache::Table->new($r, 20); #allocate 20 entries
```

set()

> *set()* takes a key/value pair and updates the table with it, creating the key if it didn't exist before, or replacing its previous value(s) if it did. The resulting header field will be single-valued. Internally this method is called when you assign a value to a key using the tied hash interface.
>
> Here's an example of using *set()* to implement an HTTP redirect:
>
> ```
> $r->headers_out->set(Location => 'http://www.modperl.com/');
> ```

unset()

> This method can be used to remove a key and its contents. If there are multiple entries with the same key, they will all be removed.
>
> ```
> $r->headers_in->unset('Referer');
> ```

The Apache::URI Class

Apache Version 1.3 introduced a utility module for parsing URIs, manipulating their contents, and unparsing them back into string form. Since this functionality is part of the server C API, *Apache::URI* offers a lightweight alternative to the *URI::URL* module that ships with the *libwww-perl* package.*

An *Apache::URI* object is returned when you call the request object's *parsed_uri()* method. You may also call the *Apache::URI parse()* constructor to parse an arbitrary string and return a new *Apache::URI* object, for example:

```
use Apache::URI ();
my $parsed_uri = $r->parsed_uri;
```

fragment()

> This method returns or sets the fragment component of the URI. You know this as the part that follows the hash mark (#) in links. The fragment component is generally used only by clients and some web proxies.
>
> ```
> my $fragment = $uri->fragment;
> $uri->fragment('section_1');
> ```

hostinfo()

> This method gets or sets the remote host information, which usually consists of a hostname and port number in the format *hostname:port*. Some rare URIs, such as those used for nonanonymous FTP, attach a username and password to this information, for use in accessing private resources. In this case, the information returned is in the format *username:password@hostname:port*.

---

* At the time of this writing, *URI::URL* was scheduled to be replaced by *URI.pm*, which will be distributed separately from the *libwww-perl* package.

This method returns the host information when called without arguments, or sets the information when called with a single string argument.

```
my $hostinfo = $uri->hostinfo;
$uri->hostinfo('www.modperl.com:8000');
```

hostname()

This method returns or sets the hostname component of the URI object.

```
my $hostname = $uri->hostname;
$uri->hostname('www.modperl.com');
```

parse()

The *parse()* method is a constructor used to create a new *Apache::URI* object from a URI string. Its first argument is an Apache request object, and the second is a string containing an absolute or relative URI. In the case of a relative URI, the *parse()* method uses the request object to determine the location of the current request and resolve the relative URI.

```
my $uri = Apache::URI->parse($r, 'http://www.modperl.com/');
```

If the URI argument is omitted, the *parse()* method will construct a fully qualified URI from $r, including the scheme, hostname, port, path, and query string.

```
my $self_uri = Apache::URI->parse($r);
```

password()

This method gets or sets the password part of the *hostinfo* component.

```
my $password = $uri->password;
$uri->password('rubble');
```

path()

This method returns or sets the path component of the URI object.

```
my $path = $uri->path;
$uri->path('/perl/hangman.pl');
```

path_info()

After the "real path" part of the URI comes the "additional path information." This component of the URI is not defined by the official URI RFC, because it is an internal concept from web servers that need to do something with the part of the path information that is left over from translating the path into a valid filename.

path_info() gets or sets the additional path information portion of the URI, using the current request object to determine what part of the path is real and what part is additional.

```
$uri->path_info('/foo/bar');
```

port()

This method returns or sets the port component of the URI object.

```
my $port = $uri->port;
$uri->port(80);
```

query()

> This method gets or sets the query string component of the URI; in other words, the part after the ?.

```
my $query = $uri->query;
$uri->query('one+two+three');
```

rpath()

> This method returns the "real path;" that is, the *path()* minus the *path_info()*.

```
my $path = $uri->rpath();
```

scheme()

> This method returns or sets the scheme component of the URI. This is the part that identifies the URI's protocol, such as *http* or *ftp*. Called without arguments, the current scheme is retrieved. Called with a single string argument, the current scheme is set.

```
my $scheme = $uri->scheme;
$uri->scheme('http');
```

unparse()

> This method returns the string representation of the URI. Relative URIs are resolved into absolute ones.

```
my $string = $uri->unparse;
```

> Beware that the *unparse()* method does not take the additional path information into account. It returns the URI minus the additional information.

user()

> This method gets or sets the username part of the *hostinfo* component.

```
my $user = $uri->user;
$uri->user('barney');
```

The Apache::Util Class

The Apache API provides several utility functions that are used by various standard modules. The Perl API makes these available as function calls in the *Apache::Util* package.

Although there is nothing here that doesn't already exist in some existing Perl module, these C versions are considerably faster than their corresponding Perl functions and avoid the memory bloat of pulling in yet another Perl package.

To make these functions available to your handlers, import the *Apache::Util* module with an import tag of *:all*:

```
use Apache::Util qw(:all);
```

escape_uri()

> This function encodes all unsafe characters in a URI into %XX hex escape sequences. This is equivalent to the *URI::Escape::uri_escape()* function from the LWP package.

```
use Apache::Util qw(escape_uri);
my $escaped = escape_uri($url);
```

escape_html()

> This function replaces unsafe HTML character sequences (<, >, and &) with their entity representations. This is equivalent to the *HTML::Entities::encode()* function.

```
use Apache::Util qw(escape_html);
my $display_html = escape_html("<h1>Header Level 1 Example</h1>");
```

ht_time()

> This function produces dates in the format required by the HTTP protocol. You will usually call it with a single argument, the number of seconds since the epoch. The current time expressed in these units is returned by the Perl built-in *time()* function.

> You may also call *ht_time()* with optional second and third arguments. The second argument, if present, is a format string that follows the same conventions as the *strftime()* function in the POSIX library. The default format is %a, %d %b %Y %H:%M:%S %Z, where %Z is an Apache extension that always expands to GMT. The optional third argument is a flag that selects whether to express the returned time in GMT (Greenwich Mean Time) or the local time zone. A true value (the default) selects GMT, which is what you will want in nearly all cases.

> Unless you have a good reason to use a nonstandard time format, you should content yourself with the one-argument form of this function. The function is equivalent to the LWP package's *HTTP::Date::time2str()* function when passed a single argument.

```
use Apache::Util qw(ht_time);
my $str = ht_time(time);
my $str = ht_time(time, "%d %b %Y %H:%M %Z");      # 06 Nov 1994 08:49 GMT
my $str = ht_time(time, "%d %b %Y %H:%M %Z",0);    # 06 Nov 1994 13:49 EST
```

parsedate()

> This function is the inverse of *ht_time()*, parsing HTTP dates and returning the number of seconds since the epoch. You can then pass this value to *Time::localtime* (or another of Perl's date-handling modules) and extract the date fields that you want.

The *parsedate()* recognizes and handles date strings in any of three standard formats:

```
Sun, 06 Nov 1994 08:49:37 GMT     ; RFC 822, the modern HTTP format
Sunday, 06-Nov-94 08:49:37 GMT    ; RFC 850, the old obsolete HTTP format
Sun Nov  6 08:49:37 1994          ; ANSI C's asctime() format
```

Here is an example:

```
use Apache::Util qw(parsedate);
my $secs;
if (my $if_modified = $r->headers_in->{'If-modified-since'}) {
   $secs = parsedate $if_modified;
}
```

size_string()

This function converts the given file size into a formatted string. The size given in the string will be in units of bytes, kilobytes, or megabytes, depending on the size of the file. This function formats the string just as the C *ap_send_size()* API function does but returns the string rather than sending it directly to the client. The *ap_send_size()* function is used in *mod_autoindex* to display the size of files in automatic directory listings and by *mod_include* to implement the *fsize* directive.

This example uses *size_string()* to get the formatted size of the currently requested file:

```
use Apache::Util qw(size_string);
my $size = size_string -s $r->finfo;
```

unescape_uri()

This function decodes all %XX hex escape sequences in the given URI. It is equivalent to the *URI::Escape::uri_unescape()* function from the LWP package.

```
use Apache::Util qw(unescape_uri);
my $unescaped = unescape_uri($safe_url);
```

unescape_uri_info()

This function is similar to *unescape_uri()* but is specialized to remove escape sequences from the query string portion of the URI. The main difference is that it translates the + character into spaces as well as recognizes and translates the hex escapes.

```
use Apache::Util qw(unescape_info);
$string = $r->uri->query;
my %data = map { unescape_uri_info($_) } split /[=&]/, $string, -1;
```

This would correctly translate the query string **name=Fred+Flintstone&town=Bedrock** into the following hash:

```
data => 'Fred Flintstone',
town => 'Bedrock'
```

The mod_perl Class

Among the packages installed by the Perl API is a tiny one named, simply enough, *mod_perl*. You can query this class to determine what version of *mod_perl* is installed and what features it makes available.

import()

If your Apache Perl API modules depend on version-specific features of *mod_ perl*, you can use the *import()* method to require that a certain version of *mod_perl* be installed. The syntax is simple:

```
use mod_perl 1.16; # require version 1.16 or higher
```

When *mod_perl* is built, you can control which handlers and other features are enabled. At runtime, *import()* can be used to check for the presence of individual features.

```
# require Authen and Authz handlers to be enabled
use mod_perl qw(PerlAuthenHandler PerlAuthzHandler);
```

If any of these features are not active, the *use* operator will fail. Here is the list of features that you can check for:

PerlDispatchHandler	*PerlFixupHandler*
PerlChildInitHandler	*PerlHandler*
PerlChildExitHandler	*PerlLogHandler*
PerlPostReadRequestHandler	*PerlInitHandler*
PerlTransHandler	*PerlCleanupHandler*
PerlHeaderParserHandler	*PerlStackedHandlers*
PerlAccessHandler	*PerlMethodHandlers*
PerlAuthenHandler	*PerlDirectiveHandlers*
PerlAuthzHandler	*PerlSections*
PerlTypeHandler	*PerlSSI*

hook()

The *hook()* function can be used at runtime to determine whether the current *mod_perl* installation provides support for a certain feature. This is the internal function that *import()* uses to check for configured features. This function is not exported, so you have to refer to it using its fully qualified name, *mod_ perl::hook()*. *hook()* recognizes the same list of features that *import()* does.

```
use mod_perl ();
unless(mod_perl::hook('PerlAuthenHandler')) {
    die "PerlAuthenHandler is not enabled!";
}
```

The Apache::Constants Class

All of the HTTP status codes are defined in the *httpd.h* file, along with server-specific status codes such as OK, DECLINED, and DONE. The *Apache::Constants* class provides access to these codes as constant subroutines. As there are many of these constants, they are not all exported by default. By default, only those listed in the *:common* export tag are exported. A variety of export tags are defined, allowing you to bring in various sets of constants to suit your needs. You are also free to bring in individual constants, just as you can with any other Perl module.

Here are the status codes listed by export tag group:

:common

>   This tag imports the most commonly used constants:

> | | |
> |---|---|
> | OK | FORBIDDEN |
> | DECLINED | AUTH_REQUIRED |
> | DONE | SERVER_ERROR |
> | NOT_FOUND | |

:response

>   This tag imports the *:common* response codes, plus these response codes:

> | | |
> |---|---|
> | DOCUMENT_FOLLOWS | BAD_GATEWAY |
> | MOVED | RESPONSE_CODES |
> | REDIRECT | NOT_IMPLEMENTED |
> | USE_LOCAL_COPY | CONTINUE |
> | BAD_REQUEST | NOT_AUTHORITATIVE |

>   CONTINUE and NOT_AUTHORITATIVE are aliases for DECLINED.

:methods

>   These are the method numbers, commonly used with the Apache *method_number()* method:

> | | |
> |---|---|
> | METHODS | M_PROPFIND |
> | M_GET | M_PROPPATCH |
> | M_PUT | M_MKCOL |
> | M_POST | M_COPY |
> | M_DELETE | M_MOVE |
> | M_CONNECT | M_LOCK |
> | M_OPTIONS | M_UNLOCK |
> | M_TRACE | M_INVALID |
> | M_PATCH | |

Each of the *M_* constants corresponds to an integer value, where M_GET..M_UNLOCK is 0..14. The METHODS constant is the number of *M_* constants, 15 at the time of this writing. This is designed to accommodate support for other request methods.

```
for (my $i = 0; $i < METHODS; $i++) {
    ...
}
```

:options

These constants are most commonly used with the Apache *allow_options()* method:

OPT_NONE	OPT_UNSET
OPT_INDEXES	OPT_INCNOEXEC
OPT_INCLUDES	OPT_SYM_OWNER
OPT_SYM_LINKS	OPT_MULTI
OPT_EXECCGI	OPT_ALL

:satisfy

These constants are most commonly used with the Apache *satisfy()* method:

SATISFY_ALL

SATISFY_ANY

SATISFY_NOSPEC

:remotehost

These constants are most commonly used with the Apache *get_remote_host* method:

REMOTE_HOST

REMOTE_NAME

REMOTE_NOLOOKUP

REMOTE_DOUBLE_REV

:http

This is a set of common HTTP response codes:

HTTP_OK	HTTP_BAD_REQUEST
HTTP_MOVED_TEMPORARILY	HTTP_INTERNAL_SERVER_ERROR
HTTP_MOVED_PERMANENTLY	HTTP_NOT_ACCEPTABLE
HTTP_METHOD_NOT_ALLOWED	HTTP_NO_CONTENT
HTTP_NOT_MODIFIED	HTTP_PRECONDITION_FAILED
HTTP_UNAUTHORIZED	HTTP_SERVICE_UNAVAILABLE
HTTP_FORBIDDEN	HTTP_VARIANT_ALSO_VARIES
HTTP_NOT_FOUND	

Note that this list is not definitive. See the Apache source code for the most up-to-date listing.

:server

These are constants related to the version of the Apache server software:

```
MODULE_MAGIC_NUMBER
SERVER_VERSION
SERVER_BUILT
```

:config

These are constants most commonly used with configuration directive handlers:

```
DECLINE_CMD
```

:types

These are constants which define internal request types:

```
DIR_MAGIC_TYPE
```

:override

These constants are used to control and test the context of configuration directives:

OR_NONE	OR_INDEXES
OR_LIMIT	OR_UNSET
OR_OPTIONS	OR_ALL
OR_FILEINFO	ACCESS_CONF
OR_AUTHCFG	RSRC_CONF

:args_how

These are the constants which define configuration directive prototypes:

RAW_ARGS	TAKE123
TAKE1	ITERATE
TAKE2	ITERATE2
TAKE12	FLAG
TAKE3	NO_ARGS
TAKE23	

As you may notice, this list is shorter than the list defined in Apache's *include/ httpd.h* header file. The missing constants are available as subroutines via *Apache::Constants*, they are just not exportable by default. The less frequently used constants were left out of this list to keep memory consumption at a reasonable level.

There are two options if you need to access a constant that is not exportable by default. One is simply to use the fully qualified subroutine name, for example:

```
return Apache::Constants::HTTP_MULTIPLE_CHOICES();
```

Or use the *export* method in a server startup file to add exportable names. The name will now become available to the *use* operator.

```
#startup script
Apache::Constants->export(qw( HTTP_MULTIPLE_CHOICES ));

#runtime module
use Apache::Constants qw(:common HTTP_MULTIPLE_CHOICES);

...
return HTTP_MULTIPLE_CHOICES;
```

While the HTTP constants generally use a return code from handler subroutines, it is also possible to use the built-in *die()* function to jump out of a handler with a status code that will be propagated back to Apache:

```
unless (-r _) {
    die FORBIDDEN;
}
```

Configuration Classes

Two classes, *Apache::ModuleConfig* and *Apache::CmdParms*, provide access to the custom configuration directive API.

The Apache::ModuleConfig Class

Most Apache Perl API modules use the simple *PerlSetVar* directive to declare per-directory configuration variables. However, with a little more effort, you can create entirely new configuration directives. This process is discussed in detail in Chapter 8, *Customizing the Apache Configuration Process*.

Once the configuration directives have been created, they can be retrieved from within handlers using the *Apache::ModuleConfig->get()* class method. *get()* returns the current command configuration table as an Apache table blessed into the *Apache::Table* class. *get()* takes one or two arguments. The first argument can be the current request object to retrieve per-directory data or an *Apache::Server* object to retrieve per-server data. The second, optional, argument is the name of the module whose configuration table you are interested in. If not specified, this argument defaults to the current package, which is usually what you want.

Here's an example:

```
use Apache::ModuleConfig ();
...
sub handler {
  my $r = shift;
  my $cfg = Apache::ModuleConfig->get($r);
  my $printer = $cfg->{'printer-address'};
  ...
}
```

The Apache::CmdParms Class

The *Apache::CmdParms* class provides a Perl interface to the Apache *cmd_parms* data structure. When Apache encounters a directive, it invokes a command handler that is responsible for processing the directive's arguments. The *Apache::Cmd-Parms* object is passed to the responsible handler and contains information that may be useful when processing these arguments.

An example of writing a directive handler is given in Chapter 8. In this section, we just summarize the methods that *Apache::CmdParms* makes available.

path()

> If the configuration directive applies to a certain *<Location>*, *<Directory>*, or *<Files>* section, the *path()* method returns the path or filename pattern to which the section applies.
>
> ```
> my $path = $parms->path;
> ```

server()

> This method returns an object blessed into the *Apache::Server* class. This is the same *Apache::Server* object which is retrieved at request time via the *Apache* method named *server()*. See above.
>
> ```
> my $s = $parms->server;
> ```

cmd()

> This method returns an object blessed into the *Apache::Command* class. The *Apache::Module* package from CPAN must be installed to access *Apache::Command* methods.
>
> ```
> use Apache::Module ();
> ...
> my $name = $parms->cmd->name;
> ```

info()

> If the directive handler has stashed any info in the *cmd_data* slot, this method will return that data. This is generally somewhat static information, normally used to reuse a common configuration function. For example, the fancy directory indexer, **mod_autoindex** and its family of *AddIcon** directives, uses this technique quite effectively to manipulate the directive arguments.
>
> ```
> my $info = $parms->info;
> ```

limited()

> The methods present in the current *Limit* configuration are converted into a bit mask, which is returned by this method.
>
> ```
> # httpd.conf
> <Limit GET POST>
> SomeDirective argument_1 argument_2
> </Limit>
> ```

```
# Perl module
use Apache::Constants qw(:methods);

sub SomeDirective ($$$$) {
    my($parms, $cfg, @args) = @_;
    my $method_mask = $parms->limited;
    if($method_mask & (1 << M_POST)) {
        ...
    }
}
```

override()

This method converts the current value of the *AllowOverride* directive into a bit mask and returns it. You can then import the *Apache::Constants :override* tag to retrieve the values of individual bits in the mask. Modules don't generally need to check this value. The internal configuration functions take care of the required context checking.

```
use Apache::Constants qw(:override);

my $override_mask = $parms->override;
if($override_mask & OR_ALL) {
    #this directive is allowed anywhere in the configuration files
}
```

getline()

If the directive handler needs to read from the configuration file directly, it may do so with the *getline()* method. The first line returned in the following example is the line immediately following the line on which the directive appeared. It's up to your handler to decide when to stop reading lines; in the example below we use pattern matching.

Reading from the configuration file directly is normally done when a directive is declared with a prototype of RAW_ARGS. With this prototype, arguments are not parsed by Apache, that job is left up to the directive handler. Let's say you need to implement a configuration *container*, in the same format as the standard *<Directory>* and *<Location>* directives:

```
<Container argument>
    ....
</Container>
```

Here is a directive handler to parse it:

```
sub Container ($$$*) {
    my($parms, $cfg, $arg, $fh) = @_;
    $arg =~ s/>//;

    while($parms->getline($line)) {
        last if $line =~ m:</Container>:i;
        ...
    }
}
```

There is an alternative to using the *getline()* method. As described in Chapter 8, when the RAW_ARGS prototype is used, a tied filehandle is passed to the directive handler as its last argument. Perl's built-in *read()* and *getc()* functions may be used on this filehandle, along with the <> readline operator:

```
sub Container ($$$*) {
    my($parms, $cfg, $arg, $fh) = @_;
    $arg =~ s/>//;

    while(defined(my $line = <$fh>)) {
        last if $line =~ m:</Container>:i;
        ...
    }
}
```

The Apache::File Class

The Perl API includes a class named *Apache::File* which, when loaded, provides advanced functions for opening and manipulating files at the server side.

Apache::File does two things. First, it provides an object-oriented interface to file-handles similar to Perl's standard *IO::File* class. While the *Apache::File* module does not provide all the functionality of *IO::File*, its methods are approximately twice as fast as the equivalent *IO::File* methods. Second, when you use Apache::File, it adds several new methods to the *Apache* class which provide support for handling files under the HTTP/1.1 protocol.

Like *IO::File*, the main advantage of accessing filehandles through *Apache::File*'s object-oriented interface is the ability to create new anonymous filehandles without worrying about namespace collision. Furthermore, you don't have to close the filehandle explicitly before exiting the subroutine that uses it; this is done automatically when the filehandle object goes out of scope:

```
{
    use Apache::File;
    my $fh = Apache::File->new($config);
    # no need to close
}
```

However, *Apache::File* is still not as fast as Perl's native *open()* and *close()* functions. If you wish to get the highest performance possible, you should use *open()* and *close()* in conjunction with the standard *Symbol::gensym* or *Apache::gensym* functions:

```
{ # using standard Symbol module
    use Symbol 'gensym';
    my $fh = gensym;
    open $fh, $config;
    close $fh;
}
```

```
{ # Using Apache::gensym() method
   my $fh = Apache->gensym;
   open $fh, $config;
   close $fh;
}
```

A little known feature of Perl is that when lexically defined variables go out of scope, any indirect filehandle stored in them is automatically closed. So, in fact, there's really no reason to perform an explicit *close()* on the filehandles in the two preceding examples unless you want to test the close operation's return value. As always with Perl, there's more than one way to do it.

Apache::File Methods

These are methods associated directly with *Apache::File* objects. They form a sub-set of what's available from the Perl *IO::File* and *FileHandle* classes.

new()

This method creates a new filehandle, returning the filehandle object on suc-cess and *undef* on failure. If an additional argument is given, it will be passed to the *open()* method automatically.

```
use Apache::File ();
my $fh = Apache::File->new;

my $fh = Apache::File->new($filename) or die "Can't open $filename $!";
```

open()

Given an *Apache::File* object previously created with *new()*, this method opens a file and associates it with the object. The *open()* method accepts the same types of arguments as the standard Perl *open()* function, including sup-port for file modes.

```
$fh->open($filename);

$fh->open(">$out_file");

$fh->open("|$program");
```

close()

The *close()* method is equivalent to the Perl built-in *close()* function, return-ing true upon success and false upon failure.

```
$fh->close or die "Can't close $filename $!";
```

tmpfile()

The *tmpfile()* method is responsible for opening up a unique temporary file. It is similar to the *tmpnam()* function in the POSIX module but doesn't come with all the memory overhead that loading POSIX does. It will choose a suit-able temporary directory (which must be writable by the web server process). It then generates a series of filenames using the current process ID and the

$TMPNAM package global. Once a unique name is found, it is opened for writing, using flags that will cause the file to be created only if it does not already exist. This prevents race conditions in which the function finds what seems to be an unused name, but someone else claims the same name before it can be created.

As an added bonus, *tmpfile()* calls the *register_cleanup()* method behind the scenes to make sure the file is unlinked after the transaction is finished.

Called in a list context, *tmpfile()* returns the temporary file name and a filehandle opened for reading and writing. In a scalar context, only the filehandle is returned.

```
my($tmpnam, $fh) = Apache::File->tmpfile;

my $fh = Apache::File->tmpfile;
```

Apache Methods Added by Apache::File

When a handler pulls in *Apache::File*, the module adds a number of new methods to the *Apache* request object. These methods are generally of interest to handlers that wish to serve static files from disk or memory using the features of the HTTP/1.1 protocol that provide increased performance through client-side document caching.

To take full advantage of the HTTP/1.1 protocol, your content handler will test the *meets_conditions()* method before sending the body of a static document. This avoids sending a document that is already cached and up-to-date on the browser's side of the connection. You will then want to call *set_content_length()* and *update_mtime()* in order to make the outgoing HTTP headers correctly reflect the size and modification time of the requested file. Finally, you may want to call *set_etag()* in order to set the file's entity tag when communicating with HTTP/1.1–compliant browsers.

In the section following this one, we demonstrate these methods fully by writing a pure Perl replacement for the *http_core* module's default document retrieval handler.

discard_request_body()

The majority of GET method handlers do not deal with incoming client data, unlike POST and PUT handlers. However, according to the HTTP/1.1 specification, any method, including GET, can include a request body. The *discard_request_body()* method tests for the existence of a request body and, if present, simply throws away the data. This discarding is especially important when persistent connections are being used, so that the request body will not be attached to the next request. If the request is malformed, an error code will be returned, which the module handler should propagate back to Apache.

```
if ((my $rc = $r->discard_request_body) != OK) {
    return $rc;
}
```

meets_conditions()

In the interest of HTTP/1.1 compliance, the *meets_conditions()* method is used to implement conditional GET rules. These rules include inspection of client headers, including *If-Modified-Since*, *If-Unmodified-Since*, *If-Match*, and *If-None-Match*. Consult RFC 2068 section 9.3 (which you can find at *http://www.w3.org/Protocols*) if you are interested in the nitty-gritty details.

As far as Apache modules are concerned, they need only check the return value of this method before sending a request body. If the return value is anything other than OK, the module should return from the handler with that value. A common return value is HTTP_NOT_MODIFIED, which is sent when the document is already cached on the client side and has not changed since it was cached.

```
if((my $rc = $r->meets_conditions) != OK) {
    return $rc;
}
# else ... go and send the response body ...
```

mtime()

This method returns the last modified time of the requested file, expressed as seconds since the epoch. The last modified time may also be changed using this method, although the *update_mtime()* method is better suited to this purpose.

```
my $date_string = localtime $r->mtime;
```

set_content_length()

This method sets the outgoing *Content-length* header based on its argument, which should be expressed in byte units. If no argument is specified, the method will use the size returned by *$r->filename*. This method is a bit faster and more concise than setting *Content-length* in the *headers_out* table yourself.

```
$r->set_content_length;
$r->set_content_length(-s $r->finfo); #same as above
$r->set_content_length(-s $filename);
```

set_etag()

This method is used to set the outgoing *ETag* header corresponding to the requested file. *ETag* is an opaque string that identifies the current version of the file and changes whenever the file is modified. This string is tested by the *meets_conditions()* method if the client provides an *If-Match* or *If-None-Match* header.

```
$r->set_etag;
```

set_last_modified()

> This method is used to set the outgoing *Last-Modified* header from the value
> returned by *$r->mtime*. The method checks that the specified time is not in
> the future. In addition, using *set_last_modified()* is faster and more concise
> than setting *Last-Modified* in the *headers_out* table yourself.

> You may provide an optional time argument, in which case the method will
> first call the *update_mtime()* to set the file's last modification date. It will then
> set the outgoing *Last-Modified* header as before.

```
$r->update_mtime((stat $r->finfo)[9]);
$r->set_last_modified;

$r->set_last_modified((stat $r->finfo)[9]); # same as the two lines above
```

update_mtime()

> Rather than setting the request record *mtime* field directly, you should use the
> *update_mtime()* method to change the value of this field. It will only be
> updated if the new time is more recent than the current *mtime*. If no time
> argument is present, the default is the last modified time of *$r->filename*.

```
$r->update_mtime;
$r->update_mtime((stat $r->finfo)[9]); #same as above
$r->update_mtime(time);
```

Using Apache::File to Send Static Files

Apache's *http_core* module already has a default handler to send files straight from
disk to the client. Such files include static HTML, plain text, compressed archives,
and image files in a number of different formats. A bare-bones handler in Perl only
requires a few lines of code, as Example 9-1 shows. After the standard preamble,
the *handler()* function attempts to open $r->filename. If the file cannot be
opened, the handler simply assumes file permission problems and returns
FORBIDDEN. Otherwise, the entire contents of the file are passed down the HTTP
stream using the request object's *send_fd()* method. It then does a little tidying up
by calling *close()* on the filehandle and returns OK so that Apache knows the
response has been sent.

Example 9-1. A Simple but Flawed Way to Send Static Files

```
package Apache::EchoFile;

use strict;
use Apache::Constants qw(:common);
use Apache::File ();

sub handler {
    my $r = shift;
    my $fh = Apache::File->new($r->filename) or return FORBIDDEN;
```

Example 9-1. A Simple but Flawed Way to Send Static Files (continued)

```
    $r->send_fd($fh);
    close $fh;
    return OK;
}

1;
__END__
```

While this works well in most cases, there is more involved in sending a file over HTTP than you might think. To fully support the HTTP/1.1 protocol, one has to handle the PUT and OPTIONS methods, handle GET requests that contain a request body, and provide support for *If-modified-since* requests.

Example 9-2 is the *Apache::SendFile* module, a Perl version of the *http_core* module default handler. It starts off as before by loading the *Apache::Constants* module. However, it brings in more constants than usual. The *:response* group pulls in the constants we normally see using the *:common* tag, plus a few more including the NOT_IMPLEMENTED constant. The *:methods* group brings in the method number constants including M_INVALID, M_OPTIONS, M_PUT, and M_GET. The *:http* tag imports a few of the less commonly used status codes, including HTTP_METHOD_NOT_ALLOWED.

We next bring in the *Apache::File* module in order to open and read the contents of the file to be sent and to load the HTTP/1.1–specific file-handling methods.

The first step we take upon entering the *handler()* function is to call the *discard_request_body()* method. Unlike HTTP/1.0, where only POST and PUT requests may contain a request body, in HTTP/1.1 any method may include a body. We have no use for it, so we throw it away to avoid potential problems.

We now check the request method by calling the request object's *method_number()* method. Like the *http_core* handler, we only handle GET requests (method numbers M_GET). For any other type of request we return an error, but in each case the error is slightly different. For the method M_INVALID, which is set when the client specifies a request that Apache doesn't understand, we return an error code of NOT_IMPLEMENTED. For M_OPTIONS, which is sent by an HTTP/1.1 client that is seeking information about the capabilities of the server, we return DECLINED in order to allow Apache's core to handle the request (it sends a list of allowed methods).

The PUT method is applicable even if the resource doesn't exist, but we don't support it, so we return HTTP_METHOD_NOT_ALLOWED in this case. At this point we test for existence of the requested file by applying the −e file test to the cached *stat()* information returned by the request object's *finfo()* method. If the file does not exist, we log an error message and return NOT_FOUND. Finally, we specifically check for a request method of M_GET and again return HTTP_METHOD_NOT_ ALLOWED if this is not the case.

Provided the request has passed all these checks, we attempt to open the requested file with *Apache::File*. If the file cannot be opened, the handler logs an error message and returns FORBIDDEN.

At this point, we know that the request method is valid and the file exists and is accessible. But this doesn't mean we should actually send the file because the client may have cached it previously and has asked us to transmit it only if it has changed. The *update_mtime()*, *set_last_modified()*, and *set_etag()* methods together set up the HTTP/1.1 headers that indicate when the file was changed and assign it a unique entity tag that changes when the file changes.

We then call the *meets_conditions()* method to find out if the file has already been cached by the client. If this is the case, or some other condition set by the client fails, *meets_conditions()* returns a response code other than OK, which we propagate back to Apache. Apache then does whatever is appropriate.

Otherwise we call the *set_content_length()* method to set the outgoing *Content-length* header to the length of the file, then call *send_http_header()* to send the client the full set of HTTP headers. The return value of *header_only()* is tested to determine whether the client has requested the header only; if the method returns false, then the client has requested the body of the file as well as the headers, and we send the file contents using the *send_fd()* method. Lastly, we tidy up by closing the filehandle and returning OK.

The real default handler found in *http_core.c* actually does a bit more work than this. It includes logic for sending files from memory via *mmap()* if USE_MMAP_ FILES is defined, along with support for HTTP/1.1 *byte ranges* and *Content-MD5*.

After reading through this you'll probably be completely happy to return DECLINED when the appropriate action for your module is just to return the unmodified contents of the requested file!

Example 9-2. A 100-Percent Pure Perl Implementation of the Default http_core Content Handler

```
package Apache::SendFile;

use strict;
use Apache::Constants qw(:response :methods :http);
use Apache::File ();
use Apache::Log ();

sub handler {
    my $r = shift;
    if ((my $rc = $r->discard_request_body) != OK) {
        return $rc;
    }
```

Example 9-2. A 100-Percent Pure Perl Implementation of the Default http_core Content Handler (continued)

```perl
    if ($r->method_number == M_INVALID) {
        $r->log->error("Invalid method in request ", $r->the_request);
        return NOT_IMPLEMENTED;
    }

    if ($r->method_number == M_OPTIONS) {
        return DECLINED; #http_core.c:default_handler() will pick this up
    }

    if ($r->method_number == M_PUT) {
        return HTTP_METHOD_NOT_ALLOWED;
    }

    unless (-e $r->finfo) {
        $r->log->error("File does not exist: ", $r->filename);
        return NOT_FOUND;
    }

    if ($r->method_number != M_GET) {
        return HTTP_METHOD_NOT_ALLOWED;
    }

    my $fh = Apache::File->new($r->filename);
    unless ($fh) {
        $r->log->error("file permissions deny server access: ",
                       $r->filename);
        return FORBIDDEN;
    }

    $r->update_mtime(-s $r->finfo);
    $r->set_last_modified;
    $r->set_etag;

    if((my $rc = $r->meets_conditions) != OK) {
        return $rc;
    }

    $r->set_content_length;
    $r->send_http_header;

    unless ($r->header_only) {
        $r->send_fd($fh);
    }

    close $fh;
    return OK;
}

1;


__END__
```

Special Global Variables, Subroutines, and Literals

As you know, Perl has several magic global variables, subroutines, and literals that have the same meaning no matter what package they are called from. A handful of these variables have special meaning when running under *mod_perl*. Here we will describe these and other global variables maintained by *mod_perl*. Don't forget that Perl code has a much longer lifetime and lives among many more namespaces in the *mod_perl* environment than it does in a conventional CGI environment. When modifying a Perl global variable, we recommend that you always localize the variable so modifications do not trip up other Perl code running in the server.

Global Variables

We begin with the list of magic global variables that have special significance to *mod_perl*.

$0

> When running under *Apache::Registry* or *Apache::PerlRun*, this variable is set to that of the *filename* field of the `request_rec`.
>
> When running inside of a *<Perl>* section, the value of $0 is the path to the configuration file in which the Perl section is located, such as *httpd.conf* or *srm.conf.*

$^X

> Normally, this variable holds the path to the Perl program that was executed from the shell. Under *mod_perl*, there is no Perl program, just the Perl library linked with Apache. Thus, this variable is set to that of the Apache binary in which Perl is currently running, such as */usr/local/apache/bin/httpd* or *C:\Apache\ apache.exe.*

$|

> As the *perlvar(1)* manpage explains, if this variable is set to nonzero, it forces a flush right away and after every write or print on the currently selected output channel. Under *mod_perl*, setting $| when the STDOUT filehandle is selected will cause the *rflush()* method to be invoked after each *print()*. Because of the overhead associated with *rflush()*, you should avoid making this a general practice.

$/

> The *perlvar* manpage describes this global variable as the input record separator, newline by default. The same is true under *mod_perl*; however, *mod_perl* ensures it is reset back to the newline default after each request.

%@

You are most likely familiar with Perl's $@ variable, which holds the Perl error message or exception value from the last *eval()* command, if any. There is also an undocumented %@ hash global, which is used internally for certain *eval* bookkeeping. This variable is put to good use by *mod_perl*. When an *eval()* error occurs, the contents of $@ are stored into the %@ hash using the current URI as the key. This allows an *ErrorDocument* to provide some more clues as to what went wrong.

```
my $previous_uri = $r->prev->uri;
my $errmsg = $@{$previous_uri};
```

This looks a bit weird, but it's just a hash key lookup on an array named %@. Mentally substitute %SAVED_ERRORS for %@ and you'll see what's going on here.

%ENV

As with the Perl binary, this global hash contains the current environment. When the Perl interpreter is first created by *mod_perl*, this hash is emptied, with the exception of those variables passed and set via *PerlPassEnv* and *PerlSetEnv* configuration directives.

The usual configuration scoping rules apply. A *PerlSetEnv* directive located in the main part of the configuration file will influence all Perl handlers, while those located in *<Directory>*, *<Location>*, and *<Files>* sections will only affect handlers in those areas that they apply to.

The Apache *SetEnv* and *PassEnv* directives also influence %ENV, but they don't take effect until the *fixup* phase. If you need to influence %ENV via server configuration for an earlier phase, such as authentication, be sure to use *PerlSetEnv* and *PerlPassEnv* instead because these directives take effect as soon as possible.

There are also a number of standard variables that Apache adds to the environment prior to invoking the content handler. These include DOCUMENT_ROOT and SERVER_SOFTWARE. By default, the complete %ENV hash is not set up until the content response phase. Only variables set by *PerlPassEnv*, *PerlSetEnv*, and by *mod_perl* itself will be visible. Should you need the complete set of variables to be available sooner, your handler code can do so with the *subprocess_env* method.

```
my $r = shift;
my $env = $r->subprocess_env;
%ENV = %$env;
```

Unless you plan to spawn subprocesses, however, it will usually be more efficient to access the subprocess variables directly:

```
my $tmp = $r->subprocess_env->{'TMPDIR'};
```

If you need to get at the environment variables that are set automatically by Apache before spawning CGI scripts and you want to do this outside of a content handler, remember to call *subprocess_env()* once in a void context in order to initialize the environment table with the standard CGI and server-side include variables:

```
$r->subprocess_env;
my $port = $r->subprocess_env('SERVER_SOFTWARE');
```

There's rarely a legitimate reason to do this, however, because all the information you need can be fetched directly from the request object.

Filling in the %ENV hash before the response phase introduces a little overhead into each *mod_perl* content handler. If you don't want the %ENV hash to be filled at all by *mod_perl*, add this to your server configuration file:

```
PerlSetupEnv Off
```

Regardless of the setting of *PerlSetupEnv*, or whether *subprocess_env()* has been called, *mod_perl* always adds a few special keys of its own to %ENV.

MOD_PERL

The value of this key will be set to a true value for code to test if it is running in the *mod_perl* environment or not.

```
if(exists $ENV{MOD_PERL}) {
... do something ...
}
else {
... do something else ...
}
```

GATEWAY_INTERFACE

When running under the *mod_cgi* CGI environment, this value is CGI/1.1. However, when running under the *mod_perl* CGI environment, GATEWAY_ INTERFACE will be set to CGI-Perl/1.1. This can also be used by code to test if it is running under *mod_perl*; however, testing for the presence of the MOD_PERL key is faster than using a regular expression or *substr* to test GATEWAY_INTERFACE.

PERL_SEND_HEADER

If the *PerlSendHeader* directive is set to *On*, this environment variable will also be set to *On*; otherwise, the variable will not exist. This is intended for scripts which do not use the CGI.pm *header()* method, which always sends proper HTTP headers no matter what the settings.

```
if($ENV{PERL_SEND_HEADER}) {
    print "Content-type: text/html\n\n";
}
else {
    my $r = Apache->request;
```

```
        $r->content_type('text/html');
        $r->send_http_header;
    }
```

%SIG

The Perl `%SIG` global variable is used to set signal handlers for various signals.

There is always one handler set by *mod_perl* for catching the `PIPE` signal. This signal is sent by Apache when a timeout occurs, triggered when the client drops the connection prematurely (e.g., by hitting the stop button). The internal *Apache::SIG* class catches this signal to ensure the Perl interpreter state is properly reset after a timeout.

The *Apache::SIG* handler does have one side effect that you might want to take advantage of. If a transaction is aborted prematurely because of a `PIPE` signal, *Apache::SIG* will set the environment variable `SIGPIPE` to the number 1 before it exits. You can pick this variable up with a custom log handler statement and record it if you are interested in compiling statistics on the number of remote users who abort their requests prematurely.

The following is a *LogFormat* directive that will capture the `SIGPIPE` environment variable. If the transaction was terminated prematurely, the last field in the log file line will be 1, otherwise –.

```
LogFormat "%h %l %u %t \"%r\" %s %b %{SIGPIPE}e"
```

As for all other signals, you should be most careful not to stomp on Apache's own signal handlers, such as that for `ALRM`. It is best to localize the handler inside of a block so it can be restored as soon as possible:

```
{
    local $SIG{ARLM} = sub { ... };
    ...
}
```

At the end of each request, *mod_perl* will restore the `%SIG` hash to the same state it was in at server startup time.

@INC

As the *perlvar* manpage explains, the array `@INC` contains the list of places to look for Perl scripts to be evaluated by the *do EXPR*, *require*, or *use* constructs.

The same is true under *mod_perl*. However, two additional paths are automatically added to the end of the array. These are the value of the configured *ServerRoot* and *$ServerRoot/lib/perl*.

At the end of each request, *mod_perl* will restore the value of `@INC` to the same value it was during server startup time. This includes any modifications made by code pulled in via *PerlRequire* and *PerlModule*. So, be warned: if a script compiled by *Apache::Registry* contains a `use lib` or other `@INC` modification statement, this modification will not "stick." That is, once the script is cached, the modification is undone until the script has changed on disk and is recompiled. If one script relies on another to modify the `@INC` path, that modification should be moved to a script or module pulled in at server startup time, such as the perl startup script.

%INC

As the *perlvar* manpage explains, the `%INC` hash contains entries for each filename that has been included via `do` or `require`. The key is the filename you specified, and the value is the location of the file actually found. The `require` command uses this array to determine whether a given file has already been included.

The same is true in the *mod_perl* environment. However, this Perl feature may seem like a *mod_perl* bug at times. One such case is when *.pm* modules that are modified are not automatically recompiled the way that *Apache::Registry* script files are. The reason this behavior hasn't been changed is that calling the *stat* function to test the last modified time for each file in `%INC` requires considerable overhead and would affect Perl API module performance noticeably. If you need it, the *Apache::StatINC* module provides the "recompile when modified" functionality, which the authors only recommend using during development. On a production server, it's best to set the *PerlFreshRestart* directive to *On* and to restart the server whenever you change a *.pm* file and want to see the changes take effect immediately.

Another problem area is pulling in library files which do not declare a `package` namespace. As all *Apache::Registry* and *Apache::PerlRun* script files are compiled inside their own unique namespace, pulling in such a file via *require* causes it to be compiled within this unique namespace. Since the library file will only be pulled in once per request, only the first script to *require* it will be able to see the subroutines it declares. Other scripts that try to call routines in the library will trigger a server error along these lines:

```
[Thu Sep 11 11:03:06 1998] Undefined subroutine
&Apache::ROOT::perl::test_2epl::some_function called at
/opt/www/apache/perl/test.pl line 79.
```

The *mod_perl_traps* manual page describes this problem in more detail, along with providing solutions.

Subroutines

Subroutines with capitalized names have special meaning to Perl. Familiar examples may include *DESTROY* and *BEGIN*. *mod_perl* also recognizes these subroutines and treats them specially.

BEGIN

Perl executes *BEGIN* blocks during the compile time of code as soon as possible. The same is true under *mod_perl*. However, since *mod_perl* normally only compiles scripts and modules once in the parent server or once per child, *BEGIN* blocks in that code will only be run once.

Once a *BEGIN* block has run, it is immediately undefined by removing it from the symbol table. In the *mod_perl* environment, this means *BEGIN* blocks will not be run during each incoming request unless that request happens to be the one that is compiling the code. When a *.pm* module or other Perl code file is pulled in via *require* or *use*, its *BEGIN* blocks will be executed as follows:

— Once at startup time if pulled in by the parent process by a *PerlModule* directive or in the Perl startup script.

— Once per child process if not pulled in by the parent process.

— An additional time in each child process if *Apache::StatINC* is loaded and the module is modified.

— An additional time in the parent process on each restart if *PerlFreshRestart* is *On*.

— At unpredictable times if you fiddle with `%INC` yourself. Don't do this unless you know what you are doing.

Apache::Registry scripts can contain *BEGIN* blocks as well. In this case, they will be executed as follows:

— Once at startup time if pulled in by the parent process via *Apache::RegistryLoader*.

— Once per child process if not pulled in by the parent process.

— An additional time in each child process if the script file is modified.

— An additional time in the parent process on each restart if the script was pulled in by the parent process with *Apache::RegistryLoader* and *PerlFreshRestart* is *On*.

END

In Perl, an *END* subroutine defined in a module or script is executed as late as possible, that is, when the interpreter is being exited. In the *mod_perl* environment, the interpreter does not exit until the server is shutdown. However, *mod_perl* does make a special case for *Apache::Registry* scripts.

Normally, *END* blocks are executed by Perl during its *perl_run()* function, which is called once each time the Perl program is executed, e.g., once per CGI (*mod_cgi*) script. However, *mod_perl* only calls *perl_run()* once during server startup. Any *END* blocks that are encountered during main server startup, such as those pulled in by *PerlRequire* or *PerlModule*, are suspended and run at server shutdown time during the *child_exit* phase.

Any *END* blocks that are encountered during compilation of *Apache::Registry* scripts are called after the script has completed the response, including subsequent invocations when the script is cached in memory. All other END blocks encountered during other *Perl*Handler* callbacks (e.g., *PerlChildInitHandler*) will be suspended while the process is running and called only during *child_exit* when the process is shutting down.

Module authors may wish to use `$r->register_cleanup` as an alternative to *END* blocks if this behavior is not desirable.

Magic Literals

Perl recognizes a few magic literals during script compilation. By and large, they act exactly like their counterparts in the standalone Perl interpreter.

__END__

This token works just as it does with the standalone Perl interpreter, causing compilation to terminate. However, this causes a problem for *Apache::Registry* scripts. Since the scripts are compiled inside of a subroutine, using __END__ will cut off the enclosing brace, causing script compilation to fail. If your *Apache::Registry* scripts use this literal, they will not run.

In partial compensation for this deficiency, *mod_perl* lets you use the __END__ token anywhere in your server configuration files to cut out experimental configuration or to make a notepad space that doesn't require you to use the # comment token on each line. Everything below the __END__ token will be ignored.

Special Package Globals

There are a number of useful globals located in the *Apache::Server* namespace that you are free to use in your own modules. Unless otherwise specified, treat them as read-only. Changing their values will lead to unpredictable results.

`$Apache::Server::CWD`

This variable is set to the directory from which the server was started.

`$Apache::Server::Starting`

If the code is running in the parent server when the server is first started, the value is set to 1; otherwise, it is set to 0.

`$Apache::Server::ReStarting`

> If the code is running in the parent server when the server is restarted, this variable will be true; otherwise, it will be false. The value is incremented each time the server is restarted.

`$Apache::Server::SaveConfig`

> As described in Chapter 8, *<Perl>* configuration sections are compiled inside the *Apache::ReadConfig* namespace. This namespace is normally flushed after *mod_perl* has finished processing the section. However, if the `$Apache::Server::SaveConfig` variable is set to a true value, the namespace will not be flushed, making configuration data available to Perl modules at request time.

```
<Perl>
$Apache::Server::SaveConfig = 1;

$DocumentRoot = ...
...
</Perl>
```

> At request time, the value of `$DocumentRoot` can be accessed with the fully qualified name `$Apache::ReadConfig::DocumentRoot`.

The next chapters show the Apache API from the perspective of the C-language programmer, telling you everything you need to know to squeeze the last drop of performance out of Apache by writing extension modules in a fast compiled language.

10

C API Reference Guide, Part I

The last two chapters of this book, Chapters 10 and 11, focus on aspects of the Apache module API that C-language programmers need to know. The majority of the API has already been covered in previous chapters, where we looked at it from the perspective of its Perl incarnation. We will briefly revisit each of the topics that we've already discussed in order to show you how the API appears in C. Topics that are specific to the C API, such as memory management, are covered in more detail.

Because the C API is so much of a recapitulation of the Perl API,[*] we won't show you as many complete examples in this chapter as we have in the previous ones, although there are still plenty of code snippets. For a complete C module skeleton, have a look at *mod_example.c*, which can be found in the Apache distribution in the directory *src/modules/example*. It implements handlers for each of the phases and writes out a log entry when each phase has been activated. For "how did they do that?" questions, peruse the source code for the standard modules in *src/modules/standard*. You'll also find a number of complete C API example modules at this book's companion web site, *http://www.modperl.com*.

This chapter covers the most common parts of the API, including the data types that all handlers must know about, functions for manipulating arrays, tables, and resource pools, and techniques for getting and setting information about the request. The next chapter describes how to define and manage configuration directives and covers the less essential parts of the C API, such as string manipulation functions, and esoterica such as opening pipes to subprocesses.

---

[*] Technically, it's the other way around.

We do our best to follow the Apache coding style guide throughout. You'll find this guide along with other developer resources at the Apache Project Development site, *http://dev.apache.org/*.

Which Header Files to Use?

Like other C programs, Apache modules must `#include` a variety of header files declaring the various data types and functions used by the API. The include files are found in the *src/include* directory beneath the top of the Apache distribution. Almost every module will want to include the following files:

```
#include "httpd.h"
#include "http_config.h"
#include "http_core.h"
#include "http_log.h"
#include "http_main.h"
#include "http_protocol.h"
#include "http_request.h"
```

In addition, modules wishing to launch subprocesses will need to include the script utility definitions:

```
#include "util_script.h"
```

More rarely used are header files required for the MD5 digest function, URI parsing, and regular expression matching. We explain which header files to include in the sections that deal with those parts of the Apache API.

Major Data Structures

Our Perl examples throughout the book have plugged into the Perl API via an object-oriented interface that blurs the distinction between data structures and function calls. For better or for worse, there is no such blurring in the C API. Data is maintained in data structures. To work with these structures, you either access their fields directly or pass them to function calls to do the work for you. In this section, we work our way through the four central data structures in the Apache C API: the `module`, the `request_rec`, the `conn_rec`, and the `server_rec`.

The module Record

Our Perl examples have plugged into the various phases of the request cycle via the various *Perl*Handler* directives. There are no such directives for C modules. Instead, all C modules contain a compiled data structure of type `module`. At runtime, all loaded modules are linked together via a linked list rooted at the Apache global `top_module`. Apache then consults each `module` table in turn to determine what phases of the transaction the module wishes to handle.

The `module` structure is usually defined at the bottom of the module's C source code file. Most module writers begin by cutting and pasting this definition from another source code file, filling in the slots that they need and `NULL`ing out those that they don't want. In this tradition, let's revisit the *mod_hello* module introduced in Chapter 2, *A First Module*:

```
module MODULE_VAR_EXPORT hello_module =
{
    STANDARD_MODULE_STUFF,
    NULL,                   /* module initializer             */
    NULL,                   /* per-directory config creator   */
    NULL,                   /* dir config merger              */
    NULL,                   /* server config creator          */
    NULL,                   /* server config merger           */
    NULL,                   /* config directive table         */
    hello_handlers,         /* [9]  content handlers          */
    NULL,                   /* [2]  URI-to-filename translation */
    NULL,                   /* [5]  check/validate user_id     */
    NULL,                   /* [6]  check user_id is valid *here* */
    NULL,                   /* [4]  check access by host address */
    NULL,                   /* [7]  MIME type checker/setter   */
    NULL,                   /* [8]  fixups                     */
    NULL,                   /* [10] logger                     */
    NULL,                   /* [3]  header parser              */
    NULL,                   /* process initialization          */
    NULL,                   /* process exit/cleanup            */
    NULL                    /* [1]  post read_request handling */
};
```

`module` is a typedef, which you will find defined in the Apache source tree under *include/http_config.h*. `MODULE_VAR_EXPORT` is a define that can be found in the platform-specific *os.h* header files. Its purpose is to export the `module` data structure from the module's DLL under Win32 systems so the server core library is able to see it. On other systems, `MODULE_VAR_EXPORT` is simply a define which does nothing, as you can see in the file *include/ap_config.h*.

While you can name the module record and its source file anything you like, you are encouraged to follow the Apache convention of naming the module *something_module* and its source file *mod_something*. This will make it easier for you and others to remember the module name and avoids conflict with *apxs* and the DSO loading system, which sometimes depend on this convention.

STANDARD_MODULE_STUFF

The first few bits of `module` structure consist of boilerplate code that is filled in by the `STANDARD_MODULE_STUFF` preprocessor macro. Although you'll probably never have to access these fields yourself, here is a list of what's there in case you're wondering:

int version

> The server API version the module was compiled with and is used to make sure that the module is binary-compatible with the version of the server. This is defined by the macro MODULE_MAGIC_NUMBER_MAJOR found in the header file *ap_mmn.h*. The *ap_mmn.h* header file also includes a list of the changes which call for a "bump" of the MODULE_MAGIC_NUMBER_MAJOR version. This value can be used by modules to provide compatibility between Apache versions.

int minor_version

> The server API minor version the module was compiled with. This value is defined by the macro MODULE_MAGIC_NUMBER_MINOR, found in the header file *ap_mmn.h*. This value is not checked by the server, as minor API changes do not break binary compatibility.

int module_index

> Holds a unique index number assigned to the module at runtime and is used for lookups by the internal configuration system.

const char *name

> The name of the module, derived from the file in which the structure was declared. This is determined at compile time by taking the basename of the C compiler's __FILE__ token.

void *dynamic_load_handle

> A void * slot which can be used to hold a handle to the module if it was compiled as a dynamic shared object (DSO) and loaded with LoadModule.

struct module_struct *next

> A pointer to the next module in the internal linked list.

You should never have to worry about these fields. Just include the STANDARD_ MODULE_STUFF macro at the top of your module structure and forget about it.

Handler and callback slots

The rest of the module structure is mostly function pointers. Each field holds the address of a routine to invoke during the server's various initialization, transaction, and cleanup phases, or NULL if there is no routine to call. Because the Apache API was developed over time, the order of handlers in the module table does not correspond to the order in which they are called during the request cycle. We will describe them in the order in which they appear in the data structure. See Chapter 3, *The Apache Module Architecture and API*, for the correct chronological perspective.

Module initialization handler

```
void module_init(server_rec *s, pool *p);
```

This handler is called during the module initialization phase immediately after the server is started. This is where modules initialize data, consult configuration files, or do other preparatory work in the parent server before any children are forked off or threads spawned.

Under Unix and other process forking systems, each child process will inherit its own copy of any data structures created during this phase. Under threading systems, module authors will need to take care of maintaining per-thread instances of such data if needed.

The initialization function will be called with two arguments: a pointer to the current **server_rec** structure (described in detail below) and a pointer to a resource pool whose lifetime ends only when the server is finally shut down.

For an example of a module that steps in during this phase, see *mod_mime*, which builds its MIME types hash table from the *mime.types* file once during initialization.

Configuration creation and merging routines (four of them!)

```
void *create_dir_config (pool *p, char *dir)
void *merge_dir_config (pool *p, void *base_conf, void *new_conf)
void *create_server_config (pool *p, server_rec *s)
void *merge_server_config (pool *p, void *base_conf, void *new_conf)
```

Modules may add their own configuration directives to the server, which will then act just like built-in configuration directives. However, the server core knows nothing about what to do with these directives, and instead passes back the preparsed directives to the module for processing.

These four slots contain pointers to optional routines for handling module-specific configuration data blocks. You are not obliged to fill in all of them, or indeed any at all. See "Implementing Configuration Directives in C" in Chapter 11, *C API Reference Guide, Part II*, for details.

Configuration directive (command) table

```
command_rec *cmds
```

The **command_table** field holds a pointer to a **command_rec** structure, which describes each of the module's configuration directives in detail and points back to configuration callbacks to process the directives.

The **command_rec** structure is described in detail in Chapter 11 under "Implementing Configuration Directives in C."

Response handlers table

```
handler_rec *handlers
```

The next field contains the module dispatch table for the response phase of the request. It can be used to map one or more MIME content types to content handlers defined within the module or to map symbolic handler names to handler functions.

Here is a slightly expanded version of our Chapter 2 *mod_hello* example:

```
static handler_rec hello_handlers[] =
{
    {"hello-handler", hello_handler},
    {"application/x-hello", hello_handler},
    {NULL}
};
```

The handler table is an array of **handler_rec** structures. The last entry in the array must be a **NULL** record. Each **handler_rec** entry in the array has the following simple structure:

char *content_type

> The first element is the content type or the symbolic handler name. As described in the introduction to Chapter 4, *Content Handlers*, Apache will dispatch on the handler name or the MIME type, depending on the current directory's configuration. In this example, the *hello_handler()* content-handling subroutine is associated both with the symbolic handler name *hello-handler* and a magic MIME type of *application/x-hello*. This means that you can arrange for the content handler to be invoked either by setting the handler explicitly in a *<Directory>* or *<Location>* block with **SetHandler hello-handler**, or by setting the handler implicitly by requesting a document of MIME type *application/x-hello* (since there is no default MIME file extension mapping for this type of document, you'll have to make one up using *AddType*).

> It is perfectly valid for several modules to register their interest in handling the same MIME type. Apache will call them from most recent to least recent until one returns a status code other than **DECLINED**. It is also possible to use wildcards in the MIME type. For example, the *http_core* default handler registers `*/*`, indicating that it will handle a request of any type that is not handled by a more specific module.

int handler(request_rec *r)

> This is a pointer to the content handler subroutine that will be invoked to process the request at response time. As with the other HTTP request time callbacks, the function is passed a **request_rec *** structure and is expected to return an integer status value. The list of symbolic status code constants can be found in the header file *httpd.h*. The constants are identical to the list given in Table 3-1.

The content handler is something of an oddball among the various handlers because it is registered indirectly through the **handler_rec**. This structure allows modules to register multiple handlers for the response phase, leaving

Apache to select one of them based on the *content_type* for a given request. As we are about to see, handlers for the other phases are plugged directly into the `module` record.

URI translation handler

```
int translate_handler(request_rec *r)
```

This is the slot where a pointer to the URI translation handler, if any, is plugged in. It receives an argument consisting of a `request_rec` pointer and is expected to return an integer status code. Unless explicitly stated otherwise, the other phase handlers have similar calling conventions.

Authentication handler

```
int check_user_id(request_rec *r)
```

This is the slot where a pointer to the authentication handler, if any, is registered.

Authorization handler

```
int auth_checker(request_rec *r)
```

This is the slot where the authorization handler subroutine, if any, is registered.

Access handler

```
int access_checker(request_rec *r)
```

This is the slot where the access control handler subroutine, if any, is registered.

MIME type handler

```
int type_checker(request_rec *r)
```

This is the slot where the MIME type checker subroutine, if any, is registered.

Fixup handler

```
int fixer_upper(request_rec *r)
```

This is the slot where the fixup handler, if any, is registered.

Logging handler

```
int logger(request_rec *r)
```

This is the slot where the logging handler, if any, is registered.

Header parser handler

```
int header_parser(request_rec *r)
```

This is the slot where the header parser handler subroutine, if any, is registered.

Child initialization handler

```
void child_init(server_rec *s, pool *p)
```

This is where the child initialization subroutine is registered. Unlike other handlers, this subroutine is not called with a request record (there is no request at this stage). Instead, it is called with two arguments consisting of a `server_rec` pointer and a resource pool. It can do any processing or initialization it needs. If the routine needs to allocate some private storage, it can allocate memory from the resource pool and store a pointer to the returned structure in a static variable. The memory contained in the pool will not be released until the child process exits.

The *child_init* function should return no result.

Child exit handler

```
void child_exit(server_rec *r, pool *p)
```

This is the slot where the child exit handler is called. The exit handler should undo everything that the child init handler did. The handler is called with a `server_rec` pointer and a resource pool and should return no function result.

Post read request handler

```
int post_read_request(request_rec *r)
```

This is the slot where the post read request handler subroutine, if any, is registered.

The request_rec Structure

The `request_rec` request record is the heart and soul of the Apache API. It contains everything you could ever want to know about the current request and then some. You should already be intimately familiar with the request record from the Perl API. This section will show you what the `request_rec` looks like from within C.

The full definition of the `request_rec` is long and gnarly, combining public information that modules routinely use with private information that is only of interest to the core server (this includes such things as whether the request is using the "chunked" transfer mode implemented by HTTP/1.1). Example 10-1 gives the full definition of the `request_rec`, copied right out of *include/httpd.h*. We give detailed explanations for those fields that module writers need to worry about and silently ignore the rest.

ap_pool *pool

This is a resource pool that is valid for the lifetime of the request (*ap_pool* is merely a typedef alias for *pool*). Your request-time handlers should allocate memory from this pool.

conn_rec *connection

This is a pointer to the connection record for the current request, from which you can derive information about the local and remote host addresses, as well as the username used during authentication. for details, see "The conn_rec Structure" later in this chapter.

server_rec *server

This is a pointer to a server record **server_rec** structure, from which you can gather information about the current server. This is described in more detail in the next section, "The server_rec Structure."

request_rec *next
request_rec *prev
request_rec *main

Under various circumstances, including subrequests and internal redirects, Apache will generate one or more subrequests that are identical in all respects to an ordinary request. When this happens, these fields are used to chain the subrequests into a linked list. The **next** field points to the more recent request (or **NULL**, if there is none), and the **prev** field points to the immediate ancestor of the request. **main** points back to the top-level request. See Chapter 3 and Chapter 8, *Customizing the Apache Configuration Process*, for a more detailed discussion of the subrequest mechanism.

char *the_request

This contains the first line of the request, for logging purposes.

int proxyreq

If the current request is a proxy request, then this field will be set to a true (nonzero) value. Note that *mod_proxy* or *mod_perl* must be configured with the server for automatic proxy request detection. You can also set it yourself in order to activate Apache's proxy mechanism in the manner described in Chapter 7, *Other Request Phases*.

int header_only

This field will be true if the remote client made a head-only request (i.e., HEAD). You should not change the value of this field.

char *protocol

This field contains the name and version number of the protocol requested by the browser, for example HTTP/1.0.

time_t request_time

This is the time that the request started as a C **time_t** structure. See the manual page for *gmtime* for details on the **time_t** structure.

const char *hostname

This contains the name of the host requested by the client, either within the URI (during proxy requests) or in the *Host* header. The value of this field may not correspond to the canonical name of your server or the current virtual host but can be any of its DNS aliases. For this reason, it is better to use the *ap_get_server_name()* API function call described under "Processing Requests."

char *status_line

This field holds the full text of the status line returned from Apache to the remote browser, for example 200 OK. Ordinarily you will not want to change this directly but will allow Apache to set it based on the return value from your handler. However, you can change it directly in the rare instance that you want your handler to lie to Apache about its intentions (e.g., tell Apache that the handler processed the transaction OK, but send an error message to the browser).

int status

This field holds the numeric value of the transaction status code. Again you will usually not want to set this directly but allow Apache to do it for you.

char *method

This field contains the request method as a string, e.g., GET.

int method_number

This field contains the request method as an integer, e.g., M_GET. The appropriate symbolic constants are defined in *include/httpd.h*.

int allowed

This is a bit vector of request methods that your handler can accommodate. Ordinarily a content handler can just look at the value of **method** and return **DECLINED** if it doesn't want to handle it. However, to be fully friendly with the HTTP/1.1 protocol, handlers may also set **allowed** to the list of methods they accept. Apache will then generate an *Allow:* header which it transmits to any browser that's interested.

Here's a code fragment from a handler that accepts the GET and HEAD methods but not POST (or any of the more esoteric ones):

```
r->allowed = M_GET | M_HEAD;
```

long bytes_sent

This field contains the number of bytes that have been sent during the response phase and is used for logging. This count includes the document body but not the HTTP header fields.

time_t mtime

This field contains the modification time of the requested file, if any. The value may or may not be the same as the last modified time in the *finfo* stat buffer. The server core does not set this field; the task is left for modules to take care of. In general, this field should only be updated using the *ap_update_mtime()* function, described later in the section "Sending Files to the Client."

long length

> This field holds the value of the outgoing *Content-length* header. You can read this value but should only change it using the *ap_set_content_length()* function, described later in the section "Sending Files to the Client."

long remaining

> This field holds the value of the incoming *Content-length* header, if any. It is only set after a call to the *ap_setup_client_block()* function. After each call to *ap_get_client_block()*, the number of bytes read are subtracted from the *remaining* field.

table *headers_in
table *headers_out
table *err_headers_out
table *subprocess_env
table *notes

> These are pointers to Apache **table** records which maintain information between the phases of a request and are disposed of once the request is finished. The tables are dynamic lists of name/value pairs whose contents can be accessed with the routines described later under "The Table API."

> These five tables correspond to the like-named methods in the Perl API. **headers_in** and **headers_out** contain the incoming and outgoing HTTP headers. **err_headers_out** contains outgoing headers to be used in case of an error or a subrequest. **subprocess_env** contains name=value pairs to be copied into the environment prior to invoking subprocesses (such as CGI scripts). **notes** is a general table that can be used by modules to send "notes" from one phase to another.

const char *content_type
const char *content_encoding

> These fields contain the MIME content type and content encoding of the outgoing document. You can read this field to discover the MIME checking phase's best guess as to the document type or set it yourself within a content or MIME checking handler in order to change the type. The two fields frequently point to inline strings, so don't try to use *strcpy()* to modify them in place.

const char *handler

> This is the symbolic name of the content handler that will service the request during the response phase. Handlers for earlier phases are free to modify this field in order to change the default behavior.

array_header *content_languages

> This field holds an **array_header** pointer to the list of the language codes associated with this document. You can read and manipulate this list using the

Apache array API (see "The Array API"). This array is usually set up during the MIME checking phase; however, the content handler is free to modify it.

The `request_rec` also contains a `char *` field named `content_language`. The header file indicates that this is for backward compatibility only and should not be used.

`no_cache`

If set to a true value, this field causes Apache to add an *Expires* field to the outgoing HTTP header with the same date and time as the incoming request. Browsers that honor this instruction will not cache the document locally.

`char *unparsed_uri`
`char *uri`
`char *filename`
`char *path_info`
`char *args`

These five fields all hold the requested URI after various processing steps have been performed. `unparsed_uri` is a character string holding the raw URI before any parsing has been performed. `uri` holds the path part of the URI, and is the one you will usually work with. `filename` contains the translated physical pathname of the requested document, as determined during the URI translation phase. `path_info` holds the additional path information that remains after the URI has been translated into a file path. Finally, `args` contains the query string for CGI GET requests, and corresponds to the portion of the URI following the ?. Unlike the Perl API, you will have to parse out the components of the query string yourself.

You can turn `path_info` into a physical path akin to the CGI scripts' `PATH_TRANSLATED` environment variable by passing `path_info` to a subrequest and examining the `filename` field of the returned request record. See "The Subrequest API and Internal Redirects" later in this chapter.

`uri_components parsed_uri`

For finer access to the requested URI, Apache provides a `uri_components` data structure that contains the preparsed URI. This structure can be examined and manipulated with a special API. See "URI Parsing and Manipulation" in Chapter 11 for details.

`struct stat finfo`

This field is a `stat` struct containing the result of Apache's most recent *stat()* on the currently requested file (whose path you will find in `filename`). You can avoid an unnecessary system call by using the contents of this field directly rather than calling *stat()* again. If the requested file does not exist, `finfo.st_mode` will be set to zero.

In this example, we use the `S_ISDIR` macro defined in *stat.h* to detect whether the requested URI corresponds to a directory. Otherwise, we print out the file's modification time, using the *ap_ht_time()* function (described later) to format the time in standard HTTP format.

```
if(S_ISDIR(r->finfo.st_mode)) {
    ap_rprintf(r, "%s is a directory\n", r->filename);
}
else {
    ap_rprintf(r, "Last Modified: %s\n"
                  ap_ht_time(r->pool, r->finfo.st_mtime, timefmt, 0));
}
```

void *per_dir_config
void *request_config

These fields are the entry points to lists of per-directory and per-request configuration data set up by your module's configuration routines. You should not try to manipulate these fields directly, but instead pass them to the configuration API routine *ap_get_module_config()* described in the section "Accessing Module Configuration Data" in Chapter 11. Of the two, `per_dir_config` is the one you will use most often. `request_config` is used only rarely for passing custom configuration information to subrequests.

Example 10-1. The request_rec Structure (from include/httpd.h)

```
struct request_rec {

    ap_pool *pool;
    conn_rec *connection;
    server_rec *server;

    request_rec *next;          /* If we wind up getting redirected,
                                 * pointer to the request we redirected to.
                                 */
    request_rec *prev;          /* If this is an internal redirect,
                                 * pointer to where we redirected *from*.
                                 */

    request_rec *main;          /* If this is a sub_request (see request.h)
                                 * pointer back to the main request.
                                 */

    /* Info about the request itself... we begin with stuff that only
     * protocol.c should ever touch...
     */

    char *the_request;          /* First line of request, so we can log it */
    int assbackwards;           /* HTTP/0.9, "simple" request */
    int proxyreq;               /* A proxy request (calculated during
                                 * post_read_request or translate_name) */
    int header_only;            /* HEAD request, as opposed to GET */
```

Example 10-1. The request_rec Structure (from include/httpd.h) (continued)

```
char *protocol;             /* Protocol, as given to us, or HTTP/0.9 */
int proto_num;              /* Number version of protocol; 1.1 = 1001 */
const char *hostname;       /* Host, as set by full URI or Host: */

time_t request_time;        /* When the request started */

char *status_line;          /* Status line, if set by script */
int status;                 /* In any case */

/* Request method, two ways; also, protocol, etc.  Outside of protocol.c,
 * look, but don't touch.
 */

char *method;               /* GET, HEAD, POST, etc. */
int method_number;          /* M_GET, M_POST, etc. */

/*
    allowed is a bitvector of the allowed methods.

    A handler must ensure that the request method is one that
    it is capable of handling.  Generally modules should DECLINE
    any request methods they do not handle.  Prior to aborting the
    handler like this the handler should set r->allowed to the list
    of methods that it is willing to handle.  This bitvector is used
    to construct the "Allow:" header required for OPTIONS requests,
    and METHOD_NOT_ALLOWED and NOT_IMPLEMENTED status codes.

    Since the default_handler deals with OPTIONS, all modules can
    usually decline to deal with OPTIONS.  TRACE is always allowed,
    modules don't need to set it explicitly.

    Since the default_handler will always handle a GET, a
    module which does *not* implement GET should probably return
    METHOD_NOT_ALLOWED.  Unfortunately this means that a script GET
    handler can't be installed by mod_actions.
*/
int allowed;                /* Allowed methods - for 405, OPTIONS, etc */

int sent_bodyct;            /* byte count in stream is for body */
long bytes_sent;            /* body byte count, for easy access */
time_t mtime;               /* Time the resource was last modified */

/* HTTP/1.1 connection-level features */

int chunked;                /* sending chunked transfer-coding */
int byterange;              /* number of byte ranges */
char *boundary;             /* multipart/byteranges boundary */
const char *range;          /* The Range: header */
long clength;               /* The "real" content length */

long remaining;             /* bytes left to read */
long read_length;           /* bytes that have been read */
```

Example 10-1. The request_rec Structure (from include/httpd.h) (continued)

```
    int read_body;              /* how the request body should be read */
    int read_chunked;           /* reading chunked transfer-coding */

    /* MIME header environments, in and out.  Also, an array containing
     * environment variables to be passed to subprocesses, so people can
     * write modules to add to that environment.
     *
     * The difference between headers_out and err_headers_out is that the
     * latter are printed even on error and persist across internal redirects
     * (so the headers printed for ErrorDocument handlers will have them).
     *
     * The 'notes' table is for notes from one module to another, with no
     * other set purpose in mind...
     */

    table *headers_in;
    table *headers_out;
    table *err_headers_out;
    table *subprocess_env;
    table *notes;

    /* content_type, handler, content_encoding, content_language, and all
     * content_languages MUST be lowercased strings.  They may be pointers
     * to static strings; they should not be modified in place.
     */
    const char *content_type;   /* Break these out --- we dispatch on 'em */
    const char *handler;        /* What we *really* dispatch on          */

    const char *content_encoding;
    const char *content_language;       /* for back-compat. only -- do not use */
    array_header *content_languages;    /* array of (char*) */

    int no_cache;
    int no_local_copy;

    /* What object is being requested (either directly, or via include
     * or content-negotiation mapping).
     */

    char *unparsed_uri;         /* the uri without any parsing performed */
    char *uri;                  /* the path portion of the URI */
    char *filename;
    char *path_info;
    char *args;                 /* QUERY_ARGS, if any */
    struct stat finfo;          /* ST_MODE set to zero if no such file */
    uri_components parsed_uri;  /* components of uri, dismantled */

    /* Various other config info which may change with .htaccess files
     * These are config vectors, with one void* pointer for each module
     * (the thing pointed to being the module's business).
     */
```

Example 10-1. The request_rec Structure (from include/httpd.h) (continued)

```
    void *per_dir_config;        /* Options set in config files, etc. */
    void *request_config;        /* Notes on *this* request */

/*
 * a linked list of the configuration directives in the .htaccess files
 * accessed by this request.
 * N.B. always add to the head of the list, _never_ to the end.
 * that way, a sub request's list can (temporarily) point to a parent's list
 */
    const struct htaccess_result *htaccess;

/* Things placed at the end of the record to avoid breaking binary
 * compatibility.  It would be nice to remember to reorder the entire
 * record to improve 64-bit alignment the next time we need to break
 * binary compatibility for some other reason.
 */
    unsigned expecting_100;       /* is client waiting for a 100 response? */
};
```

The server_rec Structure

The server record contains various bits of information about the server and its operations. There are different server records for each virtual host; your handlers will be passed the correct server record at runtime, either directly in the argument list (for example, for the *child_init* handler) or indirectly in the **request_rec**, where the record can be recovered from the **server** field.

Example 10-2 gives the definition of **server_rec** as it appears in *include/httpd.h*. As was the case in the **request_rec**, the **server_rec** contains information that is useful to module writers intermixed with information that only core server routines care about. In the descriptions that follow, we skip over the fields that serve internal functions only.

In general, the fields contained within the **server_rec** are intended for reading only. Do not change them directly.

server_rec *next

> Apache maintains a linked list of all configured virtual servers, which can be accessed with the **next** field. For example, a module initializer may want to open a different log file for each virtual server:

```
void my_module_init(server_rec *main_server, pool *p)
{
    server_rec *s;
    for(s = main_server; s; s = s->next) {
        my_open_log(s, p);
    }
}
```

char *srm_confname
char *access_confname

These two fields contain the locations of the resource and access control configuration files, usually named *srm.conf* and *access.conf.* The paths contained in these fields may be absolute or may be relative to the server root. You should call *ap_server_root_relative()* (described later) to convert them into absolute paths. The path to the main server configuration file, *httpd.conf,* is stored elsewhere in a global variable named ap_server_confname.

char *server_admin

This field contains the email address of the server administrator as configured with the *ServerAdmin* directive.

char *server_hostname

This field contains the (virtual) name of the server host. It is better to use the *ap_get_server_name()* function (described later) during a request since it takes into account the status of the *UseCanonicalName* configuration directive.

unsigned short port

This field contains the port number that the (virtual) server is listening on. If the host is listening on multiple ports, this field won't reflect that fact; however, it will always contain the canonical port number to use for redirects to the host. If you just wish to recover the port that the current request was directed to, it is easier to use *ap_get_server_port()* instead. See the section "Processing Requests."

char *error_fname
FILE *error_log
int loglevel

These three fields provide information about the server error log. The pathname of the log file, either absolute or server-root relative, can be found in error_fname, while the error_log field contains a FILE* open on this file. You can write to this FILE* indirectly via the error-logging API described later under "Error Logging" in the section "Server Core Routines." It is not a good idea to write directly to this field, as it will be NULL if syslog support is enabled.

The loglevel field holds an integer between 1 and 8 which describes the severity level of messages that should be logged. It is used internally by the error-logging API to decide which messages should be logged based on the configured *LogLevel.*

In general, you should use the error-logging API rather than access these fields directly, but there are a few exceptions. One case occurs when your application needs to know if the server configuration has enabled logging via *syslog()*. This can be accomplished with the following code fragment:

```
int is_using_syslog = !strncasecmp(s->error_fname, "syslog", 6);
```

Also, you might legitimately need to check the `loglevel` field if the operation that generates the log message introduces some overhead. It makes no sense to initiate a time-consuming operation to generate an error message that is never seen!

int is_virtual

The `is_virtual` field is a flag that is set to a nonzero value if the server record applies to a virtual host.

void *module_config

This field is a list of module per-server configuration records. You should not try to manipulate this field directly but instead gain access to it via the configuration API described in the "Accessing Module Configuration Data" in Chapter 11.

void *lookup_defaults

This is an opaque data block which contains information that the Apache core uses during its configuration process. It is actually the master copy of the `per_dir_config` vector found in each request record, and contains the list of per-directory configuration information used by each module that implements its own directives. See the section "Customizing the Configuration Process" in Chapter 11 for an example of using this field.

int timeout
int keep_alive_timeout
int keep_alive_max
int keep_alive

These fields hold the integer values corresponding to the *Timeout, KeepAliveTimeout, MaxKeepAliveRequests,* and *KeepAlive* configuration directives, respectively.

array_header *names
array_header *wild_names

These fields contain the entry points into lists of alternative names for the current (virtual) server. They correspond to the canonical name of the server plus any aliases added with the *ServerAlias* directive. `names` holds only normal names, while `wild_names` lists the alternative names that contain wildcard characters, if any. You can access the contents of these lists with the Apache array API described later.

```
uid_t server_uid
gid_t server_gid
```
These two fields contain the user and group IDs under which the server's children run.

Example 10-2. The server_rec Structure (from include/httpd.h)

```
struct server_rec {

    server_rec *next;

    /* description of where the definition came from */
    const char *defn_name;
    unsigned defn_line_number;

    /* Full locations of server config info */

    char *srm_confname;
    char *access_confname;

    /* Contact information */

    char *server_admin;
    char *server_hostname;
    unsigned short port;         /* for redirects, etc. */

    /* Log files -- note that transfer log is now in the modules... */

    char *error_fname;
    FILE *error_log;
    int loglevel;

    /* Module-specific configuration for server, and defaults... */

    int is_virtual;              /* true if this is the virtual server */
    void *module_config;         /* Config vector containing pointers to
                                  * modules' per-server config structures.
                                  */
    void *lookup_defaults;       /* MIME type info, etc., before we start
                                  * checking per-directory info.
                                  */
    /* Transaction handling */

    server_addr_rec *addrs;
    int timeout;                 /* Timeout, in seconds, before we give up */
    int keep_alive_timeout;      /* Seconds we'll wait for another request */
    int keep_alive_max;          /* Maximum requests per connection */
    int keep_alive;              /* Use persistent connections? */
    int send_buffer_size;        /* size of TCP send buffer (in bytes) */

    char *path;                  /* Pathname for ServerPath */
    int pathlen;                 /* Length of path */

    array_header *names;         /* Normal names for ServerAlias servers */
    array_header *wild_names;    /* Wildcarded names for ServerAlias servers */
```

Example 10-2. The server_rec Structure (from include/httpd.h) (continued)

```
    uid_t server_uid;         /* effective user id when calling exec wrapper */
    gid_t server_gid;         /* effective group id when calling exec wrapper */

    int limit_req_line;       /* limit on size of the HTTP request line    */
    int limit_req_fieldsize;  /* limit on size of any request header field */
    int limit_req_fields;     /* limit on number of request header fields   */
};
```

The conn_rec Structure

The connection record structure, **conn_rec**, contains information that is specific to each client/server connection but not necessarily to each request (remember that recent versions of the HTTP protocol allow browsers to make multiple requests within the same TCP/IP session by issuing a *Keepalive* header). Within handlers, the current **conn_rec** is available inside the request record's **connection** field. The same server child will process all requests that are piggybacked on the same connection.

Most of the fields in the connection record are used internally by the server. Its most common use in modules is to retrieve the user's login name during authentication and to recover the client's IP address. The definition of **conn_rec** is given in Example 10-3. As before, we skip over those fields that module writers shouldn't worry about.

ap_pool *pool

> This is a resource pool that module writers can use to allocate resources that should persist for the lifetime of the connection. This is rarely necessary, and it is usually better to use the pool located in the request record for this purpose.

server_rec *server
server_rec *base_server

> These fields contain pointers to the server records for the current and base servers. If the current connection is being served by the main server, then these two pointers will be the same. Otherwise, **server** will point to the record for the current virtual host. The current host's server record is more conveniently obtained from the request record's **server** field.

BUFF *client

> The **client** field contains a **BUFF***, which is Apache's equivalent of the familiar standard I/O **FILE***. This field is used internally to read and write data to the client and may be implemented as a plain TCP socket, an SSL channel, or some other protocol such as DCE RPC. You will never use this field directly but go through Apache's I/O routines instead. These are described in detail later in this section.

```
struct sockaddr_in local_addr
struct sockaddr_in remote_addr
```
These fields contain the endpoints of the active TCP/IP socket. You might use this information to request *identd* identification from the remote host.

```
char *remote_ip
```
The `remote_ip` field contains the dotted Internet address of the client.

```
char *remote_host
```
This field may contain the DNS name of the client. The various caveats described in Chapter 9, *Perl API Reference Guide*, for the *remote_host()* method of the *Apache::Connection* class also apply here. It is almost always a better idea to use the high-level API call *ap_get_remote_host()* than to access this field directly.

```
char *remote_logname
```
This field may contain the login name of the remote user, provided that *IdentityCheck* is turned on and that the *identd* daemon is running on the user's machine (and a host of other considerations, such as the presence of firewalls between the client and host). All the caveats listed in Chapter 9 under the *remote_logname()* method of the *Apache::Connection* class apply here as well. You are strongly encouraged to take advantage of the high-level call *ap_get_remote_logname()* rather than accessing this field directly.

```
char *user
```
If an authentication method is in use for the current connection, the `user` field holds the login name provided by the user. The password cannot be recovered from this connection record, however. To get this information, you must call the high-level routine *ap_get_basic_auth_pw()*.

```
char *ap_auth_type
```
If authentication is in use for the current connection, this field will hold the name of the authentication method. At the time of this writing, the possibilities were `Basic` and `Digest`.

```
if(strcasecmp(c->ap_auth_type, "Basic")) {
    ap_log_error(APLOG_MARK, APLOG_NOERRNO|APLOG_WARN, r->server,
            "phew, I feel better now");
}
```

```
unsigned aborted
```
The `aborted` field is set to a true value if a timeout set by *ap_soft_timeout()* occurs while reading or writing to the client (see "The Timeout API" later in this chapter). This can happen, for example, when the remote user presses the browser stop button before the document is fully transmitted.

```
if(r->connection->aborted) {
    ap_log_error(APLOG_MARK, APLOG_NOERRNO|APLOG_WARN, r->server,
            "uh,oh, the client has gone away!");
}
```

signed int double_reverse

This field contains a flag indicating whether a double-reverse hostname lookup has been performed. 0 indicates that a double-reverse lookup has not been done (yet), and 1 indicates that the lookup was performed and was successful. If the field is set to -1, it means that the lookup was tried but failed. Double-reverse lookups are only performed if the configuration variable *HostnameLookups* is *On* or if an *allow* directive is configured to limit hostnames rather than IP addresses. See also the description of *ap_get_remote_host()*.

Example 10-3. The conn_rec Definition

```
struct conn_rec {

    ap_pool *pool;
    server_rec *server;
    server_rec *base_server;    /* Physical vhost this conn come in on */
    void *vhost_lookup_data;    /* used by http_vhost.c */


    /* Information about the connection itself */

    int child_num;             /* The number of the child handling conn_rec */
    BUFF *client;              /* Connection to the guy */

    /* Who is the client? */

    struct sockaddr_in local_addr;     /* local address */
    struct sockaddr_in remote_addr;    /* remote address */
    char *remote_ip;           /* Client's IP address */
    char *remote_host;         /* Client's DNS name, if known.
                                * NULL if DNS hasn't been checked,
                                * "" if it has and no address was found.
                                * N.B. Only access this though
                                * get_remote_host() */
    char *remote_logname;      /* Only ever set if doing rfc1413 lookups.
                                * N.B. Only access this through
                                * get_remote_logname() */
    char *user;                /* If an authentication check was made,
                                * this gets set to the user name.  We assume
                                * that there's only one user per connection(!)
                                */
    char *ap_auth_type;        /* Ditto. */

    unsigned aborted:1;        /* Are we still talking? */
    signed int keepalive:2;    /* Are we using HTTP Keep-Alive?
                                * -1 fatal error, 0 undecided, 1 yes */
    unsigned keptalive:1;      /* Did we use HTTP Keep-Alive? */
    signed int double_reverse:2;/* have we done double-reverse DNS?
                                * -1 yes/failure, 0 not yet, 1 yes/success */
    int keepalives;            /* How many times have we used it? */
};
```

Memory Management and Resource Pools

If you've ever developed a moderately complex C-language program, you've struggled with memory management. It's not easy to manage memory in C: failing to deallocate a data structure when you're through with it gives rise to memory leaks, and conversely, disposing of the same data structure twice is likely to lead to a crash. It's one thing to have a small memory leak in your own program. Unless the leak is very severe, the program will probably finish execution and exit normally before memory becomes tight. However, it's quite another issue to have memory management problems in a network server, which is expected to run for weeks or months at a time. Even small leaks can add up over time, and a dangling pointer or a doubly deallocated block can make the whole server crash.

The Apache server developers were aware of the challenge of memory management, and so they devised a system to make life easier both for themselves and for module writers. Instead of managing memory directly, Apache module developers take the memory they need from one or more resource pools. An Apache `pool` structure keeps track of all module memory allocations and releases all allocated blocks automatically when the lifetime of the pool has ended.

Different pools have different lifetimes: one lasts for the lifetime of a child, one for the lifetime of a request, another for the module configuration phase, and so forth. However, the nicest feature about pools is that the programmer generally doesn't need to know a pool's lifetime. Apache passes the appropriate `pool` pointer to your callback functions during the various startup, configuration, and request phases. Depending on the context, sometimes the pool is passed directly to your subroutine as an argument, and sometimes it is tucked away inside one of the other data structures needed by the subroutine, such as the `request_rec` or `conn_rec` structures.

Most memory management is performed within the various request phase handlers. In this case, the resource pool to draw from will be found inside the `request_rec`. Any resources associated with this pool will not be released until the very end of a request (after logging). This arrangement may not be suited to certain very specialized modules. For example, the *mod_autoindex* module needs to make many short-lived memory allocations while it is generating directory listings. In this case, modules can create subpools, which are private resource pools allocated from within the main resource pool. The module can allocate blocks from within its subpool and destroy the subpool when it's no longer needed. If a module screws up and forgets to deallocate its subpool, no permanent harm is done. The subpool is deleted when its parent resource pool is cleaned up at the end of the request.

Once a memory block is allocated from a pool, there is no easy way to deallocate it. Normally you will wait for the pool to expire naturally. However, if you have created a subpool to work with, you can delete the whole subpool (and all its contained memory blocks) in one fell swoop.

Memory and String Allocation Routines

All memory-handling API routines are defined in the include file *include/alloc.h*, which is brought in automatically when you include *include/httpd.h*. The routines for allocating and freeing blocks of pool memory are all named after the familiar C library functions with the prefix *ap_p* tacked onto the front.

void *ap_palloc (struct pool *p, int nbytes)

> This function works just like using *malloc()*, but you don't have to worry about calling *free()* (in fact, you should not). The memory will be cleaned up for you when the pool reaches the end of its lifetime. You must pass the *ap_palloc()* function a pointer to a preallocated pool, such as the one recovered from the request record. In this example, we create a C string large enough to accommodate *len* characters (plus terminating byte):

```
char *string = (char*)ap_palloc(r->pool, len + 1);
```

> If there is insufficient memory to satisfy your request, *ap_palloc()* will return null. You should check for this condition and take appropriate action.

void *ap_pcalloc (struct pool *p, int nbytes)

> This works just like the standard *calloc()* function; it calls *memset()* to initialize the memory to a block of '\0' bytes. In this example, we create a `hello_dir_config` structure (defined elsewhere) that is initially cleared out:

```
hello_dir_config *cfg =
    (hello_dir_config*)ap_pcalloc(p, sizeof(hello_dir_config));
```

char *ap_pstrdup (struct pool *p, const char *s)

> This function works like the standard *strdup()* function to duplicate a string, but the new string is allocated from the indicated pool:

```
char *copy = ap_pstrdup(r->pool, string);
```

char *ap_pstrndup (struct pool *p, const char *s, int n)

> This is a version of *ap_pstrdup()*, but it only allocates and copies *n* bytes.

```
char *copy = ap_pstrndup(r->pool, string, len);
```

char *ap_pstrcat (struct pool *p,...)

> This function is similar to the standard *strcat()* function, but it accepts a variable list of string arguments to join together, returning the result as a newly allocated character string. The list of strings must be NULL-terminated:

```
char *string = ap_pstrcat(r->pool, "<", html_tag, ">", NULL);
```

char *ap_psprintf (struct pool *p, const char *fmt, ...)

This function works like the standard *sprintf()*, but it is much safer than the standard version because it allocates the requested memory from the pool, rather than writing the string into a static buffer. (Standard *sprintf()* has recently triggered a number of CERT advisories for some popular pieces of Internet software.) Here is an example of the function's usage:

```
char *string = ap_psprintf(r->pool, "<%s>", html_tag);
```

char *ap_cpystrn (char *dest, const char *source, size_t maxlen)

While this function is not tied to a pool, we list it here with the other string manipulation functions. In this version of the standard *strncpy()* function, the destination string is always guaranteed to be NULL-terminated, even if the entire source string was not copied. Furthermore, the return value points to the terminating '\0' byte rather than to the beginning of the string, allowing you to check more easily for truncation. Another difference from the standard function call is that *ap_cpystrn()* does not null-fill the string, although this will be rarely noticed in practice.

```
result = ap_cpystrn(to, from, len);
if ((result - to) == len) {
    ap_log_error(APLOG_MARK, APLOG_NOERRNO|APLOG_WARNING,
                 server_rec, "truncation during ap_cpystrn()");
}
```

int ap_snprintf (char *dest, size_t len, const char *fmt, ...)

We again list this string manipulation function here, although it is not directly tied to a pool. This is a version of the *snprintf()* function, which comes with some versions of the standard C library. Because *snprintf()* isn't available on all platforms, the Apache version provides portability.

```
char string[MAX_STR_LEN];
ap_snprintf(string, sizeof(string), "<%s>", html_tag);
```

Subpool Management

You will probably never need to manage your own subpools, since there should always be a pool available during the various phases that will be cleaned up when the time is right. However, if your module is allocating a considerable amount of memory, you may need tighter management over when pools are released. This you can do by allocating and destroying private subpools.

struct pool *ap_make_sub_pool (struct pool *p)

Given an existing pool, this call returns a subpool. You can then allocate blocks of memory from within the subpool using the routines described above. When the parent pool is released, your subpool will be destroyed along with it, or you can destroy the pool yourself using the routine described next. A new pool can also be created without a parent pool by passing in a

NULL argument. In this case, such code will be completely responsible for destroying the new pool.

void ap_destroy_pool (pool *p)

This function destroys the pool or subpool along with all its contents. Once a pool has been destroyed, be careful not to use any pointers to memory blocks that were allocated from within it!

void ap_clear_pool (struct pool *p)

ap_clear_pool() destroys the contents of the pool but leaves the pool itself intact. The pool is returned to its initial, empty state and can be used to allocate new blocks.

Getting Information About Pools

Although these functions are hardly ever needed, they are included here for the sake of completeness.

pool *ap_find_pool(const void *block)

Given a memory block, this function will return a pointer to the resource pool that it belongs to. The function will return unpredictable results if you pass it a pointer that was not allocated with the pool API.

int ap_pool_is_ancestor (pool *a, pool *b);

This function returns a true value if pool *b* is a subpool that was originally allocated from pool *a*.

The Array API

The HTTP protocol is filled with lists: lists of language codes, HTTP header fields, MIME types, and so forth. In general, it's not possible to predict the size of the lists in advance, and some of them can be quite large. In order to deal with this, Apache provides an array API that allows you to create lists of arbitrary type and length, much like the dynamic arrays provided by Perl. More complex data structures, such as the `table` type (described later in this chapter), are built on top of Apache arrays.

The array_header Type

The core of the array API is the `array_header` structure, whose definition you can find in *include/alloc.h*:

```
typedef struct {
    ap_pool *pool;
    int elt_size;
    int nelts;
```

```
    int nalloc;
    char *elts;
} array_header;
```

The fields you'll use are the `nelts` field, which holds the current number of elements in the array, and the `elts` field, which contains a pointer to the data in the array. `elts` is declared as a `char*` for the convenience of internal routines. You will need to cast it to a pointer of the correct type before you can access elements safely. You should not need to worry about the other fields, but note that the `array_header` contains a pointer back to the resource pool from which it was allocated. This means that both the array header and its contents will be freed automatically when the pool reaches the end of its lifetime.

Creating and Manipulating Arrays

Here are the API calls for working with arrays. Although array elements can be of any arbitrary type, we use `char*` strings in our examples for the sake of simplicity.

*array_header *ap_make_array (pool* p, int nelts, int elt_size)*

> This function allocates a new array from resource pool *p* with elements *elt_size* bytes in length and enough initial space to hold *nelts* elements. If successful, the call will return a pointer to a new `array_header`.
>
> If the array needs to grow beyond its initial length, the array API will resize it automatically. This means that you can safely allocate an array with zero elements.
>
> Here is an example of creating a new array with an initial length of 5 elements. Each element is large enough to hold a `char*` string pointer:
>
> ```
> array_header *arr = ap_make_array(p, 5, sizeof(char*));
> ```

*void *ap_push_array (array_header *arr)*

> The *ap_push_array()* function is used to add a new element to the end of the list. It works a little differently than you would expect. Instead of allocating the new element first and then pushing it onto the end of the list, you call *ap_push_array()* to allocate the element for you. It will create a new element of the correct size within the array's pool and return a pointer to the new element. You cast the returned `void*` to the data type of your choice and copy your data in.
>
> Here's an example in which we add a new element containing the string *text/html* to the end of the array. The call to *ap_push_array()* allocates room for a new `char*` pointer, while the subsequent call to *ap_pstrdup()* allocates room for the string itself and copies its address into the element. This example assumes that the array was created with *ap_make_array()* using an *elt_size* determined by `sizeof(char *)`.

```
char **new;
new = (char **)ap_push_array(arr);
*new = ap_pstrdup(r->pool, "text/html");

/* or in a single line */

*(char **)ap_push_array(arr) = ap_pstrdup(r->pool, "text/html");
```

*void ap_array_cat (array_header *dst, const array_header *src)*

> If you wish to add the elements of one array to another, the *ap_array_cat()* function will handle the job. It takes two **array_header** pointers as arguments and concatenates the second onto the end of the first. The first will grow as necessary. Note that the *elt_size* used to create each array should be the same; otherwise, unpredictable results may occur.

```
ap_array_cat(arr, other_arr);
```

*array_header *ap_append_arrays (pool *p, const array_header *a1, const array_header *a2)*

> This function is similar to *ap_array_cat()* but creates a brand new array in the indicated pool. The resulting array will be the concatenation of *a1* and *a2*.

```
array_header *new = ap_append_arrays(p, one_array, another_array);
```

*char *ap_array_pstrcat (pool *p, const array_header *arr, const char sep)*

> This function builds a new string using the elements of the given array. If *sep* is non-**NULL**, it will be inserted as a delimiter between the substrings.

```
char *table_cells = ap_array_pstrcat(r->pool, cells, ' ');
```

*array_header *ap_copy_array (pool *p, const array_header *src)*

> The *ap_copy_array()* function creates a new array in the indicated pool, then copies into it all the elements in *src*.

```
array_header *new = ap_copy_array(p, arr);
```

*array_header *ap_copy_array_hdr (pool *p, const array_header *src)*

> This function is similar to *ap_copy_array()* but implements a deferred copy. Initially only a new header is created which points back to the data of the original array. Only if the new copy is extended with an *ap_push_array()* or *ap_array_cat()* is the old data copied. If the array is never extended, it avoids the overhead of a full copy.

```
array_header *new = ap_copy_array_hdr(p, arr);
```

Accessing Array Elements

There are no functions in the API to fetch specific elements or to iterate over the list. However, it is simple enough to pull the array out of the **elts** field and type-cast it into a C array of the proper type. You can use the **nelts** field to keep track of the number of elements inside the array. In this example, we iterate over the entire array, printing out its contents (using the *ap_rprintf()* function, which we will discuss later):

```
char **list = (char**)arr->elts;
for(i = 0; i < arr->nelts; i++) {
    ap_rprintf(r, "item %d -> %s\n", i, list[i]);
}
```

Changing an item in the array is done in a similar way:

```
((char **)arr->elts)[2] = "transmission aborted"
```

If you wish to clear the array, simply set **nelts** to zero:

```
arr->nelts = 0;
```

The Table API

Apache provides a general API for creating and maintaining lookup tables. Apache tables are ubiquitous, used for everything from storing the current request's outgoing HTTP headers to maintaining the list of environment variables passed to subprocesses.

Tables are similar to Perl hashes in that they are lists of key/value pairs. However, unlike a Perl hash, keys are case-insensitive, and a single key may correspond to a list of several values.* In addition, Apache table keys and values are always strings; arbitrary data types cannot be used.

The table and table_entry Data Types

Currently, a table is an Apache array containing array elements of the **table_entry** data type (defined in *include/alloc.h*):

```
typedef struct {
    char *key;    /* the key */
    char *val;    /* the value */
} table_entry;
```

When fetching or setting the value of a key, Apache searches for the key using a simple linear search. Since most tables are short, this usually doesn't impose a significant overhead. You will usually not want to access the **table_entry** directly, but use API function calls to manipulate the keys and values for you. If you do read directly from the **table_entry**, a note in the include file indicates that you should check the key for null. This is because the **table_entry** may be made part of a more sophisticated hash table in the future.

---

* Despite the differences between Perl hashes and Apache tables, the Perl API allows programmers to access tables via tied Perl hashes. See "The Apache::Table Class" in Chapter 9.

The `table` structure itself is a private data type intended to be accessed via an opaque `table *`. If you want to peek at its definition, you can find it in *include/ alloc.c*. It is equally straightforward:

```
struct table {
    array_header a;
#ifdef MAKE_TABLE_PROFILE
    void *creator;
#endif
};
```

The `MAKE_TABLE_PROFILE` define is part of Apache's debugging code and is usually undefined, so `table` is really just an array header.

Creating and Copying Tables

If you need a table of key/value pairs that is private to your own module, you can use these API routines to create it. You can either create a new empty table or start with one that is already defined and make a copy of it. These functions are defined in the *include/alloc.h* file, which is automatically included when you bring in *include/httpd.h*.

table *ap_make_table (pool *p, int nelts)
> `ap_make_table()` creates a new empty table, given a resource pool pointer and an estimate of the number of elements you expect to add. If the *nelts* argument is nonzero, that number of `table_entry` tables will be pre-allocated for efficiency. Regardless of its initial size, the table grows as necessary to accommodate new entries and table merging operations.
>
> ```
> Accessitable *my_table = ap_make_table(p, 25);
> ```

table *ap_copy_table (pool *p, const table *t)
> This function takes a resource pool and an existing table and makes a replica of the table, returning a pointer to the copy. You can then change the contents of the copy without modifying the original. In this example, we make a copy of the `headers_in` table:
>
> ```
> table *my_headers = ap_copy_table(r->pool, r->headers_in);
> ```

Getting and Setting Table Values

These routines allow you to add new entries to the table, to change existing ones, and to retrieve entries.

const char *ap_table_get (const table *t, const char *key)
> Given a table pointer and a key, `ap_table_get()` returns the value of the entry at that key as a `char *`. If there are multiple values for that particular key, the function will only return the first one it finds, which will be the first entry added.

In this example, we recover the string value of the incoming *User-agent* header:

```
const char *ua = ap_table_get(r->headers_in, "User-agent");
```

To iterate through the multiple values for the same key, use the *ap_table_do()* function described later in this section.

*void ap_table_set (table *t, const char *key, const char *val)*

ap_table_set() sets the entry named by *key* to the character string in *val*. If an entry with the same key already exists, its value is replaced. Otherwise, a new entry is created. If more than one entry has the same key, the extraneous ones are deleted, making the key single-valued.

Internally, Apache calls *ap_pstrdup()* on the key and the value and stores copies of them in the table. This means that you are able to change or dispose of the original variables without worrying about disrupting the table.

Here's an example of using this function to set the outgoing headers field *Location* to the string *http://www.modperl.com/*. Because *Location* is a single-valued field, *ap_table_set()* is the correct call to use:

```
ap_table_set(r->headers_out, "Location", "http://www.modperl.com/");
```

*void ap_table_setn (table *t, const char *key, const char *val)*

This function behaves the same as *ap_table_set()*, but the character strings for *key* and *val* are not copied with *ap_pstrdup()*. You must ensure that the strings remain valid for the lifetime of the table. The previous example is a good candidate for *ap_table_setn()*, as it uses static strings for both the key and value.

*void ap_table_add (table *t, const char *key, const char *val)*

This function is similar to *ap_table_set()*, but existing entries with the same key are not replaced. Instead, the new entry is added to the end of the list, making the key multivalued.

Internally, Apache calls *ap_pstrdup()* on the key and the value, allowing you to change or dispose of the original variables without worrying about disrupting the table.

This example adds several *Set-cookie* fields to the outgoing HTTP headers table:

```
for(i=0; cookies[i]; i++) {
    ap_table_add(r->headers_out, "Set-cookie", cookies[i]);
}
```

*void ap_table_addn (table *t, const char *key, const char *val)*

This function behaves like *ap_table_add()*, but *key* and *val* are not duplicated before storing them into the table. This function saves a little time and memory if you are working with static strings.

void ap_table_merge (table *t, const char *key, const char *val)

> *ap_table_merge()* merges a new key value into the existing entry by appending it to what's already there. This is used for comma-delimited header fields such as *Content-language*. For example, this series of calls will result in a value of **en, fr, sp** in the *Content-language* field:

```
ap_table_merge(r->headers_out, "Content-language", "en");
ap_table_merge(r->headers_out, "Content-language", "fr");
ap_table_merge(r->headers_out, "Content-language", "sp");
```

> Like *ap_table_set()*, the key and value are copied using *ap_pstrdup()* before moving them into the table.

void ap_table_mergen (table *t, const char *key, const char *val)

> This function is the same as *ap_table_merge*, but the *key* and *val* arguments are not copied with *ap_pstrdup()* before entering them into the table.

void ap_table_unset (table *t, const char *key)

> *ap_table_unset()* deletes all entries having the indicated key. This example removes the *Referer* field from the incoming headers, possibly in preparation for making an anonymous proxy request (see Chapter 7):

```
ap_table_unset(r->headers_in, "Referer");
```

void ap_table_do (int (*comp)(void *, const char *, const char *),
void *rec, const table *t,...);

> *ap_table_get()* and *ap_table_getn()* work well for single-valued keys, but there are a few instances in which keys are not unique. To access all the values of these keys, you will have to use *ap_table_do()* to iterate over the table.

> As its prototype indicates, this function is more complicated than the ones we've seen before. The function's first argument is a pointer to a callback function that will be called during the iteration process. The second argument is a **void *** that can be used to pass some arbitrary information to the callback. The third argument is the **table *** itself. This is followed by a variable number of **char *** key arguments, terminated by a null. *ap_table_do()* will iterate over the table, invoking the callback routine only when a table entries' key matches a key in the given list. If no keys are given, the function will invoke the callback routine for all of the table entries.

> The callback function should have this function prototype:

```
int callback(void *rec, const char *key, const char *value);
```

> The first argument corresponds to the **void *** argument passed to *ap_table_do()*, and the second and third arguments are the key and value of the current table entry. The callback should do whatever work it needs to do (for example, copying the value into an Apache array), and return a true value. The callback can return 0 in order to abort *ap_table_do()* prematurely.

Here's a callback that simply prints out the key name and value without performing further processing:

```
static int header_trace(void *data, const char *key, const char *val)
{
    request_rec *r = (request_rec *)data;
    ap_rprintf(r, "Header Field `%s' == `%s'\n", key, val);
    return TRUE;
}
```

Here's how the callback can be used to print out the contents of the outgoing headers table:

```
ap_table_do(header_trace, r, r->headers_out, NULL);
```

And in this example, the callback is only invoked for the *Content-type* and *Content-length* fields:

```
ap_table_do(header_trace, (void*)r, r->headers_out,
            "Content-type", "Content-length", NULL);
```

Other Table Functions

Here are a few miscellaneous table functions that don't fit into the previous categories:

table *ap_overlay_tables (pool *p, const table *overlay, const table *base)
> This function takes the contents of the table at *overlay* and adds it to the table at *base*. Entries in *overlay* that don't exist in **base** are added to *base*. Entries that already exist in *base* are overwritten. You can use *ap_overlay_tables()* to perform a bulk update of a table. This example overlays the fields listed in **my_headers** onto the table of outgoing headers:
>
> ```
> table *new_table = _ap_overlay_tables(r->pool, my_headers, r->headers_out);
> ```

array_header *ap_table_elts (table *t)
> If you wish to access the contents of the table directly, you can call the *ap_table_elts()* function (it's a preprocessor macro, actually). It will return an **array_header ***, which you can then iterate through, casting each element to a **table_entry**.
>
> ```
> array_header *arr = ap_table_elts(my_table);
> ```

int ap_is_empty_table (table *t)
> This function (it's a preprocessor macro, actually) returns true if there are no entries in the given *table*, or false otherwise.
>
> ```
> if(!ap_is_empty_table(my_table)) {
>         /* this table has one or more elements */
> }
> ```

void ap_clear_table (table *t)
> The *ap_clear_table()* function clears all entries from the table. Example:
>
> ```
> ap_clear_table(my_table);
> ```

Processing Requests

Now that we've covered Apache's major data types and the API for manipulating them, we turn to the functions you'll use routinely within your handlers to process the incoming request and produce a response.

Getting Information About the Transaction

You can get most of the information about the incoming request by reading it from the request record, server record, or connection record. The exception to this rule are a handful of routines that require active participation on the part of Apache to recover information about the remote host and user.

These calls are declared in the header file *http_core.h* unless specified otherwise:

const char *ap_get_remote_host(conn_rec *conn, void *dir_config, int type)
> This routine returns the DNS name or dotted IP address of the remote host. The first argument is a pointer to the connection record, usually recovered from the request record. The second argument points to the per-directory configuration record, which can also be retrieved from the request record. *ap_get_ remote_host()* uses the directory configuration pointer to examine the value of the *HostnameLookups* directive. If you pass NULL for this argument, *ap_get_ remote_host()* will assume a value of *Off* for *HostnameLookups*, returning the dotted IP address of the remote host.
>
> The third argument passed to *ap_get_remote_host()* is an integer constant indicating the type of lookup you wish to perform. There are four possibilities:

REMOTE_HOST
> If this argument is specified, Apache will try to look up the DNS name of the remote host. This lookup may fail if the Apache configuration directive *HostNameLookups* is set to *Off* or the hostname cannot be determined by a DNS lookup, in which case the function will return null.

REMOTE_NAME
> When called with this argument, the function will return the DNS name of the remote host if possible, or the dotted decimal representation of the client's IP address otherwise. The function will also return the IP address if *HostNameLookups* is set to *Off*. This is the most frequently used lookup type and the default in the Perl API.

REMOTE_NOLOOKUP
> When this argument is specified, *ap_get_remote_host()* will not perform a new DNS lookup. If a successful lookup was done earlier in the request, the hostname cached in the connection record will be returned. Otherwise, the function returns the dotted decimal representation of the client's IP address.

REMOTE_DOUBLE_REV

> This argument will trigger a double-reverse DNS lookup. Apache will first call DNS to return the hostname that maps to the IP number of the remote host. It will then make another call to map the returned hostname back to a set of IP addresses. If any of the new IP addresses that are returned match the original one, then the function returns the hostname. Otherwise, it returns NULL. The reason for this baroque procedure is that standard DNS lookups are susceptible to DNS spoofing in which a remote machine temporarily assumes the apparent identity of a trusted host. Double-reverse DNS lookups make spoofing much harder, and are recommended if you are using the hostname to distinguish between trusted clients and untrusted ones. For this very reason, REMOTE_DOUBLE_REV is always used for access checking when hostnames are used, rather than IP addresses. Unfortunately, double-reverse DNS lookups are also more expensive.
>
> Unlike the other lookup types, REMOTE_DOUBLE_REV overrides the value of *HostNameLookups* and forces the lookup to occur if the result is not already cached.

Here is a typical example of using *ap_get_remote_host()* to return either the DNS name of the remote host or its dotted IP address:

```
char *remote_host = ap_get_remote_host(r->connection,
                                       r->per_dir_config, REMOTE_NAME);
```

const char *ap_get_remote_logname (request_rec *r)

> This function returns the login name of the remote user or null if that information could not be determined. This generally works only if the remote user is logged into a Unix or VMS host and that machine is running the *identd* daemon (which implements a protocol known as RFC 1413). Its single argument is the current request record, from which it derives both the connection record and the per-directory configuration information (unlike *ap_get_remote_host()*, which requires you to split out that information yourself).
>
> The success of the call also depends on the status of the *IdentityCheck* configuration directive. Since identity checks can adversely impact Apache's performance, this directive is off by default and the routine will return null.

```
const char *remote_logname = ap_get_remote_logname(r);
```

const char *ap_get_server_name(const request_rec *r)

> The *ap_get_server_name()* function will return the server's name as a character string. The name returned is the server's "public" name suitable for incorporation into self-referencing URLs. If the request was directed to a virtual host, it will be this host's name that is returned. Otherwise, the function result will be the main host's name, as given by the *ServerName* directive. If there is no *ServerName* directive, then the value returned will be the same as that returned by the system's *hostname* command.

*unsigned int ap_get_server_port(const request_rec *r)*

> This function returns the port number that the request was directed to, taking into account the default port and the virtual host. The port number returned by this function can be incorporated into self-referencing URLs.

*int ap_method_number_of(const char *method)*

> (Declared in the header file *http_protocol.h*.) This function returns the integer method number corresponding to the given *method* string.

```
int methnum = ap_method_number_of(method);
if (methnum == M_INVALID) {
    return "Unknown method!";
}
```

Getting Information About the Server

Several API routines provide you with information about the server's current configuration. This information tends to remain the same from request to request. For historical reasons, these routines are distributed among *http_config.h*, *http_core.h*, and *httpd.h*.

*char *ap_server_root_relative (pool *p, char *fname)*

> (Declared in the header file *http_config.h*.) Given a resource pool *p* and a relative file path *fname*, this routine prepends the path configured by *ServerRoot* to the file path and returns it as a new string. If an absolute file path is passed in, that value is returned, untouched. You can use *ap_server_root_relative()* to resolve relative pathnames to absolute paths beneath the server root directory or pass it an empty string to return the server root itself.

```
/* simply returns ServerRoot */
char *ServerRoot = ap_server_root_relative(r->pool, "");

/* returns $ServerRoot/logs/my.log */
char *log = ap_server_root_relative(r->pool, "logs/my.log");

/* returns /tmp/file.tmp */
char *tmpfile = ap_server_root_relative(r->pool, "/tmp/file.tmp");
```

*const char *ap_default_type (request_rec *r)*

> (Declared in the header file *http_core.h*.) This function returns the value of the *DefaultType* directive or **text/plain** if not configured.

```
const char *type = ap_default_type(r);
```

*const char *ap_get_server_version ()*

> (Declared in the header file *httpd.h*.) This function returns the server version string. This is the same string that appears in the outgoing HTTP *Server* header.

```
const char *server_version = ap_get_server_version();
```

const char * ap_get_server_built (void)
> (Declared in the header file *httpd.h*.) This function returns a date stamp indicating when the main server image was compiled.

void ap_add_version_component (const char *component)
> (Declared in the header file *httpd.h*.) When a module is considered a major component of the server, this function can be used to add the module name and version number to the server version string. It should be called from within a module init handler.
>
> ```
> ap_add_version_component("mod_perl/2.20");
> ```
>
> This will append a space followed by the string mod_perl/2.20 to the end of the server version string that Apache returns to clients.

Sending Data to the Client

Content handlers are responsible for sending the HTTP headers to the client followed by the contents of the document itself (if any). The functions listed in this section provide the interface for sending data to the client. In addition to handling the details of writing the information to the outgoing TCP connection, Apache keeps track of the number of bytes sent, updating the bytes_sent field of the request record each time one of these calls is made. In general, the calls return the number of bytes successfully sent to the client or EOF (-1) if the client unexpectedly closed the connection.

Because it's possible for the client to hang while accepting data from the server, you should bracket your writes with calls to *ap_hard_timeout()* or *ap_soft_timeout()* to time out broken connections or extraordinarily slow connections. See "The Timeout API" later in this chapter for more details.

The declarations for these functions can all be found in the include file *http_protocol.h*. They all begin with the prefix *ap_r*, where the "r" stands for "request_rec," a required argument for each call.

void ap_send_http_header (request_rec *r)
> This function sends the status line and all HTTP headers, building them up from the contents of the request record's headers_out and err_headers_out tables, along with various fields including content_type and content_encoding. Certain headers are generated by *ap_send_http_header()* that are not related to the request record, such as *Server* and *Date*.

int ap_rwrite (const void *buf, int nbyte, request_rec *r)
> This function will send *nbyte* bytes of the contents of the data buffer buf to the client. The function result is the number of bytes actually sent or -1 if an error occurred before any bytes could be sent.

```
      if ((sent = ap_rwrite(buffer, len, r)) < 0) {
          ap_log_error(APLOG_MARK, APLOG_NOERRNO|APLOG_WARNING,
                       r->server, "error during ap_rwrite()");
      }
```

int ap_rputs (const char *str, request_rec *r)

This function will send a string of arbitrary length to the client, returning the number of bytes actually sent.

```
ap_rputs(html_tag, r);
```

int ap_rvputs (request_rec *r,...)

The *ap_rvputs()* function works just like *ap_rputs()*, but it accepts a variable list of string arguments, which must be NULL-terminated.

```
ap_rvputs(r, "<", html_tag, ">", NULL);
```

int ap_rputc (int c, request_rec *r)

This function is used to send a single character to the client, similar to the standard I/O library function *putc()*. The function returns the character on success, EOF (-1) on failure.

```
ap_rputc('<', r);
ap_rputs(html_tag, r);
ap_rputc('>', r);
```

int ap_rprintf (request_rec *r, const char *fmt,...)

This function works like the standard *printf()* function, but the formatted string is sent to the client. In this example, the username used for authentication is incorporated into the document sent down the wire. The function returns the number of characters sent.

```
ap_rprintf(r, "Hello %s", r->connection->user);
```

void ap_send_size (size_t size, request_rec *r)

This function converts the file size given in `size` into a formatted string and sends the string to the client. The size given in the string will be in units of bytes, kilobytes, or megabytes, depending on the size of the file. This function is used in *mod_autoindex* to display the size of files in automatic directory listings, and by *mod_include* to implement the *fsize* directive.

```
ap_rputs("File size: ");
ap_send_size(r->finfo.st_size, r);
```

int ap_rflush (request_rec *r)

This call causes Apache to flush the outgoing socket connection, sending any buffered data down the wire to the client. You can use this function to display a partial page or, in a server push application, to display a new page of a multipart document. Don't use it more often than you need to, however, or overall performance will degrade.

Sending Files to the Client

As we learned in Chapter 4, sending a plain file over HTTP requires a few more considerations than one might think. Here we list the C API functions upon which the *Apache::File* module is built:

*int ap_set_content_length (request_rec *r, long length)*

This method sets the outgoing *Content-length* header based on the *length* argument. By using this method, you avoid the hassle of converting the *long* value to a string, along with saving a few keystrokes. The return value is always zero and can be safely ignored.

```
(void)ap_set_content_length(r, r->finfo.st_size);
```

*void ap_set_etag (request_rec *r)*

This method is used to set the outgoing *ETag* header, described in Chapter 3 in the section "The HTTP Protocol." Use this if your content handler is serving static files. Sending the entity tag allows HTTP/1.1–compliant clients to intelligently cache documents locally and only update them when they change on the server.

```
ap_set_etag(r);
```

*time_t ap_update_mtime (request_rec *r, time_t dependency_mtime)*

(Declared in the header file *http_request.h*.) Browsers will cache static documents locally and update them only when the server indicates they have changed. They do this by comparing the current document's HTTP *Last-modified* field to the value of this field when the document was last cached. Apache derives the *Last-modified* field from the request record's `mtime` field, which by default is set to the filesystem modification time of the requested file. This default is appropriate for a document that is a simple static file but not a document that is created dynamically, for example, a server-side include file that depends on one or more configuration files.

In such cases, you can use this function to set the `mtime` field to reflect the appropriate modification time, taking into account any of the document's dependencies on configuration files and other resources. Its two arguments are the request record and `dependency_mtime`. The `mtime` field will be updated if and only if the current `mtime` is older than the `dependency_mtime`. Therefore, if the final document depends on several configuration files, it is safe to call *ap_update_mtime()* once with the modification times of each configuration file. At the end of this series of calls the `mtime` field will be set to the most recent date, allowing the *Last-modified* field to accurately reflect the modification time of the requested document. Of course, the true modification time of the requested file as reported by the filesystem is unaffected by this maneuver.

This function's return value is the value of the updated `mtime`. If your handler is serving static files without modifying them en route, you will not need to call this function because Apache will already have set `mtime` appropriately. Before sending the headers, you should also be sure to call *ap_set_last_modified()* (discussed next) in order to use the value of `mtime` to create the *Last-modified* field in the outgoing headers table.

In the following example, we update the file's modification time from a dependency on a configuration file named *templates.conf*:

```
struct stat conf_info;
char* conf_file = server_root_relative(r->pool, "conf/templates.conf");
if (stat(conf_file, &conf_info) == 0) {
    ap_update_mtime(r, conf_info.st_mtime);
}
ap_set_last_modified(r);
```

*void ap_set_last_modified (request_rec *r)*

This method is used to set the *Last-modified* header using the value of `r->mtime`. If `mtime` is in the future, the header field will not be modified. This function should be called whenever you are serving static files or server-side include files and want the client to be able to cache the document contents locally. You might also want to use this function, in conjunction with *ap_update_mtime()*, if you are creating documents from database records and have some sort of timestamp in the records that enables you to determine when the data was last changed.

```
ap_set_last_modified(r);
```

See also *ap_update_mtime()*.

*int ap_meets_conditions (request_rec *r)*

As described in Chapter 9 in "The Apache::File Class," the *ap_meets_conditions()* function is used to implement "conditional GET" semantics.

```
if((rc = ap_meets_conditions(r) != OK) {
    return rc;
}
```

*int ap_discard_request_body (request_rec *r)*

Also described in Chapter 9, this utility function is used to throw away the request body.

```
if((rc = ap_discard_request_body(r) != OK) {
    return rc;
}
```

*long ap_send_fd (FILE *f, request_rec *r)*

The *ap_send_fd()* function sends the contents of the file pointed to by `FILE*` to the client and returns the number of bytes transmitted. This is a useful way to return a file to the client if you don't need to modify it on the fly. In this example, we open the file requested by the URI using the *ap_pfopen()* call. If successful, we send its contents, then close the file.

```
FILE *f = ap_pfopen(r->pool, r->filename, "r");
if (f == NULL) {
    return NOT_FOUND;
}
ap_send_fd(f, r);
ap_pfclose(r->pool, f);
```

long ap_send_ fd_length (FILE *f, request_rec *r, long length)

> This function works like *ap_send_fd()*, but only *length* bytes of data are sent. If you pass a negative value for *length*, the entire file will be sent, which, in fact, is what *ap_send_fd()* does internally. The function result is the number of bytes sent, or -1 if an error occurred before any bytes could be sent.

Reading the Request Body

Apache automatically reads all the incoming request header fields, stopping at the carriage-return/linefeed pair that terminates the HTTP header. This information is used to set up the **request_rec**, **server_rec**, and **connection_rec** structures. The server will not automatically read the request body, the optional portion of the request which may contain fill-out form fields or uploaded documents.

Many custom handlers will be able to do their work directly from the information stored in the **request_rec** and **server_rec**. The exception is content handlers, which frequently need to process the incoming request body submitted by the POST, PUT, and possibly other methods.

There are two complications when reading the request body. The first is the possibility that the remote client will break the connection before it has sent all the data it has declared it is sending. For this reason you have to set a timeout during the read so that the handler does not hang indefinitely. The timeout API is discussed later in this chapter. The second is the existence of the HTTP/1.1 "chunked" data type, in which the data is transmitted in smallish chunks, each preceded by a byte count. Sending chunked content data is different from submitting the request body normally because there is no *Content-length* header in the request to tell you in advance how many bytes to expect. In general, modules should request a client read policy of **REQUEST_CHUNKED_ERROR** to force the browser to use non-chunked (standard) data transfer mode.

You should set a hard timeout prior to making the first client data read by calling the *ap_hard_timeout()* function described later. To deal properly with chunked data, you will establish a "read policy" chosen from among the following constants defined in *include/httpd.conf*:

REQUEST_NO_BODY

> This is the simplest policy of all. It causes the request body API functions to return a 413 "HTTP request entity too large" error if the submitted request has any content data at all!

REQUEST_CHUNKED_ERROR

This is the next simplest policy. The request body API functions will allow the browser to submit ordinary content data but will reject attempts to send chunked data, with a 411 "HTTP length required" error. If the client follows the recommendations of the HTTP/1.1 protocol, it will resubmit the content using the nonchunked method. This read policy is the recommended method and guarantees that you will always get a *Content-length* header if there is a request body.

REQUEST_CHUNKED_DECHUNK

If this read policy is specified, Apache will accept both chunked and non-chunked data. If the request is chunked, it will buffer it and return to you the number of bytes you request in *ap_get_client_block()* (described later in this section).

REQUEST_CHUNKED_PASS

Under this read policy, Apache will accept both chunked and nonchunked data. If the data is chunked, no attempt is made to buffer it. Your calls to *ap_get_client_block()* must be prepared to receive a buffer-load of data exactly as long as the chunk length.

The Apache request body API consists of three functions:

*int ap_setup_client_block (request_rec *r, int read_policy)*

Before reading any data from the client, you must call *ap_setup_client_block()*. This tells Apache you are ready to read from the client and sets up its internal state (in the request record) to keep track of where you are in the read process. The function has two arguments: the current **request_rec** and the read policy selected from the constants in the preceding list. This function will return OK if Apache was successful in setting up for the read or an HTTP status code if an error was encountered. If an error result code is returned, you should use it as the status value that is returned from your handler.

The error codes that can be generated depend on the read policy you specify. If REQUEST_CHUNKED_ERROR was specified, then this call will return HTTP_LENGTH_REQUIRED if the client tries to submit a chunked request body. If REQUEST_NO_BODY was specified, then this function will return HTTP_REQUEST_ENTITY_TOO_LARGE if any request body is present. HTTP_BAD_REQUEST will be returned for a variety of client errors, such as sending a non-numeric *Content-length* field.

A side effect of *ap_setup_client_block()* is to convert the value of *Content-length* into an integer and store it in the **remaining** field of the **request_rec**.

*int ap_should_client_block (request_rec *r)*

Just before beginning to read from the client, you must call *ap_should_client_block()*. It will return a Boolean value indicating whether you should go ahead and read, or abort. Despite its name, this function is more useful for the information it provides to the browser than for the status information it returns to you. When the HTTP/1.1 protocol is in use, *ap_should_client_block()* transmits a 100 "Continue" message to the waiting browser, telling it that the time has come to transmit its content.

*long ap_get_client_block (request_rec *r, char *buffer, int bufsiz)*

This is the function that actually reads data from the client. You provide the current request record, a buffer of the appropriate size, and a count of the maximum number of bytes you wish to receive. *ap_get_client_block()* will read up to the specified number of bytes and return the count received. If you are handling nonchunked data, do not try to read more than the number of bytes declared in *Content-length* because this may cause the attempted read to block indefinitely.

In the code example shown in Example 10-4, we begin by calling *ap_setup_client_block()* to convert the *Content-length* header to an integer and store the value in the `remaining` field of the `request_rec`. We then use the value of `remaining` to allocate a buffer, `rbuf`, large enough to hold the entire contents. We next set up a hard timeout and then enter a loop in which we call *ap_get_client_block()* repeatedly, transferring the read data to the buffer piece by piece. The length of each piece we read is at most the value of `HUGE_STRING_LEN`, a constant defined in *httpd.h*. The timeout alarm is reset with *ap_reset_timeout()* after each successful read. When the data has been read completely, we call *ap_kill_timeout()* to turn off the timeout alarm, and return.

Notice that we call *ap_setup_client_block()* with a read policy of `REQUEST_CHUNKED_ERROR`. This makes the program logic simpler because it forces the client to use the nonchunked transfer method.

Example 10-4. Chunked Client Input

```
static int util_read(request_rec *r, const char **rbuf)
{
    int rc;

    if ((rc = ap_setup_client_block(r, REQUEST_CHUNKED_ERROR)) != OK) {
        return rc;
    }

    if (ap_should_client_block(r)) {
        char argsbuffer[HUGE_STRING_LEN];
        int rsize, len_read, rpos=0;
        long length = r->remaining;
        *rbuf = ap_pcalloc(r->pool, length + 1);

        ap_hard_timeout("util_read", r);
```

Example 10-4. Chunked Client Input (continued)

```
        while ((len_read =
                ap_get_client_block(r, argsbuffer, sizeof(argsbuffer))) > 0) {
            ap_reset_timeout(r);
            if ((rpos + len_read) > length) {
                rsize = length - rpos;
            }
            else {
                rsize = len_read;
            }
            memcpy((char*)*rbuf + rpos, argsbuffer, rsize);
            rpos += rsize;
        }

        ap_kill_timeout(r);
    }

    return rc;
}
```

No mainstream web client currently uses the chunked data transfer method, so we have not yet had the occasion to write code to handle it. Should chunked data transfer become more widely adopted, check the *www.modperl.com* site for code examples illustrating this aspect of the API.

Because POST requests are used almost exclusively to submit the contents of fill-out forms, you'd think that there would be an API specially designed for recovering and parsing this information. Unfortunately there isn't, so you'll have to roll your own.* Example 10-5 defines a function called *read_post()* that shows you the basic way to do this. You pass *read_post()* the request record and an empty table pointer. The function reads in the request body, parses the URL-encoded form data, and fills the table up with the recovered key/value pairs. It returns one of the error codes OK or DECLINED, although this is just for our convenience and not something required by the Apache API.

The example begins by defining a constant named DEFAULT_ENCTYPE that contains the standard MIME type for POSTed fill-out forms. Next we define the *read_post()* function. *read_post()* examines the request record's method_number field to ensure that this is a POST request. If not, it just returns OK without modifying the passed table. *read_post()* then examines the incoming request's *Content-type* field, using *ap_table_get()* to fetch the information from the request record's headers_in field. If the content type doesn't match the expected POST type, the function exits with a DECLINED error code.

---

* Before you do roll your own, be sure to have a look at *http://www.modperl.com/libapreq/* for a C library that provides routines for manipulating client request data via the Apache API. This library was released after this book's final manuscript submission.

We now read the data into a buffer using the *util_read()* function from Example 10-4, passing on the result code to the caller in case of error.

The last task is to parse out the key=value pairs from the query string. We begin by clearing the passed table, deleting its previous contents, if any. If a **NULL** pointer was passed in, we allocate a new one with *ap_make_table()*. We then enter a loop in which we split the buffer into segments delimited by the & character, using the handy *ap_getword()* function for this purpose (described in the next chapter). We then call *ap_getword()* again to split each segment at the = character into key/value pairs. We pass both the key and value through *ap_unescape_url()* to remove the URL escapes, and enter them into the table with *ap_table_merge()*. We use *ap_table_merge()* rather than *ap_table_add()* here in order to spare the caller the inconvenience of using *ap_table_do()* to recover the multiple values. The disadvantage of this choice is that values that contain commas will not be correctly handled, since *ap_table_merge()* uses commas to separate multiple values.

Example 10-5. Reading POSTed Form Data

```
#define DEFAULT_ENCTYPE "application/x-www-form-urlencoded"

static int read_post(request_rec *r, table **tab)
{
    const char *data;
    const char *key, *val, *type;
    int rc = OK;

    if(r->method_number != M_POST) {
        return rc;
    }

    type = ap_table_get(r->headers_in, "Content-Type");
    if(strcasecmp(type, DEFAULT_ENCTYPE) != 0) {
        return DECLINED;
    }

    if((rc = util_read(r, &data)) != OK) {
        return rc;
    }

    if(*tab) {
        ap_clear_table(*tab);
    }
    else {
        *tab = ap_make_table(r->pool, 8);
    }

    while(*data && (val = ap_getword(r->pool, &data, '&'))) {
        key = ap_getword(r->pool, &val, '=');

        ap_unescape_url((char*)key);
        ap_unescape_url((char*)val);
```

Example 10-5. Reading POSTed Form Data (continued)

```
      ap_table_merge(*tab, key, val);
   }

   return OK;
}
```

The BUFF API

All the I/O functions that were described in the previous two sections took the request record as an argument. Internally, these functions make calls to a lower-level I/O API that operates on the `BUFF*` stored in the connection record in the `client` field. There is a close parallelism between the request-oriented I/O functions and the connection-oriented ones. They have almost identical names, but the prefix *ap_r* is replaced by *ap_b*, and instead of taking a request record as their argument, they take a BUFF pointer. So, for instance, instead of calling:

```
      ap_rputs("<H1>In the Beginning</H1>", r);
```

you could call:

```
      ap_bputs("<H1>In the Beginning</H1>", r->connection->client);
```

You will probably never have to use the BUFF API in the ordinary course of events. The only exception is if your module needs to open a pipe to another process. In this case, the *ap_bspawn_child()* routine returns a BUFF stream connected to the external process.

In most cases, the function prototypes for the BUFF functions are similar to the prototypes of their corresponding request-oriented calls, except that the `request_rec*` is replaced by a `BUFF*`. But be wary: in several cases the arguments are swapped so that the `BUFF*` comes first in the argument list rather than last.

The buffer functions are defined in the header file *include/buff.h:*

*int ap_bwrite (BUFF *fb, const void *buf, int nbyte)*
*int ap_bputs (const char *x, BUFF *fb)*
*int ap_bvputs (BUFF *fb,...)*
*int ap_bputc (int c, BUFF *fb)*
*int ap_bprintf (BUFF *fb, const char *fmt,...)*
*long ap_send_fb (BUFF *fb, request_rec *r)*
*long ap_send_fb_length (BUFF *fb, request_rec *r, long length)*
*int ap_bflush (BUFF *fb)*

> These output functions are identical to their *ap_r* counterparts but take a `BUFF*` as their argument. Usually, this argument will be retrieved from the connection record by calling *r->connection->client*, assuming that `r` is the current request record.

Note that *ap_send_fb()* and *ap_send_fb_length()* correspond to *ap_send_fd()* and *ap_send_fd_length()* and are responsible for sending the contents of the file or process pointed to by the first argument.

int ap_bread (BUFF *fb, void *buf, int nbyte)

ap_bread() is a low-level input function that is used beneath the **_client_ block()* routines described in the previous section. It acts like the standard C library *fread()* function to read *nbyte* bytes from the BUFF pointed to by *fb*. If successful, the data is placed in *buf* and the byte count is returned as the function result. In case of an error, the function will return EOF (-1).

This function should never be used by a handler to read the incoming request body because it will not deal correctly with chunked data. However, it is useful when reading from a pipe created with the *ap_bspawn_child()* function.

```
int n = ap_bread(fb, buffer, len);
```

int ap_bgets (char *buf, int n, BUFF *fb)

The *ap_bgets* can be used like the C standard library function *gets()* to read a line of data into a string. It will read data into the *char* buf* until an EOF occurs, a newline is encountered, a carriage return/linefeed sequence occurs, or *n*-1 bytes have been read. The string is always NULL-terminated.

If successful, the function returns the number of bytes read, or 0 on an EOF condition. If an error occurs, the function returns -1.

```
char buffer[MAX_STRING_LEN];
while(ap_bgets(buffer, sizeof(buffer), fb) > 0) {
    ...
}
```

The Timeout API

The timeout API allows you to set an alarm that will be triggered after the time configured by the *Timeout* configuration directive. You should do this before starting any series of read or write operations in order to handle any of the myriad things that can go wrong during network I/O: the client hangs or crashes, the network goes down, or the user hits the stop button before the page is completely downloaded.

There are two types of timeout. A "hard" timeout causes the transaction to be aborted immediately. The currently executing handler is exited, and Apache immediately enters the logging phase. A "soft" timeout does not abort the transaction but does mark the connection record as being in an aborted state (by setting the **aborted** field to true). The current handler continues to run, but all calls to client input or output routines are ignored. This allows the handler to do any additional processing or cleanup that it requires. In either case, a message will be sent to the *ErrorLog*, labeled with the name of the handler along these lines:

```
[Tue Jul 28 17:02:36 1998] [info] mod_hello timed out for 127.0.0.1
```

or:

```
[Tue Jul 28 17:02:36 1998] [info] 127.0.0.1 client stopped connection before
mod_hello completed
```

Many content handlers will do a series of I/O, do some processing, then do some more I/O. Every time a series of read or write operations is completed, the timeout should be reset by calling *ap_reset_timeout()*. This sets the internal timer back to zero. When your handler has finished all I/O operations successfully, it should call *ap_kill_timeout()* in order to cancel the timeout for good:

```
ap_soft_timeout("mod_hello", r);
while(...) {
    ... do I/O ...
    ap_reset_timeout(r);
}
ap_kill_timeout(r);
```

The various resource pools are deallocated correctly when a timeout occurs, so you should not have to worry about memory leaks so long as you have been careful to allocate all your data structures from resource pools. Should you have non-pool resources that you need to deallocate after a timeout, you can install a cleanup handler. See "The Cleanup API" section later in this chapter for details. You may also protect critical sections of your code with *ap_block_alarms()* and *ap_unblock_alarms()* to prevent a timeout from occurring at an inconvenient time.

*void ap_hard_timeout (char *name, request_rec *r)*

> *ap_hard_timeout()* starts a timeout. The first argument contains an arbitrary string used to identify the current handler when the abort message is printed to the error log. If the alarm times out, the current handler will be exited, the transaction will be aborted, and Apache will immediately enter the logging phase of the request cycle.

```
ap_hard_timeout("mod_hello", r);
```

*void ap_soft_timeout (char *name, request_rec *r)*

> *ap_soft_timeout()* works in the same way as *ap_hard_timeout()*, except that when the timeout occurs the transaction is placed into an aborted state in which all requested I/O operations are silently ignored. This allows the current handler to continue to its normal conclusion.

*void ap_reset_timeout (request_rec *r)*

> This function resets the timeout to its initial state. You should call this function after any series of I/O operations.

*void ap_kill_timeout (request_rec *r)*

ap_kill_timeout() cancels the pending timeout. You should be sure to call this function before your handler exits to avoid the risk of the alarm going off during a subsequent part of the transaction.

void ap_block_alarms (void)
void ap_unblock_alarms (void)

These two functions are used to block off sections of code where you do not want an alarm to occur. After a call to *ap_block_alarms()*, the pending timeout is blocked until *ap_unblock_alarms()* is called.

```
ap_block_alarms();
... critical section ...
ap_unblock_alarms();
```

Status Code Constants

The various status codes that handlers might want to return are defined in *httpd.h*. In addition to the Apache-specific status codes OK, DECLINED, and DONE, there are several dozen HTTP status codes to choose from.

In addition to the constants, Apache provides some handy macros for testing the range of a status code. Among other things, these macros can be used to check the status code returned by a subrequest (as described in the next section).

int ap_is_HTTP_INFO (int status_code)

Returns true if the status code is greater than or equal to 100 and less than 200. These codes are used to flag events in the HTTP protocol that are neither error codes nor success codes.

int ap_is_HTTP_SUCCESS (int status_code)

Returns true if the status code is greater than or equal to 200 and less than 300. This range is used for HTTP success codes, such as HTTP_OK.

int ap_is_HTTP_REDIRECT (int status_code)

Returns true if the status code is greater than or equal to 300 and less than 400. This range is used for redirects of various sorts, as well as the HTTP_NOT_MODIFIED result code.

int ap_is_HTTP_ERROR (int status_code)

Returns true for any of the HTTP error codes, which occupy the range greater than or equal to 400.

int ap_is_HTTP_CLIENT_ERROR (int status_code)

Returns true if the status code is greater than or equal to 400 and less than 500, which is the range reserved for client errors such as HTTP_NOT_FOUND.

int ap_is_HTTP_SERVER_ERROR (int status_code)

 Returns true if the status code is greater than or equal to 500 and less than 600, which are used for server errors such as HTTP_INTERNAL_SERVER_ERROR.

Server Core Routines

We now turn to less frequently used calls that are part of the Apache C-language API. These calls allow you to create custom error handlers, to create and manipulate subrequests, and to write formatted error messages to the log file.

The Subrequest API and Internal Redirects

The subrequest API can be used to ask Apache "what if" questions. A subrequest acts just like an ordinary request, except that the response phase is never actually run. The earlier phases, including the URI translation handler and the MIME type checker, are run as usual, and you can use their output to do such things as translating URIs into filenames.

A special case of a subrequest is an internal redirect, in which the current content handler discontinues processing the currently requested URI and tells Apache to return a different local URI instead. The content handler that eventually gets run is not necessarily the same as the one that invoked the internal redirect, although you can arrange for this to happen with *ap_internal_redirect_handler()*.

These routines are declared in the header file *http_request.h*.

int ap_is_initial_req (request_rec *r)

 This function returns a true value if the current request is the initial one. It will return false for handlers invoked as the result of subrequests or internal redirects.

```
if(!ap_is_initial_req(r)) {
    return DECLINED;
}
```

 The Perl API provides a method called *is_main()* which returns true for initial requests and for requests triggered by internal redirects but not for subrequests. Although there is no direct equivalent in the C API, you can get the same information by examining the main field of the request record. If it is NULL, then the current request is the main one.

```
if (r->main != NULL) {
    return DECLINED; /* don't handle subrequests */
}
```

 You might wish to declare a macro like the following:

```
#define is_main(r) (r->main == NULL)
```

The Perl API also defines a method called *last()* which returns the last request in a subrequest chain. This can be useful in logging handlers for recovering the status code of the last subrequest. A corresponding call is not defined in the C API but can be easily reproduced by the following function:

```
static request_rec *last(request_rec *r)
{
    request_rec *last;
    for(last=r; last->next != NULL; last=last->next) {
        continue;
    }
    return last;
}
```

*request_rec *ap_sub_req_lookup_uri (const char *uri, const request_rec *r)*

The *ap_sub_req_lookup_uri()* function creates a subrequest from the given URI, returning the resulting request record as the function result. You can then examine the request record to retrieve the URI's filename, MIME type, or other information. The following example shows how you can use a subrequest to translate a URI into a physical pathname:

```
request_rec *subr = ap_sub_req_lookup_uri(uri, r);
char *filename = subr->filename;
```

*request_rec *ap_sub_req_lookup_file (const char *file, const request_rec *r)*

This call behaves similarly to *ap_sub_req_lookup_uri()*, except that the first argument is a filename rather than a URI and that Apache skips the URI translation phase while processing the subrequest. This example uses a subrequest to fetch the MIME type of the file given in `filename`:

```
request_rec *subr = ap_sub_req_lookup_file(filename, r);
char *mime_type    = subr->content_type;
```

It isn't necessary that the specified file actually exist in order to get useful information with *ap_sub_req_lookup_file()*. For example, the default MIME type lookup operation depends only on the filename suffix, not on the contents of the file.

*void ap_destroy_sub_req (request_rec *r)*

When you are through with a subrequest, you should release the memory occupied by its data structures by passing the subrequest record to *ap_destroy_sub_req()*. If you forget to do this, the subrequest will be deallocated anyway when the main transaction is complete.

```
ap_destroy_sub_req(subr);
```

*int ap_run_sub_req (request_rec *r)*

If you have already created a subrequest using *ap_sub_req_lookup_uri()* or *ap_sub_req_lookup_file()*, you can run its content handler by calling *ap_run_sub_req()*. This is sometimes used by modules that implement server-side include systems in order to incorporate a CGI script's output into the HTML page. The function will return the status code of the subrequest's content handler.

Here's the definition of a utility function called *include_virtual()*, which creates a subrequest, runs it, then destroys it:

```
static int include_virtual(request_rec *r, char *uri)
{
    int status = OK;
    request_rec *subr = ap_sub_req_lookup_uri(uri, r);
    status = ap_run_sub_req(subr);
    ap_destroy_sub_req(subr);
    return status;
}
```

And here's how *include_virtual()* might be used:

```
int status = include_virtual("/footers/standard_footer.html", r);
```

*void ap_internal_redirect (const char *new_uri, request_rec *r)*

The *ap_internal_redirect()* method will cause Apache to create a new request from the indicated URI and then run it. The effect is for Apache to send the client a different URI than the one originally requested. Unlike a formal redirect (in which Apache sends the browser a 301 or 302 redirect status code), the browser is not informed that this substitution has taken place.

The content handler for the new URI is not necessarily the same as the content handler that generated the redirect. Apache will determine which content handler to run by examining the new URI's MIME type and applicable configuration directives, just as if the browser had requested the URI directly.

```
ap_internal_redirect("/new/place", r);
```

After recalling this function, your handler should return without further processing the request.

*void ap_internal_redirect_handler (const char *new_uri, request_rec *r)*

If you wish to redirect to a new URI but continue to use the current content handler, call *ap_internal_redirect_handler()* instead of the previous function.

```
ap_internal_redirect_handler("/new/place", r);
```

The Cleanup API

As explained in Chapter 3, cleanup handlers are code subroutines that Apache invokes after the transaction is finished. These are usually used by modules to clean up data structures that could not be allocated from resource pools, such as device drivers and database handles, but can also be used for other tasks, such as deferring logging until after the transaction is completed (see Chapter 7 for a discussion of this technique).

Cleanup handlers use a different calling convention than that used by phase handlers. A cleanup handler takes a single **void*** argument and returns no function result. Its function prototype looks like this:

```
void cleanup_handler (void *data)
```

The **data** argument is provided for your convenience as a way to pass runtime information to the cleanup handler. It can be a pointer to any data structure of your choosing, or **NULL** if you don't care to pass any information. As we discuss later, the **data** argument is specified when you install the cleanup handler using *ap_register_cleanup()*.

One common trick is to pass a pointer to the current request record so that the cleanup handler has access to information about the transaction. In the examples that follow, we use a cleanup handler that simply prints a message to standard error indicating that it's been called:

```
static void my_cleanup(void *data)
{
    request_rec *r = (request_rec *)data;
    fprintf(stderr, "process %d all done with %s\n", (int)getpid(), r->uri);
}
```

Apache can accommodate an unlimited number of cleanup handlers, although few modules will need more than one. All cleanup functions are declared in the header file *alloc.h*.

void ap_register_cleanup (pool *p, void *data, void (*plain_cleanup) (void *),
  void (*child_cleanup) (void *))
  To install a cleanup handler, call *ap_register_cleanup()*. It takes four arguments: a pool pointer (usually the one stored in the request record), a block of module-specific data to pass to the routine, and two function pointers to cleanup handlers. The first function pointer is the one you will usually use. It points to the cleanup handler to be called when the transaction is terminated. The second function pointer is only used when your module forks a child process and you need a routine to perform cleanup before the child terminates, for example, closing an open file inherited from the parent process. Since it is highly unusual for a module to fork, you will ordinarily pass the "do nothing" routine *ap_null_cleanup* for this argument. Always be sure to use *ap_null_cleanup* rather than **NULL**.

  In the following example, we install *my_cleanup()* as the cleanup handler and arrange for it to be passed a copy of the current request record when it runs:

```
ap_register_cleanup(r->pool, (void *)r, my_cleanup, ap_null_cleanup);
```

void ap_kill_cleanup (pool *p, void *data, void (*cleanup)(void *))
  Should you need to unregister a cleanup function before it runs, pass the address of the routine and its data block to *ap_kill_cleanup()*. Both the

routine and the data block must match the values passed to *ap_register_cleanup()* in order for the removal to take effect.

```
ap_kill_cleanup(r->pool, (void *)r, my_cleanup);
```

*void ap_run_cleanup (pool *p, void *data, void (*cleanup)(void *))*

If you need to run a cleanup immediately, you can do so by calling this routine. The cleanup will be unregistered after it is run so that it is not run again during the ordinary cleanup period. It is unlikely that you will need to use this function, since it is easy enough to invoke the cleanup function directly.

Custom Response Handlers

As described in Chapters 3 and 4 and Chapter 6, *Authentication and Authorization*, Apache provides an API for creating custom error handlers. Modules can arrange for Apache to take special action when a handler returns a particular status code. Possible actions include displaying a static string, invoking a local URI, or redirecting to a remote URI. This is the mechanism that underlies the *ErrorDocument* directive.

As of Version 1.3.2, the Apache C-language API allows you to install a custom response handler from within a handler by calling the *ap_custom_response()* function, which is defined in the *http_core.h* header file. Here is the function's prototype:

```
void ap_custom_response (request_rec *r, int status, char *string);
```

r is, as usual, the current request record. *status* contains the status code that you wish to intercept, selected from among the symbolic constants defined in *httpd.h*. The last argument, *string*, can be a simple text message for Apache to display when the indicated error occurs, a remote URI, in which case Apache generates an external redirect, or a local URI, for which Apache generates a transparent internal redirect.

Apache distinguishes between these three possibilities by looking at the first few characters of the string. If it begins with a double quote mark, it is assumed to be a simple message string (the quote is stripped from the message before displaying it). Otherwise, if the string looks like a full URL (determined by calling *ap_is_url()*), Apache takes it to be an external URL. Finally, if the string begins with a forward slash, Apache assumes the string to be a local URI. If the string doesn't satisfy any of these criteria, then it is again treated as a simple text message.

Here is an example of using *ap_custom_response()* to set a text message to be displayed when authentication fails:

```
ap_custom_response(r, HTTP_UNAUTHORIZED, "sorry, I don't know you.");
```

And here is an example that will generate an internal redirect to the Perl script *server_error_handler.pl* when any sort of internal server error occurs:

```
ap_custom_response(r, HTTP_INTERNAL_SERVER_ERROR,
                   "/perl/server_error_handler.pl");
```

The next example will redirect the client to another site if an **HTTP_METHOD_NOT_ ALLOWED** error is raised:

```
ap_custom_response(r, HTTP_METHOD_NOT_ALLOWED,
                   "http://www.w3.org/pub/WWW/Protocols/rfc2068/rfc2068");
```

If you wish to use custom response handlers to pass information from the original request onward to the new request, there are a number of techniques that you can use to preserve headers, cookies, and other information. See "The ErrorDocument System" in Chapter 4 and "Cookie-Based Access Control" in Chapter 6 for a discussion of these techniques and their practical application. The main point to recall is that outgoing HTTP headers stored in the request record's **headers_out** field are *not* sent to the browser on an error, nor are they preserved across internal redirects. The contents of the **err_headers_out** table, however, have both characteristics.

Error Logging

At server startup time, Apache reopens the standard error file descriptor to the *ErrorLog* file.* If configured, each virtual server can also have its own error log. Modules can write messages to the error log in a simple way just by writing directly to standard error.

However, the simple way is less than desirable because it leaves a bare string in the error log, with no indication of the time or date that the error occurred or which module left the message. Apache's error-logging API avoids these problems by providing module writers with two functions, *ap_log_rerror()* and *ap_log_ error()*, both of which write nicely formatted error messages to the error log. In addition to a timestamp and a message, optional flags allow modules to include the name and line number of the C source code file where the error occurred as well as the contents of the system **errno** variable.

As of Version 1.3, Apache supports the notion of a message severity level. In this scheme, which should be familiar to users of the Unix *syslog* system,† each message is assigned one of eight severities that range from high (**APLOG_EMERG**) to low (**APLOG_DEBUG**). A log level setting, set by the webmaster with the configuration directive *LogLevel*, controls which messages actually get sent to the log file. For example, if *LogLevel* is set to *warn*, only messages with severity **APLOG_WARN** or higher will be written to the log file. Messages at a lower priority will be ignored. This facility allows your module to write lots and lots of debugging

---

* When native *syslog* support is enabled, the **stderr** stream will be redirected to */dev/null!*

† In fact, the error log API maps directly to *syslog* when native *syslog* support is enabled. See the Apache documentation on the *ErrorLog* directive for details on enabling native *syslog* support.

messages at a low severity level. During module development, you can set *LogLevel* to a low level in order to see the debugging messages. Later you can raise the log level so that the debugging messages are suppressed on the production server.

All logging constants and routines are declared in *http_log.h*:

void ap_log_error (const char *file, int line, int level, const server_rec *s,
    const char *fmt, ...)

void ap_log_rerror (const char *file, int line, int level, const request_rec *r,
    const char *fmt, ...)

ap_log_rerror() and *ap_log_error()* are the two main entry points for the Apache error log API. These calls have many arguments, and C programmers might want to define some macros in order to save keystrokes. A couple of examples of this technique are given at the end of this section.

The first two arguments are the filename and line number where the error occurred. Most modules will want to use the **APLOG_MARK** macro here. It uses the C compiler **__FILE__** and **__LINE__** tokens to automatically pass this information. The third argument, *level*, is the severity level at which to record the message. *level* should be selected from the list of symbolic constants given later. The severity level is actually a bit mask; by setting other bits in the mask, you can adjust other logging options, as we describe later. The fourth argument is different for the two calls. For *ap_log_error()*, it is the **server_rec**, ordinarily obtained from **r->server**. For *ap_log_rerror()*, it is the request record itself, **r**. Internally, the logging API uses the server record to find the error log's **FILE*** for writing, or it passes messages to the *syslog()* function if native *syslog* support is enabled. The fifth argument, *fmt*, is a *sprintf()*-style format string. It, and the variable number of arguments that follow it, are passed to *sprintf()* to generate the message written to the log file.

```
if (!(fh = ap_pfopen(r->pool, cfg->config_file, "r"))) {
    ap_log_error(APLOG_MARK, APLOG_EMERG, r->server,
            "Cannot open configuration file %s.", cfg->config_file);
    return HTTP_INTERNAL_SERVER_ERROR;
}
```

One difference between *ap_log_error()* and *ap_log_rerror()* is that the latter function can optionally write the error message to the notes table under a key named **error-notes**. This message can then be retrieved and displayed by *ErrorDocument* handlers and other error processors. The message is only written to the notes table if the message severity level is *warn* or higher, and there is not already an **error-notes** entry in the notes table. Another difference is that *ap_log_error()* includes the client's dotted IP address in the formatted error message.

void ap_log_reason (const char *reason, const char *fname, request_rec *r)

It is so common to encounter a system error while opening a file or performing I/O on the system that a special routine is provided in the API. *ap_log_reason()* takes a character string describing the problem, the name of the file that was involved in the error, and the current request record. It is also common to use this function to log unsuccessful attempts to access protected documents, since the remote host's name is incorporated into the error message as well.

Here's a typical example of using *ap_log_reason()* and the line that it writes to the log file.

```
ap_log_reason("Can't open index.html", r->uri, r);
```

```
[Tue Jul 21 16:30:47 1998] [error] access to /
failed for w15.yahoo.com, reason: Can't open index.html No such file
or directory
```

Internally, *ap_log_reason()* is just a frontend to the following call:

```
ap_log_error(APLOG_MARK, APLOG_ERR, r->server,
        "access to %s failed for %s, reason: %s",
        file,
        ap_get_remote_host(r->connection, r->per_dir_config, REMOTE_NAME),
        reason);
```

The `level` flag passed to *ap_log_error()* and *ap_log_rerror()* should be one of the severity level constants listed below, possibly logically ORed with either of the constants APLOG_NOERRNO or APLOG_WIN32ERROR.

APLOG_NOERRNO

By default, the logging API will include the contents of the system **errno** variable in the message. This feature is sometimes useful, as when you log an error that results from a failed system call, and sometimes not useful at all (and may in fact lead to misleading messages since **errno** is not reset by successful calls). Combine the severity level with APLOG_NOERRNO to suppress the automatic inclusion of **errno**.

```
ap_log_rerror(APLOG_MARK, APLOG_NOERRNO|APLOG_DEBUG, r,
        "The requested URI was %s", r->uri);
```

APLOG_WIN32ERROR

This constant, available on Win32 platforms only, will make Apache log the value returned by the *GetLastError()* system call in addition to the value of **errno** from the standard C library.

APLOG_EMERG

This severity level indicates that an emergency condition has occurred. It should be reserved for problems that render the server unusable.

```
ap_log_error(APLOG_MARK, APLOG_NOERRNO|APLOG_EMERG, r->server,
        "Cannot find lock file.  Aborting.");
```

APLOG_ALERT

This level is intended for problems that require immediate attention.

APLOG_CRIT

This logs messages at a level intended for severe problems that require immediate attention.

APLOG_ERR

This logs the message at the *error* severity level, intended for use with noncritical errors that nevertheless require someone's attention.

```
ap_log_error(APLOG_MARK, APLOG_ERR, r->server,
            "Could not open file", r->filename);
```

APLOG_WARN

The *warn* level is one step less severe than *error* and is intended for warnings that may or may not require attention.

APLOG_NOTICE

notice messages are used for normal but significant conditions.

```
ap_log_error(APLOG_MARK, APLOG_NOERRNO|APLOG_NOTICE, r->server,
            "Cannot connect to master database, using backup.");
```

APLOG_INFO

The *info* severity level is used for informational messages issued for nonerror conditions.

APLOG_DEBUG

The lowest severity of all is *debug*, used for issuing messages during the development and debugging of a module.

```
ap_log_error(APLOG_MARK, APLOG_NOERRNO|APLOG_DEBUG, r->server,
            "Filename=%s,uri=%s,mtime=%d,",
            r->filename, r->uri, r->finfo.mtime);
```

If the *ap_log_rerror()* and *ap_log_error()* calls are too verbose for your tastes, we recommend that you create a few preprocessor macros for frequently used combinations. For example:

```
#define my_error(mess) ap_log_error(APLOG_MARK,\
                        APLOG_NOERRNO|APLOG_ERROR,\
                        r->server, mess)

#define my_debug(mess) ap_log_error(APLOG_MARK,\
                        APLOG_NOERRNO|APLOG_DEBUG,\
                        r->server, mess)
```

Now you can log simple error messages this way:

```
my_error("Can't find lock file.  Aborting.");
```

The Piped Log API

Apache Version 1.3.0 introduced reliable piped log support, which allows your module to send log data to a running program.* If the program happens to die, it will be automatically restarted. Internally, this API is used when processing log file directives that begin with the | (pipe character). Everything following the pipe character is treated as a program to be run. After the program is launched, log entries are sent to the program on its standard input.

You will probably not need to use the piped log routines because this functionality is already handled in a generic way by Apache's *mod_log_config* module. However, if you wish to support this feature in a custom logging module of your own, these calls are available for your use.

The main data structure used by the piped log API is the **piped_log** record, defined in *http_log.h*. This data structure should be treated as an opaque data structure. Use *ap_open_piped_log()* to open a pipe to a new process, *ap_piped_log_read_fd()* and *ap_piped_log_write_fd()* to obtain file descriptors that you can use to read and write from the process, and *ap_close_piped_log()* to close the pipe when you're through.

*piped_log *ap_open_piped_log (pool *p, const char *program)*

Given a resource pool **p** and the path to an executable *program*, *ap_open_piped_log()* will launch the program, open a bidirectional pipe to it, and return a **piped_log** pointer if successful or **NULL** if not.

You should make this call during the module or child initialization phases. This will avoid the overhead of opening and closing the pipe for each request. If you open the pipe at module initialization time, the subprocess will be run as root, but there will be only one copy running. If you open the pipe during child initialization, it will run as the *httpd* user, but there will be one copy of the subprocess running for each child. It's your call which to use.

Here's an example of opening a log file specified by the module-specific configuration record **cfg**. If the initial character of the filename is the pipe symbol, the code opens it as a piped command. Otherwise, it opens it as a normal file. For simplicity, we've omitted error checking from this example.

```
if(*cfg->log_file == '|') {
    /* open as a command pipe */
    piped_log *pl = ap_open_piped_log(p, cfg->log_file + 1);
    cfg->log_fd = ap_piped_log_write_fd(pl);
}
```

---

* Reliable piped log support was not available on Win32 platforms at the time this was written.

```
else {
   /* open as normal file */
   cls->log_fd = ap_popenf(p, cfg->log_file, flags, mode);
}
if (!cls->log_fd) {
      ... raise some sort of error...
```

Some of the routines in this example are described in the next chapter.

*void ap_close_piped_log (piped_log *pl)*

This function closes a previously opened piped log. Conveniently, this function will be called at pool destruction time if you don't call it yourself.

*int ap_piped_log_write_fd (piped_log *pl)*

ap_piped_log_write_fd() returns a file descriptor that you can use to write to the logging process using the standard *write()* library call. Typically, you will write some form of accounting or status information, but the contents of the information you send are entirely up to you. Because all writing is done through a file descriptor, the same code routines that write to plain text files can be used to write to the pipe.

*int ap_piped_log_read_fd (piped_log *pl)*

ap_piped_log_read() returns a file descriptor that you can use to read from the logging process with the standard *read()* library call. It is far more usual to write to a logging process than to read from one, but you can do this if the process provides status information, for instance. If you both read and write from the process, beware of deadlock situations in which both your module and the logging process are waiting for the other.

Authorization and Authentication Routines

The last core routines we'll consider are those used for access control, authentication, and authorization. If you are familiar with the Perl API from Chapter 6, you'll find no surprises here.

These routines are declared in *http_core.h* unless otherwise specified:

*int ap_allow_options (request_rec *r)*

The *ap_allow_options()* call returns a bit mask containing the contents of the Perl-directory *Options* directive. You can logically AND this bit mask with a set of symbolic constants in order to determine which options are set. For example, the following code fragment checks whether *ExecCGI* is active for the directory containing the currently requested document:

```
if(!(ap_allow_options(r) & OPT_EXECCGI)) {
    ap_log_reason("Options ExecCGI is off in this directory",
                 $r->filename, r);
    return HTTP_FORBIDDEN;
}
```

The options constants are as follows:

Constant	Meaning
OPT_INDEXES	The *Indexes* option is set.
OPT_INCLUDES	The *Includes* option is set.
OPT_SYM_LINKS	The *SymLinks* option is set.
OPT_EXECCGI	The *ExecCGI* option is set.
OPT_UNSET	(See the description that follows.)
OPT_INCNOEXEC	The *IncludeNoExec* option is set.
OPT_SYM_OWNER	The *SymLinksIfOwnerMatch* option is set.
OPT_MULTI	The *MultiViews* option is set.

Also available are the constants OPT_NONE, for no options set (this is defined as zero), and OPT_ALL, for all but the *MultiViews* option set.

OPT_UNSET corresponds to a bit that is initially set to 1 in the options flag but is not otherwise used. If no absolute assignment to the *Options* directive has been made, then this bit will remain set; otherwise, it will be unset. In other words, you can test this bit to determine whether only additive and subtractive assignments to *Options* have been made. In a directory with this *Options* directive, the OPT_UNSET bit will be true:

```
Options +ExecCGI -Indexes
```

However, in a directory with this directive, the bit will be false:

```
Options ExecCGI
```

As Commander Spock would say, "Fascinating."

const char *ap_auth_name (request_rec *r)

If authentication is configured for the currently requested document or directory, *ap_auth_name()* will return the name of the current authentication realm, as defined by the *AuthName* directive. If no realm is currently defined, this function will return NULL.

Note that it is quite possible for the current request to have an authentication realm without authentication actually being active. For example, there may be no *requires* directive in the directory configuration.

```
const char *auth_name = ap_auth_name(r);
```

const char *ap_auth_type (request_rec *r)

This call returns the type of authentication configured for the current file or directory or NULL if none. The current possibilities are Basic and Digest.

```
const char *auth_type = ap_auth_type(r);

if(strcasecmp(auth_type, "basic")) {
    ap_log_error(APLOG_MARK, APLOG_NOERRNO|APLOG_WARN, r->server,
            "%s can't handle AuthType %s", __FILE__, auth_type);
```

```
        return DECLINED;
}
```

Although the information returned by *ap_auth_type()* seems redundant with the contents of the connection record's `ap_auth_type` field, there is an important difference. *ap_auth_type()* returns the authentication scheme *configured* for the current directory, whereas the connection record's `ap_auth_type` field returns the authentication scheme only if authentication is actually in use. To determine whether authentication is active, you should only trust the connection record's field.

*int ap_get_basic_auth_pw (request_rec *r, const char **pw)*

If the browser provided password authentication in making its request, the *ap_get_basic_auth_pw()* call will return the password. You pass the function the request record in `r` and the address of a character pointer in `pw`. If successful, the function will return a result code of OK and place a copy of the password in `pw`. Otherwise, the function will return one of the result codes `DECLINED`, `HTTP_INTERNAL_SERVER_ERROR`, or `HTTP_UNAUTHORIZED`. `DECLINED` is returned when the current request isn't for a directory that is protected by Basic authentication. `HTTP_INTERNAL_SERVER_ERROR` can occur when the authorization realm directive is missing. Finally, `HTTP_UNAUTHORIZED` is returned if the browser fails to provide a password or attempts to use the wrong authentication scheme.

This call is typically used by authentication handlers to recover the user's password. The username can be retrieved from the connection record's `user` field. You should then do something with the two values to validate them.

```
const char *sent_pw = NULL;
char *user;
int ret = ap_get_basic_auth_pw(r, &sent_pw);
if(ret != OK) {
        return ret;
}

user = r->connection->user;
    ...
```

*void ap_note_basic_auth_failure (request_rec *r)*
*void ap_note_digest_auth_failure (request_rec *r)*
*void ap_note_auth_failure (request_rec *r)*

(Declared in the header file *http_protocol.h.*) If authentication is required for the current directory, but the browser did not provide the required information, these three variants set the HTTP authentication gears in motion by sending an "Authentication Required" message to the browser.

ap_note_basic_auth_failure() and *ap_note_digest_auth_failure()* are used for Basic and Digest authentication schemes, respectively. The generic *ap_note_* *auth_failure()* call will dispatch to one of those two routines based on which type of authentication the current directory is configured to use.

We can now write the skeleton for username/password authentication. In this example, *check_auth()* is some routine that you provide to check that the login name and password are valid. Replace this routine with a function that always returns 1, and you have our *Apache::AuthAny* module from Chapter 6!

```
const char *sent_pw = NULL;
char *user = r->connection->user;
int ret = ap_get_basic_auth_pw(r, &sent_pw);
if (ret != OK) {
    return ret;
}
if(!(user && sent_pwd && check_auth(user, sent_pw)) {
    ap_note_basic_auth_failure(r);
    ap_log_reason("User did not authenticate", r->uri, r);
    return HTTP_UNAUTHORIZED;
}
```

*const array_header *ap_requires (request_rec *r)*

As we described in Chapter 6, after a successful authentication, Apache calls the authorization handler to determine whether the authenticated user is allowed access to the requested document. To do this, the authorization handler needs to process any and all *requires* directives in the current directory configuration. The *ap_requires()* call returns the contents of these directives in predigested form.

The function result of *ap_requires()* is an **array_header*** containing a list of **require_line** structs. The definition of this data type, as found in *http_core.h*, is as follows:

```
typedef struct {
    int method_mask;
    char *requirement;
} require_line;
```

method_mask is an integer bitmask constructed from the request methods listed in the current *<Limit>* directive, or -1 if no *<Limit>* section applies. The set bit numbers correspond to the method numbers **M_GET**, **M_POST**, and so on. For example, you could determine whether the first requirement applies to POST requests with the following code fragment:

```
int isPost = 0 != (requirement[0].method_mask & (1 << M_POST));
```

requirement is a character string containing the exact text of the *requires* directive. You will need to parse this text in order to determine what type of requirement to apply.

Example 10-6 gives a short example of iterating over the *ap_requires()* array and printing out the information it contains. You should be able to use this code in a real authorization module by replacing the various print statements

with code that performs the actual authorization checks. For real-life examples, see *mod_auth*, *mod_auth_dbm*, and the other standard authorization
modules.

Example 10-6. Processing requires Directives

```c
static char *request_methods[] = {
   "GET","PUT","POST","DELETE","CONNECT","OPTIONS","TRACE",NULL
};

#define comma_or_newline(value) \
if(value) fprintf(stderr, ", "); \
else      fprintf(stderr, "\n");

static void hello_util_requires_dump(request_rec *r)
{
   const array_header *requires = ap_requires(r);
   require_line *rq;
   int x;

   if (!requires) {
       fprintf(stderr,
               "requires: there are no requirements for this request\n");
       return;
   }

   rq = (require_line *) requires->elts;

   for (x = 0; x < requires->nelts; x++) {
       const char *line, *requirement;
       int i;

       fprintf(stderr, "requires: limited to request methods: ");
       for(i=0; request_methods[i]; i++) {
           if (rq[x].method_mask & (1 << i))
               fprintf(stderr, "%s ", request_methods[i]);
       }
       fprintf(stderr, "\n");

       line = rq[x].requirement;
       requirement = ap_getword(r->pool, &line, ' ');

       if (!strcmp(requirement, "valid-user")) {
           fprintf(stderr, "requires: any valid-user allowed here.\n");
           return;
       }

       if (!strcmp(requirement, "user")) {
           fprintf(stderr, "requires: allowed users: ");
           while (line[0]) {
               requirement = ap_getword_conf(r->pool, &line);
               fprintf(stderr, "`%s'", requirement);
               comma_or_newline(line[0]);
           }
       }
```

Example 10-6. Processing requires Directives (continued)

```
        else if (!strcmp(requirement, "group")) {
            fprintf(stderr, "requires: allowed groups: ");
            while (line[0]) {
                requirement = ap_getword_conf(r->pool, &line);
                fprintf(stderr, "`%s'", requirement);
                comma_or_newline(line[0]);
            }
        }
    }
}
```

int ap_satisfies (request_rec *r)

The *Satisfy* directive determines whether a request for a URI that is protected by both access control and authentication must pass through both phases successfully or either one or the other. If *Satisfy* is set to *all*, all access control and authentication tests must be passed successfully. In contrast, if the directive is set to *any*, then the request will be allowed if any of the checks returns OK.

Handlers involved with access control can gain access to this configuration directive using the *ap_satisfies()* function. It returns one of the constants SATISFY_ANY, SATISFY_ALL, or SATISFY_NOSPEC. The last constant indicates that the directive wasn't present at all. Each of these constants, and the declaration of *ap_satisfies()* itself, is found in *http_core.h*.

As an example, consider an access control handler that wants to write an error log message when a user is denied access, but not when SATISFY_ANY is set, because the user might still be allowed in during the authentication phase. It can do the following:

```
if (return_value == HTTP_FORBIDDEN) {
    if (!(r->satisfies == SATISFY_ANY && ap_some_auth_required(r)))
        ap_log_reason("Client denied by server configuration", r->uri, r);
}
return return_value;
```

int ap_some_auth_required (request_rec *r)

The *ap_some_auth_required()* function can be used within any handler to determine whether authentication is required for the requested document. If you are writing a module that must always run with authentication enabled (such as a password changing program), you can use this call to make sure that the module is never inadvertently run without protection. For example:

```
if(!ap_some_auth_required(r)) {
    ap_log_reason("I won't go further unless the user is authenticated",
                  r->uri, r);
    return HTTP_FORBIDDEN;
}
```

The next chapter shows you how to create configuration directives with the C API and covers less frequently used parts of the C-language API.

11

C API Reference Guide, Part II

The previous chapter covered the common parts of the C API, including the core routines for handling requests, manipulating tables, and managing memory. This chapter begins with a comprehensive guide to implementing configuration directives in C. It then turns to less essential parts of the API, including utility routines for parsing, routines for handling files, and functions for constructing and parsing URIs.

This chapter also covers several of the more esoteric aspects of the C API, such as the interface to the MD5 digest function and techniques for opening pipes to subprocesses.

Implementing Configuration Directives in C

The C-language API allows modules to install their own configuration directives. The directives' syntax and usage information are defined in a `command_rec` data structure and processed by directive handler callback routines defined within the module.

Whereas the configuration API is optional in Perl modules due to the catchall *PerlSetVar* directive, C-language programmers don't have this luxury. You'll have to create custom configuration directives in order to write any module that requires runtime configuration information.

Overview

Modules are responsible for managing their own configuration data. There are two general types of configuration data: data that apply to a particular server or virtual host and data that apply to a directory or URI. A module can maintain both server-specific and directory-specific configuration information or just one or the other, depending on its needs. Because there may be dozens of virtual hosts and hundreds of directories, the Apache API allows modules to juggle thousands of configuration records. During configuration file processing, Apache will call your module's configuration allocation and processing routines at the right time and in the right order to create the configuration data. Then, at request time, Apache will choose the correct configuration record to return to your handler when the handler requests it.

The work of creating and maintaining configuration records is done in several steps. In the first step, the module is given an opportunity to allocate storage for its private configuration settings and to create a reasonable set of defaults, if it chooses. The content of the configuration data is entirely private to your module. Apache sees it only as an opaque void*.

During the second step, which occurs during configuration file processing, the module's directives are parsed and passed back to your code for processing, along with the initialized configuration settings from the previous phase. There is one directive handler for each custom directive that your module declares. The directive handler will alter the configuration block in some way to record the meaning of the directive. Typically the handler will change the contents of a field or add an entry to a table.

The third step is the mysterious-sounding "merging" process. The idea is that configuration information is often nested. For example, a particular directive could appear in the main part of the configuration file, in a *<VirtualHost>* section, in a *<Directory>* section, and in a *.htaccess* file. When the directive appears in a nested scope, your module needs to handle the potential contradiction in some way, either by letting the nested directive take precedence over the parent directive or by merging the contents of the two somehow. Apache handles this process by calling your merge routines. These routines take the base configuration (the configuration that belongs to the parent scope) and the new configuration (the configuration that belongs to the nested section) and merge them into a new configuration block that combines them both.

The last step actually occurs during the transaction. Handlers that need access to their module's per-server or per-directory configuration settings request it from Apache. The *ap_get_module_config()* API function is able to perform a quick, one-step lookup of your module's configuration data relevant to the current transaction, no matter how many configuration blocks were constructed during server startup.

Creating and Merging Configuration Data Blocks

Your module declares its intent to maintain configuration information by filling in one or more of the slots in the `module` record labeled *config creator* or *config merger*. There are four such slots: one each for functions to create per-directory and per-server configuration settings and one each for merging per-directory and per-server data. The four functions have the following prototypes:

```
void *create_dir_config(pool *p, char *dir)
void *merge_dir_config(pool *p, void *base_conf, void *new_conf)
void *create_server_config(pool *p, server_rec *s)
void *merge_server_config(pool *p, void *base_conf, void *new_conf)
```

The *create_server_config()* function is an opportunity for the module to allocate per-server configuration data. It is passed a resource pool and a `server_rec` server structure. It may, if it chooses, allocate a data structure from within the resource pool, initialize it, and return it to Apache as a `void*`.

create_dir_config() is similar, except that it is called to create per-directory configuration information (directives contained within *<Directory>*, *<Location>*, or *.htaccess* files). In this case, the subroutine is called with a resource pool and the name of the current directory or URI. The routine may, if it chooses, allocate a data structure for the per-directory information and return it to Apache as a `void*`.

As a concrete example, consider a "traffic cop" module that regulates the flow of traffic on a server. It has two configuration settings: one which sets the maximum speed limit on the server (in bits per second, say) and one which contains a list of domains that have "right-of-way" through the server and can fetch documents at a higher maximum speed. This module could store the information in the following per-server configuration record:

```
typedef struct {
    int     speed_limit;
    table *right_of_way;
} traffic_server_config;
```

The following definition of *traffic_create_server_config()* allocates the storage for the per-server configuration information and sets up appropriate defaults. `speed_limit` is set to 55 (whatever that means in this context!) and the `right_of_way` field is initialized to point to a new empty table.

```
static void *traffic_create_server_config (pool *p, server_rec *s) {
    traffic_server_config *cfg =
        (traffic_server_config *)ap_pcalloc(p, sizeof(traffic_server_config));
    cfg->speed_limit = 55;
    cfg->right_of_way = ap_make_table(p, 0);
    return (void *)cfg;
}
```

This initial data block will be passed back to your module's directive handlers as a void* when the time comes to process a directive. The handler should typecast the pointer back to the correct data type, then make the appropriate change to the affected field.

A *create_dir_config()* routine will look almost identical to this, but instead of receiving a server_rec in the second argument, it receives a string containing the path to the relevant directory or URI.

Later on in the process, Apache may be called upon to process a directive that needs to be merged into the parent configuration. You can define up to two such merge routines. The *merge_server_config()* routine is called at server startup time to merge directives in *<VirtualHost>* blocks with the configuration for the parent server. It receives a pointer to a resource pool, a pointer to the parent server configuration, and a pointer to the child server configuration. The merge routine's job is to create a new configuration structure that combines the two and to return it to Apache as a void*.

merge_dir_config() is similar, but it happens at request time and operates on two per-directory structures: the parent directory's configuration and the current directory's configuration. It is expected to merge the two and return a new per-directory configuration structure that combines the configurations in some sensible way.

For example, here is a plausible server merge routine for the traffic cop configuration. We want to overwrite the speed_limit field so that the current virtual host's setting supersedes that of the base host. However, instead of allowing the virtual host's right_of_way settings to supersede those of the parent server, we merge the two using *ap_overlay_tables()*:

```
static void *traffic_merge_server_config (pool *p, void* base, void* new) {
    traffic_server_config *merged =
        (traffic_server_config*)ap_pcalloc(p, sizeof(traffic_server_config));
    traffic_server_config *parent = (traffic_server_config*)base;
    traffic_server_config *child  = (traffic_server_config*)new;

    merged->speed_limit = child->speed_limit ?
                          child->speed_limit : parent->speed_limit;
    merged->right_of_way = ap_overlay_tables(p, parent->right_of_way,
                                             child->right_of_way);
    return (void*)merged;
}
```

If your module does not define any merge routines, then Apache will use the configuration of the most recent server or directory configuration, ignoring any directives which previously have been defined for a block's ancestors. If your module defines no *create_server_config()* or *create_dir_config()* routine, then it will have no runtime configuration blocks. However, this doesn't mean that the module can't maintain any configuration information at all; it can still maintain some state in static variables. However, this information will be global to the module, rather than server-specific or directory-specific. This rarely works out the way you want it, nor is it thread-safe.

Rather than having the *create_server_config()* and *create_dir_config()* fill in the configuration records' fields with default values, it is often useful to have the two routines fill in the configuration fields with explicit UNSET values. This allows you to distinguish between fields that are unset and fields that just happen to have been set to the default value. It also simplifies merging because the assignment logic now becomes the following:

```
merged->attr = base->attr == UNSET ? base->attr : new->attr;
```

There is one major trap in the current Apache configuration API. If your module depends on per-server records and *<VirtualHost>* sections are in use, then at least one of your module's configuration directives must be present in the *<VirtualHost>* section or your module's *create_server_config()* routine will never be called. As a result, your module will have no chance to create its per-server configuration before its handlers are called at transaction time. There are two ways around this problem. You can simply DECLINE to handle the transaction if the per-server configuration block is NULL, or you can try to fill in the values of the configuration block on the fly.

The command_rec Structure

A module defines custom configuration directives using the *config directive table* slot of its `module` structure. This table is a pointer to an array of `command_rec` records having the structure shown in Example 11-1. Usually this array of `command_rec` data is created as a static data structure in the module source code. The last element of the array must be NULL. As a concrete example, here's a short `command_rec` definition borrowed from *mod_actions.c*:

```
static const command_rec action_cmds[] =
{
    {"Action", add_action, NULL, OR_FILEINFO, TAKE2,
     "a media type followed by a script name"},
    {"Script", set_script, NULL, ACCESS_CONF | RSRC_CONF, TAKE2,
     "a method followed by a script name"},
    {NULL}
};
```

The `action_cmds` array declares two directives: *Action*, which is processed by a handler routine named *add_action()*, and *Script*, processed by *set_script()*.

Example 11-1. The command_rec Struct (from http_config.h)

```
typedef struct command_struct {
    const char *name;          /* Name of this command */
    const char *(*func) ();    /* Function invoked */
    void *cmd_data;            /* Extra data, for functions which
                                * implement multiple commands...*/
    int req_override;          /* What overrides need to be allowed to
                                * enable this command.*/
    enum cmd_how args_how;     /* What the command expects as arguments */
    const char *errmsg;        /* 'usage' message, in case of syntax errors */
} command_rec;
```

The various fields of the `command_rec` should look familiar to the Perl API covered in Chapter 8, *Customizing the Apache Configuration Process*:

char *name

> This is the configuration directive's name, used within *httpd.conf* and the other configuration files. The name may not contain whitespace but is otherwise unrestricted in its contents. However, for consistency, you should stick to the Apache convention of making directives short phrases with the initial letter of each word capitalized. Apache processes directives in a case-insensitive manner.
>
> While processing configuration files, Apache employs a general parsing algorithm. Whenever it hits what appears to be a configuration directive, it searches through the internal module list and peeks into each module's command table until it finds the definition it's looking for. At this point, the server parses the directive's arguments and passes the information to the module's designated configuration processing routine.

const char *(*func) ()

> This is a pointer to a directive handler that Apache will call at runtime to process the directive. The prototype for the callback is determined by the `args_how` field described later in this section. Usually the callback simply sets a value in a module-specific data structure.

void *cmd_data

> If the module needs to share common information among multiple directive handlers, the `cmd_data` field allows you to pass this information around as a `void*` block. If non-NULL, Apache will pass the contents of `cmd_data` to the directive handler at runtime in the `cmd_parms` argument. One use for this would be a situation in which a single directive handler is responsible for processing multiple directives. In order for the handler to determine which directive it's responsible for, the module can leave the address of a distinguishing flag in the `cmd_data` slot.

For an example of this technique, see how *mod_autoindex* implements the various *AddIcon** and *AddAlt** directives.

`int override`

> This field indicates the scope of a directive. The scope is used by Apache to determine what parts of the various configuration files and *.htaccess* files the directive is allowed to appear in. `override` is a bit mask constructed from the bitwise OR of a set of constants which we list presently.

`enum cmd_how args_how`

> This field tells the server how it should parse the directive's arguments. It is any of 12 constants that specify the number of mandatory and optional arguments the directive takes. We explain the possibilities later in this section.

`char *errmsg`

> This field contains a short usage message that is displayed when the configuration parser encounters a syntax error in the directive. The usage message is also put to good use by *mod_info* to display modules' current configurations.

Constants for the override Field

Directives vary in their scope. Some affect low-level processes such as URI translation or the proxy mechanism and therefore belong outside of *<Directory>* and *<Location>* sections. Others control access to particular files and directories and only make sense when located within a *<Directory>* or *<Location>* section. In other cases, you might want the directive to be available to the webmaster but not allow it to appear in *.htaccess* files where it would be available to HTML authors.

The `override` field of the `command_rec` controls the scope. It is the bitwise combination of the following constants defined in *http_config.h*:

`RSRC_CONF`

> The directive can only be present in the server *.conf* files, *outside* of *<Directory>*, *<Location>*, and *<Files>* containers. Not allowed in any *.htaccess* files or other files defined by the *AccessFileName* directive.

`ACCESS_CONF`

> The directive can only be present in the server *.conf* files, *inside* *<Directory>*, *<Location>*, and *<Files>* sections. It is not allowed in *.htaccess* files.

`OR_AUTHCFG`

> The directive has the same scope as `ACCESS_CONF`, but it is also allowed in *.htaccess* if *AllowOverride AuthConfig* is configured for the current directory.

`OR_LIMIT`

> The directive has the same scope as `ACCESS_CONF`, but it is also allowed in *.htaccess* if *AllowOverride Limit* is configured for the current directory.

OR_OPTIONS

The directive is allowed *anywhere* in the *.conf* files, and it is also allowed in *.htaccess* if *AllowOverride Options* is configured for the current directory.

OR_FILEINFO

The directive is allowed *anywhere* in the *.conf* files, and it is also allowed in *.htaccess* if *AllowOverride FileInfo* is configured for the current directory.

OR_INDEXES

The directive is allowed *anywhere* in the *.conf* files, and it is also allowed in *.htaccess* if *AllowOverride Indexes* is configured for the current directory.

OR_ALL

The directive can be just about anywhere it wants to be.

OR_NONE

The directive cannot be overridden by any of the *AllowOverride* options.

Constants for the args_how Field

Directives differ in their syntax: the number of arguments they take, the number of variable arguments, and the relationship of one argument to another. Apache can handle the common syntaxes, preparsing the directive and its arguments, then presenting the results to a directive handler of your own devising.

Eleven constants, all defined in *http_config.h*, specify various syntax parsing strategies. If none of these satisfies your needs, a twelfth constant, RAW_ARGS, gives you direct access to the text of the configuration file.

In the list that follows, we give the constant and the recommended function prototype for the directive handler callback. All callbacks take at least two arguments. parms is a pointer to a cmd_parms structure, from which various information about the server and the status of the configuration process can be extracted. More details on the cmd_parms structure are given in the next section.

mconfig is a generic pointer to the module-specific per-directory configuration data that your module created earlier with its *create_dir_config()* routine. Since most directive handlers work with pre-directory configuration records, this parameter is provided as a convenience. Your handler will typecast this to its specific type, and then set the appropriate fields. Directive handlers that operate on per-server configuration data must manually retrieve the record using *ap_get_module_config()* as described later.

On successful processing of the directive, the handler should return NULL. If an error occurred while processing the directive, the routine should return a string describing the source of the error. There is also a third possibility. The configuration directive handler can return DECLINE_CMD, a constant defined in *http_config.h*

as the string \a\b. This is useful in the rare circumstance in which a module redeclares another module's directive in order to override it. The directive handler can
then return DECLINE_CMD when it wishes the directive to fall through to the original module.

NO_ARGS

The directive takes no arguments at all, for example *ClearModuleList*.

Function prototype:

```
static const char *cmd_no_args
      (cmd_parms *parms, void *mconfig)
```

FLAG

The directive takes one of the string arguments *On* or *Off*. The parser converts this argument to an integer Boolean, which it passes to the directive handler. *UseCanonicalName* is one example of this type of directive.

Function prototype:

```
static const char *cmd_flag
      (cmd_parms *parms, void *mconfig, int flag)
```

TAKE1

The directive takes one argument only, e.g., *Port*.

Function prototype:

```
static const char *cmd_take1
      (cmd_parms *parms, void *mconfig, const char *arg)
```

Here is an example of a handler for a *TrafficCopSpeedLimit* directive that takes
a single argument indicating the maximum speed at which clients are allowed
to fetch documents:

```
static const char *traffic_speed_limit_cmd (cmd_parms *parms,
                        void *mconfig, const char *arg)
{
    traffic_dir_config *cfg = (traffic_dir_config *)mconfig;
    traffic_server_config *scfg = (traffic_server_config *)
      ap_get_module_config(parms->server->module_config, &traffic_module);

    long int speed = strtol(arg, (char**)NULL, 10);

    if (speed < 0) {
        return "Speed must be a positive number";
    }
    if (speed == LONG_MAX) {
        return "Integer overflow or invalid number";
    }
    scfg->speed_limit = speed;
    return NULL;
}
```

TAKE2

The directive takes exactly two arguments, e.g., *SetEnv*.

Function prototype:

```
static const char *cmd_take2
       (cmd_parms *parms, void *mconfig, const char *one, const char *two)
```

ITERATE

The directive takes a list of arguments, each of which has the same meaning, as in *IndexIgnore*. The callback is invoked repeatedly to process each argument.

Function prototype:

```
static const char *cmd_iterate
       (cmd_parms *parms, void *mconfig, const char *arg)
```

For example, a *TrafficCopRightOfWay* directive for the imaginary traffic cop module might take a list of domains and hostnames that are allowed to retrieve documents as fast as they wish. Assuming that the list of privileged hosts is maintained as the set of keys in an Apache table, here's one way to record the configuration information:

```
static const char *traffic_rt_of_way_cmd(cmd_parms *parms,
                          void *mconfig, const char *arg)
{
    traffic_dir_config *cfg = (traffic_dir_config *)mconfig;
    traffic_server_config *scfg = (traffic_server_config *)
        ap_get_module_config(parms->server->module_config, &traffic_module);

    ap_table_set(scfg->right_of_way, arg, "t");
    return NULL;
}
```

ITERATE2

The directive takes a mandatory first argument followed by a variable list of arguments to be applied to the first. A familiar example is the *AddIcon* directive. Apache will call the directive handler once for each member of the list, passing the handler the mandatory argument and the current list item.

Function prototype:

```
static const char *cmd_iterate2
       (cmd_parms *parms, void *mconfig, const char *one, const char *two)
```

TAKE12

The directive will accept one or two arguments, as in the *AuthUserFile* directive. If the optional second argument is absent, it will be passed as NULL to your handler.

Function prototype:

```
static const char *cmd_take12
       (cmd_parms *parms, void *mconfig, const char *one, const char *two)
```

TAKE3

The directive takes exactly three arguments.

Function prototype:

```
static const char *cmd_take3
      (cmd_parms *parms, void *mconfig,
        const char *one, const char *two, const char *three)
```

TAKE23

The directive takes two or three arguments, as in *Redirect*. Missing arguments are passed to the directive handler as NULL.

Function prototype:

```
static const char *cmd_take23
      (cmd_parms *parms, void *mconfig,
        const char *one, const char *two, const char *three)
```

TAKE123

The directive takes one, two, or three arguments. Missing arguments are passed to the directive handler as NULL.

Function prototype:

```
static const char *cmd_take123
      (cmd_parms *parms, void *mconfig,
        const char *one, const char *two, const char *three)
```

TAKE13

Continuing in the same vein, directives with this syntax take either one or three arguments, but not two. Any missing arguments are passed as NULL.

Function prototype:

```
static const char *cmd_take13
      (cmd_parms *parms, void *mconfig,
        const char *one, const char *two, const char *three)
```

RAW_ARGS

This last constant is used for complex directives that the server won't be able to parse on its own. Your module must implement the parsing itself. The corresponding directive handler will be passed everything to the right of the directive name as an unparsed string. It can then use *ap_getword()* to process the string a word at a time.

The function prototype for RAW_ARGS directive handlers looks like this:

```
const char *cmd_raw_args
      (cmd_parms *parms, void *mconfig, const char *args)
```

RAW_ARGS can also be used to implement new container-style directives like *<Limit>* and *<Location>* by reading directly from the configuration file using the config_file field of the parms argument. See "Customizing the Configuration Process" later in this chapter for details on reading from this field.

The cmd_parms Structure

A `cmd_parms` structure is the first argument passed to all directive handlers. It contains a miscellaneous collection of information about the server configuration process. You may never actually need to use this argument, but it is available for certain advanced configuration tasks, such as implementing new container directives.

Example 11-2 gives the `cmd_parms` typedef, copied from *http_config.h*. The extensive (and sometimes wry) comments have been condensed to save some space.

Example 11-2. The cmd_parms Structure (from http_config.h)

```
typedef struct {
    void *info;                  /* argument to command from cmd table */
    int override;                /* same as req_override */
    int limited;                 /* which methods are <Limit>ed */
    configfile_t *config_file;   /* filehandle for reading from config stream */
    pool *pool;                  /* long-term resource pool */
    pool *temp_pool;             /* short-term resource pool */
    server_rec *server;          /* server record */
    char *path;                  /* directive path information */
    const command_rec *cmd;      /* copy of command_rec entry */
    const char *end_token;       /* end token for container directives */
} cmd_parms;
```

Here is a brief description of each of the fields in this structure:

`void *info`

This field contains a copy of the **cmd_data** field in the current directive's command record. It is typically used for passing static information to the directive handler.

`int override`

The **override** field contains a copy of the **args_how** field in the current directive's command record.

`int limited`

If the directive is contained within a *<Limit>* section, this field contains a bit mask representing the method numbers that the section applies to. This bit mask is constructed from the method numbers in the same way as described in "Authorization and Authentication Routines" in Chapter 10.

`configfile_t *config_file`

This is a filehandle-like data type from which you can read raw text from the current configuration file. See "Customizing the Configuration Process" later in this chapter for details on using this field.

pool *pool

This is a resource pool that persists for the lifetime of the server. It is only destroyed when the server is restarted or shutdown. If you wish to allocate truly long-term configuration information, this is the pool to use.

pool *temp_pool

In contrast, this pool pointer is available only within the configuration phase during server startup. It is destroyed before the first request is served. It is handy for allocating space for scratch data that your module won't need after configuration is completed.

server_rec *server

This field contains a pointer to the **server_rec** for the current (virtual) host. You will need to use it when processing server-specific configuration directives in order to retrieve the server-specific configuration record.

char *path

When the handler is called to process a directory-specific directive, the path will contain whatever is the argument of the enclosing *<Directory>*, *<Location>*, or *<Files>* section. For *<Directory>* and *<Location>*, this will be the path of the current directory. For *<Files>*, it will be the text of the regular expression or glob match. If the handler is being called to process a directive located in an access control file, **path** will contain the path to the directory containing the *.htaccess* file.

If the directive is called in a server context (either in the main part of a configuration file or a *<VirtualHost>* section), **path** will be an empty string.

The **path** field is used by two frequent idioms. One idiom is used when you want a directive to be available *only* in a per-directory context, such as a *.htaccess* file. This effect is achieved by the following fragment of a directive-processing routine:

```
static const char *foo_cmd(cmd_parms *parms, void *mconfig, ...)
{
    foo_dir_config *cfg = (foo_dir_config *)mconfig;
    if (parms->path == NULL || cfg == NULL) {
        return "foo: only valid in per-directory context";
    }
    ...
```

The other idiom is used when you want a directive to be valid for processing directives located both inside and outside of *<Directory>* sections and to operate on the per-server configuration record when outside a directory context but on the per-directory record when inside a directory context:

```
static const char *foo_cmd(cmd_parms *parms, void  *mconfig, ...)
{
    foo_dir_conf *dconf = (foo_dir_conf *)mconfig;
    foo_srv_conf *sconf = (foo_srv_conf *)
        ap_get_module_config(parms->server->module_config, &foo_module);
```

```
        if (parms->path == NULL) {
            ...configure sconf...
        }
        else {
            ...configure dconf...
        }
    }
```

const command_rec *cmd

This field points back to the **command_rec** entry that describes the directive that the current handler is responsible for.

const char *end_token

When Apache is processing the contents of a container section such as *<Directory>*, **end_token** contains the character string that will terminate the section, e.g., **</Directory>**. **end_token** is used internally by Apache's *ap_srm_command_loop()* function (described later in this chapter) but is rarely, if ever, needed by modules.

Accessing Module Configuration Data

The last piece in the puzzle is a way for modules to get access to their configuration data at request time, from within a transaction phase handler. This need is satisfied by the *ap_get_module_config()* call, and its rarely used sibling, *ap_set_module_config()*.

void *ap_get_module_config (void *conf_vector, module *m)

Modules can use *ap_get_module_config()* to fetch both per-directory and per-server configuration data. To fetch per-directory data, pass the function the contents of the request record's **per_dir_config** field as the first argument, and the address of the module's own **module** structure as the second:

```
hello_dir_config *cfg = (hello_dir_config *)
        ap_get_module_config(r->per_dir_config, &hello_module);
```

The function result is a **void***. For clarity you should cast it to correct type in order to access the configuration data structure's fields, although technically many C compilers allow you to assign void pointers to typed variables without complaining. You'll see examples of both styles in the standard Apache modules.

Do not make the mistake of using the request record's **request_config** field here. The **request_config** is a spare (and usually empty) field that a module can use to pass configuration information to subrequests. We'll touch on this shortly.

To fetch per-server data, use the configuration vector stored in the server record's **module_config** field as the first argument:

```
traffic_server_config *cfg = (traffic_server_config *)
    ap_get_module_config(r->server->module_config, &traffic_module);
```

In case you're wondering, the `per_dir_config` and `module_config` fields are actually pointers to a private Apache type known as the "configuration vector." However, this data type doesn't contain any user-serviceable parts and so is presented to the visible part of the API as an opaque void pointer.

void ap_set_module_config (void *conf_vector, module *m, void *val)

Modules don't often call this function directly, as it is called for them by the internal configuration mechanism. When a new per-directory or per-server module configuration is created, Apache saves a pointer to it in a vector of configuration records, indexed by the address of your `module`. A copy of this vector eventually appears in the server record's `module_config` field or in the request record's `per_dir_config` field. Given a configuration vector, a `module` pointer, and the configuration data block, *ap_set_module_config()* appends the configuration information to the vector for later retrieval by *ap_get_module_config()*.

Some modules, such as *mod_negotiation*, don't bother with a per-server config creator because their entire configuration consists of an "on" or "off" Boolean. Instead, the directive handlers for these modules simply call *ap_set_module_config()* to set their configuration block to `NULL` when their state is off or non-`NULL` when their state is on. This is not a recommended practice!

Another use for *ap_set_module_config()* is to pass per-request configuration data to subrequests via the request record's `request_config` field. This field usually points to an empty configuration vector, but handlers are free to append their own configuration data to the vector. The information is then available for use by subrequests and by handlers for later phases of the transaction. Any information stored in `request_config` is cleared out at the end of the current transaction.

Example:

```
ap_set_module_config(r->request_config, &my_module, cfg_ptr);
```

To see some practical examples of the `request_config` field, examine the source code for *mod_include* and *mod_mime_magic*, where the `request_config` vector is used to stash information passed to subrequests.

To pass simple string messages between different phases and between requests and subrequests, you might consider using the `notes` table instead.

"Hello World" with All the Bells and Whistles

To show you how custom configuration directives work in practice, let's go ahead and add a directive handler table to the *mod_hello* example that we introduced long, long ago in Chapter 2, *A First Module*.

We start simply by adding the ability for users to configure *mod_hello* to say hello to something other than "world," which you are surely tired of by now. Once we are done making the required modifications to *mod_hello.c*, the message "Hello world" can be changed to "Hello Dolly" by adding this line to any configuration file:

```
HelloTo Dolly
```

The complete source code for the modified *mod_hello.c* is shown in Example 11-3.

The first change over the original version is to declare the **module** structure at the top of the source file. This is to allow the C compiler to handle forward references to the structure within the calls to *ap_get_module_config()*. The new line immediately follows the **#include** lines:

```
module hello_module;
```

Next, we declare a new data type to hold our per-directory configuration data, **hello_dir_config**. Its definition has a single field only, a **char*** named **to**, which will hold the argument of the *HelloTo* directive:

```
typedef struct {
    char *to;
} hello_dir_config;
```

Now we need to add a function to create a new per-directory structure. This will be called each time Apache notices one of the module's directives in a directory or location configuration section. Our function simply allocates a new **hello_dir_config** structure and initializes the **to** field to contain the default string **world**:

```
static void *hello_create_dir_config(pool *p, char *path)
{
    hello_dir_config *cfg =
      (hello_dir_config *)ap_pcalloc(p, sizeof(hello_dir_config));
    cfg->to = "world";
    return (void *)cfg;
}
```

Now we must modify the **module** structure so that the per-directory config creator slot is occupied by our new per-directory config creator function:

```
hello_create_dir_config,  /* per-directory config creator */
```

In this case, our configuration data is so simple that there's no need to write a directory config merge function. In the absence of a merge function, Apache will use the most specific configuration record, giving us the most recent value of *HelloTo*. This is exactly what we want.

What's next? We need a function to actually handle the directive. Once Apache hits the *HelloTo* directive, it will call this function, passing it a **cmd_parms** pointer, a pointer to our newly initialized `hello_dir_config` structure, and the directive argument. The *hello_cmd_to()* directive handling function is nice and simple. It makes a copy of the argument and stores it into the configuration structure. We return NULL to indicate that all went well:

```
static const char *hello_cmd_to(cmd_parms *parms,
                                void *mconfig, char *to)
{
    hello_dir_config *cfg = (hello_dir_config *)mconfig;
    cfg->to = (char*)ap_pstrdup(parms->pool, to);
    return NULL;
}
```

In order for Apache to know about our new directive, we need to create a `command_rec` table to register it with the `module` structure. The table declares a single directive named *HelloTo* whose command handler is *hello_cmd_to()*. The directive will be available anywhere in the configuration files and will take a single argument. There's no static information to pass to the handler, so this field is NULL:

```
static command_rec hello_cmds[] =
{
    {
        "HelloTo",                       /* directive name */
        hello_cmd_to,                    /* config action routine */
        NULL,                            /* argument to include in call */
        OR_ALL,                          /* where available */
        TAKE1,                           /* arguments */
        "Who we say hello to, default is 'world'" /* description */
    },
    {NULL}
};
```

Notice that the `command_rec` table is terminated by a NULL record.

We can now add the `hello_cmds` array to the command table slot of the `module` structure. The complete module structure looks like this:

```
module MODULE_VAR_EXPORT hello_module =
{
    STANDARD_MODULE_STUFF,
    NULL,                   /* module initializer              */
    hello_create_dir_config, /* per-directory config creator      */
    NULL,                   /* dir config merger               */
    NULL,                   /* server config creator           */
    NULL,                   /* server config merger            */
    hello_cmds,             /* command table                   */
    hello_handlers,         /* [9]  content handlers           */
    NULL,                   /* [2]  URI-to-filename translation */
    NULL,                   /* [5]  check/validate user_id     */
    NULL,                   /* [6]  check user_id is valid *here* */
    NULL,                   /* [4]  check access by host address */
    NULL,                   /* [7]  MIME type checker/setter   */
```

```
    NULL,                /* [8]  fixups                    */
    NULL,                /* [10] logger                    */
    NULL,                /* [3]  header parser             */
    NULL,                /* process initialization         */
    NULL,                /* process exit/cleanup           */
    NULL                 /* [1]  post read_request handling */
};
```

The last thing we need to do is to actually put the configuration data to use. In the content handler function *hello_handler()*, we add the following line to retrieve the configuration structure:

```
hello_dir_config *cfg = (hello_dir_config *)
    ap_get_module_config(r->per_dir_config, &hello_module);
```

Now we change the call to *rputs()*, where we used to print out "Hello world", into a call to *rprintf()* that uses the configuration information to print out a customized message:

```
rprintf(r, "say \"hello %s\"?\n", cfg->to);
```

Recompile the module, restart the server, and start saying "Hello" to whomever you choose!

Example 11-3. mod_hello with a Custom Configuration Directive

```
/* file: mod_hello.c */

#include "httpd.h"
#include "http_config.h"
#include "http_core.h"
#include "http_log.h"
#include "http_protocol.h"

/* Forward declaration so that ap_get_module_config() can find us. */
module hello_module;

/* Here's our per-directory configuration data */
typedef struct {
    char *to;
} hello_dir_config;

/* This function is called to create the default per-directory
   configuration */
static void *hello_create_dir_config(pool *p, char *path)
{
    hello_dir_config *cfg =
        (hello_dir_config *)ap_pcalloc(p, sizeof(hello_dir_config));
    cfg->to = "world";
    return (void *)cfg;
}

/* This is the handler for the HelloTo directive */
static const char *hello_cmd_to(cmd_parms *parms, void *mconfig, char *to)
```

Example 11-3. mod_hello with a Custom Configuration Directive (continued)

```
{
    hello_dir_config *cfg = (hello_dir_config *)mconfig;
    cfg->to = (char *)ap_pstrdup(parms->pool, to);
    return NULL;
}

/* Make the name of the content handler known to Apache */
static command_rec hello_cmds[] =
{
    {
        "HelloTo",                /* directive name */
        hello_cmd_to,             /* config action routine */
        NULL,                     /* argument to include in call */
        OR_ALL,                   /* where available */
        TAKE1,                    /* arguments */
        "Who we say hello to, default is 'world'" /* description */
    },
    {NULL}
};

/* here's the content handler */
static int hello_handler(request_rec *r) {
  const char* hostname;
  hello_dir_config *cfg;

  r->content_type = "text/html";
  ap_send_http_header(r);
  hostname = ap_get_remote_host(r->connection,
                                r->per_dir_config, REMOTE_NAME);
  cfg = (hello_dir_config *)
        ap_get_module_config(r->per_dir_config, &hello_module);

  ap_rputs("<HTML>\n", r);
  ap_rputs("<HEAD>\n", r);
  ap_rputs("<TITLE>Hello There</TITLE>\n", r);
  ap_rputs("</HEAD>\n", r);
  ap_rputs("<BODY>\n", r);
  ap_rprintf(r, "<H1>Hello %s</H1>\n", hostname);
  ap_rputs("Here we go again...", r);
  ap_rprintf(r, "\"Hello %s\"!\n", cfg->to);
  ap_rputs("</BODY>\n", r);
  ap_rputs("</HTML>\n", r);

  return OK;
}

/* Make the name of the content handler known to Apache */
static handler_rec hello_handlers[] =
{
    {"hello-handler", hello_handler},
    {NULL}
};
```

Example 11-3. mod_hello with a Custom Configuration Directive (continued)

```
/* Tell Apache what phases of the transaction we handle */
module MODULE_VAR_EXPORT hello_module =
{
    STANDARD_MODULE_STUFF,
    NULL,                   /* module initializer                */
    hello_create_dir_config,  /* per-directory config creator      */
    NULL,                   /* dir config merger             */
    NULL,                   /* server config creator         */
    NULL,                   /* server config merger          */
    hello_cmds,             /* command table                 */
    hello_handlers,         /* [9]   content handlers         */
    NULL,                   /* [2]   URI-to-filename translation */
    NULL,                   /* [5]   check/validate user_id      */
    NULL,                   /* [6]   check user_id is valid *here* */
    NULL,                   /* [4]   check access by host address */
    NULL,                   /* [7]   MIME type checker/setter    */
    NULL,                   /* [8]   fixups                   */
    NULL,                   /* [10]  logger                   */
    NULL,                   /* [3]   header parser            */
    NULL,                   /* process initialization         */
    NULL,                   /* process exit/cleanup           */
    NULL                    /* [1]   post read_request handling  */
};
```

Handy Built-in Directive Handlers

It is often the case that a configuration directive will end up simply setting the value of a structure field without doing any additional work. There are a few directive handlers built into the Apache API to handle such common cases.

Since it isn't possible for a built-in function to know anything about the structure of a module-specific data type, these functions work by writing directly into the module's configuration data using pointer arithmetic. You calculate the correct offset into the structure using the *XtOffsetOf()* macro[*] and place this offset into the command table's **cmd_data** field.

For example, in Example 11-3 the *HelloTo* directive simply sets a string pointer in the **to** field of the **hello_dir_config** struct. Instead of writing our own handler to accomplish this task, we can use the generic *ap_set_string_slot()* call, providing the handler with the offset of the field:

```
static command_rec hello_cmds[] =
{
    {
        "HelloTo",
        ap_set_string_slot,
        (void *)XtOffsetOf(hello_dir_config, to),
```

---

[*] The name *XtOffsetOf()* betrays this macro's origins. It was cut and pasted from the X Windows source code!

```
            OR_ALL,
            TAKE1,
            "Who we say hello to, default is 'world'"
        },
        {NULL}
    };
```

The generic directive handlers and the *XtOffsetOf()* macro are declared in *ap_config.h*. The following generic directive handlers are available:

const char *ap_set_string_slot (cmd_parms *parms, char *ptr, char *arg)

> This handler is used with the **TAKE1** prototype to set a string in a configuration structure. The provided offset must point to a **char*** field. See the previous code snippet for an example of its usage.

const char *ap_set_string_slot_lower (cmd_parms *parms, char *ptr, char *arg)

> This function works just the same as *ap_set_string_slot()* but changes the value of the directive's argument to lowercase before setting the configuration field.

const char *ap_set_flag_slot (cmd_parms *parms, char *ptr, int flag)

> This function is intended to be used with a **FLAG** prototype. The structure offset should point to an integer field. For example, if we wanted the ability to turn off our "Hello world" message entirely, we could add a new **int helloOn** field to the **hello_dir_config** struct and toggle it on and off with a *SayHello* directive. An appropriate slot in the command table would then look like this:

```
    {
        "SayHello",
        ap_set_flag_slot,
        (void *)XtOffsetOf(hello_dir_config, helloOn),
        OR_ALL,
        FLAG,
        "Should we say Hello, On or Off",
    },
```

> The content handler could now test **cfg->helloOn** to determine whether to print out that annoyingly repetitive message or not.

const char *ap_set_file_slot (cmd_parms *parms, char *ptr, char *file)

> The last goodie is a built-in handler that works much like *ap_set_string_slot()* but assumes the argument is a filename. If the filename is not absolute, it is first resolved relative to the configured *ServerRoot* directory.

For example, let's say we wanted to read our "Hello" message from a file stored on disk. We could add a **char* to_file** field to the configuration struct and set it using a *HelloToFile* directive described by this table entry:

```
    {
        "HelloToFile",
        ap_set_file_slot,
        (void *)XtOffsetOf(hello_dir_config, to_file),
```

```
        OR_ALL,
        TAKE1,
        "File containing hello message, absolute or server root relative."
    },
```

With this setup, both *HelloToFile /etc/motd* and *HelloToFile conf/hello.conf* would work in a manner consistent with other Apache directives.

Accessing Other Modules' Configuration Information

Although it violates the principles of code encapsulation, there's no reason that one module can't access another module's configuration information. The module simply calls *ap_get_module_config()* with the address of the other module's `module` table in order to obtain the desired configuration information. You'll need to know the correct data type for the configuration data in order to do anything useful with it, of course.

If you happen to have a C module that needs to tap into the *PerlSetVar* configuration, you can do so by following this example:

```
#include "modules/perl/mod_perl.h"

perl_dir_config *c = (perl_dir_config *)
        ap_get_module_config(r->per_dir_config, &perl_module);
table *perl_vars = c->vars;
```

mod_perl's per-directory configuration data is simply an Apache table. You can access the *PerlSetVar* keys and values with *ap_table_get()*:

```
char *value = ap_table_get(perl_vars, "GuestbookFile");
```

Before interacting with another module, it is wise to determine if the module has been configured with the server. There are a few functions that can be used to find out if a module is accessible:

module *ap_find_linked_module (const char *name)
This function will walk the internal list of loaded modules, comparing `name` with the `name` field of each `module` structure. If a match is found, a pointer to the `module` structure is returned, `NULL` otherwise. The *IfModule* configuration directive is implemented using this function. Example:

```
if(ap_find_linked_module("mod_proxy.c")) {
    /* mod_proxy is loaded */
}
```

int ap_exists_config_define (char *name)
Apache Version 1.3.1 added a *−D* command line switch that can be used to pass the server parameter names for conditional configuration with the *IfDefine* directive. These names exist for the lifetime of the server and can be

accessed at any time using the *ap_exists_config_define()* function. For example, both *Stronghold* and *mod_ssl*'s `module` structures are defined in a file named *mod_ssl.c*, so *ap_find_linked_module()* cannot be used to differentiate between the two. However, *mod_ssl* passes a *–DSSL* parameter to the server which can be tested instead:

```
if(ap_exists_config_define("SSL")) {
    /* mod_ssl started the server with -DSSL */
}
else {
    ...
}
```

Customizing the Configuration Process

If Apache's standard configuration mechanism isn't sufficient for you, or you want to do something wild like generating dynamic configuration files on the fly (as *mod_perl* does in its *<Perl>* sections), you can reach into the internals of Apache's configuration machinery and make it do what you want. This section covers the more obscure parts of Apache's configuration system and shows you how to achieve advanced effects such as redirecting the configuration process from your own data source.

The configfile_t Structure

Apache uses a clever abstraction for its configuration process. Instead of reading the text of the configuration file directly from a `FILE*` or file descriptor, Apache interposes the concept of an abstract "configuration stream," the `configfile_t` pointer. Configuration streams are much like ordinary files, allowing your programs to read from them character by character or line by line, and they are often attached to real files. However, a `configfile_t` pointer may just as easily be attached to another process or even to a set of internal subroutines that read configuration information from a database. By creating a custom `configfile_t` pointer, your module can dynamically generate configuration text to feed directly into the Apache configuration machinery.

The `configfile_t` struct is defined in *httpd.h*. Its definition is reproduced in Example 11-4. The most important fields are the first three, which are pointers to callback functions that act like the *getc()*, *fgets()*, and *close()* standard I/O library functions. These three functions are used to implement the routines that fetch data from whatever file, process, or internal routine is attached to the data stream. The fourth field, `param`, is a `void*` that holds stream-specific data. In a configuration stream attached to a file, this might be the `FILE*`. In a stream attached to routines that read data from a database, this might be the database handle. This field is passed to the callback functions at runtime. The last two fields, `name` and `line_` number, contain a description of the data source and the number of the last-read line. These fields are used for reporting configuration syntax errors.

Example 11-4. The configfile_t Struct (from httpd.h)

```
typedef struct {
    int (*getch) (void *param);   /* a getc()-like function */
                                  /* an fgets()-like function */
    void *(*getstr) (void *buf, size_t bufsiz, void *param);
    int (*close) (void *param);   /* a close() function */
    void *param;                  /* the argument passed to getch/getstr/close */
    const char *name;             /* the filename / description */
    unsigned line_number;         /* current line number, starting at 1 */
} configfile_t;
```

Directive processing handlers can find a pointer to the currently active configfile_t stream by examining the config_file field of the passed parms argument.

Using Configuration Streams

The API calls listed in this section allow you to open configfile_t pointers on files, to read configuration data from them, and to create custom configfile_t streams that fetch their data from arbitrary sources. For the most part, you should access the configfile_t fields via the appropriate API functions listed in this section. Do not attempt to modify any of the fields directly.

The following short code fragment shows the basic outline for opening a configuration file, reading it line by line, then closing it:

```
    char line[MAX_STRING_LEN];
    configfile_t *cfg = ap_pcfg_openfile(p, file);

    if(!cfg) {
        ap_log_error(APLOG_MARK, APLOG_CRIT, s,
                    "unable to open config file %s", file);
        exit(1);
    }

    while (!(ap_cfg_getline(line, sizeof(line), cfg))) {
        if(*line == '#' || !*line) {
            continue; /* skip comments and empty lines */
        }
        /* ... do something with the line ... */
    }

    ap_pcfg_closefile(cfg);
```

*configfile_t *ap_pcfg_openfile (pool *p, const char *name)*

The most common type of configfile_t is one that is opened on an ordinary text file. Examples include Apache's *httpd.conf, srm.conf,* and *access.conf* configuration files.

The *ap_pcfg_openfile()* function takes a resource pool pointer and the path of the configuration file to open. If successful, the function fills in the stream's `param` field with a `FILE*` opened on the requested file and sets up the first three fields so as to call back to functions that read data from the `FILE*`.[*]

If an error occurs while opening the file, the function logs an error message and returns `NULL`.

*int ap_cfg_getline (char *buf, size_t bufsize, configfile_t *cfp)*

The *ap_cfg_getline()* function reads a line of data from the given `configfile_t` pointer. The arguments consist of a character buffer, (*buf*), the maximum size of the buffer (*bufsize*), and the `configfile_t` pointer itself. The function fills the buffer with a line of configuration file data up to the maximum specified in *bufsize*, and returns the number of characters read as the function result. The function returns 0 if no more data is left to read or if an error occurred.

The definition of a configuration file "line" is different from the usual one. The returned line is stripped of leading and trailing whitespace, and runs of space characters and other whitespace are replaced with single spaces, unless they are enclosed within quotes. The *ap_cfg_getline()* function also correctly handles continuation lines. Lines ending with the backslash character (\) are merged into single lines, and the newlines replaced with single spaces. For each line read, the `configfile_t`'s `line_number` field is incremented by one.

*int ap_cfg_getc (configfile_t *cfp)*

The *ap_cfg_getc()* function acts like *getc()* to return a single character from the `configfile_t` stream. The character is returned as the function result, or EOF is returned when there is no more data to be read. The `line_number` field is incremented when a linefeed character is seen, but continuation characters do *not* receive special treatment.

*int ap_cfg_closefile (configfile_t *cfp)*

Once you are done reading from a `configfile_t`, call *ap_cfg_closefile()* to close the file or release other resources.

*configfile_t *ap_pcfg_open_custom (pool *p, const char *descr, void *param, int(*getc_func)(void*), void *(*gets_func) (void*, size_t, void*), int(*close_func)(void*))*

The *ap_pcfg_open_custom()* function can be used to open and initialize a new configuration stream. The long prototype for this function may seem intimidating, but it's actually straightforward. The first argument is a resource

---

[*] Actually, the `FILE*` is not stored directly into the `param` field. Instead, it is stored into an intermediate data type called a `poolfile_t` that contains both the `FILE*` and a resource pool pointer. It is this `poolfile_t` that gets stored into the `param` field.

pool pointer, typically the pool pointer located in the server_rec passed to your module initialization handler. The second argument is a char* containing a description of the stream for use in error reporting. The third argument, param, is a generic pointer to any data you want to pass to the three callbacks. The fourth, fifth, and sixth arguments are function pointers to the callbacks themselves, corresponding to the routines that implement *getc_func()*, *fgets_func()*, and *close_func()* behavior.

The prototypes for these three callbacks are as follows:

```
int getc_func (void *param);
int gets_func (void *buffer, size_t bufsize, void *param);
int close_func (void *param);
```

The *getc_func()* should return a single character from the data stream. *gets_func()* should return a whole line or the number of characters specified in bufsize, whichever is smaller. *close_func()* should do whatever is necessary to close and deallocate the stream. Apache's core configuration routines only use *ap_cfg_getline()* to read from configuration streams, so it is possible in some circumstances to pass NULL for the *getc_func()* pointer.

The only example of using *ap_pcfg_open_custom()* in the standard distribution is in *http_config.c*, where it is used to process the Apache *−C* and *−c* command line arguments. *mod_perl* also uses this function during processing of *<Perl>* sections. You'll see an example of using this function shortly.

*const char *ap_srm_command_loop (cmd_parms *parms, void *cfgvector)*

The *ap_srm_command_loop()* function is the core of Apache's internal configuration process. The function operates on the configuration stream contained within the passed cmd_parms pointer and the vector of per-directory module-specific configuration pointers contained within the server record's lookup_defaults field. The return value is NULL if the entire configuration stream was parsed correctly or a character string indicating the error if the loop terminated prematurely because of a syntax error.

Within the function, Apache reads one line of configuration data after another with *ap_cfg_getline()*. It parses each line into directive name and arguments, searches through the modules' command tables for the handler for this directive, then locates the correct per-directory configuration pointer within the configuration vector. The command parameters, configuration pointer, and directive arguments are then passed to the handler for processing.

If your module wishes to take over Apache's configuration process and configure everything from information stored within, say, a database, it can do so. For instance, your module might declare a *ConfigFromDatabase* directive that takes a single argument, the data source from which to read the configuration information:

```
ConfigFromDatabase ODBC:ApacheConfig
```

Then, to implement this directive, the directive handler can be written like this:

```
static const char *cfg_from_db_cmd(cmd_parms *parms, db_cfg *cfg,
                                   char *dsn)
{
    db *dbhandle = db_open(dsn);
    configfile_t old_cfg = parms->config_file; /*save old config stream */

    parms->config_file =
        ap_pcfg_open_custom(p,
                            "Database config",
                            (void *)dbhandle,
                            NULL,
                            db_getline,
                            db_close);

    char *errmsg = ap_srm_command_loop(parms,
                                       parms->server->lookup_defaults);
    if (errmsg) {
        ap_log_error(APLOG_MARK, APLOG_CRIT, s,
                     "unable to config from database %s" );
        return errmsg;
    }
    ap_cfg_closefile(parms->config_file);

    parms->config_file = old_cfg; /* restore configuration stream */
    return NULL;
}
```

Your code has to supply the *db_open()* and *db_close()* routines to open and close the database handle, as well as the *db_getline()* routine. This last routine must return directive strings in exactly the same way they would appear in an ordinary configuration file, such as:

```
Group apache
```

Writing Container Directives

`cmd_parms->config_file` is also useful for implementing your own container-style directives. The logic is the same as described in Chapter 7, *Other Request Phases*. In the command table, declare the start-section directive as a `RAW_ARGS` style directive and omit the trailing > from the directive name. You should also declare the end-section directive as a `NO_ARGS` command:

```
static command_rec traffic_cmds[] =
{
    {"<TrafficCopSpeedLimits", spdlimit_container_cmd, NULL,
     RSRC_CONF, RAW_ARGS, "a district speed limit container"},
    {"</TrafficCopSpeedLimits>", spdlimit_container_cmd_end, NULL,
     RSRC_CONF, NO_ARGS, "end of speed limit container"},
    { NULL },
};
```

The command handler for the start-section directive uses a three-argument proto-type similar to this one:

```
const char *spdlimit_container_cmd(cmd_parms *parms,
                            void *mconfig, const char *args)
```

Everything to the right of the directive name will be passed in **args** as an unprocessed string. This string will include the terminal > symbol, so the com-mand handler should be careful to strip off the character. Something like this will do the trick:

```
char *endp = strrchr(args, '>');
if (!endp) {
    return "Syntax error: no terminal \">\" sign";
}
*endp = '\0';
```

The routine should then call *ap_getword_conf()* (or one of the other *ap_getword_* variants) in order to parse out the arguments and take the appropriate actions:

```
const char *pos = args;
char *nextword;
while (*pos && (nextword = ap_getword_conf(parms->pool, &pos))) {
    /* do something */
}
```

Now the directive handler will process the contents of the container. It does this by reading directly from **parms->config_file** until it finds the string that termi-nates the container. For each line it reads, it parses out the line and takes what-ever action is appropriate:

```
char line[MAX_STRING_LEN];
while (!ap_cfg_getline(line, sizeof(line), parms->config_file)) {
    if (!strcasecmp(line, "</TrafficCopSpeedLimits>")) {
        break;
    }
    /* otherwise parse the line and do something with it */
}
```

(**MAX_STRING_LEN**, defined in *httpd.h*, is used for static string buffers in various parts of the Apache core.)

Because this loop swallows the container terminator, Apache will normally never even see it. The reason for including the end-section directive in the module's command table is to catch configuration errors in which the end-section directive appears without being preceded by a matching start-section directive. The handler for this directive returns an error string:

```
static const char *spdlimit_container_cmd_end(cmd_parms *parms,
                                      void *mconfig)
{
  return "</TrafficCopSpeedLimits> without matching
          <TrafficCopSpeedLimits> section";
}
```

You can also write a completely generic end-section directive handler by taking advantage of the information stored in **parms**:

```
static const char *end_section(cmd_parms *parms, void *mconfig) {
    return ap_pstrcat(parms->pool, parms->cmd->name,
        " without matching <", parms->cmd->name + 2, " section", NULL);
}
```

We now turn to utility functions for manipulating strings, URIs, dates, and files.

String and URI Manipulation

The Apache API provides an extensive set of functions for parsing and manipulating strings and URIs. Some of these routines are functionally identical to standard C library functions but provide either a performance boost or enhanced safety. Other routines provide completely new functionality.

String Parsing Functions

While Apache's library for parsing and manipulating character strings is not nearly as rich as Perl's text processing abilities, it is a vast improvement over what's available in the impoverished standard C library.

Most of the string parsing routines belong to the *ap_getword** family, which together provide functionality similar to the Perl *split()* function. Each member of this family is able to extract a word from a string, splitting the text on delimiters such as whitespace or commas. Unlike Perl *split()*, in which the entire string is split at once and the pieces are returned in a list, the *ap_getword** functions operate on one word at a time. The function returns the next word each time it's called and keeps track of where it's been by bumping up a pointer.

All of the *ap_getword** routines are declared in *httpd.h*. The original declarations in *httpd.h* refer to the second argument as **char **line**. In the function prototypes that follow, we've changed the name of this argument to **char **string** in order to avoid the implication that the argument must always correspond to a single line of text.

char *ap_getword (pool *p, const char **string, char stop)
> *ap_getword()* is the most frequently used member of this family. It takes a pointer to a **char*** and splits it into words at the delimiter given by the *stop* character. Each time the function is called it returns the next word, allocating a new string from the resource pool pointer *p* to hold the word. The **char**** is updated after each call so that it points to the place where the previous call left off.

Here is an example of using *ap_getword()* to split a URL query string into its component key/value pairs. *ap_getword()* is called in two different contexts. First it's called repeatedly to split the query string into words delimited by the & character. Then, each time through the loop, the function is called once again to split the word into its key/value components at the = delimiter. The names and values are then placed into a table to return to the caller:

```
while(*data && (val = ap_getword(r->pool, &data, '&'))) {
    key = ap_getword(r->pool, &val, '=');

    ap_unescape_url((char *)key);
    ap_unescape_url((char *)val);
    ap_table_merge(tab, key, val);
}
```

This API also makes parsing HTTP cookies a breeze. In the following code fragment, *util_parse_cookie()* fetches the incoming HTTP cookies and parses them into a table. The incoming HTTP *Cookie* field, if present, contains one or more cookies separated by semicolons. Each cookie has the format *name=value1&value2&value3*, where the cookie's name is separated from a list of values by the = sign, and each value is, in turn, delimited by the & character. The values are escaped using the URI escaping rules in much the same way that CGI parameters are.

The code begins by retrieving the value of *Cookie*. It then splits it into individual name=value pairs using the *ap_get_word()* function. After trimming whitespace, *ap_getword()* is called once more to split each cookie into its name and value parts and again a third time to split out the individual values. The values are unescaped with *ap_unescape_url()*, and the parsed name and values are then added to a growing table:

```
table *util_parse_cookie(request_rec *r)
{
    const char *data = ap_table_get(r->headers_in, "Cookie");
    table *cookies;
    const char *pair;
    if(!data) return NULL;

    cookies = ap_make_table(r->pool, 4);
    while(*data && (pair = ap_getword(r->pool, &data, ';'))) {
        const char *name, *value;
        if(*data == ' ') ++data;
        name = ap_getword(r->pool, &pair, '=');
        while(*pair && (value = ap_getword(r->pool, &pair, '&'))) {
            ap_unescape_url((char *)value);
            ap_table_add(cookies, name, value);
        }
    }

    return cookies;
}
```

char *ap_getword_nc (pool *p, char **string, char stop)

This function is exactly the same as *ap_getword()*, but it accepts a non-*const* string pointer. Internally this routine shares all its code with *ap_getword()* and is simply provided as a convenience for avoiding a typecast.

char *ap_getword_nulls (pool *p, const char **string, char stop)

Unlike *ap_getword()*, which will skip multiple occurrences of the *stop* delimiter, *ap_getword_nulls()* preserves empty entries; that is, if the delimiter is a comma and the string looks like this:

```
larry,,curly
```

Then *ap_getword()* ignores the empty entry between the first and last words, while *ap_getword_nulls()* will return an empty string the second time it is called.

char *ap_getword_nulls_nc (pool *p, char **string, char stop)

This function is the same as *ap_getword_nulls()*, except that it accepts a non-constant string pointer.

char *ap_getword_white (pool *p, const char **string)

Because it is so common for a string of words to be delimited by variable amounts of whitespace, the *ap_getword_white()* function is provided for your use. In this case the delimiter is any number of space characters, form-feeds, newlines, carriage returns, or vertical tabs. This function is particularly useful for processing whitespace-delimited configuration directives.

```
while(*data && (val = ap_getword_white(r->pool, &data))) {
    ...
}
```

char * ap_getword_white_nc (pool *p, char **string)

This function is exactly the same as *ap_getword_white()*, but it accepts a non-constant string pointer.

char *ap_getword_conf (pool *p, const char **string)

This function is much like *ap_getword_white()*, but it takes single- and double-quoted strings into account as well as whitespace escaped with backslashes. This is the routine used internally to process Apache's configuration files.

During processing, the quotes and backslashes are stripped from the word. For example, given the following string, *ap_getword_conf()* will return `Hello World` on the first pass and `Example` on the second:

```
"Hello World" Example
```

If a backslash were present before the space preceding `Example`, the entire string would be treated as a single word and returned on the first call to *ap_getword_conf()*.

char *ap_getword_conf_nc (pool *p, char **string)

> This function is exactly the same as *ap_getword_conf()*, but it accepts a non-constant string pointer.

char *ap_get_token (pool *p, const char **string, int accept_white)

> This function is generally used to parse multivalued HTTP headers, which are delimited by commas or semicolons. If the *accept_white* parameter is non-zero, then whitespace will also be treated as a delimiter. Substrings enclosed in quotes are treated as single words, and, like *ap_getword_conf()*, the quotes are stripped from the return value. However, unlike *ap_getword_conf()*, back-slashes are not honored. Regardless of the setting of *accept_white*, leading and trailing spaces are always stripped from the return value.
>
> The *mod_negotiation* module makes heavy use of this function to parse *Accept* and *Accept-language* headers.
>
> Here is a typical example of using this function to extract all the words in the string stored in **data**:

```
while(*data && (val = ap_get_token(r->pool, &data, 0))) {
    ...
}
```

int ap_find_token (pool *p, const char *string, const char *tok)

int ap_find_last_token (pool *p, const char *string, const char *tok)

> These two functions are used for searching for particular tokens within HTTP header fields. A token is defined by RFC 2068 as a case-insensitive word delimited by the following separators:

```
separators     = "(" | ")" | "<" | ">" | "@"
               | "," | ";" | ":" | "\" | <">
               | "/" | "[" | "]" | "?" | "="
               | "{" | "}" | SP | HT
```

> *ap_find_token()* will return true if any token in the specified string matches the third argument, **tok**. *ap_find_last_token()* will return true if the last token in the string matches **tok**. Both functions match the token substring in a case-insensitive manner. This is useful if you want to search HTTP headers that contain multiple values, without having to parse through the whitespace, quotation marks, and other delimiter characters on your own. For example, this code fragment shows one way to detect the presence of a **gzip** token in the HTTP header *Accept-encoding*:

```
if(ap_find_token(p, ap_table_get(r->headers_in, "Accept-encoding"), "gzip"))
{
    /* we could do some on-the-fly compression */
}
```

String Comparison, Pattern Matching, and Transformation

The following group of functions provides string pattern matching, substitution, and transformation operations similar to (but more limited than) Perl's built-in operators.

Most of these functions are declared in *httpd.h*. The few exceptions are listed separately.

int ap_fnmatch (const char *pattern, const char *string, int flags)

(Declared in the header file *fnmatch.h*.) The *ap_fnmatch()* function is based on the POSIX.2 *fnmatch()* function. You provide a search pattern, a string to search, and a bit mask of option flags. The function will return 0 if a match is found, or the nonzero constant FNM_NOMATCH otherwise. Note that the function result is the reverse of what you would expect. It is done this way in order to be compatible with *strcasecmp()*. It may be less confusing to compare the function result to the constant FNM_NOMATCH than to test for zero.

The pattern you provide is not a regular expression, but a shell-style glob pattern. In addition to the wildcard characters * and ?, patterns containing both string sets like foo.{h,c,cc} and character ranges like .[a-zA-Z]* are allowed. The flags argument is the bitwise combination of zero or more of the following constants (defined in *fnmatch.h*):

FNM_NOESCAPE

> If set, treat the backslash character as an ordinary character instead of as an escape.

FNM_PATHNAME

> If set, allow a slash in *string* to match only a slash in *pattern* and never a wildcard character or character range.

FNM_PERIOD

> If this flag is set, a leading period in *string* must match exactly with a period in *pattern*. A period is considered to be leading if it is the first character in *string* or if FNM_PATHNAME is set and the period immediately follows a slash.

FNM_CASE_BLIND

> If this flag is set, then a case-insensitive comparison is performed. This is an Apache extension and not part of the POSIX.2 standard.

Typically you will use *ap_fnmatch()* to match filename patterns. In fact, this function is used internally for matching glob-style patterns in configuration sections such as *FilesMatch* and *LocationMatch*. Example:

```
if(ap_fnmatch("*.html", filename, FNM_PATHNAME|FNM_CASE_BLIND)
    != FNM_NOMATCH) {
    ...
}
```

int ap_is_fnmatch (const char *pattern)

(Declared in the header file *fnmatch.h*.) This function returns true if *pattern* contains glob characters, false otherwise. It is useful in deciding whether to perform an *ap_fnmatch()* pattern search or an ordinary string comparison.

```
if (ap_is_fnmatch(target)) {
    file_matches = !ap_fnmatch(filename, target, FNM_PATHNAME);
}
else {
    file_matches = !strcmp(filename, target);
}
```

int ap_strcmp_match (const char *string, const char *pattern)

Just to add to the confusion, *ap_strcmp_match()* provides functionality similar to *ap_fnmatch()* but only recognizes the * and ? wildcards. The function returns 0 if a match is found, nonzero otherwise. This is an older function, and there is no particular reason to prefer it. However, you'll see it used in some standard modules, including in *mod_autoindex* where it is called on to determine what icon applies to a filename.

```
if(!ap_strcmp_match(filename, "*.html")) {
    ...
}
```

int ap_strcasecmp_match (const char *str, const char *exp)

ap_strcasecmp_match is the same as *ap_strcmp_match* but case-insensitive.

int ap_is_matchexp (const char *string)

This function returns true if the string contains either of the wildcard characters * and ?, false otherwise. It is useful for testing whether a user-provided configuration string should be treated as a pattern to be passed to *ap_strcmp_match()* or as an ordinary string. Example:

```
if (ap_is_matchexp(target)) {
    file_matches = !ap_strcmp_match(filename, target);
}
else {
    file_matches = !strcmp(filename, target);
}
```

int ap_checkmask (const char *string, const char *mask)

(Declared in the header file *util_date.h*.) The *ap_checkmask()* function will attempt to match the given *string* against the character *mask*. Unlike the previous string matching functions, *ap_checkmask()* will return true (nonzero) for a successful match, false (zero) if the match fails.

The mask is constructed from the following characters:

@   uppercase letter

$ lowercase letter

&   hex digit

digit

~   digit or space

*   swallow remaining characters

x   exact match for any other character

For example, *ap_parseHTTPdate()* uses this function to determine the date format, such as RFC 1123:

```
if (ap_checkmask(date, "## @$$ #### ##:##:## *")) {
    ...
}
```

Because it was originally written to support date and time parsing routines, this function is declared in *util_date.h*.

int ap_ind (const char *s, char c)

This function is equivalent to the standard C library *index()* function. It will scan the character string *s* from left to right until it finds the character *c*, returning the location of the first occurrence of *c*, or -1 if the character is not found. Note that the function result is the integer index of the located character, not a string pointer as in the standard C function.

int ap_rind (const char *s, char c)

ap_rind() behaves like *ap_ind()*, except that it scans the string from right to left, returning the index of the rightmost occurrence of character c. This function is particularly useful for Hebrew and Arabic texts.

regex_t *ap_pregcomp (pool *p, const char *pattern, int cflags);
void ap_pregfree (pool *p, regex_t *reg);

Apache supports regular expression matching using the system library's regular expression routines *regcomp()*, *regexec()*, *regerror()*, and *regfree()*. If these functions are not available, then Apache uses its own package of regular expression routines. Documentation for the regular expression routines can be found in your system manual pages. If your system does not support these routines, the documentation for Apache's regular expression package can be found in the *regex/* subdirectory of the Apache source tree.

We won't try to document the complexities of regular expression matching here, except to remind you that regular expression matching occurs in two phases. In the first phase, you call *regcomp()* to compile a regular expression pattern string into a compiled form. In the second phase, you pass the compiled pattern to *regexec()* to match the search pattern against a source string. In the course of performing its regular expression match, *regexec()* writes the offsets of each matched parenthesized subexpression into an array named `pmatch[]`. The significance of this array will become evident in the next section when we discuss *ap_pregsub()*.

For your convenience, Apache provides wrapper routines around *regcomp()* and *regfree()* that make working with regular expressions somewhat simpler. *ap_pregcomp()* works like *regcomp()* to compile a regular expression string, except that it automatically allocates memory for the compiled expression from the provided resource pool pointer. `pattern` contains the string to compile, and `cflags` is a bit mask of flags that control the type of regular expression to perform. The full list of flags can be found in the *regcomp()* manual page.

In addition to allocating the regular expression, *ap_pregcomp()* automatically installs a cleanup handler that calls *regfree()* to release the memory used by the compiled regular expression when the transaction is finished. This relieves you of the responsibility of doing this bit of cleanup yourself.

Speaking of which, the cleanup handler installed by *ap_pregcomp()* is *ap_pregfree()*. It frees the regular expression by calling *regfree()* and then removes itself from the cleanup handler list to ensure that it won't be called twice. You may call *ap_pregfree()* yourself if, for some unlikely reason, you need to free up the memory used by the regular expression before the cleanup would have been performed normally.

char *ap_pregsub (pool *p, const char *input, const char *source, size_t nmatch, regmatch_t pmatch[])

After performing a regular expression match with *regexec()*, you may use *ap_pregsub()* to perform a series of string substitutions based on subexpressions that were matched during the operation. The function is broadly similar in concept to what happens in the right half of a Perl `s///` operation.

This function uses the `pmatch[]` array, which *regexec()* populates with the start and end positions of all the parenthesized subexpressions matched by the regular expression. You provide *ap_pregsub()* with *p*, a resource pool pointer, *input*, a character string describing the substitutions to perform, *source*, the source string used for the regular expression match, *nmatch*, the size of the *pmatch* array, and *pmatch* itself.

input is any arbitrary string containing the expressions $1 through $9. *ap_pregsub()* replaces these expressions with the corresponding matched subexpressions from the source string. $0 is also available for your use: it corresponds to the entire matched string.

The return value will be a newly allocated string formed from the substituted input string.

The following example shows *ap_pregsub()* being used to replace the *.htm* and *.HTM* filename extensions with *.html*. We begin by calling *ap_pregcomp()* to compile the desired regular expression and return the compiled pattern in memory allocated from the resource pool. We specify flags that cause the match to be case-insensitive and to use the modern regular expression syntax. We proceed to initialize the `pmatch[]` array to hold two `regmatch_t` elements. Two elements are needed: the first which corresponds to $0 and the second for the single parenthesized subexpression in the pattern. Next we call *regexec()* with the compiled pattern, the requested filename, the `pmatch[]` array, and its length. The last argument to *regexec()*, which is used for passing various additional option flags, is set to zero. If *regexec()* returns zero, we go on to call *ap_pregsub()* to interpolate the matched subexpression (the filename minus its extension) into the string `$1.html`, effectively replacing the extension.

```
regmatch_t pmatch[2];
regex_t *cpat = ap_pregcomp(r->pool, "(.+)\\.htm$", REG_EXTENDED|REG_ICASE);

if (regexec(cpat, r->filename, cpat->re_nsub+1, pmatch, 0) == 0) {
    r->filename = ap_pregsub(r->pool, "$1.html",
                             r->filename, cpat->re_nsub+1, pmatch);
}
```

char *ap_escape_shell_cmd (pool *p, const char *string)

If you must pass a user-provided string to a shell command, you should first use *ap_escape_shell_cmd()* to escape characters that might otherwise be interpreted as shell metacharacters. The function inserts backslashes in front of the potentially unsafe characters and returns the result as a new string.

Unsafe characters include the following:

`& ; ` ' " | * ? ~ < > ^ ( ) [ ] { } $ \n`

Example:

```
char *escaped_cmd = ap_escape_shell_cmd(r->pool, command);
```

Do not rely only on this function to make your shell commands safe. The commands themselves may behave unpredictably if presented with unreasonable input, even if the shell behaves well. The best policy is to use a regular expression match to sanity-check the contents of all user-provided data before passing it on to external programs.

char *ap_escape_quotes (pool *p, const char *string)

This function behaves similarly to the previous one but only escapes double quotes.

```
char *escaped_string = ap_escape_quotes(r->pool, string);
```

void ap_str_tolower (char *string)

> This function converts all uppercase characters in the given string to lowercase characters, modifying the new string in place.
>
> ```
> ap_str_tolower(string);
> ```

char *ap_escape_html (pool *p, const char *string)

> The *ap_escape_html()* function takes a character string and returns a modified copy in which all special characters (such as > and <) are replaced with their HTML entities. This makes the string safe to use inside an HTML page. For example, after the following example is run, the resulting string will read `&lt;h1&gt;Header Level 1 Example&lt;/h1&gt;`:
>
> ```
> char *display_html = ap_escape_html(p, "<h1>Header Level 1 Example</h1>");
> ```

char *ap_uuencode (pool *p, const char *string)

> This function takes a string, base64-encodes it, and returns the encoded version in a new string allocated from the provided resource pool. Base64 is the algorithm used by the *uuencode* program (hence the function name) and is widely used by the MIME system for packaging binary email enclosures.
>
> ```
> char *encoded = ap_uuencode(p, encoded);
> ```

char *ap_uudecode (pool *p, char *string)

> *ap_uudecode()* reverses the effect of the previous function, transforming a base64-encoded string into its original representation.
>
> ```
> char *decoded = ap_uudecode(p, encoded);
> ```

Type Checking Macros

Apache provides a set of wrappers around the standard character class macros found in the *ctype.h* header file. The reason for these wrappers is to provide correct behavior on systems that support 8-bit characters. Unfortunately, not all C libraries are fully internationalized.

Even if you don't care about 8-bit support, it is a good idea to use the *ap_* character class macros instead of the standard equivalents because they guarantee compatibility should locale support be added to Apache in the future.

These functions can be found in header file *ap_ctype.h*:

int ap_isalnum (int character)

> Returns true if *character* is alphanumeric.

int ap_isalpha (int character)

> Returns true if *character* is alphabetic.

int ap_iscntrl (int character)

> Returns true if *character* is a control character.

int ap_isdigit (int character)
   Returns true if *character* is a numeric digit.

int ap_isgraph (int character)
   Returns true if *character* is any printable character except the space.

int ap_islower (int character)
   Returns true for lowercase characters.

int ap_isprint (int character)
   Returns true if *character* is printable.

int ap_ispunct (int character)
   Returns true for a punctuation character (neither a space nor alphanumeric).

int ap_isspace (int character)
   Returns true for whitespace characters.

int ap_isupper (int character)
   Returns true for uppercase characters.

int ap_tolower (int character)
   Returns the lowercase version of *character*.

int ap_toupper (int character)
   Returns the uppercase version of *character*.

URI Parsing and Manipulation

In addition to the general string manipulation routines described above, Apache provides specific routines for manipulating URIs. With these routines you can break a URI into its components and put it back together again.

The main data structure used by these routines is the `uri_components` struct. The typedef for `uri_components` is found in the *util_uri.h* header file and reproduced in Example 11-5. For your convenience, a preparsed `uri_components` struct is contained in every incoming request, in the field `parsed_uri`. The various fields of the parsed URI are as follows:

`char *scheme`
   This field contains the URI's scheme. Possible values include `http`, `https`, `ftp`, and `file`.

`char *hostinfo`
   This field contains the part of the URI between the pair of initial slashes and the beginning of the document path. It is often just the hostname for the request, but its full form includes the port and the username/password combination needed to gain access under certain protocols (such as nonanonymous FTP). Here's an example `hostinfo` string that shows all the optional parts:

   `doug:xyzzy@ftp.modperl.com:23`

char *user

The field contains the username part of the `hostinfo` field or an empty string if absent.

char *password

This field contains the password part of the `hostinfo` field or an empty string if absent.

char *port_str

This field contains the string representation of the port. You can fetch the numeric representation from the `port` field.

char *path

This field corresponds to the path portion of the URI, namely everything after the `hostinfo`. Neither the query string (the optional text that follows the ? symbol) nor the optional `#anchor` names that appear at the ends of many HTTP URLs are part of the path. It is equivalent to `r->uri`.

char *query

The `query` field holds the query string, that is, everything after the ? in the path but not including the `#anchor` fragment, if any. It is equivalent to `r-> args`.

char *fragment

This field contains the `#anchor` fragment, if any. The # symbol itself is omitted.

unsigned short port

`port` holds the port number of the URI, in integer form. For the same information in text form, see `port_str`.

The other fields in the `uri_components` record are for internal use only and are not to be relied on.

Example 11-5. The uri_components Data Type

```
typedef struct {
    char *scheme;       /* scheme ("http"/"ftp"/...) */
    char *hostinfo;     /* combined [user[:password]@]host[:port] */
    char *user;         /* user name, as in http://user:passwd@host:port/ */
    char *password;     /* password, as in http://user:passwd@host:port/ */
    char *hostname;     /* hostname from URI (or from Host: header) */
    char *port_str;     /* port string (integer representation is in "port") */
    char *path;         /* the request path
                           (or "/" if only scheme://host was given) */
    char *query;        /* Everything after a '?' in the path, if present */
    char *fragment;     /* Trailing "#fragment" string, if present */

    struct hostent *hostent;

    unsigned short port;  /* The port number, numeric, NULL */
                          /*     valid only if port_str != NULL */
```

Example 11-5. The uri_components Data Type (continued)

```
    unsigned is_initialized:1;

    unsigned dns_looked_up:1;
    unsigned dns_resolved:1;

} uri_components;
```

In addition to the **uri_components** record located in the request record's **parsed_uri** field, you can access Apache's URI parsing and manipulation package using a series of routines variously declared in *httpd.h* and *util_uri.h*:

*int ap_unescape_url (char *url)*

(Declared in the header file *httpd.h*.) This routine will unescape URI hex escapes. The escapes are performed in place, replacing the original string. During the unescaping process, Apache performs some basic consistency checking on the URI and returns the result of this check as the function result code. The function will return **HTTP_BAD_REQUEST** if it encounters an invalid hex escape (for example, %1g), and **HTTP_NOT_FOUND** if replacing a hex escape with its text equivalent results in either the character / or \0. If the URI passes these checks, the function returns **OK**.

```
    if (ap_unescape_url(url) != OK) {
        ap_log_error(APLOG_MARK, APLOG_NOERRNO|APLOG_WARNING,
                     r->server, "bad URI during unescaping");
    }
```

*char *ap_os_escape_path (pool *p, const char *path, int partial)*

(Declared in the header file *httpd.h*.) *ap_os_escape_path()* takes a filesystem pathname in **path** and converts it into a properly escaped URI in an operating system–dependent way, returning the new string as its function result. If the *partial* flag is false, then the function will add a / to the beginning of the URI if the path does not already begin with one. If the *partial* flag is true, the function will not add the slash.

```
    char *escaped = ap_os_escape_path(p, url, 1);
```

*int ap_is_url (const char *string)*

(Declared in the header file *httpd.h*.) This function returns true if *string* is a fully qualified URI (including scheme and hostname), false otherwise. Among other things it is handy when processing configuration directives that are expected to accept URIs.

```
    if(ap_is_url(string)) {
        ...
    }
```

*char *ap_construct_url (pool *p, const char *uri, const request_rec *r)*

This function builds a fully qualified URI string from the path specified by **uri**, using the information stored in the request record *r* to determine the server name and port. The port number is not included in the string if it is the same as the default port 80.

For example, imagine that the current request is directed to the virtual server *www.modperl.com* at port 80. Then the following call will return the string `http://www.modperl.com/index.html`:

```
char *url = ap_construct_url(r->pool, "/index.html", r);
```

char *ap_construct_server (pool *p, const char *hostname, unsigned port, const request_rec *r)

(Declared in the header file *httpd.h.*) The *ap_construct_server()* function builds the hostname:port part of a URI and returns it as a new string. The port will not be included in the string if it is the same as the default. You provide a resource pool in *p*, the name of the host in *hostname*, the port number in *port*, and the current request record in *r*. The request record is used to determine the default port number only and is not otherwise involved in constructing the string.

For example, the following code will return `www.modperl.com:8001`:

```
char *server = ap_construct_server(r->pool, hostname, 8001, r);
```

unsigned short ap_default_port_for_scheme (const char *scheme)

(Declared in the header file *util_uri.h.*) This handy routine returns the default port number for the given URL scheme. The scheme you provide is compared in a case-insensitive manner to an internal list maintained by Apache. For example, here's how to determine the default port for the secure HTTPS scheme:

```
unsigned short port = ap_default_port_for_scheme("https");
```

unsigned short ap_default_port_for_request (const request_rec *r)

(Declared in the header file *util_uri.h.*) The *ap_default_port_for_request()* function looks up the scheme from the request record argument, then calls *ap_default_port()* to return the default port for that scheme. It is almost exactly equivalent to calling `ap_default_port_for_scheme(r->parsed_uri.scheme)`.

```
unsigned short port = ap_default_port_for_request(r);
```

struct hostent * ap_pgethostbyname (pool *p, const char *hostname)

(Declared in the header file *util_uri.h.*) This function is a wrapper around the standard *gethostbyname()* function. The `struct hostent` pointer normally returned by the standard function lives in static storage space, so *ap_pgethostbyname()* makes a copy of this structure from memory allocated in the passed resource pool in order to avoid any trouble this might cause. This allows the call to be thread-safe.

int ap_parse_uri_components (pool *p, const char *uri, uri_components *uptr)

(Declared in the header file *util_uri.h*.) Given a pool pointer p, a URI uri, and a uri_components structure pointer uptr, this routine will parse the URI and place the extracted components in the appropriate fields of uptr. The return value is either HTTP_OK (integer 200, not to be confused with the usual OK which is integer 0) to indicate parsing success or HTTP_BAD_REQUEST to indicate that the string did not look like a valid URI.

```
uri_components uri;
int rc = ap_parse_uri_components(p, "http://www.modperl.com/index.html",
&uri);
```

char *ap_unparse_uri_components (pool *p, const uri_components *uptr, unsigned flags);

(Declared in the header file *util_uri.h*.) The interesting *ap_unparse_uri_components()* routine reverses the effect of the previous call, using a populated uri_components record to create a URI string, which is returned as the function result. The flags argument is a bit mask of options that modify the constructed URI string. Possible values for flags include:

UNP_OMITSITEPART

Suppress the scheme and hostinfo parts from the constructed URI.

UNP_OMITUSER

Suppress the username from the hostinfo part of the URI.

UNP_OMITPASSWORD

Suppress the password from the hostinfo part of the URI.

UNP_REVEALPASSWORD

For security reasons, unless the UNP_REVEALPASSWORD bit is explicitly set, the password part of the URI will be replaced with a series of X characters.

UNP_OMITPATHINFO

If this bit is set, completely suppress the path part of the URI, including the query string.

UNP_OMITQUERY

Suppress the query string and the fragment, if any. The following example will re-create the URI without the username and password parts.

```
char *string = ap_unparse_uri_components(p, &uri,
                             UNP_OMITPASSWORD|UNP_OMITUSER);
```

File and Directory Management

Apache provides routines for opening files, reading and writing to them, and closing them. Some of these routines are wrappers around the standard operating system calls in order to provide a compatibility layer for the Unix, Win32, and other ports. Other functions are an improvement over their operating system equivalents because they take advantage of Apache's memory management system.

Pathname Manipulation

These routines are handy for parsing strings that contain filenames and paths. See the next section, "Working with Files and Directories," for functions that operate on files and directories themselves.

These functions are all declared in *httpd.h*:

void ap_chdir_file (const char *file)

> Given a pathname in *file*, this peculiar little function identifies the directory part and invokes *chdir()* to make it the current working directory. Here's an example of calling the function on the request record's `filename` field in order to *chdir()* to the directory that contains the requested file:

```
ap_chdir_file(r->filename);
```

int ap_os_is_path_absolute (const char *filename)

> This function provides a portable test as to whether a filename is absolute or not. On Unix systems, an absolute filename begins with a /, whereas under Win32 systems, an absolute filename may begin with a drive letter, a colon delimiter, and a / or \.

```
if(!ap_os_is_path_absolute(filename)) {
    ... must resolve the relative filename somehow ...
```

char *ap_make_full_path (pool *p, const char *directory, const char *filename)

> *ap_make_full_path()* will concatenate *directory* and *filename* and return the result. The function is smart about checking the directory string for a terminating slash and automatically inserting one if needed.

int ap_is_directory (const char *path)

> This function returns true if `path` exists and is a directory, false otherwise.

int ap_count_dirs (const char *path)

> Given a pathname *path*, *ap_count_dirs()* counts the number of directories contained in the path. This function merely counts the number of occurrences of the slash character in the path. It doesn't actually check that any of the directories exist.

void ap_no2slash (char *path)

> It is easy to inadvertently introduce multiple slashes into pathnames when concatenating directories and filenames. Although both the filesystem and URIs are resistant to repeated slashes, you can use this function to make constructed paths more aesthetic by folding multiple slashes into a single one. It changes the provided pathname in place and does not return a function result.

The following example will remove the double-slash from the path */home/ httpd/docs//oops.html.*

```
char *oops = ap_pstrdup(r->pool, "home/httpd/docs//oops.html");
ap_no2slash(oops);
```

*char *ap_make_dirstr_prefix (char *prefix, const char *path, int n)*

This highly specialized function will copy, at most, **n** leading directories found in **path** into the character array at *prefix*, ensuring that *prefix* will terminate in a slash. You must ensure that *prefix* is large enough to hold the resulting data—potentially the length of *path* plus one extra byte for the string terminator. The function returns a pointer to the end of *prefix*, in anticipation of your appending more data (typically a filename) onto the end of the string.

The following example shows one way to make a copy of the path to the parent directory of the currently requested file:

```
char* path = r->filename;
char* prefix = (char*)ap_palloc(r->pool, strlen(path)+1);
ap_make_dirstr_prefix(prefix, path, ap_count_dirs(path)-1);
```

In case this was less than crystal clear, here is an example input/output table:

path	n	prefix
/a/b/c	1	/
/a/b/c	2	/a/
/a/b/c	3	/a/b/
/a/b/c	4	/a/b/c
/a/b/c	5	/a/b/c

*char *ap_make_dirstr_parent (pool *p, const char *filename)*

This function returns a new string containing the parent directory in which *filename* lives. This is a much easier way to accomplish the same thing as the example given in the previous section, and probably a little faster as well. *ap_ make_dirstr_parent()* operates entirely on the string level. It doesn't actually check that any of the directories exist.

```
char *dirname = ap_make_dirstr_parent(r->pool, r->filename);
```

*void ap_getparents (char *filename)*

Passed a file path in *filename*, the *ap_getparents()* function strips out any relative path components by removing references to the `..` and `.` directories. The stripping method follows the four parsing phases described in RFC 1808. The operation is performed in place just like *ap_no2slash()*.

You should perform this operation before opening files based on user-provided input. Otherwise, it might be possible for a malicious user to trick your module into opening a file in a directory outside the document root. (Microsoft Internet Information Server has been bitten by this bug several times.)

By the time your handler finds the requested URI in the request record, Apache has already passed it through *ap_getparents()*, so there is no need to call the function a second time. However, you will still need to run the function on any paths passed in fill-out forms and possibly on paths entered in configuration variables as well.

Working with Files and Directories

Apache provides a series of wrappers around the C library routines that open and close files and directories. The main purpose of these routines is to take advantage of the resource pool API. Any files and directories that you open using the API calls will be automatically closed and their data structures deallocated when the current resource pool is destroyed.

These routines all live in *alloc.h*:

FILE *ap_pfopen (pool *p, const char *name, const char *fmode)
> *ap_pfopen()* is a wrapper around the standard *fopen()* call. In addition to ensuring that the FILE* is closed when the pool is destroyed, it provides some internal compatibility code that ensures that the append (*a*) mode works the same on all platforms.
>
> In this example, the file indicated in r->filename is opened for reading:
>
> ```
> FILE *fh = ap_pfopen(r->pool, r->filename, "r");
> ```

int ap_pfclose (pool *p, FILE *fh)
> Although files opened with *ap_pfopen()* will be closed automatically for you when the transaction is finished, you may close them sooner using *ap_pfclose()*. Be sure to use this call rather than the standard *fclose()* so that Apache will know to cancel the scheduled cleanup.
>
> ```
> ap_pfclose(r->pool, fh);
> ```

FILE *ap_pfdopen (pool *p, int fd, const char *fmode)
> This function works like the standard *fdopen()* call to create a new FILE* attached to the indicated file descriptor. Like *ap_pfopen()*, the file is automatically closed when the pool is cleaned up.
>
> ```
> FILE *fh = ap_pfdopen(r->pool, fd, "r");
> ```

int ap_popenf (pool *p, const char *name, int flags, int mode)
int ap_pclosef (struct pool *p, int fd)
> These calls are equivalent to the standard *open()* and *close()* calls. *ap_popenf()* opens the indicated file and returns a file descriptor, or -1 if the file could not be opened. *ap_pclosef()* closes the file and cancels the scheduled cleanup before pool destruction.
>
> ```
> int fd = ap_popenf(r->pool, r->filename, O_RDONLY, 0600);
> read(fd, buffer, 1024);
> ap_pclosef(fd);
> ```

void ap_note_cleanups_for_file (pool *p, FILE *fp)

If a module has opened a `FILE*` stream with a function other than *ap_pfopen()*, it can use this function to ensure the file will be closed when the given pool is destroyed.

```
FILE *fp = tmpfile();
ap_note_cleanups_for_file(r->pool, fp);
```

void ap_note_cleanups_for_fd (pool *p, int fd)

If a module has opened a file descriptor with a function other than *ap_pfdopen()*, it can use this function to ensure the descriptor will be closed when the given pool is destroyed.

```
int fd = open(tempfile, O_WRONLY|O_CREAT|O_EXCL|O_BINARY, 0622);
if (fd == -1) {
    ap_log_rerror(APLOG_MARK, APLOG_ERR, r,
                  "error creating temporary file %s", tempfile);
    return HTTP_INTERNAL_SERVER_ERROR;
}
ap_note_cleanups_for_fd(r->pool, fd);
```

void ap_kill_cleanups_for_fd (pool *p, int fd)

If a file descriptor has been registered to be closed with *ap_note_cleanups_for_fd()*, this function can be used to unregister the cleanup.

```
ap_kill_cleanups_for_fd(r->pool, fd);
```

DIR *ap_popendir (pool *p, const char *name)
void ap_pclosedir (pool *p, DIR *d)

These functions correspond to the *opendir()* and *closedir()* calls. Like the other functions in this section, directory handles allocated with *ap_popendir()* are automatically closed and cleaned up for you when the pool is destroyed. You can close the directory earlier with *ap_pclosedir()*.

In this example, we check to see whether the requested filename is a directory. If so, we open it as a directory rather than as a file.

```
if(S_ISDIR(r->finfo.st_mode)) {
    DIR *dh = ap_popendir(r->pool, r->filename);
    ...
    ap_pclosedir(r->pool, dh);
}
```

int ap_psocket (pool *p, int domain, int type, int protocol)
int ap_pclosesocket (pool *p, int sock)

ap_psocket() is a wrapper around the *socket()* system call. The socket is closed when the pool is destroyed. The *ap_pclosesocket()* function closes a socket previously opened with *ap_psocket()*, canceling the scheduled cleanup.

```
int sock = ap_psocket(p, PF_INET, SOCK_STREAM, IPPROTO_TCP);
...
ap_pclosesocket(p, sock);
```

Time and Date Functions

Several API calls give you access to Apache's routines for formatting and parsing HTTP-compliant date strings. Also see the descriptions for *ap_update_mtime()* and *ap_set_last_modified()* in Chapter 10, *C API Reference Guide, Part I*, under "Sending Files to the Client."

The declarations for these functions are scattered among several header files, including *httpd.h*, *util_date.h*, and *http_request.h*. In the following list we indicate where the function can be found:

char *ap_ht_time (pool *p, time_t t, const char *fmt, int gmt)

(Declared in the header file *httpd.h*.) Given a resource pool, a `time_t` timestamp, a character format, and a flag indicating whether or not to use GMT (Greenwich Mean Time, also known as Universal Standard Time), this function returns a character string containing the date. The character format uses the same code as the standard C library *strftime()* function, with the addition of two common extensions. The code `%Z` is substituted with the string `GMT`, and the code `%z` is substituted with `+0000`. See the manual page for *strftime()* for other codes you can use.

This example returns a string in the format `Tue, 15 Sep 1998 14:36:31 GMT`, which happens to be the HTTP date format recommended by RFCs 822 and 1123.

```
char *str = ap_ht_time(p, time(NULL), "%a %d %b %Y %T %Z", 0);
```

time_t ap_parseHTTPdate (const char *date)

(Declared in the header file *util_date.c*.) Given a `char*` containing a date in HTTP format, this routine parses the date and returns a `time_t` Unix timestamp. This routine is flexible enough to correctly handle minor variations in the date format, such as omitting the time zone and day of the week. Any text that follows the time string is ignored.

Here's an example of converting the incoming *If-modified-since* header into a timestamp. We then compare this timestamp to the requested file's last modification date and return `HTTP_NOT_MODIFIED` if the file is not newer than the browser's cached copy.

```
char *if_modified_since = ap_table_get(r->headers_in, "If-modified-since");
if (if_modified_since) {
   time_t secs = ap_parseHTTPdate(if_modified_since);
   if (secs <= r->mtime) {
     return HTTP_NOT_MODIFIED;
   }
}
```

See also *ap_meets_conditions()*.

struct tm *ap_get_gmtoff (int *tz)

(Declared in the header file *httpd.h*.) The *ap_get_gmtoff()* function calculates the current local time and returns it as a tm* function result. The offset from GMT, in minutes, is returned in the *tz* argument.

Here's an example borrowed from *mod_rewrite*, which it uses to write logging timestamps in the format [14/Sep/1998:11:01:23 -0500].

```
static char *current_logtime(request_rec *r)
{
    int timz;
    struct tm *t;
    char tstr[80];
    char sign;

    t = ap_get_gmtoff(&timz);
    sign = (timz < 0 ? '-' : '+');
    if (timz < 0) {
        timz = -timz;
    }

    strftime(tstr, 80, "[%d/%b/%Y:%H:%M:%S ", t);
    ap_snprintf(tstr + strlen(tstr), 80-strlen(tstr), "%c%.2d%.2d]",
                sign, timz/60, timz%60);
    return ap_pstrdup(r->pool, tstr);
}
```

char *ap_get_time (void)

(Declared in the header file *httpd.h*.) This function returns a date/time string in the format returned by the standard *ctime()* library call. Although this format is not compliant with the recommended HTTP header format, it is somewhat more concise and, for historical reasons, is used by the logging API for error log timestamps. Do not use it for the *Expires* header field or other HTTP headers that use dates. Use *ap_gm_timestr_822()* instead.

```
char *ctime_string = ap_get_time();
```

char *ap_gm_timestr_822 (pool *p, time_t sec)

(Declared in the header file *httpd.h*.) The unfortunately named function *ap_gm_timestr_822()* returns a date/time string that is formatted according to the RFC 822 SMTP specification. You can use this to create the outgoing *Expires* or *Date* fields. The sec argument contains the timestamp you wish to format.

In this example, we arrange for the outgoing document to expire 1 hour (3600 seconds) from the current time:

```
now = time(NULL);
ap_table_set(r->headers_out, "Expires", ap_gm_timestr_822(r->pool, now+3600))
```

time_t ap_tm2sec (const struct tm *t)

(Declared in the header file *util_date.h*.) The *ap_tm2sec()* function converts a GMT tm structure into a timestamp, the number of seconds since the start of the epoch. It is much faster than the standard equivalent *mktime()* function, and unlike *mktime()*, *ap_tm2sec()* will always return a valid *time_t()* value, which may be 0 should an error occur.

```
time_t secs = ap_t2sec(&tm);
```

Message Digest Algorithm Functions

Apache includes a version of the MD5 Message Digest algorithm distributed as freeware by RSA Data Security Inc. These routines provide the functionality of the Perl MD5 module used in Chapters 5 through 7. In fact, both the Apache and Perl MD5 implementations are derived from the same source code.

Although MD5 was originally incorporated into Apache to support Digest Authentication, you can use it for whatever purpose you desire. As we've seen in earlier chapters, MD5 turns out to be handy anywhere you need to quickly check the authenticity of a file or message.

You will find all the data types and routines described in this section in header file *ap_md5.h*.

*void ap_MD5Init (AP_MD5_CTX *context)*

To compute an MD5 checksum, you will initialize the algorithm with *ap_MD5Init()*, add one or more rounds of data to it with *ap_MD5Update()*, and retrieve the checksum with *ap_MD5Final()*. A "context" record, the `AP_MD5_CTX` struct, keeps track of the state of the algorithm throughout this process.

ap_MD5Init() takes a new, uninitialized context variable and initializes it so that the algorithm is ready to use. You do not have to worry about what's in the context struct. You can create it on the stack or allocate it from a resource pool:

```
AP_MD5_CTX context;
ap_MD5Init(&context);
```

*void ap_MD5Update (AP_MD5_CTX *context, const unsigned char *input, unsigned int inputLen)*

Once the context is initialized, call *ap_MD5Update()* as many times as you need to add data to the digest function. In addition to the context record, you provide a character buffer in *input* and the length of the buffer in *inputLen*.

```
ap_MD5Update(&context, string, strlen(string));
```

*void ap_MD5Final (unsigned char digest[16], AP_MD5_CTX *context)*

When you are done adding data to the checksum, call *ap_MD5Final()*. This signals the algorithm to flush its buffers and calculate the final digest. The digest data (in binary form) will be returned in the 16 bytes of **digest**.

Here's one way to compute the checksum of the requested file. After retrieving the digest in binary form, we transform it into a human-readable hexadecimal string and return it:

```
AP_MD5_CTX context;
unsigned char buffer[1024];
unsigned char hash[16];
unsigned int len;
char *ptr, result[33];
int i;

FILE *fh = ap_pfopen(r->pool, r->filename, "r");
if (!fh) {
    return NULL;
}
ap_MD5Init(&context);
while ((len = fread(buffer, sizeof(unsigned char), 1024, fh)) > 0) {
    ap_MD5Update(&context, buffer, len);
}
ap_MD5Final(hash, &context);
for (i=0, ptr=result; i<16; i++, ptr+=2 ) {
    ap_snprintf(ptr, sizeof(result), "%02x", hash[i]);
}
*ptr = '\0';
return ap_pstrdup(r->pool, result);
```

The following functions are handy Apache extensions to the RSA routines. They are found in *util_md5.h*.

char *ap_md5 (pool *p, unsigned char *string)

ap_md5() is equivalent to the *hexhash()* method of the Perl MD5 module. It takes a resource pool p plus an arbitrary character string, string, and returns the hexadecimal representation of its MD5 digest. For example, should you wish to implement a message authentication check (MAC) as we did in the hangman example of Chapter 5, this will do the trick (assuming that WORD, LEFT, and so on are character strings):

```
char *fields = ap_pstrcat(p, SECRET, WORD, LEFT, GUESSED, GAMENO, WON, TOTAL,
    NULL);
char *mac = ap_md5(p, ap_pstrcat(p, SECRET, ap_md5(p,fields), NULL));
```

char *ap_md5_binary (pool *p, const unsigned char *buf, int len)

The *ap_md5_binary()* function does exactly the same work as *ap_md5()* but accepts a *len* parameter for data whose length cannot be determined using *strlen()*. In fact, *ap_md5_binary()* does all the real work when *ap_md5()* is called.

char *ap_md5digest (pool *p, FILE *infile)

Given a resource pool pointer and a FILE* *infile*, this function computes the MD5 digest from the contents of the file and then base64-encodes it. The resulting character string is human-readable but is *not* the same as the hexadecimal representation more commonly used for MD5 digests. *ap_md5digest()* was designed for use with MIME MACs, which use base64 encoding.

```
char *digested_file = ap_md5digest(r->pool, infile);
```

char *ap_md5contextTo64 (pool *p, AP_MD5_CTX * context)
> Given an MD5 context, this routine calls *ap_MD5Final()* and returns the digest
> as a base64-encoded string. Example:
>
> ```
> char *encoded_context = ap_md5contextTo64(r->pool, &context);
> ```

User and Group ID Information Routines

These are a handful of routines that act as frontends to the standard Unix *getpwnam()* and *getgrnam()* functions. In addition to their role as easy-to-use wrappers, they provide portability with operating systems that don't provide these calls, such as Win32 systems.

These routines are declared in *httpd.h*:

uid_t ap_uname2id (const char *uname)
> Used internally to process the *User* configuration directive, this function will
> use *getpwnam()* to look up the given user login name and return the user's
> UID. If the name is prefixed with the # symbol, as in #501, the string is con-
> verted into integer format and simply returned. Under Win32 systems, this
> function always returns 1.
>
> ```
> uid_t id = ap_uname2id(uname);
> ```

gid_t ap_gname2id (const char *gname)
> This function behaves identically to *ap_uname2id()*, except that it operates on
> group names and group IDs, using the Unix *getgrnam()* for its lookups. Under
> Win32 systems, this function will always return 1.
>
> ```
> gid_t id = ap_gname2id(gname);
> ```

Data Mutex Locking

Apache provides a cross-platform API for implementing data mutex locking. This is a mechanism implemented on most platforms to provide serialization when multiple concurrent threads need access to global data. The API was introduced with the Win32 port of Apache and will be adapted to future multithreaded versions of Apache for other platforms. While there is no need to implement data access serialization under multiprocess versions of Apache, this API will still work in such environments and is recommended for portability.[*]

---

[*] Under multiprocess versions of Apache, such as 1.3.x under Unix, using the mutex API does not introduce any overhead, as each function is simply defined as a no-op macro.

mutex *ap_create_mutex (char *name)

    This function is used to allocate a mutex structure, which is required to implement runtime locking. This structure is normally a global variable, which is created during the module initialization phase.

```
static mutex *my_mutex = NULL;

static void my_module_init(server_rec *s, pool *p)
{
    if (!my_mutex) {
        my_mutex = ap_create_mutex(NULL);
    }
}
```

int ap_acquire_mutex (mutex *mutex_id)

    The *ap_acquire_mutex()* function will acquire a lock. If a lock has already been acquired by another thread, it will block until it is released by the other thread.

int ap_release_mutex (mutex *mutex_id)

    After locked data access is complete, the *ap_release_mutex()* function must be called so other threads are able to acquire locks.

```
static int my_handler(request_rec *r)
{
    ...
    (void)ap_acquire_mutex(my_mutex);
    /* read or modify some global data */
    (void)ap_release_mutex(my_mutex);
}
```

void ap_destroy_mutex (mutex *mutex_id)

    This function will release any resources associated with a mutex structure that was created with *ap_create_mutex()*.

```
ap_destroy_mutex(my_mutex);
my_mutex = NULL;
```

Launching Subprocesses

The last topic we discuss is the API for launching subprocesses. While we don't like to encourage the creation of subprocesses because of the load they impose on a server, there are certain modules that need to do so. In fact, for certain modules, such as *mod_cgi*, launching subprocesses is their entire raison d'être.

Because Apache is a complex beast, calling *fork()* to spawn a new process within a server process is not something to be done lightly. There are a variety of issues to contend with, including, but not limited to, signal handlers, alarms, pending I/O, and listening sockets. For this reason, you should use Apache's published API to implement fork and exec, rather than trying to roll your own with the standard C functions.

In addition to discussing the subprocess API, this section covers a number of function calls that help in launching CGI scripts and setting up the environment for subprocesses.

void ap_add_cgi_vars (request_rec *r)
void ap_add_common_vars (request_rec *r)

(Declared in the header file *util_script.h*.) By convention, modules that need to launch subprocesses copy the contents of the current request record's `subprocess_env` table into the child process's environment first. This table starts out empty, but modules are free to add to it. For example, *mod_env* responds to the *PassEnv*, *SetEnv*, and *UnsetEnv* directives by setting or unsetting variables in an internal table. Then, during the request fixup phase, it copies these values into `subprocess_env` so that the variables are exposed to the environment by any content handler that launches a subprocess.

These two routines are called by *mod_cgi* to fill up the `subprocess_env` table with the standard CGI environment variables in preparation for launching a CGI script. You may want to use one or both yourself in order to initialize the environment to a standard state.

add_cgi_vars() sets up the environment variables that are specifically called for by the CGI/1.1 protocol. This includes `GATEWAY_INTERFACE`, `QUERY_STRING`, `REQUEST_METHOD`, `PATH_INFO`, and `PATH_TRANSLATED`, among others.

ap_add_common_vars() adds other common CGI environment variables to `subprocess_env`. This includes various `HTTP_` variables that hold incoming HTTP headers from the request such as `HTTP_USER_AGENT` and `HTTP_REFERER`, as well as such useful variables as `PATH`, `SERVER_NAME`, `SERVER_PORT`, `SERVER_ROOT`, and `SCRIPT_FILENAME`.

char **ap_create_environment (pool *p, table *t)

(Declared in the header file *util_script.h*.) Among the arguments you need when *exec*ing a program with the *ap_call_exec()* command is an environment array. This function will take the key/value pairs contained in an Apache table and turn it into a suitable array. Usually you'll want to use the `subprocess_env` table for this purpose in order to be compatible with *mod_cgi* and *mod_env*.

```
char **env = ap_create_environment(r->pool, r->subprocess_env);
```

int ap_can_exec (const struct stat*)

(Declared in the header file *httpd.h*.) This utility routinely checks whether a file is executable by the current process user and/or group ID. You pass it the pointer to a stat structure, often the info field of the current request record. It returns a true value if the file is executable, false otherwise:

```
if(!ap_can_exec(&r->info)) {
    . . . log nasty error message . . .
    return HTTP_FORBIDDEN;
}
```

int ap_bspawn_child (pool *p, int (*)(void *, child_info *), void *data,
*   enum kill_conditions, BUFF **pipe_in, BUFF **pipe_out, BUFF **pipe_err)*
(Declared in the header file *buff.h*.) The *ap_bspawn_child()* function is a mixture of the Unix *fork()* and *popen()* calls. It can be used to open up a pipe to a child process or just to fork off a child process to execute in the background.

This function has many arguments. The first argument, *p*, is a pool pointer. The current request's resource pool is the usual choice. The second argument is a function pointer with the following prototype:

```
int child_routine (void *data, child_info *pinfo);
```

After forking, Apache will immediately call *child_routine()* with a generic data pointer (copied from the third argument to *ap_bspawn_child()*, which we discuss next) and a child_info pointer, a data type needed for the Win32 port. For all intents and purposes, the child_info argument is an opaque pointer that you pass to *ap_call_exec()*. It has no other use at present. The child routine should return a nonzero value on success or a zero value on failure.

The third argument to *ap_bspawn_child()* is *data*, a generic void pointer. Whatever you use for this argument will be passed to the child routine, and it is a simple way to pass information from the parent process to the child process. Since the child process usually requires access to the current request, it is common to pass a copy of the request_rec in this field.

The fourth argument is *kill_conditions*, an enumerated data type that affects what Apache does with the spawned child when the server is terminating or restarting. The possibilities, which are defined in *alloc.h*, are kill_never, to never send a signal to the child; kill_always, to send the child a SIGKILL signal; kill_after_timeout, to send the child a SIGTERM, wait 3 seconds, and then send a SIGKILL; justwait, to wait forever for the child to complete; and kill_only_once, to send a SIGTERM and wait for the child to complete. The usual value is kill_after_timeout, which is the same scheme that Apache uses for the listening servers it spawns.

The last three arguments are *pipe_in*, *pipe_out*, and *pipe_err*. If they are non-NULL, *ap_bspawn_child()* fills them in with BUFF pointers attached to the standard input, output, and error of the spawned child process. By writing to *pipe_in*, the parent process will be able to send data to the standard input of the spawned process. By reading from *pipe_out* and *pipe_err*, you can retrieve data that the child has written to its standard output and error. Pass **NULL** for any or all of these arguments if you are not interested in talking to the child.

int ap_spawn_child (pool *p, int (*)(void *, child_info *), void *data, enum kill_conditions, FILE **pipe_in, FILE **pipe_out, FILE **pipe_err)

(Declared in the header file *alloc.h.*) This function works exactly like *ap_bspawn_child()* but uses more familiar FILE streams rather than BUFF streams for the I/O connection between the parent and the child. This function is rarely a good choice, however, because it is not compatible with the Win32 port, whereas *ap_bspawn_child()* is.

void ap_error_log2stderr (server_rec *s)

Once inside a spawned child, this function will rehook the standard error file descriptor back to the server's error log. You may want to do this after calling *ap_bspawn_child()* and before calling *ap_call_exec()* so that any error messages produced by the subprocess show up in the server error log:

```
ap_error_log2stderr(r->server);
```

void ap_cleanup_for_exec (void)

(Declared in the header file *alloc.h.*) You should call this function just before invoking *ap_call_exec()*. Its main duty is to run all the cleanup handlers for all the main resource pools and all subpools.

int ap_call_exec (request_rec *r, child_info *pinfo, char *argv0, char **env, int shellcmd)

(Declared in the header file *util_script.h.*) After calling *ap_bspawn_child()* or *ap_spawn_child()*, your program will most probably call *ap_call_exec()* to replace the current process with a new one. The name of the command to run is specified in the request record's **filename** field, and its command-line arguments, if any, are specified in **args**. If successful, the new command is run and the call never returns. If preceded by an *ap_spawn_child()*, the new process's standard input, output, and error will be attached to the BUFF*s created by that call.

This function takes five arguments. The first, **r**, is the current request record. It is used to set up the argument list for the command. The second, *pinfo*, is the **child_info** pointer passed to the function specified by *ap_bspawn_child()*.

argv0 is the command name that will appear as the first item in the launched command's **argv[]** array. Although this argument is usually the same as the path of the command to run, this is not a necessary condition. It is sometimes useful to lie to a command about its name, particularly when dealing with oddball programs that behave differently depending on how they're invoked.

The fourth argument, *env*, is a pointer to an environment array. This is typically the pointer returned by *ap_create_environment()*. The last argument, *shellcmd*, is a flag indicating whether Apache should pass any arguments to the command. If *shellcmd* is true, then Apache will *not* pass any arguments to the command (this is counterintuitive). If *shellcmd* is false, then Apache will use the value of r->args to set up the arguments passed to the command. The contents of r->args must be in the old-fashioned CGI argument form in which individual arguments are separated by the + symbol and other funny characters are escaped as %XX hex escape sequences. args may not contain the unescaped = or & symbols. If it does, Apache will interpret it as a new-style CGI query string and refuse to pass it to the command. We'll see a concrete example of setting up the arguments for an external command shortly.

There are a few other precautionary steps *ap_call_exec()* will take. If *SUEXEC* is enabled, the program will be run through the setuid wrapper. If any of the *RLimitCPU*, *RLimitMEM*, or *RLimitNPROC* directives are enabled, *setrlimit* will be called underneath to limit the given resource to the configured value.

Finally, for convenience, under OS/2 and Win32 systems *ap_call_exec()* will implement the "shebang" Unix shell-ism. That is, if the first line of the requested file contains the #! sequence, the remainder of the string is assumed to be the program interpreter which will execute the script.

On Unix platforms, successful calls to *ap_call_exec()* will not return because the current process has been terminated and replaced by the command. On failure, *ap_call_exec()* will return -1 and errno will be set.[*] On Win32 platforms, successful calls to *ap_call_exec()* will return the process ID of the launched process and not terminate the current code. The upcoming example shows how to deal with this.

*void ap_child_terminate (request_rec *r)*

If for some reason you need to terminate the current child (perhaps because an attempt to exec a new program has failed), this function causes the child server process to terminate cleanly after the current request. It does this by setting the child's *MaxRequests* configuration variable to 1 and clearing the keepalive flag so that the current connection is broken after the request is serviced.

```
ap_child_terminate(r);
```

*int ap_scan_script_header_err_buff (request_rec *r, BUFF *fb, char *buffer)*

This function is useful when launching CGI scripts. It will scan the BUFF* stream fb for HTTP headers. Typically the BUFF* is the pipe_out pointer returned from a previous call to *ap_bspawn_child()*. Provided that the

---

[*] Note that the source code for *ap_call_exec()* refers to the return value as the "pid." This is misleading.

launched script outputs a valid header format, the headers will be added to the request record's `headers_out` table.

The same special actions are taken on certain headers as were discussed in Chapter 9, *Perl API Reference Guide*, when we covered the Perl *cgi_header_out()* method (see "Server Response Methods" in "The Apache Request Object"). If the headers were properly formatted and parsed, the return value will be OK. Otherwise, `HTTP_INTERNAL_SERVER_ERROR` or some other error code will be returned. In addition, the function will log errors to the error log.

The `buffer` argument should be an empty character array allocated to `MAX_STRING_LENGTH` or longer. If an error occurs during processing, this buffer will be set to contain the portion of the incoming data that generated the error. This may be useful for logging.

```
char buffer[MAX_STRING_LEN];
if(ap_scan_script_header_err(r, fb, buffer) != OK) {
    ... log nasty error message ...
```

*int ap_scan_script_header_err (request_rec *r, FILE *f, char *buffer)*

This function does exactly the same as *ap_scan_script_header_err_buff()*, except that it reads from a `FILE*` stream rather than a `BUFF*` stream. You would use this with the `pipe_out FILE*` returned by *ap_spawn_child()*.

*int ap_scan_script_header_err_core (request_rec *r, char *buffer,*
*int (*getsfunc) (char *, int, void *), void *getsfunc_data)*

The tongue-twisting *ap_scan_script_header_err_core()* function is the underlying routine which implements *ap_scan_script_header_err()* and *ap_scan_script_header_err_buff()*. The key component here is the function pointer, *getsfunc()*, which is called upon to return a line of data in the same way that the standard *fgets()* function does. For example, here's how *ap_scan_script_header_err()* works, using the standard *fgets()* function:

```
static int getsfunc_FILE(char *buf, int len, void *f)
{
    return fgets(buf, len, (FILE *) f) != NULL;
}

API_EXPORT(int) ap_scan_script_header_err(request_rec *r, FILE *f,
                                          char *buffer)
{
    return scan_script_header_err_core(r, buffer, getsfunc_FILE, f);
}
```

Your module could replace *getsfunc_FILE()* with an implementation to read from a string or other resource.

A Practical Example

We are going to say "Goodbye World" now but this time in a very *big* way. We will add a "goodbye-banner" handler to *mod_hello*. This handler will run the Unix *banner* command to print out a large, vertically oriented "Goodbye World" message. Although this is a very simple example compared to what happens inside *mod_cgi*, it does show you everything you need to write basic fork/exec code. For advanced tricks and subtleties, we recommend you peruse the source code for *mod_cgi* and *mod_include*.

The additions to *mod_hello.c* are shown in Example 11-6. At the top, we add *util_script.h* to the list of included files and hardcode the absolute path to the *banner* program in the *#define BANNER_PGM*.

Example 11-6. Additions to mod_hello.c to Launch a Child Process

```
#include "util_script.h"
#define BANNER_PGM "/usr/bin/banner"

/* Forward declaration so that ap_get_module_config() can find us. */
module hello_module;

static int banner_child(void *rp, child_info *pinfo)
{
    char **env;
    int child_pid;
    request_rec *r = (request_rec *)rp;

    env = ap_create_environment(r->pool, r->subprocess_env);
    ap_error_log2stderr(r->server);
    r->filename = BANNER_PGM;
    r->args = "-w80+Goodbye%20World";
    ap_cleanup_for_exec();
    child_pid = ap_call_exec(r, pinfo, r->filename, env, 0);
#ifdef WIN32
    return(child_pid);
#else
    ap_log_error(APLOG_MARK, APLOG_ERR, NULL, "exec of %s failed", r->filename);
    exit(0);
    /*NOT REACHED*/
    return(0);
#endif
}

static int goodbye_banner_handler(request_rec *r)
{
    BUFF *pipe_output;
    if (!ap_bspawn_child(r->pool, banner_child,
                         (void *) r, kill_after_timeout,
                         NULL, &pipe_output, NULL)) {
        ap_log_error(APLOG_MARK, APLOG_ERR, r->server,
                     "couldn't spawn child process: %s", BANNER_PGM);
```

Example 11-6. Additions to mod_hello.c to Launch a Child Process (continued)

```
        return HTTP_INTERNAL_SERVER_ERROR;
    }
    r->content_type = "text/plain";
    ap_send_http_header(r);
    ap_send_fb(pipe_output, r);
    ap_bclose(pipe_output);
    return OK;
}

static handler_rec hello_handlers[] =
{
    {"hello-handler", hello_handler},
    {"goodbye-banner-handler", goodbye_banner_handler},
    {NULL}
};
```

Skipping over the definition of *banner_child()* for now, look at *goodbye_banner_ handler()*. This is the content handler for the request. We are going to access the output of the *banner* command, so we declare a BUFF pointer for its standard output. Now we attempt to fork by calling *ap_bspawn_child()*. We pass the request record's resource pool as the first argument and the address of the *banner_child()* subroutine as the second. For the third argument, we use a copy of the request_ rec, cast to a void*. We use kill_after_timeout for the kill conditions argument, which is the usual choice. We don't care about the banner program's standard input or standard error, so we pass NULL for the fifth and seventh arguments, but we do want to recover the program's output, so we pass the address of the pipe_output BUFF* for the sixth argument.

If *ap_bspawn_child()* succeeds, there will now be two processes. In the child process, *ap_bspawn_child()* immediately invokes the *banner_child()* function, which we will examine momentarily. In the parent process, *ap_bspawn_child()* returns the process ID of the child. If it encounters an error it will return 0, and the parent logs an error and returns HTTP_INTERNAL_SERVER_ERROR.

The remainder of what we have to do in the handler is simple. We set the outgoing response's content type to *text/plain* and send the HTTP header with *ap_send_ http_header()*. Next we forward the child process's output to the browser by calling *ap_send_fb()*, which reads from the child and sends to the client in a single step. When this is done, we clean up by closing pipe_output and return OK.

The *banner_child()* function is called within the child spawned by *ap_bspawn_ child()*. We're going to set up the environment, do a little cleanup, and then replace the process with the *banner* program. We begin by recovering the request record and passings its pool and subprocess_env fields to *ap_create_ environment()*, obtaining an environment pointer. We then open the child's standard error stream to the error log by invoking *ap_error_log2stderr()*.

We want to call *banner* as if it had been invoked by this command at the shell:

```
% banner -w80 "Goodbye World"
```

This specifies a banner 80 characters wide with a message of "Goodbye World". To do this, we place the command's full path in the request record's `filename` field, and set the `args` field to contain the string `-w80+Goodbye%20World`. Individual command arguments are separated by + symbols, and any character that would have special meaning to the shell, such as the space character, is replaced with a URL hex escape.

Before we launch *banner* we should invoke any cleanup handlers that have been registered for the current request. We do so by calling *ap_cleanup_for_exec()*. Now we call *ap_call_exec()* to run *banner*, passing the routine the request record, the `pinfo` pointer passed to the routine by Apache, the name of the banner program, and the environment array created by *ap_create_environment()*. We want Apache to pass arguments to *banner*, so we specify a `shellcmd` argument of false.

If all goes well, the next line is never reached on Unix platforms. But if for some reason Apache couldn't exec the *banner* program, we log an error and immediately exit. The return statement at the end of the routine is never reached but is there to keep the C compiler from generating a warning. As noted above, *ap_call_exec()* behaves differently on Win32 platforms because the function launches a new process rather than overlaying the current one. We handle this difference with conditional compilation. If the Win32 define is present, *banner_child()* returns the process ID generated by *ap_call_exec()*. We do this even though it isn't likely that the *banner* program will ever be ported to Windows platforms!

There's only one thing more to do to make the *goodbye_banner_handler()* available for use, which is to add it and a symbolic handler name to the `hello_handlers[]` array. We chose "goodbye-banner-handler" for this purpose. Now, by creating a *<Location>* section like this one, you can give the handler a whirl:

```
<Location /goodbye>
   SetHandler goodbye-banner-handler
</Location>
```

Figure 11-1 shows our handler in action, and this seems to be a good place to say goodbye as well.

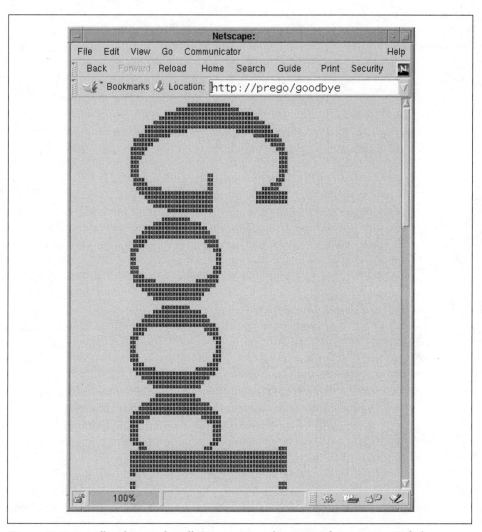

Figure 11-1. "goodbye-banner-handler" re-creates a burst page from a circa-1960 line printer.

Standard Noncore Modules

The *mod_perl* distribution comes with a number of helper classes that add specialized functionality to the package. None of them are essential to write Apache modules in the Perl API or have any equivalent in the C-language API, but they can be very handy at times.

The Apache::Registry Class

The *Apache::Registry* class is essentially a CGI environment emulator that allows many CGI scripts to run without modification under *mod_perl*.

Because there are many differences between CGI and the Apache API, *Apache::Registry* has to do a great deal of work to accomplish this sleight of hand. It loads the scripts in its designated directory, compiles them, and stores them persistently in a memory structure. Before *Apache::Registry* runs a script, *mod_perl* will set up the various CGI environment variables, provided *PerlSetupEnv* is configured to *On*, which is the default. When the *PerlSendHeader* directive is *On*, *mod_perl* monitors the text printed by the script, intercepts the HTTP header, and passes it through *send_cgi_header()*. It also arranges for STDIN to be read from the request object when the script attempts to process POST data. *Apache::Registry* also monitors the modification dates of the script files it is responsible for and reloads them if their timestamp indicates they have been changed more recently than when they were last compiled.

Despite its complexity, *Apache::Registry* is easy to set up. The standard configuration consists of an *Alias* directive and a *<Location>* section:

```
Alias /perl/ /home/www/perl
<Location /perl>
  SetHandler     perl-script
```

```
    PerlHandler     Apache::Registry
    Options         +ExecCGI
    # optional
    PerlSendHeader On
</Location>
```

After restarting the server, you can place any (well, almost any) Perl CGI script into */home/www/perl* (or the location of your choice) and make it executable. It runs just like an ordinary CGI script but will load much faster.

The behavior of *Apache::Registry* can be tuned with the following directives:

PerlTaintCheck

When set to *On, mod_perl* will activate Perl taint checks on all the scripts under its control. Taint checks cause Perl to die with a fatal error if unchecked user-provided data (such as the values of CGI variables) is passed to a potentially dangerous function, such as *exec()*, *eval()*, or *system()*.

PerlSendHeader

When set to *On, mod_perl* will scan for script output that looks like an HTTP header and automatically call *send_http_header()*. Scripts that send header information using CGI.pm's *header()* function do not need to activate *PerlSendHeader*. While scripts that use CGI.pm's *header()* will still function properly with *PerlSendHeader On*, turning it *Off* will save a few CPU cycles.

PerlFreshRestart

If *PerlFreshRestart* is set to *On, mod_perl* will flush its cache and reload all scripts when the server is restarted. This is very useful during module development to immediately see the changes to the source code take effect.

PerlWarn

If the script mentions the *–w* switch on its #! line, *Apache::Registry* will turn Perl warnings on by setting the $^W global to a nonzero value. The *PerlWarn* directive can be configured to *On* to turn on warnings for all code inside the server.

Apache::Registry has several debug levels which write various informational messages to the server error log. *Apache::Registry* scripts can change the debug level by importing *Apache::Debug* with its *level* pragma:

```
    use Apache::Debug level => $level;
```

The debug level is a bit mask generated by ORing together some combination of the following values:

1   Make a note in the error log whenever the module is recompiled

2   Call *Apache::Debug::dump()* on errors

4   Turn on verbose tracing

The current value of the debug level can be found in the package global $Apache::Registry::Debug. You should not set this value directly, however. See Chapter 2, *A First Module*, for more hints on debugging *Apache::Registry* scripts.

The Apache::PerlRun Class

The *Apache::PerlRun* handler is intended for Perl CGI scripts that depend strongly on the traditional one-process-per-execution CGI model and cannot deal with being invoked repeatedly in the same process. For example, a script that depends on a lot of global variables being uninitialized when it starts up is unlikely to work properly under *Apache::Registry*.

Like *Apache::Registry*, *Apache::PerlRun* manages a directory of CGI scripts, launching them when they are requested. However, unlike *Apache::Registry*, this module does not cache compiled scripts between runs. A script is loaded and compiled freshly each time it is requested. However, *Apache::PerlRun* still avoids the overhead of starting a new Perl interpreter for each CGI script, so it's faster than traditional Perl CGI scripting but slower than *Apache::Registry* or vanilla Apache API modules. It offers a possible upgrade path for CGI scripts: move the script to *Apache::PerlRun* initially to get a modest performance bump. This gives you time to rework the script to make it globally clean so that it can run under *Apache::Registry* for the full performance benefit.

The configuration section for running *Apache::PerlRun* is similar to *Apache::Registry*:

```
Alias /perl-run/ /home/www/perl-run/
<Location /perl>
  SetHandler      perl-script
  PerlHandler     Apache::PerlRun
  Options         +ExecCGI
  # optional
  PerlSendHeader On
</Location>
```

The *Apache::PerlRun* handler is only a small part of the picture. The rest of the *Apache::PerlRun* class provides subclassable methods that implement the functionality of *Apache::Registry*. The *Apache::PerlRun* handler simply uses a subset of these methods; other modules may override certain methods to implement the *Apache::Registry* enviroment with a few twists. However, these *Apache::PerlRun* class methods were not fully defined when this book was going to press.

The Apache::RegistryLoader Class

Ordinarily, *Apache::Registry* scripts are not compiled until they are needed. This means that the very first time one of these scripts is required by a child process, there will be a delay while the script is loaded and compiled.

Apache::RegistryLoader was designed to avoid this delay by precompiling *Apache::Registry* scripts during the server startup phase. In addition to minimizing loading time, it also reduces memory consumption because the Registry scripts are compiled into the single server *parent* process before it forks off the flock of child servers. The memory occupied by this precompiled code is then shared among the children, and although there doesn't appear to be a difference in child process size when you invoke *ps* (on Unix systems), overall memory consumption is reduced. See the *mod_perl_tuning* document in the *mod_perl* distribution for more details.

Typically, you will invoke *Apache::RegistryLoader* from a Perl startup script. A typical entry looks like this:

```
#!/usr/local/bin/perl

use MyFavoriteModule1 ();
use MyFavoriteModule2 ();
...
use Apache::RegistryLoader ();
my $rl = Apache::RegistryLoader->new;
$rl->handler('/perl/test.pl'=> '/home/www/perl/test.pl');
$rl->handler('/perl/test2.pl'=> '/home/www/perl/test2.pl');
...
```

This code creates a new *Apache::RegistryLoader* object by invoking the class's *new()* method and then calls this object's *handler()* method for each script you want to load. *Apache::RegistryLoader* is actually a subclass of *Apache::Registry* which overrides certain methods such that the *Apache::RegistryLoader handler()* method only invokes the script compliation and caching methods of *Apache::Registry*.

Notice that *handler()* requires two arguments: the URI of the script to compile and its physical pathname. The reason you can't just provide one or the other is that the task of translating from a URI to a filename is usually done at request time by a translation handler. However, at server startup time there's no request to process, and therefore no way of getting at the translation handler.

If you specify a URI only, *Apache::RegistryLoader* will try to interpret it relative to the server root. This will work only if the *Apache::Registry* directory URI is aliased to an identically named physical directory beneath the server root.

Here's an example:

```
# in httpd.conf
ServerRoot /home/www
Alias      /perl/  /home/www/perl/

# in Perl startup script
use Apache::RegistryLoader ();
Apache::RegistryLoader->new->handler("/perl/test.pl");
```

Another solution is to provide a URI translation routine to the *new()* method at the time you create the *Apache::RegistryLoader* object. The Apache translation handlers can only be run during request time, so we must roll our own during startup. The translation handler will take an argument consisting of the script URI and return the translated physical pathname to the file as its function result. The following code fragment illustrates how to precompile all *.pl* files in the directory *~www/perl/*:

```
# in perl.conf (or any other configuration file)
PerlRequire conf/preload_scripts.pl

# in conf/preload_scripts.pl
#!/usr/local/bin/perl
use Apache::RegistryLoader ();
use DirHandle ();
use strict;

sub do_translate {
  my $uri = shift;
  return Apache->server_root_relative($uri);
};

my $rl = Apache::RegistryLoader->new(trans => \&do_translate);
my $dir = Apache->server_root_relative("perl/");

my $dh = DirHandle->new($dir) or die $!;

foreach my $file ($dh->read) {
   next unless $file =~ /\.pl$/;
   $rl->handler("/perl/$file");
}
```

The Apache::Resource Class

Apache::Resource allows you to set resource limitations on the Apache server process. You can limit the amount of CPU time a child process will use, the amount of memory it allocates, the number of files it can have open simultaneously, the number of processes it can spawn, and other low-level resources. This allows you to limit the overall impact of a runaway process or to degrade processing gracefully if the server is overloaded by too many requests.

In order to use *Apache::Resource*, you must have the Perl *BSD::Resource* module installed. This module does not come installed in Perl by default. As the name implies, *BSD::Resource* will only compile on BSD-derived versions of Unix and a few close approximations. It will *not* run correctly on Win32 systems.

To use *Apache::Resource*, place the following declarations in one of your server configuration files:

```
PerlSetEnv   PERL_RLIMIT_DEFAULTS
PerlModule   Apache::Resource
PerlChildInitHandler Apache::Resource
```

This chooses reasonable defaults for the resource limits, loads the *Apache::Resource* module, and sets it to run whenever a child process is initialized.

You can further customize the module by using *PerlSetEnv* to declare more specific resource limits for CPU usage, memory, and so on. There are actually two limits you can set for each of these resources: a hard limit that can't be changed and a soft limit that can be increased by modules if they choose to do so (up to the hard limit). You can use a single number for each resource variable, in which case it will be used for both the hard and soft limits, or you can specify a pair of numbers delimited by a colon in *S:H* format. The first number is the soft limit, and the second is the hard.

The following variables are available for your use:

PERL_RLIMIT_DATA
    Child memory limit in megabytes.

PERL_RLIMIT_CPU
    Child CPU units in seconds.

PERL_RLIMIT_FSIZE
    Maximum file size in megabytes.

PERL_RLIMIT_RSS
    Maximum process size in megabytes.

PERL_RLIMIT_STACK
    Child stack limit in megabytes.

PERL_RLIMIT_CORE
    Maximum core file size in megabytes.

Within a handler, modules can examine the limits and change them (up to the ceiling specified by the hard limits) by calling the *getrlimit()* and *setrlimit()* methods of *BSD::Resource*.

The Apache::PerlSections Class

As described in Chapter 7, *Other Request Phases*, it's possible to configure the Apache server entirely via Perl scripts embedded in *<Perl>* sections. The *Apache::PerlSections* module is a helper class that provides convenient functions for this process. It provides two public functions, *dump()* and *store()*.

dump()

Called from within a *<Perl>* configuration section, *dump()* returns a pretty-printed string containing the current configuration variables. The string can be written out to a file and later brought back in via a *require*.

Example:

```
<Perl>
    use Apache::PerlSections ();
    $Port = 8529;
    @DocumentIndex = qw(index.htm index.html);

    print Apache::PerlSections->dump();
</Perl>
```

This will print out something like this:

```
package Apache::ReadConfig;
#scalars:

$Port = 8529;

 #arrays:

@DocumentIndex = (
  'index.htm',
  'index.html'
);

# hashes

1;
__END__
```

Notice that the variables are declared in the *Apache::ReadConfig* package. We give the reason for this in the next section.

store()

This is identical to *dump()*, except that the formatted string is written directly to the file path you specify.

Example:

```
<Perl>
    .....
    print Apache::PerlSections->store('httpd_config.pl');
</Perl>
```

If a relative path is given to *store()*, it will be taken as relative to the current configuration file.

The Apache::ReadConfig Class

Apache::ReadConfig is a namespace used by the *<Perl>* configuration section mechanism to store its global variables. All global variables defined in this namespace are processed as if they were configuration directives during server startup time. See Chapter 8 for detailed examples on configuring *httpd* with Perl.

The Apache::StatINC Class

When you write a script using the *Apache::Registry* mechanism, *Apache::Registry* watches the script file's modification date and reloads the script if it is more recent than the compiled version in memory. This lets you edit the script file and see the changes immediately.

However, this is not the case with Apache Perl API modules or any Perl library files that they depend on. Changing the *.pm* file does not cause the module to be reloaded automatically. You ordinarily have to restart the whole server with *apachectl restart* or *apache −k restart* to see any changes take effect.

You can use the *Apache::StatINC* to alter this behavior. Each time it runs, *Apache::StatINC* checks the contents of the Perl global %INC hash of loaded modules. *Apache::StatINC* keeps track of each module's modification time. When it notes that a module has been modified since it was last loaded, it removes the module from %INC, forcing Perl to reload and compile it.

To install *Apache::StatINC*, add the following configuration directive to *perl.conf* (or any of the configuration files):

```
PerlInitHandler Apache::StatINC
```

This directive arranges for *Apache::StatINC*'s *handler()* method to be invoked every time Apache handles an HTTP request, before any other *Perl*Handlers* are run.

Note that *Apache::StatINC* only sees the directories that were present in the @INC include path at the time the server was started. During a request, a script or module may modify the @INC path, but those changes are lost when *mod_perl* restores @INC to the same value it had at server startup time. If you wish to monitor custom directories, you should install them at Perl startup time, either by putting the requisite *use lib* lines in the Perl startup script or by defining the PERL5LIB environment variable before starting the server.

We do not recommend *Apache::StatINC* for use on a production server. It introduces significant overhead on every transaction.

The Apache::Include Class

This class provides methods to support integration between *mod_include* and *mod_perl*. It makes it possible for parsed HTML files (*.shtml*) to include *Apache::Registry* scripts with directives like this one:

```
<!--#perl sub="Apache::Include" arg="/perl/ssi.pl" -->
```

When this directive is processed by Apache's standard *mod_include* module, the *Apache::Registry* script *ssi.pl* is run and its output incorporated into the page.

Apache::Include provides a method named *virtual()* for those who wish to include the contents of another document in the output of their *Apache::Registry* scripts. It is called with two arguments: the URI you wish to incorporate and the current request object. Only local URIs can be included in this way.

Here's an example:

```
#!/usr/local/bin/perl
use Apache ();
use Apache::Include ();

my $r = Apache->request;
print "Content-type: text/plain\n\n";
print "I am including a document now:\n";
Apache::Include->virtual('/contents.txt', $r);
print "I am done.\n";
```

See Chapter 7, *Perl Server-Side Includes*, for more details on using the *#perl* element with server-side includes.

The Apache::Status Class

The *Apache::Status* class provides dynamic status and debug information about the *mod_perl* interpreter. When installed, it will display symbol table dumps, inheritance trees, lists of global variables, and other displays that may be of interest to Perl module developers (Figure A-1).

A URI to run *Apache::Status* must be installed before the module can be used. To do this, create an entry like the following in one of the Apache configuration files:

```
<Location /perl-status>
    SetHandler  perl-script
    PerlHandler Apache::Status     .
</Location>
```

After restarting the server, requests for the URI */perl-status* will display a series of pages showing the status of various Apache modules, including your own.

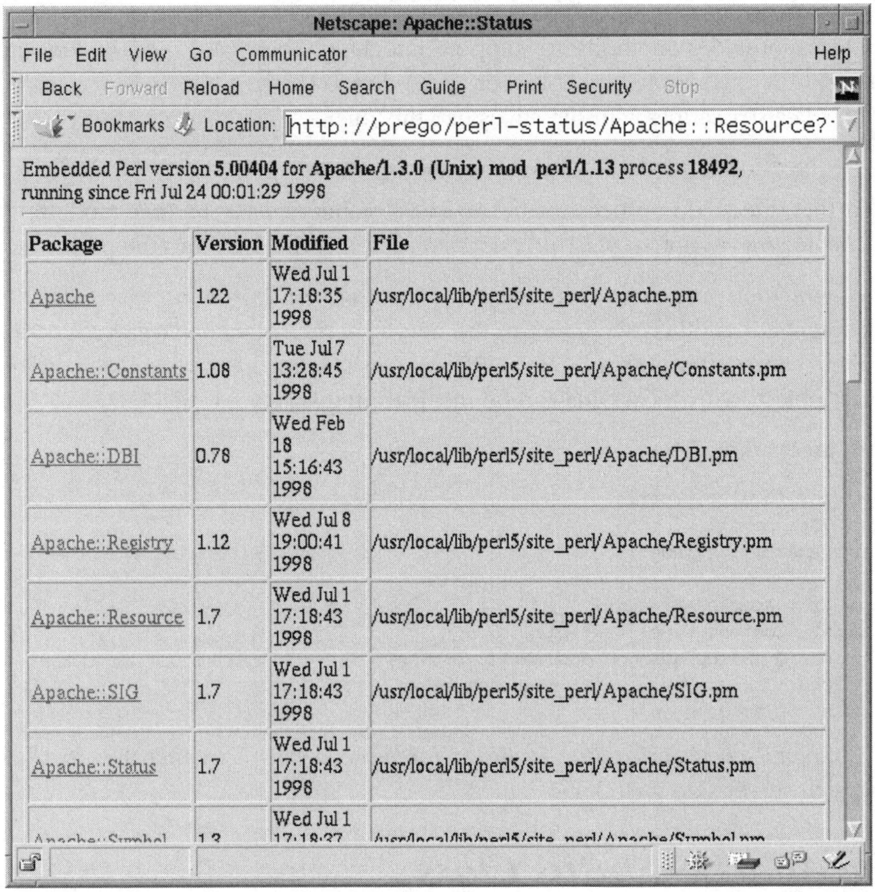

Figure A-1. The Apache::Status module produces detailed reports on the state of mod_perl.

Apache::Status requires the *Devel::Symdump* module to run at all. This is not a standard part of the Perl distribution and will need to be downloaded from CPAN and installed. Certain other features of the module are not activated unless you also install a few third party pieces. With the *Data::Dumper* module installed and *StatusDumper* set to *On*, it is possible to view the contents of global variables. Installing *Apache::Peek* and setting *StatusPeek* to *On* enables inspection of symbols the same way Perl views them internally. If *mod_perl* was compiled with Perl 5.005 or higher and the *B::Graph* module was installed, along with the *dot* program, setting *StatusGraph* to *On* enables *Apache::Status* to render GIF graphs of OP trees. The three modules can be found on CPAN. *dot* is part of AT&T's graph visualization toolkit available at *http://www.research.att.com/sw/tools/graphviz/*. Here is a sample configuration that enables all of these features:

```
<Location /perl-status>
    SetHandler  perl-script
    PerlHandler Apache::Status
    PerlSetVar  StatusDumper On
    PerlSetVar  StatusPeek   On
    PerlSetVar  StatusGraph  On
</Location>
```

Your module can add one or more custom menu items to the *Apache::Status* main page. When you click on this link, *Apache::Status* runs a subroutine defined in your module and displays the subroutine's output, usually some HTML. To install this type of custom menu item, include a code snippet like this at the bottom of the module:

```
if (Apache->module("Apache::Status")) {
    Apache::Status->menu_item('MyApp' => "MyApp Menu Item",
                              \&myapp_debug_menu);
}
sub myapp_debug_menu {
  my ($r,$q) = @_;
  push(@s,'<h2>some html</h2>');
  push(@s,'some <b>more</b> html');
  return \@s;
}
```

In this example, we first check with Apache to see if the *Apache::Status* module is present. If so, we call its *menu_item()* method. The first two arguments to *menu_item()* are the name of the current module and the descriptive title to use for its custom menu item. The third argument is a CODE reference to a subroutine to run when the menu item is selected.

In this example, the subroutine is named *myapp_debug_menu()*. On entry to this subroutine, *Apache::Status* passes it the Apache request object and a CGI object (from the CGI.pm module). The subroutine is free to do whatever it likes with these objects or ignore them entirely. The subroutine builds up an array containing the HTML it wants to display. Its function result is a reference to that array.

Good examples of creating custom menu items can be found by inspecting the source code of the *Apache::Resource* and the *Apache::DBI* modules.

B

Building and
Installing mod_perl

This appendix contains instructions for building and installing *mod_perl* using a variety of techniques. It also provides a full listing of *mod_perl*'s many configuration options.

Standard Installation

As described in the walk-through in Chapter 2, *A First Module*, the standard way to build and install *mod_perl* is to run *Makefile.PL* with the following sequence of commands:

```
% perl Makefile.PL configuration options
% make
% make test
% make install
```

This will automatically build a *mod_perl*-embedded version of Apache and install it in the standard location. The configuration options you specify give you extensive control over the building and installation process.

Makefile.PL Options for mod_perl

There are several reasons for *mod_perl*'s bewildering number of configuration options. Many of the options came to be during the early days of *mod_perl*, when new options were frequently added in an "experimental" state. As these features matured and stabilized, their activation switches remained for those site administrators who do not want to expose certain areas of the API to programmers. By turning off unwanted features, sites can also reduce the size of the Apache executable somewhat, although this overhead is small compared to the size of the Perl runtime itself.

Most first-time users of the Perl API will want to configure *mod_perl* with the `EVERYTHING=1` option in order to turn on all features. Later, when you've experimented with the API, you may decide to dispense with some features, and you can reconfigure the server with a more select set of options. Other recommended options are `USE_APACI=1`, to use the Apache AutoConf-style Interface (APACI), and `APACHE_PREFIX=/server/root`, to specify the location of the server root in which to install the *mod_perl*-enabled server and support files.

Options for controlling the build process

These options control the configuration and build process. Among other things, these options allow you to specify parameters that are passed through to Apache's configuration system.

`USE_APACI=1`

> Tells *mod_perl* to configure Apache using the flexible Apache AutoConf-style Interface (APACI), rather than the older system, which required a file named *src/Configuration* to be edited. This option is recommended.

`APACHE_PREFIX=/usr/local/apache`

> When *USE_APACI* is enabled, this attribute will specify the *--prefix* option for Apache's *configure* script, specifying the installation path for Apache. When this option is used, *mod_perl*'s *make install* will also *make install* on the Apache side, installing the *httpd* binary and support tools, along with the configuration, log, and document trees.

`APACI_ARGS="--option=val,--other-option=val"`

> Passes additional arguments to Apache's *configure* script. The argument list should be contained within single or double quotes and delimited by commas. Example:

```
% set runpath=/var/run/apache
% set logpath=/var/logs/apache
% perl Makefile.PL APACI_ARGS="--runtimedir=$runpath,--logfiledir=$logpath"
```

`WITH_APXS=~www/bin/apxs`

> Tells *mod_perl* the location of the APache eXtenSion tool (*apxs*); see Chapter 2 under "Building a Dynamically Loadable Module" and Appendix C, *Building Multifile C API Modules*. This is necessary if the binary cannot be found in the command path or in the location specified by *APACHE_PREFIX*.

`USE_APXS=1`

> Tells *mod_perl* to build itself using the APache eXtenSion (*apxs*) tool. As described in Chapter 2, this tool is used to build C API modules in a way that is independent of the Apache source tree. *mod_perl* will look for *apxs* in the location specified by *USE_APXS*. If *USE_APXS* is not specified, *mod_perl* will check the *bin* and *sbin* directories relative to *APACHE_PREFIX*.

USE_DSO=1

> Tells *mod_perl* to build itself as a dynamic shared object (DSO). Although this reduces the apparent size of the *httpd* executable on disk, it doesn't actually reduce its memory consumption. This is recommended only if you are going to be using the Perl API occasionally or if you wish to experiment with its features before you start using it in a production environment.
>
> This feature was considered experimental at the time this book was written. Consult the *mod_perl INSTALL.apaci* file for details on using this option.

APACHE_SRC=/*path*/*to*/apache_*x.x.x*/src

> Tells *mod_perl* where the Apache source tree is located. You may need this if the Apache source tree is not in the immediate vicinity of the *mod_perl* directory.

SSL_BASE=/*path*/*to*/ssl

> When building against a *mod_ssl* enabled server, this option tells Apache where to look for SSL *include* and *lib* subdirectories.

DO_HTTPD=1

> Tells *mod_perl* to build the Apache server for you, skipping the interactive prompt. If *APACHE_SRC* is also specified, *mod_perl* will use its value. Otherwise, it will search the immediate vicinity of the *mod_perl* directory and use the first Apache source tree it finds.

ADD_MODULE=info,status,proxy

> Specifies a list of optional Apache modules to configure into the server, delimited by a comma. For example, this command will enable the *mod_info*, *mod_status*, and *mod_proxy* modules:
>
> ```
> % perl Makefile.PL ADD_MODULE=info,status,proxy
> ```

PREP_HTTPD=1

> Tells *mod_perl* only to prepare Apache for building. Running the *make* command after this option is used will only build the Perl side of *mod_perl*. You will have to build *httpd* manually.

DYNAMIC=1

> Tells *mod_perl* to build the *Apache::** API extensions as shared libraries. The default action is to link these modules statically with the *httpd* executable. This can save some memory if you only occasionally use these API features. They are described briefly in this appendix and in more detail in Chapter 9, *Perl API Reference Guide*.

PERL_TRACE=1

> This option enables runtime diagnostics for *mod_perl*. You will also need to set the MOD_PERL_TRACE environment variable at runtime in order to see the diagnostics.

`PERL_DESTRUCT_LEVEL={1,2}`

> When the Perl interpreter is shutting down during server shutdown, this level enables additional checks to make sure the interpreter has done proper book-keeping. The default is 0. A value of 1 enables full destruction, and 2 enables full destruction with checks. This value can also be changed at runtime by setting the environment variable `PERL_DESTRUCT_LEVEL`.

`PERL_DEBUG=1`

> This options builds *mod_perl* and the Apache server with C source code debugging enabled (the –*g* switch). It also enables *PERL_TRACE*, sets *PERL_DESTRUCT_LEVEL* to 2, and links against the debuggable *libperld* Perl interpreter if one has been installed. You will be able to debug the Apache executable and each of its modules with a source level debugger, such as the GNU debugger *gdb*.

Options for activating phase callback hooks

The following *Makefile.PL* options enable handling of the various phases of the Apache request cycle. The significance of these phases is explained in previous chapters. Unless specified otherwise, these options are all disabled by default. Specifying `EVERYTHING=1` will enable them en masse.

`PERL_DISPATCH=1`

> Enables the *PerlDispatchHandler* directive.

`PERL_CHILD_INIT=1`

> Enables the *PerlChildInitHandler* directive.

`PERL_CHILD_EXIT=1`

> Enables the *PerlChildExitHandler* directive.

`PERL_INIT=1`

> Enables the *PerlInitHandler* directive.

`PERL_POST_READ_REQUEST=1`

> Enables the *PerlPostReadRequestHandler* directive.

`PERL_TRANS=1`

> Enables the *PerlTransHandler* directive.

`PERL_HEADER_PARSER=1`

> Enables the *PerlHeaderParserHandler* directive.

`PERL_ACCESS=1`

> Enables the *PerlAccessHandler* directive.

`PERL_AUTHEN=1`

> Enables the *PerlAuthenHandler* directive.

PERL_AUTHZ=1

> Enables the *PerlAuthzHandler* directive.

PERL_TYPE=1

> Enables the *PerlTypeHandler* directive.

PERL_FIXUP=1

> Enables the *PerlFixupHandler* directive.

PERL_HANDLER=1

> Enables the *PerlHandler* directive. (This directive is enabled by default.)

PERL_LOG=1

> Enables the *PerlLogHandler* directive.

PERL_CLEANUP=1

> Enables the *PerlCleanupHandler* directive.

Options for activating standard API features

These options enable various standard features of the API, which are described in Chapter 9. While not absolutely needed, they're very handy and there's little penalty for including them. Unless specified otherwise, these options are all disabled by default. The EVERYTHING=1 or DYNAMIC=1 options will enable them all.

PERL_FILE_API=1

> Enables the *Apache::File* class.

PERL_TABLE_API=1

> Enables the *Apache::Table* class.

PERL_LOG_API=1

> Enables the *Apache::Log* class.

PERL_URI_API=1

> Enables the *Apache::URI* class.

PERL_UTIL_API=1

> Enables the *Apache::Util* class.

PERL_CONNECTION_API=1

> Enables the *Apache::Connection* class. This class is enabled by default. Set the option to 0 to disable it.

PERL_SERVER_API=1

> Enables the *Apache::Server* class. This class is enabled by default. Set the option to 0 to disable it.

APACHE_HEADER_INSTALL=1

> Disables the installation of Apache header files. This option is enabled by default. Set the option to 0 to disable it.

Options for activating miscellaneous features

These options enable or disable a variety of features that you may or may not need. They are disabled by default unless `EVERYTHING=1` is specified.

`PERL_SECTIONS=1`

Enables *<Perl>* configuration sections.

`PERL_SSI=1`

Enables the *perl* directive in the *mod_include* module.

`PERL_DIRECTIVE_HANDLERS=1`

Enables the Perl configuration directive API, including the *Apache::Module-Config* and *Apache::CmdParms* classes. This API is described in Chapter 8, *Customizing the Apache Configuration Process.*

`PERL_STACKED_HANDLERS=1`

Enables the "Stacked Handlers" feature.

`PERL_METHOD_HANDLERS=1`

Enables the "Method Handlers" feature.

`EVERYTHING=1`

This attribute enables all phase callback handlers, all API modules, and all miscellaneous features.

`EXPERIMENTAL=1`

This attribute enables all "experimental" features, which are usually under development and discussion on the *modperl* mailing list.

Other Configuration Methods

As with everything having to do with Perl, there are many ways to build and install *mod_perl*. This section covers several of the alternatives.

Using the .makepl_args.mod_perl File

The various *Makefile.PL* options can be overwhelming, difficult to remember, and cumbersome to type. One way to save your preferences for posterity is to wrap the *Makefile.PL* command into a shell script.

Another way to save your preferences is to create a file named *.makepl_args.mod_perl*, located either in the current directory (.), the parent directory (..), or your home directory. When *Makefile.PL* runs, it scans these directories for the file, reads it in, and strips out blank lines and comments. Everything else is treated as a command line option. For example:

```
# File: .makepl_args.mod_perl
# enable all phase callbacks, API modules and misc features
EVERYTHING=1
```

```
#tell Makefile.PL where the Apache source tree is
APACHE_SRC=/usr/local/apache/src

#tell Makefile.PL to use the first source found, which will be the
#path specified above by APACHE_SRC
DO_HTTPD=1

#tell Makefile.PL to configure Apache using the apaci interface
USE_APACI=1

#specify the --prefix to give Apache's configure script
APACHE_PREFIX=/usr/local/apache

#add mod_info, mod_status and mod_proxy
ADD_MODULE=info,status,proxy

#additional arguments to give Apache's configure script
#arguments can be delimited by a comma and/or specified with multiple
#APACI_ARGS lines
APACI_ARGS=--enable-shared=mime,--enable-shared=alias
APACI_ARGS=--logfiledir=/usr/local/apache/logs
APACI_ARGS=--runtimedir=/usr/local/apache/logs
```

Now you can type the command *perl Makefile.PL* without giving any explicit options and they will be read in from the file. Any options you do supply on the command line will override those in the file.

Installing via CPAN.pm

Once you are familiar with installing *mod_perl* manually, you might want to install future updates using Andreas Koenig's awesome CPAN shell. This interactive program automatically determines the latest version of *mod_perl*, downloads it from a CPAN site, and runs the configuration, make, and install steps.

To enter the CPAN shell, type:

> % **perl -MCPAN -e shell**

If this is the first time you're running the shell, you'll be lead through a series of one-time configuration questions. The only question you need to be prepared for is the one that prompts you to type in the name of your favorite CPAN site. Refer back to the preface for instructions on finding a convenient site.

After CPAN is initialized, type:

> cpan> **install mod_perl**

and watch it fly!

Building mod_perl and Apache Separately

If you use a lot of third-party Apache modules, you may want to decouple the process of building *mod_perl* from the process of building Apache. This is only a little bit harder than the full automatic method described above.

You will first need to configure *mod_perl* using *Makefile.PL* in the manner described in the previous sections. However, answer "no" when prompted for whether to build *httpd* in the Apache source tree. Alternatively, you can disable the prompt completely by providing a configuration option of `PREP_HTTPD=1` on the command line.

You will *make* and *make install* in the *mod_perl* source directory as before. This process will build a *libperl.a* library within the Apache source tree but will not build the server itself. Now go ahead and build any third-party modules you wish to add to Apache. When you are ready to configure and install the server, enter the Apache directory tree and run the *configure* script with the following option:

```
--activate-module=src/modules/perl/libperl.a
```

This option must be in addition to any other options you wish to pass to the configure script; again, it's a good idea to run the *configure* command from within a shell script that you can edit and run again. The *--activate-module* option links the precompiled *libperl.a* library to the Apache server executable but does not otherwise interact with the *mod_perl* build process.

Building mod_perl as a DSO

If an Apache server installation is already installed, *mod_perl* can be built as a DSO without the Apache source tree handy. Example:

```
perl Makefile.PL USE_APXS=1 APACHE_PREFIX=/usr/local/apache EVERYTHING=1 ...
```

The *USE_APXS* option tells *mod_perl* to build itself using the Apache *apxs* tool. The *Makefile.PL* will look for *apxs* under the *bin/* and *sbin/* directories relative to *APACHE_PREFIX*. If *apxs* happens to be installed elsewhere, simply use the full pathname for the value of the *USE_APXS* attribute:

```
perl Makefile.PL USE_APXS=/usr/bin/apxs EVERYTHING=1 ...
```

Provided an *APACHE_PREFIX* attribute was passed to the *Makefile.PL* script, running *make install* will install and configure the *mod_perl* DSO library along with installing the Perl libraries. If no *APACHE_PREFIX* attribute was specified, simply copy the new *apaci/libperl.so* library to anywhere you choose.

C

Building Multifile
C API Modules

If you need to build a C module from several object files, or if the module requires functions defined in external library files, then you need to go beyond the simple build mechanism described in Chapter 2, *A First Module*. This appendix describes how to do so.

Statically Linked Modules That Need External Libraries

If you have a module that requires one or more external library files and you wish to link it into the *httpd* binary statically, then you have to arrange for the library to be added to the LIBS variable that the *httpd* makefile uses for the link phase. The most straightforward way to achieve this is to provide a "hint" to Apache's configuration system. You can embed configuration hints directly in the module source file, or you can place them in separate files located in the same directory as the source file.

For the purposes of this example, we'll assume we're implementing a module named *mod_compress* which requires some of the data compression/decompression functions located in the system *libz* library. We need to arrange for *–lz* to be added to the LIBS makefile variable. One way to do this is to add the following comment somewhere toward the top of the source file *mod_compress.c*:

```
/* Module configuration hints
MODULE-DEFINITION-START
Name: compress_module
ConfigStart
  LIBS="$LIBS -lz"
  echo " + using -lz for compression support"
ConfigEnd
```

```
MODULE-DEFINITION-END
*/
```

When the *configure* script runs, it scans through a module looking for lines containing the *MODULE-DEFINITION-START* and *MODULE-DEFINITION-END* keywords and passes everything between the two lines to the configuration system. Within the configuration section, the *Name:* keyword specifies the name of the module, which should be the same as the name given in the `module` declaration. This is followed by a section bracketed by the keywords *ConfigStart* and *ConfigEnd.* Everything between these two keywords is treated as a shell script and passed to */bin/sh* for evaluation. You are free to do anything in this section that you wish, including calling other shell scripts. In this case, we simply augment the **LIBS** variable by appending *−lz* to it; we then call *echo* to display a message indicating that we've done so.

An alternate way to achieve the same thing is to place the configuration information in a separate file named *module_name*.`module` located in the same directory as the module's source code. In this example, we would want to create a file named *mod_compress.module* containing the following text:

```
Name: compress_module
ConfigStart
  LIBS="$LIBS -lz"
  echo " + using -lz for compression support"
ConfigEnd
```

The contents of the file is identical to the text between the *MODULE-DEFINITION-START* and *MODULE-DEFINITION-END* lines. In either case, running *configure* with the option *--enable-module=modules/site/mod_compress.c* should now give output similar to the following:

```
Configuring for Apache, Version 1.3.3
 + activated compress module (modules/site/mod_compress.c)
Creating Makefile
Creating Configuration.apaci in src
 + enabling mod_so for DSO support
Creating Makefile in src
 + configured for Linux platform
 + setting C compiler to gcc
 + setting C pre-processor to gcc -E
 + checking for system header files
 + adding selected modules
    o rewrite_module uses ConfigStart/End
 + using -ldbm for DBM support
      enabling DBM support for mod_rewrite
    o compress_module uses ConfigStart/End
 + using -lz for compression support
 + using -ldl for vendor DSO support
 + doing sanity check on compiler and options
Creating Makefile in src/support
```

```
Creating Makefile in src/main
Creating Makefile in src/ap
Creating Makefile in src/regex
Creating Makefile in src/os/unix
Creating Makefile in src/modules/standard
Creating Makefile in src/modules/proxy
Creating Makefile in src/modules/extra
```

The relevant lines here are `compress_module uses ConfigStart/End` and `use -lz for compression support`. Together they show that the configuration hints have been correctly recognized and processed by the configuration system. If we were to go on to build *httpd*, we would see *–lz* included among the list of libraries brought in during the link phase.

Other makefile variables that you can adjust in this way are `INCLUDES`, the list of directory paths to search for header files, `CFLAGS`, the list of flags to pass to the compiler during compile phase, and `LDFLAGS`, the list of flags to pass to the linker during link phase.

This same technique can be used to create DSO modules, but there's a catch, as we explain in the next section.

Dynamically Linked Modules That Need External Libraries

Things get slightly more complicated when you want to build your module as a dynamic shared object (DSO) for loading at runtime. This is because not all Unix architectures allow you to link one shared object to another. Because both the module and the external library are shareable, this restriction causes *LoadModule* to fail at runtime with "symbol not found" errors.

Most Unix architectures don't suffer this problem, including all ELF-based systems. However, older systems that use the *a.out* binary architecture, including most BSD-derived systems, do suffer from this limitation. If this is the case with your system, you have the choice of statically linking the module with the *httpd* binary, as described in the previous section, or statically linking the whole external library into the DSO module.

Regardless of whether your system allows linking of DSOs to each other, its easiest to create modules that depend on external libraries using the APache eXtenSion (*apxs*) tool. Start out by running *apxs* with the *–g* and *–n* switches in order to create a skeleton build directory for your module:

```
% apxs -g -n compress
Creating [DIR]  compress
Creating [FILE] compress/Makefile
Creating [FILE] compress/mod_compress.c
```

Now edit the stub *.c* file to contain the handlers you need. In the case of *mod_compress.c*, we would add code to invoke *libz*'s file compression and decompression routines. To get the DSO module to link correctly, you must now edit *Makefile* so that the LIBS definition refers to *–lz*. For platforms that allow DSOs to be linked together, uncomment the LIBS line and edit it to read like this:

```
LIBS = -lz
```

If your platform doesn't support linking between DSOs, you have a few options. One option is to compile the library statically. The easiest way to do this is to locate the archive version of the library, for example, *libz.a*, and add the full path of the library file to the LIBS definition:

```
LIBS = /usr/local/lib/libz.a
```

This will cause the contents of *libz.a* to be linked in statically, just like an ordinary object file. However, there is one very large caveat! This will only work if the library archive was originally compiled with position-independent code, using the *–fpic* compiler flag or equivalent. If this was not the case, then the DSO module will fail, either when it is first built or when you first attempt to load it. If you really want to pursue this option, you can attempt to obtain the source code for the library and recompile it with the correct compiler flags.

Another option is to load the necessary shared libraries manually using *mod_so*'s *LoadFile* directive. This instructs Apache to load the symbols of any shared object file on the system, including shared libraries. You should call this directive *before* you attempt to load any DSO modules that require shared libraries that aren't linked into *httpd* itself. For example, to make *mod_compress* work on a system that doesn't allow shared libraries to be linked to DSOs, you could modify *httpd.conf* as follows (changing the paths as appropriate for your system):

```
LoadFile   /usr/lib/libz.so
LoadModule compress_module libexec/mod_compress.so
```

The last variant we will consider is when you are using a system that allows DSOs to be linked to shared libraries and you wish to build a DSO module in the Apache source tree with the Apache configuration system rather than with *apxs*. You can do so using the configuration techniques described in the previous section. However, the configuration system ordinarily won't allow a DSO module to be linked to a shared library because it is forbidden on some systems. In order to allow this to happen, you must recompile Apache with the *SHARED_CHAIN* compilation rule. This makes the way that Apache compiles and links DSO modules a little bit smarter. At configure time, the Apache configuration system examines the contents of the LIBS makefile definition. Any shared libraries in LIBS are remembered and used later when linking against DSO-based modules. To enable this feature, reconfigure Apache with the *--enable-rule=SHARED_CHAIN* option, as follows:

```
% ./configure --enable-rule=SHARED_CHAIN \
            ...other options....
```

This feature is only useful when creating DSO modules within the Apache source tree. It has no effect on modules created with *apxs*.

Shared library support is quite variable between different flavors of Unix. Be prepared to experiment a bit with loadable modules, and be aware that some combinations of loadable modules and shared libraries may just not work on certain platforms. A lengthier discussion can be found in the Apache documentation under *manual/dso.html*.

Building Modules from Several Source Files

The Apache build system is easiest to use when each C API module fits into a single source file. However, if the design of your module requires it to be spread out among a series of source files, Apache can accommodate this, albeit with a little more preparation on your part.

If you are building within the Apache source tree, the easiest way to structure the module is to place all the source files in their own subdirectory of *src/modules/*. The build scheme will be to create a library file named "lib*your_module*.a" first, and then to link this with *httpd*.

In addition to the source code files, the subdirectory will contain a file named *Makefile.tmpl* containing instructions for building the module, and, optionally, a file named "lib*your_module*.module" containing configuration hints for the module. You will also create a dummy file named *Makefile.libdir* which has no other purpose than to tell the configuration system that you have provided your own build targets in *Makefile.tmpl* and to suppress the automatic target generation that the configuration process usually performs.

As a concrete illustration, we will take the *mod_compress* example from the previous section and split it up into two source code files. *compress.c* will contain the module definition and the handler code, while *compress_util.c* will contain various utilities for compressing and decompressing files. The module will be compiled into a library archive named *libcompress.a*, and the whole set of source files and makefiles will live in the subdirectory *src/modules/compress*. It is important for the name of the library to match the name of the subdirectory in which it lives, or Apache's automatic configuration process may not work correctly.

We begin by creating the *src/modules/compress* directory and moving the appropriate *.c* and *.h* files into it. We next create the dummy file *Makefile.libdir*. It may be empty, or it can contain the following text copied from the like-named file in *mod_proxy*:

```
This is a place-holder which indicates to Configure that it shouldn't
provide the default targets when building the Makefile in this directory.
Instead it'll just prepend all the important variable definitions, and
copy the Makefile.tmpl onto the end.
```

We now create a *Makefile.tmpl* file containing the appropriate build rules and targets. The easiest way to create one is to copy an existing one from an existing multifile module (such as *mod_proxy*) and modify it. Example C-1 shows the file we created for *mod_compress*. Almost all of this was copied verbatim from the *mod_proxy*. The only things that changed were the LIB definition, which was altered to refer to *libcompress*, the OBJS and OBJS_PIC definitions, which were altered to contain the list of object files to link, and the *libcompress.a* and *libcompress.so* build targets, which were modified to refer to *libcompress* rather than to *libproxy*. In addition, the list of header file dependencies that followed the # DO NOT REMOVE line were deleted. If you are using the *gcc* compiler, you can rebuild the appropriate dependencies by issuing the *make depend* command within the subdirectory once the configuration script has been run.

Lastly, we create the file *libcompress.module* containing the configuration hints for the module. Its contents are identical to the *mod_compress.module* file discussed in the first section of this chapter:

```
Name: compress_module
ConfigStart
  LIBS="$LIBS -lz"
  echo " + using -lz for compression support"
ConfigEnd
```

To compile, link, and activate the multisource version of *mod_compress*, issue the following command at the top level of the Apache distribution:

```
% ./configure --activate-module=src/modules/compress/libcompress.a
```

libcompress.a will now be built and then linked statically to the *httpd* executable.

As an added bonus, you can request for *libcompress* to be a shared module, and it will be built correctly as a DSO. The configuration command is the same as you would normally use for other shared modules:

```
% ./configure --activate-module=src/modules/compress/libcompress.a \
        --enable-shared=compress
```

Example C-1. Makefile.tmpl for the Multifile Version of the mod_compress Example Module

```
LIB=libcompress.$(LIBEXT)

OBJS=compress.o compress_util.o
OBJS_PIC=compress.lo compress_util.lo

all: lib

lib: $(LIB)

libcompress.a: $(OBJS)
        rm -f $@
        ar cr $@ $(OBJS)
        $(RANLIB) $@

libcompress.so: $(OBJS_PIC)
        rm -f $@
        $(LD_SHLIB) $(LDFLAGS_SHLIB) -o $@ $(OBJS_PIC) $(LIBS_SHLIB)

.SUFFIXES: .o .lo

.c.o:
        $(CC) -c $(INCLUDES) $(CFLAGS) $<

.c.lo:
        $(CC) -c $(INCLUDES) $(CFLAGS) $(CFLAGS_SHLIB) $< && mv $*.o $*.lo

clean:
        rm -f $(OBJS) $(OBJS_PIC) $(LIB)

distclean: clean
        -rm -f Makefile

# We really don't expect end users to use this rule.  It works only with
# gcc, and rebuilds Makefile.tmpl.  You have to re-run Configure after
# using it.
depend:
        cp Makefile.tmpl Makefile.tmpl.bak \
        && sed -ne '1,/^# DO NOT REMOVE/p' Makefile.tmpl > Makefile.new \
        && gcc -MM $(INCLUDES) $(CFLAGS) *.c >> Makefile.new \
        && sed -e '1,$$s: $(INCDIR)/: $$(INCDIR)/:g' \
               -e '1,$$s: $(OSDIR)/: $$(OSDIR)/:g' Makefile.new \
           > Makefile.tmpl \
        && rm Makefile.new

#Dependencies

$(OBJS) $(OBJS_PIC): Makefile

# DO NOT REMOVE
```

Building Modules from Several Source Files with apxs

You may also use the *apxs* system to create a DSO module from several source files. Once again, it's easiest to start with the dummy project created by *apxs* when you use the *−g* and *−n* options. After *apxs* creates the directory tree, create the *.c* and *.h* files you need, and edit the automatically created *Makefile*. We recommend that you add a new definition named SRC to the *Makefile* with a value equal to all the source files in your module. For the *mod_compress* example, SRC would look like this:

```
SRC = compress.c compress_util.c
```

Now find the build target that corresponds to the shared module object file, *mod_compress.so* in the current example, and change it according to this model:

```
#    compile the shared object file
mod_compress.so: $(SRC) Makefile
        $(APXS) -o $@ -c $(DEF) $(INC) $(LIB) $(SRC)
```

This makes the shared object depend on the source code files and on *Makefile* itself. The build rule invokes *apxs* with the *−c* (compile) option and the appropriate library files and sources to create the DSO module.

D

Apache:: Modules Available on CPAN

There are many modules available from CPAN for use with Apache and *mod_perl*. Some are "drop-in" modules which you simply install, configure, and run with the server. Others are modules that are used by other Apache modules. In this section we will list the modules which are currently available, along with a brief description. You will find all of these modules from your local CPAN mirror at *http:// www.perl.com/CPAN/modules/by-module/Apache/*.

Other modules which might not be available yet are listed in the Apache/Perl module list, which is at *http://www.perl.com/CPAN/modules/by-module/Apache/ apache-modlist.html*.

In this appendix we only give terse descriptions of each module just to give you an idea of what the many generous and talented authors have decided to share with us. Please consult each module's documentation for more details.

Content Handling

Apache::Album

Apache::Album sets up a virtual set of photo albums, creating thumbnail images on the fly using *Image::Magick*. The dynamic layout of the album allows you to configure captions, background, table borders, footers, and more.

Author

Jim Woodgate, *woody@bga.com*

Apache::Gateway

Apache::Gateway implements a gateway based on the HTTP 1.1 draft definition of a gateway:

> [a] server which acts as an intermediary for some other server. Unlike a proxy, a gateway receives requests as if it were the origin server for the requested resource; the requesting client may not be aware that it is communicating with a gateway.

Besides the standard gateway features, *Apache::Gateway* also implements the following:

- Automatic failover with mirrored instances
- Multiplexing
- Pattern-dependent gatewaying
- FTP directory gatewaying
- Timestamp correction

Author

Charles C. Fu, *ccwf@bacchus.com*

Apache::GzipChain

Apache::GzipChain compresses the output from other Perl handlers on the fly. This is done only if the browser understands *gzip* encoding. To determine this, *Apache::GzipChain* will check both the browser's *Accept-Encoding* header and *User-Agent* header

Author

Andreas Koenig, *koenig@kulturbox.de*

Apache::Layer

Apache::Layer provides a handler to layer multiple content trees on top of each other. It is most useful for web sites where a high proportion of the site content is common.

Author

Simon Matthews, *sam@peritas.com*

Apache::Filter

Apache::Filter has similar goals as *Apache::OutputChain*, allowing modules to filter the output of each other.

Author

Ken Williams, *ken@forum.swarthmore.edu*

Apache::OutputChain

Apache::OutputChain provides a mechanism for chaining Perl content response handlers. This allows you to make filter modules that take output from previous handlers, make some modifications, and pass the output to the next handler or to a browser.

Author

Jan Pazdziora, *adelton@fi.muni.cz*

Apache::PrettyText

Apache::PrettyText will dynamically format files of type *text/plain*, so output always looks "pretty" by the time it reaches the browser window.

Author

Chris Thorman, *chris@thorman.com*

Apache::ProxyPass

Apache::ProxyPass implements *mod_proxy ProxyPass* functionality that is configurable on a per-directory basis, rather than a per-server basis.

Author

Michael Smith, *mjs@iii.co.uk*

Apache::RandomLocation

Apache::RandomLocation can be configured to serve a random URI selected from a list for the given location. This can come in quite handy for slinging advertising banners and multiplexing requests.

Authors

Matthew Darwin, *matthew@davin.ottawa.on.ca*
Randy Kobes, *randy@theory.uwinnipeg.ca*

Apache::RedirectDBI

Apache::RedirectDBI redirects requests to different directories based on the existence of a user in one or more database tables.

Author

Michael Smith, *mjs@iii.co.uk*

Apache::Sandwich

Apache::Sandwich provides a mechanism for adding headers and footers to documents on the fly, creating a document "sandwich." It does so using the subrequest mechanism, so there is no document parsing overhead involved, as there is with SSI documents.

Authors

Doug MacEachern, *dougm@pobox.com*
Vivek Khera, *vivek@khera.org*

Apache::Stage

A staging area is a place where an author of an HTML document can check the look and feel of a document before it is "published." *Apache::Stage* provides such a place that requires a minimum amount of space. It doesn't require separate servers, a mirror of the "real" tree, or even a tree of symbolic links, just a sparse directory to hold the documents being modified.

Author

Andreas Koenig, *koenig@kulturbox.de*

Apache::AutoIndex

This module is a subclassable Perl version of the *mod_dir* and *mod_autoindex* directory indexer modules.

Author

Philippe M. Chiasson, *gozer@ectoplasm.dyndns.com*

URI Translation

Apache::TimedRedirect

Apache::TimedRedirect will redirect configured URIs to another URI if the request happens within a given time period. It is intended to politely redirect visitors from a site that is undergoing some form of maintenance, such as database-driven areas of a site when the databases are being refreshed.

Author

Peter G. Marshall, *mitd@mitd.com*

Apache::TransLDAP

Apache::TransLDAP can be configured to translate requests for user directories by mapping to an LDAP database entry.

Author

Clayton Donley, *donley@wwa.com*

Perl and HTML Mixing

Apache::ASP

Apache::ASP provides an Active Server Pages port to Apache. Active Server Pages is a web application platform that originated with Microsoft's IIS server. Under Apache for both Win32 and Unix, it allows a developer to create web applications with session management and Perl embedded in static HTML files.

Author

Joshua Chamas, *chamas@alumni.stanford.org*

Apache::Embperl

See Appendix F.

Apache::EmbperlChain

Apache::EmbperlChain hooks with the *Apache::OutputChain* module to process the output of modules as *HTML::Embperl* documents.

Author

Eric Cholet, *cholet@logilune.com*

Apache::EP

HTML::EP is a system for embedding Perl into HTML and ships with an *Apache::EP* module which provides a handler for *mod_perl*. It includes session support, database handling, basic localization, and some examples such as Unix user administration and a web shop.

Author

Jochen Wiedmann, *joe@ispsoft.de*

Apache::ePerl

ePerl interprets HTML files interspersed with Perl code—one of the very first of its kind.

Author

Ralf S. Engelschall, *rse@engelschall.com*

Apache::Mason

HTML::Mason allows web pages and sites to be constructed from shared, reusable building blocks called components. Components contain a mix of Perl and HTML and can call each other and pass values back and forth like subroutines. Common design elements (headers, footers, etc.) need be changed only once to affect the whole site. *Mason* has component/data caching facilities, as well as several debugging features: requests can be replayed from the command line and the Perl debugger, and a web-based previewer shows how each piece of a page is generated.

Author

Jonathan Swartz, *swartz@transbay.net*

Apache::SSI

Apache::SSI implements the functionality of *mod_include* in Perl. *Apache::SSI* can be subclassed to implement new SSI directives or to modify the behavior of existing ones. In addition, the output of *Apache::SSI* can be hooked into *Apache::Filter* or *Apache::OutputChain* for further processing.

Author

Ken Williams, *ken@forum.swarthmore.edu*

Apache::Taco

Apache::Taco provides a template-driven system for generating web pages with dynamic content. The package comes complete with an *Apache::Taco* module for use with *mod_perl*.

Author

Ken Williams, *ken@forum.swarthmore.edu*

Authentication and Authorization

Apache::AuthenDBI

Apache::AuthenDBI authenticates users against a database using Perl's DBI. Supported DBI drivers include Mysql, Oracle, Sybase, and many more listed at *http://www.bermetica.com/technologia/DBI/*.

Author

Edmund Mergl, *E.Mergl@bawue.de*

Apache::AuthzDBI

Apache::AuthzDBI provides authorization against a database using Perl's DBI.

Author

Edmund Mergl, *E.Mergl@bawue.de*

Apache::AuthCookie

Apache::AuthCookie provides authentication via HTTP cookies. It is a base class module whose subclasses implement the methods for verifying the user's credentials and session key.

Author

Eric Bartley, *bartley@purdue.edu*

Apache::AuthenCache

Apache::AuthenCache is used to cut down on expensive authentication database lookups by caching the results in memory. It was designed with *Apache::AuthenDBI* in mind but works just as well with any authentication module.

Author

Jason Bodnar, *jbodnar@tivoli.com*

Apache::AuthLDAP

Apache::AuthLDAP implements authentication and authorization against an LDAP database. In addition to LDAP groups, authorization may be based on arbitrary LDAP attributes.

Author

Clayton Donley, *donley@wwa.com*

Apache::AuthenNIS

Apache::AuthenNIS authenticates users against an NIS database using the *Net::NIS* module.

Author

Demetrios E. Paneras, *dep@media.mit.edu*

Apache::AuthenNISPlus

Apache::AuthenNISPlus authenticates users against an NIS+ database.

Author

Valerie Delane, *valerie@savina.com*

Apache::AuthzNIS

Apache::AuthzNIS authorizes users based on NIS group membership using the *Net::NIS* module.

Author

Demetrios E. Paneras, *dep@media.mit.edu*

Apache::AuthenPasswd

Apache::AuthenPasswd authenticates users against the system */etc/passwd* file.

Author

Demetrios E. Paneras, *dep@media.mit.edu*

Apache::AuthzPasswd

Apache::AuthzPasswd authorizes users based on group membership in the system */etc/passwd* file.

Author

Demetrios E. Paneras, *dep@media.mit.edu*

Apache::AuthenPasswdSrv

Apache::AuthenPasswdSrv authenticates users against a Unix domain socket server. It includes a sample server which checks a username and password against an NIS database using *Net::NIS* and *ypmatch*.

Author

Jeffrey Hulten, *jeffh@premier1.net*

Apache::AuthenRadius

Apache::AuthenRadius provides authentication against a RADIUS server using the *Authen::Radius* module.

Author

Daniel, *daniel-authenradius@electricrain.com*

Apache::AuthenSMB

Apache::AuthenSMB uses *Authen::SMB* to authenticate users against an SMB password database. Generally it is used in Unix environments to allow interaction with Windows NT domain controllers.

Author

Michael Parker, *parker@austx.tandem.com*

Apache::AuthenURL

Apache::AuthenURL implements authentication against an external server that supports Basic authentication. The server is contacted via a configured URL, and the user's credentials are passed downstream for authentication. This module is most useful when a particular authentication client doesn't run on the same platform as the main webserver.

Author

John Groenveld, *groenveld@acm.org*

Apache::AuthenIMAP

Apache::AuthenIMAP implements Basic authentication against an IMAP server.

Author

Malcolm Beattie, *mbeattie@sable.ox.ac.uk*

Apache::DBILogin

Not to be confused with *Apache::AuthenDBI*, the *Apache::DBILogin* module authenticates against a DBI connection itself, not against a table in the database.

Author

John Groenveld, *groenveld@acm.org*

Apache::PHLogin

Apache::PHLogin authenticates against a PH database using the *Net::PH* module.

Author

John Groenveld, *groenveld@acm.org*

Fixup

Apache::RefererBlock

Apache::RefererBlock will examine the MIME type of each request. If the type is one of those listed in the configured *CheckMimeTypes*, it will check the referrer header. If the referrer doesn't start with one of the strings configured in *AllowedReferers*, a "Forbidden" error will be returned.

Author

Eric Cholet, *cholet@logilune.com*

Apache::Usertrack

Apache::UserTrack implements *mod_usertrack* in Perl and provides high-resolution timing by using the *Time::HiRes* module.

Author

Ask Bjoern Hansen, *ask@netcetera.dk*

Logging

Apache::DBILogger

Apache::DBILogger logs the same data normally sent to the *TransferLog* but writes it to a DBI database rather than a file on disk.

Author

Ask Bjoern Hansen, *ask@netcetera.dk*

Apache::DBILogConfig

Apache::DBILogConfig replicates the functionality of the standard Apache module, *mod_log_config*, but logs information in a DBI-compliant database instead of a file.

Author

Jason Bodnar, *jbodnar@tivoli.com*

Apache::Traffic

Apache::Traffic tracks the total number of hits and bytes transferred per day by the Apache web server, on a per-user basis. This allows for real-time statistics without having to parse the log files. The statistics are made available through the *traffic* script, which queries the shared memory segment or DBM file where log data is stored.

Author

Maurice Aubrey, *maurice@hevanet.com*

Profiling

Apache::DProf

Apache::DProf is a wrapper for running the *Devel::DProf* profiler in the *mod_perl* environment.

Author

Doug MacEachern, *dougm@pobox.com*

Apache::SmallProf

Apache::SmallProf is a wrapper for running the *Devel::SmallProf* profiler in the *mod_perl* environment.

Author

Doug MacEachern, *dougm@pobox.com*

Persistent Database Connections

Apache::DBI

Apache::DBI provides transparent persistent database connections via DBI.

Author

Edmund Mergl, *E.Mergl@bawue.de*

Apache::Mysql

Apache::Mysql provides transparent persistent database connections for the Mysql module.

Author

Neil Jensen, *njensen@habaneros.com*

Apache::Sybase::CTlib

Apache::Sybase::CTlib provides transparent persistent database connections for the *Sybase::CTlib* module.

Author

Mark A. Downing, *mdowning@rdatasys.com*

Miscellaneous

Apache::Language

Apache::Language provides transparent multiple language support for *mod_perl* scripts and Apache Perl modules.

Author

Philippe M. Chiasson, *gozer@ectoplasm.dyndns.com*

Apache::LogFile

Apache::LogFile provides a *PerlLogFile* directive that will open a Perl filehandle at server startup time. The filehandle can be connected to a program via Apache's reliable piped log API or simply to a file on disk.

Author

Doug MacEachern, *dougm@pobox.com*

Apache::Mmap

Apache::Mmap provides a facility for using the *mmap()* system call to have the OS map a file or Perl scalar variable into a process's address space.

Author

Mike Fletcher, *lemur1@mindspring.com*

Apache::Module

Apache::Module provides interfaces to the Apache C data structures and API that are related to a module structure, the `module`, `handler_rec`, and `command_rec` structures. The package includes two modules which use these interfaces.

Apache::ModuleDoc generates on-the-fly documentation of C modules, including Perl directive syntax. *Apache::ShowRequest* takes a URI and walks you through each of the request phases, showing which modules participate in each and what return code they produce for the given URI.

Author

Doug MacEachern, *dougm@pobox.com*

Apache::Peek

Apache::Peek is a modified version of the *Devel::Peek* module which sends peek output to the client rather than STDERR.

Author

Doug MacEachern, *dougm@pobox.com*

Apache::Request

Apache::Request, *Apache::Cookie*, and *Apache::Upload* provide a Perl interface to the *libapreq* C library (see Appendix E).

Author

Doug MacEachern, *dougm@pobox.com*

Apache::Roaming

This module is a Perl version of *mod_roaming* (see Appendix E), which provides the same functionality while adding the ability to subclass handling of user profile data.

Author

Jochen Wiedmann, *joe@ispsoft.de*

Apache::Session

Apache::Session provides data persistence for *mod_perl* applications. The data store may be disk, shared memory, a DBI database, or resident memory for Win32 systems.

Author

Jeffrey Baker, *jeff@godzilla.tamu.edu*

Apache::TempFile

Apache::TempFile generates names for temporary files which are automatically removed when the current request has been completed.

Author

Tom Hughes, *tom@compton.demon.co.uk*

Apache::Throttle

Apache::Throttle implements content negotiation based on the speed of the connection. It's primary purpose is to transparently send smaller (lower-resolution, lower-quality) images to users with slow Internet connections.

Author

Don Schwarz, *dons@xnet.com*

Apache::UploadSvr

Apache::UploadSvr implements a small publishing system for a web server with authentication, simple security, preview, directory viewer, and an interface to delete files.

Author

Andreas Koenig, *koenig@kulturbox.de*

E

Third-Party C Modules

In this appendix you will find a listing of all the C-language Apache modules that are not part of the Apache distribution but are available and listed in the Apache Module Registry at *http://modules.apache.org/*.

As with Appendix D, we only give terse descriptions of each module just to give you an idea of what the many generous and talented authors have decided to share with us. Please consult each module's documentation for more details.

Content Handling

mod_blob_pg95

This module implements URI to Postgres95 Large Object mapping.

Author

Adam Sussman, *asussman@vidya.com*

mod_CommProc

The Communications Processor (CommProc) is a set of APIs and preconstructed frameworks that build the components (clients and resources) of a message-based distributed computing system.

Author

Mike Anderson, *mka@redes.int.com.mx*

mod_fastcgi

FastCGI keeps CGI processes alive to avoid per-hit forks.

Maintainer

Jonathan Roy, *roy@idle.com*

mod_conv

This module enables you to view FTP archives using WWW conversions.

Author

Jakub Jelinek, *jj@sunsite.mff.cuni.cz*

mod_js

This JavaScript module is based on the Mozilla js interpreter.

Authors

Hypankin, *hankin@apache.org*
Magnus, *magnus@apache.org*
Jeremie Miller, *jeremie@netins.net*
The Mozilla team, *http://www.mozilla.org/*

mod_jserv

mod_jserv is an Apache module and Java class for running Java servlets with Apache.

Author

The Java Apache Project Team, *http://java.apache.org/*

mod_ecgi

mod_ecgi turns a CGI program into a dynamically loaded library and runs it without forking. This approach provides the simplicity and portability of CGI without the overhead of both a fork and exec.

Author

Nick Kew, *nick@webthing.com*

mod_fjord

Provides a Java backend processor that uses the Kaffe JVM.

Author

David Young, *dwy@ace.net*

mod_neoinclude

NeoWebScript provides a Tcl scripting extension.

Authors

Karl Lehenbauer
Randy Kunkee

OpenASP

OpenASP is an Open Source implementation of Active Server Pages (ASP).

Author

Nathan Woods

PHP

PHP provides a server-side scripting language and extensive database support.

Author

PHP Development Team, *http://www.php.net/*

mod_pyapache

This module embeds a Python language interpreter to avoid the overhead of CGI fork/exec.

Author

Lele Gaifax, *lele@integra.it*

mod_owa

This module is an Apache implementation of the Oracle Web Server PL/SQL cartridge.

Authors

Alvydas Gelzinis, *alvydas@kada.lt*
Oksana Kulikova, *oksana@kada.lt*

International Language

mod_a4c

The All4Chinese module provides online Chinese Code Translation BIG5 <-> GB2312.

Author

Brian Lin, *foxman@okstation.com*

mod_beza

mod_beza is a module and patch for converting national characters.

Author

Krzysztof Marek Matyskiel, *K.Matyskiel@ia.pw.edu.pl*

mod_charset

This module implements smart Russian code page translations.

Authors

Dmitriy Krukov, *dvk@stack.net*
Alex Tutubalin, *lexa@lexa.ru*

mod_fontxlate

This module is a configurable national character set translator.

Author

Warwick Heath, *warwick@rcc-irc.si*

MultiWeb

MultiWeb is a multilingual extension with charset conversion support.

Author

Konstantin Chuguev, *joy@urc.ac.ru*

SSI for ISO-2022-JP

SSI handling ISO-2022-JP encoding document.

Authors

Takuya Asada
Mitsunobu Shimada
Takatsugu Nokubi, *knok@daionet.gr.jp*

Security

mod_ssl

This module is a free Apache Interface to SSLeay.

Author

Ralf S. Engelschall, *rse@engelschall.com*

Apache-SSL

This module provides SSL extensions for Apache.

Author

Ben Laurie, *ben@algroup.co.uk*

Raven SSL

An SSL security module for the Apache web server.

Author

Covalent Technologies, Inc., *http://raven.covalent.net/*

mod_cgi_sugid

Sets user and group ID for CERN-like CGI execution.

Author

Philippe Vanhaesendonck, *pvanhaes@be.oracle.com*

Access Control

mod_allowdev

This module can be configured to prohibit serving files that are not on a listed device.

Author

Dean Gaudet, *dgaudet@arctic.org*

mod_bandwidth

This module implements bandwidth usage limitation either on the whole server or on a per-connection basis, based on the size of files, directory location, or remote domain or IP.

Author

Yann Stettler, *stettler@cohprog.com*

mod_disallow_id

This module can be configured to limit access based on UID and GID.

Author

Lou Langholtz, *ldl@chpc.utah.edu*

mod_lock.c

This small module allows you to conditionally lock a part of a web site by just creating a file in a predefined location. This feature is useful for system maintenance on multi-VirtualHosted systems.

Author

Lyonel Vincent, *vincent@hpwww.ec-lyon.fr*

mod_throttle

This module throttles the usage of individual users to reduce server load.

Author

Mark Lovell, *mlovell@bigrock.com*

Authentication and Authorization

mod_auth_nis

This module authenticates against an NIS database.

Author

Dirk-Willem van Gulik, *Dirk.vanGulik@jrc.it*

mod_auth_cookie

This module translates an HTTP cookie into a Basic authentication header for use with any Basic authentication handler.

Author

Vivek Khera, *vivek@khera.org*

mod_auth_cookie_mysql

This module authenticates users based on a cookie value, which is matched against the contents of a MySQL database.

Author

Mark-Jason Dominus, *mjd-mac_mysql@plover.com*

mod_auth_cookie_file

This module implements HTTP cookie–based authentication against a *.htpasswd-*like file.

Author

Dirk-Willem van Gulik, *Dirk.vanGulik@jrc.it*

mod_auth_cookie_msql

This module implements HTTP cookie-based authentication against an mSQL database.

Author

Dirk-Willem van Gulik, *Dirk.vanGulik@jrc.it*

mod_auth_dce

This module implements authentication against a DCE (Distributed Computing Environment) registry and provides DFS (Distributed File System) based access control.

Author

Paul Henson, *henson@acm.org*

mod_auth_external

This module authenticates against a user-provided function or external program.

Authors

Nathan Neulinger, *nneul@umr.edu*

Tyler Allison, *allison@mail.arc.nasa.gov*

mod_auth_inst

This module provides instant password authentication for "dummy" users.

Author

Clifford Wolf, *apache@clifford.at*

mod_auth_kerb

This module implements Kerberos authentication via Basic authentication or Kerberos mutual authentication when using a kerberized client.

Author

James E. Robinson III, *james@ncstate.net*

mod_auth_ldap

This module implements Basic authentication by mapping names and passwords onto attributes in entries in preselected portions of LDAP DSA. The UMich LDAP client libraries are required to use this module.

Author

Norman Richards, *orb@cs.utexas.edu*

mod_auth_ldap

This module implements Basic authentication against entries in an LDAP directory. The Netscape LDAPv3 SDK is required to use this module.

Author

Dave Carrigan, *Dave.Carrigan@cnpl.enbridge.com*

mod_ldap

This module implements authentication and authorization against an LDAP directory. The UMich LDAP client libraries are required to use this module.

Author

Lyonel Vincent, *vincent@hpwww.ec-lyon.fr*

mod_auth_msql

This module implements Basic authentication against an mSQL database.

Author

Dirk-Willem van Gulik, *Dirk.vanGulik@jrc.it*

mod_auth_mysql

This module implements Basic authentication against a Mysql database.

Author

Vivek Khera, *vivek@khera.org*

mod_auth_pam

This module implements authentication against Pluggable Auth modules.

Author

Ingo Lutkebohle, *ingo@blank.pages.de*

mod_auth_pg

This module authenticates users against a PostgreSQL database. The module gets the username and password pair in the standard way or from a cookie, and you can choose your preferred method.

Author

Min S. Kim, *minskim@usa.net*

mod_auth_pgsql

This module implements Basic authentication against a PostgreSQL database.

Authors

Adam Sussman, *asussman@vidya.com*
Giuseppe Tanzilli, *g.tanzilli@eurolink.it*

mod_auth_pg95

This module implements authentication against a Postgres95 database.

Author

Adam Sussman, *asussman@vidya.com*

mod_auth_radius

This module implements Basic authentication against a RADIUS server, including full RADIUS challenge-response using HTTP cookies.

Authors

Alan DeKok, *alan@cryptocard.com*
CRYPTOCard Inc., *http://www.cryptocard.com/*

mod_auth_rdbm

This module provides a lightweight but highly scalable and efficient mechanism for HTTP Basic authentication over a network. RDBM authentication is similar to DBM or DB authentication, with these added benefits:

- Multiple web servers can share a user database, without the penalties of NFS.

- Database locking is not an issue. So, for example, allowing write access to the database from CGI programs is much simplified.

Author

Nick Kew, *nick@webthing.com*

mod_auth_samba

This module implements authentication and authorization against a Samba Lan-Manager.

Author

Juha Ylitalo, *juha.o.ylitalo@ntc.nokia.com*

mod_auth_smb

This module implements authentication against a Samba LanManager.

Author

Jason L. Wright, *jason@thought.net*

mod_auth_sys

This module implements authentication and authorization against Unix user accounts, including */etc/passwd, /etc/group*, NIS, NIS+, and Shadow.

Author

Franz Vinzenz, *vinzenz@ntb.ch*

mod_auth_sys

This module implements authentication and authorization against system */etc/ passwd* and */etc/group* files.

Author

Howard Fear, *hsf@pageplus.com*

mod_auth_yard

This module implements authentication and authorization against a YARD database.

Author

Uwe C. Schroeder, *uwe@cht.de*

mod_auth_notes

This module implements authentication against a Lotus Notes database.

Author

Guillermo Payet, *gpayet@oceangroup.com*

Logging

mod_log_dir

This module implements per-directory logging to pre-existing, server-writable log-files using the config log module formatting syntax. Subdirectory logging configurations override any logging the parent directories may have configured.

Author

Lou Langholtz, *ldl@chpc.utah.edu*

Distributed Authoring

mod_cvs

This module automatically updates files in a CVS-based web tree.

Author

Martin Insulander, *martin@insulander.com*

mod_dav

This module enables Apache to understand the DAV protocol extensions to HTTP. DAV stands for "Distributed Authoring and Versioning" and is currently an Internet draft nearing completion. DAV is intended to replace proprietary authoring protocols, such as those used by FrontPage or NetFusion, but is also a complete set of protocols for manipulating a web server's files and directories and their properties. For more information, see *http://www.lyra.org/greg/mod_dav/*.

Author

Greg Stein, *gstein@lyra.org*

mod_put

This module implements the HTTP/1.1 PUT and DELETE methods.

Author

Lyonel Vincent, *vincent@hpwww.ec-lyon.fr*

Miscellaneous

mod_session

This module implements advanced session management and tracking.

Author

Adam Sussman, *asussman@vidya.com*

mod_cntr

This module dynamically counts and displays web page access.

Author

Dan Kogai, *dankogai@dan.co.jp*=head2 mod_macro

mod_macro

This module implements a mechanism for defining and using macros with the Apache configuration files.

Author

Fabien Coelho, *coelho@cri.ensmp.fr*

mod_roaming

This module enables Apache to act as a Netscape Roaming Access server. When Netscape Communicator Version 4.5 or higher is configured against a Roaming Access server, your preferences, bookmarks, address books, cookies, and other user specific data is stored on the server so that the same settings can be used from any Netscape Communicator client that can access the server.

Author

Vincent Partington, *vincentp@xs4all.nl*

libapreq

This library provides routines for manipulating client request data via the Apache API. Functionality includes parsing of *application/x-www-form-urlencoded* and *multipart/form-data* content types, along with parsing and generation of HTTP cookies.

Author

Doug MacEachern, *dougm@pobox.com*

F

HTML::Embperl— Embedding Perl Code in HTML

—Adapted and condensed from the
HTML::Embperl manual pages by Gerald Richter

HTML::Embperl is a text processor module which takes your ASCII text, extracts embedded Perl code, executes the code, and, as far as necessary, inserts the result in your text. While Embperl can also be used with non-HTML documents, it has several features that are specifically for HTML.

This appendix gives you an overview of what you can do with Embperl. It is *not* a complete description of Embperl. For detailed information, please look at the documentation provided with Embperl or at the Embperl website (*http://perl.apache. org/embperl/*).

Embperl is not the only processor for embedded Perl code. ASP used with the ActiveState Perl port provides this for Microsoft IIS, and ePerl does this job very well for all sorts of ASCII files. There are other Perl solutions around as well. PHP is a well-known solution for easily building web pages with embedded code and database connections, but it uses its own language instead of Perl.

The main advantage of Embperl is its built-in HTML awareness. It provides features for handling form data and HTML tables, along with converting log files and error pages to HTML and linking them together. It also allows for escaping and unescaping.

Embperl can be used offline (as a normal CGI script or as a module from other Perl code), but its real power comes when running under *mod_perl* and Apache. It's directly integrated with Apache and *mod_perl* to achieve the best performance by directly using Apache functions and precompiling your code to avoid a recompile on every request.

Embperl was designed to be used with a high-level HTML editor. The Perl code can be entered as normal text (the editor need not know any special HTML tags, nor is it necessary to enter special HTML tags via uncomfortable dialogs); just enter your code as if it were normal text. Embperl takes care of unescaping the HTML entities and eliminates unwanted HTML tags that are entered into your Perl code by the editor (for example, <BR> to break lines for better readability). If you prefer to use an ASCII editor for writing your HTML code, don't worry. You can configure everything that you want Embperl to do—and everything that you don't want it to do, too. Also, on the output side, Embperl correctly escapes your HTML/ URL output (as long as you don't disable it).

How can you embed Perl code in your HTML documents? There are three ways:

- [- ... -] to execute code

  ```
  [- $a = 5 -]   [- $b = 6 if ($a == 5) -]
  ```

  The code between [- and -] is executed. No output will be generated. This is mainly for assignments, function calls, database queries, etc.

- [+ ... +] to output the result

  ```
  [+ $a +]   [+ $array[$b] +] [+ "A is $a" +]
  ```

  The code between [+ and +] is executed and the return value (the value of the last expression evaluated) is output (sent to the browser).

- [! ... !] to execute code once

  ```
  [! sub foo { my ($a, $b) = @_ ; $a * $b + 7 } !]
  ```

  This is the same as [- ... -], except that the code is only executed for the first request. This is mainly for function definitions and one-time initialization.

Comments can be entered by bracketing them between [# and #]. In contrast to normal HTML comments, Embperl comments are removed before they are sent to the browser.

Embperl supports some metacommands to control the program flow within the Embperl document. This can be compared to preprocessor commands in C. The meta commands take the following form:

```
[$ cmd arg $]
```

if, elsif, else, endif

The *if* command in Embperl is just the same as it is in Perl. It is used to conditionally output or process parts of the document. For example:

```
[$ if $ENV{REQUEST_METHOD} eq 'GET' $]
   This is a GET request
[$ elsif $ENV{REQUEST_METHOD} eq 'POST' $]
   This is a POST request
[$ else $]
```

```
      This is not GET and not POST
  [$ endif $]
```

This will output one of the three lines depending on the setting of
$ENV{REQUEST_METHOD}.

while, endwhile

The *while* command can be used to create a loop in the HTML document. For
example:

```
[$ while ($k, $v) = each (%ENV) $]
   [+ $k +] = [+ $v +] <BR>
[$ endwhile $]
```

This example will display all environment variables, each terminated with a
line break.

do, until

The *do* and *until* commands also create a loop but with a condition at the
end. For example:

```
[- @arr = (3, 5, 7); $i = 0 -]
[$ do $]
   [+ $arr[ $i++ ] +]
[$ until $i > $#arr $]
```

foreach, endforeach

The *foreach* and *endforeach* commands create a loop iterating over every element of an array/list. For example:

```
[$ foreach $v (1..10) $]
   [+ $v +]
[$ endforeach $]
```

var <var1> <var2> ...

By default, you do not need to declare any variables you use within an Embperl page. Embperl takes care of deleting them at the end of each request.
Sometimes, though, you want to declare them explicitly. You can do this by
using *var*:

```
[$ var $a @b %c $]
```

Has the same effect as the Perl code:

```
use strict ;use vars qw {$a @b %c} ;
```

hidden

The *hidden* command is used for creating hidden form fields and is described
in the form field section later in this appendix.

While the Embperl metacommands give your document a more readable way of
nesting control structures and give Embperl a better chance to control and log
what's happening (as we will discuss in more detail later), you can also use Perl

control structures inside your Embperl documents. (See the Embperl documentation for more details.)

Dynamic Tables

One very powerful feature of Embperl is its ability to process dynamic tables. This feature was designed mainly to display Perl arrays (one- or two-dimensional, regular and irregular), but it can also be used in other ways.

Here is an example that displays a Perl array:

```
[- @a = ( 'A', 'B', 'C') ; -]
<TABLE BORDER=1>
   <TR>
       <TD> [+ $a[$row] +] </TD>
   </TR>
</TABLE>
```

This example simply displays a table with three rows containing A, B, and C. The trick is done by using the magical variable $row which contains the row count and is incremented for every row. The table ends if the expression that contains $row returns *undef.* The same can be done with $col for columns. You can also use $cnt to create a table that wraps after a certain number of elements. This works with TABLE, SELECT, MENU, OL, DL, and DIR.

Here is a simple DBI example that displays the result of a query as a two-dimensional table with field names as headings in the first row:

```
[-
# connect to database
 $dbh = DBI->connect($DSN) ;

# prepare the sql select
$sth = $dbh -> prepare ("SELECT * from $table") ;

# excute the query
$sth -> execute ;

# get the fieldnames for the heading in $head
$head = $sth -> {NAME} ;

# get the result in $dat
$dat = $sth -> fetchall_arrayref ;
-]

<table>
   <tr><th>[+ $head->[$col] +]</th></tr>
   <tr><td>[+ $dat -> [$row][$col] +]</td></tr>
</table>
```

Handling Forms

Another feature of Embperl is the way it helps you to handle forms. Posted form data is available in %fdat and @ffld. The hash %fdat contains the values of all form fields. The array @ffld contains the names in the order in which they were submitted.

Moreover, the HTML tags Input, Textarea, and Select take values from %fdat. If you do not specify a default value for an input tag, but a value for that input tag is available in %fdat, Embperl will automatically insert the value from %fdat and send it to the browser. This is similar to the behavior of *CGI.pm*. This means that if you post a form to itself, the browser will display the values you just entered.

Sometimes it's necessary to pass values between consecutive forms. One way to do this is to pass them via hidden form fields. The *hidden* metacommand creates hidden form fields for all fields not in another input field. This can be used to transport data through confirmation forms, for example, a wizard.

Example F-1 shows many of the possibilities of Embperl. It's a simple form where you can enter your name, your email address, and a message. If you hit the send button, you see the data you just entered and can confirm the information by hitting the "send via mail" button, or you can go back to the input form to change the data. If you confirm your input, the data will be sent to a predefined email address. The example also shows how you can implement error checking—if you omit your name or your email address, you will get a corresponding error message and the input form is shown again.

The first part is the error checking; the second part is the confirmation form; the third part sends the mail if the input was acceptable and is confirmed; the last part is the input form itself.

Depending on the values of $fdat{check}, $fdat{send}, $fdat{name}, and $fdat{email}, the document decides which part to show.

Example F-1. Input and Confirmation Form

```
[-  $MailTo = 'richter\@ecos.de' ;

 @errors = () ;
 if (defined($fdat{check}) || defined($fdat{send}))
   {
   push @errors, "**Please enter your name" if (!$fdat{name}) ;
   push @errors, "**Please enter your e-mail address" if (!$fdat{email}) ;
   }
-]
```

Example F-1. Input and Confirmation Form (continued)

```
[$if (defined($fdat{check}) and $#errors == -1)$]
[-
 delete $fdat{input} ;
 delete $fdat{check} ;
 delete $fdat{send}
-]

<hr><h3> You have entered the following data:</h3>
<table>
 <tr><td><b>Name</b></td><td>[+$fdat{name}+]</td></tr>
 <tr><td><b>E-Mail</b></td><td>[+$fdat{email}+]</td></tr>
 <tr><td><b>Message</b></td><td>[+$fdat{msg}+]</td></tr>
 <tr><td align="center" colspan="2">
    <form action="input.htm" method="GET">
      <input type="submit" name="send"
             value="Send to [+ $MailTo +]">
      <input type="submit" name="input" value="Change your data">
      [$hidden$]
    </form>
    </td></tr>
</table>

[$elsif defined($fdat{send}) and $#errors == -1$]

[- MailFormTo ($MailTo,'Formdata','email') -]
<hr><h3>Your input has been sent</h3>

[$else$]

<hr><h3>Please enter your data</h3>

<form action="input.htm" method="GET">
 <table>
   [$if $#errors != -1 $]
     <tr><td colspan="2">
     <table>
   <tr><td>[+$errors[$row]+]</td></tr>
     </table>
     </td></tr>
   [$endif$]
   <tr><td><b>Name</b></td> <td><input type="text"
                                name="name"></td></tr>
   <tr><td><b>E-Mail</b></td> <td><input type="text"
                                 name="email"></td></tr>
   <tr><td><b>Message</b></td> <td><input type="text"
                                  name="msg"></td></tr>
   <tr><td colspan=2><input type="submit"
                       name="check" value="Send"></td></tr> </table>
</form>

[$endif$]
```

Storing Persistent Data

While hidden fields are useful when working with forms, it's often necessary to store persistent data in a more general way. Embperl utilizes *Apache::Session* to do this job. *Apache::Session* is capable of storing persistent data in memory, in a text file, or in a database. More storage methods may be supported in the future. Although you can simply call *Apache::Session* from an Embperl page, Embperl can call it for you. All you need to do is to put user data in the hash %udat. The next time the same user requests any Embperl page, %udat will contain the same data. You can use this approach to keep state information for the user, and depending on your expire settings, you can also keep state between multiple sessions. A second hash, %mdat, can be used to keep state for one page for multiple users. A simple example would be a page hit counter:

```
The page is requested [+ $mdat{counter}++ +] times
since [+ $mdat{date} ||= localtime +]
```

This example counts the page hits and shows the date when the page is first requested. (See the hangman game at the end of this appendix for more examples of %udat and %mdat.) You don't need to worry about performance—as long as you don't touch %udat or %mdat, no action is taken.

Modularization of Embperl Pages

If you are working on a complete site and not just a few pages, there are always elements which occur in every page or in many pages. Instead of copying the source code to every page, you can include Embperl modules in your pages, so you'll have to write the source only once. Such a module could be a header, a footer, a navigation bar, etc. Embperl is capable of not only including such partial pages but also passing arguments. Here is an example that tells the navigation bar which element to highlight:

```
[- @buttons = ('Index', 'Infos', 'Search') -]
<table><tr><td>
[$if $buttons[$col] eq $param[0]$] <bold> [$endif$]
<a href="[+ $buttons[$col] +].html"> [+ $buttons[$col] +] </a>
[$if $buttons[$col] eq $param[0]$] </bold> [$endif$]
</td></tr></table>
<hr>
```

Now if you are on the "Infos" page, you can include the navigation bar as follows:

```
[- Execute ('navbar.html', 'Infos') -]
```

This will include the navigation bar, which is stored in the file *navbar.html*, and pass as its first parameter the string Infos. The navigation bar module itself uses a dynamic table to display one column, which contains the text and a link, for every item in the array @buttons. Also, the text that is equal to text passed as a first parameter is displayed in bold. There is also a long form of the *Execute* call, which allows you to control all aspects of executing the module.

Debugging

Debugging of CGI scripts is always a difficult task because the execution is controlled by the web server and, for the most part, you can't use a debugger. Embperl helps you debug your Embperl pages by creating a detailed log file. The log file shows you what Embperl does as it processes your page. Depending on the debug flag settings, Embperl logs the following:

* Source

* Environment

* Form data

* Evals (source and result)

* Table processing

* Input tag processing

* HTTP headers

To make debugging even easier, you can tell Embperl to display a link at the top of each page to your log file while you are debugging a page. If you follow the link, Embperl will show the portion of the log file that corresponds to that request. The log file lines are displayed in different colors to give you a better overview. With these links to the log file enabled, every error displayed in an error page is also a link to the corresponding position in the log file, so you can easily locate where things are going wrong.

Querying a Database

Often it's necessary to query a database when generating a dynamic page. We have already seen in our discussion of dynamic tables how this can be done using the DBI database interface. Since the tasks needed in a web page are often the same, there is a module called *DBIx::Recordset*, which simplifies commonly needed tasks:

```
[-*set = DBIx::Recordset -> Search ({%fdat,
                            ('!DataSource'   => $DSN,
                            '!Table' => $table,
                            '$max'    => 5,)}) ; -]
```

```
<table>
 <tr><th>ID</th><th>NAME</th></tr>
 <tr>
   <td>[+ $set[$row]{id} +]</td>
   <td>[+ $set[$row]{name} +]</td>
 </tr>
</table>
[+ $set -> PrevNextForm ('Previous Records',
                         'Next Records',
                         \%fdat) +]
```

The *Search()* method in this example will take the values from %fdat and use them to build a SQL WHERE expression. This way, what you search for depends on what is posted to the document. For example, if you request the document with *http://host/mydoc.html?id=5*, the above example will display all database records where the field id contains the value 5. The result of the query can be accessed as an array (this does not mean that the whole array is actually fetched from the database). Alternatively, you can directly access the current record just by accessing the fields, as shown here:

```
set[5]{id}    access the field 'id' of the sixth found record
set{id}       access the field 'id' of the current record
```

While normal DBI lets you access your data by column numbers, *DBIx::Recordset* uses the field names. This makes your program easier to write, more verbose, and independent of database changes.

The *PrevNextButtons* function can be used to generate a button for showing the previous record or the next record. *PrevNextButtons* generates a small form and includes all necessary data as hidden fields. To get it to work, simply feed this data to the next *Search* request.

There are also methods for *Insert, Update,* and *Delete.* For example, if %fdat contains the data for the new record, the following code will insert a new record into the database:

```
[-*set = DBIx::Recordset -> Insert ({%fdat,
                                    ('!DataSource'  => $DSN,
                                    '!Table' => $table)}) ; -]
```

DBIx::Recordset can also tie a database table to a hash. You need to specify a primary key for the table, which is used as a key in the hash:

```
$set{5}{name}    access the name with the id=5
                 (id is primary key)
```

There are more features of *DBIx::Recordset,* such as handling linked tables, which makes it useful even in pages that do not use Embperl.

Security

Another topic of interest in web environments is security. When running under *mod_perl*, all Perl code shares the same interpreter. This means that every application can access data from every other application. Embperl maintains a separate namespace for every document, which prevents accidentally overwriting other applications' data but provides no real security. You can still access anything you like if you explicitly specify a package name.

Therefore, Embperl incorporates *Safe.pm*, which makes it impossible to access any packages other than your own. This can be used, for example, to calculate something in a Perl module and then pass the results to an Embperl document. If the Embperl document runs in a safe namespace, it can access the data it has received from the browser, but it can't access data outside itself. Therefore, you can safely let different people create the layouts for Embperl pages.

Safe.pm also permits the administrator to disable any set of Perl opcodes. This gives you the power to decide which Perl opcodes are permitted for use by the page creators.

An Extended Example

Hopefully, you now have a general overview of the main features of Embperl. For more information—for example, to learn more about the many options you have in configuring Embperl or for instructions on how to configure Apache or *mod_perl*—please take a look at the Embperl web site at *http://perl.apache.org/embperl/*. Embperl is actively supported and development is going on all of the time. The web site will always contain information on the newest features.

Example F-2 shows one last example of how you can use Embperl. It's a rewritten version of the hangman game of Chapter 5, *Maintaining State*. Instead of creating its own session management, as in Chapter 5, this hangman game uses the Embperl built-in capabilities.

Example F-2. Hangman with Embperl

```
<!DOCTYPE HTML PUBLIC "-//IETF//DTD HTML//EN">
<HTML><HEAD><TITLE>Hangman with Embperl</TITLE></HEAD>
<BODY BGCOLOR="white" ONLOAD="if (document.gf) document.gf.guess.focus()">

<H1>Hangman with Embperl</H1>

<P> This is an Embperl version of the Hangman game from
<A HREF=http://www.modperl.com/>Writing Apache Modules with Perl and C<A>
     Chapter 5 </P>
```

Example F-2. Hangman with Embperl (continued)

```
<HR>

[!

use constant WORDS => 'hangman-words';
use constant ICONS => '../images';
use constant TRIES => 6;
use constant TOP_COUNT => 15; # how many top scores to show

########## subroutines #############
# This subroutines are just the same as in the hangman6.pl from chapter 5

# This is called to process the user's guess

sub process_guess {
    my ($guess,$state) = @_;

    # lose immediately if user has no more guesses left
    return ('','lost') unless $state->{LEFT} > 0;

    # lose immediately if user aborted
    if ($fdat{'abort'}) {
        $state->{TOTAL} += $state->{LEFT};
        $state->{LEFT}  =  0;
        return (qq{Chicken! The word was "$state->{WORD}."},'lost') ;
    }

    # break the word and guess into individual letters
    my %guessed = map { $_ => 1 } split('',$state->{GUESSED});
    my %letters = map { $_ => 1 } split('',$state->{WORD});

    # return immediately if user has already guessed the word
    return ('','won') unless grep(!$guessed{$_},keys %letters);

    # do nothing more if no guess
    return ('','continue') unless $guess;

    return (qq{You\'ve lost.  The word was "$state->{WORD}".},'lost')
    if $state->{LEFT} <= 0;

    # This section processes individual letter guesses
    $guess = lc($guess);
    return ("Not a valid letter or word!",'error') unless $guess=~/^[a-z]+$/;
    return ("You already guessed that letter!",'error')  if $guessed{$guess};

    # This section is called when the user guesses the whole word
    if (length($guess) > 1 && $guess ne $state->{WORD}) {
        $state->{TOTAL} += $state->{LEFT};
        $state->{LEFT}  = 0;
        return (qq{You lose.  The word was "$state->{WORD}."},'lost')
    }
```

Example F-2. Hangman with Embperl (continued)

```
    # update the list of guesses
    foreach (split('',$guess)) { $guessed{$_}++; }
    $state->{GUESSED} = join('',sort keys %guessed);

    # correct guess -- word completely filled in
    unless (grep (!$guessed{$_},keys %letters)) {
        $state->{WON}++;
        return (qq{You got it!  The word was "$state->{WORD}."},'won');
    }

    # incorrect guess
    if (!$letters{$guess}) {
        $state->{TOTAL}++;
        $state->{LEFT}--;
        # user out of turns
        return (qq{The jig is up.  The word was "$state->{WORD}".},'lost')
                if $state->{LEFT} <= 0;
        # user still has some turns
        return ('Wrong guess!','continue');
    }

    # correct guess but word still incomplete
    return (qq{Good guess!},'continue');
}


###########################
# pick a word, any word
sub pick_random_word {
    open (LIST, WORDS)
    || die "Couldn't open ${\WORDS}: $!\n";
    my $word;
    rand($.) < 1 && ($word = $_) while &lt;LIST&gt;;
    chomp($word);
    close LIST ;
    $word;
}

# End of subroutines
##############################################################

!]

[-
# change username if requested
$udat{username} = $fdat{change_name} if ($fdat{change_name}) ;

# store the score of the last game if we start a new one
# NOTE: %mdat stores data for that page across multiple requests
$mdat{$udat{username}} =    {GAMENO  => $udat{GAMENO},
                             WON     => $udat{WON},
                             AVERAGE => $udat{AVERAGE},
                             SCORE   => $udat{SCORE}}
                    if ($udat{username} && $fdat{newgame}) ;
```

Example F-2. Hangman with Embperl (continued)

```
# initialize user data if necessary
# NOTE: %udat stores data for that user across multiple requests
%udat = {} if ($fdat{clear}) ;
if ($fdat{restart} || !$udat{WORD})
    {
    $udat{WORD}                = pick_random_word() ;
    $udat{LEFT}      = TRIES;
    $udat{TOTAL}     += 0;
    $udat{GUESSED}   = '';
    $udat{GAMENO}    += 1;
    $udat{WON}       += 0;
    }

# check what the user has guessed
($message,$status) = process_guess($fdat{'guess'} || '',\%udat)
        unless $fdat{'show_scores'};

# setup score values
$current_average = int($udat{TOTAL}/$udat{GAMENO} * 100) / 100 ;
$udat{AVERAGE} = $udat{GAMENO}>1 ?
    int(($udat{TOTAL}-(TRIES-$udat{LEFT}))/($udat{GAMENO}-1) * 100)/100 : 0;
$udat{SCORE}    = $udat{AVERAGE} > 0 ?
    int(100*$udat{WON}/($udat{GAMENO}*$udat{AVERAGE})) : 0;

# convert strings to hashs
%guessed = map { $_ => 1 } split ('', $udat{GUESSED});
%letters = map { $_ => 1 } split ('', $udat->{WORD});
$word    = join (' ', map {$guessed{$_} ? $_ : '_'} split ('', $udat{WORD})) ;

# delete the the values posted as guess, so the input field will be empty
delete $fdat{guess} ;
-]

[#### show the current status ####]

[$ if $udat{username} $]
    <H2>Player: [+ $udat{username} +]</H2>
[$ endif $]

<TABLE>
    <TR WIDTH="90%">
        <TD><B>Word #:</B>   [+ $udat{GAMENO} +] </TD>
        <TD><B>Won:</B>      [+ $udat{WON} +]    </TD>
        <TD><B>Guessed:</B> [+ $udat{GUESSED} +] </TD>
    </TR>
    <TR>
        <TD><B>Current average:</B> [+ $current_average +]   </TD>
        <TD><B>Overall average:</B> [+ $udat{AVERAGE} +]              </TD>
        <TD><B>Score:</B>           [+ $udat{SCORE} +]               </TD>
    </TR>
</TABLE>
```

Example F-2. Hangman with Embperl (continued)

```
[$if !$fdat{show_scores} $]

    [#### show the images, the word and the message form process_guess ####]

    <IMG ALIGN="LEFT" SRC="[+ ICONS +]/h[+ TRIES-$udat{LEFT} +].gif"
                      ALT="[ [+ $udat{LEFT} +] tries left]">

    <H2>Word: [+ $word +] </H2>
    <H2><FONT COLOR="red">[+ $message +]</FONT></H2>

    <FORM METHOD="POST"  ENCTYPE="application/x-www-form-urlencoded">

    [$if $status =~ /won|lost/ $]

        [#### game over, if won let the user enter his name and
              ask if he like to play again ####]

        [$if $status eq 'won' $]
        <P>Enter your name for posterity:
        <INPUT TYPE="text" NAME="change_name" VALUE="[+ $udat{username} +]">
        [$ endif $]
        <P>Do you want to play again?
        <INPUT TYPE="submit" NAME="restart" VALUE="Another game">
        <INPUT TYPE="submit" NAME="show_scores" VALUE="Show High Scores">
        <INPUT TYPE="checkbox" NAME="clear" VALUE="on">Clear my score</P>
        <INPUT TYPE="hidden" NAME="newgame" VALUE="on">

    [$else$]

        [#### let the user enter a guess or give up ####]

        Your guess: <INPUT TYPE="text" NAME="guess" VALUE="">
        <INPUT TYPE="submit" NAME=".submit" VALUE="Guess">
        <BR CLEAR="ALL">
        <INPUT TYPE="submit" NAME="show_scores" VALUE="Show High Scores">
        <INPUT TYPE="submit" NAME="abort" VALUE="Give Up" STYLE="color: red">

    [$endif$]

    </FORM><BR CLEAR="ALL">

[$ else $]

        [#### show a sorted table of the best players ####]

        [-
        $maxrow = TOP_COUNT ;
        @name = sort { $mdat{$a}{SCORE} <=> $mdat{$b}{SCORE} }
                  grep (/^[^_]/, keys (%mdat))
        -]
```

Example F-2. Hangman with Embperl (continued)

```
        <TABLE BORDER="undef" WIDTH="75%">
            <CAPTION><B>Top 15 Winners</B></CAPTION>
            <TR>
                <TH>Name</TH>
                <TH>Games</TH>
                <TH>Won</TH>
                <TH>Average</TH>
                <TH>Score</TH>
            </TR>
            <TR>
                <TD>[+ $n = $name[$row]    +]</TD>
                <TD>[+ $mdat{$n}{GAMENO}   +]</TD>
                <TD>[+ $mdat{$n}{WON}      +]</TD>
                <TD>[+ $mdat{$n}{AVERAGE}  +]</TD>
                <TD>[+ $mdat{$n}{SCORE}    +]</TD>
            </TR>
        </TABLE>

        [$ if $#name == -1 $]
            <H2>No scores available, nobody won the game so far</H2>
        [$endif$]

        <FORM METHOD="POST"  ENCTYPE="application/x-www-form-urlencoded">
                <INPUT TYPE="submit" NAME="play" VALUE="Play">
        </FORM>

[$endif$]

<p><hr>

<small>Hangman for <A HREF="http://perl.apache.org/embperl/">HTML::Embperl</A>
  (c) 1998 G.Richter, Lincoln Stein, graphics courtesy Andy Wardley</small>

</body>
</html>
```

Here is a sample *srm.conf* entry to go with it:

```
    PerlSetEnv SESSION_FILE_DIRECTORY /tmp/sessions
    PerlSetEnv EMBPERL_SESSION_CLASS File
    PerlModule Apache::Session::File
    PerlModule HTML::Embperl
    <Location /hangman>
      SetHandler perl-script
      PerlHandler HTML::Embperl
      Options ExecCGI
    </Location>
```

Index

Symbols

%@ hash (Perl), 498
$$ handler function prototype, 65
$/ variable (Perl), 497
$| variable (Perl), 497

Numbers

$0 variable (Perl), 497
301 "Moved Permanently" message, 124
302 "Moved Temporarily" message, 124
304 "Not Modified" message, 120
401 "Authorization Required" code, 263
403 "Forbidden" code, 262
404 "Not Found" error, 90
500 "Internal Server Error" error, 91

A

aborted( ) (Apache::Connection), 471
aborted field (conn_rec), 525
Accept header (HTTP), 54
Accept-Charset header (HTTP), 54
Accept-Language header (HTTP), 54
Accept-Ranges header (HTTP), 56
access_checker( ), 74, 511
ACCESS_CONF constant, 400, 576
access_confname field (server_rec), 521
access control, 262, 268–282
    browser-controlled, 271–276
    C API handler, 511
    cookie-based, 304–322
    CPAN Apache:: modules for, 666
    methods for, 461–464
    third-party modules for, 679
    time-based, 270
access control phase (Apache server), 61, 74, 268
access.conf file, 20
--activate-module argument (configure), 35
Active Server Pages (ASP), 664
ActiveX technology, 7
add( ) (Apache::Table), 475
AddHandler directive, 87
AddType directive, 100
advertisements, blocking
    (example), 374–381
alert( ) (Apache::Log), 460
Alias directive, 42, 333
AliasMatch directive, 333
allocation routines (C API), 528
allowed field (request_rec), 514
allow_options( ), 461
    constants for, 484
anonymizing proxy requests, 372–373
anonymous authentication handler
    (example), 285–287
ap_acquire_mutex( ), 622
ap_add_cgi_vars( ), 623
ap_add_common_vars( ), 623
ap_add_version_component( ), 541
ap_append_arrays( ), 532
ap_array_cat( ), 532
ap_array_pstrcat( ), 532
ap_auth_name( ), 565

703

About the Author

Lincoln Stein is an assistant investigator at Cold Spring Harbor Laboratory, where he develops databases and user interfaces for the Human Genome Project using the Apache server and its module API. He is the author of several books about programming for the web, including *The Official Guide to CGI.pm*, *How to Set Up and Maintain a Web Site*, and *Web Security: A Step-by-Step Reference Guide*.

Doug MacEachern has been addicted to Perl and web servers since early 1994 when he was introduced to Plexus as student employee at the University of Arizona. Soon after returning to his home town of Boston, Massachusetts, and entering the "real world," he discovered the Apache web server, and since early 1996, he has been gluing Perl into all its nooks and crannies. His day job has consisted of integrating various other technologies with the web, including DCE, Kerberos, and GSSAPI, but Perl has been the only one he cannot let go of.

Doug has continued as a developer disguised as a consultant since the start of 1998, spending most of his time between Auckland, New Zealand, and San Francisco, California, with time at home in Boston during the warmer months.

Doug likes to spend his time away from software—far, far away, sailing on the ocean, diving below it, or simply looking at it from a warm, sandy beach where technology doesn't go much beyond thatched huts and blenders.

Colophon

The animal featured on the cover of *Writing Apache Modules with Perl and C* is a white-tailed eagle. These large sea eagles have a very large range and are therefore highly adaptable. They are mostly found in coastal areas, but can also be found in the tundra and steppes, forests, and mountains. They build huge nests in trees, bushes, cliffs, or on the ground, depending on what their environment offers.

Eagles fall into the category of bird known as "raptors," a category that also includes falcons and hawks. Like other sea eagles, white-tailed eagles have toes adapted to grasping smooth prey such as fish. Their excellent vision enables all eagles to spot prey from the air or a high perch. They frequently hunt in pairs for their favorite meal of diving birds. Keeping a sharp eye on the bird as it dives, the white-tailed eagle grabs it as soon as it resurfaces. Fish is another staple of the white-tailed eagle's diet. In fact, their diet is as adaptable as everything else about these birds. They will frequently eat fish in summer and waterfowl and carrion in winter, when fish are less plentiful.

Eagles often eat their victims while still flying, breaking them apart and discarding the nonedible parts to lighten their load. Eagles, like most raptors, often dine on sick or wounded animals.

There are more than 50 species of eagle spread throughout the world, with the exception of New Zealand and Antarctica. A pair of eagles will use the same nest year after year, lining it with green leaves and grass, fur, turf, or other soft materials and adding to it each year. The largest eagle nest ever found was 20 feet deep and 10 feet across.

White-tailed eagles are highly regarded, even revered, by many native populations of Siberia and Scandinavian fishermen. However, in other areas overhunting has almost led to their extinction. Increased awareness and limits on hunting have helped this majestic bird rebuild its population, and it is now considered to be safe.

Melanie Wang was the production editor and copy editor for this book, and Sheryl Avruch was the production manager. Sarah Jane Shangraw, Nicole Arigo, and Mary Anne Weeks Mayo provided quality control reviews. Betty Hugh and Sebastian Banker provided production support. Robert Romano created the illustrations using Adobe Photoshop 4 and Macromedia FreeHand 7. Mike Sierra provided FrameMaker technical support. Seth Maislin wrote the index.

Edie Freedman designed the cover of this book, using a 19th-century engraving from the Dover Pictorial Archive. The cover layout was produced by Kathleen Wilson with QuarkXPress 3.32 using the ITC Garamond font. The quick reference card was designed and produced by Kathleen Wilson.

The inside layout was designed by Alicia Cech and implemented in FrameMaker 5.5 by Mike Sierra. The text and heading fonts are ITC Garamond Light and Garamond Book. This colophon was written by Clairemarie Fisher O'Leary.

Whenever possible, our books use a durable and flexible lay-flat binding, either RepKover™ or Otabind™. If the page count exceeds the maximum bulk possible for this type of binding, perfect binding is used.

 # More Titles from O'Reilly

Web Programming

CGI Programming on the World Wide Web

By Shishir Gundavaram
1st Edition March 1996
450 pages, ISBN 1-56592-168-2

This book offers a comprehensive explanation of CGI and related techniques for people who hold on to the dream of providing their own information servers on the Web. It starts at the beginning, explaining the value of CGI and how it works, then moves swiftly into the subtle details of programming.

Dynamic HTML: The Definitive Reference

By Danny Goodman
1st Edition July 1998
1088 pages, ISBN 1-56592-494-0

Dynamic HTML: The Definitive Reference is an indispensable compendium for Web content developers. It contains complete reference material for all of the HTML tags, CSS style attributes, browser document objects, and JavaScript objects supported by the various standards and the latest versions of Netscape Navigator and Microsoft Internet Explorer.

Frontier: The Definitive Guide

By Matt Neuburg
1st Edition February 1998
618 pages, 1-56592-383-9

This definitive guide is the first book devoted exclusively to teaching and documenting Userland Frontier, a powerful scripting environment for web site management and system level scripting. Packed with examples, advice, tricks, and tips, *Frontier: The Definitive Guide* teaches you Frontier from the ground up. Learn how to automate repetitive processes, control remote computers across a network, beef up your web site by generating hundreds of related web pages automatically, and more. Covers Frontier 4.2.3 for the Macintosh.

JavaScript: The Definitive Guide, 3rd Edition

By David Flanagan & Dan Shafer
3rd Edition June 1998
800 pages, ISBN 1-56592-392-8

This third edition of the definitive reference to JavaScript covers the latest version of the language, JavaScript 1.2, as supported by Netscape Navigator 4.0. JavaScript, which is being standardized under the name ECMAScript, is a scripting language that can be embedded directly in HTML to give web pages programming-language capabilities.

Learning VBScript

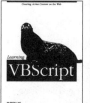

By Paul Lomax
1st Edition July 1997
616 pages, includes CD-ROM
ISBN 1-56592-247-6

This definitive guide shows web developers how to take full advantage of client-side scripting with the VBScript language. In addition to basic language features, it covers the Internet Explorer object model and discusses techniques for client-side scripting, like adding ActiveX controls to a web page or validating data before sending to the server. Includes CD-ROM with over 170 code samples.

Web Client Programming with Perl

By Clinton Wong
1st Edition March 1997
228 pages, ISBN 1-56592-214-X

Web Client Programming with Perl shows you how to extend scripting skills to the Web. This book teaches you the basics of how browsers communicate with servers and how to write your own customized web clients to automate common tasks. It is intended for those who are motivated to develop software that offers a more flexible and dynamic response than a standard web browser.

Web Server Administration

Stopping SPAM

By Alan Schwartz & Simson Garfinkel
1st Edition October 1998
204 pages, ISBN 1-56592-388-X

This book describes spam—unwanted email messages and inappropriate news articles—and explains what you and your Internet service providers and administrators can do to prevent it, trace it, stop it, and even outlaw it. Contains a wealth of advice, technical tools, and additional technical and community resources.

Web Security & Commerce

By Simson Garfinkel
with Gene Spafford
1st Edition June 1997
506 pages, ISBN 1-56592-269-7

Learn how to minimize the risks of the Web with this comprehensive guide. It covers browser vulnerabilities, privacy concerns, issues with Java, JavaScript, ActiveX, and plug-ins, digital certificates, cryptography, web server security, blocking software, censorship technology, and relevant civil and criminal issues.

Building Your Own WebSite™

By Susan B. Peck & Stephen Arrants
1st Edition July 1996
514 pages, Includes CD-ROM,
ISBN 1-56592-232-8

This is a hands-on reference for Windows® 95 and Windows NT™ users who want to host a site on the Web or on a corporate intranet. This step-by-step guide will have you creating live web pages in minutes. You'll also learn how to connect your web to information in other Windows applications, such as word processing documents and databases. The book is packed with examples and tutorials on every aspect of web management, and it includes the highly acclaimed WebSite™ 1.1 server software on CD-ROM.

Apache: The Definitive Guide, 2nd Edition

By Ben Laurie & Peter Laurie
2nd Edition February 1999
388 pages, includes CD-ROM
ISBN 1-56592-528-9

Written and reviewed by key members of the Apache group, this book is the only complete guide on the market that describes how to obtain, set up, and secure the Apache software on both UNIX and Windows systems. The second edition fully describes Windows support and all the other Apache 1.3 features. Includes CD-ROM with Apache sources and demo sites discussed in the book.

Web Performance Tuning

By Patrick Killelea
1st Edition October 1998
374 pages, ISBN 1-56592-379-0

Web Performance Tuning hits the ground running and gives concrete advice for improving crippled Web performance right away. For anyone who has waited too long for a Web page to display or watched servers slow to a crawl, this book includes tips on tuning the server software, operating system, network, and the Web browser itself.

Building Your Own Web Conferences™

By Susan B. Peck & Beverly Murray Scherf
1st Edition March 1997
270 pages, Includes CD-ROM
ISBN 1-56592-279-4

Building Your Own Web Conferences is a complete guide for Windows® 95 and NT™ users on how to set up and manage dynamic virtual communities that improve workgroup collaboration and keep visitors coming back to your site. The second in O'Reilly's "Build Your Own..." series, this book comes with O'Reilly's state-of-the-art WebBoard™ 2.0 software on CD-ROM.

O'REILLY®

TO ORDER: **800-998-9938** • *order@oreilly.com* • *http://www.oreilly.com/*
OUR PRODUCTS ARE AVAILABLE AT A BOOKSTORE OR SOFTWARE STORE NEAR YOU.
FOR INFORMATION: **800-998-9938** • **707-829-0515** • *info@oreilly.com*

Perl

Perl in a Nutshell

*By Stephen Spainhour, Ellen Siever &
Nathan Patwardhan
1st Edition January 1999
674 pages, ISBN 1-56592-286-7*

The perfect companion for working
programmers, *Perl in a Nutshell* is a
comprehensive reference guide to the
world of Perl. It contains everything you
need to know for all but the most obscure
Perl questions. This wealth of information is packed into an
efficient, extraordinarily usable format.

The Perl Cookbook

*By Tom Christiansen & Nathan Torkington
1st Edition August 1998
794 pages, ISBN 1-56592-243-3*

This collection of problems, solutions,
and examples for anyone programming
in Perl covers everything from beginner
questions to techniques that even the most
experienced Perl programmers might
learn from. It contains hundreds of Perl
"recipes," including recipes for parsing strings, doing matrix
multiplication, working with arrays and hashes, and performing
complex regular expressions.

Learning Perl, 2nd Edition

*By Randal L. Schwartz &
Tom Christiansen,
Foreword by Larry Wall
2nd Edition July 1997
302 pages, ISBN 1-56592-284-0*

In this update of a bestseller, two leading
Perl trainers teach you to use the most
universal scripting language in the age
of the World Wide Web. Now current for
Perl version 5.004, this hands-on tutorial includes a lengthy new
chapter on CGI programming, while touching also on the use of
library modules, references, and Perl's object-oriented constructs.

Learning Perl on Win32 Systems

*By Randal L. Schwartz, Erik Olson &
Tom Christiansen
1st Edition August 1997
306 pages, ISBN 1-56592-324-3*

In this carefully paced course, leading Perl
trainers and a Windows NT practitioner
teach you to program in the language
that promises to emerge as the scripting
language of choice on NT. Based on the
"llama" book, this book features tips for PC users and new,
NT-specific examples, along with a foreword by Larry Wall, the
creator of Perl, and Dick Hardt, the creator of Perl for Win32.

Mastering Regular Expressions

*By Jeffrey E. F. Friedl
1st Edition January 1997
368 pages, ISBN 1-56592-257-3*

Regular expressions, a powerful tool for
manipulating text and data, are found in
scripting languages, editors, programming
environments, and specialized tools. In
this book, author Jeffrey Friedl leads you
through the steps of crafting a regular
expression that gets the job done. He examines a variety of tools
and uses them in an extensive array of examples, with a major
focus on Perl.

Mastering Algorithms with Perl

*By Jon Orwant, Jarkko Hietaniemi &
John Macdonald
1st Edition August 1999 (est.)
484 pages (est.), ISBN 1-56592-398-7*

There have been dozens of books on
programming algorithms, but never
before has there been one that uses Perl.
Whether you are an amateur programmer
or know a wide range of algorithms
in other languages, this book will teach you how to carry out
traditional programming tasks in a high-powered, efficient,
easy-to-maintain manner with Perl. Topics range in complexity
from sorting and searching to statistical algorithms, numerical
analysis, and encryption.

Perl

Programming Perl, 2nd Edition

By Larry Wall, Tom Christiansen &
Randal L. Schwartz
2nd Edition September 1996
670 pages, ISBN 1-56592-149-6

Coauthored by Larry Wall, the creator of
Perl, the second edition of this authoritative
guide contains a full explanation of Perl
version 5.003 features. It covers Perl
language and syntax, functions, library
modules, references, and object-oriented features, and also explores
invocation options, debugging, common mistakes, and much more.

Perl Resource Kit—Win32 Edition

By Dick Hardt, Erik Olson,
David Futato & Brian Jepson
1st Edition August 1998
1,832 pages, Includes 4 books & CD-ROM
ISBN 1-56592-409-6

The *Perl Resource Kit—Win32 Edition* is
an essential tool for Perl programmers who
are expanding their platform expertise to
include Win32 and for Win32 webmasters
and system administrators who have discovered the power and
flexibility of Perl. The Kit contains some of the latest commercial
Win32 Perl software from Dick Hardt's ActiveState company, along
with a collection of hundreds of Perl modules that run on Win32,
and a definitive documentation set from O'Reilly.

Advanced Perl Programming

By Sriram Srinivasan
1st Edition August 1997
434 pages, ISBN 1-56592-220-4

This book covers complex techniques for
managing production-ready Perl programs
and explains methods for manipulating data
and objects that may have looked like magic
before. It gives you necessary background
for dealing with networks, databases, and
GUIs, and includes a discussion of internals to help you program
more efficiently and embed Perl within C or C within Perl.

Perl Resource Kit—UNIX Edition

By Larry Wall, Nate Patwardhan,
Ellen Siever, David Futato & Brian Jepson
1st Edition November 1997
1812 pages, ISBN 1-56592-370-7

The *Perl Resource Kit—UNIX Edition* gives
you the most comprehensive collection
of Perl documentation and commercially
enhanced software tools available today.
Developed in association with Larry Wall,
the creator of Perl, it's the definitive Perl distribution for webmasters, programmers, and system administrators.

The *Perl Resource Kit* provides:

- Over 1800 pages of tutorial and in-depth reference
  documentation for Perl utilities and extensions, in 4 volumes.
- A CD-ROM containing the complete Perl distribution,
  plus hundreds of freeware Perl extensions and utilities—
  a complete snapshot of the Comprehensive Perl Archive
  Network (CPAN)—as well as new software written by Larry
  Wall just for the Kit.

Perl Software Tools All on One Convenient CD-ROM
Experienced Perl hackers know when to create their own, and when
they can find what they need on CPAN. Now all the power of CPAN—
and more—is at your fingertips. The *Perl Resource Kit* includes:

- A complete snapshot of CPAN, with an install program for
  Solaris and Linux that ensures that all necessary modules are
  installed together. Also includes an easy-to-use search tool
  and a web-aware interface that allows you to get the latest
  version of each module.
- A new Java/Perl interface that allows programmers to write
  Java classes with Perl implementations. This new tool was
  written specially for the Kit by Larry Wall.

Experience the power of Perl modules in areas such as CGI,
web spidering, database interfaces, managing mail and USENET news,
user interfaces, security, graphics, math and statistics, and much more.

Learning Perl/Tk

By Nancy Walsh
1st Edition January 1999
376 pages, ISBN 1-56592-314-6

This tutorial for Perl/Tk, the extension
to Perl for creating graphical user
interfaces, shows how to use Perl/Tk to
build graphical, event-driven applications
for both Windows and UNIX. Rife with
illustrations, it teaches how to implement
and configure each Perl/Tk graphical element.